Intranets

UNLEASHED

Copyright © 1996 by IntraACTIVE, Inc.

FIRST EDITION

All rights reserved. No part of this book shall be reproduced, stored in a retrieval system, or transmitted by any means, electronic, mechanical, photocopying, recording, or otherwise, without written permission from the publisher. No patent liability is assumed with respect to the use of the information contained herein. Although every precaution has been taken in the preparation of this book, the publisher and author assume no responsibility for errors or omissions. Neither is any liability assumed for damages resulting from the use of the information contained herein. For information, address Sams.net Publishing, 201 W. 103rd St., Indianapolis, IN 46290.

International Standard Book Number: 1-57521-115-7

Library of Congress Catalog Card Number: 96-67952

99 98 97 96   4 3 2 1

Interpretation of the printing code: the rightmost double-digit number is the year of the book's printing; the rightmost single-digit, the number of the book's printing. For example, a printing code of 96-1 shows that the first printing of the book occurred in 1996.

Composed in AGaramond and MCPdigital by Macmillan Computer Publishing

Printed in the United States of America

Trademarks

All terms mentioned in this book that are known to be trademarks or service marks have been appropriately capitalized. Sams.net Publishing cannot attest to the accuracy of this information. Use of a term in this book should not be regarded as affecting the validity of any trademark or service mark.

President, Sams Publishing Richard K. Swadley
Publishing Team Leader Dean Miller
Managing Editor Cindy Morrow
Director of Marketing John Pierce
Assitant Marketing Managers Kristina Perry
Rachel Wolfe

Acquisitions Editor
Grace M. Buechlein

Development Editor
Brian-Kent Proffitt

Software Development Specialist
Cari Skaggs

Production Editor
Gayle L. Johnson

Copy Editors
Cheri Clark
Chuck Hutchinson
Marla Reece
Marylin Stone

Indexer
Gina Brown

Technical Reviewer
Dennis Teague

Editorial Coordinator
Bill Whitmer

Technical Edit Coordinator
Lynette Quinn

Editorial Assistants
Carol Ackerman
Andi Richter
Rhonda Tinch-Mize

Cover Designer
Jason Grisham

Book Designer
Gary Adair

Production Team Supervisor
Brad Chinn

Production
Stephen Adams
Debra Bolhuis
Georgiana Briggs
Jason Hand
Casey Price
Dana Rhodes
Laura Robbins
Ian Smith
Mark Walchle

Overview

Introduction **xxxix**

Part I Introducing Intranets

1. Harnessing the Power: Intranet Defined **3**
2. What Can You Do?: The Intranet in Action **15**
3. Intranets Versus Traditional Groupware **33**
4. Client/Server Basics and Theory **41**

Part II Building Your Intranet

5. An Intranet Shopping List **59**
6. Servers: Hardware Needs **73**
7. Servers: Operating Systems **81**
8. Server Software **91**
9. Starting with the Server **109**
10. Connectivity: Opening Up Your LAN **129**
11. Wide Area Networks **151**
12. Selecting an Internet Service Provider **163**
13. Client Issues **181**
14. Security: Keeping Hackers Out **205**
15. Security: Access Control **221**
16. Security: Secure Internet Data Transmission **245**
17. Training the Users **263**
18. Intranet Administration: A Critical Function **285**

Part III Using Your Intranet: Business Applications

19. Browsers: Viewing Corporate Information with HTML **299**
20. Authoring Tools **309**
21. Creating a Dynamic Site **319**
22. Creating a Functional Site **335**
23. PDF Presentations **351**
24. SGML Presentations **361**
25. Audio Presentations **367**
26. Video Presentations **381**

Part IV Using Your Intranet: Corporate Data

27   FTP: Sharing Files   **393**

28   Using Databases   **419**

29   Telnet: Direct Access   **437**

Part V Using Your Intranet: Communication

30   E-Mail: The Basic Model   **459**

31   Internet Chat Tools: An Intermediate Model   **477**

32   Internet Phones: The Advanced Model   **487**

33   CU-SeeMe: The Next Wave   **501**

Part VI Developing Intranet Applications

34   Intranet Tools   **513**

35   Creating Real-World Applications   **535**

36   Group Scheduling   **549**

37   Message Boards   **561**

38   Contact Databases   **575**

39   Alert Messaging and Real-Time Chat   **587**

40   News Feeds   **599**

41   Group Document Creation and Editing   **619**

42   Private Messaging Areas   **633**

43   Document Submission   **649**

44   Search Functions   **659**

45   Help Desk   **673**

46   Reference Desk   **687**

Part VII Administering Your Intranet

47   Integrating Existing Applications   **701**

48   Maintaining a User Database   **717**

49   Designing a Successful File Structure   **727**

50   Maintaining Security   **739**

51   Hardware and Software Upgrades   **747**

Part VIII Advanced Topics

    52   Managing and Planning for Large Web Projects   **757**

    53   The Future of Intranets   **781**

    A   Resource Guide   **803**

          Glossary   **847**

          Index   **861**

Contents

Introduction xxxix

Part I Introducing Intranets

1 Harnessing the Power: Intranet Defined 3
   Where the Internet Ends and the Intranet Begins 4
   "But We Already Have E-Mail" (and Other Misconceptions) 5
   Wresting Order Out of Chaos:
      Maximizing Value and Optimizing Utility 5
   Some Intranet Benefits 7
      Enhanced Efficiency 7
      Enhanced Effectiveness 8
   Content Is the Key 8
   Is an Intranet the Answer? Some Intranet Criteria 9
   An Intranet Checklist 10
   Setting Intranet Goals 12
   Getting Started 13
   Summary 14

2 What Can You Do?: The Intranet in Action 15
   Three Levels of Usage, Three Levels of Impact 16
      Level One: Displaying General Information 17
      Level Two: Sharing Business Data 20
      Level Three: Interactive Communications 25
   The Noncommercial Application of Intranets 28
   Summary 32

3 Intranets Versus Traditional Groupware 33
   Major Differences 34
      PCs Versus File Servers 34
   Basic Static Corporate Information 36
   Corporate Data 37
   Communication 38
   Expanding LAN Groupware
      Applications into Intranet Applications 39
   Summary 40

4 Client/Server Basics and Theory 41
   Mainframes 42
   PCs 43
   Bulletin Board Systems 44
   The First Online Services 46

	The Internet	47
	Client/Server Relationship	48
	Servers and Their Functions	49
	Server Hardware	50
	Server Software	50
	Clients and Their Functions	51
	Client Hardware	51
	Client Software	51
	The Future of Clients	53
	Middleware: The Next Step	53
	Summary	55

Part II Building Your Intranet

5	An Intranet Shopping List 59	
	Choosing Server Hardware for Your Intranet	60
	Server Operating Systems	63
	Server Software	67
	Web Servers	67
	Client Hardware	69
	Client Software	69
	Connectivity	69
	Security	70
	Summary	71
6	Servers: Hardware Needs 73	
	Examining the Organization's Needs	74
	Initial Capacity	74
	Scalability	74
	Support	75
	Examining Your Current Environment	75
	Server Options	76
	Intel-Based Servers	76
	SPARC-Based Servers	77
	Macintosh Servers	78
	Other Servers	78
	Expansion Costs	79
	The Costs of Downtime	80
	The Reality of Costs: Return on Investment	80
	Summary	80

7 Servers: Operating Systems 81
How Important Is the Operating System Decision? 82
Examining Factors in Operating System Decisions 83
    Solaris 84
    SCO UNIX and BSD/OS 84
    Linux 86
    Windows NT 86
    OS/2 88
    MacOS 88
    Other Operating Systems 89
Market Share: Who Uses What? 89
Summary 90

8 Server Software 91
Commercial Web Servers 93
    Netscape Enterprise Server for UNIX and Windows NT 94
    Oracle 95
    Microsoft Internet Information Server for Windows NT 97
    O'Reilly WebSite Server 98
    Mac HTTP from Quarterdeck 98
Freeware Web Servers 99
    HTTPd 99
    Apache 100
Mail Servers 102
    Netscape MailServer 2.0 103
    NTMAIL 103
    SLmail 104
News Servers 104
Other Software Options 105
Summary 108

9 Starting with the Server 109
Keeping a Log 110
    All Initial Parameters 111
    Emergency Startup Procedures 111
    Any Modifications to System Startup Files 111
    Installed Software 112
    Modifications to Installed Software 112
Why Keep a Log? 112
    Who Keeps the Log? 113
    How Is the Log Kept? 113
The Implementation Plan 114
    What's in the Plan 114

- Pursuing a Level of Reliability 115
- Planning for Upgrade Paths 116
- Planning the Implementation Itself 116
- Planning the Work 117
- Why Have a Plan? 118
  - Planning to Decide Appropriate Software 118
  - Planning to Foresee Expenses of Software and Hardware 118
  - Planning for Maintenance Costs 118
  - Planning for Reasonable Expectations 118
- Who Writes the Plan? 119
- When Is the Plan Updated? 119
  - The Plan's Relationship with the Log Book 119
  - The Log Book's Role During the Implementation 120
  - The Log Book as a Status Check 120
  - Work Patterns as Clues 120
- Issues During Installation 120
  - General Setup Issues 121
  - Familiarize Yourself with the Technical Issues 121
- Using Sound Engineering Practices 123
  - Prepare to Do Everything at Least Twice 124
  - Plan Lots of Extra Time into Each Task 125
  - Always Read All the Available Instructions 125
- Hardware-Specific Issues 125
  - Intel 125
  - Macintosh 126
  - Network Interface 126
  - Peripherals 126
- Operating System-Specific Issues 126
  - Windows 127
  - Macintosh 127
  - UNIX 127
- Summary 127

10 Connectivity: Opening Up Your LAN 129
- LAN Hardware Components 131
  - Connection Media 131
  - LAN Interfaces 133
- LAN Software/Network Operating Systems 138
  - NetWare 139
  - Windows NT 140
  - Windows for Workgroups 140

	LANtastic	141
	AppleTalk	141
	TCP/IP	141
	Remote and Telecommuting Access to Your LAN	142
	Modems	142
	ISDN	144
	Setting Up the Network Servers	145
	File Servers	147
	Print Servers	148
	E-Mail Servers	148
	Communications Server	148
	World Wide Web Servers	149
	Network Connectivity Hardware	149
	Summary	150
11	Wide Area Networks 151	
	Types of WANs	152
	56Kbps Digital Data Service (DDS)	152
	T-1 Services	153
	T-3 Services	153
	Frame Relay	153
	Sonet	155
	SMDS	155
	ATM	156
	WAN Implementation	156
	Connecting the LANs	157
	Bridges	157
	Routers	157
	Accessing the WAN	159
	56K Circuits	159
	T-1 Circuits	160
	T-3	160
	Frame Relay	160
	SMDS	160
	Sonet	160
	ATM	160
	Why a WAN for Your Intranet?	161
	Connectivity	161
	Security	161
	Communications	161
	Summary	162

12 Selecting an Internet Service Provider 163

- A Little Background 164
- General Considerations 165
- Types of Internet Connections 165
  - Dial-Up Analog Service 166
  - Digital PPP and SLIP Dial-Up Accounts 167
  - Dedicated and Dial-Up LAN Connections 167
- Planning and Setting Up the LAN for Internet Connectivity 169
  - Internet Addresses 170
- Hardware and Software 172
  - Routers 173
  - Workstation Software 174
  - Server Software 174
- Getting Connected 175
- Security 176
  - Firewalls and a Word to the Wise 176
- Systems Integrators as ISPs 178
- Summary 179

13 Client Issues 181

- Costs 182
  - Hardware Costs 182
  - Software Costs 183
  - Upgrade Considerations and Costs 186
  - Maintenance Costs 186
- Hardware 186
  - Macintosh 187
  - IBM Compatibles 188
- Software 193
  - Browsers 193
  - E-Mail Software 196
  - FTP 200
  - Telnet 202
  - Internet Phone and Chat 203
- Summary 204

14 Security: Keeping Hackers Out 205

- Building a Security Model File Structure 206
  - User Structure and Permission 207
  - Authentication Points 207
- Protecting the Local Area Network 208
  - What Resources Are on the LAN? 209
  - What Resources Are Available LAN-Wide? 209

	What Computers Are on the LAN?	210
	Which Users Have Access to Which Resources?	210
	Separation by Function	210
	Setting Access Limits	211
	The LAN's Access Paths	211
	Defining User Paths for the LAN	211
	LAN Access	212
	Accessing the LAN's Resources	213
	Authentication Methods	214
	Post Name Check	214
	Username Authentication	214
	Kerberos	214
	Smartcards	215
	Usernames	215
	Passwords	215
	Firewalls	216
	A True Firewall	216
	Protecting Your WAN: A Complete Security Model	216
	Usernames and Passwords	217
	Firewalls Redux	217
	Testing Security	219
	Summary	220
15	Security: Access Control 221	
	Security and the Intranet	222
	Crackers Tread Where Administrators Fail to Secure	222
	Living Large	223
	Determining Your Security Needs	224
	Battening Down the Hatches	227
	Designated Intranet Server	227
	Exorcisms	227
	Sweep and Clean	227
	User Accounts	227
	Passwords and Authentication	227
	CERN Authentication	229
	`Protect`	230
	`DefProt`	230
	Protection Setup Files	231
	Creating Users and Passwords	231
	Creating Groups	232
	Embedded Protection	234
	Examples of Protections	235

	NCSA Authentication 236
	`.htaccess` and `access.conf` 236
	Creating Users and Passwords 239
	Personal HTML Directories 240
	User Access to CGI Scripts 241
	Enabling CGI Scripts in Directories Other than `/cgi-bin` 241
	Access to Server-Side Includes 243
	Enabling Server-Side Includes 243
	Allowing Access 244
	Summary 244
16	**Security: Secure Internet Data Transmission 245**
	What Is Transmission Security? 246
	How Information Is Transmitted 247
	How Information Is Intercepted and Read 248
	Sniffing Devices 248
	Devices for Spoofing 249
	Methods of Transmissions and Their Levels of Security 251
	Encryption 251
	Why Use Encryption? 252
	Private Key Encryption 252
	Public Key Encryption 253
	State-of-the-Art Encryption and Its Future 255
	Why a Technical Solution Is Never the Whole Solution 257
	Client/Server Issues 257
	Secure Computing in Practice 258
	File Transmission 258
	Interactive Transmission 259
	How Much Is Too Much? 260
	What Level of Security Is Right for You? 261
	Summary 261
17	**Training the Users 263**
	Getting Users Connected 264
	Software 268
	Keeping Users Online 269
	New Workflow Lines 276
	Group Training Sessions 278
	Online Training 282
	Summary 283
18	**Intranet Administration: A Critical Function 285**
	Defining the Job 286
	Password and Other Access Management 286
	Usage Analysis 287

Technical Support 288
    Content and Archive Maintenance 288
    E-Mail Management 289
Coordinating Administration 291
Administrator Skills 291
    Technical Proficiency 292
    Attention to Detail 292
    Interpersonal Skills 293
Administrator Training Needs 293
    Training the Administrators 294
Summary 295

Part III Using Your Intranet: Business Applications

19 Browsers: Viewing Corporate Information with HTML 299

Browsers in General 300
An Explanation of Standard Features 302
    Netscape 302
    Internet Explorer 304
    Oracle PowerBrowser 305
Summary 307

20 Authoring Tools 309

WYSIWYG Tools 310
    Netscape Navigator Gold 312
    FrontPage 313
Near-WYSIWYG Tools 314
    HotDog Pro 314
    HoTMetaL 315
Summary 316

21 Creating a Dynamic Site 319

The Dynamic Site 320
Inputting Data 322
    Inventory Data 322
    Static Data 323
    Image and Audio Data 323
    E-Mail and FTP 325
    WWW Forms 327
Storing Data 328
    The Common Gateway Interface 328
    Flat File Databases 330
    Relational Databases 330
Summary 332

22 Creating a Functional Site   335
Manipulating Data   336
Shell Scripts   336
Perl   339
Database Interface   342
Structured Query Language (SQL)   342
Transmitting Functionality   344
Java   345
JavaScript   346
ActiveX   348
Summary   349

23 PDF Presentations   351
What Is PDF?   352
Technical Specifications   353
Uses and Advantages of Portable Documents   353
The Intranet Link   354
Differences and Alternatives: Digital Document Platforms   355
PostScript   355
Acrobat   355
Creating Portable Documents   356
Creating Your Document or Presentation   357
Viewing a PDF File   358
Distributing PDFs   358
Alternatives   359
Summary   359

24 SGML Presentations   361
How SGML Works   362
Using SGML to Preserve File Structure   363
Document Type Definition   364
Benefits of SGML   364
Increased Access   365
Information Collection and Compilation   365
Information Dissemination   365
Cost Efficiency   365
Drawbacks of SGML   365
Does Your Company Need SGML?   366
Summary   366

25 Audio Presentations   367
Bandwidth and Hardware   369
Audio Formats   370

Audio Server Software 372
    Streaming Audio Packages 372
Recording Audio 373
    Choosing Sound-Editing Software 374
The Future of Online Audio 376
    The Internet Phone 376
    Voice Recognition 377
Summary 379

26 Video Presentations   381
Producing Your Intranet Video 383
Creating Recorded Video 383
Creating Live Video 385
    Xing StreamWorks 386
    StreamWorks Network Manager 386
VDOLive 387
Playback 388
Summary 390

Part IV Using Your Intranet: Corporate Data

27 FTP: Sharing Files   393
A Brief History of FTP 394
What Does FTP Do? 394
FTP Clients Versus FTP Servers 396
FTP Commands in Detail 397
    How to Enter FTP 397
    Help from Within FTP 398
FTP: A Complex Example 402
Platform Independence: Why We Use FTP 404
What Is Anonymous FTP? 405
    What Makes Anonymous FTP So Special? 405
    Configuring Anonymous FTP 405
    Testing Anonymous FTP 408
FTP Clients 408
    UNIX/Linux 408
    MS-DOS/Windows 3.x 409
    Starting Up the FTP Client Program 409
    Windows NT/Windows 95 410
    MacOS 410
    Choosing the Right FTP Client Package 411
FTP Servers 411
    UNIX/Linux 411
    MS-DOS/Windows 3.1/Windows 95 412

		Macintosh	412
		Windows NT	412
	What Data Should Be Shared Via FTP?		413
		Over the Internet	414
		Inform Your Community	414
		What Type of Data?	414
		Some Final Thoughts on Internet FTP	415
		Within an Intranet	415
		Format Matters (and Does It Ever!)	415
	Security (or How to Share Files Smartly)		416
		File System Structure	416
		System Isolation	416
		Controlling Access to the FTP Server	416
		Using Inactivity Time-Outs	417
		Anonymous FTP Revisited	417
	Summary		417
28	Using Databases 419		
	Selecting Tools		420
	Evaluating Database Options		424
		Informix	425
		Sybase	425
		Oracle	426
		Microsoft SQL Server	427
		Paradox 7.0	428
	Advanced Intranet Database Issues		429
	Distributing Your Data Across Your Intranet		429
	Replicating Your Data Across Your Intranet		430
		Types of Data Usage	431
	Designing for Growth		432
	Implementation Examples		433
		Contact or Employee Tracking	433
		Online Inventory	434
		Time Reporting	434
		Product Requisition or Purchasing	434
	Summary		435
29	Telnet: Direct Access 437		
	What Does Telnet Do?		438
	How Does Telnet Work?		440
		Telnet Clients Versus Telnet Servers	440
		Telnet as a Part of TCP/IP	441
		Telnet Versus rlogin	441

What Is Telnet Used For? 442
  The System Administrator's Best Friend 442
  Command-Line Uses 442
  Graphic Applications: The X Window System 443
Server Issues 444
  The Number of Users 444
Process Control: ps and the Process Table 447
Connectivity Issues 450
  Problems with the Remote System 450
  Problems Getting to the Host 451
Security Issues: Transmissions Over Ethernet 451
  Raw Data Passed Via Telnet 453
  Packet Filtering 453
  Another Look at the Process Table 453
Commonsense Issues 454
Summary 455

Part V Using Your Intranet: Communication

30 E-Mail: The Basic Model   459
    A Brief History of E-Mail 460
    Making E-Mail Work 460
      E-Mail Addressing 461
      More on Domain Names 461
    Features, Functions, and Freedom: The Benefits of E-Mail 463
      Aliasing 463
      Remote Messaging 464
      Photographic Memory: The E-Mail Transcriber 464
      Bigger Ain't Better: Powerful Tool, Small Bandwidth 464
      Office Uses for E-Mail 465
      File Sharing 466
      Mailbots 467
      Mailing Lists or Listservs 467
      Wide Area Network Communication 468
      Global Communication 469
    Mail Server Issues 469
      Server Options 470
    Client Tools 472
      Pine 472
      Eudora 472
      SPRYMail 473
      GroupWise 474
      Netscape Mail 474
    Summary 476

Contents

31 Internet Chat Tools: An Intermediate Model 477
- Origins: Internet Relay Chat (IRC) 478
- How Chat Works 479
- Applications 480
- Server Issues 481
- Client Tools 483
- Comparing Chat to Internet
  Phone and Video-Conferencing 484
- Summary 485

32 Internet Phones: The Advanced Model 487
- What Is an Internet Telephone, and What Can It Do? 488
- System Resource Usage 490
- Privacy 491
- A Brief History and Barriers to Proliferation 491
- How Does an Internet Phone Work on an Intranet? 493
  - Speed Differences 493
  - Protocol Differences 493
  - Bandwidth Differences 494
- Internet Phone Uses for Intranets 494
  - Long-Distance Savings 494
  - Web-Page Voice Links 495
  - Video-Phone Use on Intranets 495
- Server Issues 496
- Legal and Regulatory Issues 497
- Client Tools 498
- Summary 499

33 CU-SeeMe: The Next Wave 501
- What Is Real-Time Video-Conferencing? 502
- Real-World Applications 503
- Server Issues 504
  - Reflector Technology 505
  - Video-Conferencing Without Reflectors 505
- Bandwidth and Video Compression 505
- Client Hardware and Software Packages 507
- First Steps 508
- Serving Video-Conferences on an Intranet 509
- Implications of Video-Conferencing Over the Internet 509
- Summary 509

Part VI Developing Intranet Applications

34 Intranet Tools 513
- Choosing Your Tools 514
  - Server-Side Includes (SSI) 515
  - Application Programming Interface (API) 516
  - Plug-Ins 518
  - The Common Gateway Interface (CGI) 518
  - Text Manipulation 520
  - Nontextual Data Handling 520
  - Database Interaction 520
- Languages 521
  - Content Tools 521
  - JavaScript 521
  - VBScript 524
  - VRML 526
  - Java 527
- Interface Tools: Perl 529
- Prewritten TCP/IP Applications 530
- Wayfarer QuickServer 532
- Summary 533

35 Creating Real-World Applications 535
- The Need for Needs Assessment 536
  - Organizational Priorities 537
  - Internal Communications 538
  - Technical Requirements 539
- Involving Users: Why, When, and How 540
  - User Input 541
  - User Participation 541
- A User Survey Example 543
- Summary 548

36 Group Scheduling 549
- Scheduling for Intranets 551
- Online Scheduling Applied 553
- Scheduling Applications 555
  - InTandem by IntraACTIVE 555
  - WebShare by Radnet 557
  - Crew by Thuridion 558
- Summary 559

37 Message Boards 561
- Message Boards on the Web 563
- Why Use Message Boards? 566

Using Internal Message Boards 566
Message Boards for Intranets 567
Group Conversation 571
Summary 574

38 Contact Databases   575
    Shared Resources 576
        Corporate Directories 577
        Contact Databases for Intranets 577
    Software for Contact Management 578
        Customized Fields 578
        Customized Phone Lists 579
        Support for Large Volumes of Data 579
        Public and Private Comments 579
        Hyperlinked Records 580
        A Search Engine with Controls 580
        Profiles 580
    Summary 585

39 Alert Messaging and Real-Time Chat   587
    Why Real Time? 588
    Alert Messaging for Intranets 589
    Real-Time Chat 591
        MOOs, MUDs, and WOOs 592
    Chat for Intranets? 594
    Summary 597

40 News Feeds   599
    Just the Facts 600
    Getting Online News 602
    News That Fits 604
    Signing Up for News 604
    News Clips 606
        Information, Inc. 608
        Individual, Inc.'s First! Intranet 610
        Grayfire 611
        Network News Corporation
            by Wave Systems Corporation 612
        NewsEDGE/Web by Desktop Data Corporation 613
        NewsAlert 614
    Summary 616

41 Group Document Creation and Editing   619
    Collaborative Documents 620
        The Exquisite Corpse 621

Online Document Collaboration 622
Document Collaboration for Intranets 623
Document Collaboration Applications 627
   IntraActive's InTandem 627
   Thuridion Crew: Locker 627
   WebFlow Corporation's
   SamePage Intranet Work Processor 629
Summary 630

42 Private Messaging Areas 633

Private Message Boards for Intranets 634
Customizing Message Board Software for Privacy 635
Conference Software for the Web 638
   Forums.com by the Media Machine, LLC 640
   Motet Conferencing by Motet 642
   WebShare by Radnet 644
Privacy Issues 646
Summary 648

43 Document Submission 649

Document Submission with FTP 650
Submitting Documents to a Database 651
Document Database Software 652
   IntraACTIVE's InTandem 653
   Livelink Intranet's Library 654
   Lotus InterNotes 655
   Netscape Navigator 656
Summary 657

44 Search Functions 659

How Search Engines Work 660
   The Range and Complexity of Search Engines 661
   Types of Searches 662
Setting Up Your Search Mechanisms 663
   AltaVista 664
   Excite 666
   Livelink and Pat Search 666
   Oracle Relational Database 668
   Sybase SQL 670
   Verity 670
   Choosing a Search Engine 671
Summary 672

45 Help Desk 673

Organizing Help 674
Writing the Help Text 678

	Developing Help 680
	Images 680
	Managing Help and Questions 681
	E-Mail Addresses 682
	Mail Routers and Chat Lines 684
	Buying Help 684
	Summary 685
46	**Reference Desk 687**
	Listing Resources 688
	Linking Your Resources 690
	Guiding Your Users 693
	Online Research 694
	Deep Sea Fishing: Six Rules of Online Research 694
	Research Rule #1: Know Your Search Sites 694
	Research Rule #2: Know What
	You Want, and You Just Might Get It 695
	Research Rule #3: Break the Maze 696
	Research Rule #4: Don't Mail Code (Unless You Want To) 696
	Research Rule #5: Build Your Bookmark List 697
	Research Rule #6: Old News Is Not Good News 698
	Summary 698

Part VII Administering Your Intranet

47	**Integrating Existing Applications 701**
	A Brief History of Modern Applications 702
	Goals of Integration 703
	Short-Term 703
	Long-Term 705
	The Current State of the Application Environment 707
	Purpose 707
	Application Ranges 707
	Frequency of Use 708
	Functionality 708
	Integration with the Intranet 711
	Inventory 711
	Focus and Implementation 712
	Feedback and Evaluation 713
	Intranet- and Internet-Enabled Applications 714
	A Commercial Application 714
	An In-House Application 715
	Summary 716

Intranets UNLEASHED

48 Maintaining a User Database 717
　Creating a Sustainable User Model 718
　　User Groups 719
　　Administrative Groups 720
　　Superusers 721
　Implementing a User Database 721
　　FTP Servers 721
　　Web Servers 721
　　Maintaining Security 722
　　Keeping Records 722
　　Monitoring Users 724
　Summary 726

49 Designing a Successful File Structure 727
　The File Structure Game Plan 729
　Hardware Issues and Disaster Planning 730
　Platform Issues 732
　　UNIX 732
　　Windows NT 733
　　Dueling Servers 733
　　Web Space 734
　　FTP Space 735
　　User Space 735
　Summary 737

50 Maintaining Security 739
　Physical Security 740
　Passwords 741
　Web Server Security 743
　Securing Applications and Functions 744
　Crack! Crack! Crack! 745
　Summary 746

51 Hardware and Software Upgrades 747
　Maintaining Compatibility 748
　Keeping Up with Technology 748
　　Testing 749
　　Ready for Prime Time? 749
　Upgrading Servers 749
　　Upgrading Server Hardware 750
　　Upgrading Server Software 750
　　Upgrading Workstations 750
　Summary 753

Part VIII Advanced Topics

52 Managing and Planning for Large Web Projects 757

Initial Plans for the Web 758
Choosing a Production Team 758
    Executive Producer 759
    Product Manager 759
    Program Manager 760
    Production Manager 760
    Design Manager 760
    Editorial Manager 760
    Internet Software Developers 761
    Internet Multimedia Designers 762
    Internet Systems Administrators 762
Formulating a Business Plan 763
    Definition of Goals 763
    Brainstorming for Concepts 763
    Critique of Concepts 765
    Mission Statement 765
    Budget, Projections, and Timeline 765
    Reality Check 766
    Project Planning 767
Developing a Site Specification 767
    Site Architecture and Features 767
    Site Content 769
    User Interface 769
    Site Technology 770
Defining Operating Procedures 770
Creating a Marketing Plan 772
Defining a Long-Term Plan 774
Emerging Technologies 775
    Java 775
    ActiveX 775
    VRML 776
    Video Streaming 776
    Audio Streaming 776
    Data Streaming 777
    Internet Phone 777
    Internet Video-Conferencing 777
    Wireless Internet Connections 777
    Intelligent Agents 777
    Online Commerce 777

	Outsourcing 778
	Summary 779
53	The Future of Intranets 781
	Business Trends 782
	Reformatting the Workforce 784
	Workplace Communications 784
	Information Economy 785
	Virtual Corporations 787
	The Global Economy 788
	Telecommuting and Hoteling 788
	Outsourcing 788
	Technology Trends 789
	Open Standards 789
	Bandwidth 790
	Wireless Communication 793
	Single-Client Applications 794
	Voice Mail and Fax Gateways 794
	Intelligent Agents 795
	The Future of Intranet Applications 796
	Extranets 801
	Summary 802
A	Resource Guide 803
	Chapter 1 804
	InTandem 804
	Chapter 2 804
	Audio and Video 804
	Databases 804
	Other Services 805
	Chapter 3 805
	Groupware 805
	Web Browser 805
	Databases 806
	Chapter 4 806
	Magazines 806
	E-Mail Clients 806
	File Transfer Programs 807
	Servers 807
	Operating Systems 808
	Other Services 809
	Chapter 5 809
	Companies with Intranets 809
	Servers 809

- Operating Systems 811
- Modems 811
- Sound Cards 812
- E-Mail 812
- Other Technology 813

Chapter 7 813
- Solaris 813
- SCO UNIX 813
- Linux 814
- Free BSD 814
- Windows NT Server 814
- OS/2 Warp Server 814
- MacOS 814
- Novell NetWare 814
- AIX 815
- HP/UX 815

Chapter 8 815
- WebCompare's Server Features Comparison Page 815
- Netscape Commerce Server 815
- Netscape Navigator 815
- Java 815
- Oracle WebServer 815
- Netscape LiveWire 816
- Microsoft Internet Information Server 816
- O'Reilly Software's WebSite 816
- Apple Internet Server 816
- NCSA httpd 816
- Apache HTTP Server 816
- Sendmail 817
- Netscape Mail Server 817
- NT Mail 817
- SL Mail 817
- Netscape News Server 817
- NNTP News Server 817
- Progressive Networks RealAudio 817
- Xing StreamWorks 817
- CoolTalk 818
- CU-SeeMe 818
- Lotus Notes 818

Chapter 12 818
- Online Services 818
- Modems 819
- Networking Hardware and Software 819

Chapter 13	821
Operating Systems	821
TCP/IP Clients	822
Browsers	822
E-Mail	823
FTP	824
Telnet	824
Voice Communication	824
Chapter 14	825
Computer Emergency Response Team	825
Chapter 17	825
Software	825
Modems	826
Internet Connections	826
Chapter 19	826
Web Organizations	826
Browsers	827
Web Technology	827
Chapter 20	828
Browsers	828
Authoring Tools	829
Chapter 23	829
Digital Document Formats	829
Chapter 24	830
Chapter 25	830
Audio Formats	830
Audio Editors	831
Audio Servers	831
Voice Communication	832
Voice Recognition	832
Chapter 26	832
Video Servers	832
Video Utilities	833
Image Tools	833
Sound Tools	833
Chapter 27	834
FTP Clients	834
FTP Servers	834
Chapter 28	835
High-Level Databases	835
Mid-Level Databases	835
Chapter 29	835

These applications will become more widespread when hardware and software become less expensive. As bandwidth continues to increase and users are able to connect at higher rates of speed, audio- and video-conferencing with an intranet will become easier and more prevalent than with legacy groupware.

Expanding LAN Groupware Applications into Intranet Applications

There are several ways to bridge the gap between legacy groupware and true intranet functionality without having to uproot your whole system. Many current groupware applications can be modified to use open standards and work in conjunction with new intranet technology. Several companies are providing ways to do this modification through new software or upgrades. Groupwise mail can be upgraded to use POP3 and SMTP inexpensively, and Lotus is working to make Notes databases accessible through the Web. Through a series of gateways, Memo has expanded its global connectivity to communicate with users of UNIX, the Internet, and a series of other protocols. Also, Netscape has recently acquired Collabra Software, which will allow current Collabra users to integrate their internal messaging and groupware systems with IP-based enterprise networks and the Internet.

Another method of developing intranet systems is to program the actual applications or modify current LAN software, instead of utilizing premade software packages. HAHT Software is giving developers and users of all levels the tools to build interactive business applications and Web sites. Thus, by starting with the existing LAN, Web design professionals and developers can design a series of applications to be used by an organization over the Internet.

Although upgrading or modifying existing software is one option for creating your own intranet, most groupware applications, even when modified to work as intranet applications, are inferior to products built with the open architecture of the Internet.

> **TIP**
>
> If you already have a file server on your LAN, it might not be very difficult to set up FTP service. By running an FTP server daemon on top of your file server, you can provide access to files using open TCP/IP architecture and with the enhanced features of FTP without giving up the security and structure of your current system. In fact, you can have both systems—the legacy groupware file server and an FTP server—running at the same time and serving the same files. It's relatively easy to find robust FTP servers for almost any operating system.

Summary

For those organizations building systems to carry them into the future, now is the time to leave groupware technology behind. Aside from the fact that groupware will not be compatible with future applications, it currently is not compatible with the Internet. In addition, with groupware, your software dictates the format in which data, information, and communications are configured. Groupware also makes changing, modifying, and updating applications difficult, as software and standards are proprietary.

For those same organizations that are looking for the most efficient ways to communicate externally with employees, business partners, and association members, all these groups must be "connected" to systems that are designed to meet and keep up with rapidly evolving technology. Remember, with an intranet, the software is built around your data, information, and communications needs; and intranets use open standards, meaning the standards of applications designed for the intranet are available to users, making communications on all levels with anyone accessible.

Client/Server Basics and Theory

4

by David Garrett

IN THIS CHAPTER

- Mainframes 42
- PCs 43
- Bulletin board systems 44
- The first online services 46
- The Internet 47
- Client/server relationship 48
- Servers and their functions 49
- Clients and their functions 51
- The future of clients 53
- Middleware: the next step 53

Introducing Intranets

Part I

Because most of the Internet technology and concepts we will be talking about are based on Internet applications and how they can be used to develop an intranet, you must first understand client/server technology—the basis on which the Internet is built. When you understand client/server technology, you will understand better many of the concepts and ideas discussed here and how to expand on them. Let's begin by discussing how computers first became connected to each other and how client/server technology grew from there.

Mainframes

Before the advent and widespread use of the personal computer (PC) in the early 1980s, businesses and government relied on mainframe computers for information technology. The mainframes had the capacity to compute but were slow and could handle only a limited number of users. Mainframe users were tied to small "dumb terminals," essentially keyboards and monitors with no capacity to compute or process information. Information was entered and received at the dumb terminals but processed on the mainframe machine. Figure 4.1 illustrates mainframes and dumb terminals.

FIGURE 4.1.
The mainframe computer processed information, and the dumb terminal served merely to enter and receive data.

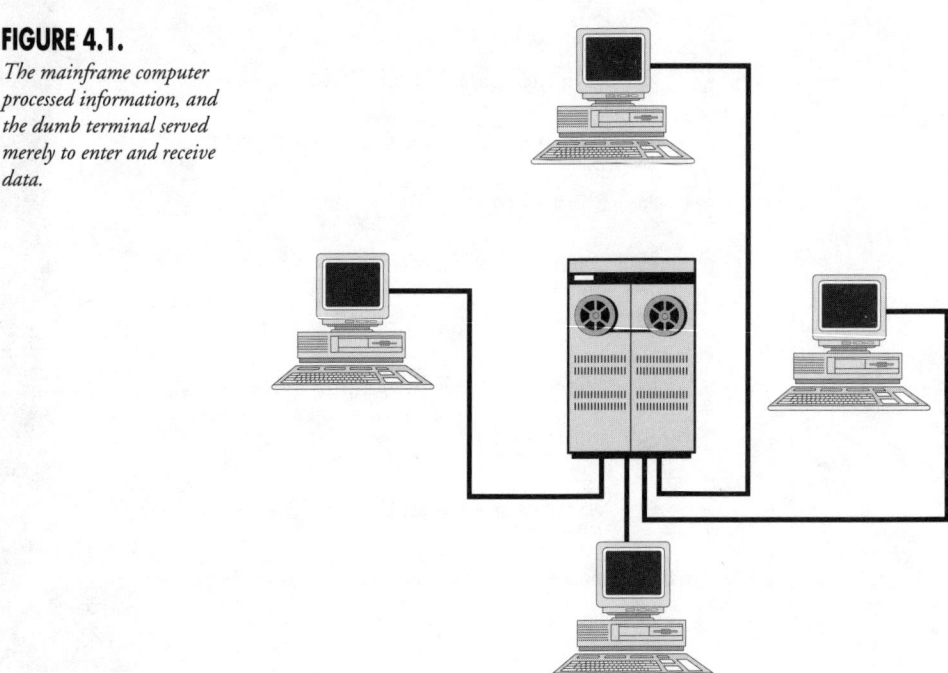

These early mainframes were large machines, often taking up an entire room. They looked nothing like today's sleek PCs or compact laptop computers, which conveniently fit into briefcases. In fact, technology has come so far in such a short time, it's likely that the operator, who in the 1960s and 1970s conducted his or her work holed up in a room with a mainframe, now performs similar work on a laptop—capable of handling and processing at least as much information—while he or she travels around the country, or even the world!

PCs

By 1985 the PC arrived in the serious business environment. This computer could perform all the functions of the mainframe—right on the desktop. PCs could process databases and spreadsheets, and their word processing features were the death knell for typewriters. These computers were fast compared with the mainframe, which usually was slowed due to the number of users logged on from the individual dumb terminals. Now, each user had his or her own machine.

But for all the new functions they could handle, the first PCs still had a long way to go. Data exchange was difficult. To share information among other PCs and users, files had to be copied onto floppy disks and then physically installed in the disk drives of other PCs. A partial solution to this drawback came with the local area network (LAN). With a LAN, computers in the same building could communicate with one another through wiring, as shown in Figure 4.2.

FIGURE 4.2.
An ethernet LAN interconnects PCs in the same building using wiring and a concentrator.

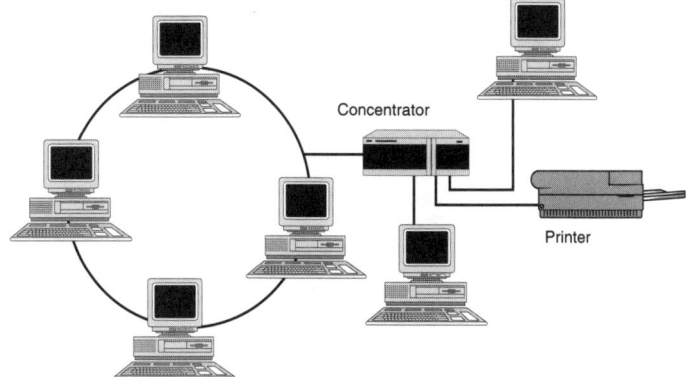

Now users could share files without having to physically install them in each PC; however, only one person could work on a file at one time. Although users could share files, they still could not easily exchange data. This was inefficient for businesses, and organizational problems arose. For example, if an organization with several salespeople wanted to track sales, each salesperson had to keep a separate sales data file. When it was time to look at the complete sales picture, each salesperson's file had to be merged with the other files to obtain effective and accurate data. Because of this inconvenience, much of the data was compiled and stored on paper, which was more expensive in materials and labor costs.

Internal communications for businesses and the government became easier with the advent of internal e-mail in the late 1980s. This eased communications within a building. But what was being done to allow these businesses and the government to communicate with other businesses or agencies across town, on the other coast, or even in another country?

Bulletin Board Systems

In the continuing evolution of computer communications, the modem arrived on the scene in the 1970s but did not gain widespread appeal until the mid-1980s. Finally, computers in remote locations—countries, coasts, or continents away—could connect with each other. This made it easy for two individuals at a time to exchange files with each other and even to chat online. This initial modem connection was linear, and therefore limited in scope, as only two users could take advantage of one connection.

Bulletin board system(BBS) software was created to enhance the modem's capabilities (see Figure 4.3). Now, individuals could connect to other computers in remote locations, albeit excruciatingly slowly and with much patience and technical know-how. Thus began the first forms of remote digital exchange. Businesses used BBS technology to provide technical support to clients and employees. Hobbyists and interest groups utilized the technology as a new, faster means of communication. Whereas the modem enabled a site-to-site or computer-to-computer connection, bulletin boards enabled computers to communicate and exchange information through this connection. Now, instead of a person-to-person connection, it was much like today's conference call, with many users from remote sites congregating in a common cyberarea.

FIGURE 4.3.

Bulletin board system (BBS) technology connects a computer to several modems communicating with other computers over telephone lines and single modems.

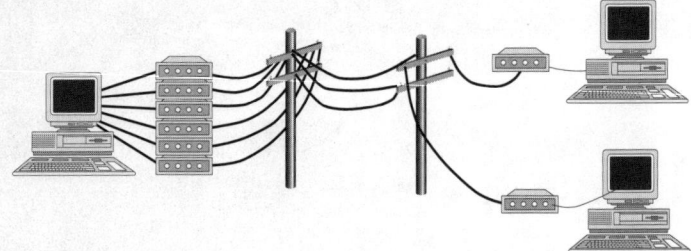

BBS software was one of the first vestiges of client/server applications. Initial client/server technology consisted of a main computer, operated by the systems operator, or sysop, which was capable of connecting several hundred modems. At the other end of the connection was the individual user's machine, with its single modem. The user dialed the BBS from its single modem and connected to one of the BBS's modems. At first, users had to type in arcane commands to accomplish everything from communicating and processing information to searching and retrieving data, as shown in Figure 4.4. Later came graphical interfaces, first with ASCII characters and then with graphic files.

Client/Server Basics and Theory

Chapter 4

FIGURE 4.4.
BBSs have a variety of interfaces, such as this ASCII interface.

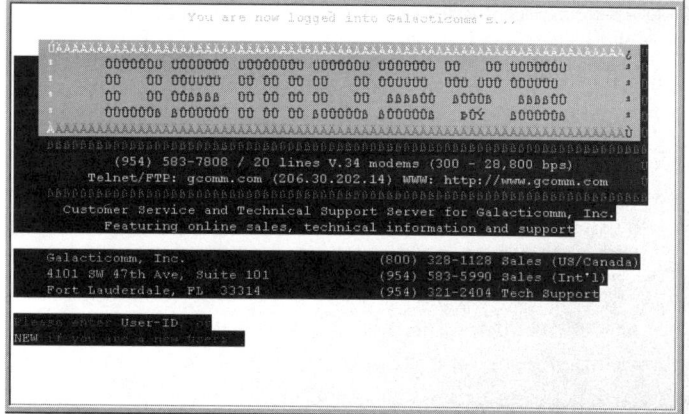

BBSs were one of the first communications tools to deal with the issues of cross-platform computing. Because there was no common operating system, or language, the BBS sysop did not know what type of computer was connecting with it. To further complicate the connection, at this time there was a larger variety of computers on the market and in use than there are today. Atari, Commodore, Amiga, Texas Instruments, as well as Apple and IBM, were all popular home PCs at that time. Each had their own operating systems and configurations. The BBS operator's task was to construct a common interface so that it could communicate with any computer. One of the first such interfaces, and one that remains prevalent in terminal connections today, was ANSI/VT-100. With VT-100, any computer anywhere could connect to a BBS and get a common interface.

The first BBSs performed only limited functions, mainly providing an area for uploading or downloading files and e-mail. As the software grew more complex, more functions were added, such as message boards. Here users carried on conversations by posting and replying to messages on a range of topics. As BBSs became more popular and host computers became more powerful, with the capability to handle more connections, users began to "chat" in real time. This allowed multiple users to "speak" with each other at the same time. Chatting in real time allowed users to have a dynamic rather than a static conversation. Some users even played games with each other over BBSs.

Businesses, mostly computer related, started using BBSs to provide computer files such as drivers, patches, and upgrades to their customers and to handle technical support. With message boards, a technical support question only had be answered once and then was posted for any user to access. Now any user could find answers to common questions without tying up phone lines or expensive human technicians. BBSs were created on a simple theory: Place a reservoir of information on a single computer, make it accessible to the world, and let it be a meeting place for the exchange of information and ideas.

Introducing Intranets

Part I

The server aspect was the key to BBSs' success in the age of the modem. It enabled users to log on once a day or once a month to retrieve their e-mail, new files, or new message board postings. The information was stored on the server for the individual user to retrieve at his or her leisure; an expensive constant or direct connection was not necessary.

Shortly after BBSs became the main avenue for computer communications, BBSs started connecting to each other and to the Internet in the late 1980s and early 1990s. Now, in addition to exchanging e-mail and files with other users on a single BBS, the Internet and multiple BBSs enabled users to perform these functions with many users (see Figure 4.5). At first, it was set up in multilevel client/server fashion. The BBS functioned as a server for its individual users but as a client for the Internet as a whole. The first BBSs to connect to the Internet did so through a modem connection to an Internet service provider that sent and downloaded the user's mail a few times a day.

FIGURE 4.5.
Two BBSs connected through the Internet serving client computers over modems.

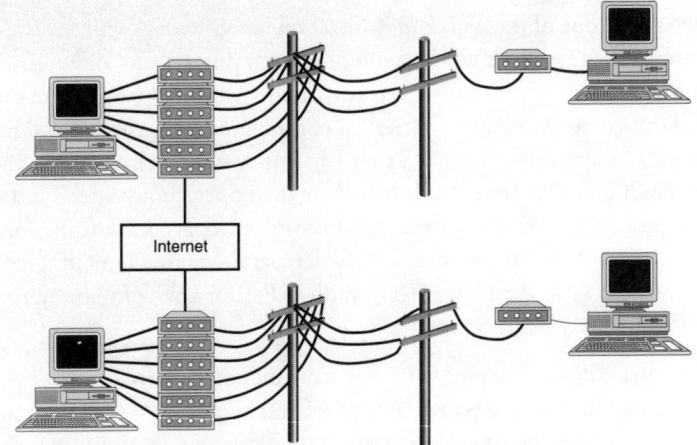

In 1995, *Boardwatch* magazine listed more than 30,000 bulletin board systems in the United States.

From the large and isolated mainframe and the first desktop PCs of limited data exchange evolved today's PCs, which allow users to create files and applications and to communicate and share those files with users worldwide. E-mail as we know it today was born from these initial BBSs.

The First Online Services

BBSs launched a desire for more sophisticated nationwide networks. In the late 1980s, services like CompuServe, America Online, and Prodigy were created to tap into the growing pool of bulletin board users. While these advanced applications began to satisfy and convert bulletin board users to their services, their other features piqued the interest of many would-be users.

With access to features like up-to-the-minute news, access to local phone numbers nationwide, a growing user base, libraries, and chat groups, people soon realized they could utilize their computers—at the office and at home—quickly and easily to communicate worldwide. Their computers offered a world of resources, literally, at their fingertips.

The Internet

While people at work and at home were scurrying to sign up with an online software program, the Internet began to expand beyond its exclusive service as a military function.

One of the Internet's first stops after its military service was in educational institutions. Universities found the Internet especially useful in exchanging research data, ideas, and papers and began exchanging files, data, and findings with other campuses worldwide.

Researchers, however, did not need to set up separate computers to host their data or to serve as a common place to store the information; they already had powerful computers that were connected to the Internet. What was needed, however, was a way to host the data and an established protocol for requesting and receiving information in an organized and efficient manner. Server computers called daemons became the hosts for an Internet protocol. The first daemons were mail and file transfer protocols (FTPs). The FTP daemon waited for the user to request a file. When a file was requested, the daemon started the processes necessary to answer a request. Somewhat like the postal worker who sorts snail mail, the mail daemon waited for mail to arrive, processed that mail, and then forwarded it to a local mailbox or a remote site, where it was delivered to the user.

The idea of an interconnected computer network capable of supporting multiple users with simultaneous access to the same information had long been proposed by scientists who recognized its research potential even before technology made it possible.

The evolution of the Internet dates from the 1960s, with the development of packet-switched networks—messages fragmented into smaller parts. These subparts, or packets, were discrete data units routed and reassembled at the other end of a transmission, permitting several users to share the same connection.

Packet-switched networks took computing from a client/server model to peer-to-peer networks, a development that would ultimately replace the large, centralized mainframe systems with the decentralized systems represented by today's PCs.

In 1969 an early packet-switched network was implemented at the U.S. Department of Defense's Advanced Research Projects Agency (DARPA). In 1982 the ARPANET, as it was called, replaced its original Network Control Protocol (NCP) with the Transmission Control Protocol (TCP) and Internet Protocol (IP). Used together, the TCP/IP suite of communications protocols connects a set of networks, now widely referred to as the Internet.

In the early 1980s, a meeting of DARPA, the National Science Foundation, and scientists from various universities yielded the development of the Computer Science Research Network (CSNET). CSNET and ARPANET were later connected through a gateway called the VAN (Value Added Network). The VAN, coupled with free access to TCP/IP, heralded the beginning of what is now known as the Internet.

Client/server architectures such as the user-created UNIX User Network (Usenet) implementing the Unix-to-Unix Copy Protocol (UUCP) and the Because It's Time Network (BITNET) also emerged in the early 1980s as homegrown alternatives to ARPANET. These networks used off-the-shelf technology in innovative ways, and their users, initially university researchers, have grown into sizable, diverse populations who exchange e-mail, engage in wide-ranging, free-style discussions and subscribe to a countless number of subject areas.

Client/Server Relationship

As PCs evolved and users became more sophisticated and hungry for even more information, there developed a need for a new type of computer: the server. A server is a piece of hardware that receives, processes, and replies to a query. It usually is or resides on a central computer. A server has the capability to handle multiple connections concurrently and from many different sources or clients. Traditionally, server hardware is in the form of powerful minicomputers. More recently, however, high-end PCs are being used as servers in many functions.

A client is a computer or software application that helps a user form and send a query and then displays the results of the queried information for the user. Practically any computer can be a client; in fact, most servers have client software installed on them as well.

Like automated teller machines (ATMs), client/server applications are based on transactions. The client sends a request to the server, similar to a customer sending a request to an ATM. Just as the outcome of the ATM transaction depends on what type of information the customer gives the ATM when prompted, so does the outcome of a client request for information from a server depend on the information given to the server.

The client sends a request to the server with the following information:

- Address for the server (Where do I ask for this information?)
- The request (What information do you want?)
- The return address for the information (Where do I send the information?)

There must be a common protocol that both the client and the server speak to communicate with one another. On the Internet that protocol is TCP/IP. The server does most of the work in the relationship: It waits for requests, processes them, and then sends the client the information requested.

Through some client/server applications, like Telnet and the World Wide Web, remote users can actually run applications on the server machine and manipulate data. For instance, remember the salespeople who were tracking sales through individual computers? Well, now they can log onto a central computer using a Telnet application and enter their individual sales figures. The sales data now can be processed together at a central location. Or, using a secure protocol and a more advanced technology, such as a Web server gateway, a user can enter the information on his or her own machine, where it is compiled and sent to the server. The connection time, therefore, only lasts as long as the transmission.

Servers and Their Functions

Depending on the needs of a business or organization, there usually is one server or a group of servers. For example, a bank would have a group of servers, one servicing each branch. The server's function is to process information requests. When a request is received by the server, that server performs one of two functions: It either answers the request and updates information or it sends the request to the right place. For example, if information is affected by the request, such as in the case of an ATM transaction, a request for a withdrawal means the account must be debited. In the case of redirecting the request, if someone is using an ATM from a bank with which he or she doesn't have an account, the server for that ATM sends the information request to the server at the customer's bank. In this case, the ATM server is actually acting as a client and the customer's bank is the server. When the information is returned to the ATM, it is "serving" the information back to the client (see Figure 4.6).

FIGURE 4.6.
ATMs are connected to a network of servers that have your banking information.

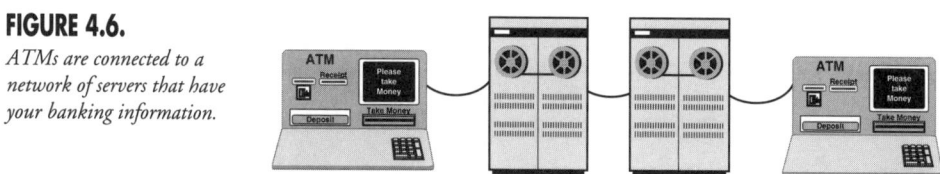

The applications for this kind of relationship in the business environment are virtually limitless. Any common source of information, from price lists and inventory to contact databases and financial data. Any data that must be accessed and modified by multiple users can be done very efficiently in this client/server model.

> ### THE ATM: A CLIENT/SERVER APPLICATION
>
> To understand the client/server relationship, consider something that most of us, for better or worse, have become accustomed to: using the ATM.
>
> Think of the ATM as the client. You utilize the ATM for various banking needs by entering your specific information request. Assume you need cash. You insert your card, from which your account number is read. When prompted, you enter your PIN (personal identification number), how much money you want, and which account to access. The ATM then sends the request to a central server machine. The server machine processes the request, matches your PIN to your account, debits your balance, and sends the reply back to the client, the remote ATM site. The client then acknowledges the result of the request by sending cash and a receipt (you hope). Because all the clients share a common server, your account is always updated.

Server Hardware

If you're going to serve information, you need a computer on which to serve it. Server hardware traditionally has been a minicomputer such as a Sun or a Cray, or a high-end IBM or DEC computer. With the new Pentium and power-PC processor, however, more PCs are being used as servers for limited uses such as a Web or a mail server, or even an FTP file server. For Telnet or database applications, however, more powerful servers are needed. For example, if a company wanted to post employee manuals, memos, and directories on a Web server, or simply serve mail to a medium-sized LAN, a Pentium computer would more than suffice. On the other hand, if a large corporation wanted to maintain an up-to-the-minute nationwide inventory supply, a more powerful computer likely would be required.

Server Software

You can have multiple software servers on one computer. In a typical intranet, an organization will want a mail server to process and deliver e-mail, an FTP server to manage file transfers, a Web server to host and serve World Wide Web documents, and possibly a database server to store and process data. Each server, or daemon, listens for a specific request. The appropriate server then answers the request. Some servers, like FTPs, file servers, and mail servers, only require a little memory. Others, such as some Web and database servers, need much more RAM to operate. A typical Pentium Web server should operate just fine with 32MB of RAM, whereas a machine running multiple servers might need as much as 128MB RAM, depending on how many concurrent users there are or how many requests must be processed at one time.

Clients and Their Functions

To understand how clients work, think about the ATM analogy. The client, the ATM, asks questions to determine the form of the query (deposit, transfer, and so on). It then arranges those questions into a query the server will understand. Next the client sends the query to the server using the correct protocol. Anyone who has programmed computers knows that computers do not respond to plain English—or Spanish for that matter. Commands must be given to the computer in a specific way. The client works along the same model. The client software knows the language spoken by the server and formats the request in a way that the server will understand.

A mail client does much the same. There is a standard mail protocol over the Internet, but dozens of clients take the information. Though your message may be entered in several ways, each client will put it in the correct format to transmit it over the Internet. So, regardless of which mail client you use, your message is sent over the Internet in the same way as all other Internet messages.

Examples of clients are Eudora for mail, Fetch or CuteFTP for file transfer, and Netscape or Internet Explorer for browsing the World Wide Web. The rich variety of clients and servers is why this technology is so important and useful; it doesn't matter what kind of computer you have or which operating system you run—as long as you can speak the basic Internet protocol, TCP/IP, you can connect to the server.

Client Hardware

Client hardware can range from an old Apple II computer to a Cray supercomputer. All the client needs is a connection to the server and the capability to run client software. Some new clients, like two-way pagers, Apple Newtons, and other personal data assistants, are clients as well. Although they can't perform many functions, they can send and receive information to and from a server.

Client Software

Most client software is available for many computers and operating systems. Client software once was all command-line software, which means it didn't do much except make the connection to the server. It looked much like a DOS prompt. The user had to know specifically what information to feed the server and in what format that information must be in to communicate with the server. Now there are graphical interfaces for most client software. Essentially graphical interfaces perform the same functions as command line software did but are

Part I

user-friendly. Users make queries by pointing and clicking, and dragging and dropping, while the graphical interface transforms those queries into a language that the server can understand. It then sends the query using TCP/IP. The graphical interface just makes it easier to construct the command if the user doesn't know the arcane protocols and procedures. Figures 4.7, 4.8, and 4.9 show three ways to send mail.

FIGURE 4.7.
Command line is run through the server.

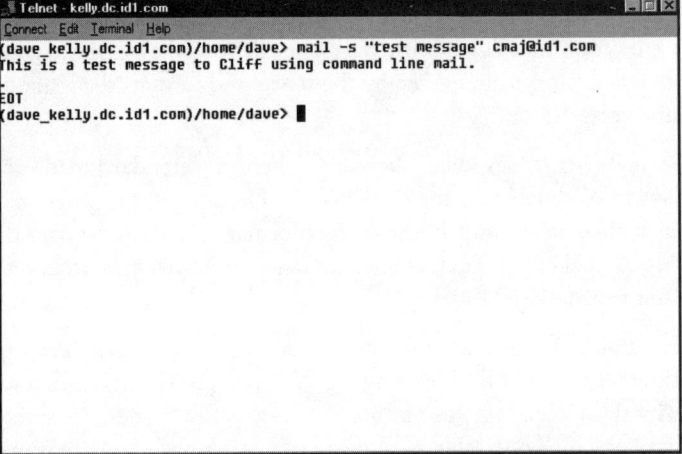

FIGURE 4.8.
Pine is a client program run on a server machine.

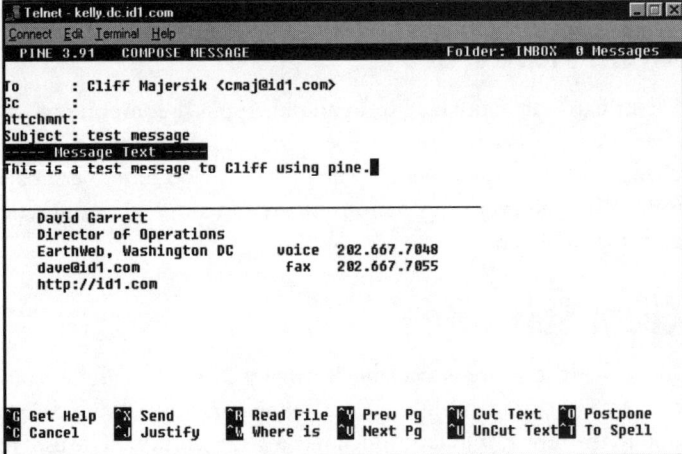

FIGURE 4.9.
Eudora is a client program run on a client machine.

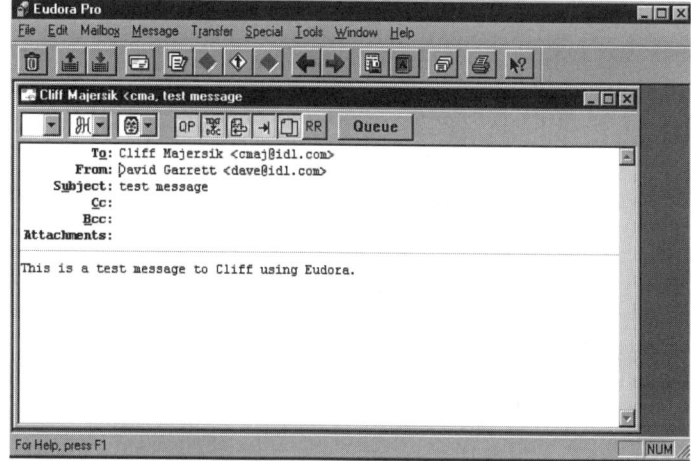

The Future of Clients

With the advent of the network terminal—a $500 PC receiving much attention among the online world and highly touted by such industry giants as Oracle and AT&T—and other similar devices, client software is likely to function as part of the operating system rather than as individual software. Netscape, the most popular World Wide Web browser, is already doing this by combining into one application mail, FTP, even Internet phone, and soon many other clients. With advancing wireless technology, it is possible that someday day soon you will send and receive e-mail and travel the information superhighway from your cellular telephone (hopefully not at the same time you are navigating the actual eight-lane highway!)

Middleware: The Next Step

Middleware is the practice of writing programs that use the computer processing capacity of both the server and the client. Right now, client hardware is not being completely utilized because of the current limitations in bandwidth. A mid-level computer, even with a very fast connection, can process data much faster than it can receive it. The goal for the next generation of client/server software is to create a program that will take information from the server, send that information to the client, let the client manipulate it, and then send the results back to the server. For example, in the case of online banking, you could download a bank data form that retrieves your personal credit and financial information from the server along with it. You then could use that application for many banking needs, including transferring funds, applying for a loan, or requesting traveler's checks. The application then would send the information back to the server, complete with all your financial data. Thus, part of the processing is done with the client, and part is done with the server.

The idea of middleware is to provide a cross-platform means of creating and distributing a software application, regardless of what kind of computer and operating system is being used by the client. In this way, an organization can create a specialized, customized piece of software built to perform specific functions.

> ### DEATH, TAXES, AND MIDDLEWARE
>
> Benjamin Franklin said that in this world, nothing is certain but death and taxes. Using middleware can ease one of these certainties by simplifying IRS tax procedures. Imagine that the IRS could combine all the past year's tax information as it relates to you. The software application would include all the information on your estimated payments and withheld taxes, as well as information from past tax years and current 1099s. The application also would include any updates or changes in the tax laws. Then, an individual could download the application, answer tax questions directly and manipulate the data, and send the completed information back to the IRS. This process could eliminate the process of organizing information from several sources (employers, banks, and so on). The application could even interface with your own bookkeeping software to make the job that much easier, as shown in Figure 4.10.

FIGURE 4.10.
Middleware software applications could greatly simplify individual tax procedures through direct links among the IRS server, bank, employer, and taxpayer's personal computer.

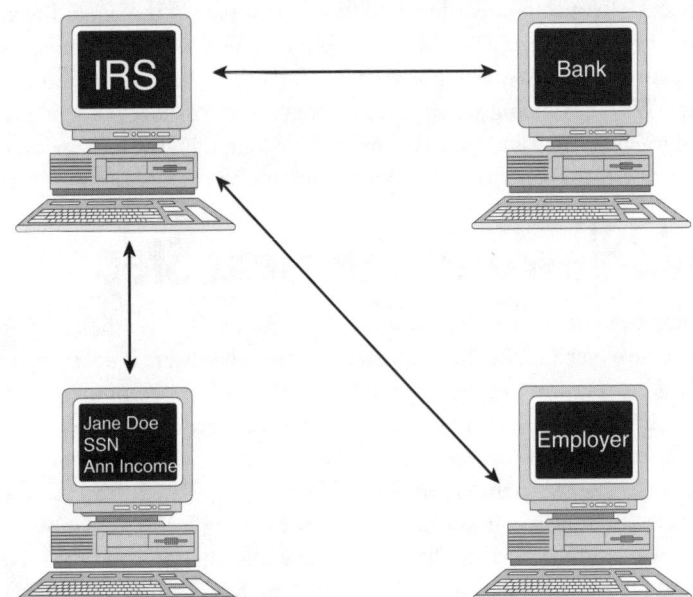

Summary

Client/server applications currently dominate the Internet and form the basis for the best tools currently available with which to build intranets. Client/server applications also provide the most flexible platform to build future applications, whatever form they might take. A basic understanding of client/server technology and applications is fundamental in understanding the concepts and functions outlined here. As you will continue to learn throughout this book, all functions you build into your intranet will be based in some way on client/server theory.

IN THIS PART

- An Intranet Shopping List **59**
- Servers: Hardware Needs **73**
- Servers: Operating Systems **81**
- Server Software **91**
- Starting with the Server **109**
- Connectivity: Opening Up Your LAN **129**
- Wide Area Networks **151**
- Selecting an Internet Service Provider **163**
- Client Issues **181**
- Security: Keeping Hackers Out **205**
- Security: Access Control **221**
- Security: Secure Internet Data Transmission **245**
- Training the Users **263**
- Intranet Administration: A Critical Function **285**

PART II

Building Your Intranet

An Intranet Shopping List

by David Garrett

IN THIS CHAPTER

- Choosing server hardware for your intranet **60**
- Server operating systems **63**
- Server software **67**
- Client hardware **69**
- Client software **69**
- Connectivity **69**
- Security **70**

Part II

Part I, "Introducing Intranets," laid out the basics:

- Where the Internet ends and the intranet begins
- What you can do with an intranet and what an intranet can do for you
- Intranets versus traditional groupware
- Client/server basics and theory

With this foundation, you are ready to build your intranet. What do you need? What do you want? What are your costs? What will you get for the money? The answer is simple—anything you want. There have been intranets built with Scotch tape and baling wire. Some intranets that work well and are functional cost only a few hundred bucks. On the other hand, large corporations, such as Ford and Silicon Graphics, have spent millions on their intranets. It really depends on your intranet dreams and wish list. Here I'll help you create a shopping list of products to make your dream intranet come true, as shown in Figure 5.1.

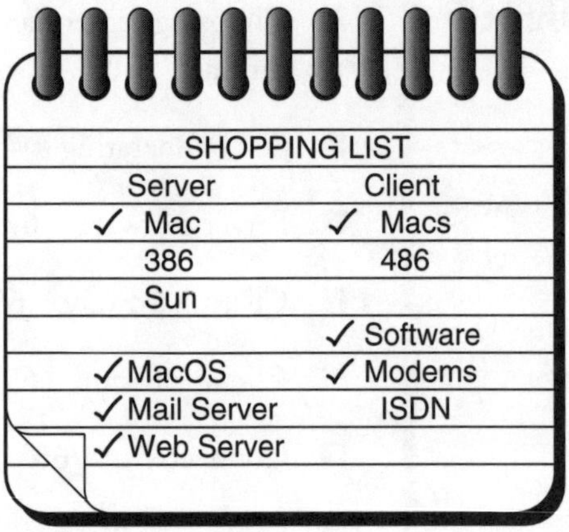

FIGURE 5.1.
Your shopping list might include categories for both server and client machines.

SHOPPING LIST	
Server	Client
✓ Mac	✓ Macs
386	486
Sun	
	✓ Software
✓ MacOS	✓ Modems
✓ Mail Server	ISDN
✓ Web Server	

Choosing Server Hardware for Your Intranet

As discussed in previous chapters, intranets are built on a client/server principal, which means to utilize an intranet you must have clients and servers in place. Chances are you probably already have client machines you can use, and perhaps even servers. Chapter 4, "Client/Server Basics and Theory," covered the differences between the two, so the first part of this chapter is devoted to the most important part of your intranet—the server machine. Depending on the size and purpose of the intranet, the server hardware can consist of anything from a 386 desktop computer to one or several Sun Sparc Ultra computers. Figure 5.2 shows some examples of server hardware you can use. It just depends on what you want your intranet to accomplish.

An Intranet Shopping List

Chapter 5

FIGURE 5.2.
You have a variety of options when it comes to choosing servers for your intranet.

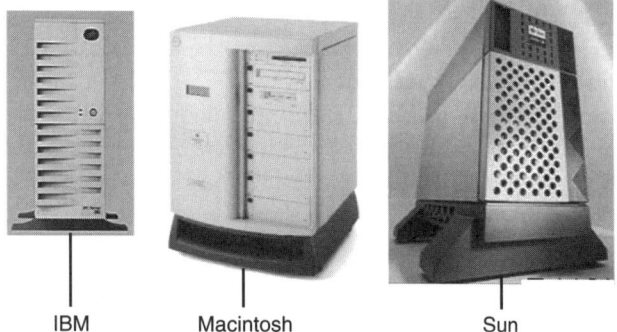

IBM   Macintosh   Sun

If your intranet goal is as simple as running a Web server to host 30 to 40 users and post HTML pages, you probably don't need much more than a 386 or 486 processor. You certainly should have a decent amount of RAM on the machine—at least 16 to 24MB. You'll also want a good-sized hard drive that is at least twice the size of all the files you plan to add in the next year. You will also need a large disk cache and an httpd. httpd stands for *hypertext transfer protocol daemon,* the program that runs on your server and responds to Web requests. httpd is just another name for a Web server.

The next level of server might include a medium-sized intranet for 50 to 75 users that hosts a Web server, a mail server, possibly a gateway into a database, and/or audio-conferencing. In this scenario, you'll want at least a 486 processor, but probably a Pentium, PowerPC, or Macintosh clone, such as a Power Computing machine. This intranet would require at least a 2-gigabyte hard drive and a minimum of 24MB of RAM.

These first two scenarios can incorporate the computers currently sitting on someone's desk. Depending on the operating system in use, it may not even be necessary to buy a new computer for a server. If the goal of either of these intranet scenarios is to perform regular mail and Web service and to communicate internally with a local area network (LAN), the intranet may require just one computer.

If you find yourself in one of these scenarios, I recommend one of two server solutions. You could designate the least-used computer as the server; then this computer would be load-balanced. With most operating systems, including Windows 95, Windows NT, and MacOS, Web and mail servers can run in the background without noticeable impact. With Windows 3.1 or Windows for WorkGroups it might slow down a bit but still probably won't be that much slower. It's similar to hooking your computers to a LAN and accessing information from another computer on the LAN; users don't really notice, unless there is a lot of activity. The other server solution is to find the person who uses his or her computer the most, such as the resident geek or the systems administrator, and run the Web server on his or her machine. In this case, you can be reasonably assured that the server will run most of the time. And, it's even possible that person will upgrade the software and make sure that server issues are dealt with immediately. It's also likely this person has the best and fastest computer. If that's the case, the effects of running the Web server likely will be felt the least. Certainly, if the organization wants to host several Web servers, such as for different departments, this can be done on different machines. The vice president of finance might have a Web server on her machine, while the vice president of manufacturing also has one on his machine. As you can see, servers come in many shapes and sizes. You may realize you can have a fully stocked server on existing desktops, or you may have to do some shopping.

The next level of an intranet might be a large corporation or trade association. An intranet in either of these scenarios typically will have several hundred users. It likely will run mail and Web servers, have a database gateway, and run advanced communications software, like message boards and scheduling. It might even have audio- and video-conferencing. A server capable of hosting this number of applications will vary widely in cost and performance.

How fancy your purchase is and how much money you put down on such a server really depends on how much use you will get out of your intranet. For example, if most users use it occasionally or a few users use it a lot, a fast Pentium processor with 24 to 40MB of RAM might serve all the intranet's needs. With any more use than this, you should move to either a dual-processor Pentium or a minicomputer, such as a Sun Sparc 5 or DEC alpha. Even a small minicomputer, like a Sun Sparc 5, will be much faster than any Pentium-based machine. Of course, it's also possible to split responsibilities between two servers: One could run the Web and mail servers, while the other could run a database. Splitting resources like this could make it possible to use two Pentium machines rather than a more expensive minicomputer.

The next level is an enormous intranet, typically a machine used continually by several thousand users working in different geographic locations. These intranets run large and busy Web servers, handling mail for several thousand people and serving database queries, as well as possibly serving audio- and video-conferencing. At this level, you'll want to start with a Sparc 20, a Silicon Graphics, or an equivalent machine.

If you find yourself on the fence between one of these levels, ask yourself some questions, such as the following:

- How many users will my intranet serve?
- How often will they use it?
- What functions do they currently need?
- What functions will they need in six months? One year?

There are some things you may want to buy today that will be cheaper tomorrow. Any machine you can't afford today may be in your price range a few months from now. If you want to get your feet wet and expand as you go, you might begin with a cheap server or use your current machine as the host. Proceeding cautiously is one thing, but be careful not to create an intranet that is so sluggish that users don't use it. Try to strike that sometimes difficult and delicate balance.

Server Operating Systems

When the time comes to shop for server software, the operating systems should be at the top of this section of the shopping list. To make it easy on you, you might be pleased to know that the operating system you choose is almost entirely a matter of personal preference. Most of the applications you will want to run on your intranet are available for many platforms. Sometimes you won't have a choice, especially if your server will sit on a preexisting machine. In this case, you must make your choices accordingly, as they must be compatible with the operating system on this machine. If you do have a choice, however, here's the rundown. (For more detailed information on operating systems, read Chapter 7, "Servers: Operating Systems.")

Windows 3.1 (Windows for Workgroups) doesn't offer too much, but it will get the job done if you only plan to run Web and mail servers. Figure 5.3 shows Windows 3.1 running httpd.

FIGURE 5.3.
A Windows 3.1 operating system running httpd.

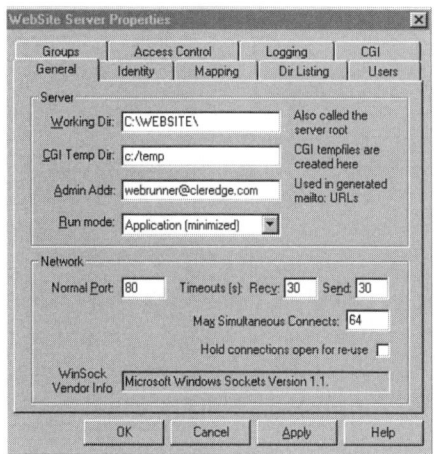

Stepping up to Windows 95, you'll find a wider choice of software availability and compatibility. Although Windows 95 is no Windows NT, most software that runs on Windows NT will run on Windows 95, as shown in Figure 5.4.

Building Your Intranet

Part II

FIGURE 5.4.
A Windows 95 operating system running Netscape FastTrack server.

If you're running a Macintosh house or you're more comfortable with Macintoshes, it's certainly an option to have a Macintosh server, although you probably won't find as many software options on the shelves. Macintosh operating systems offer true multitasking, and they have a RISC processor, which makes them fast servers. Figure 5.5 shows MacOS running httpd and a mail server.

FIGURE 5.5.
MacOS running httpd and a mail server.

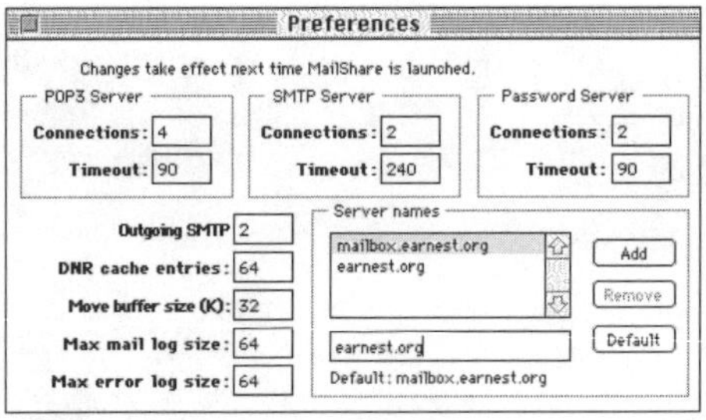

Windows NT gets the industry's nod of approval as a good choice of operating system. Microsoft is targeting the intranet for its Windows NT line of products. Windows NT comes with a mail and Web server and give users the freedom to run practically any intranet application needed. Figure 5.6 shows Windows NT running httpd.

FIGURE 5.6.
The Windows NT operating system running httpd and a mail server.

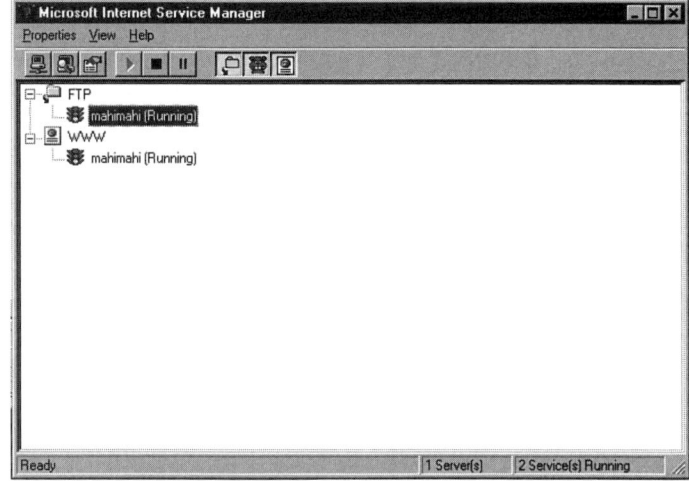

Linux is a strong competitor of Windows NT. (Figure 5.7 shows an X Window Linux desktop with a Netscape browser surfing a page hosted on a server on the machine itself.) In fact, I consider the two to be *the* choice operating systems. One great thing about Linux is that it is free; however, on the downside, there is no support (other than the thousands of users on Internet Usenet newsgroups, who seem happy to provide ad hoc support), and it's not plug and play. Unlike Windows 95 or Windows NT, you can't just slide the CD-ROM into the machine and it's up and running; Linux makes you do lots of configuring. Linux is infinitely more flexible than Windows 95 or Windows NT, allowing its users to perform almost any function and configure the machine any way they want. Like Windows NT, Linux likely will run into problems finding the right drivers or supplemental software on a less sophisticated machine. I recommend using a big brand-name computer like IBM or Toshiba if you want to run Linux. For example, I'm currently running Linux on one of my mail-order machines, but I can't seem to find the print driver.

The next level of operating system is UNIX, which Linux is based on. UNIX is very fast and has true multitasking, one of its main advantages. The processor can perform many functions easily at once. If two, or even dozens of users are making requests at the same time, it will keep up. As with Linux, UNIX offers some Internet pluses, such as the capability to establish shell accounts, which neither Windows 95 nor Windows 3.1 offers. UNIX makes it easy to set up user space, but it may not give you a nice graphical interface and an easy plug and play. If you use Sun machines, you'll have to use Sun's version of UNIX, which is Solaris.

FIGURE 5.7.
The Linux operating system with a term window running httpd.

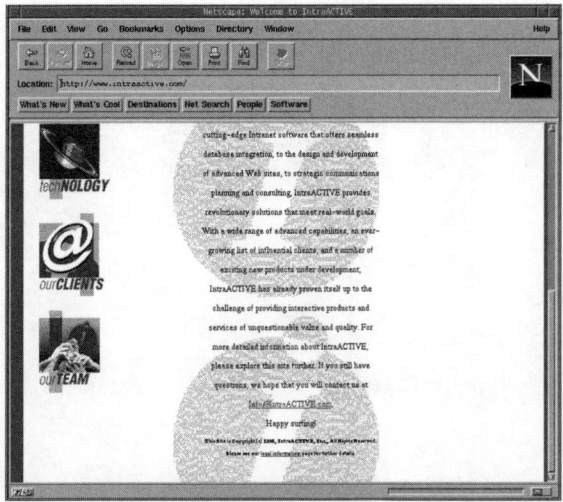

MCKEON & JEFFRIES

McKeon & Jeffries expects to have fewer than 150 users, who will use the intranet mostly for e-mail and Web service. The accounting firm wants a Web server, a mail server, and a machine to support them. The average user is expected to use the intranet a little each day, though some will never use it at all and a few will use it constantly. The users do not need secure Web transmissions, but they will need decent authentication.

The company needs an e-mail package to integrate its interoffice e-mail with Internet e-mail. It also needs a Web browser on each client machine. McKeon & Jeffries does not plan to use the intranet for audio- or video-conferencing, so it will not need to buy speakers, microphones, or cameras, but it will need to upgrade the machines of its support staff to use the Web browser effectively.

M&J also must set up an Internet connection and a way for users on the road to dial into the network. Users connecting from the road or home will need modems and software to set up dial-up connections.

McKeon & Jeffries Intranet Shopping List

Server:
       Pentium machine
       Operating system
       Web server
       FTP server
       Mail server (possibly a patch for Groupwise)
       Message Board software

> Connectivity:
>
>> New ISDN line for third office
>> ISDN line to Internet
>> Internet service provider
>> LAN modem bank
>> PPP software (client and server)
>> P-50 router
>
> Clients:
>
>> Web browser
>> Mail client (possibly Groupwise)
>> HTML editor
>
> Security:
>
>> x86 machine
>> Firewall Software

Server Software

After you have decided on a server, it's time to look at software that will serve your information. The only server software packages essential to an intranet are a Web server and a mail server. If you want real-time audio, you must also choose a streaming audio server or some other audio server. You may need a streaming video server as well if you plan to utilize real-time video or video-conferencing. You also may need to run a database on your server.

Web Servers

If you want a basic Web server, almost any will do. For instance, if you merely want to serve HTML pages and images, without secure transmissions or complex authentication, you can use any Web server. Regardless of the operating system you're using, you can find a free Web server. The NCSA (National Center for Supercomputing) makes a Web server that can be used by almost any operating system; it's free on the Internet at http://hoohoo.ncsa.uiuc.edu/. Of course, Netscape, Oracle, O'Reilly, Apache, Microsoft, and dozens of other companies are in the running for your server dollars. If you're using Windows NT, UNIX, or Linux, you definitely have a mail server built in and possibly a Web server as well. However, the NT mail server will need software upgrades in order to send Internet mail. Mail servers also are available for every operating system, and these also are free and quite functional. Perhaps now or down the road, you will want to add other servers, such as audio and video. (For detailed information on audio and video servers, read Chapter 8, "Server Software.") If you're considering audio and video servers, be prepared to put down some bucks. Also, if you want Web servers with special features that talk to your database or provide secure transmission, be prepared to spend some serious money. Secure Web servers can run as high as $10,000, and audio and video streaming servers can cost several thousand dollars, depending on quality.

THE SPORTING GOODS AND APPAREL ASSOCIATION

The SGAA expects to have 300 to 500 users, about half of whom will be heavy users. The SGAA expects to provide secure Web service with a heavy daily load. The intranet will need to run a database on the server, as well as real-time audio-conferencing and possibly video-conferencing. It also will need high-level authentication.

The SGAA will need to recommend a Web browser to their users, but purchasing the software will be the responsibility of each individual user or the sponsoring member company. Also, the administrative staff will need speakers, microphones, and cameras for audio and video privileges.

The SGAA will need a fast connection to the Internet, as most of its users will be accessing the site through their own Internet connections. The connectivity of this intranet must support many concurrent users accessing the site.

The SGAA's Intranet Shopping List

Server:
- Sun machine
- Operating system
- Mail server
- Web server
- Database
- Streaming audio server

Connectivity:
- T-1 line
- Internet service provider
- Modem for Sun machine
- PPP software (client and server)
- CSU/DSU

Clients:
- Mail client
- FTP client
- Telnet client
- Web browser
- HTML editor
- Streaming audio client

Security:
- Security testing software
- Firewall software

Client Hardware

As an intranet developer, your biggest task is to make sure your user group has adequate machines. Many users might connect from home, and it's likely they'll have good machines. Of course, if your users are connecting from home, they will need a modem. I wouldn't suggest anything slower than a 28.8Kbps for surfing Web sites. If the user just needs to connect with the mail server, a 14.4 should do. At this time, 28.8 is the fastest available.

However, don't worry about the home users so much; it's the users who have ancient corporate LANs you should think about. For example, it's not uncommon to find 386 DOS-based computers without color monitors on the desktops in many corporate LAN environments. Obviously, there is no longer a whole lot these poor users can accomplish with this antiquated technology. The basic minimum needed for an intranet client is a 486 with a color monitor and 8MB of RAM, and this is bare bones. If you plan to do audio- or video-conferencing or use Java, your users will need a fast 486 or a Pentium with at least 16MB of RAM. If you plan to incorporate even basic audio- and video-conferencing, you must consider sound cards, microphones, speakers, and cameras. These peripherals are not cheap. You can expect to pay for a sound card and speakers about what you'd pay for a decent home-stereo system. If you plan to use a microphone for audio-conferencing, don't waste $10 on a cheap one; spend a few more dollars and buy a decent one.

Client Software

An enormous amount of client software is available for free or for very little money on the Internet, and some of it is even fairly good. You will probably need a Web browser and assorted plug-ins, a mail client, an FTP client, a Telnet (or terminal) client, and possibly streaming audio or video clients. Many Web browsers' beta and preproduction versions are free; of course they don't have all the bells and whistles of commercially available software, but they are functional. These are adequate for getting started. There also are several free mail clients available, such as Eudora and Pine. Also, it is certainly possible to integrate your intranet or Internet mail with your existing LAN mail. Your Groupwise mail can route your Internet and intranet, but you'll have to get a patch for a nominal fee.

Connectivity

Most intranets will not be self-contained within one environment. Several locations, be they offices, homes, or mobile offices, will be hooked together, either by direct connections with one another or through the Internet. This means you must provide for connectivity between the client and the server. This is not a big challenge on a typical LAN, as everything is already connected. If your intranet is going to be self-contained within the LAN, there already is an existing ethernet, or possibly ARCnet, system linking the LAN. After you've determined where your intranet server will reside, the next step is to add modems so users from outside the LAN can dial in. In this case, you'll probably need a Shiva or other brand of network modem system. If you want to connect to the Internet or connect two offices in different geographic locations through direct connection, you'll need an outside connection, or bandwidth.

There are a few different levels of bandwidth. If you just want to use e-mail or a program like Freeloader to surf the Internet, you can get away with a 28.8 modem for your office and a dial-up account. This is probably enough to handle Internet mail and light surfing for an office of up to 10 users. If you have more than 10 users, Internet use is greater, or people are reaching your intranet through the Internet, you will want something like an ISDN line, which is 128 KB/s. You could use an ISDN to connect a few offices. If you had three small offices with a limited number of users, the offices could be connected with an ISDN line and data could be exchanged at a high rate of speed; it also could handle audio- and video-conferencing. But if these offices had hundreds of users, the line would jam immediately. In this case, I recommend a T-1 (1.5 MB/s) or T-3 (10 MB/s), which are established data lines—but this is an expensive solution. A direct connection like this either to the Internet or to another location is a permanent high-speed data connection. Unlike a modem, these lines are always running, are digital, and can transport data very quickly. However, if you're connecting two or three offices or want a big pipe to the Internet or lots of surfing, a T-1 is necessary. A T-3 is only necessary if your intranet requires audio- and video-conferencing at high rates of speeds or if thousands of users regularly access the site.

To minimize bandwidth usage, consider using Freeloader or a similar program. Freeloader software goes out on the Internet on a regular basis and downloads favorite sites so your users can surf them locally. This lets them surf frequently visited sites quickly using minimum bandwidth.

Security

You must start considering security at the earliest stages of planing your intranet. First, consider the physical security of your computers. Dead bolts, cipher locks, and card key entry systems are all things to consider. Also, special rooms, cages, and metal doors might be necessary, depending on how sensitive the data on your intranet is.

After your computers have been physically secured, you must look carefully at the electronic security. Keeping unauthorized people out, keeping your data out of the wrong hands, and protecting your transmissions are all important considerations. To keep unauthorized people out, consider a firewall. A firewall restricts and monitors network traffic so that you can choose who and what to allow in, yet still be able to spot intruders. The Eagle Raptor and Gauntlet products are both good examples of commercial firewalls. To keep your data safe from prying eyes, you need a file system that keeps careful track of permission and ownership. Windows NT, UNIX, and Novell NetWare are all examples of such systems. Windows 95 and MacOS are examples of insecure file systems. Finally, when considering the security of your data when transmitted from computer to computer, you must look at encryption. Encrypting your transmissions ensures that they are useless to an interceptor. PGP, pretty good privacy, is a freely available encryption program that you can use for your e-mail, among other things. Secure Web servers can also encrypt any data you share over the Web. See Chapters 14 through 16 for more details about securing your intranet.

Summary

This chapter should have given you enough basic information to begin penning your intranet shopping list. Remember, though, the information provided here is just a guide to send you in the right direction in search of the building blocks of your intranet. Consider the shopping list in this chapter as an outline with just the basic food groups. Chapters 6 through 13 are designed to help you select the most appropriate foods and ingredients to fatten your shopping list.

Servers: Hardware Needs

by Mike Mazan

IN THIS CHAPTER

- Examining the organization's needs 74
- Examining your current environment 75
- Server options 76
- Expansion costs 79
- The costs of downtime 80
- The reality of costs: return on investment 80

A server can be the solid foundation of an intranet, or it can be the thorn in the side that renders an intranet virtually useless. An intranet is normally an extension of a corporation's internal network. When you're adding a server, a little bit of planning can go a long way toward successful implementation. In this chapter, we'll take a realistic look at what it takes to support a growing intranet. We'll begin by examining an organization's needs, including the current environment and infrastructure, as well as future needs. We'll also examine costs as this chapter outlines the necessary considerations to effectively plan an intranet's foundation.

Examining the Organization's Needs

Many intranets start out as experiments within one department of an organization. Generally, this means that someone has set up a spare computer, loaded it with free software, and plugged it into the corporate network, which is usually a Local Area Network (LAN). While this "build-up" is relatively simple for most organizations, it works only on a small scale, perhaps only for that department. Rolling out a sophisticated or even simple intranet to an entire organization requires much more than a spare computer and a free software program. Knowing an organization's server needs inside and out requires focusing on three areas: initial capacity, scalability, and support.

Initial Capacity

An intranet provides a type of "information central" to an organization—whether it be corporate, educational, nonprofit, or otherwise—that was never before available. Predicting its use and, therefore, the capacity you need, is a challenging task. A pilot project involving a select user group will help ascertain the users' level of technological ability and the usefulness of an intranet to this user group. The usage of the pilot group must take into account how much the users have been encouraged to use the new system, which in some cases may go hand-in-hand with the users' level of computer ability. If you haven't implemented a pilot project, the scalability and support areas become more critical.

Scalability

Scalability is the most important factor in an intranet server. The success of any new project is based on its usage, and an intranet is no different. After a successful project is created, you have to respond with a higher level of server service. Many servers can reach new levels of performance easily if you add more resources, such as processors, disk space, and memory. Other servers can be upgraded to new higher-performance servers without changing any of the software. It is far better to install an intranet server that is at the low end of its capacity than one that's at the top end. This allows you to respond to increased usage by adding resources—upgrading hardware or software. For example, if you are using a Windows 95 solution, you have a relatively low upper limit as far as the number of users and server capacity goes, because you are stuck with a Pentium-based machine. With Windows NT, you can upgrade to a much faster processor, like a DEC Alpha, without changing your software.

Often you can increase server performance simply by adding more servers to support each different application. Some companies, such as Federal Express, have more than 60 internal intranet servers. This method also improves the robustness of the intranet over a large single server by giving each application or group of applications its own server. Thus, one corrupt application that crashes its server will not affect any of the other servers or their applications. For example, FedEx has several servers that serve just their database, while others serve different parts of their Web site.

Support

Support is the last area to examine when determining organizational needs. Support plays an important part in server selection. A server should be geared to serve data to the intranet but still be compatible with existing systems and staff knowledge. For example, if the rest of your organization is running on Scaleable Processor Architecture (SPARC) servers, an Intel-based server is probably not the best choice. Using a server type that is already supported in your organization allows current staff resources to be maximized.

In the area of support, don't overlook the server's availability needs. If an organization's server runs 24 hours a day, consider installing redundant server features such as RAID (Redundant Array of Inexpensive Disks) in case of drive failures, and redundant power supplies for protection against power supply failures. A RAID server is a group of disks that automatically copy one another so that if one goes bad, the data remains intact. A redundant power supply provides power to the servers in case of emergency. If the intranet continuously serves hundreds of users simultaneously, the organization can't afford for the server to crash.

Examining Your Current Environment

In examining your current environment, keep in mind that an intranet is not much more than another application server running on your corporate network. However, because of its heavy use, this application server could cause network performance degradation, leading to slow network response. Make sure that the network administrators and planners are aware that these new application servers are being installed so that they can plan for the server's network bandwidth needs appropriately.

Network protocols in the current environment also play a significant role in the success of an intranet. Intranets are popular because they allow many machine platforms to share graphical data, which was not an option prior to intranets. Because TCP/IP (Transport Control Protocol/Internet Protocol) is the main common protocol between most computer platforms, most intranet servers and software use it. If you choose to use other protocols, such as AppleTalk (an Apple-specific protocol) or IPX (a Novell-specific protocol), your server and software choices will be limited.

Server Options

You can choose from a variety of server platforms when selecting a new server. Many companies are releasing packaged or bundled servers that have components that are optimized for a Web server, including the bundling of server specific software. Most of the new servers fall into the following categories. In late 1994, Sun Microsystems released its Netra line of Web-specific servers, which currently dominate the Web server market. Intel-based servers offer the most choices in operating systems and server software and are responsive and flexible. However, because the components are not always assembled and tested by a single manufacturer, Intel-based servers can create configuration and compatibility problems between components that are supposed to work together but do not. MacOS touts an easy user interface but lacks some of the flexibility and horsepower of other server platforms.

When selecting a server platform, keep in mind that the basic purpose of an intranet server is to move data from storage to the network. Make sure that any server you plan to purchase has robust data I/O capability on the disk controller as well as the network controller. Many network and disk controllers are geared for workstation use but are not suitable for use in an environment that handles a large number of concurrent requests. In disk controllers, this means using a SCSI (Small Computer Systems Interface) instead of an IDE (Integrated Drive Electronics) interface, both of which are commonly used in most computer platforms and are the gateways that provide communication between the devices and the processor. In networking controllers, this means using a network that has some on-board intelligence.

The next sections include a rundown of the different server families and their respective advantages and disadvantages.

Intel-Based Servers

An Intel-based server can be either "home-built" (designed by the user) or built and configured by the manufacturer, as shown in Figure 6.1. An Intel-based server runs on most operating systems, including Windows NT, Windows 95, UNIX, and Solaris. The Intel platform represents a growing share of the Web server market. Because of Intel's edge in the market, many new server technologies will be available for the Intel platform before they are for other platforms.

A downside of the Intel platform is that the numerous combinations of internal components can make it difficult to isolate a specific problem. These different components can cause conflicts, or they could turn out to be incompatible with one another. For example, a combination of the BIOS (Basic Input/Output System), including the network card and disk controller, could crash the server. BIOS is the core system that tells the computer how to react to problems. But with each manufacturer pointing at another manufacturer, pinpointing the problem on the intranet server is anything but straightforward. However, to minimize this drawback, select a manufacturer or integrator that assembles and tests all components of the server together for the specific application at hand.

Servers: Hardware Needs
Chapter 6

FIGURE 6.1.
An Intel-based server, manufactured by Hewlett-Packard.

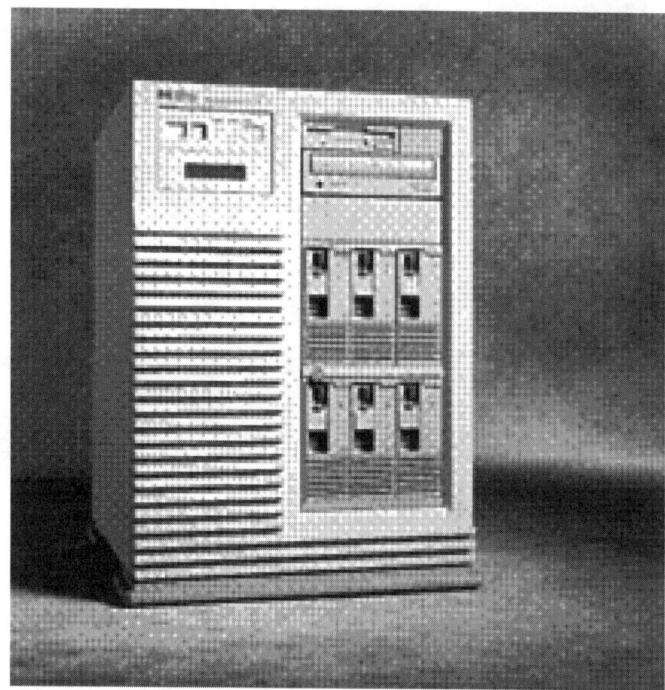

An Intel-based system can start as low as $2,000 for a low-end Pentium system with 16MB of RAM and 1GB of disk storage and go as high as $8,000 to $12,000 for a Dual Pentium Windows NT system with 128MB of RAM and 4GB of RAID storage.

SPARC-Based Servers

SPARC servers made by Sun, SGI, and others claim the largest market share of Web server platforms for good reason. In the Solaris UNIX environment that runs on a SPARC server, shown in Figure 6.2, the TCP/IP protocol is an inherent part of the operating system—not an added protocol. In addition, the SPARC processor is specifically suited to handle the many concurrent requests that are required by a busy intranet server.

Sun has built its market share by adding valuable features, such as bundling the servers with appropriate software to create, run, and administer Web sites, in its Netra line of servers. Many other companies are now providing similar bundling with their servers.

Cost is the main deterrent to choosing a SPARC server. A SPARC system with 32MB of RAM and 4GB disk storage costs from $4,000 to $6,000; with multiple processors, the price quickly can jump to more than $20,000.

FIGURE 6.2.
A SPARC server, manufactured by Axil Computer.

Macintosh Servers

The Macintosh remains a strong contender in the Web server market because of its user-friendly interface and easy-to-configure TCP/IP and Web administration tools. However, it cannot support the number of simultaneous users that other platforms, such as SPARC or Intel-based servers, can.

A Macintosh, such as the one shown in Figure 6.3, offers perhaps the least expensive server option at about $2,500 to $3,500 for a PowerPC or Quadra-based computer with 32 RAM and 2GB disk storage.

Other Servers

Alpha-based platforms outshine all other platforms, and if cost is not an issue, I recommend an Alpha server. However, because processor speeds can be as high as 233MHz, you should expect to pay about three to four times more for an Alpha platform than for an Intel-based platform. Also, the Alpha-based systems generally run Windows NT, locking the user into a specific operating system.

MCKEON & JEFFRIES

McKeon & Jeffries chose a Pentium-based server because they anticipated fewer than 200 users with light usage. They decided on a high-end machine with 64MB of RAM and a 4GB hard drive. As they planned to run Windows NT, they purchased a name-brand machine to facilitate getting NT drivers for their hardware. Their server cost just under $10,000.

FIGURE 6.3.
A Macintosh Internet server.

THE SPORTING GOODS AND APPAREL ASSOCIATION

The SGAA had much different hardware needs. They planned to support many more users performing more complex functions than McKeon & Jeffries. They wanted to run a high-end database on the server that could support several hundred users, at times with very heavy usage. The SGAA decided on a Sun SPARC 20 as its server because of its scalability and power. They purchased 96MB of RAM and an 8GB RAID hard drive system. This system would give the SGAA and its users a high level of reliability and speed and a wide variety of software choices. Most intranet and Internet software is available for Sun machines. The SGAA spent just under $35,000 for its server.

Expansion Costs

Most server platforms have numerous expansion capabilities. All accept additional memory and disk space, and some take additional processors. With most platforms, upgrades are cost-effective ways to increase the server's performance. For some servers, the best way to increase performance is to replace the whole server itself. In addition to significant replacement costs, installing a new platform requires downtime that should be factored into the cost.

The Costs of Downtime

When an intranet is a pilot project with few users, a downed server won't create too much turmoil among those selected users. However, when an entire organization depends on the information and resources available on the intranet, downtime has a significant cost. High-reliability features are a small price to pay for a robust, dependable server. Converting from basic disk storage to basic RAID storage to protect against disk failures should cost no more than about 25 cents per megabyte. For example, 4GB of disk storage might cost $2,000, while 4GB of RAID storage would cost about $3,000. The difference is a small price to pay for protection against drive failure and data loss.

An often-overlooked cause of server failure is overheating problems that can show up just about anywhere and can be challenging to solve. Overheating can also affect your server's performance. Many processors lose 20 to 30 percent of performance with just a 20-degree temperature increase. Most systems will support additional cooling devices at a cost of $25 to $50. Adding an extra power supply or upgrading to a load-sharing power supply is another modest cost in the $200 to $400 range.

I recommend adding cooling features when setting up the server, because they will cover the majority of hardware-based system failures at a price much lower than the toll attached to a server failure.

The Reality of Costs: Return on Investment

We all know of projects that should have succeeded, could have succeeded, and might have succeeded but were bogged down with server problems. Without a well-planned server at the core of your intranet, any return on investment will be much harder to realize. You should plan on spending a lot of time choosing and setting up your server hardware, and you should plan on it being a significant cost. You will find it much less expensive to plan carefully and purchase a server that will perform reliably and will be scaleable to support all the users you anticipate for quite some time. Realize that even the cheapest server hardware will probably cost you more than $5,000. Some businesses or organizations might spend six figures.

Summary

In the future, main server platforms will begin to share more similar features than they currently do. At this time, I recommend choosing a server platform to support all your organization's resources and make sure the server has plenty of expansion capability.

The payback of pre-implementation planning is enormous. The bottom line should be clear. Just as most firms wouldn't hire a second-rate CEO to lead the company, intranet administrators shouldn't "hire" a weak server foundation to support the organization's intranet.

Servers: Operating Systems

7

by Mike Mazan

IN THIS CHAPTER

- How important is the operating system decision? **82**
- Examining factors in operating system decisions **83**
- Market share: who uses what? **89**

The server operating system is the "middleware" of the server system. In many cases, the choice of hardware drives the choice of operating system, but some servers allow for many choices. This chapter explores popular operating systems and what factors to consider when choosing an operating system.

How Important Is the Operating System Decision?

The operating system, as the middleware of the server system, is the program or interface between the actual hardware and the application programs. Because the operating system is a key component of the server solution, selecting one wisely is important, and there are several important considerations. The operating system comprises all the tools that allow the server to be configured, maintained, and backed up, as well as the interface that allows the hardware to connect to the intranet. In many cases, the choices are minimized when the hardware has been selected. Other server hardware requires a decision to be made on the operating system. For example, if your server machine is a Sun computer, you likely will be forced to use Solaris, Sun's version of UNIX. On the other hand, if your server is a Pentium-based machine, you have many options from which to choose. In these cases, a well-selected operating system can be almost transparent to the operation of the server.

When deciding which operating system will run on your server, first turn to your hardware. Some hardware runs only with specific operating systems, as specified in Table 7.1. For example, SPARC-based or Macintosh server hardware has specific operating systems written by the hardware manufacturer. In some ways, these operating systems are a great choice, because they are designed, engineered, and supported specifically for the hardware selected. This eliminates many issues relating to drivers when installing and configuring the server. On the other hand, if you choose Intel-based server hardware, it is refreshing to know that you can select from several operating systems. However, the fact that you can use anything from a 386-based machine to an SGI minicomputer as your server makes the server hardware and software choice more difficult.

Table 7.1. Some hardware limits your choice of operating systems, whereas other hardware does not.

Operating System	Pentium	Macintosh	SUN	DEC
Windows NT	■			
Windows 3.1	■			
Windows 95	■			
Solaris	■		■	
UNIX	■	■	■	■

Operating System	Pentium	Macintosh	SUN	DEC
Linux	■	■		
MacOS		■		
SUN OS			■	

One of the important factors to consider is the level of technical competency of the systems administrator or whoever will be tending to the hardware and software needs of your intranet. If your resident techie is a master at troubleshooting MacOS or Windows problems but has never touched a UNIX box, you should consider using a MacOS or Windows version as the operating system for your server. On the other hand, if you have a UNIX specialist on staff, you can get away with a slower server running a version of UNIX, which is much faster than Windows or Mac.

Your operating system choice also is important for the future of your intranet. If you decide later that your intranet is too large to run on your Windows 95 or MacOS machine, it could be tough to translate some of your custom applications to a UNIX machine.

Examining Factors in Operating System Decisions

Many veteran intranet server installers swear by UNIX. It is available for just about all types of servers and in many flavors. UNIX has a long history with the Internet, as much of the Internet was first developed and run on UNIX servers. To this day, the majority of servers on the Internet are UNIX-based. UNIX generally includes TCP/IP as an integral part of the operating system. It also can provide significant performance on less powerful server equipment. Many UNIX systems can run on a small Intel-based 486 server, but UNIX also has the flexibility to run on almost every hardware platform.

A key to UNIX's success in the Internet world is that there are so many knowledgeable UNIX professionals. Some good places to find UNIX administrators (usually) are in Usenet newsgroups. For example, in Washington, D.C., there is a proliferation of them lurking on dc.jobs.

Although UNIX is still the leader in Web sites on the Internet, newer revisions of existing operating systems such as MacOS and Windows NT are quite robust for many sites and deserve a good look. Also, the base of knowledgeable staff available for these newer operating systems is continually growing.

The following sections help you narrow your decisions when it comes to choosing an operating system for your intranet.

Solaris

Solaris was developed by Sun Microsystems as a more open option of SunOS for its SPARC-based servers and workstations. Sun machines are popular, powerful, and expensive computers built for serving information to many PCs or dumb terminals. Their processors are RISC-based and can perform several tasks simultaneously, as shown in Figure 7.1. Many universities and large corporations use Sun machines to serve information on their networks.

FIGURE 7.1.
Solaris's OpenWindows is a graphical interface for Sun's brand of UNIX.

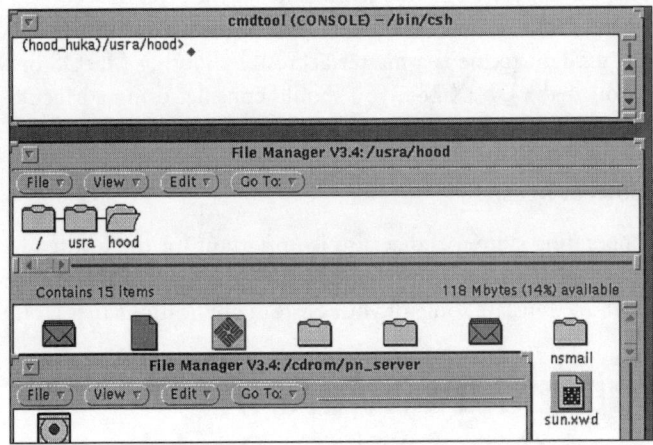

Currently, Solaris has the largest share of the Internet market, mostly because Solaris is the most popular version of UNIX, and Sun has aggressively marketed Internet solutions. Sun spun off the group that developed the operating system into a separate group, Sunsoft. Sunsoft also has ported Solaris into the Intel environment, but with little sales success, mainly because it is difficult and confusing to set up and maintain. It is rare that you will see a 486 machine running Solaris except as an administration tool for a Sun machine. The biggest audience for this operating system is a large corporation or organization that plans on heavy traffic on the intranet. Some of the most poplar sites on the Internet reside on Sun servers. Unless you have an enormous number of users performing complicated tasks constantly, you shouldn't have any trouble with your server slowing down. Another potential audience for Solaris-based servers is companies and organizations that already use Sun machines to run a database or some other network application. For example, if your Oracle database already is running on a SPARC-20, it may be a trivial matter to put a Web server on the machine and use that as your server.

SCO UNIX and BSD/OS

SCO UNIX and BSD/OS are the two most popular commercially available UNIX versions for the Intel platform. The Santa Cruz Operation's SCO UNIX started as a Xenix operating system and was developed and upgraded to the current release called OpenDesktop and OpenServer. These latest releases have graphical user interfaces that prove more friendly than the traditional character-based UNIX operating systems. But don't despair; they are still rooted in the UNIX core and still support character-based commands and use, as shown in Figure 7.2. There are many potential users of these operating systems, from the smallest intranet to the most advanced. The typical user is the organization that wants to make the most of its hardware dollars. A bare-bones UNIX will run well on an Intel 386 machine, and you will be surprised at the performance. If your plan is to run a simple Web server and mail for fewer than 20 users, you should have no problem with the performance of a 386, assuming you have at least 12 to 16MB of RAM.

FIGURE 7.2.
There are many graphical variants of UNIX, but the base of UNIX is still the character-based environment.

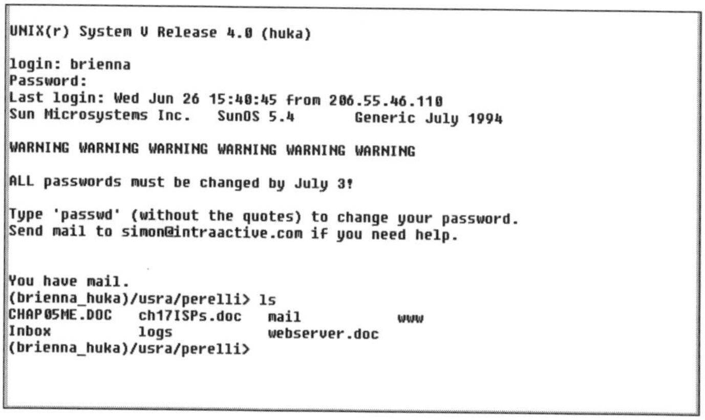

```
UNIX(r) System V Release 4.0 (huka)

login: brienna
Password:
Last login: Wed Jun 26 15:40:45 from 206.55.46.110
Sun Microsystems Inc.    SunOS 5.4         Generic July 1994

WARNING WARNING WARNING WARNING WARNING WARNING

ALL passwords must be changed by July 3!

Type 'passwd' (without the quotes) to change your password.
Send mail to simon@intraactive.com if you need help.


You have mail.
(brienna_huka)/usra/perelli> ls
CHAP05ME.DOC     ch17ISPs.doc    mail              www
Inbox            logs            webserver.doc
(brienna_huka)/usra/perelli>
```

By the same token, if you have a very busy intranet site serving mail to 100 or more users but don't want to bear the added expense of the hardware, software, and administration of using a Sun or SGI minicomputer, you can squeeze more performance out of a Pentium machine running UNIX than one running Windows 95 or Windows NT. Some intranet developers might want to use UNIX because it provides users with some of the Internet features not available with Windows and MacOS servers. Finger, plan, and vacation mail are standard UNIX features you won't see with many operating systems. Also, UNIX allows for users to have a shell account on the server and server space. If you want your mail to reside on the server and users to read it directly from there, UNIX is the only way to go.

Another nice thing about UNIX is that it is the only operating system that can run on almost any computer. Say you build your intranet on a 386, need to expand to a 486 or Pentium the following year, need to upgrade to a DEC Alpha to handle the traffic the next year, and then possibly a SPARC Ultra. You will have no problem picking the site off one machine and plunking it down on the next.

BSD/OS has seen increasing growth since releasing its product in 1993. BSD, developed by Berkeley Software Design, is based on variations made to the UNIX operating system by students and staff at the University of California. The variations are mostly to the user shell and some functionality; you probably won't notice the difference between versions of UNIX unless you are a serious programmer or UNIX specialist. BSD has targeted the Internet and intranet markets and has a product that is now used to support some of the largest and most popular Web sites on the Internet, such as Adobe and Intel. BSD also has released some gateways to allow its servers to interact easily with sites running Novell Netware.

Linux

Linux, shown in Figure 7.3, started in early 1991 as a project by Linus Torvalds, a student in Finland, to test the capabilities of the Intel 386 architecture. By the end of that year the operating system was being distributed free on the Internet and is still free today. To find out where to get various versions of Linux, see http://www.linux.org. It has many proponents, including a large technical user base, but it suffers from a lack of commercial backing, mostly because it is free. Some companies are starting to get into the business of packaging various versions of Linux and distributing it free with books and installation guides.

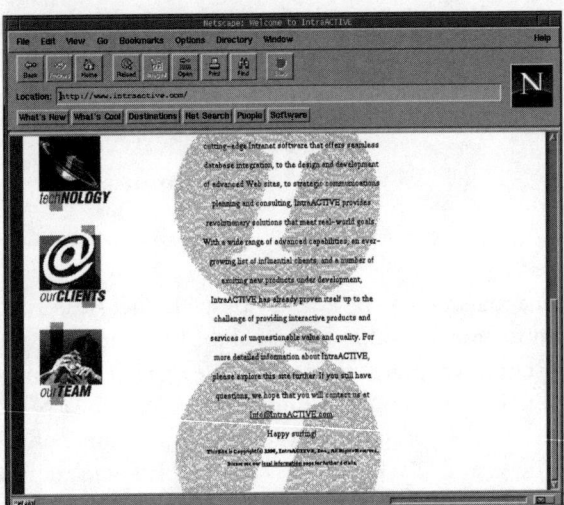

FIGURE 7.3.

Linux is a shareware UNIX platform built especially for Intel-based machines.

Most of Linux's success is due to its amazing flexibility. Users can modify and customize almost anything in Linux. Imagine being able to design your own operating system and customize it so it is perfect for your needs—this is Linux. If you can learn how, you can do almost anything with Linux. If you are looking to put a site online with little cost and have staff knowledgeable in Linux, it might be the perfect answer.

Windows NT

Windows NT, shown in Figure 7.4, has been in development since the late 1980s, when Microsoft decided that the then-recent release of OS/2 wouldn't cut it as the operating system of the 1990s because of its lack of portability: OS/2 was written specifically for the Intel architecture. Microsoft hired a former DEC engineer and started on the road to an object-oriented, portable operating system.

FIGURE 7.4.

Windows NT 4.0 brings Windows 95's easy-to-use interface to NT.

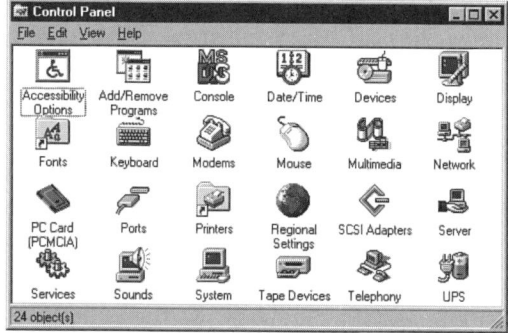

In its early releases, Windows NT didn't live up to Microsoft's marketing hype as the be-all, end-all operating system, but its latest release has been regarded as stable and robust. It also has begun to receive media and market attention. In the past, Windows NT was available only for servers based on the Intel architecture, but with the latest release, Windows NT has been ported to different server architectures, such as the Alpha, which was developed by DEC. This gives the user who wants to use Windows NT as the operating system more hardware choices. This recent attention has moved Windows NT toward the top of the operating system ladder. As its market share has grown, most system manufacturers now provide Windows NT drivers for their products, and a large base of application developers are porting their products to Windows NT.

Like the UNIX operating system, Windows NT breaks its modules down into two modes: kernel and user. This separation allows the operating system to be more stable, as a module or program running in the user mode is not likely to crash the whole system.

Looking toward the future, Microsoft has released Windows NT 4.0, which includes additional tools that specifically benefit its use as an intranet server operating system, such as IIS 2.0 with NT Server. Time will tell if those tools are based on Microsoft's marketing or if they will actually be useful tools.

Windows NT is likely a good fit in medium to large organizations that plan to have medium to large intranets. These organizations may not be interested in having a UNIX specialist on staff to take care of a single machine. Many companies use Windows NT now as a server for their LAN or WAN. If you already have a Windows NT administrator on staff, it certainly makes sense to use NT as the operating system for your intranet.

OS/2

OS/2 began with high expectations. In 1987 IBM and Microsoft released it to become the successor to MS-DOS. Within a few years, Microsoft had pulled out of the jointly developed product, and IBM took over all development and marketing. In the early 1990s, OS/2 had developed into a fair platform for client-server computing, and some application developers started using some OS/2 features to gain a foothold in the growing client-server market. In its latest release, OS/2 Warp, IBM has delivered a solid operating system with many features, such as networking and name service built in. Although OS/2 Warp hasn't gained market penetration, it remains a strong robust operating system. The only folks likely to use OS/2 are companies or organizations that are already using it on their LANs or WANs.

MacOS

In the mid-1980s, Apple developed a new operating system focused on its ease of use: MacOS. To this day, arguably, it offers users the easiest interface of all operating systems. MacOS, shown in Figure 7.5, is the second most-used operating system (as discussed in the section "Market Share: Who Uses What?"). As a Web server, MacOS provides some neat features, including easily configured TCP/IP and Web administration tools. The MacOS also has a strong knowledgeable user base. The main reluctance in using MacOS as an intranet server operating system is in its capacity. As a server, it doesn't efficiently handle more than 50 or so simultaneous users. However, if you are starting with a small pilot in an organization that already has strong MacOS knowledge, MacOS is a good choice.

FIGURE 7.5.

The MacOS has a strong, knowledgeable user base.

Other Operating Systems

There are other operating systems that provide the necessary middleware for supporting an intranet server. Most of these choices, however, are good matches only if your environment is specific to their servers. For example, Novell has released some Web server solutions that allow for supporting a Web site on Novell NetWare. This could be a match for a company with a large investment in Novell servers and Novell's underlying network protocol, IPX.

Other choices might be based on the knowledge factor or existing equipment, as discussed in the previous sections. Such choices might include AIX, IBM's UNIX variant, which runs on IBM's RS/6000 line of servers, or HP/UX, Hewlett-Packard's UNIX variant, which runs on Hewlett-Packard's HP9000 line of servers.

Market Share: Who Uses What?

For years, Internet servers have been running UNIX almost exclusively. Again, this is because it is available for just about every type of hardware and there is a large base of knowledgeable UNIX administrators, installers, and programmers—more so than any other operating system. In addition, UNIX is the basis of the beginnings of the Internet.

However, recently, while the cost of technology has been continually decreasing, there has been a consistent increase in the use of easy-to-use graphics-based operating systems. These are highlighted by MacOS and Windows NT, which have been growing faster than any other operating system but still lag far behind Solaris and UNIX. The capabilities of these newer operating systems have been growing to the point that the current release of Windows NT can handle the same loads that were previously only handled under UNIX. However, as you can see in Figure 7.6, Sun Solaris has by far the largest market of Internet servers. Over the next few years, expect to see the difference between the top three or four operating systems narrow as features and benefits become similar among the operating systems and in-house knowledge becomes a larger factor in selecting the operating system.

FIGURE 7.6.

Operating system market share according to a 1995 Internet site survey.

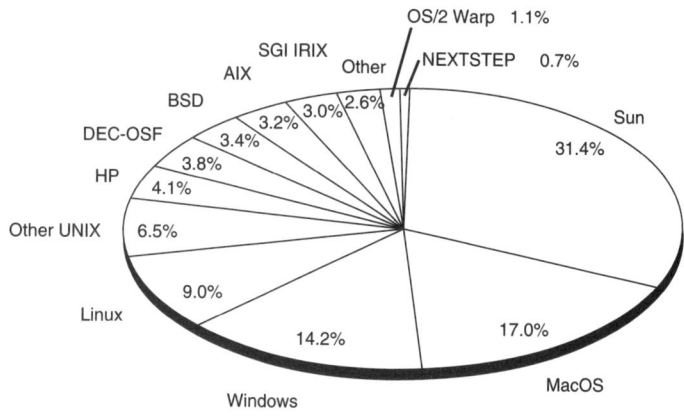

This Internet site survey was created by Jim Fetters of Arizona State University and administered between April and August 1995; it included more than 600 responses. The 1996 version of this survey currently is underway and should be available at http://www.mirai.com by the time this book is published.

MCKEON & JEFFRIES

Choosing an operating system for its intranet was a fairly easy task for McKeon & Jeffries. Their systems administrator was very familiar with Windows NT, and the accounting firm was using Windows NT to serve files and the database.

M&J managers believed that, with 150 users, it was unlikely that they would have more traffic than a Pentium-based machine running NT could handle, and if it does increase, they plan to upgrade to a multiprocessor Pentium or a DEC Alpha. Also, because their database was already running on an NT machine, it would be less difficult to create a gateway from the intranet to the database.

THE SPORTING GOODS AND APPAREL ASSOCIATION

The SGAA had less of a choice in the matter. Because SGAA decided on the Sun SPARC-20 as the server for its intranet, Solaris was the only choice. The association hired a consultant to help its manager of information services install the machine and customize it, as well as teach the staff the basics of UNIX administration.

Of course, by using a UNIX-based operating system, the SGAA had a wide range of choices for individual applications to run on its system, including freeware and shareware.

Summary

In most cases, the server hardware selected for a system drives the choice of operating system. So, with your hardware in place, begin narrowing your operating system choice based on that hardware and the relevant knowledge base of your current staff; but remember, sometimes this choice should be based on the functionality of the operating system.

Server Software

8

by Eric Ashman

IN THIS CHAPTER

- Commercial Web servers **93**
- Freeware Web servers **99**
- Mail servers **102**
- News servers **104**
- Other software options **105**

Part II

To create a fully functioning intranet, you must determine what kind of server software packages to install on your main platform. Besides choosing a Web server package, you should consider other server software, such as software that will provide your intranet with e-mail and possibly audio. This chapter discusses the types of server software available and the features of each package. You don't have to incorporate all the features covered here; just as not every person needs a graphics program or a telecommunications package on their personal computer, not every organization needs every available server feature.

The most important software running on your intranet is the Web server software. A Web server answers requests for Web documents. For example, if you want to access a requested document on IntraActive's server at http://www.intraactive.com, the server answers your request—assuming it is in the right directory and the permissions are configured. In other words, you define what documents you want to make available by the commands you give. In UNIX, a Web server runs in the background, along with the other server processes like FTP and mail.

All Web servers do the same thing: They listen to requests and process them. Like any piece of technology—CD players, portable cassette players, VCRs, cellular telephones—the manufacturer's reputation and the available features will drive your purchase choice. All Web servers will send out the requested documents, but the difference in Web servers is noted in their features: How easy is it to install and configure? How fast can it send out pages? Is it secure, and when it sends back requests, can it do so in a secure manner?

Keep the following features in mind when choosing your Web server on the basis of the functionality you want to have with your intranet:

- Speed: How many users will be accessing files at the same time? And when they access those files, how much processing does the server need to do? For example, if 10 people are accessing one simple HTML file with no images at the same time, this is roughly equivalent to two people accessing an HTML file with five images, which is roughly equivalent to one user accessing a database through the Web server. A Web server such as Oracle WebServer 2.0 will not serve static HTML files and images as fast as the National Center for Supercomputing Applications (NCSA) or Apache server but will provide much swifter access to a database.

- Setup and maintenance: Keeping your Web server up and running at all times will no doubt be important to the success of your intranet. It might be worth a little extra money or even a little less speed to have a Web server that has an easy-to-understand interface, like O'Reilly's WebSite or the Netscape server.

- Keeping track of users: Depending on what kind of intranet you are running, it might be important to know where your users are going, who's logging on, and how long they're staying. Or, it might not matter at all. Authentication is also an issue. Do you need a complex and sophisticated authentication system, or is a simple user ID and password enough?

- Security: Does your intranet need to encrypt transmissions between the server and the user? Or do you need to prohibit access by any particular user or group? Some Web servers, like the Oracle server, allow for complex security procedures, and some are very basic.
- Other features: You may want to talk to a database; you may want to run Windows applications from your server; you may want a powerful search engine included. Of course, there is also the matter of cost. And obviously, you'll need to get a server that can run on your intranet's platform.

Commercial Web Servers

The capability of Web server software to make fast and efficient transactions should be your main concern when shopping for software. Each time one of your users requests a page, the server will have to respond to that request—the faster the better. Each transaction could consist of many different server actions. For instance, if a Web page has several images or an embedded CGI script, the server would have to perform a separate function for each of those elements each time a user requested that page. In essence, your Web server is acting as a fulfillment center for your intranet. Every time you click an icon or type in a URL, the Web server is assembling all the pieces of that page and sending them to the user. For basic HTML, this can be done quickly and easily by almost any Web server. However, if the Web server needs to query a database or perform other dynamic functions, it must be more powerful. For example, if the Web server has to query an authentication table and hunt through hundreds of usernames and passwords for every page it returns, it must be more powerful in order to serve your pages quickly and efficiently.

It also is important to consider how well the package works with other packages, as you want to avoid conflicts and downtime at all costs. Remember that your intranet's functions will depend on the server software's reliability. When choosing software, keep in mind the method by which you will install the server software: It should be simple and quick. While getting your server up and running, you'll want as few headaches as possible so that you can focus on selecting the other types of software needed for your intranet.

Your Web publishing needs should be another criteria for selecting a Web server package. As the main hub of your intranet, the Web server should be easy to administer, well-supported, highly effective, and flexible enough to grow with your intranet. There are Web server packages with all kinds of administration tools. Some of the most basic Web server packages are administered by configuration files only, meaning the administrator must be technically knowledgeable and be able to troubleshoot configuration problems.

Other packages come with configuration tools. For example, many Microsoft Windows 95 and Windows NT Web server packages have a separate Windows application that allows administrators to set up and make changes to the Web server options. Some of these are very easy to use; however, it must be considered that with these types of servers, the administrator must have the tool on the machine from which he or she would administer. This makes it difficult for administrators to make updates or changes to the Web server from a remote location, such as home or on the Web. Yet another, and possibly the most popular administration interface, is as a Web page itself. Most new servers' configuration scripts are written so that users from any location can use a simple Web browser to update and modify the Web server configuration. However, this particular method can sometimes be less than reliable. Along the analogy of a doctor healing him or herself, if your Web server is having problems, it might be difficult to use the Web server itself to troubleshoot and reconfigure. The Web server package should be supplemented with comprehensive printed documentation and contact phone numbers. For an excellent online reference of Web server software, visit WebCompare's Server Features Comparison page at http://www.webcompare.com/server-main.html.

Although the process of installing Web server software is more technical than installing a word processing or drawing program, you don't have to be a computer whiz to do it. Keep the manual that came with your package close by. (Each Web server software package has its own installation method, so I haven't included step-by-step instructions.) The following sections review the advantages and potential disadvantages of some popular server software packages.

Netscape Enterprise Server for UNIX and Windows NT

If securing the information on your intranet is of primary importance to you, you'll want a server software package that offers top-notch security features. The Netscape Enterprise Web server software for UNIX and Windows NT won't let you down. It is advantageous to intranet builders because it allows for encrypted transmissions both internally and externally. The encryption key is especially useful if you have secure information on the corporate local area network (LAN). This software also supports the Java environment. To read specific Netscape Enterprise product description information, visit this site:

http://home.netscape.com/comprod/server_central/product/enterprise/index.html

When installing the Netscape Enterprise Server, configure and administer your machine using the Netscape Navigator browser. You might find that this method is an advantage for you, as you're likely to be familiar with the Netscape Navigator browser. The Web-based interface includes remote maintenance features and real-time performance measurement tools; it also allows you to set up an automatic directory tree, which means that you can choose a recursive document route anywhere on your machine. The user interface is forms-based and very simple to use.

The Netscape Enterprise Server, shown in Figure 8.1, is rich with features. It allows users to serve several different Web sites using the same server on the same machine. It uses the standard NCSA log format. It can measure performance, tell you what kind of browser was used and where the user came from, and track individual users as they maneuver through the site. It has built-in image maps (NCSA) and supports the Windows CGI interface.

FIGURE 8.1.
When installing the Netscape Enterprise Server, you are greeted with this window.

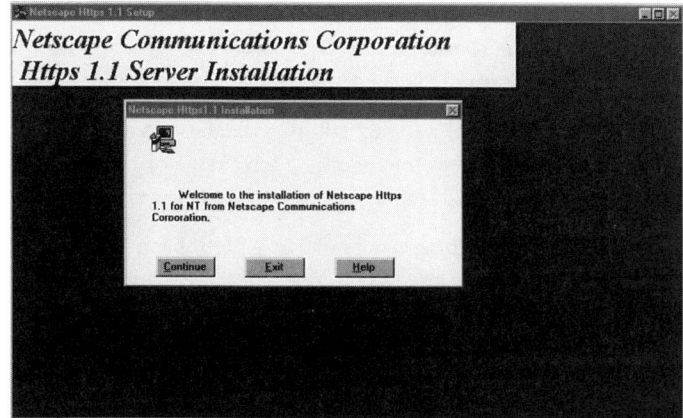

The Enterprise Server also has relatively secure authentication. You can prohibit entire realms of the Internet from accessing the site, or you can prohibit specific individuals. You can require a password on the individual level and even show different individuals different parts of static Web pages. You can configure groups of users so that you can provide different levels of access to a whole group instead of an individual. The server supports SSL (Secure Sockets Layer), versions 2 and 3, but does not support S-HTTP.

The server also comes with a search engine and has a direct link to some database protocols. However, Netscape will not provide the source code for the server, so you are limited by the level to which it allows you to customize. This commercial server is one of the most expensive available today.

Oracle

The Oracle server is much like the Netscape server in that it is relatively easy to install and has a browser interface, which means that after you install it, you can configure your server using a Web browser. Instead of relying on arcane configurations, Oracle's configuration site already is set up. However, I've found that this built-in configuration site isn't always stable; it's actually more stable and safe to configure the server myself by editing the configuration files with a text editor. When I set this server up, it erased my configuration file. This has happened to me three or four times, although it has not been reported as a known problem. Another drawback is that the pre-established configuration does not do a backup, something I always do as part of configuration.

The Oracle server is secure, however. It supports a secure socket layer key, so when data is transferred between the server and browser, it can be encrypted. The Oracle Web Server 2.0 currently supports SSL version 2, but not version 3. It does not support S-HTTP. For authentication the Oracle Web Server not only can have individual and group-based password authentication but can match a username and password with a specific IP address or subnet. In this manner, a user attempting to gain access to the site not only must have the correct username and password but must be accessing the site from a specific computer or group of computers. This feature unique to the Oracle Web server provides an additional layer of security. Users also can be authenticated via the Oracle7 database.

Oracle allows the user to natively talk to a database so Web server requests can be queried by the database. This allows Oracle to take advantage of the power and flexibility of a database, whereas most servers just "serve" HTML pages, images, and applications.

For example, if I want to serve a book on a Web, I can take each page and turn it into a Web page. I can do this using any Web server. However, assume I want to create a site using some data that remains constant and some that is changing, such as keeping an inventory online. The spec sheets and product information would stay static, but the number of products I had on hand would change; in other words, the number of products on hand would relate to the information about that product. To serve this information on the Web, I would want to use a relational database. Because it is relational, there is no redundancy with the Oracle database.

Currently no other server programs can draw information from a database in this way. Netscape's LiveWire is the next closest software and may develop into a more dynamic application, but currently it is not up to snuff. Certainly, users can always write their own gateways, but Oracle is really the strongest commercially available product. Oracle runs on Solaris and Windows NT but not on Windows 95, and it supports the native Java environment.

The Oracle Web Server, shown in Figure 8.2, currently runs on UNIX or Windows NT. It can serve several sites with the same Web server and the same machine, but each distinct site will leave a larger footprint on your machine than will additional sites with other servers. Oracle logs files using the NCSA common format, but log files cannot be automatically archived. In general, the logging for the Oracle Web Server is not as good as with other Web servers; you can't tell what kind of Web browser is accessing the site, you cannot track individual users, it does not report referrer logs, and there are no performance measurement logs at all. However, using PL/SQL, pages that are dynamically generated from the database can be logged with a great deal of detail. Time, date, user ID, and reference page can all be captured and logged into the database, where very sophisticated statistical information can be generated. This will take some fairly advanced programming, but if you're willing to spend the time, you can actually get much better and more concise logs using the Oracle database.

FIGURE 8.2.

The Oracle server configuration is Web-based.

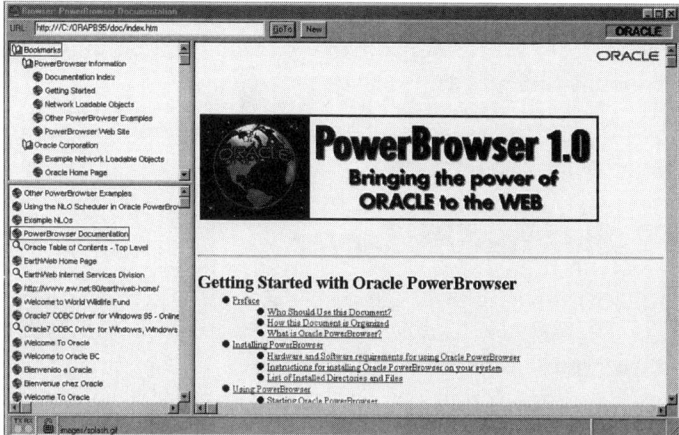

This is also a very expensive commercial server and is not quite as far along for more traditional Web service than are some others. However, the database support is phenomenal. The database itself is also very expensive. However, organizations that are already running an Oracle database and want to serve that information to their intranet, or build a gateway to that database for their users will find that Oracle Web Server is an ideal solution.

You can find an online brochure about the Oracle7 Workgroup Server at `http://www.ksi.co.za/prodinfo/wgs.html`.

Microsoft Internet Information Server for Windows NT

The Internet Information Server (IIS), Microsoft's version of a Web server, is hard to ignore. It can't handle a large amount of traffic because it runs on Windows NT, but it's a stable choice for a small intranet. Organizations that already use Windows NT solutions will find that setting up and running IIS is a relatively easy and functional Web server. The most recent version of IIS—version 2.0 at this writing—only runs on Windows NT Server 4.0, so if you're using an older version of Windows NT, you'll have to use version 1.0 of the Web server.

Currently, the server supports SSL version 2, but not version 3 or S-HTTP. Also, prohibiting users is not as effective or easy as with other Web servers. You can use user and password authentication, and you can set up user groups for security. A security advantage of the IIS is that it allows the administrator to control password length, uniqueness, and how often a password must be changed. This Web server can even disable a password if it is typed incorrectly a specified number of times. This is the only Web server I know of with this feature.

This server does not use an NCSA common log format, which means that programs that have been written specifically to create statistics from log files, such as WWWStat, cannot be used. IIS cannot generate referrer logs, tell what kind of browser the client is using, or track additional users as they maneuver about the site.

The server comes with an administration tool that is now, unfortunately, only available for Windows NT, which means that any administration must be done on an NT machine. Microsoft is currently writing a version for Windows 95.

A home page for users of the Microsoft Internet Information Server is at `http://www.microsoft.com/infoserv`.

O'Reilly WebSite Server

O'Reilly has strategically designed its Web server package for intranets to be run on Windows NT or 95. The package, called WebSite, has access control features that can be implemented with passwords. WebSite allows you to use a CGI program to run programs like Excel and Visual Basic from within a browser. A feature called WebView provides a tree-like palette in which you can map out documents, links, statistics, and icons. WebSite will work with Windows NT or Windows 95 running TCP/IP. Although it probably is the least expensive Web server on the market, it's not secure and not as fast as many Web servers. The new version, due out soon, will be SSL compliant.

WebSite does allow for user authentication and user groups, and can easily prohibit users from any domain name or subnet. However, this is the extent of its security features. It does come with a Windows 95 administration tool that can be used from any Windows 95 machine. It comes with a built-in search engine and image map handling.

WebSite uses standard NCSA log formats and can generate referrer logs as well as report the user's browser. It cannot track individual users.

An excellent home page to get more information on O'Reilly's WebSite is at the following address:

`http://www.ora.com/gnn/bus/ora/ads/ws1-cat.html`

Mac HTTP from Quarterdeck

The Mac HTTP is relatively comparable to O'Reilly's. The fastest machine the Mac HTTP can run on is a PowerMac, which is certainly as fast as a Pentium—but it's not a DEC Alpha. This server is ideal for a small office that uses a Macintosh server, especially if it's an all-Macintosh house. Like O'Reilly's WebSite, it cannot talk to a database.

This low-level server does not create common log formats and cannot generate any information about referrers, browsers, or individual users. In addition, the server can serve only one site at a time.

Mac HTTP does provide authentication by username and password and can prohibit by domain name and subnet. However, you cannot create user groups or hierarchical permissions for directories of documents.

This server has no graphical interface and is relatively difficult to configure. For more information on Mac HTTP, visit www.starnine.com.

Freeware Web Servers

One factor undoubtedly on your mind as you weigh the advantages and disadvantages of various Web server software is cost. You might be surprised to find that many Web server software packages are free. That's right, free; all you have to do is download. You're probably asking, "What's the catch?" In many cases, there is no catch. The reason that many server software packages are free is because the whole business of developing and distributing them is a very new one. The companies that are developing server software are still establishing a competition with each other. Therefore, many of them have decided (especially the ones who already are making lots of money from other products) that it's best not to charge right now. However, things won't be free forever. Server software developers intend to charge for their products in the future, and about 30 percent of the developers already do.

You'll usually find that there's very little technical support available for freeware packages and that some are not very user-friendly. Free packages are frequently written by development teams or university departments (another reason why they're free), who assume that the packages' users will be technically savvy. If you trust your intuition, or that of whoever administers your intranet's Web server, you might find a freeware package adequate for your needs, not to mention cost-effective. If you're hesitant about the quality of a freeware server, testing it first always is an option.

If you plan to take advantage of the free-for-all server software packages, here are two to consider.

HTTPd

HTTPd, offered by NCSA, is a popular freeware package designed by the software development group at the University of Illinois at Urbana-Champaign. It is fast and offers the basics. HTTPd, shown in Figure 8.3, is available only for UNIX-based operating systems. It can serve multiple sites from one server using one machine with very little footprint on your system. Of course, it uses the NCSA common log format and can generate referrer and browser logs.

You can authenticate by user ID and password, and users can be grouped. Specific domain names and IP addresses can be barred from the site. The server is not SSL or S-HTTP compliant.

One of the best features of this Web server is that the source code comes with it. You can make customizations or modifications as you deem necessary and if you possess the skills.

An HTTPd home page is at http://hoohoo.ncsa.uiuc.edu.

FIGURE 8.3.
The HTTPd configuration file.

```
#==============================================================
# NCSA HTTPd (comments, questions to httpd@ncsa.uiuc.edu)
#==============================================================
#
# This is the main server configuration file. It is best to
# leave the directives in this file in the order they are in, or
# things may not go the way you'd like. See URL http://hoohoo.ncsa.uiuc.edu/
# for instructions.
# Do NOT simply read the instructions in here without understanding
# what they do, if you are unsure consult the online docs. You have been
# warned.
# Thanks to A. P. Harris for some of the organization and explanations
# contained here-in.
#
#
#==============================================================
# Server Operation
#--------------------------------------------------------------
# ServerType is either inetd, or standalone.
# Set to 'inetd' to run from inetd, or 'standalone', to run as a daemon.
# Default: standalone
```

Apache

Apache is based on NCSA's HTTPd but claims to have fewer bugs. In fact, the name Apache comes from the fact that it is a series of patches incorporated onto the NCSA server—hence, "a patchy server." This is also the only server available for the OS/2 operating system. Apache offers multiple methods from which to customize error messages and the capability to customize other key needs, such as text responses and local and external URL redirection. Like HTTPd, it requires that you understand how to configure it with your operating system. Apache will soon introduce a commercial version, which should have SSLs.

Apache supports standard NCSA log formats, can create referrer and browser logs, and can track users. It allows for authentication based on user ID and password, and can prohibit access from specific domain names and IP addresses. It is one of the fastest servers available but must be set up and maintained by editing the configuration files. There is no graphical interface.

For more information Apache, visit `http://www.apache.org`.

Freeware Web server packages often provide all you need to develop a smoothly functioning hub for your intranet; so consider these when making your choice. Also, look at what packages other intranets have selected, and query their administrators about their experience. Table 8.1 offers information about the Web server packages of selected companies.

Server Software
Chapter 8

Table 8.1. A comparison of what various Web servers offer users.

	Apache	Mac HTTP	Microsoft IIS	NCSA	Netscape Enterprise	Netscape FastTrack	WebSite
Operating system(s)	Most UNIX, OS/2	MacOS	Windows NT (Intel, MIPS)	UNIX	UNIX, Windows NT, Solaris	UNIX, Windows NT, Solaris	Windows NT (Intel)
Can serve multiple domains	■	■	■	■	■	■	■
CERN/ NCSA common log	■			■	■	■	■
Can generate referrer logs	■			■	■	■	■
Built-in image map handling	■		■	■	■	■	■
Supports authentication	■		■	■	■	■	■
Prohibits by domain name	■	■		■	■	■	■
Supports SSL			■		■	■	
Web-based setup			■	■	■	■	■
Web-based maintenance			■		■	■	■
Remote maintenance	■		■		■	■	■
Includes full source code	■			■			
Search engine		Apple search		Internal NCSA and WAIS support			Built in, with indexer

MCKEON & JEFFRIES

For M&J, the Web server choice was an obvious one. The firm needed limited security and limited authentication, it wasn't worried about user logs, and it could only work with a Windows NT solution. For the cost, O'Reilly's WebSite was the perfect answer. It allowed quick and easy setup, and it came with a Windows 95 administration tool that allowed the system administrator to maintain the site from any location. Setting up the Web server took a matter of minutes, and maintaining it just a few minutes a week.

THE SPORTING GOODS AND APPAREL ASSOCIATION

The SGAA's choice was also obvious, but for different reasons. It needed a server that could talk fluidly and quickly with a powerful backend database. It also needed very complex security and authentication solutions. The plan was to give different users the ability to see different areas of the site, determined by their user ID. The Oracle Web server, though expensive, was the perfect option. Setup and configuration was a long, complicated process mostly performed by its consultants. However, maintenance of the site thereafter was done using Oracle's Web-based maintenance tool.

Mail Servers

In addition to Web server software, you'll also want mail server software. Your intranet would be severely limited without it, as electronic mail is such an integral part of the Internet and intranets. Before you choose a mail server, do your homework; you'll find notable differences in the installation processes and features of various mail server programs.

If you have a UNIX system, the mail server Sendmail probably was pre-installed on your machine. Sendmail, a popular, free (for UNIX users), and powerful software program is extremely complex: The configurations are endless. Sendmail uses SMTP (simple mail transfer protocol) and is considered one of the most difficult UNIX utilities to learn. However, many of the functions you'll need, such as mail forwarding, are already configured for you. If you want to customize Sendmail, get a good manual, because not only is it hard to configure, but there is a dearth of experts and consultants to advise users. The O'Reilly company offers one in its Nutshell series; to order the book, visit http://www.ora.com/www/item/sendmail.html.

If Sendmail is not your first choice, talk to your operating system vendor about other packages available for your platform. There may be less powerful but easier-to-configure mail server software packages available specifically for your machine. As far as UNIX is concerned, I've heard rumors that other mail server software is available, but I must confess I don't know anyone who uses anything other than Sendmail.

Before I look at some of the other mail server software programs available, I'll explore how a mail server communicates with its clients. When a user sends a message, a mail server accepts the message and requests to put the mail in someone's mailbox. If the user to whom the message is addressed does not have an account, the server will tell the machine sending mail to return the mail. This procedure is performed by one of two protocols: SMTP or POP (Post Office Protocol). The protocol used depends on the mail server package. Sendmail uses SMTP, but other packages, some of which I'll look at here, use POP. Because POP is basically the protocol that delivers mail on your system, whereas SMTP is what delivers the mail across the Web, users can utilize SMTP without POP, but they cannot use POP without SMTP. Think of SMTP as the central distribution point and POP as the local carrier. Sendmail basically delivers mail as far as the individual machine and POP delivers it to the individual user.

When looking at the various mail server packages, pay attention to the features that differentiate them. First, consider the ease with which you can install and configure a particular package. Mail servers are notorious for being cryptic and difficult to install. Second, check each mail package's capability to control the individual parameters of the users. If some of the users of your intranet are not too technical, you might want to have a preferences panel on the mail program that will allow them to configure their options. Central configuration files can help tailor an "average user's" configuration. Finally, as always, make sure that your mail server package comes with manuals and technical support contacts. A few mail server software programs and their main features follow.

Netscape MailServer 2.0

Netscape's mail server is easily configured through the Netscape browser interface but also can be used with several server programs, as it is completely distinct from any Web server. The package is designed to appeal to intranet administrators whose primary concern is security. The encryption tool, S/KEY, prevents network eavesdropping. Netscape's MailServer is a good choice for any organization transmitting a heavy flow of mail. For more information, see the following Web site:

http://home.netscape.com/comprod/server_central/product/mail/index.html

NTMAIL

NTMAIL is a package of programs and services designed specifically for Microsoft's Windows NT—both the server and the workstation. Both SMTP and POP3 (Post Office Protocol version 3) are offered. NTMAIL is a stable mail server. It comes standard with the NT server as well as an interface tool. It seems to have excellent technical support. A home page is at http://www.mortimer.com/ntmail/index.htm.

SLmail

Like many mail servers, Seattle Lab's SLmail handles mail though the SMTP and POP3 protocols. For intranet e-mail, all that is needed is a functioning LAN that uses the TCP/IP network protocol. For Internet e-mail, you need an Internet connection. SLmail is a good choice for a small to medium mail user base. It has no security layer. For more information, visit `http://www.seattlelab.com`. Remember, servers generally all perform the same basic functions, so carefully consider their features and interface capabilities. Making a careful choice about mail server software will keep your mail systems running smoothly. To talk to people who have had experience with a particular mail server package, look for a Usenet newsgroup such as `comp.mail.misc` and post a query.

News Servers

Usenet—the Internet news forum—is a completely distributed system that never dies. Just as a Web server serves up information and resources from the Web, Usenet distributes and provides an orderly format for message boards. The protocol used to transmit Usenet posts is Network News Transport Protocol (NNTP), and a news server spools newsgroups off the Internet. News servers talk to each other and distribute and update messages by replicating themselves across newsgroups; when one news server gets a new post to a group, every other news server with that group makes a copy of it. News servers are especially useful in filtering redundant messages so they aren't distributed more than once. For example, a team of technical support users may have a discussion of a particular problem, possibly finding a solution. Later, that discussion can be used by others who have encountered the same problem, thus saving them time.

If you want to provide your intranet's users with access to particular Usenet groups or create internal newsgroups, you should select and install a news server. Your own news server will give you more control over user access to newsgroups and a faster connection to the newsgroups to which you are subscribed. The news server controls newsgroups subscribers and delivers articles to other machines. A news reader, which is connected to the server, allows users to read and post news. Many browsers, such as Netscape Navigator, have news reading options. But if you have detailed configurations for your intranet's news access, you should look into installing a news reader as a supplement to a news server.

Newsgroups often are a worthwhile addition to your intranet, but you'll have to decide the way in which to provide them. If you decide to install your own news server, you can establish internal newsgroups for your intranet. Internal newsgroups are composed of postings only from members of your intranet and are accessible only to users of your intranet, whereas external newsgroups from Usenet are composed of Internet users from around the globe. Both internal and external newsgroups are great tools for instigating communication about key internal issues and for creating project workgroups, sales discussions, and online customer support. Another benefit of having your own news server is that you can set up intracorporate newsgroup discussion lists. Such an internal list can promote pertinent and relevant organization-related discussions among all employees who otherwise would not have such a forum.

There are few commercially available newsgroup products, and I don't expect this market to grow in the future. Most of the functions that newsgroups perform now are handled by the Web, in most cases making newsgroups unnecessary. However, if you want reliable messaging without writing your own custom software or purchasing expensive message board software, or if your users are used to the Usenet format, a news server might be the way to go. There are many freeware news servers floating around on the Internet, but the only one we found to be easy to configure and stable was the Netscape News Server.

Netscape News Server, shown in Figure 8.4, is designed especially for intranets, but it handles both Internet and internal newsgroups. It allows intracorporate newsgroups and an SSL technology, which can be used to encrypt newsgroup postings. Another feature provides the means to set user access to particular newsgroups with passwords. These password-protected newsgroups are then available only to subscribed members. For an FAQ about the Netscape News Server, visit the following Web site:

http://home.netscape.com/comprod/server_central/support/faq/news_faq.html

FIGURE 8.4.
The Netscape News Server.

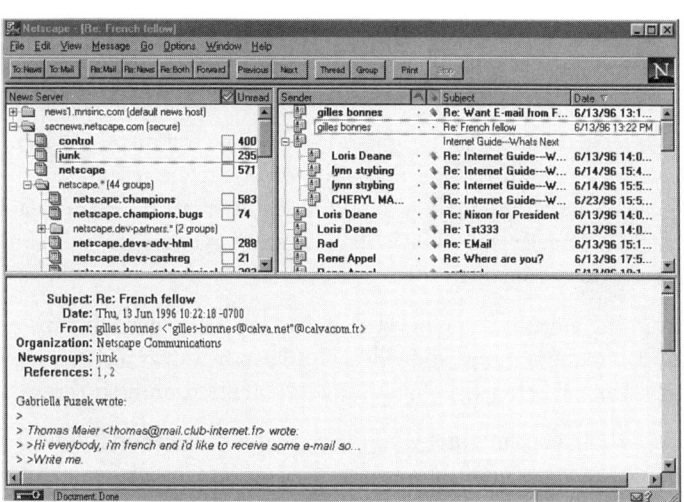

Other Software Options

Besides mail and news software, you'll find a variety of other software packages that might be useful to your intranet. In fact, one of the advantages of building an intranet is that you always have the option to implement new features as they become available. Let's look at some Web utilities, tools, and applications of both the past and present.

Perhaps you've heard about Gopher. Maybe you've noticed that some Web sites use a Gopher as a means for storing information. Do you want to put a Gopher on your intranet? Not anymore. Gopher is an older, text-based system that has been replaced by the Web. I don't know of anyone currently setting up Gopher sites; most people are translating Gopher sites into Web sites. Before the Web, the Gopher was a menu-driven, point-and-click, linear program that provided a means to thumb your way through information. With Gopher, if you had 1,000 documents that you wanted to make available and easily accessible to your readers, users had to click from page to page until they found the document they wanted. Unlike Gopher, the Web has documents connected, so users can jump around instead of tediously clicking from one document to the next. In addition, the Web includes formatting, sounds, pictures, and an expanding host of multimedia options. Gopher-based information is best read on a text Web browser called Lynx. Today, if you find a page that is operating a Gopher, it's likely that you'll also find that the information is in the process of being converted into HTML to be transferred to a Web server.

You've probably also heard about IRC (Internet Relay Chat). It's doubtful that any intranet seriously needs IRC, as it is primarily an entertainment forum in which Internet users worldwide gather for miscellaneous conversation. It's true that a chat environment (ideally) might be useful for meetings or brainstorming sessions, but usually the connection is too slow to allow for spontaneous conversation. As a result, the "chatters" often wind up discussing mechanics of the Internet or problems with their modems or computers rather than the topic around which the session was originally created.

To develop the structured, topic-oriented conversations you'll want for your intranet, consider installing a software package that will allow you to create and play streaming audio. With streaming audio, an audio file is compressed into a small amount of data that can be transferred in real time. The streaming file is about as small as a text file but is ordered so that you listen to it as it arrives at your site.

Streaming video is being developed, but because video contains more information than does audio, it requires more bandwidth. Until bandwidth availability increases, the quality of streaming video will be relatively poor, unless you are running it through a LAN.

Establishing your intranet with the capacity for streaming audio (and video) is a good idea. As the Web becomes more interactive, you'll want to install the tools needed to participate in audio- and video-conferences and to create online presentations. (See Chapter 25, "Audio Presentations," and Chapter 26, "Video Presentations.") One popular streaming audio package is Progressive Networks' RealAudio.

RealAudio is the company that first developed streaming audio. RealAudio is set up so that it sends the audio message to a RealAudio player and as the audio comes in, it gets uncompressed and is fed to the player. This allows the user to hear the audio even while it's still being downloaded. This may not sound that useful; however, imagine that someone has a microphone. As he or she speaks, the voice is being compressed, sent, and played to the recipient. It's possible with RealAudio for someone to deliver a speech online in real time. There are several radio stations that broadcast on the Internet using RealAudio. To visit the RealAudio home page, go to `http://www.realaudio.com`.

Other commercially available streaming audio packages include Xing Streamworks and Netscape CoolTalk; both work with Web servers.

Xing Streamworks was created by Xing Technologies and is distributed by Hewlett Packard. It provides live and on-demand audio and video services. Xing Streamworks is a newcomer to the market so it is not yet widely used, but with its backing from Hewlett Packard, it's worth looking into.

Netscape CoolTalk is distributed by Netscape and provides audio streaming with the streaming client integrated into the browser, but not video streaming. Unlike RealAudio, CoolTalk doesn't have to start a new application every time a user accesses a new Web page, because CoolTalk does it for you. This is an ideal program for those interested in a complete Netscape solution.

Along with streaming audio, your intranet might benefit from the potential of video-conferencing. As the quality progresses, streaming video technology will be used for electronic meetings (both internal and intracorporate), sales presentations, training, and documentation. Think of streaming video as something to work toward as you select the software servers to include on your intranet.

CU-SeeMe, shown in Figure 8.5, is a high-quality intranet video-conferencing package developed by Cornell University that streams video and audio and works with the Macintosh, Windows 3.1, Windows NT, and Windows 95. The freeware is impressive, but currently special hardware is needed to run it.

FIGURE 8.5.
CU-SeeMe.

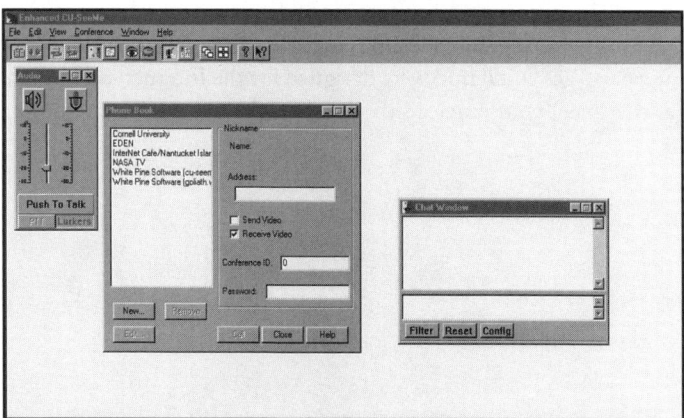

Whether to stock your intranet with the tools for real-time audio and video capacities is an issue worth some thought. If you currently don't have a need for real-time conferencing, you might want to wait until the technology develops further. It's highly likely that, as the Web develops into a media-rich environment, your intranet will require at least some plug-in players for real-time audio and video. Usually these players are free and can be downloaded from their developers, but to create your own multimedia presentations, it's likely you'll have to purchase a package.

Summary

Selecting server software for your intranet is not an easy task. Be sure to educate yourself on all the options. Remember that many packages are available only for specific systems (such as Sun, Windows NT, or SGI). It is important to choose your hardware on the basis of the software you use and the performance the software will give your application. Before purchasing any packages, list the goals you want to accomplish. For example, here are some questions to consider:

- How many users will you serve, and with what frequency (how many hits)?
- What kind of authentication do you need?
- Do you need to transport documents securely?
- Do you need a database gateway? What kind?
- Do you need a GUI administration interface?
- What platform do you use?
- What is your budget?

Do some research about the kinds of server software used by companies similar to yours, and query the administrators about their experience.

Software developers usually offer beta or demo versions. Download these samples from the Web, or call the company directly about getting a sales presentation. Above all, remember that many of the packages you'll find were designed for the Internet rather than an intranet. To find packages that meet your exact needs, use the Web as your research tool.

Starting with the Server

by Richard Simon

IN THIS CHAPTER

- Keeping a log 110
- Why keep a log? 112
- The implementation plan 114
- Planning the implementation itself 116
- Planning the work 117
- Why have a plan? 118
- Who writes the plan? 119
- When is the plan updated? 119
- Issues during installation 120
- Using sound engineering practices 123
- Hardware-specific issues 125
- Operating system-specific issues 126

Building Your Intranet

Part II

This chapter covers the planning and implementation steps necessary to set up a server. Taking the time to develop a thorough setup plan before getting started will help ensure your success. Recording a detailed log throughout both the planning and implementation processes will help keep the setup process in order and serve as a road map for work on the setup. So, begin by starting your log, then plan the implementation, then do the actual work.

The planning and record keeping may seem, at first, too exhaustive. However, nowhere more than in the initial stages of setting up is it possible to find and correct problems quickly and, most importantly, cheaply. Pinpointing these problems is possible only if you plan first and act later. If you fail to do so and server problems do creep up later, you'll be forced to backtrack your way into solutions—an inefficient way to work and usually a costly price to pay.

Keeping a Log

In deciding what you should keep in your log, you must define a *log umbrella*, as shown in Figure 9.1. This means you must determine two types of boundaries: which computers are logged and which procedures are logged. To make this judgment, begin by establishing which computers are most important. Many of the other decisions about which procedures to log will be determined by what operating systems are running on the important computers. You should keep records for any machines that are important or large enough to have a premium placed on their reliability. This includes computers that perform any file, print, Web, security, or application service. It also should include any backup devices or large electronic storage devices such as RAIDs, which provide a redundant array of hard disks that are simultaneously updated on a system.

FIGURE 9.1.
An example of a log umbrella. Note the computers that fall inside and outside the umbrella. Also note the services that sit under the umbrella.

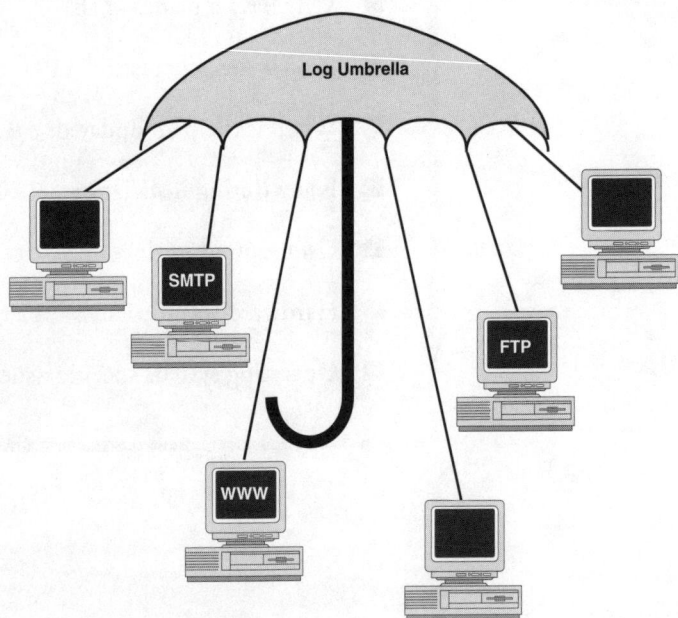

You should keep records on any software that requires user modification. This is often the case with UNIX, but certainly not exclusively. Software on all platforms often requires attention to certain details. These details must be logged, as is discussed in the section "Installed Software."

All system administrators should keep a log of problems and their solutions. When a systems administrator notices a problem with any computer or software that is under the umbrella, he or she should log it immediately so it can be tracked. This means that all system problems fall under the umbrella.

All Initial Parameters

Keep logs of the initial parameters of any software or computer under the umbrella. Having software version numbers, Ethernet address, and initial configuration files at your fingertips will save you hours.

Emergency Startup Procedures

One of the most important components of the log is a list of emergency startup procedures. When an important component of your system will not restart, nothing is more essential than regaining control. Having any necessary procedures written down will shorten this process considerably and make it less frenetic. This should include not only steps to take but also the locations of any useful startup disks.

For both Windows 95 and Windows NT computers, the emergency repair disk is absolutely essential.

Any Modifications to System Startup Files

Log any modifications to system startup files for all computers under the umbrella. This applies to any operating system.

For Intel-based computers running Windows, copies of the configuration files (config.sys, autoexec.bat, win.ini, system.ini, and protocol.ini) should be on disk, with the disk's location in the log. Do the same for Windows 95 computers, and keep a copy of the registry.

For Macintosh computers, keep a list of the extensions and control panels that load together to make a working system, and note any unusual preferences, as shown in Figure 9.2.

For UNIX-based computers, document any modifications to the startup files, and keep copies of all the original configuration files. Also, write down the locations of any relevant log files; make sure they are easily accessible.

FIGURE 9.2.

The Macintosh Extensions Manager Control Panel allows you to turn extensions on and off to assist your troubleshooting.

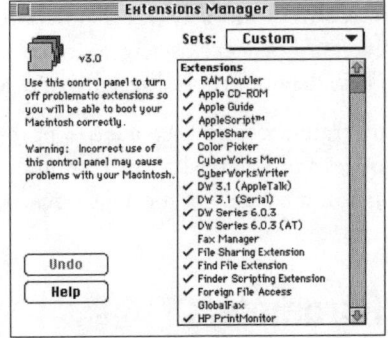

Installed Software

Also keep logs of important attributes of any installed software; this is true of important software even if it is not currently running on a machine within the umbrella. This information should include the location of the installed software (the full pathname) as well as the location of and any modifications to configuration files for the software.

Other important software information includes the location of the original source. Whether this is a set of disks, a CD-ROM, or a compressed archive file, this original and untouched source is extremely valuable.

Modifications to Installed Software

After the software has been installed, make sure log entries are made each time the software is modified. Document any alterations to Windows-style .INI files, Mac preference alterations, or adjustments to UNIX make or configuration files.

Why Keep a Log?

All this log keeping is not just an organizational drill. Keeping a log is a key component of system administration, not to mention an important part of sound engineering principles.

Logs provide an important record when it becomes necessary to troubleshoot. These logs provide a chronological record of changes that will help determine when a problem started. Logs also can provide a list of suspects for problems. A log entry provides the troubleshooter with valuable leads when he or she is trying to determine why the system is malfunctioning.

Logs, especially logs of the troubleshooting process, can serve as a knowledge base far superior to any other manual or guide. Logs provide lists of problem symptoms and solutions that can be reviewed for similarities. Logs also provide an initial knowledge base for training new systems administrators. This knowledge base is specific to your system, so it provides a much more relevant body of information.

Who Keeps the Log?

When determining what goes into the log, it is equally important to determine who will keep the log. Those responsible must agree on what will be kept and why. Simply telling those working on the server that they must keep a log will be insufficient. Keeping a log is often an unpleasant, time-consuming task. It often involves deliberately slowing down progress on a problem just for the sake of "paperwork." Being able to keep a log during a real crisis is a very difficult skill, but it is essential for preventing the crisis from recurring.

All Systems Administrators

All system administrators must be scrupulous record keepers. The system administrators are most responsible for the overall health of the system, and they will be the ones who have the task of restoring it to health when its gets sick. Thus, system administrators are responsible to both themselves and the organization to keep good records.

Users with Root Access

Any users who have system-level access to a computer or software under the umbrella must know what actions are to be logged. Anyone who has system-level access may make adjustments that can affect the system as a whole. These adjustments are all relevant to the logs. Again, it is important that anyone in a position to perform functions that should be logged agrees to update the logs as appropriate. A tradeoff to receiving root access is an understanding that logs must be kept.

How Is the Log Kept?

The method used to keep the log is in some ways as important as the log itself. Electronic solutions give the advantage of retrievability, but they lose out on convenience. If the staff is particularly meticulous about the records, an all-electronic solution may work, as shown in Figure 9.3. Otherwise, solutions may be more low-tech, such as a notebook next to an important computer.

FIGURE 9.3.
How an online log book should look.

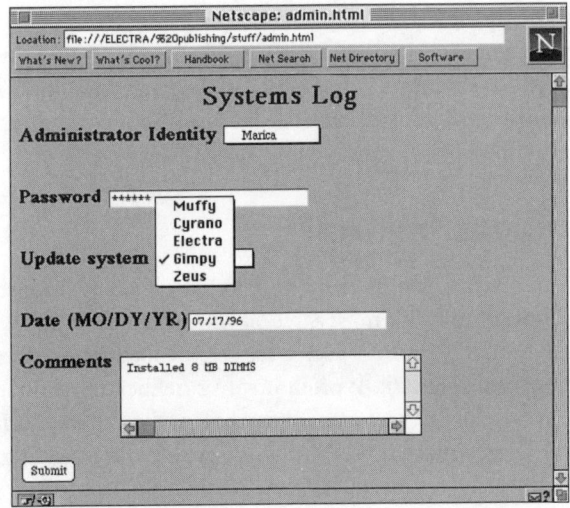

The Implementation Plan

After making arrangements for keeping a log, you must plan the implementation of your server. Now it's time to plan the server's place in your operation, as well as the steps to get the server up and running.

What's in the Plan

Begin the planning process with a top-down perspective on the business. The plan should be driven by concerns for the business, not concerns for the technology. To develop the plan, you should have previously determined what products and services the system will offer. Do not alter your plans on the basis of what the technology offers; rather, decide what you want to accomplish and then find the appropriate tools to do it. Set priorities and then focus on what products fit those ideas.

When drawing up the plan, spend most of your time determining what hardware and software best fit your needs. As you plan the server setup, you will discover that technology will only solve so many, if any, problems.

Remember, choosing hardware determines what operating system you can use. And, when the operating system is chosen, you will have set some limits on software options. The choice of software, of course, limits the functions your server can perform, so concentrate on doing things in the right order. When making these choices, proceed in the order from most general (operating system) to most specific (software packages). Although you must make choices in a specific order, making all your choices at the same time can translate into an optimum package. Remember not to focus on just one aspect of the system; instead, view the system as a whole.

An important aspect of planning is planning for maintenance. Support and maintenance often are the most costly aspects of a server, so don't forget to factor these costs into the overall plan.

Pursuing a Level of Reliability

The most important aspect of the plan is determining how much reliability is necessary. You must decide between cost and reliability, probably the most direct tradeoff you will face when planning. Money will buy you more redundancy, better equipment, and more comprehensive coverage. It will not buy you reliability, however, unless your planning and execution are solid.

You must determine how important avoiding downtime is. When your applications are not time sensitive, the cost of downtime is not so severe. So don't make the mistake of overestimating the cost of downtime. High reliability is costly and creates numerous support headaches. If you don't have to go through it, don't. It's also important to remember that the last 10 percent of reliability costs the most.

Another important aspect of planning reliability is to understand what role other factors play in your downtime. Your Internet provider can easily be the source of most of your downtime. No matter how good your system is, it is as good as down if it cannot reach the Internet.

Also consider technical support. Sometimes a problem will be beyond the scope of your in-house technical staff. There are many companies that provide hardware and software support for companies of all sizes. Having your hardware supported means getting a replacement disk or CPU in a matter of hours. Having your software supported means getting immediate answers to critical questions and reducing the time it takes to identify and solve problems.

You also must determine the dollar value of your data. Data is prone to loss, damage, and theft, so plan ahead for these risks. When your data consists mostly of casual e-mail, data loss is not so critical.

Evaluate the necessary security level of your data. That is, how much of the value of the data is lost if an unauthorized user sees it? Everyone uses passwords and file permission structures to secure their data, but do you need more than that? How physically secure is your network? This determination is critical in deciding how secure your transmission must be.

Transmission security means how secure your data is when it moves from place to place. Transmission security is often a weak link that people ignore. When determining the costs and benefits of security measures, never forget to consider the cost of restricted access. Remember that the computer exists so users can access data. If the access to the data is too restricted, you have decreased the value of your whole system. Evaluating and handling security threats are discussed in more detail in Chapters 14 through 16.

Planning for Upgrade Paths

A further important consideration when planning the server is how that server will be upgraded. All aspects of a computer system quickly become obsolete. Never trust that the computer you buy today will be exactly the same a year from now. It's likely you will buy a completely different piece of hardware three years from now. To maximize the value of your investment, you want a computer that can adapt to change. To find this beast, you must think carefully about your business.

Take time to consider seriously where and how the business will grow. Simple, less expensive systems often are not very scaleable, meaning they have little capability to grow. For instance, Microsoft Access is a fine database as long as you are dealing with a very simple table structure, a few forms and reports, and fewer than 15,000 records. To reach a larger scale, you need a tool with more power.

When planning a server, consider the following:

- Look at the number of users you must support, and try to guess how that number will change.
- Examine the services offered and consider how those services will evolve and change.
- Evaluate all these variables in dollar terms and see how much additional money must be invested for this level of change.
- Ask yourself how scaleable your system is.
- Ask yourself where the investment increments are. Sometimes a few dollars more will get you to the next tier, where there is a lot of room to grow.

Planning the Implementation Itself

When you've finally gotten around to planning the actual work of installing and configuring the server, you must think on a pragmatic, straightforward level. The more carefully you plan here, the less likely it is that you'll have a Phillips head in your hand at midnight wondering how it happened. At the center of a good plan are the equipment manuals and software you will need. With these in hand, first decide what you need immediately. This should include the following:

- Emergency items, such as boot or emergency disks and instructions on how to bring the system back up after a disaster
- Dire emergency items, such as original copies of any system software, tools for any hardware work, and the phone number of a consultant who knows more than you
- Preferred items, such as original copies of all software you intend to install and all manuals you will need

Now you are ready to plan for the stage of implementation that will occur next month.

This list might include the following:

- Cables
- SCSI terminators
- Connectors
- Replacement parts for incompatible parts

In six months you will probably be well into your first major upgrade. It's likely you will have attempted or experienced some of the following tasks:

- Added disk space
- Completed at least one upgrade, if not more, of a critical software package
- Contemplated upgrading your operating system
- Witnessed bottlenecks in your server performance
- Witnessed a failed or crashed system

Each of these events and transitions must be understood and planned for in terms of both service losses and cost.

In spite of everything else that has been said, don't overplan. Seeing a year into the future of your system requires a crystal ball. Within a year, expect to be looking for more capacity to deliver your services. Expect to have had a second six months full of more change than the first six months, and expect to be dissatisfied with your current server's capabilities.

Planning the Work

When scheduling the initial sessions of setup and configuration, don't underestimate the time it will take. If you have had some experience with the system you will be setting up, you should be able to make some good estimates about the time it will take. If there are any aspects of the system you are unfamiliar with, expect to be surprised by how many new variables it adds.

Two rules should be uppermost in your mind when planning:

- Always schedule extra time for each task.
- Don't roll it out until it's ready. Never expect to deploy any system of any kind without testing every important function.

Technology that doesn't work decreases your credibility with everyone involved. When you set up a system, it's no good if it doesn't work, and making adjustments is ten times harder after users are on board. Before you roll it out, you can restart a server as many times as you want. After you roll out the server, these things all have to be scheduled well in advance.

Why Have a Plan?

Everyone involved in the plan must understand the importance of planning. Convincing everyone of the validity and importance of the plan is as important as the plan itself. A plan is of no value if no one follows it.

Planning to Decide on Appropriate Software

When ready to purchase software, take time to draw up a shopping list. Such a list is valuable in determining where the overlapping functions are. You can use your software plan to build redundancy into your system. A shopping list also will allow you to spot potential conflicts of versions or features.

Planning to Foresee Expenses of Software and Hardware

Cost is always a driving force in business decisions, so you must plan to make accurate cost assessments. Without a plan of what you will buy when, cost assessment is not possible. Also, when planning the purchases, you can compare competing proposals directly.

Planning for Maintenance Costs

Another important aspect of planning is that it allows you to factor in things often left out, such as maintenance costs. Maintenance is an important expense, and it must be added to the cost of each system component. This includes hardware and software. Planning out these extra expenses gives you a more accurate estimate of the cost of each piece. Also, planning for maintenance costs means that maintenance can be effective from the minute you start up the system.

Planning for Reasonable Expectations

A final benefit of planning is that users, customers, and technical staff can all form reasonable expectations about the system. If you write out what steps will take place when during implementation, the staff involved will know what's expected and prepare for it. Laying out the completion dates for various projects lets the users know when to expect what services. And working out the costs beforehand lets the managers of the project plan a budget. All these expectations will prevent anyone from demanding more than you can give before you can give it.

Who Writes the Plan?

You must make decisions from the outset about who will be involved in the planning process. Too few people will produce a plan with too narrow a focus; too many people involved and the plan's too wide. Be sure that there are both technical and nontechnical people involved. Never let the system administrators do all the planning. Even though they have a firm grasp of all the technical issues, other perspectives should be heard as well. The system is set up not for the ease of the administrators, but for service to the customers. The system should always plan to adapt to the customers' needs. Ease of administration should always be the last concern and never the first.

Those who direct the company will have to provide the initial priorities. Again, let the business pick the technology. The systems administrators must plan out the actual implementation. Systems administrators included in the planning stage must be sure they don't let the technology pick the business.

When Is the Plan Updated?

The plan, like everything else in your system, must be changed periodically. Deciding when and how this change takes place is an important part of making your plan. Always review the plan when new functions are proposed to look for foreseeable conflicts. Look back at what you envisioned the server to do; if adding a new function will impair delivery of the old services, you should review the plan to remember why you set up that way in the first place. The plan will provide a stable body of knowledge about what your servers do and why. Use this to judge proposed changes.

Review the plan on a regular basis for bottlenecks, and make sure the plan includes an estimate of system limits at any particular time. Regular reviews of the plan should be compared with estimates of user and customer needs. Evaluate the plan's relevance to its goals before it becomes inadequate, and use the plan to predict upgrade paths.

Before making purchases, check them against current and future paths. Implementation scheduling will be simpler based on the plan. Business can be structured around the planned introduction of services. Acquisition of new business should be coordinated with the technical bottlenecks.

The Plan's Relationship with the Log Book

The plan and the log book are not completely separate entities. Use them together. Remember that the primary function of the plan is to provide a framework for making decisions about the system. The function of the log book is to keep track of what is actually happening. If the plan does not include disk space expansion, but the log book notes many errors due to lack of disk space, there is a problem with the plan that appears first in the log book.

The Log Book's Role During the Implementation

The log book and the plan are never closer together than during the implementation phase. During the actual implementation of the server, the entries in the log book should follow the plan exactly. If that is not the case, note the variations. Pay careful attention to elements of the plan that cannot be implemented. If the Web server you have chosen does not install because it is not compatible with your operating system or it conflicts with a database, revise the plan and record the specific reasons for this in the log of the session during which this was discovered.

A second way in which the plan and log book will work together is in scheduling. Your plan includes your proposed schedule, but the log book will tell you when it actually happened. Comparing your estimates with actual time spent helps your current activity and lets you plan more precisely for future upgrades.

The Log Book as a Status Check

The server setup plan is used to familiarize someone with the context in which your system is operating; therefore, the log book should relate all the details of the setup to someone unfamiliar with it. Staff working on the system should be cognizant of where their activity fits into the plan. When this is the case, simple notations can tie pages in the log to specific line items in the plan. This helps keep the log book current through every change or tweak, large or small.

Work Patterns as Clues

The log book will provide insight not only into individual line items in the plan, but also into your planning process as a whole. The log book will point out deviations from the plan, possibly revealing a pattern from those deviations. You may notice that you often fail to see hardware incompatibilities or that you're always underestimating the time it takes to complete certain tasks. Examine your log book periodically to understand where the shortcomings are in your planning process.

Issues During Installation

At last, you get to the real job. If you've read and followed the advice in the previous sections, installation will be much easier. During this stage your efforts will take fruition. This also is the part of the job that absolutely must go right. Poor planning and inconsistent log keeping may still produce a working system, but poor implementation will never do so.

General Setup Issues

There is no substitute for technical knowledge. No matter how good you are at following instructions, reading manuals, or troubleshooting systems, the technical knowledge of the system you are working with is extremely valuable and, in many cases, irreplaceable. You must do your homework on the things you will be installing and the concepts governing your system well before you try to set it up. Much of this you will discover as you try to plan, but there will still be many technical details with which you must become familiar. Take your implementation plan and figure out each aspect of it. Try to visualize what you will be doing and how. This process of trying to pin down every step will help you remember to have crucial items when you begin implementation.

Familiarize Yourself with the Technical Issues

The following technical terms and areas are some of the most basic concepts needed to set up an intranet. If there is anything in the following list that you cannot at least define, you have more reading to do.

Hardware
- NIC
- Ethernet
- CPU
- RAM

Networking
- Theory
- OSI model
- Internetwork
- Protocols
- NetBIOS
- TCP/IP
- IPX

Communication
- ISDN
- SLIP
- PPP
- T1

The following list contains some terms often presented in contrast to one another. Understanding what each term means and how it relates to its counterpart is essential for understanding your intranet. You should understand the meanings of and the differences between the following:

- Analog and digital
- LAN and WAN
- Internetwork, the Internet, and intranet
- Routers, bridges, and hubs
- Server and client
- Operating systems, such as DOS, Windows NT, UNIX, and MacOS
- File systems, such as FAT, NTFS, UFS, CDFS, and HFS
- Web Browser and Web Server (httpd)

MCKEON & JEFFRIES

M&J's server plan was relatively simple. The systems administrator was very familiar with the operating system and the server's procedures were not complex. Also, the server was not expected to receive a lot of traffic right off the bat. The accounting firm was in no hurry to initiate its intranet's entire audience at once; it planned to slowly introduce its users to the site.

To organize the initiation process, M&J started two separate log books: The first was for the systems administrator and her assistant, the second was for the administrators in charge of developing content on the site. The first log held all the pertinent information on how to start up and shut down the server, including where application and configuration files were stored and a record of problems solved or outstanding with the software or hardware. The second log kept all the information pertaining to the actual site itself: file naming conventions, times and processes for regular updates, templates for standard pages, usernames and passwords for administrative areas and e-mail, and the instructions for such basic administrative processes as setting up new message boards, adding a new user, and creating new folders on the FTP site.

THE SPORTING GOODS AND APPAREL ASSOCIATION

The SGAA needed a much more complex plan than M&J did. The new systems administrator worked closely with the consultants that built the back-end software to create a comprehensive reference document for future use. From the first time the server was turned on to the last piece of software installed, each configuration and modification was logged in a notebook. The notebook was eventually converted to HTML and used as an online reference vehicle for the systems administrator.

> In developing the plan for the server, one of the first steps was to map out the hard drive space and decide what would go where on the drive. The consultants and the systems administrator simply mapped it out on paper, leaving space for expansion and placing system files, applications, and configuration files in logical and secure places. Several other steps were included to ensure that the file structure for the Web server and the database was secure.
>
> Finally, the plan was implemented slowly. Over two weeks the server was configured and each function was tested. The security was tested completely before the server went online for the first time.

Using Sound Engineering Practices

After you are conversant on the technical issues, you must adopt an engineer's attitude. Each person working on the implementation must understand and religiously follow a few basic principles:

- Never throw anything away. No manual, disk, paper, or connector is insignificant enough to toss. Often the hastily written notes of someone else or the one-page errata sheet that came with the manual has exactly the information you're looking for. Don't throw out accessories until you no longer own the product.

- Always make a copy. No file is too inconsequential, no storage space too full that you cannot make a copy. Any file you edit, especially any configuration or system file of any kind, should always be copied first. For files you modify often, create a directory just below them in the tree that contains all the old versions. Often an error made in a system file won't show up until another change is made. If you only have the last version, the error is still there. Copy first, edit later.

- Have all the relevant materials with you before you begin. Nothing makes a job more frustrating than finally figuring out how to solve the problem and then realizing that it involves leaving what you're doing to get the part you need. Always imagine a very broad scope for any problem you're working on and get all materials you might need.

- Always prevent disaster. A physician takes an oath to do no harm; engineers should take an oath to always prevent disaster. Make sure that whatever you do to the system, you will not make it any worse. Also, ensure that regardless of what you do to the system, you're still capable of restoring it to its present level of operation. Not having a path back to where you were can easily get you lost in the labyrinth of the system.

- Troubleshoot by science, not voodoo. If you are unfamiliar with the scientific method, read up on it. Nothing is more embarrassing than naming the cause of the problem and eliminating it, only to have the problem recur. If you have a hypothesis, test it. If you believe you have found the cause and solution to the problem, cause and solve it again (assuming that you can do this without too much disruption). Never assume that because you were working on the problem and the problem went away that you actually solved it.

- Don't create voodoo for someone else. If a problem goes away and you are not sure that you solved it, don't insist that others follow your methods. If you have not tested a patch or method, do not insist that it really does what you say. People have a way of following procedures that make no sense, so try to avoid creating procedures that in reality do nothing.
- Test first; implement second. Any changes you are going to make to any system should be tested first if at all possible. Either set up a special system as a test platform or isolate the part of the system you will use and use it to test. No amount of hassle in setting up a testing area can be compared to the aggravation of trying to repair the damage from an untested product.
- Create an isolated test area. Remember that any test area you create must be isolated from causing damage to the system as a whole.
- Eliminate single points of failure. Identify functions outlined in your plan and list the system components involved in delivering those functions. Use that list to identify "single points of failure"—that is, any place where the failure of a single component will end that function. In other words, if a single disk crash will stop all of your Web service, that disk is a single point of failure. You would need a second disk to use in an emergency and backups of the failed disk.

Prepare to Do Everything at Least Twice

If this is your first time dealing with any component, you should expect to do everything at least twice. The first time you will often make mistakes, and only on the second try will you have the chance to correct those mistakes. Often only a third try will let you know if you really corrected your original mistakes. Don't get hung up on doing it right the first time. Expect to make the mistakes, and go ahead and make them. Doing an initial install presents a unique opportunity to make and learn from your mistakes. You won't ever know what those options do until you try them. Just make sure you follow some basic guidelines:

- Test it until it's right. Never leave a system half done. Test every function you have listed in your plan and make sure it all works. If something doesn't work, log it.
- Make sure it's still right after you fix it. During your testing you may find and fix a problem. Make sure you really fixed it.
- Plan to have it fail. Be realistic about your prospects for making a perfect computer system. Be prepared to deal with the problems when they appear.
- Try to make it fail. You cannot say you truly understand a problem until you can make it happen. Whenever re-creating the problem will not cause any damage, make it happen.

Plan Lots of Extra Time into Each Task

Make sure that your important tasks have extra time built in. Never rush the jobs that require concentration; you'll only have to pay for it later. Plan for your new system to fail repeatedly. If it holds together, be pleasantly surprised. Expect to be lost. Expect to be confronted with a problem that baffles you, and expect this problem to eat up your planned extra time. Another reason to plan extra time is that you don't just make a problem go away. You must understand the problem first. If you never understand it, you may never solve it.

Always Read All the Available Instructions

An old computer expression is "RTFM," which means "read the manual." Nothing gives you as high-quality information as reading the manuals that come with your hardware and software. You should never be tempted to call or ask anyone a question until you have read the relevant sections in the manual. You should read all relevant materials and reread whatever is definitely relevant. Just as important is reading the supplements that come with the manuals. Supplements provide information that is too recent to have made it into the manuals. As such, supplements often provide the most relevant information to your problem. You must make sure that you keep any supplements.

Even more late-breaking and often far more useful are the so-called README files, which contain information too recent to be included in the supplement. Often READMEs are included with software retrieved from online. In this case, sometimes the README is the only manual you have. Another important aspect of READMEs is that they often contain the most candid information. Often a README will contain lists of shortcomings, bugs, and limitations that a company would never allow into a manual.

Hardware-Specific Issues

The following is a brief smattering of issues that seem to crop up almost every time. This list is by no means an exhaustive compilation, but only a sample for those who may be dealing with an unfamiliar product for the first time. Many neophytes will find this useful, and many old hands will nod knowingly.

Intel

The broad class of Intel or Intel-clone computers, also known as PCs, have several idiosyncrasies. With the advent of Plug and Play, this has diminished somewhat, but many are still there. Here are a few:

- ■ IRQs, I/O addresses, and DMAs: You will rarely have to deal with these with new systems, but on old ones they are your primary concern when any peripheral, mouse, modem, disk drive, monitor, CD-ROM drive, or sound card doesn't work. Any good

book on DOS can explain these parameters and how to adjust them. Also, be sure to see the manual of the device that is having trouble.
- **UART 16550:** The chip that controls your serial port must be a UART 16550 to communicate at high speed. All computers made within the last year have this chip, but always check to make sure.
- **ISA, EISA, and PCI:** These are the three types of I/O slots available. Know what you have, which ones they are, and which cards go in them. Consult your computer's manual, the manual for any special cards, or your computer manufacturer.

Macintosh

The Macintosh, or Mac, was once the exclusive property of Apple Computer, but now some other companies such as Radius have been allowed to make Mac clones. Macs are known for their easy setup and forgiving nature. Still, there are a few nuances to be aware of:

- **NuBus or PCI:** Macintoshes also might have one of two types of I/O buses. Know which one you have and what works with it.
- **Multisync monitors:** Macintosh monitors must be a certain type and be hooked up in a certain way to change resolutions at will. Always ask about this when planning to buy a Macintosh for its display capabilities.

Network Interface

Make sure you have the right network card or adapter for the cabling scheme you plan to use. Multi-interface cards are often not much more expensive than single interface.

Peripherals

Peripherals are devices you connect to your computer through an external port, such as extra disk drives, scanners, tape drives, and printers. Here are a few issues to keep in mind:

- **SCSI:** Termination, termination, termination. Every SCSI chain must have an ending point with a terminator. This is the most common problem; check it first, always.
- **SCSI IDs:** Each device needs its own.
- **Tape backups:** Always test your tape restore *before* you have to depend on it. Develop a real, redundant backup scheme.

Operating System-Specific Issues

This section lists some of the most common operating systems and one or two of the most common problems specific to those systems.

Windows

Even with the advent of Windows 95, these systems are still plagued with nagging problems. Luckily, the operating system is simple, and even the most serious problems can usually be fixed in a matter of an hour or so.

Here are a few tips: Always have a boot disk specific to each computer. When having problems, start removing drivers and features until your system works. Never assume that it is impossible that some component could be causing the trouble. Rebuild slowly to find the troublemaker. Windows systems are easy to strip to the bone. Doing this will give you a clear picture of where the trouble starts.

Macintosh

Even though the Macintosh enjoys a reputation as a trouble-free system, this is only a relative statement; you can still expect to be confronted with vexing mysteries. Sometimes the Mac's hands-off nature works against it, as there are no obvious fixes for the user to try.

Incompatible extensions are the source of a large number of problems. Know how to boot with extensions turned off, and always keep clean copies of the system handy.

UNIX

Anyone who has a UNIX system already knows what troubleshooting is all about. Problems seem to crop up with UNIX systems more regularly than other, simpler systems, but with UNIX it always works out in the end. The answer is often only a Web search away.

Know how to reboot in single-user mode in the event of catastrophic failure. Have a kernel handy that you know works and know how to boot with that kernel.

Be aware of exactly which version of which flavor of UNIX you are using.

Summary

With a concrete plan and a log book in hand, you'll soon be ready to set up a server! Use these two tools together, and don't even consider setting up a server without both of them. After arranging your priorities under your log umbrella, you're ready to begin creating your road map to the server. Remember that the primary function of your plan is to provide a framework for making decisions about the server system. Use this chapter as a framework for your system, and you'll be on your way to setting up a successful server.

Connectivity: Opening Up Your LAN

10

by Jim Noland

IN THIS CHAPTER

- LAN hardware components **131**
- LAN software/network operating systems **138**
- Remote and telecommuting access to your LAN **142**
- Setting up the network servers **145**
- Network connectivity hardware **149**

A local area network (LAN) at its simplest is comprised of two or more computers connected with cables and network operating software (NOS), which allows all the computers to talk to each other through the cables. Maximizing computer resources and making files and applications easier to share are just some of the reasons for implementing a LAN. If you have two or 502 computer users creating documents and spreadsheets that they want to print, you don't need two or 502 printers. You can share as few or as many printers over the LAN as you choose. The same is true for the applications that the computers use. Instead of buying 502 word processing applications, you can buy one or two copies with the appropriate number of licenses for each user and share the single copy of the application over the network. Many businesses, government offices, schools, colleges, and even some home computer users utilize local area networks to get the most out of their available resources.

Selecting the best LAN for a particular environment is a lot like choosing a car. You must determine the basic functions you need and then work your way down to the details. For example, first you must decide what type of car to purchase. Once you determine that a Chevy Suburban will meet all your needs, you then begin to consider the important, but somewhat minor details, such as the color, type of interior fabric, and rear door options, right down to the type of radio you desire. The same is true for LANs, beginning with choosing the appropriate operating system and the cable connection, as well as choosing which services users may access and at what time they may do so.

Assume that you need to purchase printers for a LAN. Consider the following questions: How many users are on the network? How many printers are necessary for these users? Do any staffers need a personal printer to receive confidential figures? The type of network an office uses to share word processing documents across the room is not necessarily the best network to share medical CAT scan images across a hospital campus.

Determining your needs, the technology to meet those needs, and then setting up a LAN can be a daunting task. In many cases, it may seem as though you have too many options for some products and services, while in other cases, you may have only an option or two. Some background reading on today's trends and tomorrow's predicted trends is worthwhile before you begin laying the foundation for the LAN that will hold your intranet.

This chapter explores computer and network connections and the various hardware and software systems that are available for LANs. Additionally, I'll discuss the services these systems provide and how these services are useful for remote and telecommuter access.

Just as any good architect wouldn't design a "dream home" without getting to know her clients, you must first understand the needs of your LAN clients before you begin designing the LAN architecture. After fully accessing your users' needs, including their capabilities, the function of their work, and whether those functions might change in the future, you will be ready to start designing the LAN best suited for this group of clients.

Connectivity: Opening Up Your LAN

Chapter 10

LAN Hardware Components

Consider first what hardware comprises a LAN. Because the ultimate goal here is to connect all the computers via cables to form the LAN, exploring cabling options is a good place to start.

Connection Media

This section defines the physical cabling and connection techniques used to connect computers into a network. You will find at least one of these connection types in all LANs. In some cases, you will find multiple connection/cabling types. For instance, you may see fiber optic cables in one part of the LAN (perhaps a recently installed segment) and in another area find twisted pair cables. These two different media types cannot be directly connected. They are joined through a device that converts fiber optic signals to twisted pair signaling, such as a router. You'll read more about routers later. For now, let's look at the connection media in detail.

Coaxial Cable

Only a few types of cabling are used in LANs. We'll begin with coaxial cable. The first generation of local area networks utilized coaxial, or coax, cable to connect computers. Coax cable includes a center wire called a conductor, which is usually made of copper. The center conductor is then surrounded by an insulating foam or plastic covering. A foil or wire braid surrounds the insulation. The entire cable is then covered in a plastic sheath. The center conductor is the path for the electric signals (that is, data) on the network, while the foil or sheath is the ground for the electric signals. An example of coax cabling is cable TV, which generally uses this type of connection.

In fact, some local area networks are used for both cable TV and computer data. An advantage of coax cable is that the grounding foil or braid protects the electric signals on the cable from interference created by other electric sources. Electrical radiation from such sources as lights and air-conditioning units can corrupt the data signals as they travel down the cable. A disadvantage of coax is that the connectors can be difficult to install, and the cable itself can lose some of its transmitting quality if it gets squished or kinked, similar to the way a garden hose loses water pressure. Coax cable is still found in many network environments but is being replaced more often by twisted pair.

Twisted Pair

Twisted pair cabling is just that, a pair of wires each with a plastic coating that are twisted around each other and surrounded by an outside sheath. This is the same type of wire that brings phone service into your home. Twisted pair cables are easy to assemble and not as sensitive to kinks as coax cable. The main disadvantage of twisted pair cable is that it is more susceptible to electrical interference from other electric cables and systems and therefore has a lower transmission rate (that is, how fast the data can travel through the wire) than coax cable. However, to improve the transmission rates, a series of better insulated sheaths has been developed. These different categories of more efficient cables are referred to by their level of insulating properties. Category 1 cable, or Cat 1, has less insulating properties, while Cat 3 cable has better insulation; Cat 5 cable has even more insulation. These various levels of insulation for twisted pair cables allow for transmission rates comparable with coax cable, and in some cases, exceed the coax transmission rate.

Generally, the faster your LAN transmission rate is, the higher the category cable you will need.

Fiber Optics

A fiber optic cable is a very thin rod of flexible glass fiber surrounded by a plastic coating. Instead of electrical signals traveling down a wire as with coax or twisted pair cables, fiber optic cable uses light to transmit data. The most basic format of all computer "talk" is binary, a term represented in computer data as a 1 or a 0. Transmissions on a fiber optic cable take the form of either "light is on" to represent a 1 or "light is off" to represent a 0. In contrast, coax and twisted pair cable must represent ones and zeros with varying electrical voltages on the wire; for example, +5 volts for 1 and -5 volts for 0. Since the fiber optic transmission is light, and not an electrical voltage, it is subject to no electrical interference. This provides a much more reliable transmission rate even in electrically "noisy" environments. The downside to fiber is that it is expensive to implement, sometimes costing several times what coax or twisted pair cabling costs. The skill level required to fabricate the fiber optic LAN cable is also greater. For instance, the glass fiber must be cleaved and polished just right for the fiber optic connection to work properly. Twisted pair connectors on the other hand are simply fastened to the cable.

Wireless

Wireless LANs use a Radio Frequency (RF) transmitter and receiver at each computer instead of a cable. Each computer broadcasts and receives data to and from the other computers through the air much in the same way a radio works. This may seem like the easiest and most advanced way to connect computers to a LAN, especially with no unsightly wires and the ease of relocating workstations. Indeed many in the industry thought that wireless LANs would be the wave of the future. However, some issues must be considered with wireless technology.

The first consideration is that computers using wireless LAN technologies are broadcasting through the air to the other workstations on the LAN, as well as to anyone else who may be "listening." The data sent and received could easily be picked up and decoded by someone other than the recipient for whom it was intended. The reverse is also true. Your LAN may be subject to unwanted access attempts from someone who isn't even in the building or "connected" to the LAN. If doubtful, just listen to the numerous news reports of unauthorized persons acquiring cellular phone access codes who then use the codes to place thousands of dollars in phone calls. Cellular phones and wireless LANs both use RF signals, and more people are listening than you might expect.

Also consider that the airwaves are cluttered with TV, aircraft, police, CB, and many other radio signals. It is plausible that any of these RF sources could render your wireless LAN transmissions less than reliable or altogether impossible. Despite these drawbacks, there may be a place for wireless LAN applications—for users who face certain connectivity problems that would otherwise leave them unconnected.

These four connection technologies—coax, twisted pair, fiber optics, and wireless—make up virtually all the LAN connection techniques. The type of cabling used in a LAN is determined by such factors as environmental considerations, type of network operating system, transmission rate requirements, and even ease of maintenance. In the future, fiber optic cables will become more and more commonplace in local area networks. As the price of fiber optic connections decreases, they will replace twisted pair and coax cabling with increasing frequency, but coax and twisted pair will be with us for a long time to come.

There is some flexibility in terms of which cabling you can use in your LAN design. For instance, some LAN technologies may require twisted pair exclusively, while others can run over several different types of cabling. In the next section, we will look at the different types of networks that run over these cabling systems.

LAN Interfaces

Having discussed the basics of LAN cables, now I will explain how the cables actually connect to the computers. Typically the physical connection to the LAN is made through a Network Interface Card (NIC). This card also is sometimes called a Media Access Control (MAC) card. The MAC card is installed in the computer much the same as a video graphics adapter card or a CD-ROM controller card is. Some computers come with built-in network cards. A laptop computer can access a LAN with a PCMCIA LAN card or even through a parallel port adapter, which allows the computer to talk on the network through the computer's printer port.

Again, the functionality remains the same whether the computers use a parallel port adapter, a PCMCIA card, or a standard LAN card. The network card, in whatever form, provides a path for the data to travel from the computer to the LAN cabling. Four general types of network interface cards are used today in local area networks, and a few more new technologies are gaining popularity. The primary differences between them are in the way they "package" and transmit the data to the cable and the speed at which they transmit.

Ethernet/802.3

The Ethernet, or 802.3, network is probably the most commonly used network interface card. Ethernet networking was first developed by the DEC corporation. A variation on DEC's Ethernet technology was defined by the Institute of Electrical and Electronic Engineers (IEEE) in the IEEE 802.3 standard. The Ethernet card can transmit 10 million bits (a bit is a binary 1 or 0) per second on the LAN cable. Ethernet is sometimes called a 10 megabit per second (Mbps) LAN owing to this transmission rate. Recent advances in Ethernet technology have produced the 100Mbps Ethernet LAN, which supports the growing number of applications that need greater transmission rates.

Ethernet and 802.3 are sometimes used interchangeably, but there are differences in the way the two standards package the data, called *frames,* to be transmitted on to the network. In this discussion, I will use the term Ethernet to describe the 10Mbps network card whether it is sending DEC's Ethernet frames or 802.3 frames. Other frame types also can be transmitted with the Ethernet card, such as 802.2 (another IEEE standard) and SNAP II.

All of these frames can be transmitted at 10Mbps over an Ethernet card. The Ethernet network is a Carrier Sensing Multiple Access Collision Detection or CSMA/CD system. This means that the Ethernet cards in the computers constantly listen to the network cable to determine whether other computers are using the line. If a computer has data to send, the CSMA/CD system checks to see whether there are any current transmissions. If there is no activity on the line, the computer can transmit. If the line is busy, the computer waits until the line is free. If two computers talk at the same time, a collision warning is sent out on the network, and all the computers time out for a fraction of a second before trying to transmit again. The speed of the time-out and retransmit function is on the order of milliseconds, and typically, you will only experience delays of a second or so even in a very busy network. Ethernet is somewhat like an open discussion: If you want to talk, you need to wait until no one else is speaking.

Ethernet uses either a bus or a star topology. The bus topology is essentially a term that describes a single-cable LAN with all the computers connected to it. It is very easy to implement. The bus topology comes in two versions—thin coax cable and thick coax cable. Ethernet was originally implemented with thick coax cable, but the development of thin coax, also called "cheapernet," proved much easier to install because of its thinner, more flexible properties. The coax cable bus topology is a single cable that runs throughout the office or whatever area is being networked. You simply run the cable past each computer, add a connector to the cable, connect it to the computer and continue on with the cable to the next computer. The advantages of a bus cabling topology are that you only run one cable and that the coax cable used in the bus network is more resistant to electrical interference. The disadvantage of the bus network is also the single cable. If the single cable becomes damaged in any one place, all the workstations on the LAN will be affected.

The star topology uses twisted pair cable. In this topology, each computer has its own twisted pair cable that connects the Ethernet card to a connection port on a hub or concentrator, as shown in Figure 10.1. Inside the hub is the equivalent to the single coax cable which connects all the hub ports. Technically speaking, the twisted pair LAN is still a bus, but from the actual layout of the cable, it looks to be a star. The advantage of using a star topology is that if any one cable that runs to a computer is damaged, the other computers can still communicate over the LAN. The only real disadvantage is that you must run a separate cable for each workstation. Many LAN designers feel that the benefits of the twisted pair star far outweigh the disadvantages, and the twisted pair hub approach to Ethernetworking is very widely used.

FIGURE 10.1.
An Ethernet network of the star topology type.

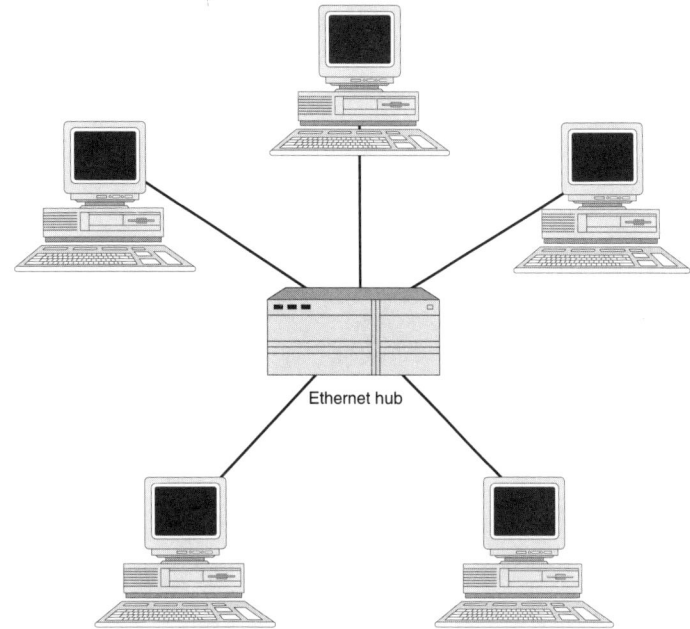

Token Ring

Token Ring was developed by IBM and is found mainly in mainframe or IBM AS/400 environments. Token Ring comes in two different versions: the 4Mbps and the 16Mbps version. As with Ethernet, Token Ring has an IEEE equivalent in the 802.5 standard, but they differ slightly in the way they package data into frames for transmission onto the network. The IBM Token Ring uses twisted pair cables and is set up in a star topology with each computer connected to a hub or concentrator. The 802.5 Token Ring also operates over twisted pair cables and can be in a star topology or an actual ring where each computer is connected to the next and the last computer is connected back to the first to close the ring, as shown in Figure 10.2. Unlike Ethernet, the communications over the Token Ring network are moderated by means of an electronic *token*—hence the name. Each computer on the network must wait to transmit data until it receives the token. Using this method, there is no possibility of data collisions created when two computers "talk" at the same time.

ARCnet

ARCnet was developed in the late 1970s by the Datapoint Corporation. ARCnet uses a combination of Token Ring and Ethernet known as a *token bus*. The IEEE standard for token bus is 802.4. ARCnet transmits data at 2.5Mbps and can run over many different cables, including twisted pair and coax cables. The ARCnet technology is not used often in office networks but rather in factory and warehouse LANs. The ARCnet network is very forgiving in terms of the quality of the connectors used and in how far you can run the cables. Ethernet and Token Ring cables' limitations are measured in hundreds of feet as where ARCnet cable runs may exceed 20,000 feet. Due to the lower transmission speeds, many administrators faced with implementing a new network choose faster technologies that cost the same to install. In addition, many data product manufacturers do not provide ARCnet network equipment. For these reasons, I do not recommend ARCnet as a good solution for contemporary LANs.

FIGURE 10.2.
A Token Ring network.

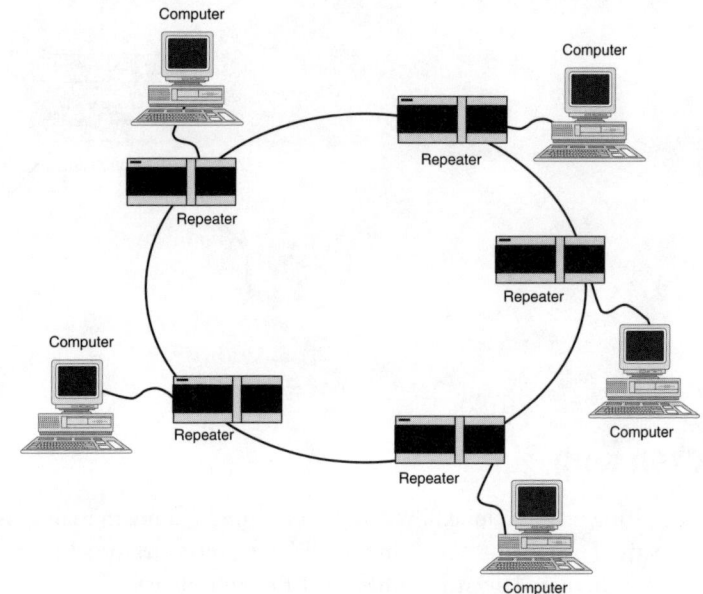

FDDI

The Fiber Distributed Data Interface, or FDDI (pronounced "fiddy"), networking technology is a product of the American National Standards Institute. It is a 100Mbps LAN that uses a token-passing access scheme with a dual ring topology. The FDDI LAN has two fiber optic cables that connect to each workstation. This dual cable implementation provides redundancy in the event that one cable should fail or become disconnected. The FDDI network connection comes in two variations, as illustrated in Figure 10.3. The Dual Attached Station (DAS) connects to both fiber optic cables. The Single Attached Station (SAS) connects to only one of the FDDI cables.

Obviously, the SAS connection does not have the redundancy a dual station has. A FDDI LAN has many advantages. Because it includes no electrical signal in the cable, the data on a FDDI network is immune to interference from lights and other electrical sources. The data traveling down the fiber can't be "tapped" or monitored because the signal is light and doesn't radiate from the cable where it could be "picked up."

FIGURE 10.3.
A FDDI network.

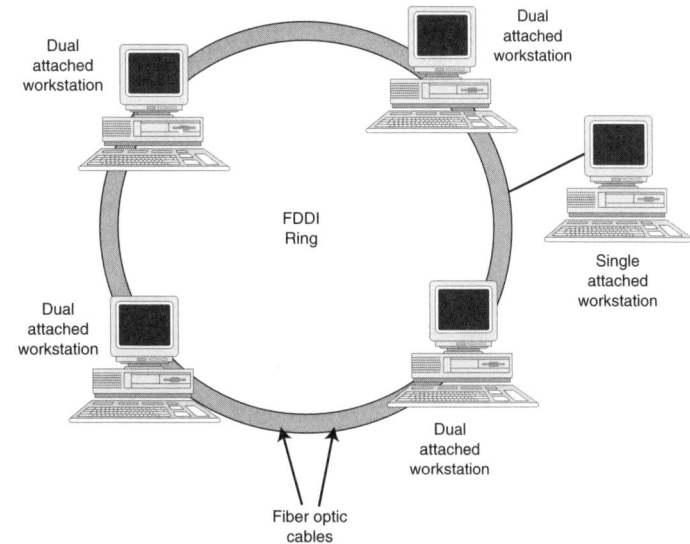

Indeed this security feature has sold FDDI into many government and commercial environments where security is a primary concern. The speed of transmission is also a major plus. Although with the new 100Mbps Ethernet technology, speed does not distinguish FDDI exclusively. FDDI also can be used as a Metropolitan Area Network (MAN), and some phone companies have begun marketing the FDDI technology to create what amounts to very large LANs for telephone customers. The main drawback of FDDI is the cost of implementing it over fiber optic cables. However, FDDI can be run over twisted pair cabling. In this environment it is called CDDI (Copper Distributed Data Interface).

ATM

Asynchronous Transfer Mode (ATM) is still largely uncharted territory because the technology is still in its infancy. The ATM implementation standards are still being defined. ATM is delivered over fiber optic cabling and has transmission speed capabilities in the 155 to 600Mbps range. ATM is a cell-switching transport service that packages data transmissions in small, fixed-size groups instead of variable-sized packets as in Ethernet or other LAN (and WAN) protocols. Using small, fixed-size cells over fiber optics allows for incredible transmission speeds. Some companies, including IBM, are rolling out ATM LAN applications, but for the most part, the cost of ATM is still prohibitive for most LAN applications. There are some ATM implementations in place supporting Wide Area Networking (WAN) and hospital or engineering labs that support medical imaging or computer-aided design applications. ATM is the future of LAN-based applications and services that require greater and greater transmission speeds.

Increasingly, more and more video teleconferencing, distance learning, voice communications, television, and graphic imagery will be running over local area networks, and we will need the transmission rates that ATM can provide. This kind of speed is crucial to supporting video and imagery data.

We have covered many different aspects of local area networking, including what kind of cabling and types of media access techniques can be employed to provide connectivity. As a rule, transmission rates of current LAN technologies are always being pushed to the limits as more and more speed-intensive applications find their way on to our computers. We will rely more and more on our computers for making voice calls, conducting videoconferences, and making bank and shopping transactions. The local area network will be tasked increasingly with these transactions.

In planing for the future, you must weigh the benefits of leading-edge technologies against the costs and decide whether you need the capabilities they bring. If you know that you will have to support computer design and modeling applications or video on the LAN in the next two years, you may want to look at ATM. Even though it will be more expensive initially, it may be cheaper in the long term versus installing an Ethernet only to dismantle it and upgrade to ATM later. We have discussed the prominent technologies, but by no means every type involved in local area networking. For the most part, these discussions cover a little of the past, the present, and the future of the local area network.

Any of these LAN networking techniques can be used in the building of an intranet. You must keep in mind, however, that you will be connecting LANs and that compatibility and end-to-end functionality is an issue. For instance, if you spend a tremendous amount of money installing 155Mbps ATM LANs in your offices to move huge imaging files around but can only afford a relatively slow T-1 (1.54Mbps) from the phone company to connect to your ATM LANs, you will have a bottleneck in your intranet, and the money you spent on ATM may be a waste. As with many things, your intranet may only be as fast as its weakest link.

LAN Software/Network Operating Systems

Now that we've covered how to connect all these computers and provided a way for them to talk to each other, we need to give them something to talk about. This section explores some of the different network operating systems (NOSs) that I mentioned earlier in this chapter. A network operating system performs the same function for the network that a Disk Operating System (DOS, UNIX, Mac, O/S, and so on) performs for a computer. The computer's operating system is the director of the computer's resources. It takes the data entered at the keyboard, displays it on the monitor, and then reads and writes files on the disk drives. When a file is printed, it feeds the data to the printer port. The computer operating system knows just where all of these resources are stored, how to identify the resources, and how to access the resources. Network operating systems perform the same functions but for many computers across a LAN. As mentioned previously, it's likely a group of users will share a printer, an application, or even a fax machine. To logistically ease the backup procedure, files generated by all the users usually are stored in one place on the network. The files necessary for the sales department to access are different from the files the accounting department needs, so certain users' access should be restricted, while setting permissions for other users will be necessary. Each of these procedures is directed through the network operating system.

The kinds of services you will find in a local area network, such as shared directories and printers or e-mail, varies from LAN to LAN. The primary services computer is called a *file server*, and all LANs have one. A file server is usually a computer much the same as all the other computers across the LAN. The file server, however, usually has a faster processor than the computers it serves, as it must "serve" the system's resources to all the computers. In addition to the basic file and printer sharing capabilities, a LAN can provide e-mail, group scheduling, World Wide Web access, and remote access. Providing these services to users often is as straightforward as loading software on the LAN.

Some of the more popular network operating systems are Novell, Banyan Vines, LANtastic, AppleTalk, and Windows NT. All of these operating systems provide the basic local area network services, such as sharing printers, directories, and files; they also allow access to other common resources, such as modems and faxes. In addition to the basic features, specific network operating systems often have advanced features or capabilities particular to that software. These more specific features may determine which NOS is utilized for each LAN. Some of these network operating systems are examined in more detail in the following paragraphs.

LAN operating systems basically fall into one of two groups. The first group is client/server. The client/server environment is distinguished by having one or more computers run software that provides the services for the LAN (for example, a file server or a print server). In the client/server group, LAN computers are loaded with software that allows them to access the server applications, hence the term client. The other class of LANs are called peer-to-peer networks. In a peer-to-peer network, any computer on the LAN can be serving applications or acting as the print server.

If you are planning to set up a LAN for 10 users so you can share files and printers, a 10Mbps Ethernet running a peer-to-peer operating system would be fine. If you are planning on getting 300 engineering, accounting, and management staff all connected to common resources, some with access to payroll or credit card accounts, you might consider a client/server operating system running on a FDDI network.

NetWare

NetWare is a network operating system designed by Novell, Inc. It actually is based on a networking technology developed by the Xerox Corporation called the Xerox Network System or XNS. NetWare first appeared in the early '80s with its early versions providing basic connectivity for desktop personal computers, which were just becoming popular. The LANs of that time were small, usually consisting of all the same type of computers with little requirement or at least support for PC to Macintosh or UNIX system access. Typically, the office PCs needed to share files and printers, and interconnectivity between dissimilar computers or even security and auditing features were unheard of in LAN network operating systems. NetWare has undergone many revisions since then and is now a dominant force in the LAN industry, holding perhaps as much as 70 percent of the market share. NetWare is a client/server LAN system and can support Macintoshes.

The advantage of Novell is the capability to support many users and services. You could use Novell to connect different offices across the hall or across the country. Novell NetWare has the capability to support many different types of computers including DOS/Windows, Macintosh, and UNIX systems. NetWare also has options for accessing the local area network by dialing in with a modem and for setting up the TCP/IP protocol for access to the Internet. It is ideal for mid-size to large size LANs and LANs with all different types of computers. The disadvantage of NetWare is that it takes a while for both the LAN administrators and users to become proficient in using all this functionality. NetWare can be run over Token Ring, Ethernet, ARCnet, and FDDI LANs.

Windows NT

Microsoft's Windows NT is the latest LAN operating system to appear on the market. Windows NT is a client/server operating system designed to support LAN connectivity in much the same fashion as NetWare. Windows NT has many of the same features that NetWare has and is NetWare's biggest competitor. Windows NT supports dial-in access to the LAN and Internet access support. Advantages of Windows NT are that it is fairly easy to become proficient in, and in many cases, it is less expensive. It doesn't have the long-term track record that many of the other operating systems have, but it is enjoying a very enthusiastic and growing loyal customer base. Windows NT can also be run over Token Ring, Ethernet, ARCnet, and FDDI LANs.

Windows for Workgroups

Windows for Workgroups is Microsoft's peer-to-peer networking environment. This NOS is good for small LANs that need to provide very basic connectivity and services, such as shared directories, printing, and application serving. Windows for Workgroups is very inexpensive compared to client/server LAN packages but again does not provide specifically for the more advanced features, such as security auditing and tracking that the larger client/server LANs offer. Windows for Workgroups runs over Token Ring, Ethernet, ARCnet, or FDDI LANs.

LANtastic

LANtastic is a peer-to-peer LAN that actually uses some of the NetWare protocols to communicate over the network. This is another NOS that is good for small LANs. Basic connectivity and services such as shared directories, printing, and application serving are supported. LANtastic is inexpensive and easy to set up compared to client/server LAN packages but again, does not provide as many service options as the client/server LANs, or even as many as Windows for Workgroups. LANtastic runs over Token Ring, Ethernet, ARCnet, and FDDI LANs.

AppleTalk

AppleTalk is a peer-to-peer LAN that is specific to Macintosh computers. AppleTalk is good for small Macintosh LANs. It supports basic connectivity and services such as shared directories, printing, and application serving. AppleTalk has no support for systems other than Macintosh. It is inexpensive because it is part of the Macintosh computer operating system and is easy to implement.

TCP/IP

TCP/IP is the "language" of the Internet. It is a networking technology developed by the United States Government Defense Advanced Research Project Agency (DARPA) in the 1970s. It is most commonly employed to provide access to the Internet but can be and is used by many people to create a LAN that may or may not connect to the Internet. In many aspects TCP/IP is a client/server-type LAN, but many manufacturers of TCP/IP software have applications that allow the "clients" to serve files or even applications.

TCP/IP has, from an architectural standpoint, some of the same qualities as NetWare, but TCP/IP is truly an open systems protocol. This means that no one manufacturer creates the product—any computer running TCP/IP software can connect to anyone else who has TCP/IP software (provided the user has an account and security permissions), regardless of who made the particular version of software. For instance, the FTP Software company's version of TCP/IP, called PC/TCP, is completely compatible with the Wollengong company's version. Novell also makes a version of TCP/IP software to provide Internet access functionality for their client/server NetWare LAN, and a version of TCP/IP is completely compatible with the PC/TCP software from the FTP company. TCP/IP is an ideal intranetworking protocol. If you have two different type of LANs such as Windows NT and NetWare which do not "talk" to each other, you could run TCP/IP in addition to the NT and NetWare software to get interoperability. TCP/IP runs over all networks, including Token Ring, Ethernet, ARCnet, and FDDI LANs.

These are the more popular LANs in use today. Support for these networks is widespread with many publications, Internet discussion groups, and certification programs for those who install and maintain these networks. Novell and Microsoft have established Certified Network Administrator and Certified Network Engineer programs.

Other LAN operating systems include

- DECnet, Digital Equipment Corporation's client/server LAN package
- XNS, the Xerox's network system that is the basis for Novell client/server LAN NetWare
- The Open Systems Interconnect, or OSI LAN system, which is another open systems LAN architecture that provides the same type of interoperability that TCP/IP offers
- Microsoft's LAN Manager, a NOS designed to run with IBM's OS/2 operating system
- The Banyan Vines network, a TCP/IP-based LAN package

None of these other LAN systems have had the impact that NetWare, TCP/IP, and Windows NT have had on local area networking. There are certainly large numbers of DECnet or Banyan Vines LANs being used today, but many consider the serious client/server LAN to be a "neck-and-neck" contest between NetWare and Windows NT.

Remote and Telecommuting Access to Your LAN

I have described some of the services found in the local area network, such as the file serving, print sharing, or e-mail in brief, and I have put these services into the context of a local environment, such as an office. One of the services mentioned is the remote access of the LAN resources—in other words, dialing into the LAN with a modem from a remote location to share files or perform administrative tasks. The idea of remote access has long been a part of LAN services, but with recent advances in the speed of modems, new protocols such as PPP (Point-to-Point Protocol), and phone company services, such as Integrated Services Digital Networking or ISDN, remote access functionality has improved dramatically. Just a few years ago, a remote user would dial into a computer on the LAN at 2400bps and log into the file server from the computer on the LAN. The remote user could only see text displayed through this kind of link, and the types of transactions performed were limited because the connection was very slow. Today, a remote user can log into the LAN and perform virtually all types of transactions as if he were actually in the office. In this section, we will discuss these different types of connections and how the LAN can be expanded or opened to provide remote access service.

Modems

Modems have been used in computer communications for many years now. A modem is a *mo*dulator/*dem*odulator. It takes the binary ones and zeros that all computers "speak" and turns them into a series of audible tones that can be sent over standard phone lines. (Standard phone lines are also referred to as plain old telephone service or POTS lines.) Modems are phones for computers, and they basically work in pairs just as phones do: the modem you are using to call and the modem that is answering your call. You can connect to any computer in the world that has a modem, just as you can call any house in the world that has a phone.

A modem is connected to a computer's communications port, known as a *comm* port (such as COM1 or COM2), and also plugs into a telephone outlet the same way a phone does. Modems are also available as a card that plugs into the computer in a manner similar to a LAN card. The computer is loaded with software, such as Datastorm's Procomm or PC Anywhere, which operates the modem and allows you to dial up the modem (that is, computer) with which you wish to communicate. Modems modulate and demodulate the data bits (1s and 0s) very slowly. If you recall, the Ethernet transmission rate is 10 million bits per second. The maximum modem transmission rate over phone lines is 28,800bps. This limits the type of transactions that can be performed over a modem, particularly in terms of accessing LAN services that are designed to be served at much faster speeds.

If you are retrieving a business letter from the file server to your home computer with a modem, the transmission rate is probably acceptable. If, on the other hand, you are trying to use the LAN word processor application on the file server through a modem connection, the transmission rate will be slow enough to make the process a very tedious venture. Modems are very inefficient for computer transmissions. All the modulating and demodulating takes time to perform; this is one of the reasons modems might never be able to exceed 28.8Kbps.

Traditionally, remote users have used a modem to access the on-site LAN by calling one of the LAN's computers, which has modem for such a purpose. This computer is called a *communications server* or *gateway,* and it gives the remote user access to the LAN by using the comm server's LAN software and network connection. The comm server is really just another LAN workstation, except it has a modem and modem software on it. One of the disadvantages of this type of access is that you must first load any files you wish to send to the file server on to the comm server through the modem connection and then from the comm server to the file server.

The file server doesn't recognize your home computer through a modem connection as a LAN client. You must use the comm server to act as a LAN client on your behalf. You could set up the file server as the comm server to gain direct access to applications and files, but this bypasses the client-to-server connection process (called a *login*) and poses definite security risks. You may not have network security concerns per se, but it is still a good idea from a network administrator's point of view to have a dedicated comm server.

As you may already have imagined, it can become a bit of a headache setting up a comm server that can support dozens or even hundreds of dial-in users. The idea of one LAN workstation with a few modems attached to it is functional for a very small LAN, but would be nothing short of a nightmare for a LAN that supports 120 dial-in users.

Another approach to dialing in with modems is the modem bank and terminal server. In this scenario, the comm server still uses modems, although they are modular or rack mountable in design versus a desktop or internal PC type modem. This allows you to add new modems in an orderly fashion as the demand grows. The modular modems are mounted in an equipment rack where each is connected to a phone line and to the communications server, which for this type of connection is actually a device called a *terminal server*. The terminal server is not a computer per se as in the earlier scenario. The terminal server does provide access for the incoming call to the LAN, but it also adds the ability to negotiate a more sophisticated type of connection.

In the modem bank/terminal server type of connection, the computer dialing in can be assigned an actual LAN identity or address. This allows the computer to converse directly with the LAN servers and resources. This method of connecting is called *remote client access* because the dialed-in computer becomes a LAN client as if it were actually on the LAN. This type of connection is negotiated using a protocol called PPP or Point-to-Point Protocol. Both the terminal server and the user's home computer must have the PPP software to establish this connection. Although the speed of the connection is still limited to the transmission rate of the modem, PPP is still a more "graceful" connection and is far more streamlined than having a comm server act as a "middleman" in the connection.

ISDN

You may have heard of the phone company's ISDN, or Integrated Services Digital Network. This type of networking provides a digital or binary (all 1s and 0s) transmission service that can be dialed just as a standard phone (POTS) line can be dialed. The advantages of ISDN for LAN access are extensive: Your computer doesn't have to have its binary "talk" modulated into tones for transmission over phone lines as modems do. The data stays digital from your computer through the phone lines to your LAN. The slowest ISDN speed is 64,000 bps or 64Kbps. The higher ISDN speeds exceed one million bps. ISDN generally comes in two forms. The first is the Basic Rate Interface or BRI. BRI is two 64Kbps channels called *bearer* or *B* channels. Both these B channels can be used together to form a 128Kbps connection. The second type of ISDN service is the Primary Rate Interface or PRI. A PRI is a 1.5 million bps line (1.5Mbps) that is made up of 23 B channels.

ISDN requires different equipment than POTS lines. A modem will not work with an ISDN circuit, because the ISDN service is all digital, whereas the modem is designed to turn digital "talk" into sounds or analog "talk." The type of equipment used to access ISDN depends on whether it is a BRI or PRI service. For the BRI service, you need a terminal adapter or TA. A TA connects your computer to the ISDN line. As with modems, you also need software to dial over the ISDN service. PRI service, on the other hand, is a more sophisticated and complicated kind of service that requires something called a *channel service unit*, or CSU, to help sort out the 23 channels of data that make up the PRI service.

The ISDN access technique at it simplest is much the same as it would be with a modem connection. One ISDN-connected computer dials another ISDN-connected computer—only the speeds involved are much faster. You can buy an ISDN card that installs in the computers or an ISDN TA that sits on the desk just as a modem does. This is a typical implementation for simple connectivity between computers. Using ISDN, you would dial directly to the file server, which would also be equipped with an ISDN card to access services in this way, but the number of incoming calls to the LAN would be limited by the number of ISDN cards in your server.

A more secure and functional method for connection to the LAN would be the ISDN terminal server solution. This solution also uses the Point-to-Point Protocol, but the phone line is the higher speed ISDN. An ISDN terminal server with PPP provides dial-in users with the feel of actually being directly connected to the LAN. The response time in accessing LAN resources is greatly improved with this solution.

The use of ISDN is expanding every day. In previous years, only very expensive digital services were available from the phone companies, and companies leased the digital line on a full-time (24 hours a day) basis whether they used the line or not. The leased 56Kbps is an example of the full-time digital line. ISDN has brought users the "dial on demand" services that allow them to dial the connection when they want it and pay per use. Even the most basic ISDN service (BRI or 128K circuit) provides a better transmission rate than the slower, more expensive 56Kbps service.

Setting Up the Network Servers

There are many things to consider in setting up the network. After you have determined the number of users and what type of LAN technologies you will use, you must select the types of hardware (that is, which computers, cables, and network cards). A fair amount of these decisions can be based on cost, but you must also consider the reliability of the equipment. If your file server keeps breaking down, it is hard to justify having saved $300 on the purchase when you've spent twice that much time fixing it. Furthermore, as soon as your users are acclimated to the LAN and using its services, even the shortest downtime will generate tons of phone calls to your office. Spending a little more on better equipment helps reduce problems in the long run.

You must also decide how to route the cabling through your facility. You could simply lay the cables around the floor, but this isn't pleasant to look at and will probably cause problems with people tripping over the cables and disconnecting them. You could place the cables up in the ceiling, but that could also cause problems because this puts the network cables close to electrical cables, possibly causing data transmission problems. If a lot of network cables are necessary to connect all your computers, you may not be able to trace or isolate a cable problem if the cables are jumbled together.

Some advanced planning is in order for the layout of the cabling. You may want to have a structured cabling system installed. A structured cabling system is a generic cabling system that can be used to connect data video and voice lines throughout your facility. It is a little more expensive for a LAN implementation only, but if in the near future you'll need to install a new phone system to support your growing business, you may be able to kill two birds with one stone and install a cabling system that supports both.

After you have decided what your users need to do and what LAN systems support those requirements, you may want to have an independent consultant look at the design to confirm your plan. A few hours time spent with someone knowledgeable about LANs and the applications that operate over them may be well worth the money. At the very least, you can confirm your LAN design skills, and if your design is incomplete, you have the opportunity to gain some valuable information.

After you are satisfied that your LAN design is adequate, you must evaluate the three issues surrounding the actual implementation of the LAN. The first is determining whether you really have the resources "in house" to perform the installation of all the network cards and cables. The second is setting up the software on the servers and client workstations and getting them to work together. The final issue is the administration of the network. Are you prepared to handle all the trouble calls and requests for additional services?

The server must have routine maintenance check-ups, and data files must be backed up periodically in the event of a system failure. All this day-to-day operations "stuff" is a full-time job and then some. You may very well want to contract out the installation, integration, the administration, and even the LAN design to someone with experience in networking. Many organizations, both commercial and in government, do just that.

You could have the administration portion of the network staffed by contractors until you have hired a few people into your staff to take over. When selecting contractors for the installation and administration of your network, make sure they have experience with the network you are installing. The same applies for those you hire as LAN support technicians. They should be able to answer detailed questions and demonstrate a clear understanding of the LAN systems you have implemented. Never allow one person to become the sole caretaker, administrator, or technician for your network. If that one person leaves your organization or if that person is away on vacation and the network goes down, you may find yourself with a network that doesn't work, and no one who knows what the cause might be.

At a minimum, your network will have one server (even in a peer-to-peer network), which will be hosting the applications or files. More often than not, a LAN has several servers to provide all of the services your users will require. You will more than likely be using an Intel-based computer (this would be the kind of computer with the Intel processor chip in it) and running DOS and Windows. The specific LAN software you select will have specifications for the minimum system requirements, and it is recommended that you exceed them where possible. If the LAN package requires a 486 66MHz computer with 8MB of RAM, you should probably go ahead and get a Pentium 90 with 16MB RAM, just to be on the safe side.

Network servers can be located anywhere on the network; however, the servers should be located off the beaten path. That is to say, you shouldn't have the servers located where people are going to be bumping into them or setting their morning coffee on top of them. These machines are the most important pieces of your LAN. You'll want to purchase a good uninterruptible power supply (UPS) to protect your server against power surges or outages. Locate the servers in a cool, environmentally controlled room. You may need air conditioning if the room has a great deal of equipment and is warm or not well-ventilated. In large LANs, rooms with many servers are referred to as server farms, and they often have not only air conditioning systems, but also humidity control and fire control systems.

Servers need to have their data backed up regularly. This typically involves a cassette tape-like system that is installed in the server, similar to a floppy or CD-ROM drive. A copy of the server files are made with the tape backup every day or every other day depending on the amount of data being created. If you are selling widgets by the thousands every day and the accounting for the business is on the LAN, you want to back up the accounts payable and receivable, as well as the inventory database every day. Then once a month, back up the entire server, applications and all. In fact, make two copies of your backups. Store one in the LAN administrator's office and the other off site. In the event of a fire or other disaster, having a backup at your house will save a lot of suffering. Some administrators deposit monthly server backups in safe-deposit boxes at two different banks in addition to the two office copies. If you are serious about your LAN, take your backups seriously.

The next few sections contain some information on the different types of servers you will find in a LAN. They are not necessarily different computers. The file server may also be the print server or the e-mail server. The different servers are listed by the services they perform to help define the roll they play in the LAN.

File Servers

The file server is the heart of the LAN. It has the applications that the users need and the files that are shared. It is usually divided into sections that the users can access, such as their own directories or shared directories, and the sections that are restricted to administrative access, such as security directories and operating system files. The computers with client software can view a list of servers on the network and select the one to which they will connect. Often each department, such as engineering, accounting, or sales, has its own server. Users may or may not have connection or login privileges on every server. Someone in engineering may have no reason to have an account on the accounting server. The servers also need to be serviced periodically. Running a disk optimizer program or utility to check the health of the disk is recommended. Norton Utilities is an example of a system diagnostic/preventive maintenance package that is widely used on DOS-based computers. Many network operating systems have their own disk maintenance programs.

Print Servers

Print servers are the servers that have a printer or printers attached to them. In a LAN environment, a computer prints to a network printer over the LAN cabling. You could make the file server also the print server, but you'll want to locate the file servers some place out of the way. You'll need to have a server that will satisfy the printing requirements located near the users. A print server is just that. The software in the client computers redirects the print jobs that would normally go to the LPT port out on the user's computer out to the network print server.

If your network is small—say, 20 users—you probably just need one print server with one printer. If your network is sixty people on two different floors, all printing documents and some printing color slide presentations, you probably want three or four print servers with five or six printers. A print server accepts the print jobs in the order in which they are sent and stores the files. This is called *spooling a job*. As soon as the printer can accept a new job, the file is sent out the print server's LPT port to be printed.

E-Mail Servers

E-mail is quickly becoming the way businesses communicate. It has in many cases replaced voice mail. E-mail comes in two basic formats: the version that is designed to work within your LAN using your LAN's software protocols (such as Novell's Groupwise Messaging System), and a TCP/IP based system that allows Internet e-mail as well as internal LAN mail. The Simple Mail Transfer Protocol, or SMTP, is an example of the TCP/IP e-mail service. The e-mail found on the Internet is largely SMTP mail. Many LAN operating systems such as Novell's Groupwise Messaging have add-on packages that allow access to Internet e-mail by creating gateway services. A gateway takes one kind of application, such as the Groupwise Message e-mail, and converts it into the SMTP e-mail format so it can be sent out to the Internet. The e-mail server can be located on the file server, consolidating the backup process.

Communications Server

We've talked about users dialing into the network to access services. The communications server is the one that provides that functionality. Again, this type of server for dial-in services is only really practical for the smaller or mid-size LANs. Larger LANs may require a modem bank and terminal server for the more sophisticated access discussed earlier. However, a comm server can provide a very useful service in addition to dial-in support—namely, dial-out. You may want to fax documents right from the desktop across the LAN through the comm server. With a fax modem attached to the server and some fax software, your users never need to walk over to the fax machine. The reverse is also true. A user can receive faxes into his or her own mailbox through the comm server. Support for this type of functionality varies with the different LAN operating systems, so you may want to make this an element of your LAN software selection process.

The communications server can also be used to perform EDI transactions. EDI, or Electronic Data Interexchange, is an electronic commerce application that allows organizations to share business information via computer systems rather than mailing large documents, such as proposals and contracts, through the postal system. You simply post the information on your comm server and other computers can dial in to retrieve a copy. The reverse application would be configuring your comm server to automatically dial into another organization's EDI comm server to fetch the latest documents. EDI is an effective way to gather or disseminate information to large numbers of people with minimum effort.

World Wide Web Servers

Many organizations are using the Internet World Wide Web (WWW) service to provide information about their organization's services and products. The WWW format displays electronic documents or pages with graphics that can be accessed using the TCP/IP protocol. The WWW service uses a protocol called Hypertext Transfer Protocol or HTTP. This page layout is useful in displaying pictures of products, places, or people, and the accompanying text can be set up to link one page or Web site to another page or site. As you view the page, the link text is highlighted so that when you click on the text with your mouse, you jump to the other page or Web site automatically.

Typically, a Web server is accessed across the Internet, but it can be used within a LAN without Internet connectivity. You still must have TCP/IP software running on the workstations. A Web server can be set up on your file server, but if the Web site becomes extremely busy (particularly if it is connected to the Internet), the serving of files and other services to your users may slow down.

Network Connectivity Hardware

There is some additional hardware that you can use in local area networking, some of which I mentioned earlier. This includes the hubs that are used in the twisted pair Ethernet LAN. The hub is the device to which all the twisted pair LAN computers are connected. These hubs come in a variety of makes and models, and selecting one can be based largely on price. However, as with the servers, you probably don't want the cheapest one in your LAN. A good rule is to eliminate the cheapest and the most expensive models and what's left will probably serve the average LAN pretty well.

A variation on the hub concept is the switch. A switch has ports just as the hub does, but the switch is smarter than a hub. The switch learns all the addresses (the unique network identifying numbers that are on each network interface card) of all the computers on the LAN. The switch knows what address can be found on each of its ports. When you issue a login or connect request to a server, the switch sees the request and connects the calling port directly to the called port. This is similar to the phone company's switching. The advantage is that the connect request doesn't have to circulate around the network looking for the right address. The switch knows which port the server is on and connects you directly.

Because the switch is handling all the connections, fewer transmission problems occur, and more time is spent sending data instead of collision messages. Switches were first used for Ethernet networks, but now there are switches for Token Ring LANs as well. If you are supporting the heavy-duty applications, such as Computer Aided Design and Software Engineering packages on your LAN, or if your LAN is simply very busy with several users, you may be a candidate for a switch. If users are complaining that it takes forever to send and receive data and that the collision lights on your equipment are constantly flickering, you may need a switched LAN.

There is a lot of leeway in the day-to-day operations of the local area network. Every little connector and cable need not be the same type or engineered down to the micrometer. Every workstation need not be set up exactly the same in terms of operating system and hardware performance. Establishing solid maintenance schedules and backup routines will go a long way in keeping things running smooth.

Summary

You've just gotten through an overview of one of the more intimidating aspects of intranets—the network hardware. This is a subject that whole books are written on (try *Understanding Local Area Networks* or *Understanding Data Communications, 5th Edition*, both from Sams Publishing), so you have some more learning to do.

But by now you should have more than a little knowledge of LANs. In the next chapter, you'll expand upon this knowledge and learn the principles of taking your LAN out into the big, wide world to meet other LANs—forming a wide area network.

Wide Area Networks

11

by Jim Noland

IN THIS CHAPTER

- Types of WANs **152**
- WAN implementation **156**
- Connecting the LANs **157**
- Accessing the WAN **159**
- Why a WAN for your intranet? **161**

In the previous chapter, I discussed the basics of setting up a local area network (LAN) and providing access and services for in-the-office and remote users dialing in by modem. This chapter discusses how to connect one or more LANs over a large geographic area to create a wide area network (WAN). Generally, a WAN is created when you utilize the phone company's data networking services to link LANs together. Some LANs are so huge that they would seem to be a WAN; I have worked on LANs that consisted of miles and miles of cabling, but here I am talking about actually connecting two or more LANs together with a phone company circuit, not just installing a large LAN. In some situations, you could connect two LANs together across a large university or hospital campus using two modems connected to servers. This could be considered a WAN, but for purposes of this discussion I am referring to the high-speed digital services usually offered by the local and long distance telephone carriers.

A WAN provides other LAN users in distant locations with the same information and services that your local LAN users have. If you have offices across town or across the country that must share services, such as inter-office e-mail or database information, you need to link the LANs over a WAN. Many companies have found that e-mail is a great way to pool resources, share ideas and distribute information about the company's business. If you maintain a central database or other applications, like shared documents that all personnel must access, you will need to set up a WAN, especially if you intend to expand your offices into other cities.

Types of WANs

There are almost as many WAN types as there are LAN options. A very basic WAN is nothing more than two computers calling each other over a modem connection. A more complex WAN may involve connecting hundreds of offices together with high-capacity digital circuits. Usually a WAN takes the form of something between these extremes. The actual circuits and services used to build a WAN are determined by the type of applications being shared across the WAN link. The speed of the circuit used for wide area networking may be driven be the number of users sharing that line and/or the type of LAN traffic (that is, applications) sent over the line. The kind of circuit is usually based on the number of sites connected and the applications shared over the link. In the following section I discuss the most prominent WAN services in use today and describe the services in some detail.

56Kbps Digital Data Service (DDS)

The 56Kbps DDS has been the standard in WAN connections for many years. Many organizations have used this type of circuit to connect offices together. As the name implies, this type of circuit can transmit data bits (1s and 0s) at the rate of 56,000 bits per second. The 56K circuit is a point-to-point circuit; this means it connects one site to another or one LAN to another. It can be a permanent, or *nailed*, circuit between two sites, or it can be a switched circuit that is dialed up as needed to other compatible 56K services. This type of circuit is sufficient for passing files or e-mail and even for running applications on the server for a few users. However, if you have 80 users all accessing a database over this circuit and sending e-mail, the 56K circuit is too slow; users will experience long delays in sending and receiving data.

T-1 Services

A T-1 (also called DS-1 or Digital Signaling-1) is a grouping of 24 64Kbps channels that create a 1.5-megabit-per-second circuit. Like the 56K circuit, a T-1 is a point-to-point service. T-1 circuits are widely used and make up a large percentage of both data and voice and video WANs. A T-1 is ideal for linking offices together at near-LAN speeds. If you are running an ethernet LAN at 10Mbps, the T-1 service will provide better than one-tenth of your LAN transmission rate. This may seem slow, but considering an average ethernet LAN only runs at about 20 percent or 30 percent capacity, the T-1 is actually closer to one-third of your LAN transmission speed. A T-1 can be nailed or switched, as with a 56K line. In addition, the T-1's channels can be divided among multiple sites. For example, your Washington, DC office could have eight channels in the T-1 going to Chicago and the remaining channels going to New York. This WAN effectively would tie all three office networks together.

T-3 Services

A T-3 (also called DS-3 or Digital Signaling-3) is a grouping of 28 T-1s to create a 45Mbps circuit. This type of service is expensive and is employed primarily when a large-capacity data transmission path is required. In a typical WAN implementation, you will not need this service, but you may hear it discussed as part of a T-1 network implementation. T-1s are multiplexed, or *bundled*, together into a T-3 for easier routing through the phone company's network.

Frame Relay

Frame relay is a service designed to operate on a 56K or a T-1 type circuit. It provides many virtual channels inside the circuit. You could take a 56K circuit and use frame relay to create several channels to other sites so that instead of one 56K circuit going from Washington, DC to Chicago and another going from Washington to New York, you would simply install one 56K frame relay in Washington with virtual channels to the other locations. This is one advantage to frame relay. Another advantage is that it is typically cheaper than standard point-to-point circuits.

The disadvantage is that the actual through-put in a 56K frame relay circuit is less then 56K. The phone companies will offer a committed information rate (CIR) to guarantee the minimum through-put. You may be able to send bursts of data above the CIR but not for sustained periods of time. You will always have the minimum transmission speed guaranteed by the CIR rate you purchase.

EVN RECORDS INC.

EVN Records has offices in three states on the East Coast. These offices currently share demographics and sales information over the phone and through the postal system. It recently has begun working with a firm in California to set up its artists' touring schedules. Meanwhile, upper management wants to reduce the long-distance phone expenses among the three East Coast offices; with their new West Coast associates, the long-distance costs will skyrocket. Upper management is interested in using the Internet to set up web pages for their artists. The network managers have convinced upper management that the information among the East Coast offices can be shared electronically by e-mail and that linking their Windows NT networks over a WAN will cost less than EVN's current long-distance telephone charges. The California office only needs to share e-mail with the East Coast offices; it doesn't need to be linked to the WAN. Because the three East Coast offices only have a few users on each LAN, it is decided to use 56K Frame Relay to link the three East Coast office LANs. These three offices each have a Windows NT workstation, and these networks will be bridged together into one LAN using the NT server at the main office. The main office also will have a fractional T-1 connected to a local Internet provider for e-mail and putting the Web pages online. The other East Coast offices will share the fractional T-1 connection out of the main office to the Internet. The California office is already connected to a local Internet provider, and the Internet will serve as the WAN for the transfer of e-mail between California and the East Coast offices (see Figure 11.1).

FIGURE 11.1.
A WAN implementation with Internet access.

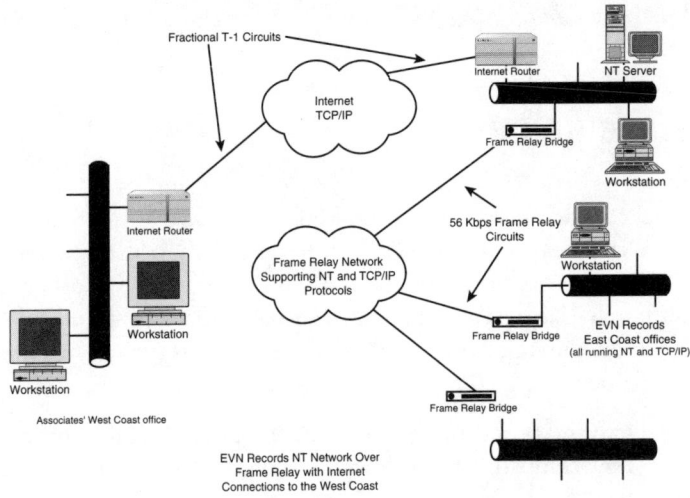

Sonet

Sonet (Synchronous Optical Network) is the latest in high-capacity fiber optic WANs. Sonet transmission rates usually start at the OC-3 (Optical Carrier-3 level), which is roughly the equivalent of 3 T-3s or a 155Mbps rayed circuit. Sonet can be deployed at the OC-12 level, which would be in excess of 600Mbps. Services like Sonet are deployed in environments such as medical imaging, intensive computer-aided design applications, or combinations of video, voice, and high-bandwidth LAN applications. There is little justification for using Sonet even if you are linking two 100Mbps LANs together, as the cost of Sonet versus the performance benefits is usually prohibitive unless your applications demand it. In any event, the deployment of Sonet service integration to your LAN is outside the scope of this document. If you have a requirement for such high transmission rates, speak with a network consultant about Sonet services.

SMDS

SMDS (Switched Multimegabit Data Service) is somewhat like frame relay in that it provides multiple virtual channels within a single SMDS service so that each can be routed to a different location. One of the main differences between frame relay and SMDS is that SMDS transmission rates start at the T-1 level (roughly 1.5Mbps) and go up to the T-3 level around 45Mbps. If you have a high-bandwidth data application that is being shared among three sites at T-3 transmission rates, SMDS is probably a good choice.

GOODBODY COMMUNITY HOSPITAL

Goodbody Hospital is a small hospital outside of the city. The two larger hospitals in the city have agreed to share their medical imaging staff expertise with Goodbody Hospital, but the doctors in the city do not have time to drive out to Goodbody Community Hospital just to review CAT scans. Therefore, the doctors decide to deploy a high-speed WAN that will link the LAN at all three locations. The WAN service must support the transmission of CAT scan images from Goodbody over to the other two hospitals' networks, where the images can be analyzed and compared against other CAT scans stored on the file servers at the two city hospitals. The CAT scan images are huge files that can be hundreds of megabytes or gigabytes each. A T-1 would be far too slow for the efficient transmission of these size files. A standard point-to-point T-3 would be effective, but to link all three hospitals the doctors would need several T-3s, which is an expensive option.

In this case, the SMDS service was the solution. With this service, the hospitals could switch the full T-3 bandwidth of 45Mbps among the three sites as needed. The hospitals needed to purchase a router for each site to direct the LAN traffic over the SMDS network. The phone company is providing the SMDS access equipment as part of the service (see Figure 11.2).

FIGURE 11.2.
An SMDS network directs LAN traffic among three locations.

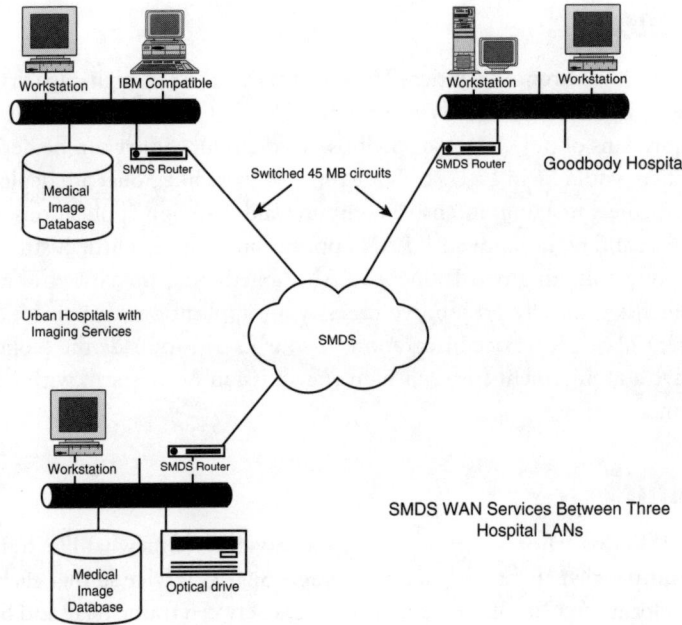

ATM

ATM (Asynchronous Transport Mode) is a transport service that will run over Sonet networks. In the previous chapter, I discussed ATM as a LAN technology; however, it makes the transition to WAN service easily. Indeed, using ATM to connect the average LAN workstations is somewhat like using a 747 jet to transport a letter to a nearby town: You could do it, but it isn't generally necessary. In large campus LANs, ATM provides a good backbone used to link multiple FDDI LANs together into one larger LAN. For those environments that need to extend the high-bandwidth capacities over greater distances than just a campus LAN, ATM is an excellent way to integrate and share not only LAN services but audio- (phone systems) and video-conferencing. ATM is still not being used widely for WANs, but many phone companies are offering some type of ATM WAN. In the future, ATM may become the standard delivery method for all computer communications, including transmissions headed into the home; television, Internet access, banking, shopping, and video phones may all be sent via ATM.

WAN Implementation

After you have determined that you need a WAN service, you must decide what applications will be running over the WAN circuit and how many people will be using them. If you have a Novel network of 200 users in one office and you want them to share e-mail and a database with a 50-user Novel LAN across town, you must figure the number of users accessing the database and sending mail simultaneously across the WAN. If only 5 users of the 50 in the remote office will be accessing the database at any given time, a 56K WAN circuit may be adequate. However, if all 50 users will be accessing the database at the same time, plus sending e-mail, you should plan for a T-1 or a fractional T-1, which is only 512Kbps or 768Kbps. There are no hard and fast rules about how fast a WAN circuit should be. It may require that you talk to the users of the applications to ascertain what their usage patterns are before you size the WAN circuit. A good general guideline is 128Kbps per 25 frequent users.

Connecting the LANs

Connecting the WAN to the LAN is usually accomplished in one of two ways for data traffic that you will find in a LAN: bridging or routing. Both of these networking services are achieved by means of a hardware device installed on the connecting LANs. The bridge or router equipment is connected to your LAN just as the computers are connected to the LAN. The bridge or router also is connected to the WAN and acts as the "server" providing a path to the other LAN at the far end of the WAN.

Bridges

A bridge is a device that passes all data on the ethernet, token ring, or whatever type of LAN you have over the WAN to the other LAN. Essentially, the LANs that are bridged over the WAN appear to be all one LAN. The advantage to this type of networking is that you can set up all the devices in both LANs as if they were all local to one another. All the numbering used to provide computers on the LANs with unique network addresses reflects a single LAN. Having a single network may simplify administration, as there is only one network to "look after." However, the disadvantage is that there may be data being sent over the bridge that should stay local, thus taking up valuable "space" on your WAN circuit. Bridges use filtering and a bridging algorithm to learn which network addresses are on the LAN and which are on the WAN, but there generally is more traffic passing through a bridge than with a router. Bridging is appropriate for small networks on either side of the WAN, but if you have large networks on either side of the WAN, you probably should use a router.

Routers

Routers are devices that are installed on the LAN much as bridges are; a router connects to both the WAN and the LAN. The difference between a router and a bridge is in the way it handles the data it receives. In the bridging world, data bits on the LAN (called packets) are passed across the WAN with minimum effort on the bridge. The bridge doesn't look at the packets very closely to examine the data, because it doesn't care what the data is; it just passes the packets over to the other side of the WAN. Routers, on the other hand, examine the data sent in the packets to see whether it needs to go over the WAN or if it should stay in the LAN. Think of a data application, e-mail for instance, as if it were a letter being sent over the LAN. It is put into a Novell or TCP/IP envelope (or whatever network you have), which is addressed by Novell or TCP/IP to show you sent it and who the recipient is. That envelope (or packet) is then "stuffed" into an ethernet or token ring envelope (whatever type of network you have) and is addressed again by the ethernet card to show from which computer it came. A bridge doesn't care about the Novell or TCP/IP addressed packet; it only looks at the ethernet or token ring address. A router, however, will "open up" the ethernet envelope to see the addressing on the packet inside the ethernet packet. The router provides an additional criteria for deciding where a particular packet should be sent. This is less important in a small network, but in a large network this function is critical to efficient use of both WAN and LAN resources. If you are connecting your network to the Internet, you must have a router. The network addresses you set up on your LAN to get on to the Internet will be unique to your network and must be routed as a separate network to the Internet, not bridged.

ABC WIDGETS, INC.

The ABC company makes widgets. ABC says it doesn't produce your run-of-the-mill widgets, but rather one-of-a-kind, top-of-the-line widgets. ABC's business has really taken off, and it has decided to open an office in Normal, Illinois, to facilitate the growing orders for widgets in the Midwest. All the company's inventory and shipping information is stored on the Novell LAN file servers in the main office in Fort Lee, New Jersey. The new Illinois office has a Novell LAN but needs access to all the information at the headquarters LAN. ABC has decided to implement a WAN so it can be linked to corporate headquarters.

The administrators found, after talking with upper management, that the ten-user LAN in Illinois will grow to more than 50 in the next six months. The users on the LAN in Midwest office will spend most of their time entering orders into the database in Fort Lee. The orders for widgets must be checked against the existing stock, ordered, and shipped using information stored in the central database with little delay. The administrators decide to purchase a point-to-point fractional T-1 from a long-distance company. The T-1 will provide a 256Kbps transmission rate initially and, with a simple call to their provider, the administrators can up the bandwidth to 512Kbps or higher when the additional employees join the Illinois office.

Because the Novell network in Fort Lee is already set up, another Novell purchase is planned for the Illinois office. This new Novell network is a separate network with its own numbers so the administrators in Illinois can number the computers on their LAN with out having to check whether a particular address is already in use by a computer in Fort Lee. Because these are separate networks, they cannot be bridged, so administrators have selected a router with an internal CSU/DSU so they can connect directly to the WAN circuit. The router also supports Novell protocol routing (called IPX routing) (see Figure 11.3).

FIGURE 11.3.
A Novell network with a WAN in place.

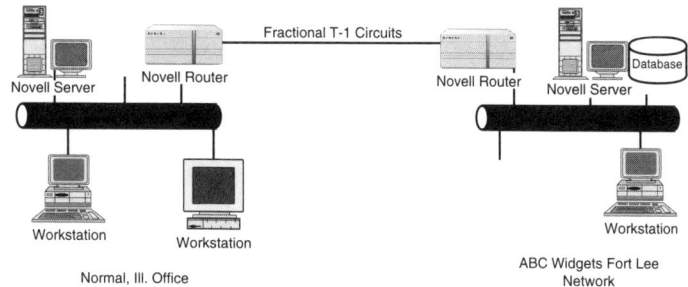

ABC Widgets WAN Connecting Two
Separate Novell LANs

Accessing the WAN

To access any WAN service with a router or a bridge, you will need an access device. This equipment will vary with the type of WAN service you use. Each WAN service requires some hardware device, and some services, such as frame relay, requires software as well. The access equipment connects to the bridge or router with a V.35 cable, for example, and then connects to the WAN circuit using whichever cable the WAN service requires, like a fiber or twisted pair cable. When you purchase your bridge or router you must know the type of WAN service you will be using and make sure you have technical support for that service. Frame relay, as an example, can be delivered over a 56K circuit, which almost any bridge or router can support, but frame relay access requires software on the router or bridge; so you must match the equipment to both the circuit and possibly the service on that WAN circuit. Your WAN service provider should know how the WAN circuit will be delivered (that is, on fiber or twisted pair) and what access equipment you will need. Many phone companies will rent or provide the access equipment as part of the service. You then only need to supply the router or bridge with the appropriate WAN port option, such as V.35, RS-449, EIA-530 or RS-232 and software, if required.

56K Circuits

For accessing a 56K circuit, use a DSU (data service unit). The DSU connects to your router or bridge and to the phone company's circuit. The DSU formats the data from the bridge or router so it can be transmitted over the 56K line. Each bridge or router that connects to a 56K circuit must have a DSU-type access device. The DSU can usually be purchased through the vendor that sells the router or bridge. Many routers and bridges come with a 56K DSU-type interface so the WAN circuit can be directly plugged into them.

T-1 Circuits

To access T-1s, you need a CSU/DSU (channel service unit/data service unit). This device provides access to all 24 channels on the T-1, and like the DSU, the CSU/DSU formats the data from the bridge or router so it can be transmitted over the line. Many routers and bridges now come with internal CSU/DSU-type interfaces so you can plug them directly into the T-1.

T-3

To access a T-3 you will probably need a fiber optic access device. Most T-3 services are now delivered on fiber optic cable, and the access device will be a fiber interface on the WAN side and more than likely a V.35 connection on the LAN side. Most routers and bridges do not support T-3s directly and require a separate access device.

Frame Relay

Frame relay services typically are accessed over T-1s or 56K lines and require the appropriate DSU or CSU/DSU. Again, many routers and bridges support direct 56K or T-1 connections; however, the router or bridge you choose must support frame relay service in its operating software.

SMDS

To access SMDS, you will probably need a fiber optic access device. SMDS is usually delivered over a T-3 or fractional T-3 using fiber optic cable, and it requires the appropriate SMDS/T-3 access device on the WAN side. Like frame relay, you need a router that supports SMDS in its software. You need the support of the SMDS provider, which may furnish the SMDS access device, in making this connection.

Sonet

Sonet WANs also require a fiber optic access device. This device is specific to the Sonet WAN, and if it is not supplied by the Sonet access provider directly, your provider should know where you can get a unit that will interface with your LAN and the Sonet service.

ATM

ATM is usually delivered over Sonet in WAN applications, so you will need the Sonet access equipment described in the "Sonet" section. ATM has been deployed over T-3s in some environments, though, and in those instances, the appropriate T-3 access equipment is used. ATM is somewhat like the frame relay or SMDS services in that it is a networking service delivered using another networking technology. Accordingly, just as with frame relay or SMDS, you need a router or other system that provides the software support for ATM.

Why a WAN for Your Intranet?

After you have decided on what kind of connectivity you want, what speed you need, and what kind of hardware and software you need to accomplish that speed, the issue remains: What do I do with a WAN?

The nice thing about a WAN is that, when it is set up correctly, it functions almost exactly like your LAN. You can set it up so that the difference between connecting to a computer across the country is not all that different from connecting to a computer down the hall. The only difference might be the speed of the connection.

For the purposes of your intranet, a WAN can help you solve several problems at once.

Connectivity

A WAN can help you to improve connectivity among the offices as well as a connection to the Internet. If you have two or more offices connected by high-speed data lines, only one needs a connection to the Internet. The other offices can connect through that single connection.

Security

With a WAN, your intranet server can be located inside your own private network. Technically you don't even have to be connected to the Internet for several offices to share documents or communicate by a web or e-mail interface. Even if you have an Internet connection, your web server can be located inside your firewall and can be made accessible only to users on the WAN; in this way you can make your intranet information very secure.

Communications

It also is possible to use these lines for telephone and fax communications among two or more offices. It is possible that your organization will save more money in long-distance phone charges with your WAN than the data lines cost.

The bottom line is that when you have a working WAN in place and are running TCP/IP, setting up an intranet Web site for those machines is pretty easy—as easy as installing Web server software on a machine and giving the computer a name. Instant intranet!

MCKEON & JEFFRIES

M&J had had a WAN up and running for some time. The Philadelphia office and the Washington, DC office had been connected by an ISDN line for more than a year. The WAN needs were twofold. First, to connect the Raleigh office to the WAN, and second, to connect the three offices to the Internet.

To connect the Raleigh office to the WAN, the simplest and least inexpensive alternative was to run an ISDN line directly to the Washington, DC office. This option did not provide the best performance but was the least expensive. The performance was hurt because the intranet server, as well as the Internet connection, were both in the Philadelphia office, so to access either one, the Raleigh employees had to go through the Washington, DC office. It was decided that this was the best option because Raleigh had the fewest employees and was not likely to have too much problem with the speed of the connection.

The Internet connection from the Philadelphia office was a little more difficult to set up. Finding a local service provider and getting the line installed was easy, but configuring the router was a little more difficult. It took several days to get the connection to work right with M&J's system.

THE SPORTING GOODS AND APPAREL ASSOCIATION

The SGAA's WAN needs were very simple: a T-1 connection to the Internet. Their Internet service provider (ISP) installed the CSU/DSU and their local telephone company installed the line itself. It took a couple trips by the ISP techie and a little tweaking from the consultants hired to build the intranet to get it to work right, but it wasn't too much of a problem.

Summary

Anyone who maintains a central database or a central resource center and who needs to service offices that are located geographically apart from each other should consider utilizing a WAN. If you begin with a clear goal of what your WAN needs to accomplish, the WAN will began to build itself. Use the information in this chapter as a reference guide to making the most beneficial choices for your WAN. With a grasp of the framework and a knowledge of the basic connecting tools, your WAN soon will allow you and your users to perform your jobs more efficiently.

Selecting an Internet Service Provider

1

by Jim

IN THIS CHAPTER

- A little background **164**
- General considerations **165**
- Types of Internet connections **165**
- Planning and setting up the LAN for Internet connectivity **169**
- Hardware and software **172**
- Getting connected **175**
- Security **176**
- Systems integrators as ISPs **178**

This chapter covers some of the more important elements of getting your LAN connected to the Internet. As you may recall from Chapter 11, "Wide Area Networks," using the Internet as a wide area network (WAN) to connect two or more LANs together is a cost-effective way of linking separate LANs together. If you have offices around the country and you want the LAN users to share e-mail and other applications, connecting each office to a local Internet provider and using the Internet as a WAN is more cost-effective than paying a phone company for a cross-country data circuit. This chapter discusses some of the hardware and software associated with establishing Internet access and some of the issues that surround connecting a LAN to a network of millions of computers, which is exactly what the Internet is.

A Little Background

In its early years, the only way you could get access to the Net was through a university or government agency—or possibly a research organization. There were virtually no businesses on the Net, and the only dial-up users were those dialing into the universities or government networks to access a computer that was connected to the Net. All through the 1970s and early 1980s, the Net was very small in terms of the actual number of users. When companies like UUNet and PSI began building Internet network systems that could be connected to the existing Net, the first commercial access to the Net began. Even just a few years ago in the early 1990s the applications and types of connections used to access the Net were very limited. A user with dial-in access, for instance, would be accessing the Net through a shell account, which is all text based; no graphical access existed for Internet services.

Since that time, the Net has grown exponentially with millions of users all around the world. We have yet to witness the potential growth of the Internet. At least half of all U.S. business organizations have not provided dial-up business accounts for their employees or connected their LANs to the Net, and many individuals who will have personal dial-up accounts have yet to join in.

This incredible growth has spawned thousands of Internet providers. The big players that have joined or are planning to join the ISP ranks include AT&T, MCI, and some of the Bell companies. Even a few of the larger cable systems such as Jones Communications and TCI are implementing cable TV connections to the Internet that promise to deliver higher speed access than is possible with a modem over phone company lines—although this type of service is still largely underdeveloped at this time. Aside from the major players like the PSIs and UUNets, there are so-called online services that not only offer Internet access but also fancy bulletin board systems to provide information content, such as America Online and CompuServe. You may have seen advertisements for one of these online services in which a "user" is talking about all the things he or she can do with this service and concludes, "I even have access to the Internet." These companies are offering a dial-in connection to their customized networks that also have a connection to the Internet; but you are not necessarily connecting to the Internet when you dial into their service.

In addition to the big ISPs and the online providers, there are numerous small ISPs that have come out of the woodwork; these are sometimes called "mom-and-pop shops." Five years ago a provider could buy a 56Kbps digital circuit to a large ISP, such as UUNet, hook some modems together, and set up shop. For the most part, we have seen that this kind of ISP is disappearing because of either serious competition from larger, less expensive ISPs or the lack of service they offer. Most mom and pop shops either get smaller and collapse because of these larger providers or, if they survive and grow, typically are bought out by the larger ISPs.

General Considerations

This section discusses the factors to consider when selecting Internet access providers. My first suggestion may disappoint you: If the providers offer freebies, such as hats, stickers, or any other neat paraphernalia when you sign up, find another service provider.

If you are simply looking for dial-up modem service, you have many options from which to choose. There are hundreds of choices that adequately satisfy dial-up service requirements. This route provides an acceptable method of connection to the Internet if you are connecting just a few computers that will do little more than browse the Web and send some e-mail.

If, on the other hand, you have many users who will browse, send e-mail, share documents consistently by e-mail, and perhaps host your company's Web site, you will need to connect your LAN to the Internet. For this type of connectivity, your options are greatly reduced. Most of the large ISPs (not the "online" providers but actual ISPs) have some sort of dedicated LAN to Internet service. UUNet is one of the largest ISPs that specialize in dedicated LAN-to-Internet access. PSI is another large ISP with dedicated access services. Numerous regional providers are also stepping up to the plate. Many of these providers offer dedicated connections to the Net but may require more than just a dedicated "pipe." You may want support from the provider in configuring your network for Internet access or assistance with e-mail and Web page support. This will narrow the field of providers even further. If you are just getting a "pipe" to the Net, you may be responsible for setting up your own news, e-mail, and Web servers. I cover these issues later in this chapter; now let's look at Internet connections.

Types of Internet Connections

Before considering the type of Internet connection for your network, you first must decide what kind of service you will provide to your users. I already have mentioned the idea of connecting a LAN to the Internet rather than just utilizing modems. Now let's consider in more detail some of the pros and cons associated with the different types of Internet services and the application of those services as they relate to your organization's needs. What follows is a general description of different types of Internet services, what they provide, and how they may fit into your plans for Internet access.

Dial-Up Analog Service

Dial-up analog service is for users who have modems connected to their computers. This dial-in user can access the Internet in two ways. Again, both of these methods use a modem to allow the computer to speak over the telephone lines. The modem takes the bits—or the 1s and 0s that the computer "speaks"—and turns them into sounds that can be sent over the telephone lines. These sounds are sometimes heard, depending on the modem, as a series of squeals and beeps when you first dial into the ISP's modems. The fastest speed at which a user can access the Internet with a modem is 28,800 bps. Slightly faster speeds may be achieved, but basically this is the maximum speed that the analog telephone lines can support. If you use modems to connect to the Internet, you will have to maintain a modem on each computer or set up a communications server to support a pool of modems that the users can access over the LAN. The modem pool is considered by some (myself included) to be more of a hassle than it's worth, particularly with the speedier and consolidated direct LAN-to-Internet services available from most ISPs.

Shell Accounts

The first of these modem connection methods is generally called a shell account. A shell account is accessed with a software package, such as a Windows terminal, Procomm, or PC Anywhere. A user dials into the ISP's modems and, after he or she is connected, logs into (connects) to a computer that is directly connected to the Internet in the ISP's facility. This computer, called a server, has its own unique Internet address. The user uses the server's Internet applications, such as e-mail or Telnet, to get around on the Internet. The shell method is the way users originally accessed the Internet through modems.

The main drawback to this type of connection is that there are no graphics associated with it. A user browsing the Web from a shell account will be using a program, such as Lynx, that allows the user to read the text on the Web but without graphics. The advantage to this account is that user can access many applications and programs located on the server that take up too much space or are too expensive to be stored on an individual's computer. Many Internet "power" users and novices alike use shell accounts as a method of Internet access.

SLIP and PPP Accounts

Recently, there has been an explosion of SLIP and PPP accounts to access the Internet. These types of accounts have led directly to the widespread use of the Internet by thousands of users who otherwise might not have ventured onto the information superhighway. Like a shell account, a PPP or SLIP user dials into the ISP to connect to the Internet. Unlike the shell account, however, the SLIP/PPP user connects to the ISP with a SLIP or PPP software package, such as a Winsock, Chameleon, or Netscape dialer, and gets an Internet address assigned directly to his or her computer. Then he or she can use the e-mail, Telnet, and Web browser applications located on the computer to communicate or search for information. Because the computer is directly connected to the Internet with its own address, the user can browse the Web in graphical mode. In most cases, users will get an Internet address assigned dynamically each time they connect to the ISP. This means nothing in terms of the functionality. For example, a user's e-mail address always will be the same, but the numerical address of the computer will be different each time he or she dials in. Most ISPs elect to dynamically assign addresses to dial-up customers from predefined pools of addresses for easier management.

Digital PPP and SLIP Dial-Up Accounts

The phone companies' recent development of ISDN (Integrated Services Digital Networks) has brought the capability to dial a digital call into an affordable price range. ISDN is an all-digital service. This means that binary (1s and 0s) that computers speak can be directly transmitted over the phone lines without having to change the 1s and 0s into sounds as a modem does. The result is much faster transmission speeds, and that means faster connections to Internet sites. The minimum speed of an ISDN phone call is 56Kbps. With just an ISDN Basic Rate Interface (BRI), users can reach dial speeds up to 128Kbps. This type of speed brings a much more functional and practical access to the Internet than even the fastest modem.

ISDN allows the user to search out and retrieve information two to four times faster than an analog modem. The ISDN service allows the user's computer to transmit a totally digital signal all the way through the phone company's network to the ISP. A modem, on the other hand, is extremely inefficient, and as a result, modem transmission speeds are limited. Obviously, the ISP must have ISDN network connections to support this type of service. Users can place ISDN calls with the help of a device called a terminal adapter (TA). Think of the TA as a modem for digital computer calls. This is not accurate technically because there is no modulating of the computer's digital "talk" into sounds, but the TA is attached to the computer in the same way as a modem. Subscribers use dial-up software that allows them to dial a PPP or SLIP connection over the ISDN line. This account also will get an address assigned when dialing in.

Dedicated and Dial-Up LAN Connections

The LAN-to-Internet connections come in two versions; both use a router to connect the LAN to the ISP and require a TCP/IP software package on each computer to access the Internet. This software is different than the software used to dial into the Internet with a TA or modem. The LAN TCP/IP software allows the computer to "talk" over the LAN through the router to the ISP and out to the Internet (see Figures 12.1 and 12.2).

FIGURE 12.1.
LAN dial-up and direct connections to the Internet.

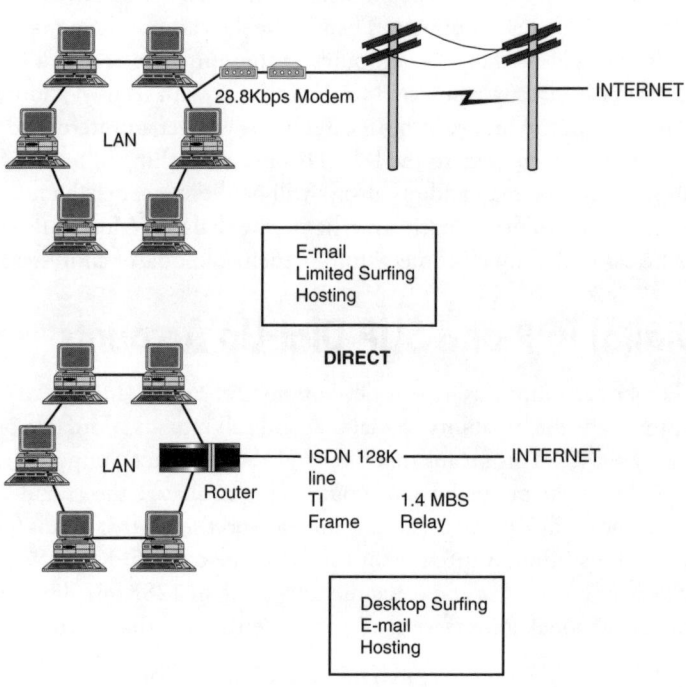

FIGURE 12.2.
Individual dial-up and single desktop connections to the Internet.

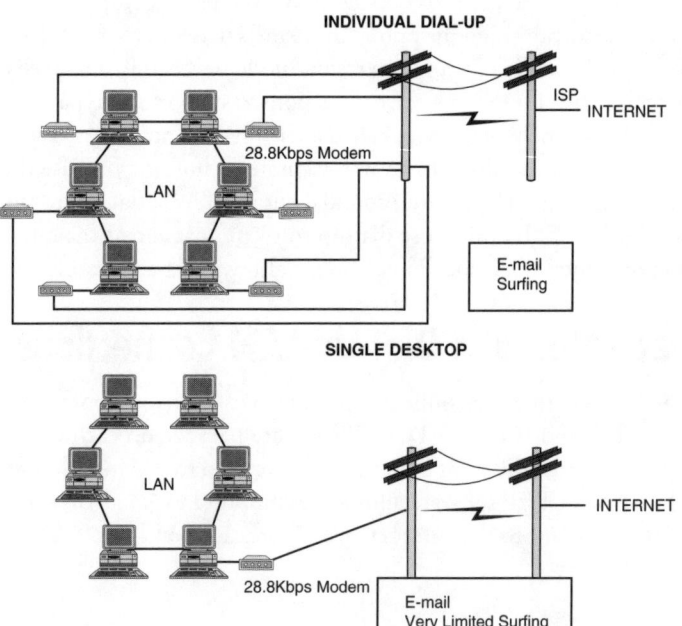

Dedicated LAN Connections

With a dedicated LAN connection, the router's connection to the Internet is "nailed up" or dedicated, meaning a path or circuit over the telephone company's network to the ISP is established 24 hours a day, seven days a week. This is an ideal connection for users who host their own Web page servers. Typically, the ISP will provide some support with mail and news servers, allowing users access to their servers. The LAN is available all the time on the Internet. This type of connection is best suited to mid- and large-size LANs with 25 or more users. The speeds of dedicated LAN connections range from 56Kbps to 45Mbps or higher, the average being the T-1 dedicated phone company service that operates at 1.5Mbps. The types of dedicated connections supported will depend on the local telephone company and the ISP.

LAN Dial-Up Connections

The other option is the dial-up circuit to the Internet. In this scenario, the circuit to the Internet is dialed up whenever one of the computers issues a connect request to the Internet, such as opening the Web browser and connecting to a site or sending out some e-mail. The router brings up the connection to the Internet when needed and then drops it when there is no traffic to the Internet. ISDN is the most common method of dialing up a LAN-to-Internet connection in high-population areas. In the Midwest, 56K or T-1 is more common than ISDN. This type of service is ideal for small LANs in which there is sporadic use of the Internet. This is not a good connection method, however, if you are planning to serve a Web site, because the connection is typically dialed from the LAN to the ISP in one direction only. The connection would not be initiated through the ISP when a user on the Internet tries to access the home page.

Planning and Setting Up the LAN for Internet Connectivity

Certain systems must be placed to support your LAN-to-Internet connection. I will assume first that there already is a LAN installed in your facility. Before you begin, ask several providers about the pricing structures of their service options. Make sure you choose a provider that has a point of presence (POP) local to your facility. Because the telephone company charges for your dedicated circuit likely will be based on mileage (the distance from your facility to the ISP over the phone lines), you don't want a provider who is across the state; you will be paying for both the telephone company lines and the connection charge to the ISP.

> **NOTE**
>
> The acronym POP is used for both Point of Presence and Post Office Protocol. Be careful not to get them confused. It's a little easier now that Post Office Protocol has been upgraded to version 3. Now it's usually called POP3.

Some ISPs will bundle the telephone company circuit charge into their billing so you only pay the ISP, but there is a charge for this service. Some ISPs also charge for the amount of data that the site receives (and in some cases transmits) across the circuit. An average price for a T-1 connection to an ISP is about $1,500 per month plus phone company charges. There are ISPs that will charge for data packet transmissions in addition to this fee, up to $6,000 a month. In my opinion, this is excessive and potentially could make budgeting your Internet connection difficult because your data packet transmission levels typically go up and down depending on what the users are doing on the Net. If a user is just Web browsing for a few days and then begins to download large files from the Net, your usage of the circuit goes up. One month you could get a $1,500 bill from the ISP, and the next month you could get a $3,500 bill.

Internet Addresses

Another planning consideration is how to set up the network to accommodate the Internet service. It's likely you will be given a group or block of TCP/IP addresses that you must assign to each workstation and server that will access the Internet.

The address block looks something like this:

```
192.188.199.0
```

192.188.199.0 is the network block, and within this block you have 254 individual addresses to assign to each computer. Each class of IP address has the numbers 1 through 256 (1 and 256 are typically reserved for specific machines). Therefore, if you see an IP address number higher than 255, it's probably incorrect.

You have a list of computers with addresses that look like this:

```
Jim's computer: 192.188.199.1
Bob's computer: 192.188.199.2
Marcia's computer: 192.188.199.3
```

These addresses are 32 bits long and are divided into 4 groups of 8 bits. Each byte (eight bits) has a value between 1 and 256. You may see addresses that look like this:

```
12.1.1.2 or 221.221.23.1
```

You will not see addresses that look like this:

```
322.198.620.8 or 914.2.832.1
```

Each computer on the Internet must have a unique address. No two computers on the Internet anywhere in the world can have the same address. The addressing of Internet computers is set up into network blocks. These blocks are then assigned to ISPs, government agencies, large corporations, and ultimately smaller companies and organizations through ISPs or the government. There are three types of address blocks: Class A, Class B, and Class C. The biggest difference is the size of the blocks or the number of individual addresses in each block. A Class A block, for instance, has over 16 million individual addresses. The kinds of organizations that can get a Class A block are limited to governments, the really big ISPs (for example, PSI, UUNet), and groups with more clout than the rest of us. If you want to hear unbridled laughter, tell your ISP you need a Class A address block; all the Class A addresses are already assigned. Class A addresses start with a first byte value of 1 and run up to 127. An example of a Class A network block would be the following:

```
22.0.0.0
```

The first byte (22) is the network number, and the other three bytes are for individual computer addresses. The individual addresses available would then be assigned as follows:

```
22.0.0.1, then 22.0.0.2, and so on
```

Class B addresses start at 128.0.0.0 and run up to 191.0.0.0, so a Class B network block would look like this:

```
131.11.0.0
```

Note that the first and second byte now make up the network number and the remaining two bytes are for individual computer addresses, such as the following:

```
131.11.0.1 or 131.11.0.2
```

A Class B address has more than 65,000 individual addresses in it. Class B addresses are rare; not as rare as a Class A, but if you ask your ISP for a Class B you will still get a chuckle. At this point, no Class As, and very few Class Bs, are left.

The last type of address block is the Class C. More than likely you will get this type of network block for your LAN. Class C addresses start at 192 and run through 223. An example of a Class C network address would be the following:

```
192.188.199.0
```

Notice that the first three bytes now make up the network block with only 254 addresses available for the individual computers. There are still a fair number of Class C addresses, but they are being assigned at a rapid rate to ISPs. The address blocks are assigned to everyone by the Network Information Center (NIC). Every address block on the Internet is registered with the NIC. Don't bother applying to the NIC for your own address block; the assignment of network addresses occurs in groups of blocks rather than individual network numbers. The NIC is sort of a wholesale distributor of addresses.

You will get your addresses from an ISP when you sign up for service. You must use the addresses assigned by the ISP. If you change providers, new addresses will be issued, and computers will have to be renumbered.

Back in the olden days of the Net (you know, the 1970s and 1980s), before the explosion of users and ISPs, you could actually apply for and receive your very own address block. Some organizations are using these addresses today. They are addresses such as Class A and B networks and in some cases Class C addresses that start with 192. The number of TCP/IP addresses seemed to be unlimited, so the NIC assigned them freely. Now, however, there is a real crunch for addresses, and they are assigned only with great review as to how they will be utilized after assignment. There is currently a plan to unleash the Next Generation IP addressing scheme. This addressing will have to be in addition to, not a replacement of, existing addresses if it is going to be practical. There are no new TCP/IP addresses in use commercially at this writing.

Although individual users or clients don't need to have static IP addresses because they can be shared, Internet hosts must have a permanent address assigned. That address is what tells Internet users where to find the host. Just a few years ago, there were fewer than 10,000 Internet hosts. Now, with every company, organization, and even some individuals gobbling up hosts at a rate of hundreds of thousands per month (see Figure 12.3), the Internet community will breathe a lot easier when a new system is put into place.

FIGURE 12.3.
This timeline illustrates the rapid growth of Internet hosts.

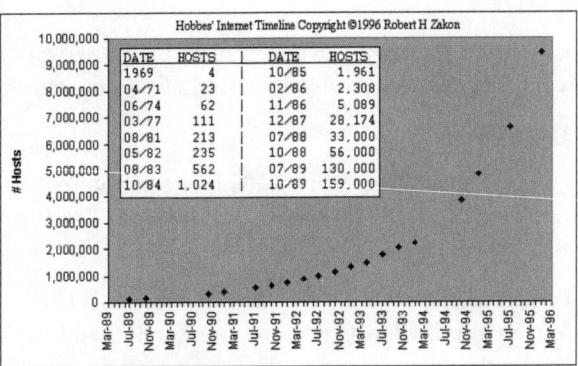

Hardware and Software

To complete your Internet connectivity, you will need specific router hardware and TCP/IP software. There is a vast array of routers available, including those from Bay Networks, Cisco, Ascend, and 3Com, just some of the major router manufacturers. Basically, all routers perform the same functions, but there are specific features that your ISP may look for or that your WAN circuit will require, such as dial-up ISDN on demand. Make sure you size a router appropriately for your network. If you have 75 users in your LAN and a T-1 to your Internet provider, a Cisco 7000 router is definitely overkill; a Cisco 2500 might be a better choice. If you have a small office with 10 users and want a dial-up LAN service, an Ascend Pipeline 50 would be a good solution.

The TCP/IP software is another important piece. If you will be responsible for the administration of your Internet (TCP/IP) LAN configuration, a good reference book on the nuts and bolts of TCP/IP is essential. O'Reilly publishes *TCP/IP*, which is generally considered *the* book on TCP/IP. (It also is referred to as the "crab book" because there is a big crab on the cover. I have no idea why there is a crab on the cover, nor do any of my associates, but we have all read it and agree that it's the best around.)

Routers

You will need a router to connect your LAN to the ISP via an ISDN line or some other direct connection. Of course, you can always connect your LAN to an ISP using merely a modem, but your bandwidth is limited to 28.8Kbps. Some ISPs will rent you the equipment you need for the connection. This is a good way to minimize your initial startup costs, and you will not have to worry about configuring the router or maintaining it. The router provides the LAN-to-WAN link. You will, for instance, have your Ethernet LAN connected through the router to a T-1 circuit that goes over to the ISP. This router must be capable of routing the TCP/IP protocol. You will find this feature listed as IP routing in the technical specifications for the router.

There are dozens of routers that will satisfy the connection to the ISP. The biggest name is Cisco, which has been making some of the finest routers for more than a decade. Its affordable 2,500 series can provide suitable basic TCP/IP connectivity from a single LAN to an ISP for about $3,000. Cisco also has a more flexible router at the intermediate level: the 3000 and 4000 series, which are modular chassis platforms that allow you to add different LAN interface cards in the same router (such as a token ring and ethernet) as well as connect multiple WANs together. If your facility is going to connect to one of your remote offices and to the Internet, you will have two WANs at your facility, and a Cisco 4000 might be a good choice. Cisco also makes the Cadillac—actually the tractor-trailer—of routers with their 7000 series. This router is the kind of system that your ISP (or your ISP's ISP) uses to connect to other ISPs on the Net; you do not need a Cisco 7000 for the scenarios discussed here. You cannot go wrong with a Cisco. Any ISP worth a hill of beans will be familiar with them.

Cisco routers are by no means the only choice for connecting your LAN to the Internet, however; 3Com routers are another option. 3Com has some low-cost routers, such as the 224 and the 227 series, that are roughly the equivalent of the Cisco 2500 series. 3Com also has the modular chassis systems, called Netbuilder II, which provide multiple LAN and WAN Interfaces. Pricing for these systems are fairly comparable to the Cisco systems.

Ascend is another router manufacturer with a reputation for Internet connectivity. Ascend's claim to fame has been primarily in the dial-up access for ISDN and modem users more so than dedicated LAN connections; however, the Ascend Pipeline 50 is a low-cost (about $1,400)

IP and IPX router that can be used with some dedicated ISDN applications and is ideal for dial-up LAN connections to the Internet. Ascend also has a new product, the Pipeline 130, that provides IP and IPX routing over T-1 WANs. This product costs about $2,000, making it a very inexpensive router for T-1 Internet access. However, the Pipeline 130 is new, and no real feedback on its performance is available.

There are other routers that can provide Internet access as well. Bay Networks, Wellfleet, and Proteon are all routers that have been used to provide TCP/IP routing, although they do not have the widespread recognition that the previously mentioned routers have. There are probably still other systems available from companies outside the United States that are just not as well known here. Basically any system that can route TCP/IP can be used for Internet access.

Workstation Software

You need TCP/IP software for all the computers that will be accessing the Internet. There are many packages from which to choose. Many LAN operating systems, such as NetWare and Windows NT, have either inherent or add-on TCP/IP support. You can also purchase TCP/IP software packages such as Netmanage's Chameleon, FTP software's PC/TCP, or Wollengong's Pathways IP software. These packages run under Windows and provide TCP/IP applications such as e-mail and Telnet over the LAN. Macintosh computers have software such as MacTCP that provides the TCP/IP over LAN functionality. These software packages allow the TCP/IP to "talk" over the ethernet, token ring, FDDI, or whatever LAN you have. You must be sure that the package you select is designed to run over your particular network because the workstations are probably already running a protocol such as NetWare's IPX. You will have to set up the LAN interface (NIC) cards with different frame types to allow your LAN operating system protocols and the TCP/IP protocols to coexist on the same NIC. Refer to your LAN operating system and the NIC card specifications for more detail.

Server Software

The servers will require a little more sophisticated software than will the workstations. A server's function is twofold: It must connect other services on the Internet and allow incoming connections to access files, such as Web pages. The service in TCP/IP that allows for these incoming connections is called a daemon (pronounced *demon*), or sometimes just the server portion of the TCP/IP software. If you are going to set up a mail server for Internet you must have the POP (Post Office Protocol) and the SMTP (Simple Mail Transfer Protocol) to route incoming and outgoing mail. The same is true for a Web server: you must have the HTTPd (Hypertext Transfer Protocol Daemon) running to serve your Web pages to other users.

If you are running a UNIX system as your Internet server, these services are probably part of the operating system and can be configured for your network specifically by editing the parameters of each server application. A UNIX server is the most common platform used on the Internet to offer these services. SUN Microsystems makes a UNIX Internet server called Netra that has all of the Internet services preinstalled—you simply enter the addresses you get from your ISP and information about the users on your LAN for e-mail accounts. To run another software package for your mail and news, many LAN operating systems such as NetWare or NT now come with some Internet server components installed that you can add to your existing network to provide SMTP and Web services. SMTP, News, POP, Web, and all other TCP/IP-based Internet applications are based on the TCP/IP protocol standard. Any TCP/IP-compliant server software you select will be functional for Internet services. To work on the Internet, you must have a TCP/IP-based server component. Figure 12.4 shows a possible "shopping list."

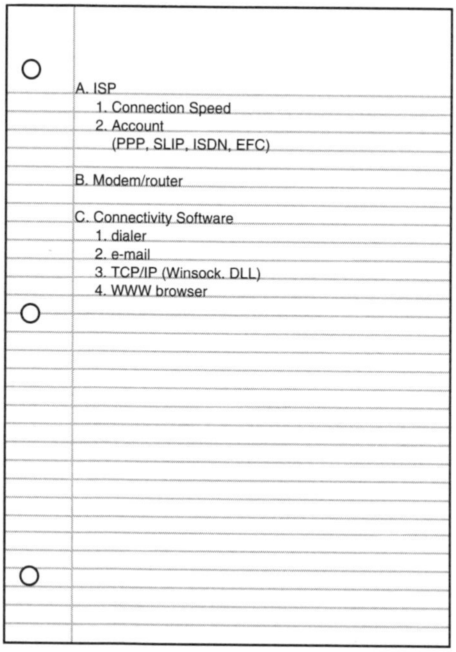

FIGURE 12.4.

An Internet server software connectivity shopping list.

```
A. ISP
   1. Connection Speed
   2. Account
      (PPP, SLIP, ISDN, EFC)

B. Modem/router

C. Connectivity Software
   1. dialer
   2. e-mail
   3. TCP/IP (Winsock. DLL)
   4. WWW browser
```

Getting Connected

After you have decided on a provider and chosen the type of service necessary for your network, the provider should be able to assist you in getting the WAN circuit ordered. This should not be a major issue for the provider; if it is, I would have serious reservations regarding the ISP's experience level. The WAN circuit must be connected to the router and configured with the appropriate information to support your LAN and the connection to the ISP. Your computers must be loaded with TCP/IP software and configured with the correct information, such as addresses and domain names. When all this is configured correctly and the WAN is connected to the LAN, you should be able to access the Internet and other Internet users should have access to your site.

This sounds too easy, right? Well, in most cases there is in fact a fair amount of tweaking and fine-tuning to sort out bugs, find the addresses that were entered incorrectly, and troubleshoot the WAN circuit that doesn't seem to work. This is all fairly typical for a job that involves getting so many pieces together. Depending on the provider you choose, you may very well be responsible for a great deal of this headache. Even if the WAN circuit and the router are provided by the ISP, you likely will have to support the LAN yourself.

The provider should issue the addresses you need and give you information on the addresses' domain name server. A domain name server is the service that advertises your organization's name and addresses to the rest of the net; your_business.com or your_group.org are examples of domain names. TCP/IP speaks in numbers, which are the addresses we discussed earlier. Domain name servers associate names with numbers so you can Web browse to www.netscape.com instead of 192.188.199.5. You can register your own domain name through your ISP. This will give you a your_business.com address so your business can have its own Web and e-mail names.

Security

Before you have your WAN circuit installed, your router up and running, and all the servers and workstations set up correctly to access the Internet, you should consider the implications of connecting the network to the rest of the world. Security is a big topic of conversation around the Internet, and with good reason. The TCP/IP protocols and all the associated applications are well studied by thousands of users. Consequently, thousands of people are intimately familiar with how the TCP/IP protocols work and how to manipulate them. Most of these users are honest networking and programming types. A small portion of the Internet population, however, is not so honest, and if this group finds an opportunity to dig around in your network, these users will take it. So let's look at the problem of Internet security.

Firewalls and a Word to the Wise

"Firewall" is the latest buzzword in the networking community. It is almost as worn out as "interactive multimedia." Firewalls are hardware devices like routers that keep the bad guys out of your network. Generally, the actual threat and the appropriate security precautions for networks are largely misunderstood, and so the firewall frenzy abounds. The idea of a firewall is that you can filter out specific addresses or protocols so that they cannot be used to gain access to your network. The firewall can be configured to allow only specific source and destination addresses access to and from your network. Another function prevents an intruder from acquiring an address from your TCP/IP network (called "spoofing") and then using it to gain access to your network servers while looking like a local computer in your network.

There are numerous important, U.S. government-controlled networks that have been accessible over the Internet and have never had a firewall router installed. That's because there is a very clear relationship between the security level of the data and the level of access to the data that a good security administrator needs to know.

The need to classify and protect data basically comes in two forms: data that is so important to your organization that its compromise would be disastrous, and data that is perhaps important but wouldn't be the end of the world if someone gained unauthorized access to it. Within government agencies there are additional levels of classified security, but these two categories will suffice for our purposes. The bottom line is this: If the data falls into the really important category, *don't put it on the Internet*—regardless of what the firewall specs promise.

If you have a Novell server on your LAN that stores customers' credit card numbers, don't load TCP/IP on it and use that server for a Web page server. Not loading TCP/IP on the server reduces the probability of hacking by a thousandfold. As far as the Internet is concerned, if a network doesn't have a TCP/IP address on it, the network doesn't exist. Now there are still ways that the hacker can gain access to the TCP/IP systems on the network, attempt to spoof a NetWare address, and hack into the Novell server, but if you configure your servers and routers carefully, you will close the openings even further, reducing the possibility of hacking.

If you contend that the data on your system is of global or life-threatening importance, don't even put the server on the same LAN as the TCP/IP systems. Even here you still must maintain the highest security configurations and procedures. The Internet is not the real issue in terms of security; it's the integrity of your users and your administrative/security skills that count.

In many cases, the routers and UNIX servers that you purchase, coupled with the security features inherent in a good LAN operating system, will be more than adequate to secure your LAN and still provide reasonable access to the authorized users without the need for a $25,000 firewall that still is not a cure-all for the issues of security. There are people who will argue this issue ad infinitum and will tear this argument to shreds; they are probably people who have read a lot of the hype in the trade magazines or are trying to sell you a firewall.

In all fairness to some of the better firewall systems, there are a few that provide some encryption, transforming the data you send over the Internet to appear as a scrambled mess of characters instead of a coherent data stream. At the receiving end, the system unscrambles the data so the server and the user can read it. This feature can be accomplished with software packages that cost much less than a firewall router, so the issue of protecting your systems comes down to education, awareness of what is already available, and segmenting and classifying your data accordingly.

MCKEON & JEFFRIES

M&J's connection to the Internet was a difficult decision, the major factor being the lack of connectivity of the Raleigh office. The Philadelphia and Washington, DC offices had been connected by an ISDN line for some time. The question was, Should the Raleigh office be connected to the WAN through a direct connection—a dedicated ISDN line, for example—or should it connect to the intranet through the Internet? The firm already had determined that it wanted Internet access for all its employees, for the communications and research benefits.

The decision was finally made to connect the LAN in the Raleigh office to Washington by an ISDN line. In turn, the Philadelphia office set up an ISDN line to the Internet. The reason for this was mostly cost. Even though the ISDN connections were moderately expensive, they provided a less expensive alternative than connecting both offices to the Internet, mainly because the Philadelphia connection would need at least a fractional T-1 to handle the incoming traffic from the Raleigh office, as well as the outgoing traffic from the other two offices. Of course, security also was a factor in the decision. With this method, M&J could keep the intranet behind its firewall, making it more difficult to break into. With the other alternative, the Web server would need the capability to access from the Internet.

THE SPORTING GOODS AND APPAREL ASSOCIATION

The SGAA's choice was much easier. The SGAA knew it needed a big pipe to the Internet because all of its users will be connecting via that route. It also needed a fast connection so the staff could comb the Internet for information and resources for members. The SGAA decided on a T-1 because the technology had been proven and because it seemed to provide the perfect level of connectivity to give their 300 users a fast interface to the SGAA's intranet.

Systems Integrators as ISPs

As you have seen in this chapter, the issues surrounding Internet access are many, and some require careful consideration to implement them with minimum problems while providing all the functionality the Internet has to offer. There is a merger of Internet, video, voice, LAN, and groupware systems occurring that is a challenge to providers and consumers alike.

Users are beginning to see the emergence of systems integrators as ISPs. A system integrator is an organization that provides engineering expertise in making discreet systems work together. Many customers are finding that they may have one of the finest ISPs available to provide access for their LANs, but if there is a problem getting NetWare and TCP/IP running together, the ISP will say, "Sorry; we don't do windows." When it comes to getting a LAN connected to the Internet, you are talking about a variety of different protocols and services that must come together in just the right way to be functional. Just getting a comprehensive view of the networking capabilities you currently have and what you will need to add to get your LAN on the Internet is a formidable task.

A good systems integrator first provides consultation and insight as to what your options are and then helps you make decisions on hardware or software that is appropriate for your environment. Most systems integrators resell equipment and software, but a good one is vendor independent, meaning they will provide you with information and solutions and recommend systems that fit your needs. There are still only a few systems integrators in the ISP businesses but that is changing slowly. It is difficult to find a company with experience in installing and getting many diverse systems to work together; there must be a very adept core of engineers at its heart. You will know a good systems integrator by its list of projects and clients, many of which should be outside of or unrelated to the Internet business. You want an integrator who has done more than connect people to the Net. Ask for references from the integrator's client list that can be contacted to verify that the integrator is in fact a source for resolving problems and designing solutions for customers.

You certainly do not need a systems integrator to connect your LAN to the Net or even as your ISP, but you may find the additional depth of expertise invaluable. The process of getting your LAN on the Internet is much more involved than establishing a dial-up account. The distinguishing qualities and criteria to be considered in finding a good provider should be networking experience and service reputation—more so than cost. If you are looking for reliable service for your organization and support for your LAN systems, expect to pay a little more for it. As with many purchases, you can almost always eliminate the highest and lowest bids and find a good provider (maybe even a systems integrator) somewhere in the middle.

The diversity of phone company services and new products available can be overwhelming, and having the knowledge base of a competent consultant can save you money and time. There are many kinds of services and products that may be appropriate for your network, especially if you are integrating dial-in access to your LAN for telecommuters or linking several LANs and providing Internet connectivity at the same time. Often these capabilities can be combined and delivered with a single system instead of two or three different systems. A systems integrator will know how to get the most out of networking systems to help you meet your objectives.

Summary

This chapter discussed the issues involved in connecting your WAN or LAN to the Internet. We talked about the different types of connections and the equipment you need to create the connection. However, by far the most important decision you will make in this area is the people or companies you will get to assist you. Whether it is an ISP, a systems integrator, or both, you will need some help getting on the Internet. Your decision as to who will get you there probably will make your experience either very simple or incredibly frustrating and time-consuming. In my experience, the best intranet investment you can make is in a competent consultant who can help get your company connected.

Client Issues

13

by David Garrett

IN THIS CHAPTER

- Costs **182**
- Hardware **186**
- Software **193**

Part II

While contemplating the necessary decisions regarding your server or servers, including what connections to set up for your machines, keep in mind what clients you will connect to the intranet. This chapter will help you develop the basis for your current client infrastructure, and, if you already have client applications in place, it should help you narrow down your shopping list of upgrades. The client hardware currently in use (or that will be used) likely will dictate what server hardware and software you choose. This chapter discusses various client hardware and software options and shows how these options influence server and connectivity applications. Becoming knowledgeable about the myriad options available to build an intranet will determine your intranet's functions and ultimate purpose.

Costs

The largest cost of building your intranet probably will be for client hardware, software, and upgrades. The types of server hardware and software, as well as the functions you include on your intranet, will likely be based on the client hardware on hand.

For users working on a contained LAN or WAN only, this assessment means a simple inventory. There will be more considerations for users who are planning to open their LAN or WAN to remote users and for users who are building an intranet specifically for remote users. Whatever the case, the client hardware will require one or possibly several definite minimum levels of compatibility with the server software. All users should be able to access and understand the functions at the basic level. An additional, more advanced level is recommended for more advanced users to utilize the intranet more fully.

Hardware Costs

As you build the foundation for your intranet with upgrades and purchases, carefully consider the display, processor speed, memory, storage (hard drive space), and peripherals, because these factors determine how complex and functional your server software will be. As you choose your framework, keep upward compatibility in mind. For example, a 386 or 486 computer with a slow processor usually doesn't require more than 12 to 20 MB of RAM (memory). More memory after that won't make the system as fast as upgrading to a faster processor would. As a client machine, a 486 or slower processor should have at least 4 MB of RAM to perform any of the applications discussed here. A 486 or slower processor is most effective with 12 to 20 MB. At the other end of the speed spectrum, a faster processor, such as a Pentium, will operate with 8 MB but would be more effective with 16 to 24 MB.

If you're working in a Macintosh environment, consider that a Performa or Quattra with 6 to 16 MB of RAM is roughly equivalent to the minimum PC machine just discussed. A PowerMac or clone should have at least 16 MB of RAM for optimal performance.

Likewise, when you're considering multimedia applications to add to your intranet, client costs will play a significant role. For example, even though installing server software that incorporates sound and/or video into your intranet can be relatively inexpensive, equipping all the client machines with multimedia peripherals can be very expensive. Although some personal computers sold within the last two years have sound and video capabilities, many do not. Also, Internet-based phone conferencing requires a high-quality microphone and speakers. Additionally, video conferencing requires a high-quality video card and a fast processor. Client machines expected to handle video conferencing should have Pentium or faster processors, as well as video cards with at least 1 MB of video RAM. The cost of preparing and maintaining a user base of qualified machines is a primary factor to consider when you're building your intranet.

Software Costs

Client-side software costs will vary widely, depending on the functions you want to perform on the intranet. Most new operating systems come prepackaged with several TCP/IP clients. Windows 95 comes with a Telnet client, a command-line FTP client, a mail client, and a Web browser. OS/2, MacOS, and Windows NT also come with various clients.

Also, many TCP/IP clients are available on the Internet for free or for less than $50 per license. Some cost as little as $10 or $15. These applications—known as *freeware* or *shareware*—typically aren't quite ready for commercial sale, either because they don't have as many features as commercially available software, or because they aren't as visually attractive (but still are acceptable clients for many users). The availability and cost of these clients are neither steady nor consistent. Intranet administrators might find that some users will want to use different clients, depending on the users' own preferences, skills, and job functions. Therefore, allowing users to utilize a basic freeware client and then find and install their own personal favorites might be a good option. Typically, no technical support is available for freeware or shareware.

Of course, if you want to purchase a full suite of products for your users, many such suites are available. Netcom, SPRY, Chameleon, FTP Software, and many other large Internet Service Providers (ISPs) and software makers offer such suites, as well as the suites available with operating systems such as Windows 95, Windows NT, OS/2, and Linux. This will probably reduce your technical support and training costs but will increase your up-front software costs. These suites can run as much as $150 to $350 per license, but they come with free or inexpensive technical support. In fact, with some of these suites, you wouldn't need a full-time systems administrator. Figure 13.1 shows an example of a suite of products.

Part II Building Your Intranet

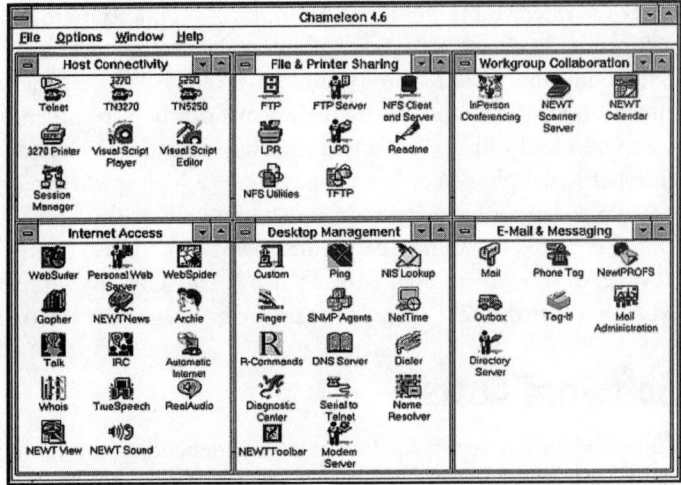

FIGURE 13.1.
Chameleon's suite of products.

The following is a list of a few suites and their contact information:

Distinct

12901 Saratoga Ave.
P.O. Box 3410
Saratoga, CA 95070
Telephone: (408) 366-8933
Fax: (408) 366-0153
ftp.distinct.com
www.distinct.com

EveryWare Development Corp.

7145 West Credit Ave.
Building 1, Suite 2
Mississauga, Ontario L5N 6J7
Canada
Telephone: (905) 819-1173
Fax: (905) 819-1172
info@everyware.com

Chapter 13 — Client Issues

FTP Software, Inc.

100 Brickstone Square
Andover, MA 01810
Telephone: (508) 685-4000
Fax: (508) 794-4488
```
ftp.ftp.com
gopher.ftp.com
www.ftp.com
```

NETCOM On-line Communications, Inc.

3031 Tisch Way
San Jose, CA 95128
Telephone: (408) 983-5950 or (800) 353-6600
Fax: (408) 241-9145
```
info@netcom.com
www.netcom.com/support
```

NetManage, Inc.

10725 North De Anza Blvd.
Cupertino, CA 95014
Telephone: (408) 973-7171
Fax: (408) 257-6405
```
sales@netmanage.com
ftp.netmanage.com
gopher.netmanage.com
```

SPRY

CompuServe Internet Division
3535 128th Avenue SE
Bellevue, WA 98006
Telephone: (206) 957-8000
Fax: (206) 957-6000

Spyglass, Inc.

1240 E. Diehl Road
Naperville, IL 60563
Telephone: (708) 505-1010
Fax: (708) 505-4944
```
www.spyglass.com
```

Upgrade Considerations and Costs

When you're adding new functions to your intranet, an important consideration is the cost of upgrading your client hardware and software. Keep in mind the lowest common denominator—the least technologically savvy machine that will utilize the new functions and the cost of running the application on this machine. Consider the cost of the software, whether the client will require new hardware such as speakers or a new video card, and how much it will cost to install any hardware. Also, consider other hardware upgrade requirements, such as memory, hard drive storage space, and a faster processor. Is an operating system upgrade or replacement necessary? If so, how will a new or upgraded operating system affect other uses for the client machine? For example, some TCP/IP software isn't made for Windows 3.1 anymore, and some Windows 3.1 products don't run well or at all on Windows 95. Upgrading your operating system to lower costs for TCP/IP solutions might increase your costs if you need to upgrade a whole range of other products in order to be compatible with the new operating system.

Maintenance Costs

Finally, don't forget the necessary evil: How much will it cost to maintain this new hardware and software? Who will provide technical support for the hardware and software? Do you have the infrastructure in place to handle calls from remote users who are having problems? Keep in mind that there are companies that provide technical support on a contract basis.

Hardware

Although it's likely that the biggest factor in the client arena is software applications, it might make sense, especially if an infrastructure doesn't exist, to weigh the benefits and drawbacks of the different hardware platforms at the same time. One of the most challenging tasks in building an intranet can be connecting clients, but hardware and operating system choices can be important factors in easing that challenge.

MCKEON & JEFFRIES

McKeon & Jeffries runs a Windows for Workgroups operating system almost exclusively. In deciding which client software to incorporate, one of the biggest issues was cost. This company intends to eventually upgrade to Windows 95, so free or cheap clients that work well on Windows 3.1 are a good short-term answer because of the expected use of Microsoft Explorer, which comes free with Windows 95.

The accounting firm wanted a feature-rich but inexpensive browser. The answer seemed to be NCSA's Mosaic. For 150 users, the cost of equipping each machine with Mosaic saved thousands of dollars over Netscape's price and didn't lose a lot of features. Of course, users at home were encouraged to use whatever browser they wanted to purchase or download. NCSA Mosaic was very easy to install, and it left a very light footprint on the client machines, so memory upgrades weren't necessary. (A *footprint* is the amount of system resources, such as memory and processing power, that a program takes up on your computer.)

For some time, McKeon & Jeffries had been using Groupwise mail for internal e-mail, and with an inexpensive add-on, they could continue to use it with the new intranet.

The firm decided to use the freeware of CuteFTP to transfer files to and from the server. A feature-rich FTP program, CuteFTP lets users configure multiple hosts, meaning that they can easily put files in their own space on the server, in public space, or in a specific area with just a click of the mouse.

Macintosh

Although the Macintosh enjoys much less popularity in the business environment, it's much more popular in educational institutions, where the basis of TCP/IP and client/server applications originated. Many of the best and most user-friendly client applications were made originally or exclusively for the Macintosh environment. The MacOS 7.0 and upgrade versions come with an easy-to-use and stable TCP/IP stack that gives the user almost plug-and-play connectivity that is far superior to IBM-compatible PCs. As an example, when I was preparing a demonstration for a conference, I set up 12 Macs in a TCP/IP network with fully functioning clients in two hours. The following weekend, when I set up a two-computer LAN in my home, it took me more than 20 hours to get the network up and running. Macintoshes are currently a little more expensive than PCs, but prices have been getting closer to PC standards over the past year as a result of Apple's trying to increase its position in the home PC market.

The Macintosh is no doubt the simplest computer system to connect to the Internet or an intranet, because most models come with network and modem ports. Users can merely plug in a modem or a network cable, follow some simple instructions, and be networked in no time. The Macintosh makes it relatively easy to add hardware such as modems, additional hard drives, SCSI devices, speakers, and microphones—as long as that hardware is external. However, adding internal memory or additional video or sound cards internally is more difficult than with the average PC. Macintoshes offered sound capability long before PCs, and they seem to have a better grasp of how to integrate sound and video into the operating system. However, Macintosh sound and video quality is no better than on high-end PCs.

One drawback of choosing a Macintosh system is the limited availability of commercial software. At most computer superstores, the Macintosh section is relegated to a remote corner. Also, Macintosh's parent company, Apple Computers, has experienced financial and management problems lately, and its future remains uncertain. One good sign is that Apple has finally licensed its operating system and chip set to clone makers. Now users don't have to rely on a single source for OS and hardware upgrades, or even new machines. It's unlikely that the Macintosh will go away anytime soon, but finding software applications won't get any easier. Macintoshes have been able to create a Windows environment and run Windows programs with limited success.

MacOS is a very stable operating system, and System 7.0 runs well on 8 MB of RAM. A Macintosh Powerbook that I use with increasing frequency has 8 MB of RAM, but I wouldn't dare try that on a Windows 95 machine. It does allow for multitasking, meaning that users can perform several operations at once. Its multitasking is much better than that of Windows 3.1, and a little better than Windows 95, but not quite as good as Linux or Windows NT.

IBM Compatibles

IBM compatibles, commonly referred to as PCs, are by far the most common business environment in existing computer infrastructures and are probably the most common hardware platforms of remote clients. This is because a number of operating systems are available for IBM compatibles—all with some form of TCP/IP compatibility. However, they aren't without disadvantages. Until about a year ago, it was unusual for PCs to be sold with sound capabilities, and it's still possible that many remote users won't have sound or high-quality video capabilities. Also, it's much more difficult to set up a network socket with a modem, although some operating systems provide for much easier local network connections (on a LAN). Plan to spend some serious time supporting remote users who attempt to connect using a Windows 3.1 or Windows 95 client and a modem. Troubleshooting network sockets on these two operating systems is difficult. Dozens of factors, including hardware, network software, extraneous software, and operating system configurations, can get in the way of setting up a remote network connection.

When it comes to internal upgrades, including internal hard drives, video cards, and memory, IBMs are much easier to upgrade than Macintoshes. However, upgrading with SCSI devices, sound, and incoming video is more difficult on the PC. Keen competition for hardware, accessories, and software in the PC market keeps prices lower and the selection fatter than for similar products for the Macintosh.

Operating Systems

There are many operating systems for use with IBM-compatible machines. Some are more limited than others, and some have specific strengths regarding TCP/IP applications. Depending on what applications will be used, it's possible for certain users to work on one operating system while others utilize another. For example, someone who is administering an intranet might want to use Linux, while a casual user who requires a suite of other products might want to use Windows 3.1 or Windows 95. For instance, a user whose primary occupation is accounting or word processing might want to use Windows, MacOS, or OS/2 because of the strong applications for those uses. However, a user who spends most of her time using intranet or Internet applications might choose Linux because of its flexibility and stability, even though the word processing and spreadsheet applications aren't as rich.

Windows 3.1

Although Windows 3.1 (shown in Figure 13.2) is without a doubt the most widely used operating system in the corporate environment, it's relatively archaic by modern software standards, especially given the difficulty it has creating network connections through modems and LANs. However, much software and many support services are available for Windows 3.1. Although it's a relatively unstable platform (it's been known to freeze up when confused, as anyone who is familiar with General Protection Faults will tell you), Windows 3.1 runs well on 386 or 486 machines with 4 MB of RAM. It is a 16-bit operating system that doesn't offer true multitasking, meaning that you can't perform more than one operation at once effectively.

FIGURE 13.2.
A Windows 3.1 desktop.

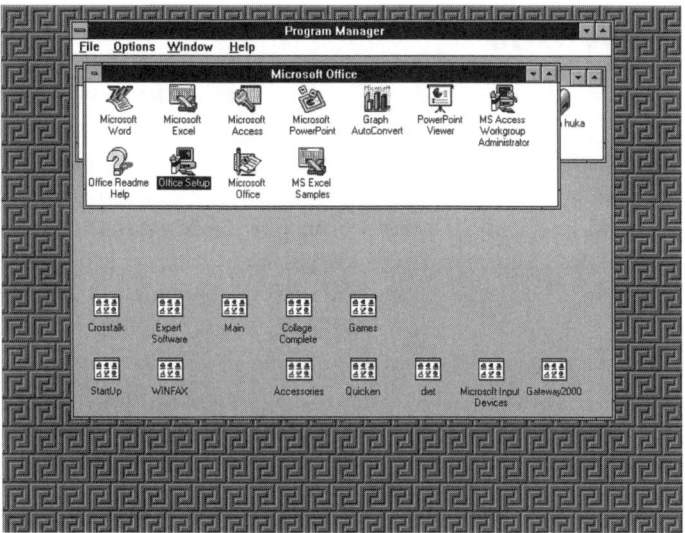

Windows NT

Windows NT, shown in Figure 13.3, is used primarily by high-end users on high-end machines. It's a 32-bit operating system that requires a minimum of 16 MB of RAM to run efficiently. It's been around since 1993 and is the parent of Windows 95. It has exceptional multitasking capabilities, and it can run most Windows 95 software. Some of its drawbacks, however, include its difficulty in configuring for networking and its lack of technical support, except for expensive support packages. It's very expensive, and it requires a proficient systems administrator to maintain. NT is currently a favorite of network administrators and high-powered users with high-end machines. Microsoft seems intent on supplanting Windows 95 with Windows NT. In fact, NT 4.0, released in August 1996, uses Windows 95's interface and NT's features.

FIGURE 13.3.
A Windows NT desktop.

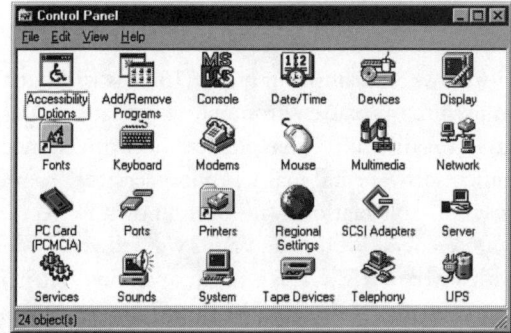

Windows 95

Windows 95, shown in Figure 13.4, is probably the most prevalent operating system for current TCP/IP network clients. By the time you read this book, there probably will be more clients that work on Windows 95 platforms than on all the other platforms combined. Windows 95, a 32-bit operating system, has reasonable multitasking and connects fairly well to TCP/IP networks on a LAN. It's a little more difficult to configure Windows 95 for dial-up networking than for direct networking. In fact, many Internet Service Providers have complained that Windows 95 makes it difficult for users to configure modem connections for networks other than the Microsoft Network. Although Microsoft claims it can run well with 8 MB of RAM, I have found that it's unbearably slow with less than 12. Windows 95 probably will be the prevalent operating system for the next five to 10 years.

FIGURE 13.4.
A Windows 95 desktop.

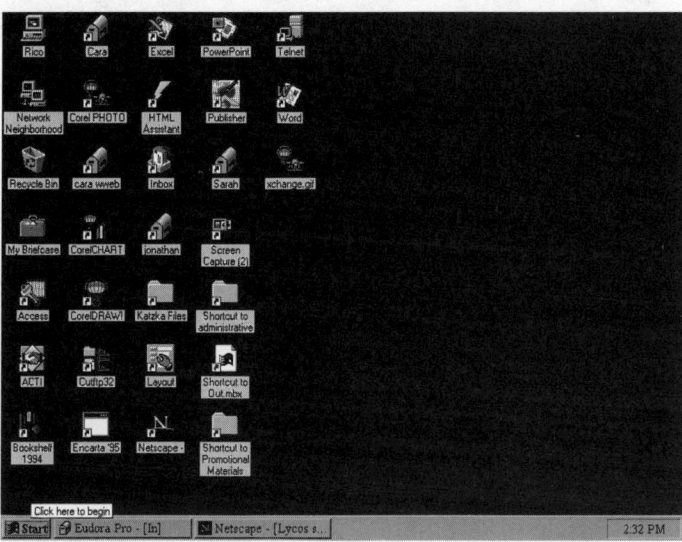

OS/2

IBM's OS/2 is a little-used but versatile operating system. It's 32-bit, runs well on 8 MB of RAM, and has excellent multitasking capabilities. It's difficult to configure, but it comes with a stable TCP/IP stack that works with many ISPs when configured correctly. OS/2 has its own mail, FTP, Telnet, and Web browser client, and many Windows 3.1 and Windows 95 clients work well (although slowly). This operating system lacks supporting software applications, which is why it's not widely used. However, for those who would rather line the pockets of Big Blue than Bill Gates, OS/2 is an acceptable alternative.

Linux

Linux is a versatile noncommercial operating system created mainly by Internet users, who are constantly upgrading it. It runs efficiently on a 486 with 8 MB of RAM. It's a true 32-bit multitasking OS, and it's the most popular graphical interface for UNIX currently in use. It's available on the Internet for free (even though some publishers have packaged it with books). Linux is supported by a vast network of users on Usenet newsgroups. Although non-UNIX experts find Linux difficult to configure, it's the operating system of choice for many programmers and systems administrators. For people who know what they're doing, Linux is the fastest and most easily customized operating system available. You can find Linux itself, along with useful installation information, at the Linux Home Page, located at `http://www.linux.org`.

> **NOTE**
>
> Linux was originally developed several years ago by Linus Torvalds, who was looking for a version of UNIX that could be more easily configured, that was able to run on x86 machines, and, most of all, that was free. Linux was built with UNIX in mind. In fact, many users would be hard pressed to tell the difference. This UNIX system has been developed and debugged as a group effort by volunteers—no single organization is responsible. Anyone with a new convention can send it to Torvalds, who will test it and possibly include it in the next version. Here is his contact information:
>
> Home address:
>
> Linus Torvalds
> Pretarinkatu 2 A 2
> 00140 Helsinki
> Finland
>
> Work address:
>
> PL 26 (Teollisuuskatu 24)
> 00014 Helsingin yliopisto
> Finland

> Telephone number:
>
> +3580 70844265
>
> Home e-mail address:
>
> `torvalds@kruuna.helsinki.fi`
>
> Work e-mail address:
>
> `Linus Torvalds@helsinki.fi`

Other Operating Systems

A whole host of other operating systems are options for intranet clients, from archaic Amiga machines to Sun Sparc stations and Silicon Graphics workstations. Client machines range in price from less than $1,000 per workstation to more than $20,000 per workstation. However, unless a systems administrator has extensive knowledge of the hardware and software being considered, it's probably not wise to choose an operating system or hardware configuration that isn't widely used. Although I know that there is an extensive and fiercely loyal network of Amiga users on the Internet, they probably don't use their machines for the reliable transmission of important corporate data.

> **THE SPORTING GOODS AND APPAREL ASSOCIATION**
>
> The SGAA had very little decision-making authority over what client hardware and software their users would implement to access the intranet. The ISP with whom the SGAA coordinated to provide access to members who needed it also provided a rudimentary suite of TCP/IP applications. Basic Telnet, FTP, Web browser, and mail clients were included. However, it was recommended that—due to the additional features that are available in these applications—users purchase Netscape as a Web browser, Eudora for mail, and WSFTP for PC users and Fetch for Mac users as the FTP client.
>
> The differences between the applications that come in the rudimentary suite and the other applications can be likened to the differences between Microsoft WordPad and Microsoft Word. Although WordPad is a capable word processor, it doesn't have the full features of Word, which means that the user just doesn't get much out of it. For example, with the basic Web browser, users can't view pages in the same style in which Netscape lets them view pages. With FTP, you can do preconfigurations with WSFTP that you can't do with rudimentary FTP. And, with Eudora, users get an easier and more efficient mail program than those that come with basic packages, which mainly tout their functional attributes. Also, because the SGAA's users work on many platforms, the company wanted applications that were available on both Windows and Macintosh operating systems.

Software

As soon as you've chosen client hardware and a network connection, it's time to consider client software needs. Client software is what interacts with the server to complete a TCP/IP transaction. All the software packages discussed here translate requests or input into a language the server can understand and communicate with the server via TCP/IP protocol.

Browsers

If your intranet will host a Web server, users will need a Web browser client. The Web browser's function is to send file requests to the Web server and display the information to the client. Browsers typically show text and images. Some can transfer sound, video, and other files to the client machine. Many browsers also can send information back to the server using embedded forms. Users also can utilize a browser by typing data into online forms to transmit to the server. New browsers can even run certain applications, such as Java or ActiveX.

Netscape

Netscape (shown in Figure 13.5) has been, and probably will be for some time, the single most popular TCP/IP application available. It's available for MacOS, Windows 3.1, Windows 95, Windows NT, and most UNIX platforms, including Linux. It runs well on 8 MB of RAM, and because it incorporates FTP, e-mail, and a newsreader into the browser, it requires fewer applications to run simultaneously when performing several functions. Netscape costs about $50 per user and can be downloaded from the Internet. Beta versions typically are available for free downloads, although these beta versions expire occasionally, leaving thousands of users scrambling to get on the server to download the latest version.

Netscape incorporates Sun's Java language into its browser so that Java applications (or applets) may run inside the browser, which means that regardless of what operating system the client is using, an applet can be written to work equally well. Java is like running an application using Netscape as the operating system.

Explorer

Explorer, shown in Figure 13.6, is Microsoft's answer to Netscape. It has many of Netscape's features (see Chapter 19, "Browsers: Viewing Corporate Information with HTML"). It is free with Windows 95, and it runs efficiently on 12 MB of RAM. There is little argument that Netscape is the better browser by almost any standard. It's fast, it has many features, and it offers more flexibility to Web content providers. However, Explorer is catching up. The Web world is still watching to see which application will dominate the market. Although Explorer has all the power of Microsoft behind it, some users think it will go the way of eight-track tapes.

FIGURE 13.5.
Netscape's home page.

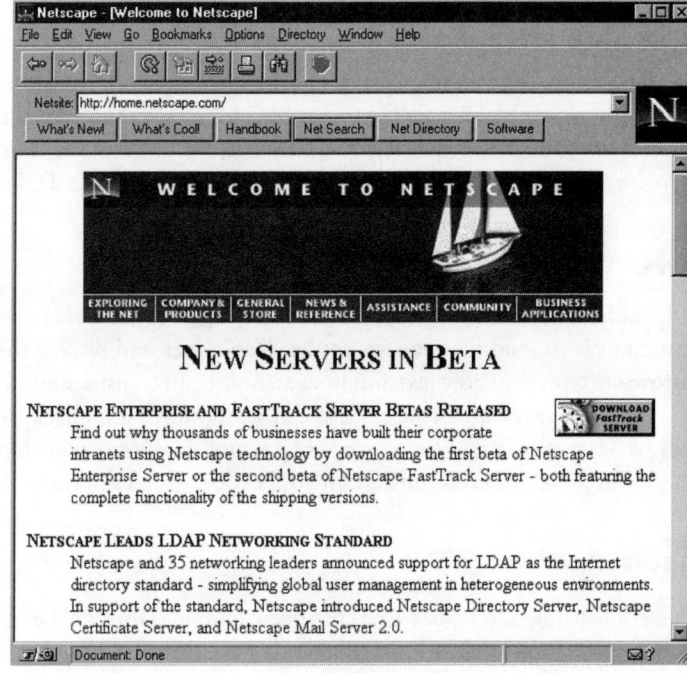

FIGURE 13.6.
Explorer's home page.

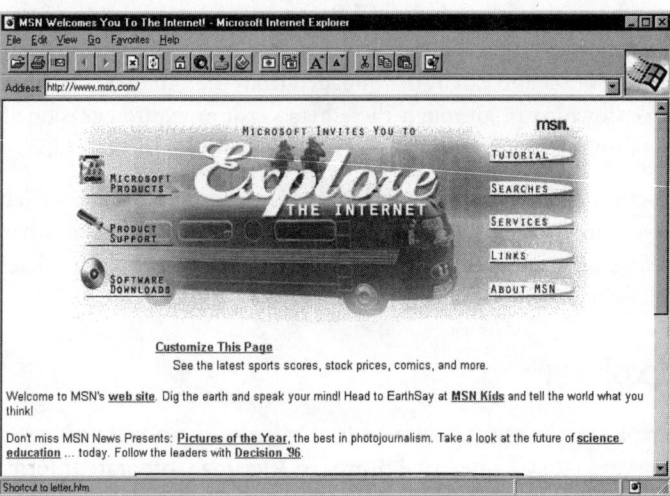

Client Issues

Chapter 13

OS/2

The OS/2 browser is free with OS/2 and runs efficiently on 8 MB of RAM. It's primitive compared to Netscape and Explorer (see Figure 13.7), but it's the only browser to run natively on OS/2.

FIGURE 13.7.
OS/2's home page.

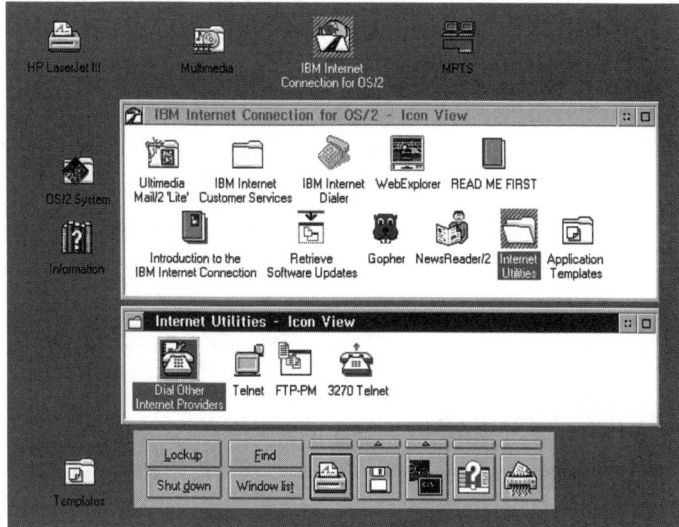

Mosaic

The National Center for Supercomputing Applications' (NCSA) Mosaic is a relatively full-featured low-end browser (see Figure 13.8). It's rich enough to cover all the basics, and it runs well on 4 MB of RAM. Mosaic is the basis for many browsers that come with commercial TCP/IP stacks. It's available on the Internet and costs about half as much as Netscape. Comparing Netscape to Mosaic is like comparing Microsoft Word to Microsoft Works: Although Netscape offers more features and extras, some users just don't need them, and therefore will find Mosaic suitable.

FIGURE 13.8.
Mosaic's home page.

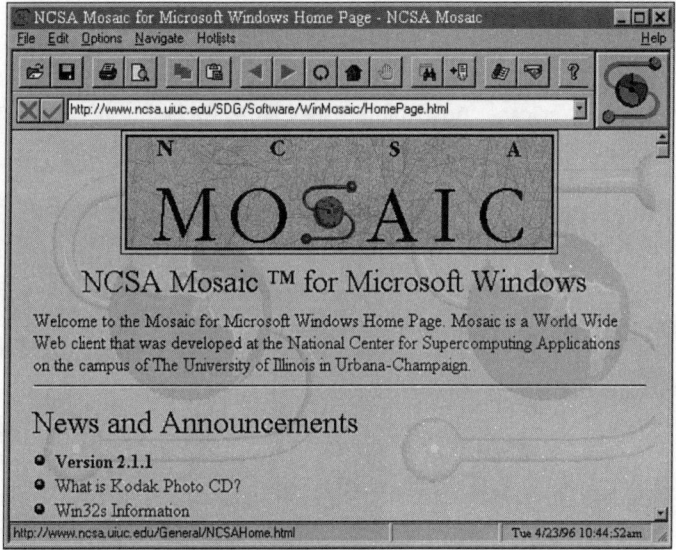

E-Mail Software

Probably the most important piece of client software is the e-mail client. E-mail, used to exchange messages and files, already has established itself as a commonplace application in many work environments. The differences among e-mail packages are mainly in their interface capabilities. All Internet mail is exchanged via Simple Mail Transfer Protocol (SMTP), a common format for sending mail messages and files. Most e-mail software uses little of a system's resources, and some e-mail programs run on the server computer. Applications running on the client computer download the mail onto the client computer and allow the user to compose mail locally and then send it to the server. The current standard for mail servers is Post Office Protocol 3 (POP3), a mail server that holds mail in an inbox spool on the server to be either downloaded to the client machine or read by a server mail tool such as Pine. Pine is an application that resides on the server and that can be accessed using Telnet.

The next standard for mail, which is still relatively new, is Interactive Mail Access Protocol (IMAP). IMAP allows a remote client to manipulate mail messages in remote folders on the server. Currently, using POP3, only the inbox on the server can be accessed by the remote client. IMAP is more useful than POP3 because it lets remote users manipulate their mail on the server in a graphical environment using cut-and-paste features on any client while storing mail on the server instead of on a single client machine.

Eudora

Eudora, shown in Figure 13.9, is the most popular TCP/IP e-mail package on the market. It's feature-rich and flexible. (See Chapter 30, "E-Mail: The Basic Model.") A freeware version of Eudora is available, but to access most of the advanced features, you must purchase the software. Eudora is available for both the Macintosh and various Windows environments.

FIGURE 13.9.
Eudora's mail package.

Netscape

Netscape's Web browser comes with a mail reader included at no extra charge. It isn't as feature-rich as Eudora, but it does provide the basics, such as message composition and storage, address books, message sorting, and mailbox compression (see Figure 13.10). Netscape's plus is its savings in system resources, especially if the user plans to utilize mail and Web browser applications concurrently. Netscape's Web browser is available for the various Windows operating systems, the Mac, and most UNIX operating systems.

FIGURE 13.10.
Netscape Mail.

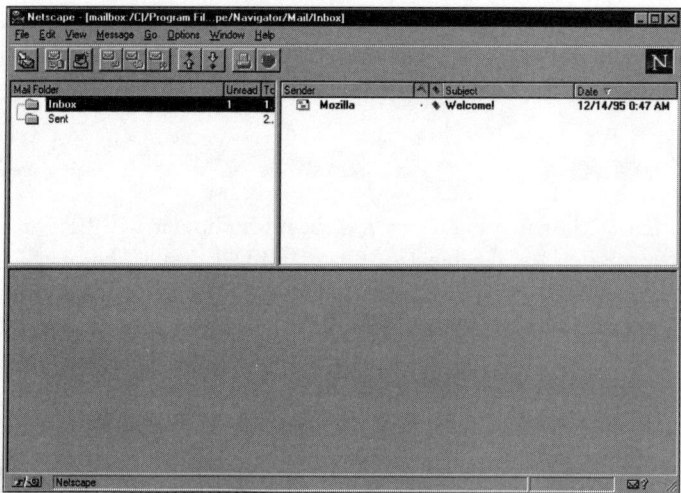

Groupwise

Groupwise, shown in Figure 13.11, is a popular LAN e-mail system that has a simple add-on for Internet mail. For offices currently using Groupwise mail, it's easy and relatively inexpensive to incorporate Internet mail into LAN mail. Groupwise isn't recommended for offices without established Internet e-mail because of its lack of features and its inability to conform to new standards as they evolve. Currently, it's available only for Windows 3.1 and Macintosh systems.

FIGURE 13.11.
Groupwise mail.

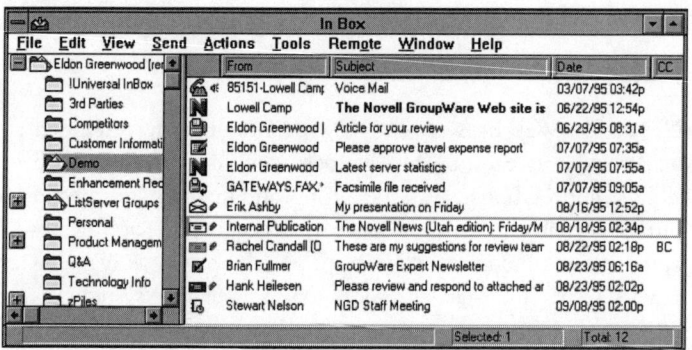

SPRY Mail

SPRY Mail, shown in Figure 13.12, is the mail client that comes with the popular Internet in a Box software. It is a fairly good mail client, boasting speed and ease of configuration. It has many of the same features as Eudora but works only with the Internet in a Box TCP/IP stack. One of its strongest features is its capability to view the inbox remotely, meaning that you can delete unwanted messages without downloading them. I recommend SPRY Mail for organizations that purchase a full suite of TCP/IP applications for users. SPRY Mail is available only for Windows 3.1 and Windows 95.

FIGURE 13.12.
SPRY Mail.

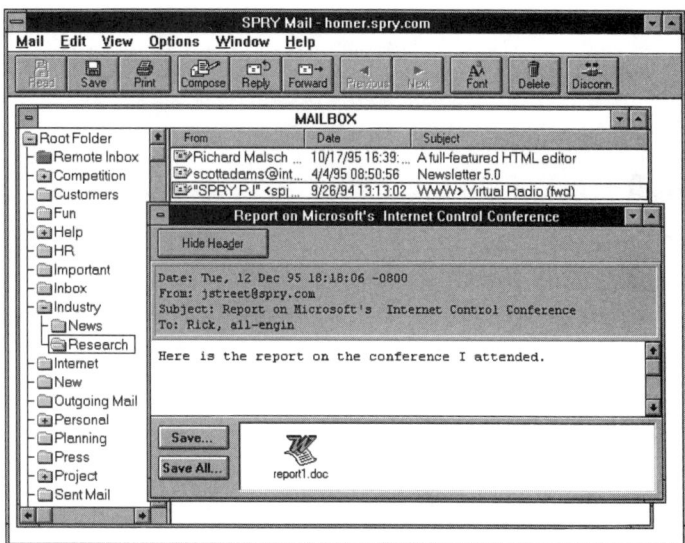

Pine

Pine, shown in Figure 13.13, isn't really a mail client. It's actually a program that resides on the server and is standard with many UNIX-based servers. It gives users the ability to read and send mail from almost any Internet connection. The mail remains on the server and can be saved in folders. Pine has many of the same features as the popular client-side mail tools, such as address books, search tools, and the ability to attach documents, and it has the added bonuses of being free and allowing users access to their mail from almost anywhere.

FIGURE 13.13.
Pine.

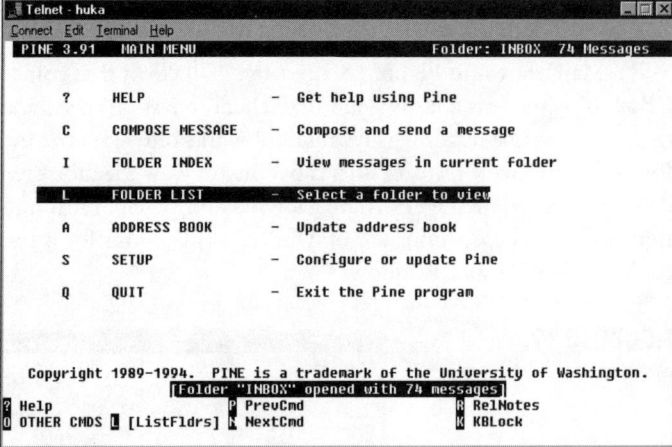

FTP

File Transfer Protocol (FTP) is a method of transferring files from a client to a server or vice versa. As with e-mail, files are transferred over the Internet using TCP/IP protocol. The only difference between graphical FTP clients and command-line FTP is the point-and-click features. Additionally, FTP clients use few system resources.

CuteFTP

CuteFTP, shown in Figure 13.14, is a shareware/freeware program available on the Internet. It has many features and is used widely. CuteFTP provides an interface that looks much like a standard file manager, with the remote file system on one side of the window and the local file system on the other. Users can simply drag and drop files from the server to their machine or from their machine to the server. CuteFTP is available for Windows 3.1 and Windows 95 systems, but it isn't yet available for the Macintosh.

Fetch

Fetch, shown in Figure 13.15, probably is the most popular FTP client available. It's available only for the Mac, and it has many features. Although PC users have a wide variety of FTP clients available to them that offer comparable applications and features, Fetch currently is the best FTP client available for the Macintosh. I don't know of anyone using another FTP client on a Mac. Fetch has a premium freeware version available on the Internet. Like CuteFTP, Fetch works much like a typical file manager, showing the remote file system and letting users browse their local drives for files and/or directories. One notable feature of Fetch is that it lets you upload and download entire directory trees.

FIGURE 13.14.
CuteFTP.

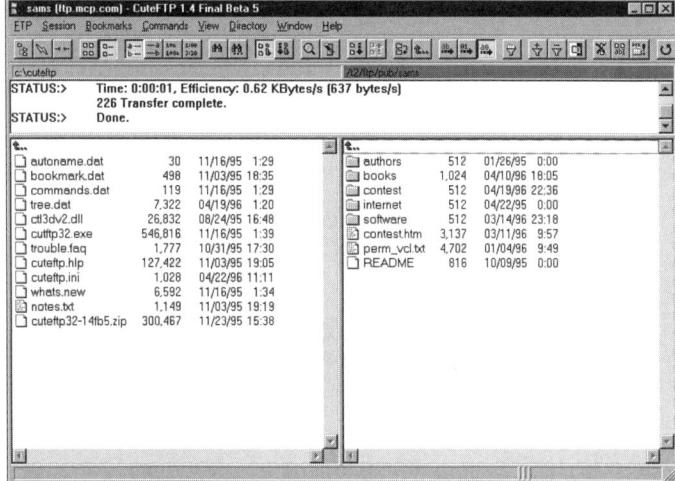

FIGURE 13.15.
Fetch.

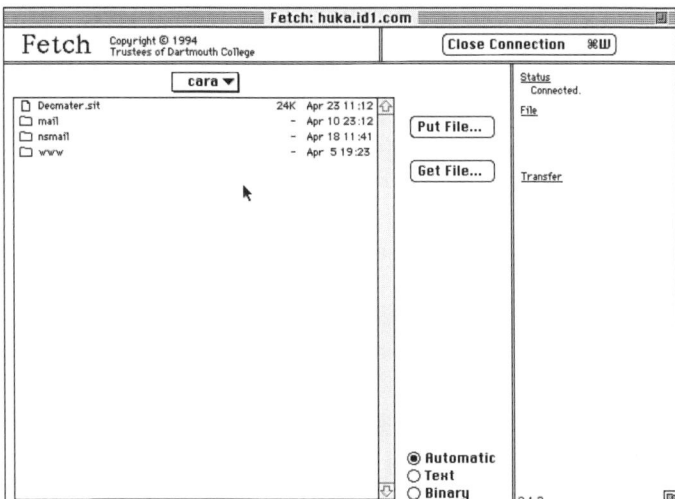

Command-Line FTP

Windows 95, Windows NT, and all UNIX operating systems come with a command-line FTP client. Because it doesn't have a graphical interface, the user must know arcane commands. See Figure 13.16.

FIGURE 13.16.
Command-line FTP.

```
(cara_huka)/usra/cara> ftp
ftp> open ftp.id1.com
Connected to ftp.id1.com.
220 ftp.id1.com FTP server (Version wu-2.4(26) Mon Oct 30 21:05:14 CST 1995) ready.
Name (ftp.id1.com:cara): anonymous
331 Guest login ok, send your complete e-mail address as password.
Password:
230 Guest login ok, access restrictions apply.
ftp> binary
200 Type set to I.
ftp> get Decmater.sit
200 PORT command successful.
150 Opening BINARY mode data connection for Decmater.sit (24451 bytes).
226 Transfer complete.
local: Decmater.sit remote: Decmater.sit
24451 bytes received in 2.2 seconds (11 Kbytes/s)
ftp> quit
221 Goodbye.
(cara_huka)/usra/cara>
```

Telnet

Telnet clients are used to directly access the server. Users need a UNIX account on the server to access Telnet. Telnet lets users edit files and run applications on the server but demands few system resources. Dozens of Telnet applications (also called terminal applications) are available on the Web as freeware and shareware. I'll discuss the two most common Telnet applications—Windows 95 Telnet and NCSA Telnet.

Windows 95 Telnet

This Telnet comes with Windows 95 and Windows NT. It's free but has few features (see Figure 13.17). (See Chapter 29, "Telnet: Direct Access," for reviews of popular terminal applications.)

FIGURE 13.17.
Windows Telnet.

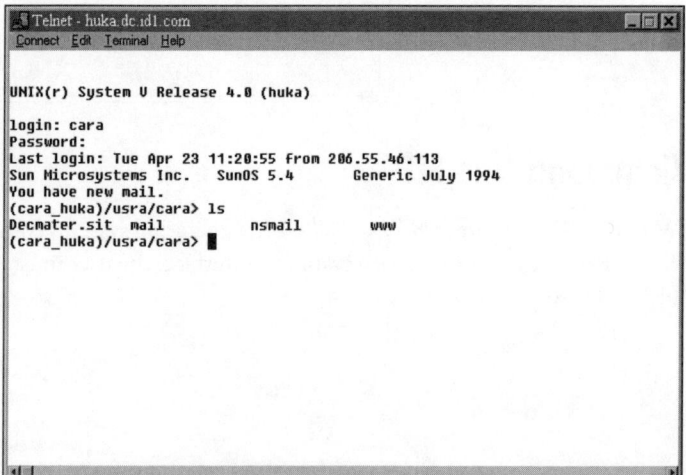

NCSA Telnet

NCSA Telnet, shown in Figure 13.18, is freeware and is a universally popular Macintosh Telnet client. It is feature-rich and uses almost no system resources.

FIGURE 13.18.
NCSA Telnet.

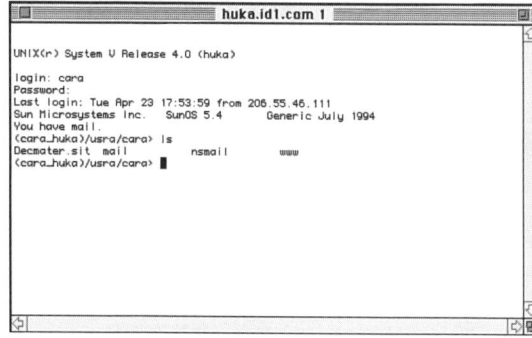

Internet Phone and Chat

A couple of the most exciting new applications on the Web are Internet Phone, which lets users talk, real-time and free of long distance charges, over the Internet, and Chat, which lets users carry on conversations real-time by typing messages back and forth (like chat rooms on America Online or forums on CompuServe). New clients are arriving on the market on a daily basis to perform both Internet Phone and Chat functions. Netscape is currently developing both an Internet phone plug-in in conjunction with InSoft, Inc. and Chat functions for use with its browser. (See Figures 13.19 and 13.20.) IBM and Microsoft likely will follow suit.

FIGURE 13.19.
Netscape Chat.

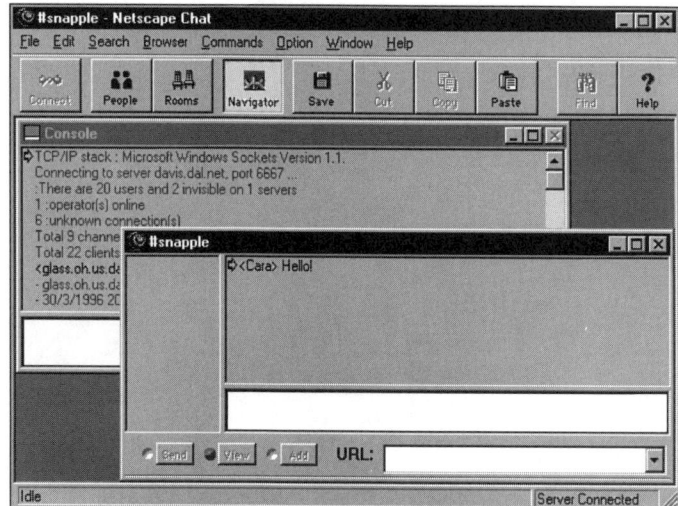

FIGURE 13.20.
Netscape's CoolTalk plug-in.

Summary

Now that you know which materials you need for a solid server, client, and connectivity foundation, you should have a better grasp of how you will begin to build your intranet foundation. Because it's much more expensive and time-consuming to upgrade client software and hardware than server software and hardware, many of your decisions probably will be based on an assessment of your current infrastructure. At this point, you might want to take an inventory of your current infrastructure or, in the case of remote users, attempt to gain insight into how technologically savvy your users are. Keeping in mind the current state of your infrastructure will help you make decisions as you continue through this book.

Security: Keeping Hackers Out

14

by Richard Simon

IN THIS CHAPTER

- Building a security model file structure **206**
- Protecting the local area network **208**
- Authentication methods **214**
- Firewalls **216**
- Protecting your WAN: a complete security model **216**
- Testing security **219**

In this chapter, you will learn how to maintain a secure system. A system is simply a collection of computers, applications, data, and people. A secure system, on the other hand, is a system that includes only authorized people performing authorized functions with specific applications to properly accessible data.

Secure systems are different from secure data, which involves making sure that when, where, and how data is stored is secure. Secure means inaccessible by unauthorized people who would otherwise alter or view that data. Secure systems also differ from secure transmissions, which involve transmitting data so that it is safe from prying eyes. Because the concepts are different, dealing with them all at once is, in the planning stages, inappropriate. Deciding which users to let use your main database will only be clouded if you are also trying to decide what encryption scheme to use. This confusion will result in the creation of incomplete security models and thus compromise the effectiveness of your security as a whole. The process of creating secure systems is about setting up a network, intranet, or any computer system, and assuring that the people who are not supposed to access it cannot gain entrance as a trusted user of the system.

Keeping a system secure means careful planning of a sound system that takes all threats into account. During this planning, you must keep dangers in perspective. Your danger from unknown outside threats is, in computers as in life, very remote. The big dangers are from those people you know and who know you. The important thing to remember about security is that all threats come from people and all threats must be stopped by people. Computers can make the monitoring easier, but they cannot counter an attack.

Building a Security Model File Structure

Knowing how to design a security model is important. Begin by making a model of where your important files are stored. Draw out what computers store these files and to which computers they can be transferred. If anyone has access to those files and access to another file system, it is safe to assume that that person will transport the files from one file system to another. If one file system is secure and the other is not, you have a problem, so make sure that data cannot be transferred.

Look at the connections. Sometimes these connections run through user accounts; in other cases they don't. Connection routes are not always readily apparent. They run through particular users, using particular computers at particular times in particular ways. That is, even one user/computer/time/application combination can be a security hole large enough to compromise the system, as you can see in the illustration shown in Figure 14.1. Note how paths of access are formed by different combinations of each element. Note also that some unusual combinations could be formed to allow possibly unintended access. Some longtime UNIX users may remember that GNU EMACS could give clever users on certain computers system-level access to entire networks.

FIGURE 14.1.
A computer network and a security plan that includes users, times, and applications.

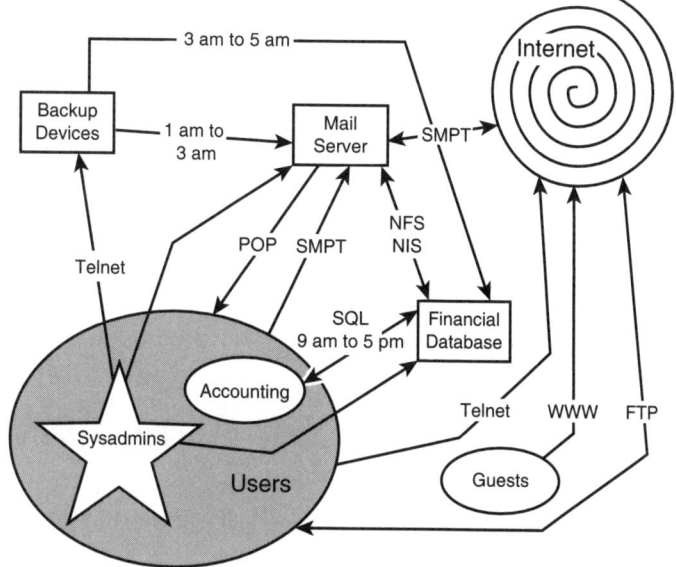

Once you have created a list of where the files are and how they are stored, you must make a list of who has access to these areas. Such a list should include the names of individuals who have access to each file system and each branch of the file system and how they are accessing it. Can they only access it through FTP or can they actually mount it as a file system on their computers?

Don't always be concerned with malicious damage. The biggest problem could be inadvertent damage or transfer of files, which is just as dangerous as someone purposely intercepting the data.

User Structure and Permission

With the user structure, define the levels of access. Someone has top-level access, and you must determine who has it. Top-level access lets these users create and destroy user accounts and read any users' data; it also provides access to the complete system. Anyone with this privilege needs to be aware of that power.

Authentication Points

For all the data and file systems, how many authentication points does a user pass through to access these systems? Are users required to pass through a firewall? If so, what are the requirements or barriers to get through that firewall? Could anyone access that firewall? You must decide the answers to these questions and determine who has read and write access as well. The ability to read and write in general is determined when you're deciding access levels, but you also need to decide if authentication will take place at the actual read-write moments. Does someone have to be authenticated to read the data or to write the data, and can the person writing the data destroy the data?

To maintain a secure system, users should be required to prove who they are at least a couple of times and in a couple of ways. When sitting down at a workstation for the first time, for example, users should at least be required to type in a password. When accessing sensitive files, users should have to put in or have already put in enough information so that their identities can be logged along with anything done to the file. Whenever connecting to a network from a remote location, users should always have to prove their identities either through a username-password exchange or through more secure methods such as s/key or kerberos, explained later in this chapter.

Protecting the Local Area Network

Any plan to protect your computer systems must begin with their physical security. The most important thing about a local area network (LAN) is its physical security. Physical security is important because on most LANs all messages are transmitted to all workstations. That is, local networks transmit messages from one computer to one other computer only from a logical perspective. From a physical standpoint, the electrical signal that constitutes the message is received by every computer connected to the wire. Additionally, most LANs are set up to trust the hosts (computers) directly connected. So anyone who can tap into your LAN's wiring or anyone who can access one of your LAN's existing computers has access to various data and resources. System administrators should investigate card or combination door locks to the most sensitive areas. Additionally, it is imperative that the systems administrator be aware of how secure the whole building is as well as be aware of the level of security in any room with computers connected to the LAN.

To protect your LAN from nonphysical threats, consider the following nine questions:

- What resources are on the LAN (for example, CD-ROMs, software, UNIX workstations, printers, data)?
- What resources are available LAN-wide (for example, databases, Web pages, printers, e-mail)?
- What computers are on the LAN?
- Which users have access to which resources?
- What are the paths running into and out of your LAN?
- Which users are allowed on the LAN?
- When are the users allowed access to the LAN?
- What resources are accessible during users' access to the LAN?
- What resources does the LAN include?

The level of security on the LAN depends on what computers, software, applications, data, and resources the LAN contains. Additional concerns to consider include the following:

- Will files be shared across the network?
- Will users be able to access other computers physically or electronically?
- Will printers be shared?
- Will sensitive information be printed on shared printers?
- What databases will be in use?
- How will users access databases?

Each of these questions requires a decision about security, and each of these resources needs its own security measures and influences the security of the system as a whole. The following sections further explore each of the nine questions.

What Resources Are on the LAN?

This first question (What resources are on the LAN?) refers to the resources located on the LAN but not necessarily shared. The response is a consideration for system administrators whose users access the LAN electronically. File systems available LAN-wide, workstations that accept connections across the LAN, and databases that accept requests from other LAN computers are all potentially vulnerable. Just as vulnerable are any file systems, workstations, or databases on the LAN that are not shared but are also not protected against sharing. All resources must have specific security measures, such as local password protection for all workstations. Other needed measures include preventing computers from being rebooted to evade security, preventing file systems not meant to be shared from being shared by a user, and password-protecting sensitive files no matter on which disk they reside.

What Resources Are Available LAN-Wide?

Can users access all information on the servers or are certain areas restricted within the LAN, such as certain functions, printers, file systems, backup devices, CD-ROM drives, or administrative applications? You must decide where restricted resources will be stored and create secure areas for them. You need to store backup tapes and backup devices, for example, with the same security as the computers. Programs set to be run by the system at certain times need to be guarded carefully so that only the system—and not some user—runs them. You need to secure printers on which certain sensitive data will be printed and to prevent others from sending jobs to that printer.

Shared File Systems

An area that deserves special consideration is shared file systems such as Network File System (NFS), which is commonly implemented under UNIX. Operating systems often include a method for broadcasting certain areas of the file system to be mounted by other computers. Clearly, using NFS and other sharing schemes increases the security exposure of a particular computer. Other important concerns for UNIX environments are authentication and system file distribution.

For Sun System users, it is important to decide whether to use Network Information System (NIS)—previously known as Sun Yellow Pages. NIS is used to share among a number of hosts common lists that are important to the system, such as the username password list, the NFS mounting tables, and trusted hosts. Using NIS, you can distribute those files so that all the systems on your LAN can use the same user lists. This capability is convenient but dangerous, because it is important not to send out copies of your password list to the wrong system. If you're using NIS or any other system of distributing system files, make sure that no one can intercept these distributions.

What Computers Are on the LAN?

The types of computers on the LAN greatly influence your security measures. Computers running the UNIX operating system have many built-in security features, whereas computers running Windows 95 and Windows 3.x have almost no security features. Examine each computer on your LAN for vulnerability. Each type of computer and each different operating system requires a different set of protective measures. To protect the LAN adequately, you must set restrictions on the types of data and applications that can be run on specific computers. If you are using a database server, for example, you may want to restrict the access that Windows 3.x clients have because the security on these clients is so poor.

Which Users Have Access to Which Resources?

When you're considering a security model, you need to consider compartments. Visualize compartments by making a diagram of all LAN resources and drawing circles around the items that should be secure. Creating compartments is a method of keeping systems separate from one another, data separate from other data, and keeping applications separate from certain systems.

Separation by Function

When you're considering compartments, be sure to decisively divide areas that should not be intermingled. Determine whether you can separate your LAN users by function, such as accounting, design, or administration departments. Determine whether they can be completely separated in the kind of data and applications that they need to access or if different departments need to share common resources. You should put the system administrators in a completely separate group so that they can get at everything in the other compartments but not have anyone get back at those same file systems or same computers.

Setting Access Limits

You may find that some systems and certain computers should be accessible only to specific users. A server with financial data, for example, should be kept separate from the rest of the network so that general users cannot access confidential financial data. If any of the data is off-limits, you should place it on a file system that is accessible only from certain systems, making those systems off-limits to general users.

All the systems, access paths, and data should be classified into particular groups. You should create groups for all resources, including a group for unsecure systems. You also should define each access path, workstation, file system, printer, database, or any other item and place it in a particular group.

The LAN's Access Paths

Another facet to consider in the security model is the paths of access. Paths should be well-defined, laying out the routes of access, who can access these routes, where and when access can occur, and how these routes are protected. When you're compartmentalizing everything, you should make sure that the paths from compartment to compartment are well-defined. Define those paths; even if no path exists from one compartment to another, the model should indicate the path's intentional absence.

Defining User Paths for the LAN

If you plan to offer paths into and out of your LAN, you need to decide who will travel these paths. If possible, restrict this list to a specific set of users. Make a list of these users, and keep it current. If you must allow access to users in groups, keep a list of the groups and keep strict guidelines for admission to each group. If you are going to allow *universal access*—access to people who have not been pre-approved—you always need to be cognizant of this use.

Also, you must define subordinate levels of access. Who is actually allowed to work on any part of the system? Should someone be allowed to create user accounts who doesn't receive the remaining route privileges? With Novell, this option is common, especially where you can define administrators who create and destroy certain accounts with a certain level of power.

You also must define levels for ordinary users who get access. In defining these users, determine what they will do with the system. Deciding by function makes it easier for you to define to which resources users get access. A person who does graphic development, for example, needs to browse on the Web and access testing sites. The system administrator's knowledge of the file areas for the designers, the graphic design tools they use, and computers the designers need access to makes it easier to fit these users into a file structure list.

Don't forget to define a guest level and anonymous access. If there is no guest or anonymous access level, be sure to define the system that way. In addition, make sure that, if you are restricting the system to no guest level access, no guest level access occurs. Test the system to make sure.

Don't make access levels too complicated. Choose a few levels and types of users, and stick with them. Individually tailoring security to each person is a big hassle, and these types of haphazard choices are destined to go wrong. The more complicated the security, the more likely problems will occur, and someone will be unable to access the system when he or she needs to access it.

A system is designed to give people access to data and perform functions, but if the security is too tight and users can't do what they are supposed to, the system can't be used. The result is a security system that is not workable.

When you're thinking about how to give access to the LAN, you need to decide where the authentication will take place, define gates, and draw circles around compartmentalized systems. This modeling exercise will give you a tight list of action items for securing your system. Draw circles around the compartments that are supposed to be secure, define gates into those compartments, and create barriers to entry. Any secure system needs a gate in front of it, and knowing what kind of authentication is taking place at that gate is important. If you don't want users to access certain file systems, for example, make sure that username and password authentication takes place before the users can access these systems. To avoid having users from outside coming into your LAN and doing anything but Telnet connections, make sure that at these connections authentication is taking place and that no other connections are possible.

What if more than one authentication process exists? Generally, users on a system become angry when they are asked to enter usernames and passwords several times. How many times and in how many ways do people have to prove that they are authorized to access certain file systems, applications, and computers? Security frequently involves a balance between security and access. You must make a decision about how secure the system should be versus how easily users can access it. If the system is easily accessible, it will not be very secure. With only a little hassle for the user, however, the system can be very secure.

LAN Access

What data can your LAN users access on other systems? If they are turning to other LANs to access resources that require more connections to other systems, such as accessing files directly on the file system as opposed to simple FTP, these connections require a lot of trust between two hosts. Do your LAN users need to go out and get this access? If so, you will need to more carefully plan and monitor your connections to other systems.

Knowing when users can go in and out of your LAN means not only knowing what times, but also knowing under what circumstances (see Figure 14.2). That is, are users aware of situations that may cause the paths to be closed, such as maintenance, upgrades, or off-hours? Channels you use to communicate these situations also can be used as security checks. Announce that you're closing some systems down, and see who doesn't get the message. By keeping careful track of when users can access the LAN, you can spot intruders more easily.

FIGURE 14.2.
A full LAN security model.

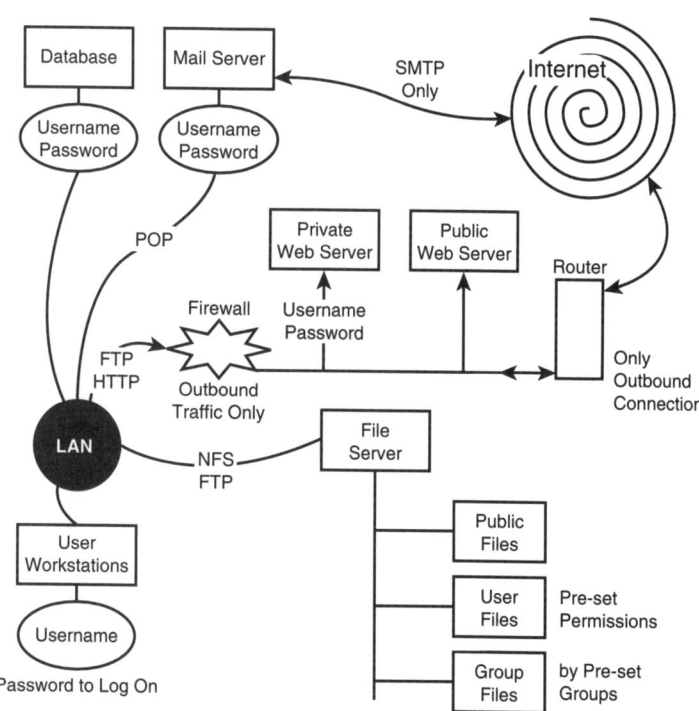

Accessing the LAN's Resources

Keep lists of resources that users are allowed to access from outside the LAN. Any item that is not on your list needs to be carefully protected from outside access. Part of designing a security model for your LAN includes creating a combined list of the users and groups, when they can access the system, and what they can access. This combined list and any explanatory or supplementary material *is* your security model.

Authentication Methods

Your system has no security without authentication. Authentication means proving your identity. Authentication does not always have to be electronic. Locks, guards, and cameras can all provide authentication of some kind. None of these devices, however, are as constantly vigilant, carefully discriminating, or as fully reviewable as electronic methods are for protecting computer systems.

Post Name Check

The first and most simple type of authentication method is a *post name check*. The system checks where the user is coming from and uses that information to authenticate the user. In other words, the system has a secure list of trusted hosts, and anyone attempting to gain a connection from the trusted host can gain access, but users not from the trusted host are not allowed access. This method does have drawbacks, however, because it depends only on the physical security of one of the trusted hosts. If anyone can gain access to a trusted host, that user can then gain access to an individual computer in the system. In the early days of the Internet, this type of security was common.

Username Authentication

A slightly more secure method is *username authentication* in which the user merely types in his or her username; if the name is on the list, he or she is given access to the system.

An even more secure method, however, is *username and password authentication*, which allows the user to enter the username and password combination. This information is compared to a list that the computer has, and the user is then given access to the system if this information is the proper combination. You can use various twists on this arrangement to encrypt either part of that pair or both parts of the pair to make the system somewhat more secure. One example is the way in which UNIX stores passwords; in this approach, the username is stored in plain text, and the password is stored encrypted so that a user cannot steal the list and use it to gain access to the system. Encrypted passwords are very difficult to decrypt. Keep in mind that usernames and passwords need to be updated and changed every three months, because eventually they may be decrypted.

Kerberos

Another authentication method includes *kerberos*. The name comes from the mythical name of the three-headed dog that guards the entrance to Hades. This method, primarily implemented under UNIX, is used to overcome problems with secure transmissions. It allows the user to be authenticated locally—that is, on the workstation—but to use network resources.

In the kerberos system, the user puts in his or her username and password, and then the workstation itself authenticates the user. The workstation then requests from the kerberos server a secret ticket for the user. This ticket is then used as a credential for any network resources. It is unique to the user for a specific time and situation. Transmitting this ticket is possible when the user wants to access certain resources that are protected. It is very secure because the user never transmits the username and password. Any eavesdroppers cannot steal the username and password, but instead get only an unusable ticket.

Smartcards

Smartcards, smartkeys, and what is known as a *challenge-and-response system* are protection methods similar to kerberos. These systems create one-time usernames and passwords, which are the most secure. Challenge-and-response systems conduct all authentication on the local computer, avoiding transmission of passwords. Like kerberos, challenge-and-response systems create one-time passwords, but unlike kerberos, they do not require a special server.

Usernames

Keep in mind that usernames are not security. As I mentioned previously, keeping a list of usernames can be a method of authentication. Expecting usernames to remain secret is not a good idea. It is like a lock on a door that doesn't have a deadbolt: The lock isn't particularly safe; someone could kick the door in. But you need that lock in place so that someone can't simply walk in. With a username list, someone can't just get on a system, but it is not to be considered the final word in security.

Passwords

There are guidelines for making passwords that people repeat over and over again much like a mantra.

Remember, when you're making a password list, don't use a word in the dictionary. Not only could someone guess that word by trying a few combinations, but the words could be subjected to a dictionary attack. In UNIX, passwords are stored in encrypted form. A password file contains the username and the encrypted password. Breaking that encryption is difficult, but a list of dictionary words could be encrypted and the encrypted string then compared to the encrypted passwords in a username and password file. If a match occurs, the password is known. The list has a limited set of words, and if that set of words matches a particular password, that account has been compromised. At that point, whoever is breaking into the system can go in as a trusted user and access the system. So the effort to keep the system secure has failed.

Using simple strings of numbers as passwords is also not a very good idea, because these strings could be subject to the same kind of attack. Letter-number combinations are harder to crack. Using special characters is a good idea; they help to increase the number of possible combinations. As you add characters to a list that you use for any passwords, the security of those passwords is increased exponentially.

Another important rule about passwords that is rarely followed is to never write down the password—not on paper, tape, or under someone's desk. Anyone who can gain access to the space is going to read the password. Any password that is written down can be read by everyone that enters the space and sees the password.

Never put passwords on e-mail, and never send them over e-mail. Users with administrator access to the system can read all e-mail on the system. E-mail is in plaintext, and users can simply scan through the file, find the password, and then use it.

Firewalls

A *firewall* is a device, set of devices, or combination of hardware and software that protects the systems on one side from systems on the other side. "Firewall" has become somewhat of a buzzword, and so people often do not realize that this term can mean many things and is really a concept, not a product. Hence, the definition includes broad terms such as "protect," "system," and "side." The definitions of these words depend on the purpose of a firewall.

A True Firewall

The firewall concept applies to an internetwork. An internetwork is a network with internal barriers. These barriers can be firewalls—that is, barriers designed to protect—or they can be barriers designed to better administrate or engineer the network. These barriers can be Ethernet or IP address barriers; that is, they can restrict traffic from one side of the barrier to the other based on Ethernet or IP addresses. They also can be based on names of computers or on the type of communication; they might allow Web traffic to pass, for example, but not file transfers. The barrier therefore allows only certain computers to communicate with certain other computers in certain ways. If these barriers exist only for security reasons, they are called "firewalls."

Protecting Your WAN: A Complete Security Model

Protecting a wide area network (WAN) or internetwork means embracing a complete security model. A WAN is made up of individual LANs and users. The LANs serve as compartments for the process of security planning. A LAN model for any particular compartment in this WAN should be completed before you determine how they interact. Plan out LAN-to-LAN access; in other words, decide how users will connect from one to the other. Decide how outside users will access each LAN compartment. Pick the services that can travel over those paths between LANs, such as Telnet, FTP, or HTTP. When you're choosing services, also decide what protocols such as TCP/IP or IPX will be allowed and whether you will use network addresses as the basis to create barriers. Know what applications will be used across the network such as network monitoring or Web browsers. List what files users will access between LANs. Plan out all these paths, where they lead, to what system, what applications, and what file systems.

Does your WAN include the Internet? Are you accessing pieces of your network across the Internet? Can people from the Internet access your network? If so, this access makes the model more complicated. Assume that everyone on the Internet will want to gain access to your WAN. Protecting against these threats is important. If you're going across the Internet to get to another part of your WAN, anyone on the Internet may be able to do the same. You need to understand how users could get access and decide what specific measures you will take to prevent this access.

Usernames and Passwords

With a WAN, you must consider a password exchange model: how will you get usernames and passwords available to users? Passwords should be transmitted only over verifiably secure means. This could mean nonelectronic transmission or encrypted electronic transmission. Consider methods such as challenge-and-response and kerberos, which allow distributed authentication and no password transmission. Also consider authenticating the recipient of the username and password. When you pass authentication credentials to someone, you need to know that they go to the right person. You also must know that the right person is actually authorized to this access.

Firewalls Redux

A firewall is a particular computer system—sometimes hardware, sometimes software, sometimes both—that stands between a secure system and an insecure system, and it allows only privileged traffic to flow through. You can build a firewall in many ways, such as a bridge that discriminates against certain Ethernet addresses (which happens to be the simplest firewall to develop). Every network interface card has an address. A bridge can discriminate and say that it does not accept traffic from certain addresses and only accept traffic from certain addresses on the other side of the bridge. With this method, faking an Ethernet address is somewhat difficult.

One level up is to restrict access and resources on the basis of IP address, but this approach is vulnerable to fake IP addresses or "IP spoofing." Giving your computer a network address belonging to another, for example, would allow you to get traffic that is bound for that address. Routers help to prevent this situation. Routers and bridges are lower-level firewalls. Often they act only as agents of network engineering and organization and are not designed to protect. Because they operate at such low levels, they are subject to many kinds of sophisticated attacks.

Another type of a firewall is an application-level firewall, which lets only predetermined traffic and packets through. A firewall of this type denies all traffic except for certain services that you enable. You can also restrict traffic so that it goes only to certain computers. Packets sent to other computers just never get there. This firewall is particularly secure and also can be used as a proxy. People inside the system send out packets that go to the firewall. The firewall claims the packets as its own and keeps records of where the packets came from; it then sends them out to where they are going. When the packets are received on the other end, the remote system believes that they were sent from the firewall, and this system sends all return packets there. The packets then get back to the firewall, where the firewall routes them back to the inside computer that originated the connection. Because the firewall acts as proxy in this way, people outside the network can see only the firewall, and anyone analyzing the packets sees only the firewall's address and ports. This type of firewall is particularly secure because it presents only the firewall to the outside system.

MCKEON & JEFFRIES

McKeon & Jeffries set up a fairly routine security system for their intranet based on the fact that, besides Web connections from inside the firewall, no one but the systems administrator and the intranet administrator would have access to the Web server. The firewall was set up at the one point of contact with the Internet, which was the ISDN line going out of the Philadelphia office. It sits on an old 486 machine with 32MB of RAM and a 200MB hard drive. This machine runs Windows NT and Eagle Raptor firewall software, which keeps out any users trying to access computers inside the firewall from the Internet, including the Web server. The accounting firm's Web server is only accessible via the Ethernet LAN and the WAN set up between the three offices.

Because the server is a Windows NT platform that does not run remote services (Telnet or FTP), it is only accessible to the systems administrator and intranet administrator when they are physically at the machine or dialed in through remote access via a modem. Thus, security for the server is not too much of a concern.

> **THE SPORTING GOODS AND APPAREL ASSOCIATION**
>
> The SGAA's security plan included using the Sun server and the router to set up a custom firewall. The router passed data packets to only one machine, the Sun server. That machine in turn looked at the packets and, via proxy servers, passed packets for authorized services onto the other machines on the LAN only.
>
> The consultants who helped build the intranet software also helped the association set up this security system. Throughout the setup, the consultants instructed the systems' administrator, who carefully documented every step of the setup. The systems administrator keeps careful track of new security developments.

Testing Security

When you're setting up a secure system, following sound engineering principles is important. One such principle is testing the system. When you're testing the system, you can use any of several methods. For example, try to break into the system from the outside. Use varying levels of knowledge of the system to simulate every potential attacker from a random hacker to a trusted insider. You also can consult one of the many security analysis firms that make a business out of helping companies ensure secure networks.

When you're testing your security, find some standard attacks that people use, and guess some usernames and passwords. Try a dictionary attack on the password file. Some programs that explain how to do a dictionary attack on the system are available. Checking passwords is a good method of keeping users aware of what the vulnerabilities are.

Examine your security model, look at the paths that you are explicitly denying, and be sure that the paths are explicitly denied. System administrators often believe that their systems are secure from certain attacks, when in fact some file has been erased and some setting has been altered. When that path is tested, it turns out to be wide open. Make sure that the holes are plugged in your system.

Finally, no security can be complete without subscribing to the CERT Mailing List. The Computer Emergency Response Team (CERT) puts out regular bulletins on vulnerabilities in various systems; you should check these bulletins regularly. CERT was formed in association with the Software Engineering Institute and Carnegie-Mellon University. Their home page, where you can find all the information you need, is located at www.cert.org.

As an overall concept, pay attention to and recheck the simple security risks, because often this is the place where the security holes are. Simple security risks include the easiest ways for people to access your system—passwords written in e-mail or on paper; services offered to the network that are unnecessary or unsafe; a failure to change the system password; giving out the system password; or not plugging known security holes. If you attend to these risks, little can actually happen. Minor awareness and careful attention to detail will tighten security considerably, making it less important for you to worry about the fancy high-tech items. Keep an eye on the important bridges, and this will cover the system.

Security is always a balance between ease of access and security. It is important to figure out what the balance is. If the system must be especially secure, the people who are using it must understand that. If the users know that they must jump through hoops to access the system, they should understand that these measures will make the system more secure. Overall, the system must look secure to users as well as intruders.

Summary

A secure system requires the cooperation of everyone involved: the system administrators, the system designers, and the users. The security is only as good as each person's commitment to it. No amount of high-tech firewalls, guard dogs, and transaction logging can protect you if your trusted users are writing down their passwords for the janitors to steal. Therein lies the real danger: Far more breaches of security have been caused by careless or, just as often, malicious employees. Preventing an angry employee from wreaking havoc on the system is the most difficult but most important security job. By comparison, hackers are a remote and easily controlled threat.

System security is both the foundation and the summation of all security. Data and transmission security has no value if the system is insecure. System security depends on data and transmission security. For most modern businesses, the computer system is the business. If the system doesn't work, the business doesn't work. The security of the computer system, then, is the security of the business. Good employees don't leave their financial statements or the keys to the file cabinet lying on their desks, but many employees leave their passwords to the same computer files or disks containing that information. Despite the thousands of books and articles written on the subject, the "it won't happen here" attitude is just as widespread as ever. Take precautions.

Security: Access Control

15

by Jerry Ablan

IN THIS CHAPTER

- Security and the intranet **222**
- Battening down the hatches **227**
- Passwords and authentication **227**
- CERN authentication **229**
- NCSA authentication **236**
- Personal HTML directories **240**
- User access to CGI scripts **241**
- Access to server-side includes **243**

One of the final tasks of configuring your intranet server is access control. This entails determining your security needs, designing a security mechanism, and implementing your planned approach. Depending on your needs, this can be simple or complicated. Running an intranet site for 15 different clients is far more detailed than running one for your business alone.

This chapter walks you through the steps necessary for configuring your server's access control. The topics that are covered include the following:

- Determining your security needs
- Security mechanisms
- Implementing your plan
- Client configurations

In this chapter, you'll use a sample Web site, `www.snookums.com`. The administrator of that site, Spider, has just added a new domain, `sweetie.com`, to his list of served domains. I'll guide you through the process of setting up security and discuss what Spider did for his two domains.

Security and the Intranet

Web servers by nature are dumb. They do exactly what is requested of them: serving files stored on your system to any system that requests them. Before implementing your intranet server, you should consider the data that is being offered and to whom it should be served.

The default Web server installation provides virtually no security. Anything that you place into your server's document root directory is fair game for any Web surfer, both internal and external. Unprotected and misconfigured servers are open to cracking and the loss of important data.

CGI scripts also are a big security risk. If one of your scripts contains bugs, or was created to harm your system, you can run into trouble. Scripts should be carefully debugged and tested before being installed on your server.

> **TIP**
>
> For some excellent intranet and general Web security information, see the WWW Security FAQ:
>
> `http://www-genome.wi.mit.edu/WWW/faqs/www-security-faq.html`

Crackers Tread Where Administrators Fail to Secure

More and more movie companies are promoting their films on the Internet these days. It is a relatively inexpensive way of notifying the public of what is coming. Before MGM/UA released the motion picture *Hackers*, it put up a Web site promoting the film. The movie, which did not look appealing to real hackers, was a good target for mischief. Hackers were insulted by the connotations summoned up by the film.

> **NOTE**
>
> There is a common misnomer when it comes to hackers.
>
> A *hacker* is someone who *hacks* code. Generally systems programmers, hackers feel that they can code just about anything. If they don't know how to do it, they will find out. Hackers are good.
>
> *Cracker*, on the other hand, is the term that truly defines the mischievous and sometimes destructive person who is out to beat the system. Crackers are the kind who will try to break into systems, use stolen long-distance access codes and credit card numbers. Crackers are bad.

The *Hackers* site opens with an image of the movie poster that is displayed at theaters. The following URL displays what the site looked like before it was hacked:

http://www.mgmua.com/hackers

A group of crackers downloaded the picture and HTML file and modified it to suit their whims. The resulting picture and Web page were left for new visitors to see at

http://www.mgmua.com/hackers/inventory/hacked/index.html

The crackers were able to do this because the administrator at MGM/UA left the HTTP PUT method unsecured. Anyone with the inkling could overwrite any file that was there.

This break-in was not malicious. But while the site was unprotected, you can only imagine the things that could have been done—files deleted, accounts compromised, even the complete destruction of all data. This is why access control is so important to every Web administrator.

Living Large

It has been proven all too often that software programs contain bugs. This is not to say that all programs are buggy, but many popular programs on the market today have bugs. A majority of these bugs go unnoticed by the user and are fixed with the next release. Some bugs do affect users.

The general feeling in the security community is that the larger the program, the more likely it is to have bugs. Bugs can cause security holes. There is no greater example of this than the infamous sendmail debug bug that spawned the *Internet Worm*.

> **NOTE**
>
> There was a bug in `sendmail`, a UNIX mail handler, that allowed a savvy cracker to run programs on the host machine. This bug involved the use of `debug` mode. You could `telnet` to the SMTP port of any machine running `sendmail`, and if not disabled, `debug` mode would be active.
>
> In 1988, a student named Robert Morris, Jr. exploited this and other UNIX daemon bugs, and released what is now known as the Internet Worm. The worm was thought, at first, to be a virus spreading wildly through the Internet. It was found to be a program that replicated itself and then used `telnet` to reach other systems and replicate itself again using the same `debug` mode bug in `sendmail`, among others.
>
> The Worm was a small program; however, it had several bugs. One of those bugs was the reason it crippled part of the Internet. If it had run properly, the Worm would not have spread as quickly.
>
> For interesting Internet Worm information, check out the following URLs:
>
> http://www.ee.ryerson.ca:8080/~elf/hack/iworm.html
> http://www.alw.nih.gov/Security/first-papers.html

A Web server is a very complex program consisting of many lines of code. It is therefore susceptible to security breaches because, by its nature, it contains bugs. The best defense against these bugs is a good offense.

Determining Your Security Needs

The first step in securing your site is to determine your security needs. These needs might range from none to top secret, but only you can decide the sensitivity of your data.

Access Control Schemes

There are three approaches to securing your intranet site. The first is the "anything goes" approach. This is a Web site with minimal restrictions. Perhaps it lives on the outside of your corporate firewall and you don't care if it lives or dies.

The second is the Draconian approach: all access to your site is cut off. You then enable bits and pieces until you attain the desired access level.

The third and final approach is somewhere in the middle. This is probably the most commonly used approach and the most difficult to keep secure. Because you are going to allow access to some parts of your site, but not all, this can cause conflicts in the configuration options. With proper planning and design, however, these conflicts can be eliminated and your site can be very secure.

Security: Access Control

Chapter 15

Mapping Your Site

In order to better understand the layout of your site, you should first map out the entire site. Make a physical and a logical map using your favorite drawing or design program. Make a flow chart or diagram, whichever you prefer. The important thing is that you, as the administrator, completely understand the extent of your Web structure. This will not only help you see the big picture, but will also enable you to concentrate better on security design. Visual aids always help designers think things through more carefully.

Figure 15.1 is the logical map that Spider (our fictitious Web administrator) made for www.snookums.com.

FIGURE 15.1.
The www.snookums.com *site map.*

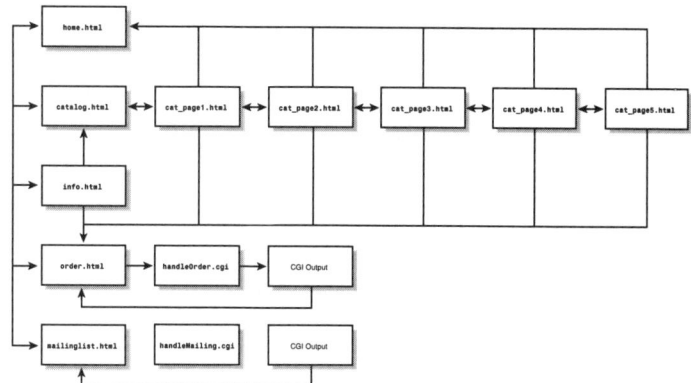

Snookums, Inc. sells many different products, and the company wants to showcase its product line and take orders online. To do this, it has set up a five-page catalog with some additional company information. The pages are as follows:

- home.html: The home page. Links are provided to all of the top-level pages.
- catalog.html: This is the catalog main page. From here you can go to any catalog page or any other top-level page.
- info.html: This is the company information page. From here you can get to any top-level page.
- order.html: This is the order page. This page provides a form to place orders for widgets. The form calls a CGI script that handles the order.
- mailingList.html: This page allows a visitor to join a mailing list for new information from Snookums, Inc.

Spider's map shows lines with arrows. These represent the pages you can access from any given page. Spider now has a better understanding of the layout of his site. Armed with this information, he is ready to begin securing the site.

Special Access Considerations

After you have mapped your site, you should think about any special access that you need to allow. Think of these as the *whos* and the *whats*.

The *whos* are the remote hosts to which you will grant access. Most Web sites have no restrictions on who can access their site. However, some visitors can become abusive or destructive and measures might need to be taken. If you want to block access for any hosts, make a note of those sites.

> **TIP**
>
> You might want to block access to your site from Web crawlers, spiders, and worms. These `robots` scan the Web for information and catalog their findings. They then allow their users to search the database that was constructed with this information. It is possible to block out these Web insects. For more information, check out the following URL:
>
> `http://info.webcrawler.com/mak/projects/robots/robots.html`

The *whats* are the pages at your site. They are what you are serving. You need to determine which hosts can view what data. Again, most Web sites grant the same access to all remote hosts. If you have any special considerations, now is the time to think of them. Some examples are

- Employee access: Perhaps you have an intranet page set up that is only for employees of your company to view from home.
- Special clients: You might have a extra special client that gets its own page on the intranet.
- Robots: You might want to block robots from getting to some pages on your site. This is not an issue for a totally isolated intranet.
- Users and passwords: You can configure any page to require a user name and password. You can even configure your entire site to require these.

In any event, you should make a note of the items that you want to provide special access.

File Permissions

One of the last things you'll need to check is the permissions for your files. Your files should never be *world-writeable*—this would allow anyone to overwrite them.

Battening Down the Hatches

If you are running your intranet server on a UNIX system, there are several precautions you should take. These precautions will limit the potential security holes that might exist. They are simple to implement and can be undone quickly in a pinch.

Designated Intranet Server

If at all possible, make your intranet server only an intranet server. Try not to use it for purposes other than an intranet. Combining an intranet server with a mail server or with a Usenet news server is just asking for trouble. These other servers can have security holes that will give a wily cracker access to your machine and its data. Also, if your Web server is compromised, you'll lose the services provided by that machine (like news or mail).

Exorcisms

Physically remove all daemons from your system that are not used or wanted. If these programs are on your server, the potential for abuse is there. For example, if you are not running a mail server on your system, remove all of the mail servers. Likewise, if FTP is not provided, remove the FTP daemon. When you have deleted the unwanted rascals, be sure to modify your `inetd.conf` file so the daemons are never called.

Sweep and Clean

Physically remove all unused language interpreters, command shells, and compilers. If these programs are not used, they don't belong on your system. If someone was able to compromise your system, the tools could help the invader build a more permanent home.

User Accounts

Keep user accounts on your intranet machine to a minimum. Only grant access to the machine on an as-needed basis. The fewer login accounts and passwords that exist on your server, the better. Any user who has an account on the intranet should use a good password. Good passwords contain a mixture of numbers and upper- and lowercase characters. These types of passwords are nearly impossible to crack.

Passwords and Authentication

It is possible to configure your server to serve documents only to users that it can authenticate. These configurations allow flexibility in the way they are set up. They also allow you to restrict access to certain parts of your site on a user-by-user basis.

Building Your Intranet

Part II

Both the CERN and NCSA servers provide a method of user authentication. Both involve a user file and a password file. These files are created with either a text editor or a supplied program. These programs can be called from CGI scripts, allowing you to register people online.

Figure 15.2 shows how the Netscape browser accepts a user-supplied user name and password.

FIGURE 15.2.
Netscape Navigator's User/Password dialog box.

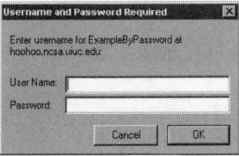

Figure 15.3 shows the same window filled in. Notice that the password is not displayed.

FIGURE 15.3.
Supplying a user name and password

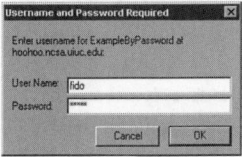

These user and password files are in no way connected with the system's own password file. Those intranet server password and user files are maintained by the administrator and are not connected. Conversely, one does not need an account on an intranet server to be granted access through password authentication.

Figure 15.4 shows successful entry to the protected page.

FIGURE 15.4.
Success!

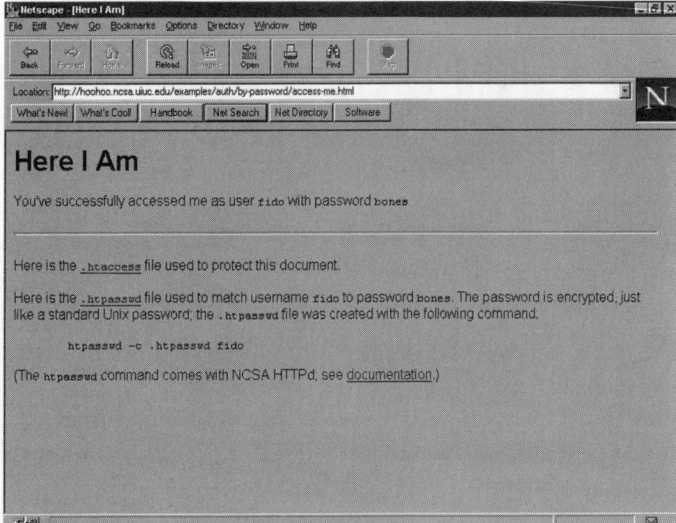

Figure 15.5 shows the message that is displayed when the user is not granted access.

FIGURE 15.5.
Failure!

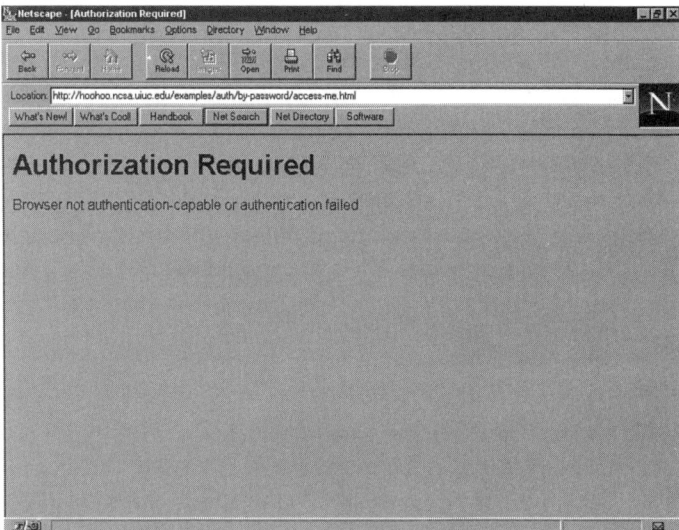

CERN Authentication

The CERN server can be configured for password authentication in many different ways. The `Protect` directive allows you to define the protection setup file for an URL or set of URLs. You can also configure the server to run as different users for different documents.

The most flexible method is to combine the use of the `Protect` directive with an *Access Control Listing*, or *ACL*, file. This file lives in the directory where your files live. It provides more detailed access rules for those files. This file is called `.www_acl`. If you use this method, no further modifications are required once your `Protect` directive is placed in your configuration file. All of the changes now go in the `.www_acl` file.

> **TIP**
>
> If you use the `Protect` or the `Protection` directives in your configuration file, the directives must be placed before any `Pass` or `Fail` directives. These directives use the URLs that are *requested* of your server, not the physical file locations on your hard drive.

Protect

The `Protect` directive enables you to specify an URL or set of URLs that are protected by an ACL file. The format of this directive is as follows:

```
Protect <template> <setup_file> [<uid.gid>]
```

`<template>` is the URL template defining the URL or set of URLs that you wish to protect.

`<setup_file>` is the full path and file name of the actual file that contains the protection rules.

`<uid.gid>` is an optional parameter. When you first configured the CERN server, you specified the user and group that the server should run as. In the examples, I chose www and www for the user and group, respectively. The `<uid.gid>` parameter lets you specify the user and group to run as for an URL or set of URLs. This is a very nice feature.

Here are some sample `Protect` statements:

- `Protect /Private/Snookums/* conf/snookums.setup`: This defines the file snookums.setup in the /usr/local/etc/httpd/conf directory as the setup file for any URL requested from the /Private/Snookums tree.
- `Protect /spider/private/* conf/spider.setup spider.www`: This defines the file spider.setup as the setup file for any URL requested from the /spider/private tree. Also, when these documents are served, the server is instructed to run as the user spider and the group www.

DefProt

You also can configure a default setup file for your `Protect` statements. The `DefProt` directive allows you to provide the file's name when it is omitted from any `Protect` statement.

For example:

```
DefProt /Private/* conf/private.setup
Protect /Private/Snookums/* conf/snookums.setup
Protect /Private/Spider/*
Protect /Private/Sweetie/*
```

The `DefProt` defines the default setup file as conf/private.setup. This file is the setup file for all files under the /Private tree.

The first `Protect` statement defines conf/snookums.setup as the setup file for the /Private/Snookums tree. The file is specified and, therefore, the default is ignored.

The second and third `Protect` statements, however, have no setup file specified. This is where the `DefProt` statement kicks in. These two statements will have the conf/private.setup file used as their protection setup files.

Protection Setup Files

Specifying the `DefProt` and `Protect` directives for your URLs is only half the job. The other half is creating the *protection setup files*. These files define the authentication scheme, password and group files, and the password server's ID.

These items are specified through directives. Here is a sample protection setup file:

```
AuthType        Basic
ServerId        SnookumsSetup
PasswordFile    /usr/local/etc/httpd/admin/passwd
GroupFile       /usr/local/etc/httpd/admin/group
```

As you can see, there are four basic directives:

- `AuthType <auth_scheme>`: This specifies the authentication scheme. Currently, only `Basic` is supported.
- `ServerId <name>`: This specifies the name of the password server. This name is nothing more than an identifier that is sent to the client. This allows smart browsers to remember your password when pages are revisited. This can be the same for your entire site or different for each protection scheme. It is up to you.
- `PasswordFile <filename>`: This specifies the full path and filename of the password file.
- `GroupFile <filename>`: This specifies the full path and filename of the group file.

The following are additional directives that can be used for embedded protection:

- `UserId <user>`: The user to run as.
- `GroupId <group>`: The group to run as.
- `GetMask <group syntax>`: This sets the group of entities that are granted access.

Creating Users and Passwords

The password file is created with a utility program called `htadm`. This program is bundled with the server when you download it. The `htadm` program has the following options and parameters:

- `htadm -adduser <passwordfile> [<username> [<password> [<realname>]]]`: This command adds a user to the password file `<passwordfile>`. `<username>` and `<password>` are optional. If they are not specified, you are prompted for the information. `<realname>` is an optional parameter to specify the user's real name.
- `htadm -deluser <passwordfile> [<username>]`: This command deletes user `<username>` from the password file `<passwordfile>`. `<username>` is optional. If it is not specified, you are prompted for the information.

- `htadm -passwd <passwordfile> [<username> [<password>]]`: This command changes the password of user `<username>` to `<password>` in `<passwordfile>`. `<username>` and `<password>` are optional. If they are not specified, you are prompted for the information.

- `htadm -check <passwordfile> [<username> [<password>]]`: This command checks a user's password in a password file. `<username>` and `<password>` are optional. If they are not specified, you are prompted for the information. `htadm` returns zero if the password is correct, and non-zero if it is not correct. The program will also write the words `Correct` or `Incorrect` to standard output.

- `htadm -create <passwordfile>`: This creates an empty password file `<passwordfile>`.

> **CAUTION**
>
> `htadm` should never be used to add users to your system password file. The format of the files is different. The results could be bad.

Creating Groups

You can configure your server to serve files only to people who belong to a certain group. These groups are maintained in the file called a *group* file. If used, this file—like the password file—can exist in any directory you wish. The format is similar to that of the password file:

`<group name>:<member1> <member2> ... <membern>`

`<group name>` is what you want to call the group. The `<member#>` is the user name or mask that you wish to be part of the group. This user name is from the Protect password file, not the system passwd file. You can specify multiple members per group.

The following is a list of the entities that can be members of groups:

- User name: *Any* user's name.
- Group name: You can specify another group to be a member of a group.
- IP address: You can specify an IP address or partial IP address as a group member.
- User or group at an IP address: You can specify a user or group of users at an IP address or partial IP address.

The best way to understand the group file syntax is to see one. This is the sample group file used in the CERN documentation for the server:

```
authors: john, james
trusted: authors, jim
cern_people: @128.141.*.*
hackers: marca@141.142.*.*, sanders@153.39.*.*,(luotonen, timbl,
       ↪hallam)@128.141.*.*, cailliau@(128.141.201.162, 128.141.248.119)
cern_hackers: hackers@128.141.*.*
```

You can specify a group of users at an IP address by surrounding them with parentheses. Also, note that the last group, `cern_hackers`, is made up of the group `hackers`, further restricted by an IP address. These files can become quite complex.

> **TIP**
>
> As corny as it might sound, remember to check and test your work thoroughly after any change in the group or password files. These configurations can get pretty hairy. A single misplaced asterisk could open up your site to anyone.

There are two predefined groups:

- `All`: This specifies all users who have an entry in the password file.
- `Anybody`, `Anyone`, and `Anonymous`: This specifies any user from any host.

.www_acl

It is possible to specify even more protection than the `Protect` statement provides. This is done with the `.www_acl` file. This file specifies the files, methods, and users allowed access inside a directory. The format of the file is as follows:

```
<filespec> : <method1,method2,etc.> : <user1,user2,group1,etc.>
```

Here is a sample `.www_acl` file:

```
secret*.html : GET,POST : trusted_people
*.html : GET,POST : snookcust
```

The first line allows the `GET` and `POST` methods for all files that match `secret*.html` to the users in the group `trusted_people`.

The second line allows the `GET` and `POST` methods for all files that end in `.html` to the users in group `snookcust`.

> **CAUTION**
>
> This file processes all lines in the file. Translation does not stop when a match occurs. This behavior is exactly like the `Map` directive. Be careful how you set up your `.www_acl` files. In the preceding example, all HTML files would be available to anyone in the `snookcust` group, even if they were not in the `trusted_people` group.

Embedded Protection

Instead of using protection setup files, you can embed your protection setup into your configuration file. This is done with the `Protection` directive. The format is as follows:

```
Protection <protname¦template> (
directives…
}
```

Any of the directives listed earlier in the Protection Setup Files section can be used in this protection *block*. This enables you to keep all of your configuration in one place. The `<protname>` is a name that you give to the protection block. You then can use the name in a normal `Protect` statement instead of the setup file. For example:

```
Protection    SpiderWeb {
    UserId        spider
    GroupId       www
    AuthType      Basic
    ServerId      SnookumsSetup
    PasswordFile  /usr/local/etc/httpd/admin/passwd
    GroupFile     /usr/local/etc/httpd/admin/passwd
    GetMask       @(170.137.254.*)
}
    Protect    /Private/Snookums/*    SpiderWeb
```

Note that the name of the protection block is `SpiderWeb`. This name is used instead of the protection setup file name in the `Protect` statement at the end of the block. It is possible to combine the two lines into one, as well. If you do not wish to use the protection name in any other `Protect` statements, simply place the URL template where the protection name would go. Here's an example:

```
Protection    /Private/Snookums/* {
    UserId        spider
    GroupId       www
    AuthType      Basic
    ServerId      SnookumsSetup
    PasswordFile  /usr/local/etc/httpd/admin/passwd
    GroupFile     /usr/local/etc/httpd/admin/passwd
    GetMask       @(170.137.254.*)
}
```

CAUTION

The CERN documentation warns that the server is not very robust in parsing the `Protection` directive. The developers ask that you make sure to place a space between the URL template and the curly brace. They also ask that the ending curly brace be alone on a line.

Examples of Protections

This configuration might seem a bit difficult at first. However, working through a few examples could help you better understand the nature of CERN protection.

Restrict by IP Address or Domain Name

The following is an example of protecting an entire directory tree for a particular IP address. This can be used to prevent a certain set of hosts from accessing part of your site. The example will allow only hosts from `snookums.com` and `sweetie.com` into the directory tree /Private/Secret. Note that there is no password or group file involved in this type of setup. It is a simple restriction based on an IP address. Therefore, the user will never be prompted for a user name or password.

```
Protection      IPRESTRICT {
    UserID          www
    GroupID         www
    AuthType        Basic
    GetMask         @(*.snookums.com,*.sweetie.com)
}

    Protect         /Private/Secret/*      IPRESTRICT
```

Restrict by User

The second example builds on the first. In addition to IP address protection, you're going to add user protection. Only certain users at `snookums.com` or `sweetie.com` are allowed access to the /Private/Secret tree.

```
Protection      USERRESTRICT {
    UserID          wwwadmin
    GroupID         www
    AuthType        Basic
    ServerID        AdminPassword
    PasswordFile    /usr/local/etc/httpd/admin/passwd
    GroupFile       /usr/local/etc/httpd/admin/group
    GetMask         admins@(*.snookums.com,*.sweetie.com)
}

    Protect         /Private/Secret/*      USERRESTRICT
```

Restrict Individual Files

The final example shows how to use the .www_acl files to restrict access to individual files. I'll build on the last two examples for this one. So far, you have restricted access to the /Private/Secret directory tree to only administrative users from `snookums.com` or `sweetie.com`. You can do the same thing using the ACL files. To do this, simply move a portion of the GetMask from the main configuration down to the directory of the files.

For your example, the configuration file would look like the following:

```
Protection          USERRESTRICT {
      UserID        wwwadmin
      GroupID       www
      AuthType      Basic
      ServerID      AdminPassword
      PasswordFile  /usr/local/etc/httpd/admin/passwd
      GroupFile     /usr/local/etc/httpd/admin/group
      GetMask       @(*.snookums.com,*.sweetie.com)
}

      Protect       /Private/Secret/*       USERRESTRICT
```

You then place the following into your `.www_acl` file:

```
*.html  : GET : admins
```

NCSA Authentication

The NCSA server can be configured for password authentication on a directory basis only. To do this, you must create a hidden file called `.htaccess` in the directory where the files are that need to be secured. You can also create a global access file called `access.conf.` and place it in your configuration directory.

`.htaccess` and `access.conf`

The `.htaccess` file can be configured many different ways. These directives are as follows:

- `AuthUserFile`: This specifies the location and name of the file from which to read passwords.
- `AuthGroupFile`: This specifies the location and name of the file from which to read groups. You can combine users into groups and allow access by group.
- `AuthName`: This specifies the identification of this screen, which is displayed at the client end.
- `AuthType`: This specifies the method of authentication. These types can be `Basic`, `PEM`, `PGP`, `KerberosV4`, `KerberosV5`, or `Digest`. `Basic` is the most commonly used method because it requires no special software on the client.
- `Limit`: This describes the allowed or denied HTTP methods (`POST`, `GET`, and so on) and remote hosts.
- `Options`: This describes which server features are supported.

The following `.htaccess` file is from the Web page shown in Figure 15.4. It is from the NCSA Web site. This page allows access only to the user `fido` with a password of `bones`.

```
AuthUserFile    /X11/mosaic/public/auth-tutorial/examples/by-password/.htpasswd
AuthGroupFile   /dev/null
AuthName        ExampleByPassword
AuthType        Basic

<Limit GET>
require user fido
</Limit>
```

From the configuration file, you can see that the password file is stored in

/X11/mosaic/public/auth-tutorial/examples/by-password/.htpasswd

You can also see that there is no group file, and the page requires user `fido`.

Here is the file from the preceding configuration:

/X11/mosaic/public/auth-tutorial/examples/by-password/.htpasswd

It is similar to the UNIX password file, but contains less information:

`fido:h5HhgnhegqFIw`

You have the option to place the entirety of this file in the global access file. To do this, you use the `Directory` directive. This is a blocking or sectioning directive. The format is as follows:

```
<Directory dirname>
directives
</Directory>
```

To move the preceding example to the `access.conf` file, simply add the following to it:

```
<Directory /usr/local/etc/httpd/htdocs/private>
AuthUserFile    /X11/mosaic/public/auth-tutorial/examples/by-password/.htpasswd
AuthGroupFile   /dev/null
AuthName        ExampleByPassword
AuthType        Basic

<Limit GET>
require user fido
</Limit>
</Directory>
```

Limit

The `Limit` directive is by far the trickiest one of the bunch. It is similar to the `VirtualHost` directive in format. This directive format encloses other directives into a *block* of configuration code. The format uses begin and end tags. These tags look like this:

```
<Limit method>
directives
</Limit>
```

You might notice the similarity to HTML code. It uses similar tags.

The following directives are allowed to be used inside a `Limit` block:

- `allow from <host1 host2...hostn|All>`: This defines the host or hosts from which access is allowed. host can be an IP address, complete host name (that is, www.snookums.com), partial host (that is, .snookums.com), or All.
- `deny from <host1 host2...hostn|All>`: This defines the host or hosts for which access is denied. host can be an IP address, complete host name (that is, www.snookums.com), partial host (that is, .snookums.com), or All.
- `order <deny,allow|allow,deny|mutual-failure>`: This defines the order in which the *allow* and *deny* statements are processed.
- `require <user|group|valid-user>`: This defines the users and groups that are required to access this directory.

Options

The `Options` directive controls the server features that can be done in your directory. These features are as follows:

- `FollowSymLinks`: This allows the following of symbolic links.
- `SymLinksIfOwnerMatch`: This allows symbolic links to be followed only if the target file or directory's owner matches that of the link.
- `ExecCGI`: This allows the execution of CGI scripts.
- `Includes`: This allows server-side include files.
- `Indexes`: This allows a user to request indexes of this directory. Disabling this feature only stops the server from generating the index. If an index file exists (specified by the `DirectoryIndex` directive), it will still be sent.
- `IncludesNoExec`: This allows server-side includes, but disallows the exec feature of them.
- `All`: This allows all of the features listed here.
- `None`: This allows none of the features listed here.

> **CAUTION**
>
> If you do not specify an `Options` directive in your configuration file, the server defaults to `All`. This might not be what you want. Be sure to check your configuration carefully.

Creating Users and Passwords

The password file can be created with a utility program called `htpasswd`. This program is bundled with the server when you download it. The syntax of the `htpasswd` program is as follows:

```
htpasswd [-c] <file> <user>
```

`<file>` is the path and name of the password file to work with. `<user>` is the user to create the password for. The `-c` option will create the file if it does not exist.

When run, this program asks you to enter the password for the user specified. You must enter it a second time to verify. The record is then written to the file specified. This new file can then be used for user authentication.

.htgroup

You can configure your server to serve files only to people that belong to a certain group. These groups are maintained in the file `.htgroup`. If used, this file—like the `password` file—can exist in any directory you wish. The format is similar to that of the `password` file:

```
<group name>:<member1> <member2> ... <membern>
```

`<group name>` is what you want to call the group. The `<member#>` is the user name that should be part of the group. This user name is from the `.htpasswd` file, not the system `/etc/passwd` file. You can specify multiple members per group.

Here is a sample `.htgroup` file:

```
snookcust: ren stimpy sven
```

In the group `snookcust`, there are three users: `ren`, `stimpy`, and `sven`.

Here is a sample `.htaccess` file using groups:

```
AuthUserFile    /usr/local/etc/httpd/passwords/.htpasswd
AuthGroupFile   / usr/local/etc/httpd/passwords/.htgroup
AuthName        Password
AuthType        Basic

<Limit GET>
require group snookcust
</Limit>
```

This requires the user to be in the group `snookcust`. Therefore, only the users `ren`, `stimpy`, and `sven` are allowed access.

Personal HTML Directories

If you are running an intranet site that enables users to have their own home pages, you need to configure your server to allow this. Both the CERN and NCSA servers have the `UserDir` directive. This directive enables the server to jump to a user's home directory when only the user's name is specified with a preceding tilde (~). On a UNIX system, you can reference any user's home directory by placing a tilde in front of that user's name. For example, to list the files in the home directory of the user `teddy`, the command would be

```
munster@honey:~$ ls -l ~teddy
```

Your intranet server can be configured to do the same thing. When a request comes in for the home page of the user `teddy`, it will usually look like the following:

```
http://www.snookums.com/~teddy/home.html
```

The `UserDir` directive enables the server to look for user files in a special subdirectory in its home directory tree.

The format of the `UserDir` directive is as follows:

```
UserDir <directory>
```

`<directory>` is the directory under the user's home directory tree to search for documents. It is similar to automatically specifying a sub-`DocumentRoot` for each user.

On the CERN server, you must specify the `UserDir` directive to enable this feature.

The NCSA server, on the other hand, enables this feature and by default points to the directory `public_html`. To disable this feature on the NCSA server, you must use the following command:

```
UserDir DISABLED
```

Here are some examples:

- `UserDir /`: If a request for `/~teddy/index.html` was received, the file `~teddy/index.html` would be served.
- `UserDir public_html`: If a request for `/~teddy/stuff.html` was received, the file `~teddy/public_html/stuff.html` would be served.

> **TIP**
>
> To enable the entire users' home directory, use a single slash (/). This will resolve to the users' root directory. This can be dangerous, however, if user file permissions are not set properly.

Be sure to inform your users to take the same precautions that you use to secure your files in the server's root directory tree: make the files readable and writeable only by themselves.

User Access to CGI Scripts

Your users might request that they be allowed to create their own CGI scripts. Besides the management headache that this causes, you probably don't want users writing programs that run on your server. Any script the user creates could potentially run as the root user and wreak major havoc on your system.

Only you know the capabilities of your users, but, generally, most systems have a mix ranging from gurus to newbies. Although you might not be worried about your gurus writing CGI code, your newbies will probably be the ones that ask for it. Unfortunately, these little snippets of code need to be as secure as your intranet server itself.

There are two ways to allow users access to your CGI scripts. Both methods are simple. The first is to restrict script directory access to a certain group of people (that is, admin users). Then, simply add users to that group so they can then create and test their own scripts.

> **TIP**
>
> It is better to store all of your CGI scripts in one place. This way, if someone were to compromise your system and place a CGI file out there, it would have to be placed in your CGI script directory. This would make it easy for you to detect.
>
> If you were to allow CGI scripts in any directory, it would be very difficult to detect changes in all of them.
>
> For some excellent CGI security information, check out the CGI security FAQ at the following URL:
>
> `http://www.cerf.net/~paulp/cgi-security/`

The second method is to enable scripts in that user's directory.

Enabling CGI Scripts in Directories Other than /cgi-bin

To configure your server to enable CGI scripts in directories other than the main /cgi-bin directory, you need to add more configuration directives. This differs slightly between the CERN and NCSA servers.

CERN Configuration

The `Exec` directive is used to map URLs to scripts. When you place executable scripts on your server, the server needs to know where the scripts are and the fact that they are executable. The format is as follows:

```
Exec <template> <result>
```

This directive differs in its use of wildcards. The `Exec` directive must include wildcards in both the `template` and the `result`. This is because many scripts take arguments that are passed along at the end of the URL. If no wildcard was used, the arguments would not be passed on properly.

Here is an example of the `Exec` directive:

```
Exec      /cgi-bin/*      /usr/local/etc/httpd/cgi-bin/*
```

This will inform your server that any URL beginning with `/cgi-bin` is an executable script that it can be found in this directory:

```
/usr/local/etc/httpd/cgi-bin/
```

Simply use this directive for each place that you want to allow scripts to execute.

NCSA Configuration

The `ScriptAlias` directive specifies a directory where executable scripts live on your server. Multiple `ScriptAlias` directives can be used in the `srm.conf` file. The format of the `ScriptAlias` directive is as follows:

```
ScriptAlias <template> <path>
```

When used, the `ScriptAlias` directive effectively remaps the location of `template` to `path`.

Here is an example of the `ScriptAlias` directive:

```
ScriptAlias    /cgi-bin    /usr/local/etc/httpd/cgi-bin
```

All requests for documents that begin with `/cgi-bin` will be rerouted through `/usr/local/etc/httpd/cgi-bin` and the output of the script will be returned to the requesting client.

Simply use this directive for each place that you want to allow scripts to execute.

> **TIP**
>
> If you want to allow CGI script execution here and there, use the `Options ExecCGI` directive in the ACF for that directory. You need to make scripts automatically execute, however.
>
> To do this, you will need to add a new MIME type to your global configuration or to your local directory ACF. This should look like the following:
>
> `AddType application/x-httpd-cgi .cgi`
>
> This will make all files ending in `.cgi` scripts. You also can add `.sh` and `.pl` as in the following:
>
> `AddType application/x-httpd-cgi .cgi .sh .pl`
>
> This will allow for the automatic execution of PERL and shell scripts as well.

Access to Server-Side Includes

Server-side includes, or *SSIs,* are a way to include other programs or HTML files into a document before it is served to the client. This allows for customization of the file on-the-fly. Types of information that you can provide include the following:

- current date and time
- Last modification date and time
- Remote user
- Remote host
- Hit counts

Allowing SSIs can be costly to your server's performance. It slows your server down to parse through a second HTML file while sending the original. To reduce this performance cost, you should only allow SSIs with files of a certain extension. This will cause the server to only parse the included file, not both files. If you don't care about the performance, this restriction is not needed.

Enabling Server-Side Includes

To enable SSIs, you first need to add a MIME type to your global configuration or local directory configuration file. This will inform the server of the extension that you wish to use for all SSIs. The server internally uses the magic MIME type of `text/x-server-parsed-html` to identify these types of documents. You must bind an extension to this MIME type. Use the `AddType` directive to do so:

`AddType text/x-server-parsed-html .shtml`

This specifies that files ending in .shtml will be the only candidates for inclusion.

Alternatively, if you don't care about server performance, use this AddType directive instead:

```
AddType text/x-server-parsed-html .html
```

Allowing Access

By default, all users have access to SSIs. You might want to restrict access to a few people or only allow SSIs from certain directories.

If you do not want to allow access to server-side includes, you must modify the Options for the global access file, access.conf. By default, all options are enabled for all directories. You must make an entry in your global access file or your directory's .htaccess file. See the earlier section regarding the format.

Summary

After reading this chapter, you should have a better understanding of the methods available to you for securing your intranet site. These include restrictions based on user, IP address, and domain name. You also should have some ideas about what you want to allow users to do. You now might or might not want to let them have access to CGI scripts or server-side includes. Hopefully, I've offered enough insight for you to make these decisions.

Security: Secure Internet Data Transmission

16

by Richard Simon

IN THIS CHAPTER

- What is transmission security? **246**
- How information is transmitted **247**
- How information is intercepted and read **248**
- Sniffing devices **248**
- Devices for spoofing **249**
- Methods of transmissions and their levels of security **251**
- Encryption **251**
- Why a technical solution is never the whole solution **257**
- Client/server issues **257**
- Secure computing in practice **258**
- How much is too much? **260**
- What level of security is right for you? **261**

In the two preceding chapters we examined ways in which to keep your data safe, mainly from within an organization. I discussed the best ways to keep hackers out of your intranet and how to protect actual data from viruses and human error as well as the physical security of your software and hardware. Now that you've secured your tools and applications physically and have taken all precautions internally to keep data safe, it's time to consider how safe your data is during transmission. This transmission from one computer to another could be within your LAN, within your intranet, or over the Internet.

This chapter's topic, secure transmission, explores the security risks involved with data transmission, such as eavesdropping and decrypting. It discusses why and how to establish secure channels as well as ways to prevent or foil attacks on these secure channels. It's aimed primarily at anyone who is trying to design a fully secure system of computers and data or for anyone interested in encrypting data for transmission. Any individual involved with transmitting sensitive data—whether in a business that exchanges confidential information, either inside its corporate headquarters or with customers, or in an organization that exchanges any sensitive data between just two computers—should not skip this chapter. This includes banks; corporations with offices in different geographical locations that share proprietary information, regardless of whether it's public or private; or individuals doing business on the Internet, including selling products and conducting business transactions.

What Is Transmission Security?

Transmission security is the capability to send a message electronically from one computer system to another computer system so that only the intended recipient receives and reads the message and the message received is identical to the message sent. The message would not be identical if it was altered in anyway, whether transmitted over faulty channels or intercepted by an eavesdropper. Transmission security translates into secure networks. Although many people regard networks as computers connected by wires, this definition of a network, while technically correct, misses the point. Rather, networks are transmitted data, the data flowing over wires.

All transmissions can be intercepted. And the cautious user looks at all transmissions as if they will be intercepted. You can minimize the risks of transmission interception, but you can never, under any circumstances, completely rule it out. After all, it is people who design and put wires in their place, and people can get to them. Accessing wires is somewhat comparable, although much more difficult, to accessing a transmission sent over airwaves, as on a CB radio. For example, as a ham, you may have a message intended only for other hams. Although hams are the main communicators on these frequencies, anyone with the right radio equipment can tune in and listen, so it's likely your message will be received and heard by other listeners who pick up the frequency, whether you want them to hear it or not.

Similar risks occur with cellular phones, even though most transmission takes place over wire and not air. One risky transmission occurred between Prince Charles and his mistress Camilla Parker Bowles when an eavesdropper intercepted a now infamous cellular phone conversation between the two.

So, like it or not, networks are our transmissions. If you ascertain that security is too high to risk over networks and you decide not to transmit over networks, throw your computer systems away; you've wasted your money. Unfortunately, transmission interceptions are inevitable; it's likely they will occur at times. Designing a 100 percent transmission-secure network is akin to designing a car that can't be broken into; no matter how secure the car is, someone can always break the windows. This doesn't mean you should sit back and wait for the interception, however; instead, build your system to deter people from attempting to break in, and make it costly for the hacker to enter.

How Information Is Transmitted

Most networking schemes involve data transmission over certain whole sections of the network. Most network transmissions don't go directly from computer A to computer B. Ethernet networks, for example, involve transmission to all directly connected computers on the local network. Two computers are "directly connected" if there is no device between them that filters the transmission based on its destination. So if computer A sends a message to computer E, computers B, C, and D will receive the message but will ignore it, because it is not intended for them, as shown in Figure 16.1. Many other types of networks, including Token Ring, FDDI, and some switched ethernets operate on the same idea: Transmitted packets go to many devices on the network and expect the recipients to ignore messages destined for other computers. This is much like radio or television transmission, in which signals are sent out in every direction, but radios and TVs not on the correct station don't use the signal.

FIGURE 16.1.
This is where every message travels on an ethernet network.

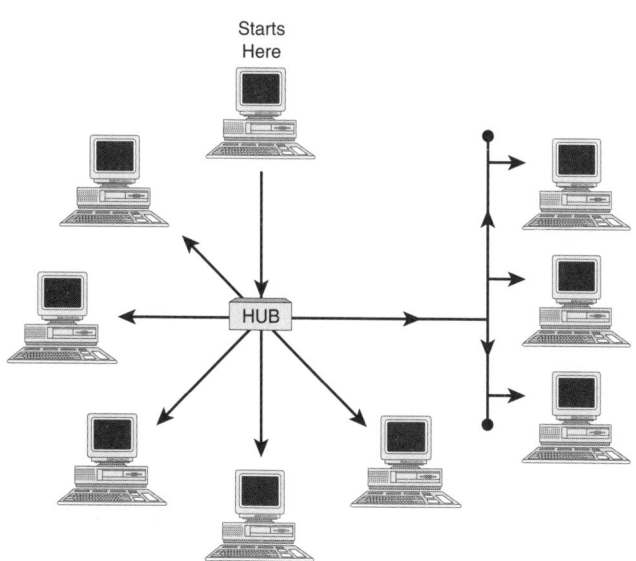

How Information Is Intercepted and Read

Any computer with access to the physical network wire or in the vicinity of over-air transmissions, however, could be instructed not to ignore the signals intended for other computers. This is the essence of electronic eavesdropping.

Information is considered intercepted when someone other than the intended recipient receives the information. Data can be intercepted in many ways, such as electronic eavesdropping or by using the recipient's password. It can occur anywhere, including in a chat room or through an e-mail exchange.

The tools required to read the transmission depend on how the information is intercepted. If an intruder is stealing transmissions at the most basic level (stealing the data packets straight off the wire or out of the air), the interloper will need something that translates electronic signals from voltage changes to the numbers and letters that those changes represent. Computers for which the transmission is intended do this automatically, because they are expecting the signal and already know its characteristics, how to decode it, and what to do with it. A much simpler method would be intercepting a message by just looking over someone's shoulder to read what they have written. Again, the legitimate user already has a context in which to interpret the on-screen information. The snooper, however, still has to interpret the message, and this isn't always so simple.

Sniffing Devices

There are troubleshooting programs and devices designed to analyze LAN traffic. These are commonly referred to as *packet sniffers,* because they are created to "sniff" packets of data for the network engineer. As mentioned in the preceding section, all transmissions are broadcast over all the wires. When one computer wants to communicate with another, it sends out an electrical signal through the network, which could be copper wire, fiber optic cable, or air. The signal travels over this whole section of the network until it reaches the end of its signal strength in the air, the end of the wire or cable, or a network device that turns the packet back because the packet's destination is not on the other side of the device. At each point along this journey that the signal encounters a network interface, that interface examines the signal. If the interface sees the signal is for someone else, it ignores it. If the interface recognizes a signal for it, it reads it and gives it to the other parts of the computer for interpretation and use.

The nice thing about LANs is that the systems administrator can use a sniffer to tap into the wire to examine it. A systems administrator should occasionally examine these lines to check on the raw material going over the LAN. This is where packet sniffers are helpful. Packet sniffers will instruct your computer to look at every signal over the wire or only signals that meet certain criteria. This allows the systems administrator to analyze and actually read electrical signals. However, anyone with malicious intent also can use packet sniffers for analyzing and reading network traffic.

Now, you might think there are users out there maliciously using packet sniffers to read data worldwide, continuously. It's true that there may be many users with malicious intent snooping around networks, but it is not as simple as just purchasing a packet sniffer. There are devices—generally referred to as *internetworking devices* and more specifically referred to as *routers* and *bridges*—that actually filter the electrical signals sent out as data packets. These devices filter signals logically, which means that any data passing through a bridge or router must be intended to go through that bridge or router; the destination of the data must be on the other side of the internetworking device to get through the filter. If the destination of the data is not on the other side of the filter, the internetworking device won't pass the signal; and if it doesn't pass the signal, someone on the other side is unable to sniff the information, as shown in Figure 16.2. Anytime you have a network that requires any sort of logical divisions, you need an internetworking device. If you are connected to the Internet, you have an internetworking device. If your local network spans a large physical distance, you have some sort of internetworking device.

FIGURE 16.2.
This sniffer cannot smell packets on the other side of the router.

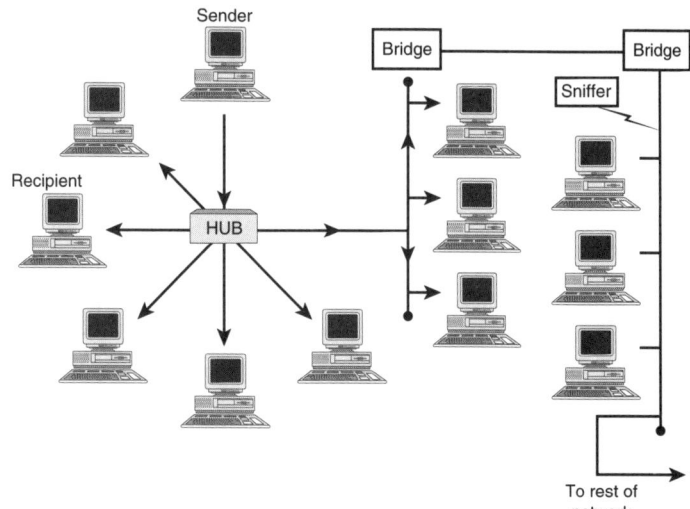

Devices for Spoofing

Spoofing is somewhat of an overrated threat. *Spoofing* means getting your computer to pretend it is a different computer. The user forces the computer to present credentials to the network that are false. To do so, the user doesn't need tools but rather information to make those credentials realistic. The Internet identifies computers by numbers: Every computer has a unique number on the Internet. Some computers will grant access to systems they are charged with protecting or resources that they guard on the basis of the identification number presented to them by another computer. In this way, if a computer presents a fake identification number, the computer that requested the number could be fooled.

These are generally difficult attacks to carry out because of how information is transmitted from computer to computer. When information is transmitted, it must follow a route based on your address. If you are using a fake address, the information returning to you will look for your fake address and thus take a route that does not lead to you, as shown in Figure 16.3. For example, if you send mail to someone but you want them to think you are someone else, you put someone else's return address on the envelope. When they write back to the person at the return address, the mail carrier delivers the message to that address and not back to you. The Internet equivalent of the dutiful mail carrier is termed "forbidding source routing" and is easy to enable. You can't get return messages, so the attack is difficult to carry out. In addition, firewalls know the difference between inside and outside, and a firewall will ignore messages from outside by computers claiming to have an inside address. Similarly, the mailroom at IBM will view suspiciously any internal company mail brought in by a mail carrier. These simple safeguards make it difficult to carry out a spoof attack from the outside.

FIGURE 16.3.

Spoofed packets reach their destination but not their origin.

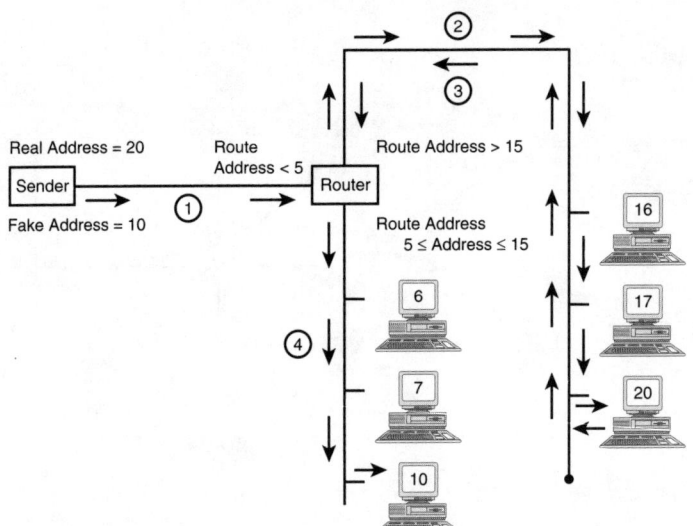

A drawback of a spoof attack from inside the company is that if a computer on the Internet at any time detects any other computer on the Internet with the same Internet address, both computers will complain. In this case, if someone is spoofing you by pretending to be you and your computer is on or being monitored, the trick would be detected easily because your computer will tell you that there is another computer on the network with the same address.

Still another drawback of a spoofing attack is that every network interface on any computer has a unique identifying number. Anyone trying to spoof your IP address on a local network could disable the computer he or she is spoofing, avoiding the earlier mentioned conflict. This would fail, however, if any other computer on the network were using the address routing protocol (ARP). The address routing protocol matches Internet addresses to the number given to a network card. Therefore, turning off your computer would eliminate the IP conflict, but the interface card number mismatch would require either stealing the network card, making a special one, or adjusting the ARP on the third computer.

Attacks in which individuals pretend to be another user can occur on several levels. The attacker can pretend that his or her network interface is one that it isn't by manufacturing a network card with a fake address. The user then might pretend to have the Internet address of another computer and thus steal that computer's transmission or create transmissions under the guise of the impersonated computer. A user could also pretend to be a different person by stealing that person's username and password in one of about a billion ways. In addition, a user could steal information simply by gaining access to a computer whose data was not protected against direct physical intrusion.

Methods of Transmissions and Their Levels of Security

At the most basic level transmission occurs over wires or in the air; every electrical signal travels one way or the other. Transmission is more secure over wire because an eavesdropper or hacker must be physically near the wire, whereas an interception of an air transmission can occur anywhere in reach of the signal.

An attempt to intercept a transmission traveling via fiber by tapping into the cable would be more easily detected than a tap into copper wire, because the tapper could easily damage or impair a particular segment of the network, which should be easy to spot. Detecting an interception that took place over the air would be nearly impossible.

Encryption

There are two aspects to consider when planning for transmission security. The first aspect, discussed in the preceding paragraph, is how transmissions are physically sent (that is, over wire or air). The impossibility of preventing physical interception should now be clear. The second aspect of secure transmission relates to the content that is being transmitted. Securing the content of the message is done through encryption.

Encryption involves transforming messages to make them legible only for the intended recipients. *Encryption* is the process of translating *plain text* into *ciphertext*. Human-readable information intended for transmission is plain text, whereas ciphertext is the text that is actually transmitted. At the other end, *decryption* is the process of translating ciphertext back into plain text. (Figure 16.4 demonstrates the process.) *Encryption algorithm* refers to the steps that a personal computer takes to turn plain text into ciphertext. A *key* is a piece of information, usually a number, that allows the sender to encode a message only for the receiver. Another key also allows the receiver to decode messages sent to him or her.

FIGURE 16.4.

Plain text is encrypted to produce ciphertext. Ciphertext is decrypted to produce plain text. Keys are used for both encryption and decryption.

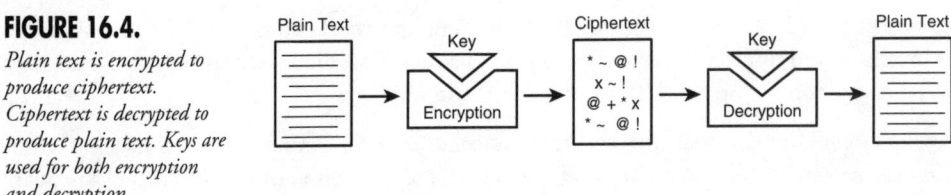

Now that you have the basic encryption jargon down, let's look at why and how encryption is essential for secure transmissions.

Why Use Encryption?

As you've learned by now, your transmissions can have only so much physical security. It is reasonable to assume that at some point someone may intercept your transmissions. Whether you expect an interception or whether you just generally suspect that interceptions may occur, you should transmit your information in a format that is useless to any interceptors. At the simplest level, this means when transmitting a message to someone, you use a coded message or slang (nicknames) that no one else understands. When Ulysses S. Grant captured Vicksburg during the Civil War, he sent a coded but predetermined message to Abraham Lincoln that read "The father of waters flows unvexed to the sea," meaning that the Union now owned the whole Mississippi river. Perhaps a good plan at the time, but still, Grant and Lincoln (or their advisers/confidantes) had to communicate a predetermined message and the message's meaning. A more recent example of a coded message might involve the use of nicknames. For instance, you and your sister give nicknames to family members whom you discuss unfavorably. Should a malicious family member decide to intercept a transmission, you would hope he wouldn't understand which family members you and your sister refer to in your messages. The obvious drawback of this coded message, like the Grant-Lincoln message, is that you and the recipient must establish a system of code before you begin transmitting messages.

A better system is one that allows you to send any message, even one you had not anticipated, to anyone without fear of interception. This is why an encryption system is so valuable; it allows any message to be transmitted that will be useless to anyone who intercepts it.

Private Key Encryption

Another rather simple form of encryption is commonly known as private key or symmetric encryption. It's called private key encryption because each party must know before the message is sent how to interpret the message. For example, spies in the movies always have a sequence of statements that they exchange to be sure of each other's identity, like "the sun is shining" must be followed by "the ice is still slippery." This is an example of encrypting so that only the person for whom a message is intended will understand it.

Other systems have been developed so that information can be encrypted in a general way. Again, using history as an example, one encryption method is commonly referred to as Caesar's code. According to history, Caesar would send messages that were encoded by replacing each letter in the message with the letter three places higher in the alphabet (A was replaced by D, B by E, and so on). The recipient just had to change the letters back to find out what the message said. An enemy who intercepted the message and did not know the method of encoding it would be unable to decipher it. Clearly though, this encoding method is not terribly difficult to break. This is called private key encryption because the method of encryption must be kept quiet. Anyone who knows the method could decode the message. It also is called symmetric because the same key is used to both encrypt and decrypt the message. Other private key methods have been devised to be more difficult to break.

Data Encrypt Standard (DES) is a private key system adopted by the U.S. government as a standard very secure method of encryption. An even more secure private key method is called a *one-time pad*. A one-time pad involves sheets of paper with random numbers on them: These numbers are used to transform the message; each number or sequence of numbers is used only once. The recipient of the message has an identical pad to use to decrypt the message. One-time pads have been proven to be foolproof—without having a copy of the pad. Supposedly, mathematicians can prove that a one-time pad is impossible to break.

The drawbacks to private key systems, however, are twofold. First, anyone who learns the method of encryption and gets the key, or a number or sequence of numbers or the sequences' equivalent of numbers that are used as a random input into the encrypted system, can break the key. Second, keys must be exchanged before transmission with any recipient or potential recipient of your message. So, to exchange keys you need a secure method of transmission, but essentially what you've done is create a need for another secure method of transmission.

Public Key Encryption

To overcome the drawbacks of private key systems, a number of mathematicians have invented public key systems. Unknown until about 30 years ago, public key systems were developed from some very subtle insights about the mathematics of large numbers and how they relate to the power of computers. Public key means that anyone can publish his or her method of encryption, publish a key for his or her messages, and only the recipient can read the messages. This works because of what is known in math as a trapdoor problem. A trapdoor is a mathematical formula that is easy to work forward but very hard to work backward. In general it is easy to multiply two very large numbers together, but it is very difficult to take a very large number and find its two prime factors. Public key algorithms depend on a person publishing a large public key and others being unable to factor this public key into its component parts. Because the creator of the key knows the factors of his or her large number, he or she can use those factors to decode messages created by others using his or her public key. Those who only know the public key will be unable to discover the private key, because of the difficulty of factoring the large number. (Figure 16.5 shows the difference between private and public key encryptions.)

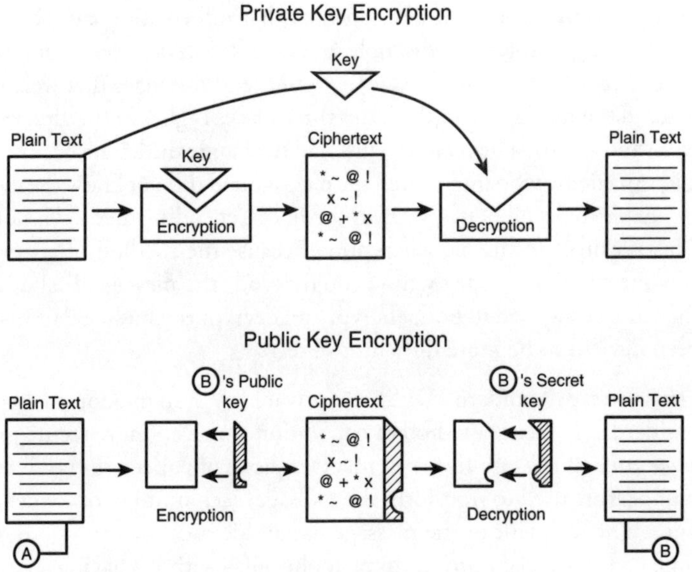

FIGURE 16.5.

Private key encryption uses one key to go both ways. Public key encryption uses one key to encrypt (the public key) and one key to decrypt (the secret key).

Public key methods vary, but one of the most common, and also free, is PGP (pretty good privacy). This is a public key encryption method that allows you to exchange messages with anyone that will send you his or her key. When you receive a key from someone, your PGP software can use that key to encode a message that only that person can interpret. The PGP method also allows you to encode a signature that only can be decoded using your public key, ensuring that it was you who sent the message. There are many free software packages that allow users to encode e-mail and other files they send. These software packages also will generate a public key for you. The software, along with the source codes, are available for almost all common operating systems.

Public key encryption works because users can send any message to any person without first meeting them or exchanging secret keys or secret encryption schemes. This obviously makes an extremely powerful tool in commerce for transmission of confidential customer information between buyers and sellers. In addition, public key encryption is extremely secure because decrypting public key encryption methods is a matter of time. If someone had enough time, that person could decipher your message. With commonly used methods, however, even an entire nation of hackers with the most powerful computers would take many years to decipher encrypted messages.

Now that I've told you about what many in the world of computer security consider the most secure method of transmission, I must tell you that there are times when public key encryption doesn't work. When the method used for encryption isn't secure, the message isn't secure. Because the methods of encryption are usually public, anyone who is interested in finding a hole has all the information necessary to find any holes. Holes often are discovered in methods previously thought to be secure. The fact that the algorithm is public makes the method more secure over the long term but less secure over the short term. In the long term all the flaws will be discovered and fixed, but over the short term flaws will be discovered and perhaps exploited. A second insecurity of public key methods in general is that public key encryption won't work when a recipient has no method of authenticating the sender. If someone sends you his or her public key, you can use that to encode a message for that person only—but it doesn't mean they are who they say they are.

Services of certifying authorities, such as Verasign, Inc., are needed to ensure the authenticity of correspondence. These certifying authorities use common identification methods to authenticate the identity of their subscribers. When verified, the authority issues a digital certificate to the subscriber. The subscriber then can use this certificate in his or her Web server to carry on secure communications with those browsing the Web site. Individuals who want to use public keys for their correspondence or companies that wish to prove their identity in electronic correspondence also can get an identity service from a certifying authority. Certifying authorities aim to overcome the aforementioned weakness of public keys being only as authentic as the user who sends it. The service only removes the dilemma one level, however, because the authority's services are only as good as their methods of authenticating subscribers.

Public key also doesn't work if your private keys are compromised. Keeping your private key secure is essential to the security of the system. Remember that the security of a public key system depends on no one being able to get your private key by knowing your public key. Your private key is what you use to decode messages sent to you and to prove your identity to others to whom you send messages. If someone is able to gain possession of your private key, that person could read your messages and forge messages from you.

State-of-the-Art Encryption and Its Future

Encryption has often involved making a choice between public and private key security methods. Public key encryption involves a heavy computing load, meaning that transmission with a public key takes more time and resources. Private key systems are less cumbersome but also less secure and less versatile. To overcome the drawbacks of both security methods, users have combined public and private key systems, such as an exchange of DES keys using a public system and then using those keys for the private DES system. Remember that private key systems can be stronger because it is possible to make an unbreakable private key system. A public key system is not theoretically unbreakable; it's just too difficult to do it in real life. The weak point in a private key system is the exchange of keys, so the very secure public key method can be used to exchange keys, and then the completely secure private key system can be used to do the actual transmission. A second advantage is that public key systems require a big commitment of computing power for every message. Private key, by comparison, is far less computing intensive and therefore cheaper and more efficient overall for transmission.

This combination likely will continue and become more common in the future, but it's unlikely that most systems will become public key. As computing resources advance to make public key encryption easier, the resources for cracking those keys also advance. This means that keys will become longer while the calculations will become bigger.

MCKEON & JEFFRIES

McKeon & Jeffries didn't foresee a lot of need for secure transactions. Its entire Web site would be behind the firewall on its network. Outside access would be available only by dialing into the network.

One of the future projects the accounting firm is planning for its intranet, however, will allow the firm's clients to access specific information through the Internet. M&J wants to allow its clients to review specific company and general financial news. In addition, the firm wants to provide clients with limited access to the file server and message boards. This would provide M&J's clients with a way to exchange files quickly and easily with the company and give the clients a vehicle to communicate with staff through the message boards. For this project, the firm is considering a public key encryption method through a secure Web server. A decision is on hold, however, as implementation of the project is about a year away and both technology and pricing will have changed considerably.

THE SPORTING GOODS AND APPAREL ASSOCIATION

The SGAA had much different security concerns. Originally, the only information that needed to be kept secure was financial transactions between the members and the organization. Paying dues and purchasing other services were done online with credit-card purchases. The association decided to implement a system that would allow secure transactions between members (that is, manufacturers selling to distributors, and distributors selling to resellers). Concern was also raised about manufacturers and resellers posting confidential and sensitive price lists on the site.

To meet these concerns, the SGAA decided to place the entire site on a secure server. Using Oracle Webserver 2.0 and a public key from Verasign, transmissions from the site were encrypted. Oracle was chosen for its noted ability to encrypt data between server and client and for its secure socket layer compatibility.

Security: Secure Internet Data Transmission

Chapter 16

Why a Technical Solution Is Never the Whole Solution

This topic cannot be discussed enough. No matter how good your solutions are, no matter how many guards are around your computers or how many passwords or encrypted materials you have, if the people in your organization don't follow good security policies or if you don't have a clear security policy, your network is not secure. Remember, the goal to good security is to keep information away from other people, not from other computers. Throughout history people have gotten information in basically the same ways. For example, disgruntled employees often can be sources of information leaks to competitors. This happens about 100 times for every one time a hacker intrudes. Of course you must have the right technical solutions for your network, but they just aren't important compared with the human concerns. All the important information is really in someone's head, and it doesn't take packet sniffers to pull it out. (For a complete discussion on good security policies, see Chapter 14, "Security: Keeping Hackers Out.")

Human history is full of spy stories about stolen information; these stories are never about how someone used a computer to get the information. Of the many recent incidents of breaches of national security—Aldrich Ames, who gave details of espionage operations; the Walkers, who sold Navy code books; the Rosenbergs, who gave away atomic secrets—almost none involved strictly computer-based breaches. The reason this rarely occurs is that all the data is handled by humans—they're the ones who put data in computers—and humans have far less strict security than computers do.

Client/Server Issues

A group known as the computer emergency response team (CERT) at Carnegie-Mellon University makes it their business to find security holes in the Internet and then to make the public aware of these holes. CERT especially concerns itself with computer-Internet connections using TCP/IP protocol and maintains a list of Internet-related security holes. To find the information about CERT, look for their home page at http://www.cert.org.

Reading information about holes and keeping abreast of security issues will give you information about old holes, including what holes have been discovered, allowing you to plug your system. Usually hackers are aware of old holes and search systems for those holes, creating havoc on private or public networks. Exploiting unplugged known holes is overwhelmingly more common than finding a new, undiscovered hole. After an intruder has used a hole to eavesdrop your transmissions, that person can use any information you transmit. A hacker could sell your marketing plans, reschedule your meetings, steal product orders, or provide your customers with inappropriate or wrong information. Most users don't keep themselves up-to-date on security holes, exposing themselves to holes anyone else, including hackers, might know about.

In a way, anyone setting up a server or client is creating his or her own security hole. By its nature, a Web server or a file server is a machine that invites other computers to visit and use its resources; this basis itself is insecure. The challenge now is to prevent people from using anything but the resources you have set up for them to access. On the client side, you are always asking for people to be interactive. A good example is Java. With Java the user asks the server for a LAN executable file. This means your computer is specifically taking direction from another computer. Suppose that the server directs your computer to reconfigure its own hard drive; this is an example of a security hole. This could happen inadvertently if you have an incompetent programmer who has written a Java application that damages the computer, or it could be malicious intent. Although both Java and JavaScript have extensive safeguards, there are still lingering doubts about how secure they truly are. Never dismiss the inadvertent and never overemphasize the malicious; they are both equally dangerous.

Secure Computing in Practice

Almost all network computing involves one of two types of transmission: file transfer or interactive transmission. File transfer involves one computer transferring a block of data and expecting nothing in return other than acknowledgment of reception. Interactive transmission involves two computers that have meaningful transmissions flowing in both directions. With file transmission, only the file to be transferred must be encrypted. Anyone who intercepted the transfer would only know that something had been transferred. Because only that file must be encrypted and the file must be ready before transfer, encryption can take place at any time before transfer. Interactive transmission, however, often involves spontaneous messages and must occur on both ends.

File Transmission

In practice, there are several types of file transmissions most users perform, including the transmission of files through FTP (file transfer protocol), submitting forms by a Web server, and sending e-mail.

Information transferred in this way should be encrypted before transmission. Transferring unencrypted files with these methods means the files travel as plain text, ready to be intercepted and interpreted by anyone. Clearly, encrypting files for transmission adds a level of inconvenience, but to secure the transmission, this inconvenience is unavoidable. Unfortunately, security decisions always involve a trade-off between security and convenience.

Using encryption in these cases is simple. Many shareware PGP programs exist to allow a user to encrypt a file. Other stronger methods exist for purchase, including products made by RSA security. The advantage of using these programs is that the encryption can be tested before the file is sent, ensuring its usefulness.

Interactive Transmission

To use any computer system over a network interactively, users must overcome two security exposures. First, users must authenticate themselves, and this exposes the authentication process to interception. Anyone sending out his or her password over the network is often sending that password out in clear text, which means anyone eavesdropping can pick up the password and username and use them. Stolen password and username combinations are the most common problem of interactive transmission. The other problem occurs while the user is using the system. The information being typed in is most likely going out in plain text, which can be intercepted. There are a few systems designed to limit the security risk in using a remote system interactively.

One method is called Kerberos, shown in Figure 16.6. When a user logs into a workstation, that workstation authenticates the user so that the user's password is never sent over the network in any form. That workstation then contacts the Kerberos server, which issues the user a ticket; that ticket contains encrypted information used to authenticate the user of other network computers. It's secure because the username and password are never transmitted over the network. The local machine does all the authentication, and then it uses a secure method of transmission to authenticate itself to the Kerberos server. The server then passes an encrypted ticket back to the user, who sends that ticket over the network, as opposed to using his or her password and username. For example, if the user's Telnet is somewhere, the user contacts the remote computer, which then asks the user for his or her username and password. It then transmits both across the network.

FIGURE 16.6.
Two computers using Kerberos for authentication require a third computer as a Kerberos server.

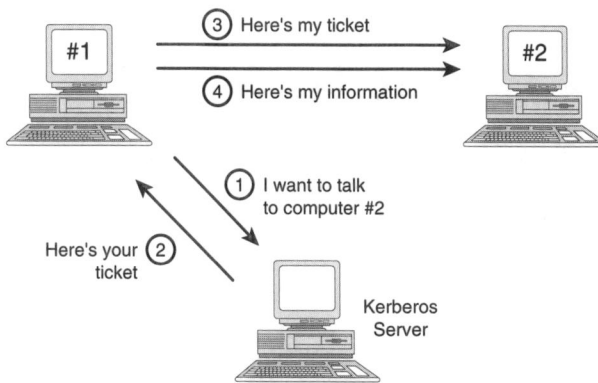

With a Kerberos server this never happens. The user is authenticated locally, and all the exchanges with the network are encrypted and completed. However, a drawback is that every machine you want to send information to or any applications or services you wish to use must be "Kerberized" so that the machine will accept your credentials. A second drawback is that if the Kerberos server is ever compromised—that is, if an unauthorized person ever gains access to the Kerberos server—then the integrity of the entire system is compromised.

If you are interacting a lot across the network, that information is insecure. With Kerberos, the transmission between the machines is not encrypted, just the authentication process is. So someone couldn't use passwords to gain access; but if all they wanted was to look at the information you are sending, they could do so. For example, if you log into a financial system and type in account numbers and financial data, an eavesdropper could get this information without actually getting on the system.

Secure RPC (Remote Procedure Call) is another method of reducing network security exposure. The difference between RPC and Kerberos is that after you authenticate yourself to the local machine, which has your private key stored on it, all your transmission across the network is encrypted. You can then authenticate yourself to other machines and transmit all your transactions over a secure channel. Like Kerberos, the main drawback is that any machines you want to interact with must be equipped with the proper decrypting software, which is a hassle. Also, because RPC is a public key encryption method, you take a performance hit because all the encryption and decryption must be done before sending out anything across the network, which takes a lot of time and computational power.

The final encrypted transmission method is SSL (secure sockets layer). SSL is a method of encrypting all the communications between computers. It is used to encrypt and decrypt communications between a Web browser and a Web server. Whenever you use URLs beginning with `https://`, you're using SSL. SSL is included with security capable Netscape browsers. SSL uses technology based on the commercially available public key encryption products of RSA, Inc. SSL itself is an open standard, and the algorithms are free to all. SSL libraries can be used to encrypt all traffic among computers, because the encryption occurs at a level that makes it transparent to both the user and any programs he or she is running.

How Much Is Too Much?

Security always involves a trade-off between the security of your data and the ease with which that data is accessible. Like any computer system or any amount of data, you must look carefully at the dollar value of secure transmissions. Encrypting a transmission so that it is too slow to be of any value must be weighed against the danger of having the transmission intercepted. The point of having a network is to transmit important data in a timely fashion. If these functions are impaired, your security measures are costing, not saving, you money. When implementing transmission security, your concern must be the amount of time and resources that someone would have to apply to decipher your transmissions. The simplest measure of this security is the length of the keys used in your encryption algorithm. Usually the particular software package that does your encryption will recommend a particular key length. These are usually sufficient enough to ensure your security, and longer ones are often merely an additional burden.

What Level of Security Is Right for You?

I cannot stress often enough that security costs money. If you are implementing complicated security measures for data that is not valuable, you are wasting money. When deciding on security measures, make the dollar-smart decision. That is, if you must upgrade all your computer hardware to handle the public key software, you should make sure that the cost of the upgrade matches the value of the data that will be encrypted. Clearly those selling products over the Internet would benefit greatly from extremely secure communications and need to spend accordingly. On the other hand, a company that uses the Internet only to disseminate catalogs and price information will not need to have such secure transmissions. Also, a company that wishes to send out confidential contracts will probably need some sort of secure e-mail capability, but it may not be necessary to pay a certifying authority for the service of verifying the company's identity to all its customers. That is, the likelihood of someone intercepting the transmissions and supplying a false contract seems not only slim but also easily detectable. It should be relatively simple to look at the times and manners in which your company needs secure transmission. After this has been determined, choose the encryption tools that cover these paths.

Summary

When it comes to security, secure data transmission fills out the final third of the security equation, right behind (or before, depending on how you look at it) security of data storage and security of the physical technology and the location of that technology. Assuming you've satisfied the first two-thirds of the security equation, before setting out to secure your data during transmission, first determine the value of that data and *then* spend accordingly to secure it. Valuable data with little or no security can prove as costly as unvaluable data with too much unnecessary security.

After determining the value of your security, consider the most appropriate options for transmitting data and then explore the various encryption methods necessary for protecting your specific data transmissions. And, finally, I can't reiterate enough that a technical solution is never the whole solution. Data originates from individuals, not from computers, so implementing strong security policies and procedures is as important as choosing all the physical and technical barriers to your data.

Training the Users

17

by David Garrett and Matthew Benson

IN THIS CHAPTER

- Getting users connected **264**
- Software **268**
- Keeping users online **269**
- New workflow lines **276**
- Group training sessions **278**
- Online training **282**

The acid test for any intranet is the degree to which it is actually used. In most cases, the intranet is intended to supplement traditional methods of intra-organizational communication. If the intranet has been properly designed, it should reflect your organization's baseline competency without imposing unreasonable demands on the user. Even so, gaining users' acceptance and weaning them away from old habits can pose a significant challenge, one that technical experts, in particular, often underestimate.

The goal of training the users is to get them comfortable and accustomed to using the intranet in their daily tasks. The intranet can save money, time, and resources, but only if it is used by the people it is meant to help.

The key to effective user training is relevance. Effective training should start with a clear, unbiased understanding of the users—their knowledge base, their technical skills, their working patterns. Without such an understanding, training can easily miss the point, either by emphasizing the wrong benefits or by under- or overestimating training needs. An in-depth discussion of online video-conferencing or other advanced applications, for example, may be wholly irrelevant (not to mention tedious) to a user group that is barely acquainted with the WWW. In the same vein, technically sophisticated users neither need nor want a half-day session on "What is the Internet?"

This chapter defines various levels of user training as it applies to different categories of intranet users and outlines components to consider in developing an overall training program.

Most users are far more concerned with the intranet utility and its capacity to improve their work than the underlying technology or the elegance of its architecture. So regardless of the content, user training should emphasize what the intranet does rather than what the intranet is. I'm not saying that training should discourage broader or deeper discussion of the intranet, but rather it should indicate the importance of a consistent focus on user requirements, expectations, and benefits.

Getting Users Connected

Establishing connectivity is one of the first tasks required in implementing a new intranet. For most organizations, getting connected is a critical first step, and the array of options can be daunting.

Regardless of the method selected, users probably will need help establishing connectivity and using new software. For some users, an instruction sheet may be sufficient. Others may require formal, step-by-step instructions, like the ones shown in Figure 17.1, and follow-up handholding. The level of connectivity training should parallel the level of the users' familiarity. You do not want to frighten beginning users during the training with subjects over their heads.

FIGURE 17.1.
An instruction sheet should have step-by-step instructions on how to set up a connection and who to contact if users have problems.

> **For Windows 3.1 Users**
> For help, contact Danny: x1397
>
> 1. Close all applications.
> 2. Put disk in disk drive.
> 3. Run setup program.
> 4. Type Cursor 7 in form.
> 5. If address = 122.22.22.222
> 6. Dial-up phone # = (202) 555-1234.

Keep in mind that user habits start early, so it is important to follow up, especially with new users, to determine

1. Are they using the connections properly?
2. Are they using connections at all?
3. How are they using the connections?

By following up, your organization can reinforce or redirect intranet training while user habits are forming rather than correct undesirable usage after the fact.

Setting up an intranet on a corporate LAN is as easy as having the system administrator install the software on everyone's machines and making sure that the right protocols are being used. People dialing in from home or satellite offices, however, may be connecting to the intranet through the Internet, which means that establishing the connectivity may be more difficult. A trade association, for example, might have an intranet hosted on a server in which everyone who connects does so through the Internet.

A corporate LAN environment is generally an IPX network. An IPX network is the current standard protocol under which most LANs work. For a corporate LAN to use an intranet, it needs to have the TCP/IP protocol installed so that the LAN machines can talk to the intranet server. A TCP/IP network is the protocol on which the Internet works. It assigns a specific number to each computer, and then it assigns a name to each number. Computers use the TCP/IP protocol to link to each other on the Internet and on your intranet.

For more modern systems, such as Windows for Workgroups, Macintosh networks, or Novell, you can set up TCP/IP relatively easily to run instead of, or in tandem with, IPX. You might want to keep the IPX protocol in place for some operations, like accessing a file server on the LAN, and use the TCP/IP protocol for accessing the Web server. You can perform many of the same tasks with TCP/IP as you can with an IPX network. Teaching users how to use the new system to perform old tasks, however, might require some training.

After establishing connectivity, you should install Web browsers or other intranet applications. Such applications include a mail client, video-conferencing, audio-conferencing, or whatever applications your organization plans to offer.

Users from outside the LAN (for example, a traveling sales staff) who need to dial in to access the intranet need to be set up on a modem system. Shiva makes a good system to attach modems to a LAN. Shiva was one of the first companies to make network modems and really is the industry leader for these products. Users can dial in directly to the LAN to connect to the TCP/IP network. If your users are dialing into the LAN to use TCP/IP applications, like Web browsing, however, the connection needs to use Point-to-Point Protocol (PPP) or Serial Line Interface Protocol (SLIP). These protocols assign an address to the client computer so that the server knows where to send the information. Of course, if users are using the Internet for access, their machines simply need to have Internet access through any Internet Service Provider (ISP).

If users are connecting with a laptop, connectivity is as easy as having them bring in their machines and having the system administrator configure them to dial up and connect to the network. If a user is connecting from home, setting up connectivity might be very difficult. No two PPP or SLIP connections are the same. Connecting to another computer with these protocols involves a relatively complicated process. Not only does the client computer need to identify itself to the host with a user ID, password, and IP address, it needs to know where to look on the host computer for various services, such as domain name service and the route to the Internet, if necessary. Using a Macintosh is easier than using Windows, as you can see in Figures 17.2 and 17.3, but companies are starting to make this process easier. Chameleon and Internet in a Box have been creating software that simplifies this process, but until a PPP or SLIP connection script becomes adopted as a standard, configuring a connection will remain relatively difficult.

FIGURE 17.2.

Windows 95 users need to configure TCP/IP in the TCP/IP Properties dialog box.

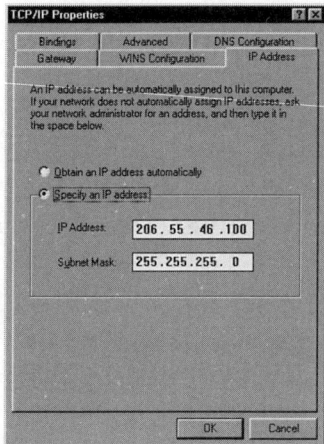

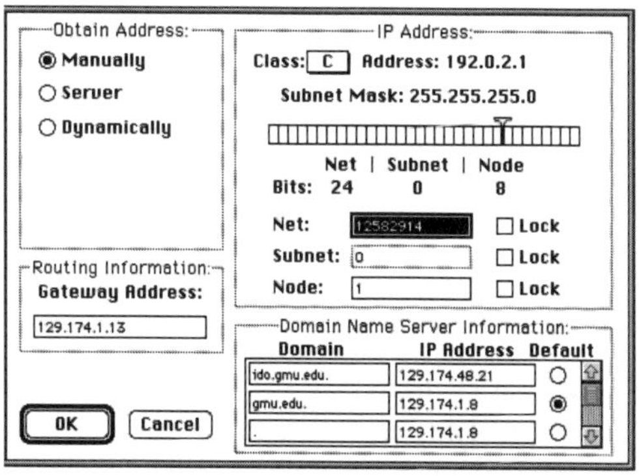

FIGURE 17.3.
MacOS users need to configure TCP/IP in the MacTCP control panel.

Supplying users with a step-by-step instruction booklet or manual is an effective means of communicating all the variables involved with configuring and connecting to different platforms. A manual should include at least the common platforms, such as Windows 3.1, Windows 95, and Macintosh operating systems. It also could include frequently asked questions and an instruction sheet for dial up.

Another avenue of connection could be through an ISDN line. An ISDN line is a direct connection, either to the Internet or to your company's LAN or WAN. Unlike a phone line, ISDN provides a digital connection and transfers data at much greater rates of speed. If you thought setting up a PPP connection was tough, however, setting up an ISDN line is nearly impossible for the average user. An organization needs a professional to set up the proper hardware. Usually the local phone company or ISDN providers can do the job for you.

Allowing access to your intranet via the Internet is relatively simple. You don't have to set up PPP, phone lines, or Shiva. The only necessary connection is that of your server to the Internet. This strategy makes it a little easier for users to get connected from home or other remote locations only because so many ISPs are willing to help users get connected. Many software programs are also available to help users get online. Chameleon and Internet in a Box are two that can be used regardless of what ISP is chosen. Also, many ISPs have their own connection software. With Windows 95, users may have some problems getting a PPP or SLIP connection with ISPs other than The Microsoft Network. Many ISPs have complained that the socket software that comes bundled with Windows 95 does not work with their connection software, although most have written new connection software that will work.

Some users, such as members of trade and professional associations, already may have connections to the Internet through their organizations or companies. With membership organizations, users already may be set up with Internet connections at home, leaving them only to point their browsers in the right direction. In these cases, the intranet administrators don't have to provide specific instructions as to how to connect to the Internet.

If users are coming in through the Internet, your organization may want to talk to a national provider to find the least expensive avenue of connection. (See Appendix A for a list of national and regional Internet Service Providers.) If your organization has a traveling development team that visits different cities nationally and internationally, for example, a national or international service provider with local phone numbers in the areas where the development team travels would make sense. But if the users are all in the region, using a regional provider may be less expensive.

Software

When you're training the users how to use the intranet, your users should have a basic knowledge of two facets involving software. They include both client and server software. Using the client software involves knowing how to use the dialer, if connecting from home; the e-mail package; the Web browser; and, if necessary, video-conferencing or audio-conferencing software. On the server side, if your intranet uses message boards, calendars, or other functionality, users need training on these individual software applications within the scope of a Web browser. If your intranet has a message board system, for example, the users need to know the ins and outs of connecting to the server and how to use the Web browser software. Additionally, after they get to the message board, they must know how to use it.

Knowing in what areas to train the users is the easy part; knowing how to train them can prove difficult. One advantage of using Web-based interfaces is that hypertext is fairly intuitive. For most applications, the users simply have to point and click in the right places. For other applications, you may need to add a few paragraphs in the manual describing how functions work and encouraging the users to try them out. In the example of the message board system, you might want to take your users through a typical conversation on the message board—how messages are posted and replied to and what the message board structure is like. Including a diagram also might be helpful.

In reality, you can train users on new software in only two ways: Train them in a group where they can sit at a machine and try out the software, or let them learn by trial and error on their own. If your software is easy enough to use, they will use it; if it is confusing, they won't.

MCKEON & JEFFRIES

For McKeon & Jeffries, getting users connected wasn't too much of a problem. After the system administrator installed TCP/IP and the Netscape browser on all the computers in the office, it was a simple matter of configuring all the laptops to dial into the network from the road or from home and writing an instruction sheet for users who wanted to configure their home machines for dial-up networking. Because all the machines in the offices used Windows for Workgroups, the administrator easily set up dial-up networking using Trumpet Winsock.

Writing the manual for users to connect at home was a little more difficult because the system administrator had to try to emulate problems users might have connecting with a Macintosh, a PC running Windows 3.1, and a PC running Windows 95. The most trouble came with writing the configuration instructions for Windows 95 because users had to use the built-in Winsock instead of Trumpet.

THE SPORTING GOODS AND APPAREL ASSOCIATION

The SGAA had a little more difficulty than M&J did. They had two classes of users to connect: their employees and their members. Because their employees were local on the LAN, getting users connected was just a matter of installing TCP/IP and Internet Explorer on their machines. For their members, the task was not quite so easy.

Because all their members connect through the Internet, the SGAA had to provide an instruction sheet on how to get an Internet connection. Many of their members have Internet access in their offices in one way or another, either through a single dial-up connection or a direct connection with access from the desktop. The rest of the members, mostly the retailers, however, needed instruction as to how to go about finding an ISP and configuring their machines, as well as how to get to the site when they did get online.

The SGAA decided to write a connection guide to send out to all its members. Before sending out the guide, the SGAA staff did some research to find an international ISP that had local access numbers in all the areas where SGAA members are located. From there, the SGAA ordered installation disks and instruction sheets from the ISP to send out with the connection guide. That way, if members didn't know how to find an ISP, they could use the one provided for them. The ISP was happy to send the disks out for free and helped the SGAA staff write the instruction manual.

Also in the instruction manual were the address, or URL, for the site, the user's ID and password, and simple instructions to enter the site.

Keeping Users Online

After users are connected to the intranet, the most important part of the training process is keeping them online. This part is essential for the success of your intranet. An intranet is interactive and cannot exist in a vacuum, especially if the organization is using it for communications. It is a classic Catch-22. If there is no content, no one will come. In the case of message boards, calendars, or other interactive applications, if no one uses them, there is no content. The trick is to get your users used to the idea of contributing to the intranet at the same time that you get them used to finding information and utilizing all its resources.

Often, users need a new mind-set in approaching their everyday tasks. Instead of calling the Human Resource Department to find out how many sick days an employee has left, he or she can find this information on the intranet. Instead of pulling out the employee handbook to learn about the summer flex-schedule, employees can click on the intranet. Instead of leaving their desks and doing research in the library, employees can, once again, go to the intranet. If you want to keep users online, they need to view the intranet as a helpful partner and resource in accomplishing their jobs. They also need to become as familiar with it as they are with the word processing program they use every day.

Adding the intranet to an organization means making fundamental changes in even extraneous tasks. Successful training is important so that the users get re-programmed to use the intranet as the resource and solution to their questions, challenges, problems, and everyday needs. Any training of the users should include getting them in the mind-set to use the intranet.

As an organization's intranet becomes more functional and has more applications in everyday work, the host organization should be prepared to continue training users on new developments and new capabilities. Expect apprehension and resistance from some users, as some individuals and institutions will have a difficult time embracing and adapting to the technology. Be prepared for rejection of the technology, and be aware of the users who jump right in thinking it will change their lives right away. The people who are excited and immediately start using the intranet may be disappointed when the information out there is not updated or new. These users may never come back.

In preparing and training the users to keep them online, slowly move nonessential work material to the intranet. This material might include the employee handbook, corporate directory, contact database, and company benefit packets. These items are important to users but perhaps are not utilized for everyday tasks. Employers don't need to sneak around and hide all the printed employee handbooks to force the users to use the intranet; posting the handbook online encourages users to use the intranet instead of digging through their junk drawers to find the ragged employee handbook with the coffee stains on it.

The next step may be for your organization to stop printing employee handbooks and to make updates and revisions only on the intranet, as shown in the example in Figure 17.4. This approach won't force the users to use the intranet every day, but it will encourage them to use it on occasion when they want to read the latest information. At this point, users will begin to understand that the organization is indeed serious about its intranet and that it is more than an optional information center.

FIGURE 17.4.
An intranet page of an employee handbook.

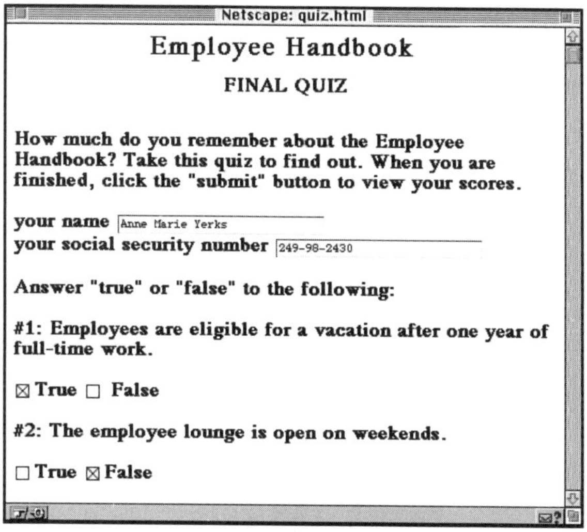

```
┌─────────────────── Netscape: quiz.html ───────────────────┐
│                                                            │
│                    Employee Handbook                       │
│                       FINAL QUIZ                           │
│                                                            │
│   How much do you remember about the Employee              │
│   Handbook? Take this quiz to find out. When you are       │
│   finished, click the "submit" button to view your scores. │
│                                                            │
│   your name  [Anne Marie Yerks        ]                    │
│   your social security number [249-98-2430]                │
│                                                            │
│   Answer "true" or "false" to the following:               │
│                                                            │
│   #1: Employees are eligible for a vacation after one year │
│   of full-time work.                                       │
│                                                            │
│   ☒ True  ☐ False                                          │
│                                                            │
│   #2: The employee lounge is open on weekends.             │
│                                                            │
│   ☐ True  ☒ False                                          │
│                                                            │
└────────────────────────────────────────────────────────────┘
```

The revised corporate directory might be created online rather than printed. Users still will have the old copies, but if they want the newest information, they have to find it online. If users are brought on to the intranet slowly, the people who are overly enthusiastic will not experience any disappointment. On the other hand, if an intranet is rolled out with all kinds of whiz-bang features and interactive tools, and no one uses it right away, bringing people back a second time might be tough.

If a goal of your intranet is to phase out widely accepted communication vehicles, such as newsletters like the one shown in Figure 17.5, corporate directories, or policy information, the host organization can set up a transition plan using strategic timing. For a newsletter, for example, the timing could include putting up the online version before delivering the hard copy. Later, the intranet version of the newsletter could have additional stories that the printed version does not have (although it would be beneficial for the printed version to have a footnote guiding the reader to use the intranet to read further information or new stories on the cyber-newsletter). The last deadline might be the day that the newsletter is no longer printed.

Unlike real estate, which boasts the three most important aspects of a property—location, location, location—for the intranet, the three important elements of consistent use are content, content, and content. Information, therefore, must be current and useful. A message of the day can encourage users to go to the intranet at least once a day. News and other features can keep users logging on. Announcing, via the intranet, new software programs or additional applications new to the intranet is one way to keep users updated. If your content is not useful, interesting, and easy to use, however, keeping users coming back will be difficult.

FIGURE 17.5.
A newsletter posted on an organization's intranet.

In the first sessions of training new users on the intranet, you will find some redundancy of information. Your organization wouldn't want to turn on the intranet and immediately stop sending memos. Doing so could alienate many potential users as well as be the source of many unread memos. One suggestion is to post information online in advance of releasing it in traditional print form. This way, no one is penalized, but the users online get the bonus of receiving the information before the other people. Getting left out of the loop could spur the nonusers to get online more often.

An incremental transition is almost always preferable, even though it takes more effort on the front end. Proceeding in stages requires some orchestration and planning; otherwise, the efforts easily can turn into chaos. One volunteer organization started by posting its newsletter to its new intranet, as shown in Figure 17.6, while mailing a hard copy the same day. Users who accessed the electronic version not only received their news faster, but they also were invited to interact with the editor and to provide e-mail comments to her directly. The organization invited users to choose between electronic and postal delivery (and emphasized the rising costs of postage); within several months, the newsletter print run dropped from thousands to hundreds. This cost savings enabled the organization to publish electronic news more frequently and include readers' views, questions, and contributions in a more timely manner.

FIGURE 17.6.
An online newsletter offers readers a timely avenue to voice their opinions to the editor.

Letters to the Editors

The "Letters to the Editors" section of *HeartWeb* is intended to provide a forum for readers to pose questions and comments to *HeartWeb* readership. All reasonable and ethical questions and comments on clinical, technical and basic issues and their responses will be posted on *HeartWeb*. Queries will not necessarily receive an answer from *HeartWeb* editors or staff as they are intended for widespread reading. Correspondence intended for privacy should not be submitted as a "Letter to the Editors".

Date sent: 04/Mar/1996:01:59:08

What is the mortality rate for a 46 year old man having
a ross procedure for aortic valve replacement?

Some organizations post contests or incentives to encourage online use. One consumer products company, for example, solicited user anecdotes—first-person success stories highlighting efficiency, discoveries, or achievements. Then it launched a contest, asking users to submit documentation of ways in which their use of the intranet had produced savings of time or money. Modest prizes were awarded monthly, culminating in a grand prize—a new laptop—to a sales representative who won a major new account by organizing a sales presentation on the company's intranet.

After a while, important messages should be sent only via e-mail, forcing the cyber slackers to use the intranet to read and respond to their e-mail. If employees feel like they are missing out on important communications, they will use the intranet.

The final area to examine in keeping users online is log reports. Just as an advertising kit reveals the demographics of a medium, log reports reveal the "user graphics" of your user base—which users came on? what did they look at? what did they not look at? and who is not logging on at all? The appropriate person, perhaps the system administrator, should talk to these users and find out why they're not using the intranet. Can they not log on? Have they forgotten how? Do they have a connectivity problem? Or have they logged on but become bored with the information posted? Depending on the response, your training program may need some tweaking to better meet the needs of these users.

Also, as the intranet is used more and the functions expand, the sponsor should publicize these functions within the user group and offer function-specific training and troubleshooting for the users, as shown in Figure 17.7.

FIGURE 17.7.
Function-specific training can occur online.

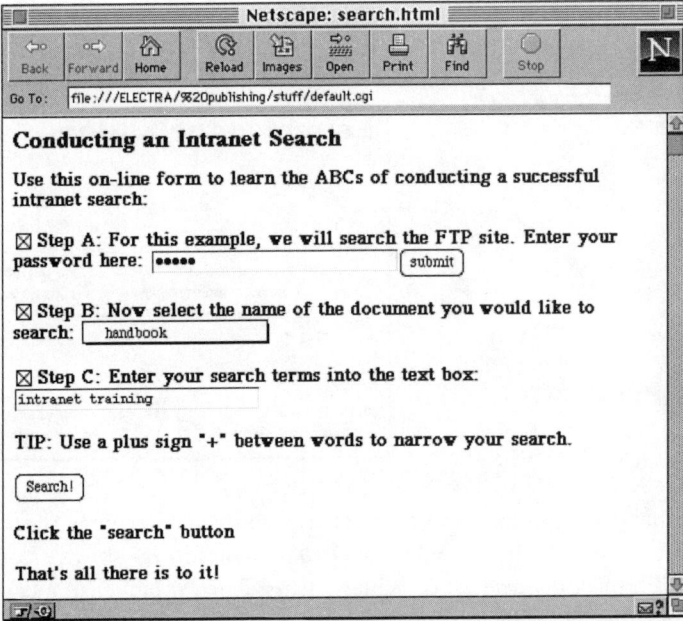

MCKEON & JEFFRIES

McKeon & Jeffries developed a simple strategy for keeping its users online. Because of its relatively small number of users, shifting to a digital format for interoffice information and communications was a short process. As hard copies of documents became more and more scarce, it became imperative for employees to use the intranet to get information on everything from memos to corporate policy to research materials.

The communications part of the intranet was a little trickier. The accounting firm first put a few beta testers on the message boards to test them and to get content up on the site. At first, the discussions tended to be centered around what was wrong with the message boards and how they could be changed, but as the beta testers became more and more familiar with the software, they started having real conversations.

The schedule for M&J's move to the intranet looked a little like this:

Day 1 through Day 30: Content is posted on the site. Memos and other interoffice communication is put on the intranet and distributed in printed form. Ten beta testers play with the message boards. Research materials, the employee handbook, and the firm directory are put on the site.

Day 31 through Day 60: Memos are put up on the site the day before they are delivered in hard copy. Information such as meeting minutes or other regularly distributed materials are put on the site, with few hard copies available. All modifications to the firm directory and employee manual are done only online. Employees are welcomed to the message board areas.

Day 61 through Day 90: No hard copies of memos or other communications or information are created or distributed. Users are required to log on to the site daily to check for new information.

THE SPORTING GOODS AND APPAREL ASSOCIATION

The SGAA developed a similar strategy for getting users online and for keeping them there. It developed a schedule as well, but instead of forcing members online, they were enticed with announcements or alerts. It also was very important that the association be completely operational when the switch was turned on, so the beta testing phase was carried out well before the site was opened to the members.

The SGAA's schedule for creating and utilizing the intranet looked like this:

Day 1 through Day 30: Thirty beta testers were invited to test the navigation and communications on the site. The audio-conferencing functions, the message boards, interactive scheduling, contact database, and chat functions were thoroughly tested.

Day 31 through Day 60: Connection manuals are sent out, and users are logging on for the first time. The association staff works hard to make sure that users are greeted with new information every day. Instead of the weekly 10-page faxes that the association usually sends to members with news, members now receive a single page with headlines and the URL to find the news on the site. The newsletter is put up on the site and is sent in the mail; the online version is more detailed, and the mailed version has URLs pointing to the online version. Logs are checked weekly to see who is logging on and who isn't.

Day 61 through Day 90: The SGAA staff continues to put content on the site, the newsfeed is implemented to bring users up-to-the-minute news, and more message boards are added. Weekly faxes are sent only to users who do not log on a regular basis. The newsletter is available online only.

New Workflow Lines

The intranet can provide a totally new way to deal with workflow. Memos, sticky notes, and highlighted sections of a paper document all can be replaced using the intranet for work projects.

For traditional groupware, the most important item is the software itself and the information it provides. The file server, print server, fax server, and database server all can operate in a vacuum; if only one person uses it, it doesn't make a difference. But for the intranet, the user is key. Employees must use the technology of the intranet for it to work. It is therefore vital that employees are connected to and can access the intranet and that they are satisfied with their experience. If they are not satisfied, they will not come back, they will not put projects on the intranet to work with other employees, and the intranet will not perform to its potential.

For a project with many facets, an intranet can offer an excellent alternative to changing the workflow lines, provided that the users are properly trained and willing to use the technology. A national organization, for example, wants to create a new membership brochure. The employees involved include the editor, the copy writers, the designer, the printer, the membership and legal departments, the executive director, and the executive committee, who are located throughout the country. Many people who must meet staggered deadlines and who are in different geographical locations perform numerous tasks.

The traditional method of creating a printed brochure might end up with a dozen sticky notes and five people saying the same thing on different copies, or the original might be held up or lost in express mail, left at home, or in the briefcase of an unreachable executive committee member. Additionally, redundant comments, phone calls, overnight mail charges, faxing, re-faxing, and deadline changing are part of the process.

With properly trained users on an intranet, new workflow lines can be implemented. Through e-mail or document management applications, the text can be forwarded to all the people who need to see it. Employees can alter it at any time and create updated versions. If your intranet has good version control, no comments, suggestions, or versions will be lost.

Group scheduling can help the team meet deadlines. If one deadline is missed, instead of a group of fast and furious phone calls to rearrange the rest of the schedule, the team could change a single group calendar instead, like the one shown in Figure 17.8. Because the calendar is in a central location, all users working on the project are aware of changed dates or any alterations.

FIGURE 17.8.

Group scheduling on the intranet offers up-to-the-minute scheduling revisions without redundancies.

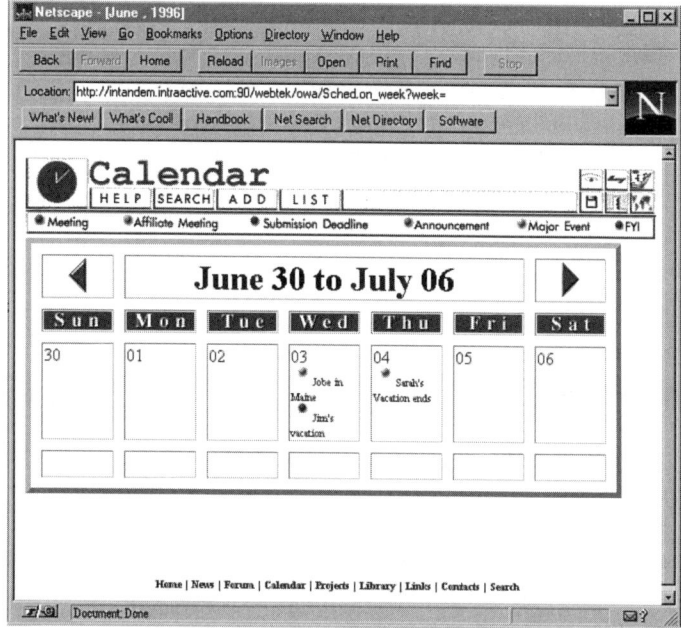

Train users to stay out of their Rolodexes, calendars, and paper memos and instead use the intranet for improved workflow. The intranet is more cost-efficient, more time-efficient, easier, and takes fewer resources than the traditional manner of working on a project like a membership brochure. This also is the case with most projects completed on an intranet. But again, ensuring that the target audience is using the intranet is the most important aspect of the training.

Another workflow change example is human resources. Inevitably, the HR department continually answers the same questions from different employees. Typically, employees call or visit the HR offices, which can be time-consuming for the HR staff.

Using the intranet, the HR department can post the most commonly asked questions—for example, what is included in the health care plan, when the new raises are slated to come through, and what the options are with the 401K plan. This kind of information might be posted to a message board. If someone e-mails a new question to the HR department and it is something in which other employees are interested, this conversation could be posted and revisited by other employees in the future, instead of the HR department continually answering the same questions.

MCKEON & JEFFRIES

McKeon & Jeffries' intranet primarily was developed to provide information online rather than to assist in workflow. After a few months, however, other uses of the intranet soon became apparent. Users started exchanging files by putting them up on the site and downloading them rather than putting them on a disk and express-mailing them or sending them via regular mail—or even instead of walking them to another floor in the office. By keeping the firm directory and other information resources online, users are encouraged to use the intranet.

THE SPORTING GOODS AND APPAREL ASSOCIATION

Because of the level of interactivity of the SGAA intranet, over time it fundamentally changed the dynamic of how SGAA worked with its members. Before the intranet, the SGAA reported news and information to its members, typically in the form of a weekly fax and a monthly newsletter. Now news appears on the site immediately as it happens; also, members are invited to post information that other members might find useful. Additionally, before the intranet the only chance the members had to communicate with one another was either individually or at the yearly convention. Now members can easily carry on conversations on the message board, update contact information on the contact database, and carry on online meetings, as well as listen to addresses and conversations of various committees.

Also, the SGAA staff are able to perform their work better. Instead of spending half their time communicating information, they can spend more time creating information and making it accessible to everyone online. The intranet helps everyone be more efficient by allowing the administrative tasks to be handled automatically.

Group Training Sessions

To the extent possible, user training should be hands-on—with real equipment and a fully functioning intranet site—and conducted in a group setting. Most instructors combine lectures, demonstrations, and practice, and ideally the trainer-trainee ratio should not exceed 1:10. In some cases, users may need training in specific skills (such as HTML markup, using various search engines, and so on), which may be offered either in conjunction with group training or as a further module.

Interactive training sessions provide the opportunity to learn by doing, and a group format helps to underscore the fundamental purpose of the intranet itself—improved collaboration and teamwork. These sessions should encourage discussion and interaction but should be conducted against a basic outline to assure focus. The following is a sample outline. In addition, you should never overlook the "cheerleader" function in intranet training. In other words, trainers should love their work and clearly convey their enthusiasm. Intranets derive their value from their use, which means recruiting and retaining users. For many people (that is, prospective users), training often provides their first direct exposure to a new intranet, and first impressions count.

1. Introduction to your intranet
   A. Purpose
   B. Functions
2. How to use a Web browser
   A. The interface
   B. Introduction to HTML
   C. Local versus remote
3. How to use intranet functions
   A. Specific applications
   B. Adding information
   C. Finding information
4. Security
   A. Authentication
   B. Keeping your password safe
   C. How to change your password
5. How to connect
   A. From the office
   B. From home
   C. From the road
6. Workflow
   A. New lines of communication
   B. Adopting information technology

Training curricula and content should be designed for maximum impact, especially on the front end. In particular, you should closely review content and presentation, not just for clarity but also for excitement. You also should select the trainers not only for their technical skills, but also for their ability to engage and intrigue training participants. In short, intranets need selling to succeed, and training—like every contact with potential users—should be seen as a sales opportunity.

As a practical matter, taking advantage of this opportunity often means involving a range of disciplines in designing and delivering intranet training. In one multinational pharmaceutical company, for example, the product marketing, human resources, strategic planning, and MIS departments joined together to determine the primary components of their intranet training curriculum and enlisted "faculty" from each of their divisions to conduct the program. This approach helped further two of the company's primary intranet objectives—collaboration and information exchange—early in the process. Moreover, it enabled user trainees to see a real commitment to these objectives, in the form of a multidisciplinary training experience.

It's important to sit down and physically show users how to use applications on the computer screen and how to best perform certain functions. As anyone who has tried to call technical support for his or her computer needs knows, learning these skills on the phone or from a manual is very difficult. But after users are shown the first steps, they find that later functions become easier to perform.

To actually set up the group training, your organization should put all the participants in one room and bring in enough computers for each participant. Keeping the numbers low (10 to 12 people) helps users get the time and space they need to learn the new technology of the intranet. More important than the low number is that each participant has his or her own computer. The intranet is interactive technology—the users need to learn using the technology. If training is set up for two people per computer, the one with more technological background tends to dominate or make the other feel inadequate or rushed when it is his or her turn.

A large screen should be set up in front so that the participants can watch as the trainer accesses different applications. Aside from the instructor, a person with a technological background should be on hand to wander through the room and help people one-on-one because, as the trainer goes through the different information, some people may go ahead, and others may lag behind.

Training should be as interactive as possible. The trainer may want to put up a calendar and have each participant put up his or her birthday, his or her next two meetings, or his or her anniversary with the organization. This way, the site has instant content, and the participants can see something they helped create, which also helps them feel more comfortable with the technology.

The trainer should walk through a whole task or project with the group. They could do a sample project, for example, using the membership brochure. The trainer could assign various roles to the participants and have them work through creating a brochure. Reminding them to keep it simple with "normal" roles, they could act as a CEO, a copy writer, a lawyer, and a designer.

In training, people need to learn about the functions of the intranet in terms of actual everyday work that they do so that they will further understand how the intranet can help them and why it is important for them to learn and use it.

Content should already be on the site before the training begins. Participants shouldn't view the intranet as an empty shoe box to put things in and then store under their bed, but rather they should view it as a useful resource they can add to instead of building from scratch. The site may include reference materials, an employee directory, old press releases, the employee handbook, and officer biographies—information that all your users would want or need to use. Participants should see the information and recognize its relevance to the organization or company. They should be able to glimpse the information but not go through it all.

The trainer also should have handouts prepared. They might include a list of frequently asked questions, information on how the site is arranged, directions on how to navigate through a project, a user manual, or troubleshooting information.

MCKEON & JEFFRIES

McKeon & Jeffries handled group training in an organized and systematic way. The system administrator simply borrowed laptops from several of the partners and placed them in a conference room, attached to the network. She also rented a large monitor to use for display purposes. Then, to eight at a time, she demonstrated the intranet and showed all the users how to access information, use the browser, send e-mail, and exchange files. She presented a handout to help users refer to specific areas of training. The system administrator also trained the staffs of the other two offices.

THE SPORTING GOODS AND APPAREL ASSOCIATION

Because of the geographical diversity of SGAA members, the group training for users was done at the annual convention. Users from each of the member companies were invited to the conference and assigned to a training session. The expense of renting computers and setting up an Internet connection for the conference was prohibitive, so the SGAA staff did the training as a slide presentation. The process of showing a screenshot and describing the function was not quite as effective as hands-on training, but users became familiar with the interface.

A user manual was distributed to users at this point so that users would have a reference guide to use in the future. It also was a way for users to take notes at the presentation on the screenshots in the manual.

Online Training

One of the uses of an intranet is training users. You can use it to provide continuing education for a CPA, to train someone on how to create a contract, or simply to train people how to perform certain functions within an organization. Message boards, for example, are useful for questions and answers about new technology, how it works, and how it can work, as shown in Figure 17.9. Although an organization is developing a new product, it could have a message board available to the users for online training about the product.

FIGURE 17.9.
A message board facilitates a question-and-answer discussion.

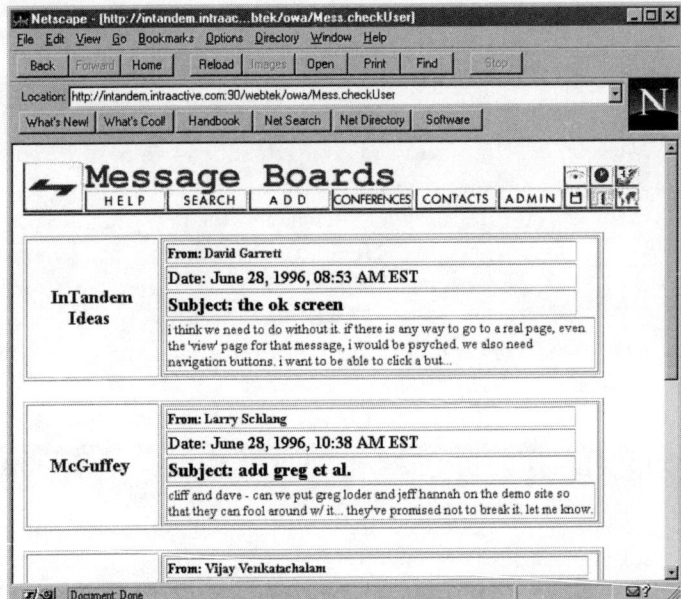

If the intranet has video online conferencing, you could use it to show users how to perform certain functions—such as filling out a check request or using a new phone system—or provide front-line customer service training.

The trainer also could take screenshots of certain application functions and show them on the Web during an online presentation to show how a function works, the steps taken to perform the function, and what the screen would look like as those steps were completed. These shots would traditionally be the same ones used on an overhead projector during a traditional training session.

Verbal instructions might accompany a screenshot presentation for users. With a RealAudio server, for example, you can show the screenshots of the images, and with each click of the new shot, the sound with the explanation can come through, providing an audio and visual presentation.

MCKEON & JEFFRIES

M&J uses its intranet to provide training, not just intranet training, but for continuing education testing on its employees. Using simple HTML pages and forms, screenshot images, and simple CGI scripts, the accounting firm uses the intranet not only to test, but also to track scores.

THE SPORTING GOODS AND APPAREL ASSOCIATION

The SGAA schedules online video conferences monthly to train members on how to use new functions and to offer assistance on existing functions. Because all the members have varying levels of computer and intranet experience, the membership department solicits training requests, and one week before the scheduled training sessions, the membership department determines what areas of the intranet the members are most interested in learning about. Some months, the responses are overwhelmingly for basic intranet instruction; at other times, the requests are overwhelmingly for higher-level training in areas such as contact databases or Telnet.

Summary

The success of your intranet depends on the users. They must be adequately trained on how to connect and access the intranet, why they should use it, and how it can help them. Trainers need to look at this new technology from the users' desks to help facilitate the transition to full usage of the intranet. Your organization may have to end "traditional" manners of communication to force users to get online.

Your organization must reach the users online and keep them online. The best training is the training users do themselves, and the only way they are going to do it is if they are properly trained in the beginning and if they deem worthwhile the content posted on the intranet.

Intranet Administration: A Critical Function

18

by David Garrett and Sweth Chandramouli

IN THIS CHAPTER

- Defining the job **286**
- Coordinating administration **291**
- Administrator skills **291**
- Administrator training needs **293**

Any consideration of administrative functions must derive from broader decisions concerning user access, intended usage, and data security. After these decisions are made, intranet administrators arguably play the single most important role in the successful implementation of this medium. The administrator's job is by definition multifaceted and includes information management, troubleshooting, conflict resolution, and technical support. An intranet administrator is the person who controls the flow of information on the site, and on any given day may act as traffic cop, librarian, enforcer, confessor, arbiter, moderator, or quick-fix artist.

All these tasks suggest that selection and training of administrators should be integral to the overall process of intranet implementation. Whether responsibility resides with a single (harried) individual or is shared throughout the organization, intranet administration requires structure, definition, and adequate preparation. This chapter offers a range of options for defining administrative roles, managing intranet administration, and identifying and addressing training needs.

Defining the Job

Certain administrative functions are necessary to maintain virtually any intranet site. Some of these functions are discussed in the following sections.

Password and Other Access Management

The administrator is the person who adds new users to the intranet and provides them with user IDs and passwords. A user ID is public, but the password is usually private and only for a specific user. The ID could be something as simple as a person's name. The password allows the user access to the intranet. The security of the site is the factor in deciding the password. If the intranet is high security, for example, the user passwords may be jumbled with letters, numbers, and underscores to make access difficult for others.

The style of the intranet is material to selecting and training an administrator. It can be a fundamentally dictatorial system where the administrator is all powerful and runs the intranet according to clear and strict protocols, or the style may be more of an organic relationship between the administrator and users. In the first situation, in which security is high, the administrator may assign passwords and not allow users to change them. In a more interactive and bottom-up organization in which security is not as high, the users may be allowed to pick their own simple passwords, like "dog," "jerk," or "schatzie," and change them routinely.

Access management is the act of controlling user accessibility of certain applications on the intranet. Some users may have more access than others in different areas. If a conference is scheduled, for example, access would be limited to those involved. The users involved in the conference would be privy to the subject matter and the date and time of the conference, but other users on the intranet would not.

The administrator also can set limits accessing intranet documents, allowing one set of users to access documents to make edits or any other changes while giving another group of users read-only privileges.

An organization wouldn't want works in progress to be disseminated prematurely—whether a policy analysis or technical paper—for competitive or legal reasons. So, in some cases only the users who are involved in the editing and decision-making progress of a document should be allowed to see it. Of this group of users, only some should be allowed to access the actual document, whereas others should have read-only access. Administrators heed caution: Too many cooks will spoil the broth.

In other situations, administrators may need to set up many levels of access. One group might draft an initial document. During the next step, the document is edited by another group of users. The document then might move through yet another group, who will approve the document. Finally, it reaches the broad group of recipients. In some circumstances, the administrator's job may seem like the technological equivalent of "pushing paper."

A range of employees who all wield a slightly different level of power are likely to be working on the intranet. Remember, most organizations do not need every user to have access to everything each staffer is working on. Just as in any office, each employee does not have access to every conference, decision-making session, conversation, or memo.

The administrator should have access to all data in any area of the intranet, using either the ID of the user or an administrator password. This capability is necessary for checking problems and troubleshooting.

Usage Analysis

Usage analysis is the log of information about users and their activity on the intranet: when they log on, how often they log on, what pages they access, and for how long they are on. It gives the administrator an idea of the activity on the site.

Usage analysis is helpful because it tells the administrator what is going on from a user standpoint. Additionally, it tells something about the users, such as which part of the site is most popular or which sections are rarely utilized. The analysis also can serve as a checklist of sorts, showing what pages need maintenance or edits or what needs to be archived. The administrator can use this information to make decisions about current and future applications that might be planned for the intranet.

If the usage analysis shows the administrator that the mission and vision pages are seldom accessed by the users, but the CEO really wants users to view those pages, for example, the administrator should bring it to the attention of editorial staff or content providers. In fact, they might work together to add something new or different to enhance the pages and draw more users. If the analysis shows that users never check the minutes from board meetings, the administrator might suggest having the minutes edited for content or archiving them in another area of the intranet.

Usage analysis also can be used to monitor the success of a mailing. Assume that the administrator wants to gauge the interest of new users. He or she sends out introductory packets and then monitors when the new users log on. Allowing for mail time, the administrator can find out how eager the new users were to log on and how long it took them to get involved. The same strategy can be used from time to time on the site with existing users. Sending out a mail message about a new feature or even pointing to some exciting news and then watching the usage closely can provide an administrator valuable information about user interest.

Usage analysis has analytic features that administrators can use to perform surveillance functions—for example, to detect unexpected entry from either a user on the intranet who doesn't have access to the particular area or from a stranger who has intruded. If administrators are regularly checking usage, they can quickly spot anomalies in the usage patterns, which may signify intruders on the intranet.

Technical Support

An integral job of the administrator is the technical support he or she provides to the users. If the user cannot access the intranet or does not understand how to access the intranet, the intranet in these situations is not an asset to the organization. It is therefore vital that the administrator be accessible to the users. The administrator can use usage analysis to check to see if all the users have even logged on for the first time after they are provided "how-to" information.

Technical support is both the nuts and bolts of physically going to the users to assist them or demonstrate a new application and interacting with the users to find out what they're thinking. This interaction allows the administrator to see eye-to-eye with the users and thus better understand what the job of the administrator is in maintaining the site.

The administrator needs to gauge users' interest continuously and encourage feedback from them. If half of the should-be users are not logging on, the administrator's job is to find out why. The administrator needs to make sure they are connected.

If users don't have fast connectivity because they're using a 9600 baud modem, for example, this creates problems with the slow speed they're accessing information from the intranet. If they find it faster to call or use e-mail instead of the intranet for communication, again the intranet is not an asset to the organization. With the knowledge of this situation, however, the administrator can recommend a solution, such as an upgrade for more satisfaction and a faster connection; or the administrator might recommend that the host put different information on the intranet so that it takes less time to access.

Content and Archive Maintenance

The purpose of content and archive maintenance is to make life easier on the users. It's a house cleaning of sorts. Depending on how administrators approach this maintenance, it can be either a full-fledged spring cleaning or a list of weekly chores. Maintaining the intranet may mean taking information not frequently accessed by users and archiving it, upgrading and changing files to make them timely or more attractive to the user, cleaning up a file so that it operates more efficiently, or creating subdirectories. The users' needs and wishes drive the maintenance. When maintaining content, the administrator needs to ensure that the pages are interesting to the users; otherwise, they won't use those pages.

The more data that is added to the site, the more difficult it is to manage and the more critical it becomes for the administrator to keep it updated and tidy. If the administrator edits a site or revises a page, he or she also needs to take down the old page to ensure that users don't accidentally access and use the old page as up-to-date information. Old information should be archived or deleted.

As an organization works on an intranet, the sites get fatter with more files to manage. The administrator might need to shift fields and directories and create new subdirectories so that information is more easily retrieved by the users. If many international legislative documents are listed on one page, for example, the administrator might create subdirectories for each country with legislative documents.

After the subdirectory is created, the Uniform Resource Locator (URL, which is the complete address of a Web site) for that information changes, so the administrator needs to revise or edit all the links to those pages to reflect the new URL. Every page has a specific URL, so the deeper the user goes into the site, the longer the URL is. If the user is in a subdirectory of a subdirectory, all those addresses are included in the URL. One of the duties of the administrator is to ensure that these pages are organized consistently in those directories.

Intranets may contain hyperlinks to other parts of the Internet, which let the user just click the URL to view the related pages. It is important that the administrator keeps a current file of those sites and their corresponding URLs. If the URL is wrong, the link won't work, and the users will get a message to see their system administrator.

E-Mail Management

Although exchanging information on a bulletin board for different users to view is one solution to more open communication among employees and business partners, giving users the ability to communicate with each other in a more dynamic setting provides an even better channel of communication. When it comes to managing e-mail, the administrator's function is to configure and update the links of e-mail addresses for all the users. It's a good idea to create an e-mail address on the site that all users can utilize to alert the administrator of problems or to get general questions answered.

The precise scope and nature of intranet administration are largely determined by the complexity of the site and the degree of its interactivity. If the site is intended primarily to display static information from a single source, for example, archive maintenance is a key administrative function. By contrast, if the intranet is designed to encourage interaction, the administrator may play an important role in moderating online discussions and in managing multiple postings. Of course, many sites or intranets emphasize both or more of these objectives, thus requiring a more sophisticated management team. In other words, the scope really depends on the goal of the intranet. The responsibilities of the administrator become heavier depending on the functionality of the site. The more functional it is for the user, the more labor-intensive it is for the administrator.

If all the users are dealing with one simple issue, such as the market price of a single commodity, for example, any publicly available market information is accessible to all the users. If several larger groups belong to the Society of Sweet Sugar Growers of the World, they likely would need additional and diversified information on the raw material. This group probably depends on specific information to guide their business decisions, such as current market prices, competition, global sugar production, import and export issues, legislative activity, or global distribution. In this case, the administrator's challenge is to create different subsections of the intranet that will provide the specific information for the large audience.

In the first example, the administrator must make sure that all pages are current and that all users are accessing the information without any glitches. In the second example, the administrator must maintain the different sites of the intranet so that individual groups can access the specific subsections that are beneficial to them. The administrator also must make sure that unauthorized users are not accessing any of the sites.

Defining the administrator's job requires answering some key questions about how the intranet will be utilized and by whom:

- What is the overall purpose of the intranet? Is it used for disseminating institutional information, encouraging interdisciplinary or interdivisional collaboration, or expediting data flow, for example?
- What kinds of information are appropriate for posting to the intranet? Some organizations tightly restrict content, whereas others encourage informal interchange. This information may include newsletters, newspaper articles related to the organization's mission or purpose, speeches, studies, meeting agendas, schedules for conferences, and calendars.
- Who are the intended users? Keep in mind that a given intranet may include multiple user access levels. These access levels include conference, bulletin board, shared access to documents, read-only, ability alter, and save.
- How is each user group expected to use the site? Will the groups, for example, read or download information, exchange documents internally, edit or coauthor materials, post new content, or schedule meetings?
- Who will provide content? Will the marketing group decide the important content to be shared? Will the communications group provide it? Or will each department separately provide information depending on the issue?

Coordinating Administration

After a company knows what will be distributed via the intranet, it must consider how all the information will be administered and distributed. The organization has spent much time planning and creating the intranet, but all the information and resources will be rendered useless unless the data is organized and current. Some companies may choose to centralize administration with a single individual or department as a means of assuring control of site content. In these cases, all input to the intranet is funneled through a single channel for posting. Depending on the technical proficiency of the content author(s), input may be forwarded in HTML or may require translation by administrative staff.

In addition, an administrator's level of authority and internal reporting should be considered in advance of assigning these tasks. Many organizations distinguish between sectors of their intranet sites such that certain areas are restricted to read-only content (for example, permanent, or official, information like the mission, vision, and biographies of officers), whereas others are dedicated to interchange (for example, conferences, bulletin boards, and online publishing). Depending on volume, these organizations may assign different individuals to administer specific sectors.

One significant advantage of segmenting intranet administration is that it helps the sponsoring organization safeguard against potential abuses of power. The trade-off here is between centralized and distributed control, but neither approach is perfect.

A growing number of companies—in response to concerns about employee privacy, among other issues—believe that oversight of their intranets should be shared, however, rather than investing sole authority in a single individual (such as the corporate security director). Depending on the organization and the intranet, an organization may have two administrators: one to handle the technical functions, like support and access, and the other to handle the political end—who in the organization has access to what conference rooms, newsletters, discussion groups—and to moderate discussions held on the intranet.

Regardless of whether the organization decides to work with one administrator or distributed administrators, all intranet administrators must understand and respect the potentially sensitive nature of their roles. By definition, they have regular access to a broad range of company information, often in draft or prospective form that is not intended for general distribution. Users must trust the administrator, or they will be leery of using the intranet. If users lack confidence in their administrator's discretion, they will not use the intranet, which means a great deal of time and money wasted.

Administrator Skills

In considering various options for assigning the administrator role, thinking in terms of technical requirements as well as of interpersonal skills is useful. Very often, an organization may treat this role as an afterthought, on the presumption that some generic support staffer or research assistant can take on these duties in addition to his or her regular job. In the early stages of intranet implementation, and given the right set of skills, this approach may actually work. As the intranet evolves, however, the administrator's job becomes more complex and demanding, and it's wise to think ahead.

In an ideal world, an intranet administrator already has a number of skills and traits, including technical proficiency, attention to detail, and interpersonal skills.

Technical Proficiency

Obviously with something as new and rapidly evolving as the intranet, an organization needs to have an administrator who has an extensive technology background and can understand how and why things happen in a computer system. The administrator needs a thorough background and proficiency with the Internet because the intranet is so similar.

A technically proficient administrator can save time and effort running the intranet. An administrator can automate a task, making it easier to perform in the future. If a user wants to create a conference, the administrator creates a script. A script is a form set up by the administrator to create something on the intranet that is used more than once, such as a conference. For a conference, the administrator may set up the script for the user to enter the subject of the conference, the names of the participants, and the time and date of the conference. The script means that the user doesn't have to go through the administrator each time for a repeating function, freeing up both the administrator and the user.

The administrator needs to have a firm understanding of connectivity (which is how the computer is connected to the large network of the Internet), the hardware connection, and the software requirements that enable the user to browse the World Wide Web and surf the Internet.

The administrator also must understand the Internet inside and out, allowing him or her to utilize it fully for the benefit of the organization. It's advantageous for an administrator to understand and be aware of other developments in other sites that are relevant to the intranet; he or she should be continually looking out for other developments.

The administrator needs to have knowledge about the World Wide Web, the latest Web browsers, and what kind of features they support. Netscape, for example, produces a table if it uses specific HTML commands, but Mosaic doesn't support tables. If the organization sees a use for tables, it needs a Web browser that will create them.

Attention to Detail

One of the jobs of the administrator is to keep URLs and links up-to-date so that they work properly. The administrator therefore needs to enter all this information exactly. This information has to be precise; the exclusion of a period or quotation mark or bracket can completely mess up a document. If an organization has a dynamic site, one that is frequently changing, for example, the link could soon be outdated. The administrator's job is to keep these links current; otherwise, the users will hit dead ends.

Interpersonal Skills

For many users, the administrator is their personal guide to the intranet. The users must feel like they can communicate with the administrator. If they don't like or trust the administrator, they won't come to him or her with questions. The administrator has to be patient, even if the same user calls with the same question for the tenth time. The administrator needs to remember that, for some users, especially the "green" users, this cutting-edge technology can be frightening.

The administrator must communicate—in layperson terms—with the users. If the users can't understand the administrator, they won't ask questions or seek help. A fine line exists between a computer support person and a user support person; technical know-how doesn't mean anything if the administrator can't communicate well with the users.

The administrator must be able to put himself or herself in the users' shoes and must understand the importance of the intranet for the users. In many ways, the administrator is a politician who has to be in touch with constituents—the users. If not, the administrator is going to lose the election because he or she doesn't understand the needs, concerns, and questions of the users. Many computer geeks can perform miracles on the machines but cannot communicate with users in a friendly and accessible way. Stay away from these self-proclaimed administrators.

Obviously, a certain level of technical speak is necessary so that the administrator can function as the organization's techno-salesperson. In addition to talking technology in simple, everyday terms with intranet users, the administrator should be versed in some techno-speak so that he or she can secure the most appropriate applications and technology that the organization is counting on.

Finally, the administrator must approach an organization's intranet with sensitivity, especially regarding some of the more confidential activities on the intranet. Many functions accessible via the intranet are considered private, closed-door meetings. The administrator should be trustworthy and able to keep sensitive issues private.

Administrator Training Needs

Obviously, intranet administrators require far more extensive training than users. Front-end investment in administrator training pays off in efficiency and user acceptance, and training content should be considered early in the intranet development process. Training content reflects both the intranet design and functions and the expectations of the sponsoring organization. Depending on the skills of the trainees, a training curriculum may combine customized content with commercially available courses in specific technologies—for example, courses on HTML, connectivity, high-tech courses on the Internet, and courses on Web servers. In addition, administrators also should know their way around the users' different client hardware and software, as well as the server hardware and software. If the company uses a database, database administration should be a priority.

Subscribing to and reading different publications on the Internet, technology, and computer applications also provide useful training for the administrator because the intranet is so new that few courses or books are yet available on the subject.

Administrators also play an important role in user training. Involving administrators in training brings them closer to the "customers" and helps them understand users' needs, which in turn helps them do their jobs better. In addition, "train-the-trainer" programs often yield significant time and cost savings.

Training the Administrators

After a company decides what functions it wants the administrators to provide, it must choose them and train them. Deciding who should administer the site depends largely on the roles the company wants that person to fill and the degree of complexity of the intranet. If a company wants the administrator to be a Webmaster for a largely static HTML site, for example, it does not need someone with as much technical know-how as for, say, a site with mostly dynamically generated pages and a back-end database. Learning how to manage an HTML Web site and even writing HTML could take an administrator just a few days. Learning advanced programming languages or how to use database gateways could take months or years. The company should find out what its needs in an administrator are and fill the position based on that. Too often I have seen organizations choose who will manage the site before deciding what the site will be, which can leave an administrator vastly under- or even over-qualified.

The real trick is to teach administrators how to shape and mold the intranet into a useful (and used) device for the organization. The administrator therefore must not only be able to construct the site, train and assist users, and manage the flow of information both from the intranet to the user and from the user to the intranet, but also must learn how to manipulate the site to make it as efficient and attractive as possible for users.

After a company carefully selects administrators, the next step is to familiarize them with the process of the intranet—where the files are, how the Web server works, who the users are, and who is responsible for providing content. The administrator also should learn about any applications that run on the intranet. If there are message boards, he or she should know how to create new message boards and edit existing ones. Perhaps the company wants the message boards moderated. If so, the administrator needs to know how to delete messages from the message board and when to do so. In essence, administrators need to learn everything about the day-to-day maintenance and upkeep of the site.

One of the easiest ways to train administrators is to give them space of their own on the server to experiment with new ideas and techniques. Even if just provided space for a personal home page or pages, users will be more apt to engage more interesting and new HTML tags or applications if they know their work is not going to be seen by all their coworkers right away. I have known several administrators who have learned everything from Java to RealAudio to VRML just by puttering around in their own Web space.

In essence, because of rapidly changing technology and because of the instantly flexible nature of an intranet, most of the learning process for the administrator is likely to be on the job. Administrators should be ready to adapt to the changing nature of this medium and ready to accept new technology and methods and scrap those that are outdated or unused.

MCKEON & JEFFRIES

McKeon & Jeffries selected only one administrator for its intranet. The administrator is a former administrative assistant at the company's Philadelphia office with experience using HTML. Involving the administrator in the project from the beginning eliminated the need for much of the training that would otherwise be required. M&J's administrator is in charge of collecting information for the site from various sources throughout the organization and publishing it on the site. The administrator also is in charge of providing training and support for the users of the intranet, although most technical questions are referred to the firm's systems administrator.

THE SPORTING GOODS AND APPAREL ASSOCIATION

The SGAA hired a corps of administrators specifically for maintaining its intranet. Three individuals are charged with handling three distinct responsibilities. The first deals with user issues—from handling technical support questions and working with users to designing and updating the graphical interface of the site. This administrator is responsible for creating help text and user manuals, as well as gauging user interest by carefully watching the logs. Another administrator is in charge of creating content. This individual collects information and publishes it on the site. Serving almost as a librarian, this administrator has the responsibility of keeping track of the information on the site and knowing what is there and where to find it. The third administrator is in charge of the software on the site; her responsibilities include developing new applications as well as fine-tuning and fixing existing ones. In all, these three administrators make the intranet a constantly changing and up-to-date information and communications source for the association.

Summary

The administrator must understand an organization's goal for its intranet. He or she is the one who will continue to build the intranet and plan for its future. A good administrator will keep discussion groups on task, help facilitate easier access of information, understand and troubleshoot user problems and needs, and be personable enough that any frustrated user feels comfortable e-mailing him or her with the most benign question.

Before selecting an administrator, an organization must define what the goals of the intranet are and how the administrator position will be responsible for keeping the intranet's goals on track. An administrator should have a grasp of the organization as a whole so that he or she can make the most appropriate decisions regarding site maintenance. The individual should have a technical background as well as a patient and open approach in dealing with users.

The administrator role can go to one or more persons, again depending on the organization of the intranet, the goals of the intranet, and the setup of the host organization.

IN THIS PART

- Browsers: Viewing Corporate Information with HTML **299**
- Authoring Tools **309**
- Creating a Dynamic Site **319**
- Creating a Functional Site **335**
- PDF Presentations **351**
- SGML Presentations **361**
- Audio Presentations **367**
- Video Presentations **381**

PART III

Using Your Intranet: Business Applications

Browsers: Viewing Corporate Information with HTML

19

by Hal Herzog

IN THIS CHAPTER

- Browsers in general **300**
- An explanation of standard features **302**

In this chapter, you examine the basics of applications most commonly known as *browsers*. Included among the information is a brief history of the World Wide Web, as well as a look into the evolution of the products involved. You look at the standard features, as well as features that are poised to become standards in the near future. You also review individual products, with emphasis placed on how each product's features will be of benefit to an organization's intranet strategy.

The browser is the window that lets your users access the information or communications on your intranet. The browser is used to display information using HTML and images and to collect information using forms. With advanced programming, the browser can let users manipulate data or run miniapplications.

Browsers in General

Whether sheepishly contemplating or dashing onto the World Wide Web (WWW), anyone who wants to explore the Web must first choose a browser. A browser is an application that is used to access the information on the Web. Perhaps you are more familiar with browsers by their product names—Netscape Navigator, Internet Explorer, or Mosaic.

The browser's original job was to access the Web and display in a useful format the information stored on the remote server in HyperText Markup Language (HTML), the language of the Web. HTML, a subset of Standard Generalized Markup Language (SGML), tells the browser what type of information to display (list, heading, link) and then lets the browser determine the best way to display the information. This process allows the user a great deal of flexibility in determining the most suitable way to access information, while at the same time allowing the content provider to focus on the most important thing, the content. As with many new technologies that have been produced in the twentieth century, the creators of the Web did not envision all the eventual applications for their technology. As new uses for the Web have risen to prominence, browsers have changed to accommodate the new goals of the users of the Web.

The World Wide Web was first conceived in 1980 at the European Laboratory for Particle Physics by Tim Berners-Lee of CERN, who was looking for a better and faster way for the scientific community to communicate. Nothing much came of it until 1989, when he submitted a formal proposal for Information Management to CERN. When it was resubmitted to CERN management in 1990, the name World Wide Web was chosen as the designation for the project.

By December 1990, the first browser had been written, using the NeXTStep platform. By 1993, more work had been done on the structure of how the Web worked, and it began to take off. By the end of that year, browsers were available for all the major platforms (Windows, Macintosh, UNIX). In January of 1993, about 1 percent of Internet usage was related to the Web.

In March of 1994, Marc Andreessen left his team of programmers at the University of Illinois to form Mosaic Communications Corporation, named after the browser he helped create. Today,

Mosaic is still being developed at the university without Andreessen. By the end of the year, the company, which changed its name to Netscape Communications Corporation, released the browser that is now known as Netscape Navigator.

Don't let the fact that Netscape came out with the first commercial browser fool you into thinking that it is the final stage in the history of the Web. The first version of Netscape did not amount to anything more revolutionary than the fact that it crashed much less than Mosaic did. Other companies soon released similar products. Spry's Internet in a Box software included Air Mosaic, and Navisoft released Internet Works. Around this time, all the products offered equal functionality, and the choice of browsers was left up to the personal preference of the user. The virtual landscape, however, was changing.

Netscape had introduced a few extensions in its browser to HTML to make documents more visually appealing. Browsers that did not support the proprietary extensions did not properly display documents using the extensions. As more and more users chose Netscape as their platform for "surfing" the Web, the people who were making Web pages felt it prudent to take advantage of the added features of Netscape. This use quickly made all other browsers sub-par and further increased Netscape's market share.

When Microsoft released Windows 95, it included a rudimentary browser, Internet Explorer 1.0. The industry did not think much of it from a technical standpoint, but the fact that Microsoft had integrated a browser into the operating system made everyone take notice of the Web in a big way. Most products were still made for Netscape's browser, though. Soon after the release of Windows 95, Microsoft released Internet Explorer 2.0, which had a few proprietary enhancements of its own. At this point, the so-called "browser wars" began. Each company, Microsoft and Netscape, began touting its respective browsers as the way to go. Hence, many sites on the Web have icons denoting that they look better in Netscape or Internet Explorer.

Netscape, meanwhile, licensed from Sun the Internet language Java for use in Navigator 2.0. This way, Web designers could add interactivity to their sites that could not be accomplished through conventional HTML. The specifics of the language are not important for the discussion here, but the fact that it made Navigator strikingly better than Internet Explorer is. Web pages that employed Java would have gaping virtual holes where the Java application was supposed to run if the user was running Internet Explorer. On its end, Microsoft released specs for VBScript, which directly competed with Java and left just as gaping a hole in Netscape browsers.

If determining how to display information is the browser's only purpose, why are so many different brands available? This question seems legitimate, in the same way that you might wonder why so many different brands of cars are made. They all have the same general purpose, to get you where you're going. The differences, though, appear in the extra features. Some features, such as airbags on cars, often become so useful to the public that they become standards. In the browser realm, each manufacturer tries, with varying degrees of success, to customize its browser to be the choice platform for navigation of the Web.

An Explanation of Standard Features

Many features in the browser realm are so pervasive that they are considered standards. The most basic level of compatibility is HTML compliance. HTML is a constantly evolving standard that controls the appearance of documents viewed on the Web. All current browsers support HTML 3.0, which may be an official standard by the time you read this book. Version 3.0 can be supported without it being "official" because the draft specifications of Internet standards are always public to ensure that all the concerned parties get a chance to comment on the new standard.

HTML provides a wide assortment of text formatting capabilities. Two fonts of the user's choice, usually Times Roman and Courier, are available for display. Text can be bold, blinking, and italicized. The size of text can be specified both in absolute terms or in relation to other text in a document. Unless specifically set up not to do so, text conforms to the width of the browser window, even after a user resizes the window.

Images play an important part in conveying ideas and are an integral part of the capabilities of any browser. Images come in many different formats, but most browsers support all of them. GIF87 and GIF89 (Graphic Interchange Format, versions 1987 and 1989) are the formats used for storing images of few colors, like company logos or graphical buttons. The GIF89 format supports a feature for storing more than one image in a file, which, when played back in rapid succession, provides a quick way of creating simple animation. JPEG or JPG (Joint Photographic Experts Group) files are usually high-quality images, like photographs. Both formats support *interlacing* (in JPEG files it is called *progressive rendering*), which is a way of storing the image in a format that appears to load faster by displaying the image in intervals, instead of line-by-line, while loading. Over slow connections, such as a modem, interlacing is an important feature.

Tables are particularly important to intranet users. Corporate information on sales, projections, or anything that involves a chart will naturally be in table form. All browsers support a variety of methods for controlling the layout of information contained in tables. These methods include vertical and horizontal alignment, border width, cell width, and cell padding. A relatively new feature that has become standard is the ability to determine the color of each individual cell, an important step in conveying information as fast as possible.

Netscape

Netscape Communications Corporation is currently the dominating force in the browser wars. Netscape's browser (a term the company says is too limiting) is called Navigator. You may know it as Netscape Navigator, Netscape, or Navigator.

In late 1994, Netscape was the first company to successfully improve the "original" browser, NCSA Mosaic. Mosaic was not the first browser in existence, but it was the first widely known one. When comparing the Navigator to Mosaic, the two programs look very similar. This is no accident. Netscape was founded by Marc Andreessen and James Clark. Andreessen headed the team that designed Mosaic. Andreessen and Clark were so sure that the public would only identify with the name Mosaic that they called their company Mosaic Communications Corporation. The computer industry, however, is always looking for the "killer application" for a given market, and because the Web was the killer environment for the Internet, Mosaic Communications Corporation named their product Mozilla. The Mozilla name was to little avail, as users seemed to like and identify with the name Netscape much better. The corporate name Netscape quickly held and most users today have never heard of Mozilla.

The Internet continues to advance and develop rapidly. In fact, Internet years are even longer than dog years. Navigator is currently marketing version 3.0, which the Netscape Corporation has called "Atlas"—presumably to symbolize the holding of the entire Net, much like the Titan Atlas held the entire world on his shoulders. To distinguish itself from the competition, Navigator includes many applications and plug-ins that were previously separate programs. Audio players and video players, for example, are now built into Navigator. The advantage of plug-ins is that they allow the content provider a standard way of adding usability to a Web site. At the time of this writing, approximately 50 plug-ins were available for free use, accessible from the Netscape Web site:

http://home.netscape.com/comprod/products/navigator/version_2.0/plugins/index.html

This site is shown in Figure 19.1. In the rare instance that a plug-in is not available to augment the capability of the browser to do a specific task, which is highly unlikely, creating a plug-in, while not an easy project, is a fairly straightforward project for a seasoned programmer. The Software Development Kit (SDK) is free to all. It includes all the code and information to write a plug-in for a specific intranet task.

FIGURE 19.1.
Netscape's plug-in registry.

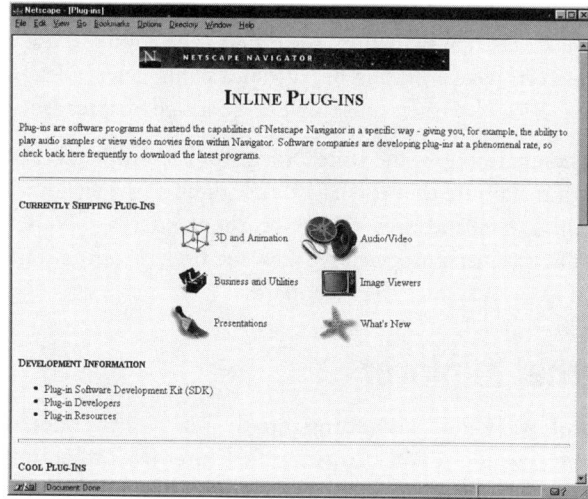

Live3D, developed by Paper Software but purchased by Netscape, conforms to the Netscape/Silicon Graphics-endorsed specification for Virtual Reality Markup Language (VRML) version 2.0, also known as Moving Worlds. The competing specifications from companies such as Microsoft do not enjoy as wide an industry support as the Moving Worlds proposal; it likely will be the standard. Tightly integrated with Java, it allows objects to be live links as well as contain many other Java-related objects. The advantage here is that Moving Worlds makes VRML more than just a "gee-whiz" technology and allows the content to be linked to other content on an intranet. The 3-D navigation of databases and files is just one of the many possibilities with this technology.

CoolTalk is a Voice Over Network (VON) technology that allows two users to conduct a voice conversation over a network, from anywhere in the world. Many users refer to products in this category by the name of a competing product: Internet Phone by VocalTec, or Iphone. Internet Phone is the most popular of this class of products, but it is not free, whereas CoolTalk comes free with Navigator. The technology of CoolTalk is quite good. It even allows you to have a digital network answering machine for those times when you are not at your desk. Compared to other similar products, CoolTalk's main drawback is its lack of a conference call mode. A future version is likely to include this feature. Also, CoolTalk is an entirely separate application from the browser, which may not be intuitive to some users.

The browser portion of Navigator has changed little from 2.x, the previous release. Netscape's specific enhancements include inline support for AVI (Audio Video Interleave is the format Windows uses to store animation) files, as well as built-in WAV, AU, MIDI, and AIFF format audio file playback capabilities. You get no cost benefit here, because applications to view and listen to these files are free. The value lies in the fact that WAV, AU, MIDI, and AIFF—traditionally tricky to set up—are integrated into Netscape.

What sets Netscape apart from the others is its ability to use tables to their fullest. Each cell of the table can have a unique background color. Such a feature is particularly useful to those intranet users who often must look at a barrage of spreadsheet data.

When compatibility is the issue, Navigator is considered the standard. Authors of Web pages check to make sure that the pages look right on Navigator. Most manufacturers of browsers know this as well and strive to support the standards of Netscape. For instance, Frames, which originally was just a proprietary Netscape trick, is now a standard feature and is on its way to becoming an official HTML standard.

Internet Explorer

Microsoft was a little late getting into the realm of Internet products, but it has brought out a very effective and useful browser called Internet Explorer. Currently, at version 3.0, it is a direct competitor of Netscape Navigator. Although it doesn't encompass the add-ons that Netscape offers, Internet Explorer itself is excellent in its speed, stability, and included features.

The Netscape home page looks pretty much the same in Explorer. Microsoft's main marketing campaign is that Explorer is free, and that may very well be its biggest selling point against Navigator, but the evaluation should not end there.

To compete with Java and JavaScript, Microsoft has introduced Visual Basic Script, also known as VBScript, which is essentially a scaled-down and packaged-for-the-Internet version of Visual Basic 4.0. Visual Basic Script does offer the advantage to users in Rapid Application Development (RAD) using Visual Basic. No such comparable product is available for Java (this may change with Visual Age for Java, IBM's authoring tool, and some others).

Microsoft has licensed Java from Sun and plans to build Java into its browser, much like Navigator, but currently the feature is not yet available. Navigator style frames are also implemented, to support as wide a range of style as possible. Plug-ins are also supported, but they tend not to work quite as well as plug-ins do in Navigator.

A slew of new technologies, packaged under the name ActiveX, also are included in Internet Explorer. ActiveX is the new name for OLE Controls, and some of ActiveX undoubtedly comes from Microsoft's canceled "Blackbird" project. This group of technologies is designed around bringing multimedia information to the user in an effective and efficient manner. ActiveX controls also allow programmers to add Internet functionality consistently and easily (from a programmer's point of view) to a product. For intranets that will have programs developed for them, these controls will enable software developers to shorten the time it takes to move from conception to a working application.

Oracle PowerBrowser

Oracle's PowerBrowser has all the standard features any good browser should have. (Figure 19.2 shows the Netscape home page as viewed in PowerBrowser.) It also can deal with frames and tables, although the documentation does not stress HTML 3.0 compliance. It does not support Java in the 1.0 release, but Oracle has stated that a Java-enabled PowerBrowser is on the way. It is undoubtedly a quality product for which Oracle will continue to meet users' demands. The main disadvantage with the Oracle PowerBrowser is that it is among the slowest browsers available. As faster computers hit the market, however, PowerBrowser's slow speed may no longer be a problem. Keep in mind, though, that users left waiting for data are unproductive users.

I should add that Oracle is a database company and, therefore, it is no surprise that the PowerBrowser shines in the area of databases. It includes a Database Wizard that makes interfacing with ODBC-compliant databases relatively effortless compared to Common Gateway Interface (CGI) programming. Another Oracle advantage is Oracle BASIC, which can automate many common tasks that would have required CGI, such as form validation and math calculations.

FIGURE 19.2.
The Netscape home page as viewed in Oracle's PowerBrowser.

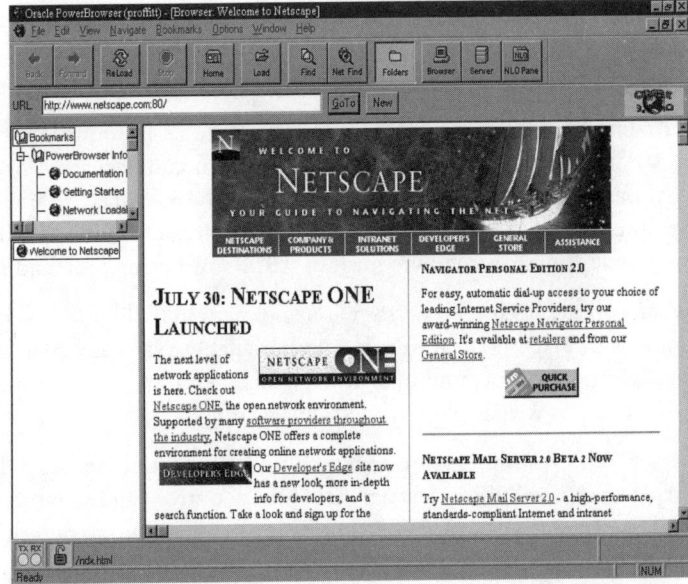

MCKEON & JEFFRIES

M&J found that the easiest course of action was to use NCSA Mosaic on their Windows 3.1 machines and Internet Explorer on their Windows 95 and Windows NT machines. These free products fit M&J's budget, and as far as features go, McKeon & Jeffries lagged far behind the industry in their need for advanced functionality. They hoped to have everyone using the latest Internet Explorer after everyone had upgraded to Windows 95.

THE SPORTING GOODS AND APPAREL ASSOCIATION

The SGAA needed to buy only a few browsers for their administrative personnel. They chose Netscape for its features and seeming commitment to making swift improvements. Also important was the broad range of operating systems that Netscape was available on. They couldn't control what computers or operating systems their members used. They recommended Netscape to all their users because of its availability and ease of use.

Summary

With all the options available, which browser is the best? That's like asking which kind of car is the best. The answer depends on your needs and intended use. If a major function of an intranet is interfacing to databases, Oracle's PowerBrowser may be the best option. If all-around functionality is required, Navigator is the best option. Meanwhile, custom application programmers will appreciate the controls available in Internet Explorer. You should consider all these browsers and each program's unique features when you or your organization begins building an intranet.

Authoring Tools

20

by Hal Herzog

IN THIS CHAPTER

- WYSIWYG tools **310**
- Near-WYSIWYG tools **314**

The tools that allow a provider to create useful and attractive Web pages were once limited to Windows Notepad, Simpletext, or another text-only editor. This limitation meant that, if you wanted to create a page, you had to remember many obscure tags and adhere to the style of HTML. Fortunately, just as yesterday's early word processors have bloomed into today's full-featured applications, authoring tools have bloomed into powerful and feature-rich applications. But you still can find authoring applications that offer little more than Notepad does. Choosing which authoring tool to use depends on your authoring style. Of course, you shouldn't be surprised that Microsoft and Netscape have greater compatibility with their browsers than other products, but other vendors provide extremely useful and user-friendly tools.

Authoring tools for the Web can be divided into two categories: WYSIWYG (What You See Is What You Get) and Near-WYSIWYG. Because they all allow the previewing of a document in any browser, the Near-WYSIWYG category is not a hindrance. In fact, because of the decreased load on a machine, some providers may choose to use Near-WYSIWYG tools to increase performance at the development stage.

When you're evaluating which tool to use, consider which features will be the most useful and necessary. If you constantly update documents by replacing selective previous information or tacking new information on to old sites, multiple search-and-replace is an important feature. If you frequently need tables, assistance with table creation is a must. Additionally, the ability to work from a standard template is useful in order to facilitate a consistent look.

WYSIWYG Tools

Internet Assistant for Word, shown in Figure 20.1, is a low-powered and free add-on from Microsoft for users of Microsoft Word 6.0 and 7.0. This authoring application is best suited for users who readily handle many documents stored in a compatible format that traditionally would be distributed as paper handouts or packets. Loading a document in Internet Assistant (IA) and then saving it as HTML using the standard Save As dialog box produce documents that, when viewed with a browser, look much like the original document. Even tables retain much of their original look, which is impressive.

Documents created with Internet Assistant often look much better when viewed with Internet Explorer than with Navigator or other products because Internet Assistant places some Internet Explorer-specific HTML code, or tags, into its output. This may be a non-issue by the time you read this book because Netscape and Microsoft are both becoming adept at copying each other's HTML tags.

The Internet Assistant does have some pretty impressive features. If you have embedded images, even PCX or BMP images, IA converts them to GIF format (the format compatible with most Web browsers) and saves them in the same directory as the HTML file. You also can create complicated tables easily by using the table tool. IA also allows you to color-code HTML tags within a document. This coding doesn't affect the appearance of the document but does help you to keep your document organized and troubleshoot problems if your document doesn't turn out the way you like it. With many editors, sorting out the tags when fixing problems in your page is sometimes difficult.

FIGURE 20.1.
Internet Assistant for Word is simply a template for Microsoft Word 6.0 or greater.

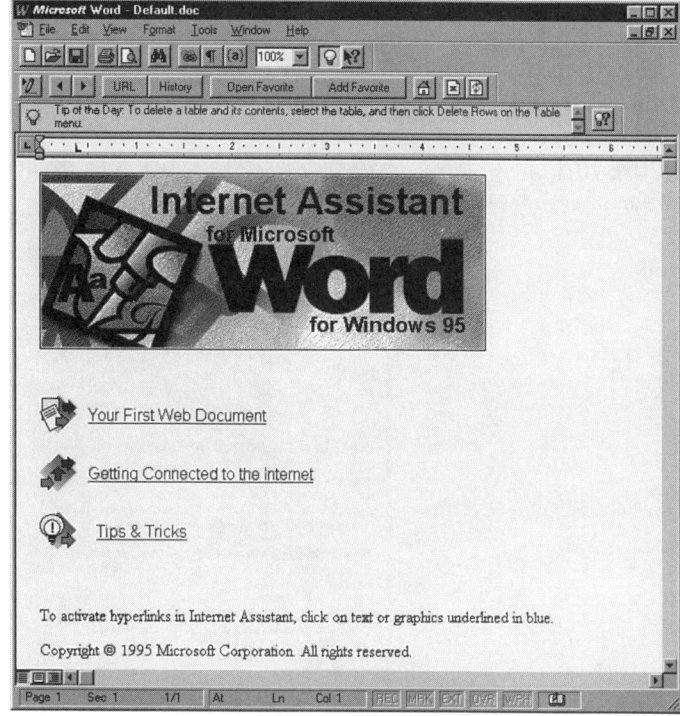

I recommend IA for any users converting lots of large documents from a word processor format, such as MS Word or WordPerfect, to HTML. The converter still doesn't work as well as it should. It tends to throw in lots of extra tags, like
s for line breaks, but using IA is an easy way to build usable HTML pages fast.

Microsoft also produces Internet Assistants for Access, Excel, PowerPoint, and Schedule+. These products perform functions similar to Internet Assistant for Word, which is to format content for use on the Web. Internet Assistant for Access allows for the creation of HTML form database information for use on the Web. Internet Assistant for Excel converts Excel tables into HTML with as little effort as a few points and clicks. The PowerPoint version converts PowerPoint presentations and slides into HTML (Microsoft has also released an ActiveX control that views PowerPoint presentations without conversion). Internet Assistant for Schedule+ takes calendar information and formats it for viewing on the Web. These products, while functional, are not as commonly used as Internet Assistant for Word, and therefore when people refer to Internet Assistant, they usually mean the one for Word.

Using Your Intranet: Business Applications

Part III

Netscape Navigator Gold

Netscape Communications Corporation does not have an entire office suite available to help with its Internet strategy. What it does have, however, is the leading market share for the browser market with Navigator. Navigator Gold is essentially the latest version of Navigator with an editor attached and integrated into the program. Figure 20.2 shows the newest Navigator. It comes with a free trial period from their Web site.

FIGURE 20.2.
Netscape's Navigator Gold.

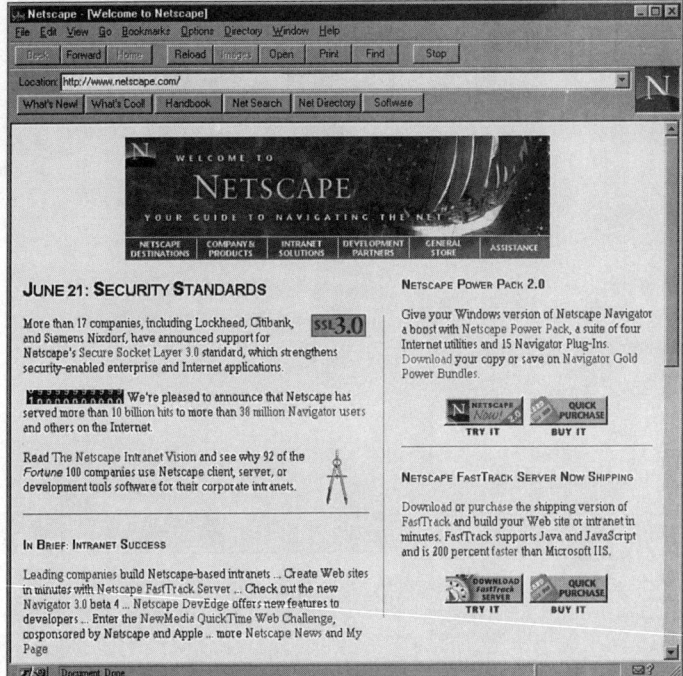

Gold is positioned as a competitor of Internet Assistant. It is the editor most capable of approximating the look of a true browser while editing because its preview mode is, in fact, Navigator. Image editing and general site management are easier than with Internet Assistant, and table support is quite good. Gold, however, does not support many of the tags that made Navigator so popular, especially the frames tag. Generally, Netscape Gold is suitable for those people who feel comfortable within the Netscape environment and who want instant editing capabilities for documents currently being browsed.

One nice feature is Gold's instant editing feature. If you are surfing a page on a remote computer and want to edit it, clicking the Edit button instantly downloads the HTML and all the images for the file to your machine. Gold also offers a great multi-level Undo feature that helps users who are not as proficient with HTML. The best feature by far, however, is Gold's Publish feature, which uploads the document to the server with the click of a button, without your having to launch a separate FTP application. This feature is great for users who edit documents on a UNIX or Linux server from a Windows or Mac environment. Gold is also a good editor for Web publishers in the UNIX or Linux environment, where good editors are few and far between.

FrontPage

FrontPage, shown in Figure 20.3, is a high-quality product that provides a dizzying array of features that help create an entire Web presence. Every HTML 3.0 tag and Microsoft-specific tags are supported to the fullest extent. What will be the most important aspect of FrontPage to Web developers is the ability to map out a site visually in a flowchart style, as opposed to having to write on scraps of paper, like many programmers do. The editor auto-verifies links on the page to make sure that they are not dead links and changes the HTML for links if you change the name or location of a file. The editor also contains a built-in "To Do" list, which allows you to keep track of what needs to be done to finish a page or site. As this product matures with version updates, it will be able to automate the task of adding Java applets and ActiveX controls, further easing the process of site creation and management.

FIGURE 20.3.
FrontPage.

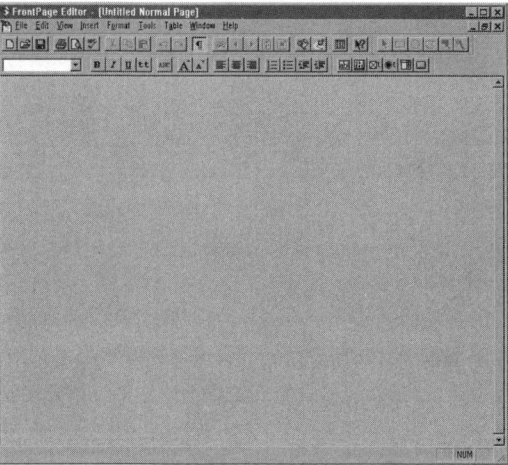

The frame support in FrontPage is better than many other editors. The process of creating frames is never fully intuitive, so any help offered is appreciated. FrontPage includes a Frames Wizard, which can help you make your frames work if you have the patience. You also can create custom templates if many pages on the site will have similar formats. This editor is better for users who have a working knowledge of HTML and plan to use advanced coding on their sites.

Near-WYSIWYG Tools

If you have some skill with HTML, if you like to be precise, or if you just want to get into the guts of your pages to make them work, near-WYSIWYG editors are what you want. This kind of editor lets you edit the actual HTML instead of manipulating text and images with icons and the mouse. The following are among the best near-WYSIWYG editors.

HotDog Pro

A classy name does not always mean a classy product. The reverse is also true. One of the best programs in the area of Near-WYSIWYG is HotDog Pro, published by Sausage Software. Aside from a juvenile-sounding name, it is a top-quality application from a company that is very prompt about updating its product as new HTML features become available. HotDog Pro, shown in Figure 20.4, includes an easy-to-use search-and-replace interface, as well as a customizable toolbar for common functions. Anything that can be automated by the use of questions in a dialog box has been, including color, font, and background attributes, as well as the final publishing of code to a site.

FIGURE 20.4.

HotDog Pro in action.

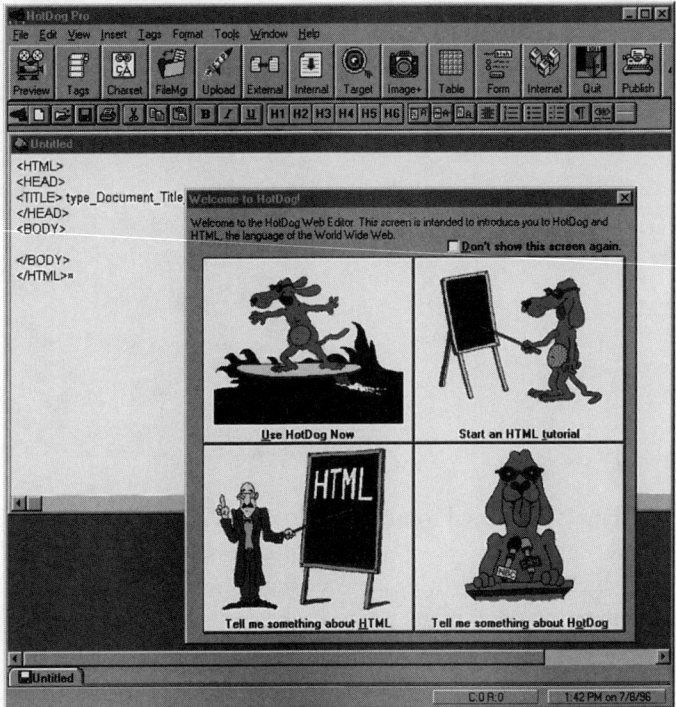

The form and table support in this editor is phenomenal. You can write complex HTML in seconds. HotDog Pro offers drag-and-drop support for images, links, and text files right into the body of the document. HotDog automatically saves your work and creates backups whenever it saves. It comes with excellent built-in tutorials and examples. This editor is great for beginners and experienced HTML publishers.

HoTMetaL

HoTMetaL, shown in Figure 20.5, is another editor that allows you a little more control over the Web page by having direct access to the HTML tags. Using the powerful toolbars, you can create pages and insert tags quickly. In fact, with HoTMetaL, you can import not only Microsoft Word but also Word Perfect, Ami Pro, and many other documents directly into the editor and convert them to HTML automatically. The tables and forms support is adequate, though a little clunky. You can view your tables right in the editor.

FIGURE 20.5.
HoTMetaL.

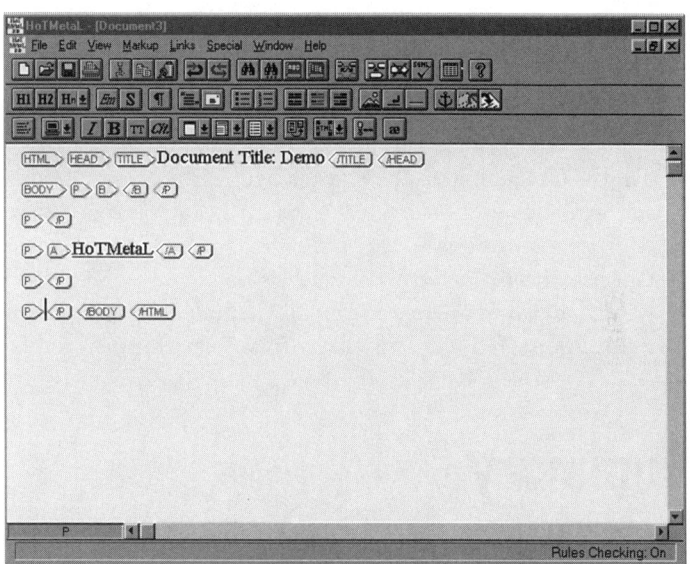

One nice feature of HoTMetaL is the ability to perform simple image editing from right within the editor. You can resize or reduce the number of colors in an image for faster download or do some special effects like embossing borders or making your buttons 3-D. HoTMetaL is also one of the only editors available with true support for frames. HoTMetaL is for users who want to create basic pages quickly and who have a working knowledge of HTML.

MCKEON & JEFFRIES

Most of the information McKeon & Jeffries wanted to put up on its intranet was documents created in Microsoft Word. For this reason, and because the firm eventually planned to use Internet Explorer on all its machines within one year, the most economical and efficient HTML editor to use was Internet Assistant. The intranet administrators merely had to install the program and then save all the files they wanted to publish in the new format. After that, combing through the documents and inserting links where appropriate was a simple matter. Most of the several hundred pages of information was converted and ready to go within a few hours.

For future projects, however, the systems administrator has purchased HotDog Pro. She likes the Windows 95 interface and the ability to perform easy searches and replaces when making a change. She also likes the table support, which is very important for an accounting firm, whose needs often include producing complex columns of figures.

THE SPORTING GOODS AND APPAREL ASSOCIATION

The SGAA had less need for an HTML editor, as most of the pages on their intranet site are dynamically generated. To produce template pages for the consultants to work with as they wrote the code for the site, however, the SGAA staff likes HTML Assistant best. It provided a simple and fast interface for them to tweak pages any way they wanted, down to the smallest nuance. Although most editors tried to guess what they wanted done, HTML Assistant let them experiment with different solutions with ease.

Summary

Like the rest of the industry surrounding intranets and the Internet, the editor market is rapidly changing and growing. New products seem to be introduced almost as fast as you can learn the old ones. Because new products are introduced does not mean that you must upgrade to the latest and greatest products. If a 1.0 product version works well in an organization, for instance, you may find no pressing need to move on to 2.0. A single person or a group of people within an organization's intranet structure should be responsible for evaluating new products as they come out. Newer products, much like new versions of word processors, have features to ease the creation of content and make it more visually appealing. Much of the innovation is in the form of shareware or trialware that you can download from the Web for a free evaluation period. Do not disregard these products even if they come from new companies or even from computer hobbyists.

As for your decision to use WYSIWYG versus Near-WYSIWYG, the authoring tools industry is moving toward a more graphically oriented model, so WYSIWYG products will see the most innovation. The decision regarding which product to use is in important one, but fortunately, if you decide that a product is not powerful enough for your needs, you suffer no real penalty besides the cost of buying a new editor. The free offerings are good enough if most of your work is simply reformatting existing documents for Web use. If you must do more detailed work, FrontPage or HotDog is your best bet.

Creating a Dynamic Site

21

by Matthew Handy and Matthew Baird

IN THIS CHAPTER

- The dynamic site **320**
- Inputting data **322**
- Storing data **328**

When building your intranet, keep in mind that you want your site to be dynamic and interactive. Making your site dynamic will make it more functional and lively to the users. The users should have the ability to interact with the site by adding and extracting data. This chapter focuses on creating a dynamic, rather than static, site. Static information has been predetermined by the site developers and exists only in the form determined by them. For example, HTML text files and graphics that don't integrate with the user's data input are static.

A dynamic site might be administered by a team or an individual, but its structure and its functions encourage and allow users to manipulate the data and to communicate with other users. Your goal should be to offer the opportunity for interaction, data manipulation, and communication, while still keeping the site operational and secure. It's a challenge, but your intranet won't be fully realized unless you work hard to incorporate some dynamic functions.

The functions that will make your site dynamic are all functions you've used previously or that you read about in earlier chapters. But now is the time for some creativity. This is where you should determine your intranet's functions and limits. The exciting part of building an intranet is that you can create a site that is entirely specific to the needs and the goals of your company. If you employ the right techniques and functions, your site will express your company's style, not just through graphics, but through user interaction. Your intranet should be as unique as your company.

The Dynamic Site

Let's look at an example of the development of a dynamic intranet. The board of directors of a floral company with stores in 10 different locations has decided to redesign its current Web site, which is a simple home page listing the names, addresses, and phone numbers of the stores in a static HTML file. The directors have decided that the site should be expanded to allow more options, not only for the public, but for the employees as well.

The primary internal goal is to allow the employees of the 10 stores to use the site to communicate with each other. The stores employ clerks, managers, delivery persons, and floral designers. The needs of each class (or type) of employee should be incorporated into the site. First, I'll look at the needs of each type of employee, and then I'll talk about what techniques and tools are available for meeting the goals of the board of directors and the needs of the employees.

Clerks will use the site to record financial data about the stores' sales and to update the product inventory (because they are responsible for maintaining a steady stock of greeting cards and gifts). Along with all the inventory, clerks might also record the number of hours they work each week; the site would take the place of the time-clock system currently in use. Clerks also could use the site to communicate with clerks from the other locations. Because some of the stores are near one another, employees—especially the clerks—shift from store to store as necessary.

The managers will use the site to administer payroll for all the employees and to create weekly schedules (all the employees will be entering requests for days off into the site). Managers also will use the site to keep the employees up-to-date with the amount of work and the type of work that will be needed for particularly busy times of the year, such as holidays. For example, because Mother's Day is one of the more lucrative holidays for florists, managers will want to send information to the employees about the strategies for handling the influx of business during that week. More than the data used by the others, the data manipulated by the managers will need to be secured so that sensitive data such as salaries and time-off requests will not be accessible to everyone. Therefore, a password system needs to be implemented for the databases that the managers will be accessing.

The site will be especially useful to delivery personnel. Directions and maps to office buildings of frequent clients will be posted on the site, and they will be easily available to delivery personnel when they are training new drivers. The status of delivery personnel would be updated regularly throughout the day. For example, the destination of a delivery person is entered into the site when the clerk who receives the order fills out the invoice. By means of a CGI (Common Gateway Interface) script, or program communicating with a database, the current location of a particular delivery person can be tracked throughout the day. Managers could track this information by taking a "snapshot" of the delivery operations at particular times of the year (or even the day) and could use this information as a reference for developing employee schedules.

The stores' floral designers will benefit from the site as well. Diagrams and photographs of specialty bouquet arrangements will be available through either postings or downloadable files. The board of directors also wants to establish a designers' bulletin board so that "tips of the trade" can be communicated from the design team in one store to design teams in other stores. When one designer creates a specialty design for a particular holiday, the site will allow for an immediate posting of a photo, a diagram, and written instructions, all of which will allow designers in other stores to implement the new arrangement immediately.

All of this sounds wonderful, and the advantages are obvious. But what disadvantages are there to developing an intranet like the one the floral board wants to create? For one thing, the intranet administrator must learn the technicalities and techniques of establishing and maintaining such a dynamic site. Issues of quality, security, technical ability, and expertise are important. The bottom line is that the intranet has to be useful, not only in its operations, but in its psychological appeal. Otherwise, the employees won't participate, leaving the site static.

Another concern for the board and the site developers is how to draw a division between the internal site, which will be used by the employees, and the public site, which will be used by individuals who want to place orders or simply learn about the company. Because some of the information, such as a customer order or complaint, will traverse from external to internal, the public and the private must be united, and the site developer must determine a way to allow unity without jeopardizing security.

A secure dynamic intranet that unites public and private access can be established if the intranet builder is creative and knowledgeable about what operations to include on the site. In fact, a dynamic intranet should be more secure than a static one, because the contents of the pages are determined by the users and the scripts. The pages do not exist as files on the server, vulnerable to break-ins. In fact, the pages do not exist until the user requests them, and they cease to exist when the user has obtained the needed information and logged off the server. Another advantage of creating a dynamic intranet: its nature requires that the developers use databases as a means of organizing the data. Having information in a database makes it easier to manipulate later should you change platforms, redevelop the site, or expand company operations. It increases your flexibility in terms of how you capture, manage, and analyze data. The way in which you choose to store your data is important: what you do now will affect the stability, security, and potential of your intranet.

Inputting Data

A dynamic intranet depends on the steady flow of data, the bulk of which is input by the users. Let's go back to the floral shop. If the model that the board wants to see is developed, the employees will be entering quite a bit of important data into the site every working day. Information about costs and assets, employee hours, customer orders, and inventory cannot be put to risk by a faulty computer operation. An intranet that is entrusted with such information must be able to accept and organize the data securely and efficiently.

Begin by thinking about what types of data the users will input. Most likely, your intranet will contain the three types of data input methods outlined here, including data from e-mail and message boards. The floral-shop model allows the employees to communicate with one another and with the managers, not only by e-mail but also through electronic bulletin boards, which the Internet community refers to as discussion databases or listservs. Commercially available programs will give site developers what they need in order to establish a discussion database on an intranet. Think of these as group Web pages. In the floral shops, employees from each division have a discussion database geared especially for their questions and needs. The data travels from the user to the database and then potentially out to all users. The data can be archived as text files. It's possible to develop an archive of the static messages and postings and integrate them into a dynamic page. For example, the employees on the floral-design bulletin board could access the archive for a listing of Mother's Day bouquet samples from previous years. Look for software that allows you to establish a discussion thread so that you will have a means of organizing the text.

Inventory Data

These datasheets list available product stock or any other type of inventory or employee information; they can be organized with a spreadsheet program, like Microsoft Excel. The floral shop requires that each of the 10 stores keep an individual inventory datasheet, but the board wants to build a common inventory database for the company intranet. This way, a clerk would access the site when looking to see whether a product not available in his store is available in another. The clerk then could immediately post a message requesting the needed product. Your intranet should allow employees to input inventory data. How the data will be stored and manipulated is discussed later in this chapter.

Static Data

Even the most dynamic intranet will contain a fair amount of static data, such as the employee handbook or memos that likely would be in text or HTML files. The problem with static data, however, is that discerning old data from new data can be difficult. For this reason, you should establish a way to tag or mark static data with a time stamp or date indicator that can be posted on the site. In the floral shop, the delivery personnel's directions and the bouquet diagrams for the designers, such as the one shown in Figure 21.1, are examples of static files.

FIGURE 21.1.
An HTML static file with the floral designer's instructions on creating a bouquet.

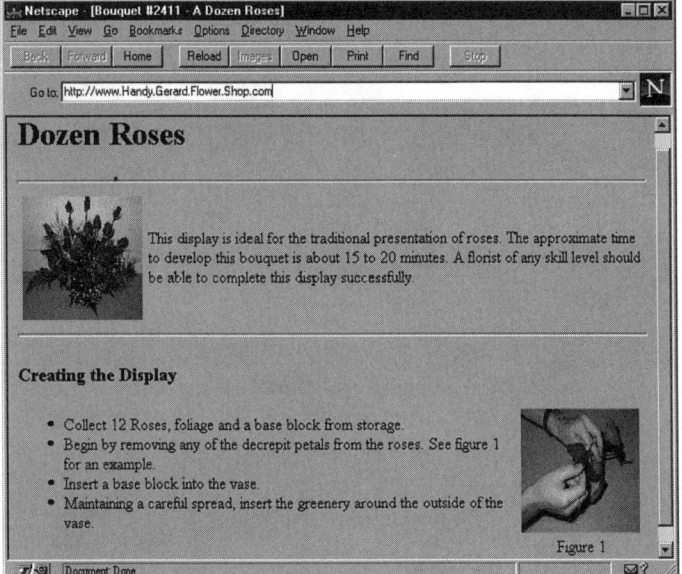

Image and Audio Data

In addition to the data input listed previously, users might input other types of data onto the company intranet. Images or audio files are an example of user-input data that could dynamically enhance your site. The creation and manipulation of image and audio files are getting easier. Many companies have computer cameras, which operate in a way that's similar to Polaroid cameras. After taking a snapshot, the battery-powered camera is connected to the computer workstation through a serial port. By means of a simple software application, the image usually can be pulled up and saved as a JPEG (Joint Photographic Experts Group) file, like the one shown in Figure 21.2, or a GIF (Graphics Interchange Format) file, like the one shown in Figure 21.3. The entire process of taking a photo and creating a file that can be input into an intranet is often less than 10 minutes. Image input is especially useful for creating easily updatable catalogs. The designers at the floral shop might post GIFs or JPEGs to their bulletin board as a way to exhibit newly designed arrangements or to show examples of particular breeds of flowers.

FIGURE 21.2.

A JPEG image of a flower arrangement.

FIGURE 21.3.

A GIF visual diagram of constructing a flower arrangement.

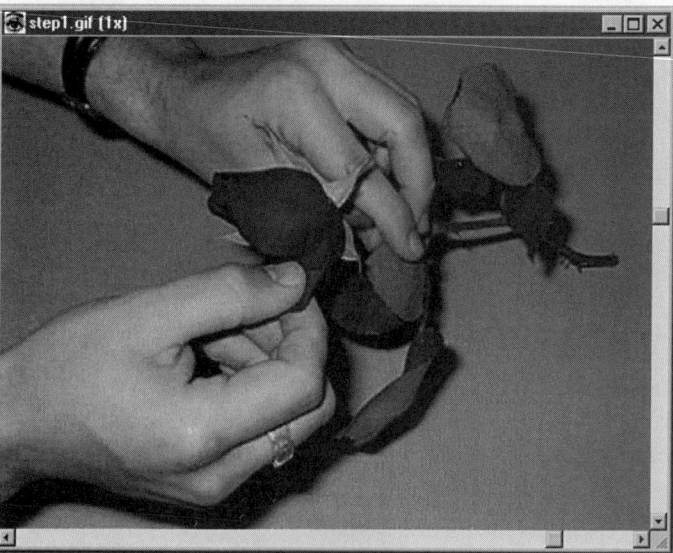

Audio and video files can also be captured and transformed into Web-compatible files. Many commercially available software programs give instructions on how to make files that can be easily input into a Web server. RealAudio (http://www.realaudio.com) has developed a plug-in player that will play audio files from a browser as fast as they are captured. Audio files are especially useful for companies that want to make conference speeches available on their intranets. Both image and audio files can be input in ways similar to the methods used for text files. A dynamic intranet will incorporate all types of user data input and will have the flexibility to incorporate new file types as they come along.

Above all, remember that your goal is to have all the users of the site interact with it by inputting data. The more user input you have, the more potential you have for developing a site that is truly dynamic. Encouraging user input means making input easy for people who do not have much computer experience. Therefore, you'll want to be selective about the applications and functions you include on your intranet. Let's go over what's available to you.

E-Mail and FTP

You will most certainly have an e-mail system operating on your intranet. E-mail is the heart of Internet communication. It's a function many people feel comfortable using and want to use. Its popularity stems from its capability to communicate directly without interrupting the recipient. Users are notified when e-mail arrives and are left to decide when they want to read it. Besides setting up every user with an e-mail account, you'll want to encourage e-mail communication by creating mail-oriented functions such as topic listservs, which are e-mail implementations of discussion databases. Various software programs exist on the different network platforms, and listserv functionality often is included with Internet mail servers, along with standard e-mail functionality.

In the floral shop, the clerks might have a listserv group in which they communicate with one another about events taking place in the stores. Listservs almost always revolve around a specific topic, so you might set them up in a way to encourage discussion on topics that will help to develop employee creativity and, in turn, morale. A delivery driver might note that a stretch of highway has been closed for construction. Another driver (or any member of that listserv group) could suggest an alternative route. This conversation would be seen by all members of the group, so all drivers would know that the highway was closed and would learn of possible alternative routes.

These messages received at the listservs can be archived by the site operators and easily can be used to create dynamic pages about the topic when need arises. For example, if the managers at the floral shops are having a meeting to plan the Christmas season, quick access to the listserv discussions from the year before would be helpful. If the clerk listserv has been active, the managers will be able to access the entries, read them, and consider the previous Christmas seasons' challenges and successes when developing the new company strategy. But if the discussion list has not been active, very little data will be available, and the managers might be less likely to look for similar data as a reference for future meetings. Therefore, it's important to utilize the information gained from the listservs and to reinforce their value within your organization to encourage use.

Besides e-mail and listservs, you'll want the users of your intranet to put data and files onto the server so that the server can process them, or so that other users can access or download them. For example, the datasheets containing daily customer figures for each floral shop can be saved to the server by the clerks at specified times during the workday. Later, the managers can incorporate the files into the common datasheet along with maintaining the individual store datasheet. The transfer of these files from the clerk to the manager can be performed by FTP (file transfer protocol), which is covered extensively in Chapter 27, "FTP: Sharing Files." For large documents, you'll want the users to use FTP as opposed to HTTP (hypertext transfer protocol) forms, because FTP is faster. FTP moves data in a raw data stream from point A to point B with no need for interpretation (as opposed to HTTP forms, which require interpretation). For example, the 10 floral shops all keep their inventories in an Excel spreadsheet. On the main server, the data is compiled into one big spreadsheet. Each store (point A) uses FTP to upload spreadsheets to the common location on the main server (point B). After the data has arrived at point B, it is secured in the server, accessible only to those who have the appropriate passwords. When the server has idle time, or at a preselected time, the server can process the datasheets and generate the company datasheet. The site administrators have the job of assigning users different levels of access when using FTP.

FTP is not the only means by which a user can send files across the Internet. Most mail programs and Web browsers have an attach-file feature. File attachments arrive with e-mail messages. The users of your intranet might use the attach-file feature to send files to one another as well as to the server for site maintenance. For instance, one of the designers in the floral-shop chain could send instructions on the care of a particular plant variety to a designer in another shop. Along those same lines, downloadable files should be made available to users. The administrator would want to create topic-specific FTP directories from which users can download information. It's easiest to facilitate FTP downloads through the Web browser. This makes FTP transparent to the user. Making the files accessible to anonymous users makes it easier to administer the site but also limits the data that is available to users. Anonymous FTP allows users to access areas with a password. It is important to realize, however, that without a password requirement, anyone can access the information. This is why you must evaluate your needs and apply the appropriate levels of security. In the case of the flower shop, the appropriate access might be write access with no ability to read. This level of security would allow all users to drop off files but not read or access any of the files already there. This is similar to a night deposit box. For security reasons, when you configure your server, don't put the upload directory in a place where the user can later execute a file he uploaded. If you do, a malicious user could upload an application that formats your hard drive and then execute it remotely. The directory should be separate from your hypertext documents and your CGI program. Remember that most "anonymous" accounts without specific settings are a two-way street (send and receive) allowing full access to all users.

WWW Forms

You can best develop the dynamic potential of your intranet with the use of forms. Most likely, you have visited Web sites that provide forms for user input. Surveys, orders, and customer complaints and comments all can be input via an online form like the one shown in Figure 21.4. Creating such forms is not as difficult as you might think, and almost all browsers support them. You will find commercially available programs that make the generation and execution of forms simple. Features such as radio buttons and pull-down windows can be incorporated at your discretion. Forms can be static or dynamic. When you use a form to capture information, clicking submit on the screen sends the information to the server. The developer of the intranet must then handle the arrival of this information. Some Web servers allow you to link a form directly to a database. In most cases, you will want to perform some kind of action with the data besides just storing it. To do this, you will have to write a script or a program that communicates with the form by using a standard called the Common Gateway Interface.

FIGURE 21.4.
A Web browser with a floral form.

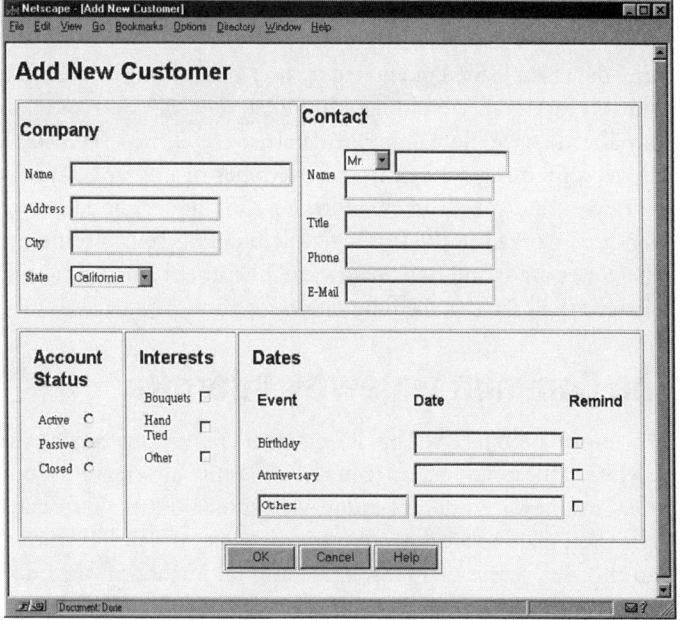

Forms have an advantage over e-mail in that you have more control over the way in which the data arrives to the site administrators. This ensures that the correct information is captured in the right places. Enhancements like JavaScript even allow the developer to check the user's input before submitting it. This is generally called *masking* data. Creating a database with forms is easier than creating one from e-mailed information or uploaded files, because all users of the form enter the data in the same manner. You might, however, lose some ability to process the data at the server's convenience. Because forms are connection oriented, the data they transmit must be dealt with immediately, so you'll want to have a CGI-based program generating the form response.

Successful use of forms requires that you determine what needs your company has that are best suited for online forms. Surveys are an example of a user-input function that works well with forms, because they usually require only the entry of single letters or numerals, which can be easily transformed into database fields. The floral shop chain might use forms in the employee intranet not only for surveys, but as a "suggestion box" or even a means by which to enter requests for days off or special assignments. The point is to use forms creatively for your company's needs and to develop them so that users will be able to input data successfully. Forms offer many ways to collect input and are the easiest to use for end users. As with many computer-related issues, however, taking responsibility away from end users increases the demand on the developers, but the scripts and programs required to capture the data from the forms are the trade-off.

Storing Data

After data is uploaded or entered by users, it must be stored. Several data-storing methods are available for intranet-building. Most likely you will store your data in a database, and you probably already have more than one database established. The floral shops have an inventory database containing a stock list of the types of greeting cards and gifts. They also have an employee database of names, addresses, and phone numbers for the people who are working or who have worked in the stores. While building your intranet, you should consider how and where user input and static data should be stored, and you also should consider what types of databases will serve as the foundation for your intranet.

The Common Gateway Interface

Any information received by the server will require instructions at the server on how to process it. Most of the functionality required to capture information is built into the Web server. These programs, however, do not know what to do with the information after they receive it. Programs that manipulate files received through e-mail or FTP run separately from the Web server and thus can receive data through common methods from a dedicated server. (In the case of e-mail, it could be a Simple Mail Transfer Protocol (SMTP) server or a Post Office Protocol (POP) server.) Programs that work with stored data from listservs also gather information via a dedicated server. The only different development challenge associated with intranets is the use of the Common Gateway Interface standard to communicate between an HTML form and the program residing on the server that manipulates the data. The data from the HTML form isn't delivered directly to the processing software (the CGI). Rather, it is parsed into a common format that every CGI-compliant Web server can read. The following is an example of CGI data encoded in a URL that a Web server would understand:

```
http://www.abc.com/cgi-bin/test.exe?First_Name=Stacey&Last_Name=McKellar
```

The CGI formatted data is then fed to the script/program, which then handles that data and returns the results to the Web server. The Web server formats the returned data as requested and returns the document to the client (browser).

The Common Gateway Interface is a series of platform-independent rules that govern how information received by a Web server from a form is handed over to a program or script for processing. In turn, it also defines the rules by which the script or program communicates with the server and, ultimately, the user at the other end. These rules are not particularly complicated, but without them, every Web server would communicate differently with programs. To ensure that scripts (and programs when possible) can be used in different computing environments, the CGI was established. This multiplatform capability means, however, that the solution might not be ideal for all operating systems. Most popular Web servers have their own specific implementation of the CGI, but all support the international CGI as well.

Taking information from a database and displaying it works in several steps. First, through a search system, you must locate the desired information in the database. You can either buy search system software or develop your own. Often SQL (simple query language) inside a CGI script or program can achieve this objective. After the information is located, it must be presented. If the data is timely, the correct information from the database should be put into HTML dynamically and sent to the user. This approach creates "virtual" HTML files, which are sent but never stored. On the other hand, if other people might be interested in the same information, the HTML file could be generated and then stored for later access. A good example of this is working through the results of the discussion databases and turning the comments and questions into HTML.

Storing information in a database can be as simple as developing a Web form that uses a CGI program to place information into a database. It also could involve a program that receives e-mail and extracts the important data and then communicates with the database through a program or script. These methods require some programming or scripting and are specific to the type of database in use.

At some point, you will likely be faced with the job of integrating old databases into a structure that is more appropriate for intranet functions. Database administration can sometimes be a difficult and complex job. Moving data has many rules and restrictions, but at a very high level, an intranet developer could get information from existing databases in several ways. The simplest way would be to access the data from the old system directly by using a CGI between the server and the database. This method is convenient provided that the data you have is easy to access and that it supports a script or programming language that can access the data. If, however, your database is older and doesn't support such features, export the data from the old system into a type supported by the new system, and then access it using a CGI program or built-in methods. This works if you can find a database type to which the old file will export and the new system will import. The newer your original system, the easier this job will be.

Another slightly different option is exporting the data from the old system into a commonly used data type, then importing it into the new system and accessing it using a CGI or built-in methods.

Flat File Databases

When working with databases, keep in mind the distinction between flat file (ASCII-based) databases and relational databases. A flat file database consists of simple ASCII text. All data in these files is nonrelational. Consider them a collection of information within a file rather than in a database. Flat file databases work in much the same way as the "merge fields" function on popular word processors like WordPerfect. The delimiting factors (such as commas or tabs) are the only indicators for how the fields should be meshed together. The following is a flat file containing contact information for three separate people in comma-separated value format:

```
"Smith","Mike","J.","202-555-1234","134 A Street","Washington","DC"
"Baron","Ed","","703-555-3164","1616 Mary St.","Fairfax","VA"
"Franklin","Stacey","L.","301-555-1143","34 Palace St.","Bethesda","MD"
```

Flat file databases came about as a way to manipulate text files around a hard drive. From a performance point of view, adding to them sequentially is fairly quick, but you don't want to take things out of them, and you don't want to search through them. It's easy and inexpensive to program for a flat file database. But these types of databases are slow to search through. The advantage of flat file databases is that they can function as a prototype for analyzing data, but generally only in a single-user environment. Another advantage is that they are portable and can easily cross platforms, making it simple to mail flat file databases electronically.

The main drawback with flat files is you must deal with locking them. Basically, only one person can write to a flat file at a time. Imagine an airline ticket system that could sell two people the same seat but only record one name. To prevent this problem, a flat file database must have some way of locking records. Because multiple CGI programs can be running at the same time and because they generally do not communicate with each other without substantial programming, using a scripting language or a development language to implement locking is tough. But if locking isn't implemented and two people write to the file at the same time, the file becomes corrupt.

Relational Databases

The other type of database is the relational database. Relational databases contain a minimal amount of data to which another database can relate. Try Microsoft Access for an inexpensive, user-friendly relational database, an example of which is shown in Figure 21.5.

Some important aspects of a relational database system are the existence of a primary key and the relationships between tables. A primary key is an important constraint of uniqueness on a field. Since every value in this field is guaranteed to be unique, you can use it to relate to other tables. Choosing your primary key is important, because it should never change. A good primary key for a table containing data about a person would be a Social Security Number—it is guaranteed to be unique and unchanging.

FIGURE 21.5.

A complicated relationship as viewed in Microsoft Access.

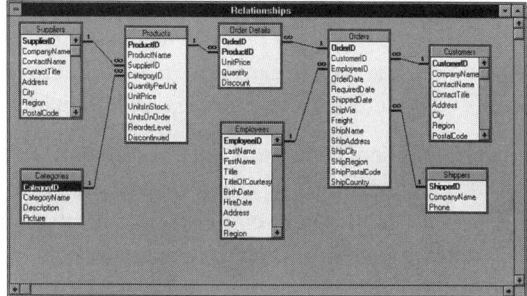

The relationship between tables describes how records in one table link to another. Consider a flower shop vendor list in which a company table has a primary key called COMPANY_ID and the contact information is kept in a different table with a primary key called CONTACT_ID. Each of these fields ensures that every company and contact is distinct. Linking a contact to a company requires an additional field in the contact table that points to the correct company. This field, called CONTACT_COMPANY_ID, would contain the corresponding COMPANY_ID value from the Company table. This means that if IBM had COMPANY_ID = 5, and you added a new contact for IBM, the new contact would have the field CONTACT_COMPANY_ID = 5.

One ideal use of a relational database is a situation in which the same information must appear in multiple places—such as a vendor list. Suppose that every contact you enter in your database also stores the name of the company, and multiple users are entering this information. If one of the users spelled the company's name wrong when entering it, a query wouldn't find all the company's employees. However, using a relational approach, you would create one instance of a company and link all the contacts to that company. If the company's name changes, it changes for all contacts. Likewise, if the address changes, and the address is associated with the company, only one record changes, but all contacts will have the newer address. This is the principle on which relational databases are built.

Relational databases should be used if you have a database existing in multiple tables (the flat file equivalent would be multiple files). There is little you can do with a relational database that you can't do with a flat file and a lot of programming. Relational tables allow for a multiple index (you can sort by names or by any other factor you've established). Indexes make searches faster than those performed through a flat file database, and make searching specifically for something like a name or phone number possible. Indexes also decrease the speed of updates and deletes. The use of indexes is something best left to a competent database designer.

Security is always an issue with corporate data, even on an intranet. Remember to integrate security into the database. Flat files don't inherently support security. You could develop your own custom code, but why reinvent the wheel? Most relational database systems handle security superbly, even down to a per-column privilege level. One drawback of using a relational database is that it requires that the person who's designing it have a thorough understanding of what he or she is doing. A poorly designed database could cause data corruption or data loss. Because there is only one copy of each piece of data, developing correct relations between tables is essential. It's integral that the primary key be an unchanging value.

Another advantage of some relational database systems is that they allow the storage of binary data and pictures and sound clips, which are called BLOBs (binary large objects). The Oracle RDBMS is an example of a high-end relational database system that supports BLOBs. The company has developed a Web server that integrates closely with its database. The Oracle Web server provides a fast gateway between the Oracle database and a Web browser. Instead of using the CGI, Oracle moves data by using code specific to that product. This method is very quick, but Oracle-specific; the Oracle Web server, however, supports the slower (but standard) CGI. Another RDBMS product to consider is Illustra, which is an object-relational database that is good at handling object-type inputs beyond standard text and numbers. Illustra can serve audio or video files, and it is especially useful for companies that work with multimedia. Illustra's big advantage is that it can serve video clips. Different segments can be pulled from the clip as instructed by a CGI script. Illustra's architecture is based on plug-ins; for example, you can develop and "plug in" a custom Web server interface. Illustra's plug-in system makes it very easy and inexpensive to upgrade; even third parties can write the plug-ins. The plug-in structure supports additional data types and provides new services. These could be data types and services that aren't yet available.

Deciding how to store your intranet's data is an important concern. Not only will your data-storing methods affect the operation of your intranet, but they also will determine your intranet's potential to incorporate technological developments as they become available.

Summary

To make an intranet more valuable, it is ideal to include as much dynamic information as possible. Dynamic development of a Web site means that the screens are generated when they are needed, not necessarily ahead of time. This means the information is current—and currency is critical.

Dynamic sites, which are built around data, are more complicated to build but are far more valuable than static sites. To build a successful site, one must not only display data but capture it as well. Keep in mind when communicating that the type or format of information being communicated will determine how it is communicated. FTP is an ideal choice for transferring information that is in a file or in a specific format generated by an application, whereas e-mail is a better choice for transmitting informal information that does not need to be processed. If input control is required and information must be processed and stored, WWW forms are the best choice.

After this data is captured, it should be stored in a database. If information is received from e-mail or FTP, processing all received information whenever the computer isn't busy is fine. For more complicated file transfers that must be dealt with immediately, WWW forms utilizing the CGI are ideal. However you access the database, you must choose the right application for the job. For simple cases that require minimal access and poor performance, I recommend flat file manipulation. For more complicated situations, relational databases offer great power and compatibility at a reduced price. Finally, some databases also are integrated into Web servers, making them particularly useful.

Remember that each problem has its own solution. No two problems are alike. But understanding the key issues about working with dynamic information—whether displaying it, capturing it, or storing it—allows you to make the right decisions as tough questions arise.

Creating a Functional Site

22

by Matthew Handy and Matthew Baird

IN THIS CHAPTER

- Manipulating data **336**
- Transmitting functionality **344**

In Chapter 21, "Creating a Dynamic Site," you learned how to generate and store data. If you're encouraging users to input data, and you're thinking carefully about how to store that data, eventually you will want to do something with all the information. This chapter focuses on methods in which you can creatively manipulate your data with a set of tools. To create a functional site, you need to know what is available in the world of Web languages and development application programs. You also need to know a little about how those languages and programs work so that you can choose the tools that will best suit your needs. Additionally, you need to know what kinds of programs and applications are currently under development because any of them might affect the future of your intranet. After reading this chapter, you should have a good understanding of the tools and techniques necessary to manipulate both the static and dynamic data of your intranet effectively.

Manipulating Data

Proper handling of the data generated by and input into your intranet requires that you work (or at least familiarize yourself) with the programming languages available to your system and with other applications that are especially useful for Web development.

Shell Scripts

If your server uses a UNIX operating system, you can manipulate its functions with the shell. A *shell* is like a series of operating system command-line instructions put into a single file for execution all at once. This is known as *batch processing* and is similar to a DOS .BAT file. Of the many examples of shells, the more popular include Bourne, C, BASH, POSIX (Windows NT), and Korn. If you are unsure which shell is installed on your UNIX server, refer to your original documentation or ask your system administrator.

> **TIP**
>
> In order to effectively use shell scripts, you must know which shell you are using. Type the following line and press Enter:
>
> ```
> echo $RANDOM
> ```
>
> The Bourne shell will return a blank line. The C shell will return the following:
>
> ```
> RANDOM: Undefined variable
> ```
>
> Both the Korn shell and BASH return a random number. To further discern between the Korn shell and BASH, type `help`. BASH will return a list of command descriptions.

Each shell reads your commands and processes them. Each shell has variables as well as sequence, selection, and repetition structures; the shell itself is not UNIX. Many shells are built on one another, so after you learn the commands for one, the others will be easier to learn. *Shell scripts* are the simplest programs to write; they are text files containing scripting commands that will—when executed—transmit data. Listing 22.1 shows a simple shell script. One common use of shell scripts is to allow a system administrator to schedule unattended reboots or shutdowns of an operating system. Other types of functions also can be performed with shell scripts. You can, for example, write a script that lists the process information for a user who is logging into the system. Knowing which user is currently logged on to your intranet lets you dynamically serve data to him based on his user profile. In the case of department-specific data, you could group the users and present data—such as news items—differently to the marketing department than to the research and development team. The intelligent delivery of information quickly becomes important when you're dealing with large amounts of data. Shell scripts are quick and dirty. You are somewhat limited, however, to the commands that are allowed by the shell (for example, you can't use programming methods such as abstract data types).

Listing 22.1. A simple shell script.

```
echo Content-type: text/plain
echo
echo "CGI/1.2 (POSIX shell, args.sh) report:"
echo
echo $# "args:"
echo $1 $2 $3 $4 $5 $6 $7 $8
echo
echo environment variables:
echo REQUEST_METHOD:    $REQUEST_METHOD
echo SCRIPT_NAME:       $SCRIPT_NAME
echo QUERY_STRING:      $QUERY_STRING
echo PATH_INFO:         $PATH_INFO
echo PATH_TRANSLATED:   $PATH_TRANSLATED
if $REQUEST_METHOD = "POST" then
    echo CONTENT_TYPE:     $CONTENT_TYPE
    echo CONTENT_FILE:     $CONTENT_FILE
    echo CONTENT_LENGTH:   $CONTENT_LENGTH
    echo
    echo ---- begin content ----
    cat
    echo
    echo ----- end content -----
    echo
fi
echo -- end of report --
```

In building your intranet, you will need to be aware of which shell or shells are on your server, as well as which shells you would like to add. In doing so, consider how much time you can dedicate to learning the language of a shell. Also consider what types of functions you want a shell to perform. You can find charts and tables offering information about the commands available for different shells online. You can find Usenet newsgroups revolving around particular shells, and you can always do a search through your Web browser. Adding the acronym "FAQ" to your searches is often helpful; for example, you might do a search for KORN shell FAQ. FAQ stands for "Frequently Asked Questions." Each newsgroup on Usenet has a FAQ.

After you are familiar with your server's shells, you may want to write scripts yourself. When you're designing scripts to be used for your intranet, you might use the language of your shell, or you might choose another scripting language. It is crucial that your scripts be robust and secure, because they will be exposed to a multitude of users every day. Writing your scripts to elegantly handle errors and deliver clear, concise, user-friendly error messages will educate the user as to the cause of the error and show him how to avoid the error in the future. Likewise, error messages provide invaluable information for the site administrator and developers, which will allow easier debugging of scripts. There is nothing more frustrating for a user than to have the Web browser return a page that says

```
HTTP: Web Server unable to handle request (37x938), have a nice day!
```

You're probably wondering how the client's browser submits all this data to the server, seeing as how there are so many different hardware and software platforms. The Common Gateway Interface (CGI) handles all cross-platform communications.

The CGI works by handling information requests and returning appropriate documents or creating documents generated by a script, translating incoming messages into a standard format that the Web server can parse. A gateway is necessary when the two languages communicating have no native method of communication. Gateways belong to a class of software known as "middleware." Middleware is a blanket term for any distributed software that supports the interaction of clients (in this case, the Web browser) and servers (for example, the HTTP server). It is important to note that middleware, and thus the CGI, does not include the software that processes the actual request or service; that is the script's job. Middleware does not support the user interface; that is the browser's job. The simplest gateway is a repeater that takes a message and repeats it: it solves distance problems but cannot translate. Aside from the Common Gateway Interface (CGI), the most common gateway you will come across is a mail gateway.

CGI is a standard that defines the format of data being passed from client to server. CGI scripts, many of which are written in Perl (you learn about Perl later in this chapter), are especially useful for the Web because they can return a variety of documents to the client. A script or program that uses the CGI to move data between the client and the server is often referred to as a CGI. Through complicated programming, CGIs can transmit images and audio clips. However, they excel in both performance and ease of programming when they are returning simple character data—for example, a page of HTML. It is important to note that CGIs are server-intensive. Many CGIs executing on one machine can bog down performance.

One prerequisite for this dynamic exchange is that the client (the one "asking") must know what type of document the host (the one "giving") is sending so that it can be presented in the appropriate usable format, perhaps as an HTML file.

Currently, the CGI is the most popular way to create dynamic HTML documents. The CGI can use almost any scripting language, but again, Perl is the most common. Other languages used to write CGIs include C, C++, Visual Basic, and even Java. CGI programs are independent processes; they go into action every time your server receives a request from a client (the

Web browser). An excellent site on the Web for learning about the CGI is

http://inwfdux1.rug.ac.be/cgi/primer.html

You do not have to be an expert programmer or have a Ph.D. in computer science to manipulate data with scripts. What you do need, however, is knowledge about the languages with which functional Web-compatible scripts can be written and some good instruction. If you already have some knowledge about scripting and want to learn more, then you might refer to online tutorials for additional guidance. You can find a UNIX and C Shell tutorial, for example, at

http://www.eng.hawaii.edu/Courses/C.unix/page-09.html

Perl

In this section, you will take a more in-depth look at one of the most popular scripting languages for the Web, one that is considered to go hand-in-hand with CGI: Perl (which stands for Practical Extraction and Report Language). Perl was developed by Larry Wall, who originally wanted to write a language with which to manipulate data gathered from Usenet newsgroups into reports (hence the name). His idea caught on, and Perl is now a key language for manipulating data from the Internet. Currently, Web developers use Perl to write CGI scripts that run on Web servers.

Perl, which is an interpreted language, is slow in comparison to a compiled language such as C/C++. An interpreter performs the operations implied by the source program. Unlike interpreted languages, compiled languages such as C++ use a *compiler*, which is a program that reads a set of commands written in one language—the *source* language—and translates it into a binary executable that can be used only by the target platform. You cannot reverse this process. Once compiled, an executable cannot be translated back into source code. Therefore, remember to archive all your source code in a safe place if you'll want to alter the executable in the future. Perl always exists as a text file, making it easy and quick to modify. A compiled program written in C exists on the server as a machine language executable, which is unreadable to most humans. To make a change to a compiled program, you must have access to the source code. After you modify the source code, you must recompile to generate the new executable. Compiled programs may sound like too much trouble, but the performance gains can sometimes far outweigh the overhead required for compiling the executable. Use a compiled program when the functionality isn't going to change, or the CGI will be used frequently.

Another advantage of Perl is its ability to cross platforms. A Perl script can usually run on UNIX, Windows NT, Apple Mac, or other operating systems with equal success. Although this cross-platform capability is generally true, some machine- and OS-specific Perl libraries do exist.

A thorough knowledge of Perl is advantageous for intranet developers. Although the popularity of various scripting languages (especially when the Internet is concerned) is always fluctuating, you can rest assured that a Perl community will exist on the Web for quite a while. Four different Usenet newsgroups are dedicated to discussing its intricacies, and you can find a well-maintained Perl home page at

`http://www.perl.com/perl/index.html`

If you choose Perl as your CGI scripting language, be sure to check out cgi-lib.pl, the definitive CGI library for Perl, at

`http://www.bio.cam.ac.uk/cgi-lib/`

In addition, a number of specialty Perl tutorials are available online. Do a Web search to find one that best suits your needs.

The basic concept of Perl is similar to that of the shell programs. Like a shell script, a Perl script is a listing of Perl statements and definitions gathered into a text file. Listing 22.2 provides an example of what a simple Perl program looks like. For an output of this listing, visit

`http://www.wavelength.com/cgi-bin/envs.pl`

Listing 22.2. A simple Perl script that shows environment variables.

```perl
print"Content-type: text/html\n\n";
print"<pre>";
foreach (keys(%ENV)) {
    print "<BR>";
    print ("$_\t$ENV{$_}");
}
print "</PRE>";
```

Once you get the hang of writing Perl, you can use it to write scripts for the functions of your intranet. Forms are a common, yet powerful, example of a function that you can implement with Perl. Listing 22.3 shows a sample form written in Perl. For an output of this script, visit

`http://www.wavelength.com/cgi-bin/testform.pl`

Listing 22.3. Writing forms with Perl.

```perl
#!/perl -w- # -*- Perl -*-
# Author: M.Baird (baird@id1.com)
# Copyright (c) 1996 by Matthew J. Baird
#?Error Messages
$ErrorNoContent[0] = "Error: No Message Content";
$ErrorNoContent[1] = "All the message fields were blank.";
&main;
# Purpose: The main function of the program
sub main
{
    if($ENV{'CONTENT_LENGTH'})
    {
        &GetInputFields;
        if(!&VerifyInputFields)
        {
            exit(0);
        }
```

Creating a Functional Site
Chapter 22

```perl
            &FillOutForm;
        }
        else
        {
            # Argument to SendHeadOfDocument is the title
            &SendHeadOfDocument("Test Form");
            &SendForm;
        }
}
#?SendHeadOfDocument($title)
#
# Purpose: This sends a header back to the browser in preparation to display
# some kind of response to what the server did.

sub SendHeadOfDocument
{
    local(
            $title # The title of the response document
            ) = @_;
        print("Content-type: text/html\n\n");
        print("<head><title>$title</title></head>\n");
        print("<body>\n");
}
sub SendForm
{
    print("<BODY>\n");
    print("This is a test of a PERL form.<br>\n");
    print("<pre>\n");
    print("<hr>\n");
    print("<H1>Test Form</H2>\n");
    print("<FORM ACTION");
    print("=\"http://www.wavelength.com/cgi-bin/testform.pl\" METHOD=\"POST\">\n");
➥print("<p>\n");
    # User info
    print("<b>Print your name:</b>\n");
    print("<pre>\n");
    print("First:\t");
    print("<INPUT TYPE = \"text\" NAME = \"First\" SIZE = 30>\n");
    print("Middle:\t");
    print("<INPUT TYPE = \"text\" NAME = \"Middle\" SIZE = 30>\n");
    print("Last:\t");
    print("<INPUT TYPE = \"text\" NAME = \"Last\" SIZE = 30>\t");
    print("</pre>\n");
    print("<HR>\n");
    print("<INPUT TYPE=\"submit\" VALUE=\"Test Form\"></FORM></pre>\n");
}
#?GetInputFields(void)
#
# Purpose: Gets and sets all the fields sent from the browser to the server
sub GetInputFields
{
    local(
            $i,
            $length,
            $input,
            @input,
            $field,
            $value
```

continues

Listing 22.3. continued

```
        );
    $length = $ENV{CONTENT_LENGTH};
    $input = getc;
    for($i=2;$i<=$length;$i++)
    {
        $input .= getc;
    }
    @input=split(m¦&¦, $input);
    for($i=0;  $i<=$#input;$i++)
    {
        $input[$i] =~ s¦\+¦ ¦g;
        $input[$i] =~ s¦%(..)¦pack("c", hex($1))¦ge;
        ($field, $value) = split(m¦=¦, $input[$i]);
        # Stop people from using subshells to execute commands
        $value =~ s/~!/ ~!/g;
  #     $InputField{$field} = $value;
    }
    # continue to process information here.
}
```

Database Interface

If you choose to use Perl as a means for incorporating dynamic functions into your intranet, you might want to take advantage of Database Interface (DBI). DBI is a *database interface* for Perl, an extension that allows it to access databases, including relational databases. Generally, when people talk about databases these days, they are referring to relational databases. The DBI is just a library that gives the programmer a set of instructions he or she can use to access a database programmatically. A number of available libraries enable Perl to do complex math, graphics, and other extended operations; the DBI is simply another one of these libraries for database access.

Besides Perl and its extensions, you can use many other languages for writing scripts. If you want to write a script in a particular language, you should check on that language's capacity to function on the Web. Likewise, if you have work written in a language that's not as Web-compatible as you would like, consider rewriting it in a language like Perl. For a language to be used on the Web, it must be able to accept data via the STDIN and write to the STDOUT (C/C++-centric terms). CGIs were originally written on UNIX machines, which use the CGI. Calling this type of program a "CGI" is actually a misnomer because it isn't a type of program; rather, it's a format to receive data over the Internet.

Structured Query Language (SQL)

For writing scripts, you might also research other languages, such as the Structured Query Language, known as SQL. The disadvantage of SQL is that it is not a language that you can use to write CGIs directly. A CGI can use SQL, however, to query data out of a database and return that data in the form of a Web page. SQL talks strictly to databases.

SQL is a comprehensive database language; it has statements for data definition, query, and update. It is both a Data Definition Language (DDL) and a Data Manipulation Language (DML). You can embed SQL in Perl, C, or whatever language you're using for your CGIs.

Originally, SQL was called SEQUEL (for Structured English Query Language) and was designed and implemented at IBM Research as the interface for an experimental relational database system called System R. Currently, the ANSI standard is SQL2. Following are the query and results of an SQL call using the Oracle RDBMS:

```
SELECT    BDATE, ADDRESS
FROM      EMPLOYEE
WHERE     FNAME = 'Matthew' AND MINIT = 'J' AND LNAME = 'Baird'
```

The words in bold are SQL reserved words. The SELECT keyword precedes an attribute list, which is a list of attribute names whose values are to be retrieved by the query. The FROM keyword specifies a table list, which is a list of the relation (table) names required to process the query. The WHERE clause is a conditional (Boolean) search expression that identifies the tuples (a fancy word for row) to be retrieved by the query. Inside the WHERE clause you can use ANDs, ORs, and other conditional modifiers. This particular query retrieves the birthdate and address of the employee whose name is Matthew J. Baird. This query results in the following table with one row of data:

```
BDATE             ADDRESS
01/28/72          123 Fore St. Washington DC
```

Listing 22.4 is the skeleton of a CGI written in C that would submit an SQL query to the RDBMS.

Listing 22.4. A form that accesses a database using SQL.

```
int main ( int argc, char * argv[] )
{
    CString method = getRequestMethod();
    cout << "Content-type: text/html\n\n" << endl;
    if ( method != "POST" )
    {
        report_error(POST_ONLY);
    }
    else
    {
        SQLStatement = " SELECT BDATE, ADDRESS FROM EMPLOYEE
            WHERE FNAME = 'Matthew' AND MINIT = 'J' AND LNAME = 'Baird'";
    }
    return(0);
}
```

If you are interested in learning more about SQL, you can find information about it on the browse page at

```
http://heasarc.gsfc.nasa.gov/docs/xray/lx_user_guide/node46.html
```

Additionally, the site http://www.creditunions.com/callahan/cusearch/ shows a form accessing a database back end to deliver over 250 megabytes of data via the WWW. The WWW-RDBMS interface CGI was written in C++ and uses Microsoft Access as the RDBMS. Access is an excellent and inexpensive RDBMS for the end-user, but it doesn't have nearly the performance of the Oracle RDBMS. This CGI's excellent performance, considering the large amount of data, is partly attributable to the proper design of the database, as well as the efficient coding of the CGI.

When you're considering what languages to use to write scripts, you should build on your knowledge; use what you already know as your starting point. As you develop your intranet, you will learn more about how to move your data from point A to point B using both current and future languages.

Transmitting Functionality

As you probably already know, corporate use of the Internet has grown rapidly in the past few years. With that growth has come a demand for applications and databases that both internal and external intranet users can access easily and securely. Most corporations want to link employees, customers, and vendors together into a custom online network, while not risking the exposure of private information. At the same time, you want to keep your intranet safe from corrupt data that might be accidentally or intentionally sent to your site.

> **TIP**
>
> The Internet can provide an authoritative source of information for customers, but be cautious of the numerous informational pages available. Finding information on an IBM product at the IBM Internet site is more likely to be right than at "Joe's IBM Information Page o' Fun."

Fortunately, some application developers have taken on the task of providing the means by which corporations and organizations can build intranets that are secure and functional, as well as flexible to developing Web technology. These developers have handled their task by creating what could be considered a new genre of application programming, which is the subject of this section. In earlier chapters of this book, you learned about some of the increasingly sophisticated e-mail and discussion groups that you can include on your intranet. As the application technology develops, anticipate that you will be able to provide your intranet users with the ability to communicate designs for product plans, documents, and schedules, both functionally and securely. Electronic forms will automate even the most bureaucratic of processes, including the filing of purchase orders, health insurance claims, and order forms. Production tools such as spreadsheets and drawing and mapping programs will be made available in less cumbersome file formats, allowing for quick and safe exchange.

As the WWW has increased in popularity, it has become increasingly more TV-like. Just look at the growth of animated pages, more of which appear on the WWW every day. Some users think that the Web will develop into a media-rich forum that might surpass television in its capacities. For this to happen, Web developers will be concentrating on creating tools that will make sites more interactive and animated. The following sections focus on the types of Web applications and application resources that already are available and on how to incorporate them into an intranet.

Java

Java: A simple, object-oriented, distributed, interpreted, robust, secure, architecture neutral, portable, high-performance, multithreaded, and dynamic language.

—from "The Java Language: A White Paper," Sun Microsystems, Inc.

By now, you've most certainly heard about Java. Despite its trendy name, Java is truly a complete programming language—one that you should take seriously if you want to build a functional intranet. What's unique about the Java programming language is that it is both interpreted and compiled. In fact, it's as close to a compiled program as you can get without its being platform-dependent. Java works on any platform, be it Windows NT, Apple Macintosh, or others that have Java interpreters. The Java interpreter is generally part of your browser.

From the programming side, Java is object-oriented, like C++, and is virtually impossible to program using any other methodology (that is, it is procedural). Although it has been termed such, Java is not necessarily "the language for non-programmers." Much debate has ensued about the possibility of individuals without technical backgrounds learning Java's ins and outs. If you aren't enthusiastic about the idea of learning Java, be assured by the fact that Java's developer, Sun Microsystems, is willing to help you and everyone else in the learning process. To see a well-designed and helpful tutorial, visit

http://www.sun.com/sunsoft/Products/Developer-products/java/Workshop/index.html

Among the many things that differentiate Java from other programming languages is that the term "Java" is not an acronym. The original name of Java was "OAK," named after the large tree outside the developer's window. The Java moniker was given to make it a more "hip" and thus more marketable product. And, not surprisingly, the name was picked by the developers during a coffee break. You might be surprised to learn, however, that Java's origins are not rooted in the World Wide Web. The conception of Java came to one of its founders, Bill Joy, in the late 1970s—long before the Internet began to resemble its present self.

Java was supposed to be instrumental in the making of smart appliances, and it is still being touted as such. It also may be the language of choice for set-top boxes. Set-top boxes are often thought of as the next progression of the Web. A piece of hardware (the box) will sit on top of your TV set and will let you access information, movies, and games through your TV over the Internet.

As Java developed as a language, it became increasingly clear that it would be a key resource for developing Web application programs. Java programs produce *applets*, a cute term for an application that can be embedded within another application. You can include an applet in an HTML document to provide interactive, executable content on a Web page. To learn more about applets, how they work, and how you can include them on your intranet, go to EarthWeb's Gamelan page at http://www.gamelan.com.

Java applets are becoming popular, but they do have limitations. Applets are currently being used to produce high-end, glitzy graphics, sound, animation, and text formatting. Beware of poorly written or functionally useless "crapplets" that eat up bandwidth and take time to download. An applet on a home page, for instance, can flash as soon as mail arrives. You could use Java to write complex software packages such as relational database management systems or word processors. File input and output are generally restricted on applets, which means that a Java applet you view on someone's home page cannot read, write, delete, rename, or create a file on your local system. When you're running a local applet, however, the Web browser may relax many of these restrictions because local applets are deemed more trustworthy than network applets. You can alter browsers to allow intermediate applet security policies. This capability is of great interest if you're on an intranet because you could write an applet viewer that would place fewer restrictions on applets loaded from the intranet than those loaded from the Internet.

JavaScript

Whether or not you decide to learn Java, you'll no doubt deal with it at some point if you want to incorporate online applications into your intranet. But you might find yourself first working with a spin-off of Java called JavaScript. (Listing 22.5 shows a sample JavaScript in action.) JavaScript has a similar structure to Java, but the comparison ends here. Designed to handle events within an HTML screen, JavaScript can manipulate the appearance of the browser. JavaScripts can change the look of frames and windows. For example, you've probably seen those messages that run like LED displays in the bottom scroll bar of your browser. Those messages are examples of what JavaScript can do. Like Java, JavaScripts are also platform independent, but they can act only on objects within the browser window. Think of JavaScript as an HTML enhancement language: it is entirely a scripting language and therefore cannot create objects like the Java language.

Listing 22.5. JavaScript in action.

```
<!--JavaScript Code-->
<SCRIPT LANGUAGE="JavaScript">
function scrollit_r21(seed)
{
        var c1   = "Wow, this javascript sure is easy!";
        var c2   = "And it lets me add lots of functionality to my intranet.";
        var c4   = "Can anyone learn how to use it?";
        var c5   = "Pretty much.  Remember to check the on-line tutorial.";
```

```
                var msg=c1+c2+c4+c5;
                var out = " ";
                var c   = 1;

        if (seed > 100) {
                seed--;
                var cmd="scrollit_r2l(" + seed + ")";
                timerTwo=window.setTimeout(cmd,100);
        }
        else if (seed <= 100 && seed > 0) {
                for (c=0 ; c < seed ; c++) {
                        out+=" ";
                }
                out+=msg;
                seed--;
                var cmd="scrollit_r2l(" + seed + ")";
                    window.status=out;
                timerTwo=window.setTimeout(cmd,100);
        }
        else if (seed <= 0) {
                if (-seed < msg.length) {
                        out+=msg.substring(-seed,msg.length);
                        seed--;
                        var cmd="scrollit_r2l(" + seed + ")";
                        window.status=out;
                        timerTwo=window.setTimeout(cmd,100);
                }
                else {
                        window.status=" ";
                        timerTwo=window.setTimeout("scrollit_r2l(100)",75);
                }
        }
}
<!-- End of JavaScript code -->
</SCRIPT>
```

JavaScript is easy to learn even if you are not a programmer, and it functions superbly as a CGI substitute for performing simple calculations traditionally managed by CGIs. JavaScript, as opposed to CGIs, moves the processing from the server to the client. Having 1,000 users request a page with JavaScript on it is a lot less server-intensive than having 1,000 users submit the same CGI. JavaScript can enhance the capabilities of Web forms, for example, by triggering immediate feedback to the user, eliminating the need for a network roundabout. You can return results without having to submit a form back to the server and then wait for a response. JavaScript works well in conjunction with forms because you can use it to check the validity of inputs (for example, make a mask on a telephone number *(xxx) xxx-xxxx*) before the information is submitted to the CGI.

Many Web developers claim that JavaScript will replace CGI scripts. Microsoft has responded to the Java craze by developing Visual Basic Script (VBScript), which functions in much the same way as JavaScript. You can anticipate that JavaScript and similar scripting tools will be at the forefront of Web development in the future.

You also can anticipate that Java will be enhanced, supplemented, and sometimes replaced with plug-in modules. If you've ever worked with graphics programs such as Adobe Photoshop or Adobe Illustrator, you're probably familiar with how plug-ins work. Or maybe you already have worked with some browser plug-ins (like Macromedia's Shockwave). Another example of a plug-in is ExCITE's NCompass. The NCompass team created a plug-in that allows OLE controls to work inside Netscape 2.0. This plug-in mimics the functionality of Microsoft's ActiveX.

ActiveX

ActiveX is Microsoft's first attempt to break some ground on the Internet by giving developers the means to create distributed software components based on the Component Object Model (COM). COM can be thought of interchangeably with the term "OLE" (Object Linking and Embedding), because OLE is unified by the inner workings of COM (which handles object creation and local/remote transparency services).

OLE has grown over the last five years and is now a set of interfaces and services for building reusable object-oriented software components.

An intranet developer can embed ActiveX components into an HTML page to be downloaded and run when the page is viewed. A page with an ActiveX object embedded might look like this:

```
<HTML>
<HEAD>
<TITLE>Matthew Baird's ActiveX Test Page</TITLE>
</HEAD>
<BODY>
<H1>Matthew Baird's ActiveX Test Page </H1>
<OBJECT WIDTH="400" HEIGHT="400"
     CODEBASE="http://www.wavelength.com/ActiveX/ocx/test.ocx"
     <EMBED SRC="test.ods"
     CODE="http://www.wavelength.com/ActiveX/ocx/test.oc
➥#Version=4,0,0,0" WIDTH="400" HEIGHT="400">
</OBJECT> </BODY>
</HTML>
```

For further examples, visit the ActiveX gallery at http://www.microsoft.com/activex/gallery/.

Why is ActiveX important to your intranet? ActiveX allows your in-house and/or contract developers to build software components that interface in a common way with other software components. By using the standard OLE interfaces, your development team can create their own specific components that can plug into other teams' components. The development cycle for a large project can be split into small component projects that will integrate seamlessly into the larger project.

As you can well imagine, there are security issues to consider when you download software from the Internet. Microsoft has addressed code security and authenticity via its "code-signing" system. When Internet Explorer hits a page that needs to download component code, the code-signing capability is activated, and Internet Explorer recognizes the authenticity of signed code.

Users can give automatic authentication rights to components from recognized sources via a pop-up message box. Obviously, download security is much more of an issue for the Internet, where you don't know who developed the code. However, intranet users will be relieved to know that company-developed code can be digitally signed and automatically installed without any user intervention.

The ActiveX SDK (Software Development Kit) beta 2 is available from Microsoft. It requires Windows 95 or Windows NT 4.0 SUR beta, beta 2 of Internet Explorer 3.0 (http://www.microsoft.com/ie/iedl.htm) or higher, the latest release of the Win32 SDK (dated after May 1996 and available on MSDN Level II), and a compiler (Microsoft Visual C++ 4.1 is the most tested). Actual code listing of ActiveX applications goes beyond the scope of this book, but the SDK includes well-documented sample code developed by Microsoft.

Incorporating applications into your intranet offers you the flexibility needed to run a feature-rich system. Besides the resources discussed in this chapter, other means of transmitting functionality are underway. One example is Netscape's LiveMedia, which transmits real-time audio and other media to the Web. Another quickly developing resource is Virtual Reality Modeling Language (VRML), which promises to be a handy tool for application designers who want to bring more 3-D to the Web. To get a taste of the potential of VRML, visit Worlds Inc.'s AlphaWorld at http://www.worlds.net/alphaworld.

Summary

Data arriving at and leaving your intranet means you need to master the task of manipulating that data. Begin the process by first making sure that you understand your system's programming languages. Familiarizing yourself with the server's shells will soon have you writing your own shell scripts. Remember that compatibility and functionality with the Web are the key components of a fully workable script. Familiarizing yourself with the ways in which the Web transmits (both now and in the future) functionality will help you create a secure, vibrant, and smoothly operational intranet. Don't forget that online resources will help you, too. Not only will you find FAQs and *white papers*—white papers generally explain the overlying and general technology behind the product, but not enough to clone it—you'll also be able to download tools that will help you achieve your goals.

PDF Presentations

23

by Jobe Doody

IN THIS CHAPTER

- What is PDF?   **352**
- Technical specifications   **353**
- Uses and advantages of portable documents   **353**
- The intranet link   **354**
- Differences and alternatives: digital document platforms   **355**
- Creating portable documents   **356**
- Distributing PDFs   **358**
- Alternatives   **359**

Anyone who has browsed the World Wide Web knows that, as a communications medium, it is very different from conventional publications like print magazines, newspapers, and paper documents. Its purpose—to deliver information to a target audience—is the same, however.

Until recently, converting prepared documents—the ones painstakingly formatted with type, layout, and design—to be posted on the Web usually had been an unforgiving task. It required learning HyperText Markup Language (HTML) codes, a primitive process of editing text when you compare it to the graphical user interfaces (GUI) of today's Microsoft or WordPerfect word processors. Graphics had to be converted separately, if possible, to low-resolution and restrictive color palettes. Add low-network bandwidth requirements, audiences with low-resolution monitors, half a dozen or so different Web browsers, and you're left with a process that was often frustrating with results that were disappointing.

A new age and suite of document presentation applications has arrived, however. Software companies, mostly those involved in engineering applications for conventional media publishing, have developed digital document formats that allow formatted documents to be published electronically via the Internet or through non-network digital media such as CD-ROMs or ubiquitous floppy disks. The purpose of this chapter is to introduce you to digital document formats (DDFs) and quickly get you started with using them and incorporating their use into intranets.

What Is PDF?

PDF, or portable document format, is a document format that allows you to view complex documents using a simple viewer. In essence, a PDF document contains all the elements of that document in and of itself. If you create a document in Microsoft Word, for example, anyone else who has Microsoft Word can view that document. If that person has only Microsoft Works or WordPerfect, however, he or she would have a difficult time viewing the file.

Although in recent years, most good word processing applications such as Microsoft Word and WordPerfect have filters for each other and other popular formats, they are still not perfect. When a document is saved in Microsoft Word, some of the elements of that document are communicated or symbolized by Microsoft Word itself. The fonts, embedded images, columns and tabs, or other complex formatting procedures are saved in a special Microsoft language. This language can be understood by Microsoft Word, and sometimes can be translated by a Microsoft Word filter. To get a better idea of this example, try opening a Microsoft Word document in Notepad. You see a lot of special characters, and all the document's formatting is gone, as shown in Figure 23.1.

A PDF file, on the other hand, is self-contained. All the formatting, fonts, images, and every other part of the file are saved with the file, and you can view them by using a simple viewer.

FIGURE 23.1.
On the left is a document in Word, and on the right is a document in Notepad. The special characters represent the formatting.

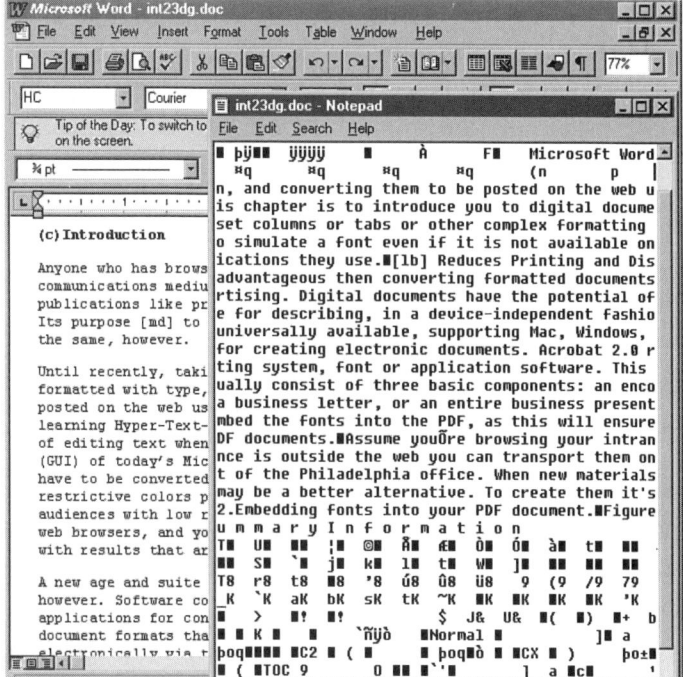

Technical Specifications

The PDF file format uses only the printable subset of ASCII, which means that the formatting, images, or fonts that are used in your document are described to the reader in that language.

A PDF file can simulate a font even if it is not available on the viewer's machine. You therefore can use whatever font you want when you create the document, and anybody who has a reader can view the font almost exactly as it would appear if the reader had the font installed on his or her system.

PDF files use a sophisticated means of compression to reduce file size. This compression is great for an intranet because PDF files use less bandwidth when you transfer files.

Uses and Advantages of Portable Documents

PDFs have introduced a wide range of new features to electronic publishing, intranets in particular. With PDFs, you can do the following:

- Transform paper documents for electronic publishing
- Use them with your favorite applications such as PageMaker, Word, Quark Express, and WordPerfect
- Put documents on the Web with virtually no re-authoring time
- Let employees, clients, and potential clients view, search, and print documents with no loss of original formatting and feel, regardless of the applications they use
- Reduce printing and distribution costs
- Incorporate hypermedia features into your documents

Anyone who needs to distribute documents to a large audience should find PDFs useful, especially if you have to publish documents electronically. The *New York Times,* for example, uses Adobe Acrobat's Portable Documents (PDF) to publish its *Times Fax,* a daily synopsis of the day's events. Before, *Times Fax* was available only through fax subscription but is now available through Acrobat on the Web. See for yourself at http://nytimesfax.com/altfax.html. The IRS has PDF tax forms that you can download, and numerous companies now are using PDFs to distribute product catalogs and literature. Interested in more examples? On its WWW site, Adobe maintains a page of other sites that use its PDF format. You can visit that site by pointing your browser to http://www.adobe.com/Acrobat/PDF sites.html.

Using PDFs is simple (as simple as sending a document to the printer) and in many cases more advantageous than converting formatted documents for the Web. They transform paper documents for electronic publishing and can be used with most publishing applications such as PageMaker, Quark Express, Microsoft Word, WordPerfect, Adobe Illustrator, and many more regardless of the operating system (that is, Macintosh, Windows, DOS, or UNIX). PDFs can be distributed through a range of applications, including the World Wide Web, e-mail, Lotus Notes, CD-ROM, corporate networks, and print-on-demand systems. PDFs eliminate many printing and distribution costs and are environmentally friendly, reducing trips to the photocopier and the offset printer.

The Intranet Link

Just as digital documents add features for distributing documents on the Web, they add features to intranets as well. With digital documents, you can post frequently used documents. Imagine, no more having to look for the employee handbook. The company newsletter is right there online. Want a second opinion on something? E-mail your proposal to Jim in advertising. Digital documents have the potential of making the office paperless.

Don't stop there. You can probably think of many valuable ways to use PDFs on an intranet. Here are some other examples:

- Updates on company objectives and progress
- Training information and documentation
- New employee orientation guides
- Employee annual reports
- Employee handbooks, summary plan descriptions, and policy/procedure guides
- Telephone directories
- Articles by employees
- Corporate newsletters
- Job postings

Differences and Alternatives: Digital Document Platforms

Publishers have a variety of digital document formats from which to choose. Among the most widely used are PostScript (.PS), Adobe Acrobat (.PDF), and WordPerfect Envoy (.EVY).

PostScript

The father of digital document formats, Adobe's PostScript has been around since 1985, when Apple Computer introduced the LaserWriter, the first PostScript laser printer. By definition, PostScript is an interpreted, stack-oriented language for describing, in a device-independent fashion, the way in which pages can be composed of characters, shapes, and digitized images in black and white, grayscale, or color. Documents created in PostScript therefore can be used by almost any computer platform or printer that supports the PostScript language. Concerning the text and graphics field, PostScript is now the most widely used printer controller in the industry. It gives computer users total control over text, graphics, color separations, and halftones.

Though PostScript has a wide-felt presence in the paper document publishing area, it lacks in the digital document market. Its files are usually very large, wasting bandwidth on the Internet. Sometimes, converting and viewing the documents require some technical knowledge about the language. Besides simple viewing and printing, PostScript lacks many features available in Adobe Acrobat and Envoy, such as document indexing, text searching, and markups. PostScript is, however, universally available, supporting Mac, Windows, OS/2, and UNIX platforms.

Acrobat

When it was first introduced, Acrobat, also by Adobe Systems, was hyped as the first step toward the paperless office and the most important document-imaging technology since

PostScript. It is truly a much newer solution, and Adobe boasts its features as ideal for intranets. It's easy to see why. As a digital document format, Acrobat includes text and graphic linking, searching, and indexing. You don't find these features available in PostScript. Because of its PostScript heritage, however, you can use Acrobat to do everything PostScript can do, including converting PostScript to Acrobat.

The Adobe Acrobat family actually consists of three products designed to bring electronic document solutions to a wide range of users:

- Acrobat 2.0 includes all the software a user requires for creating electronic documents from common desktop applications such as WordPerfect and Microsoft Excel. Included in Acrobat 2.0 are Acrobat Exchange and PDF Writer for creating electronic documents. Acrobat 2.0 requires reader applications in order to view PDF documents. Macintosh and Windows Readers can be freely distributed to anyone. DOS and UNIX readers are also free, but they can be distributed only within your organization.

- Acrobat Pro includes all the components of Acrobat 2.0 plus Acrobat Distiller. Distiller allows you to convert any PostScript language file into PDF. As such, PostScript can be converted locally on Macintosh computers or over a network file system, allowing PostScript documents to be converted by any number of users on your network.

- Acrobat for Workgroups includes everything a workgroup of 10 requires: 10 licenses of Acrobat Exchange for Macintosh and Windows, Acrobat Distiller, and Acrobat Catalog. Acrobat Catalog allows PDF files to be incorporated with indexes for full-text cross-document searches.

Adobe's PDF format allows intranet users to pass documents back and forth between Adobe Acrobat software, regardless of computer, operating system, font, or application software. Documents can be passed onto another computer without losing their formatting information. PDF, therefore, is an ideal way to transfer highly visual documents over the Web.

Why use PDF instead of PostScript? Size is a big concern; PostScript files are significantly larger than the same files saved as PDFs. Also, the Web browser market is leading electronically formatted documents in the direction of PDFs. Netscape, creators of Netscape Navigator, the Web browser that holds nearly 85 percent of the total browser market share, has made an agreement with Adobe to include a built-in PDF viewer in upcoming releases of Navigator. You therefore will no longer have to install Adobe's PDF viewer plug-in to view PDF documents. You will still have to install viewers for every other type of digital document format.

Creating Portable Documents

Digital document format systems usually consist of three basic components: an encoder, an editor, and a player. The encoder is the software that actually creates the portable file. Encoders come in two forms: utilities that emulate a printer driver to capture and convert print output, and stand-alone programs that convert more complicated PostScript documents.

For this tutorial, you use Adobe Acrobat. For more information on obtaining a copy of Acrobat, consult your local software dealer or visit Adobe's Acrobat Web site at http://www.adobe.com/acrobat/main.html.

Creating Your Document or Presentation

After you install the Acrobat software, the next task is to create the document for use on your intranet. You have a lot of flexibility here: you can create a simple static document, such as a business letter, or an entire business presentation to share with another user or group of users. You are limited only to the capabilities of your authoring software (PageMaker, PowerPoint, Quark, Word, and so on) and your imagination. In most cases, the process is the same: you create or scan documents to output from your authoring software to Acrobat's PDF Writer or Distiller.

As an example, consider a company profile created in PageMaker. This file contains important information that is useful to fellow employees or a potential customer. Converting this document to a PDF is almost as easy as printing it. Simply select the PDF Writer prior to printing (the print setup in Windows and the Chooser option on a Macintosh).

From here, fine-tune your PDF settings by selecting the fonts used in the original document, as shown in Figure 23.2, and graphic compression settings, as shown in Figure 23.3. Embedding the fonts into the PDF is especially important, as doing so ensures that the layout of the PDF does not change when viewed by a user who does not have the same fonts that are used in the document installed in his or her computer. The graphic compression settings allow you to shrink the memory requirements of your PDF, but you should be careful. If you choose a compression setting that is too low, this setting may sacrifice graphic quality.

FIGURE 23.2.

Embedding fonts into your PDF document.

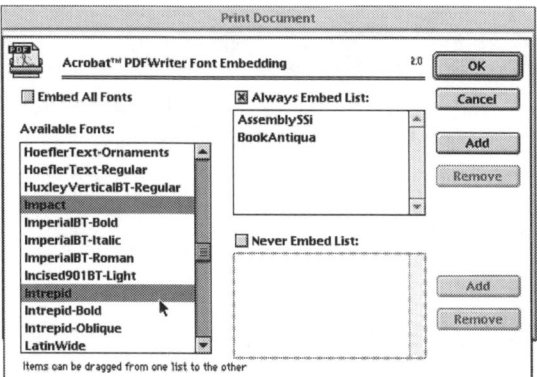

Next, select the view PDF file. Making this selection automatically opens the Acrobat viewer after the PDF is created. View the file to make sure that the PDF was created error free.

FIGURE 23.3.
Selecting the appropriate graphic compression for your PDF document.

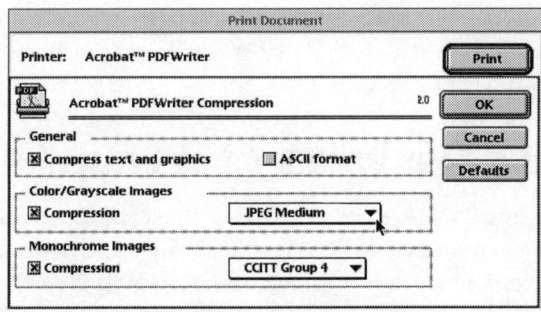

Finally, choose Print from the PDF Writer menu. You are prompted to enter a filename for the PDF and to select the directory in which you want to create the PDF. Your file is then converted to a PDF. This process may take a few minutes.

Viewing a PDF File

Viewing a PDF file is even easier than creating PDF documents.

Assume that you're browsing your intranet's Web site with Netscape, and you come across this year's year-end report, which hasn't hit the printer yet. Simply click the link to download the PDF. As long as the Acrobat software is correctly installed, the viewer automatically opens the downloaded PDF.

You can view the file by placing the PDF you created on your intranet and downloading it, or by opening it locally from the viewer. After the viewer loads the document, you can browse, search, or print the document.

> **NOTE**
>
> Netscape and Adobe struck a deal to embed PDF viewer capabilities in all new versions of Netscape. Look for this capability in all upcoming versions of Netscape. If you don't use Netscape, don't worry. The viewer will continue to be available to you from Adobe's Web site at `http://www.adobe.com/acrobat/readstep.html`.

Distributing PDFs

You can distribute PDFs in many ways. If you're online, you can put them on the company's Web or FTP servers. If your target audience is outside the Web, you can transport them on a floppy disk or CD-ROM. Or you can add a personal touch by sending a PDF through e-mail.

Alternatives

Some other PDFs work in many of the same ways that Adobe Acrobat does. One such alternative is WordPerfect Envoy. Although it's identical in many ways to Adobe Acrobat, the differences between the two products are best explained by their origins. Acrobat originated as an outgrowth of Adobe's PostScript printing language. PostScript was designed for printing pages one at a time on printers. By contrast, Envoy was designed to address the problems of electronic document distribution, specifically online viewing, flexible navigation, efficient searching, annotation, printing, and transmission. Many of Envoy's features are showing up in Adobe's new Acrobat "Amber" PDF format, the next generation of Acrobat software.

MCKEON & JEFFRIES

M&J uses the PDF format very rarely. Their main production person who creates marketing materials and brochures works in the Philadelphia office. When new materials are created, they are posted to the intranet in PDF format so that they can be reviewed by partners and interested parties who are either in the two other offices or on the road. Because most of the decision-makers work in the Philadelphia office, however, walking the files down the hall is typically much easier and more efficient.

THE SPORTING GOODS AND APPAREL ASSOCIATION

The SGAA uses the PDF file format fairly often. Whenever new marketing materials for the association are created, they are placed on the intranet in PDF format. Advertisements, new membership documents, and even the annual report are distributed to key association members in this manner. This format allows for a quick and easy method for review, especially if approval is needed to publish the documents.

Summary

The Web is a great medium to publish information; however, if the material you want published comes from formatted documents, PDFs may be a better alternative. Creating them is as easy as printing, and you can distribute them via almost any form of digital media. But don't take my word for it; get online and see what PDFs can do for you!

SGML Presentations

24

by Jim Miller

IN THIS CHAPTER

- How SGML works **362**
- Using SGML to preserve file structure **363**
- Document type definition **364**
- Benefits of SGML **364**
- Drawbacks of SGML **365**
- Does your company need SGML? **366**

Ever since computer technology has been available in multiple platforms, one of the problems that has plagued users has been the difficulty, or downright impossibility, of transferring documents from one computer system or software program to another.

The beginning of the cure for this plague came about in 1986 when the Standard Generalized Markup Language (SGML) was adopted by the International Organization for Standardization (ISO) as a standard for the exchange of data worldwide. Since that time, use of SGML has increased rapidly, particularly among the defense, aerospace, automotive, electronics, and telecommunications industries.

How SGML Works

SGML is a standard language for "marking" or coding electronic documents and files that allows users to access information regardless of the system or platform they are using. SGML works by treating the content, format, and structure of a document as three distinct elements, as shown in Figures 24.1 and 24.2.

FIGURE 24.1.

SoftQuad's Panorama, showing an SGML document.

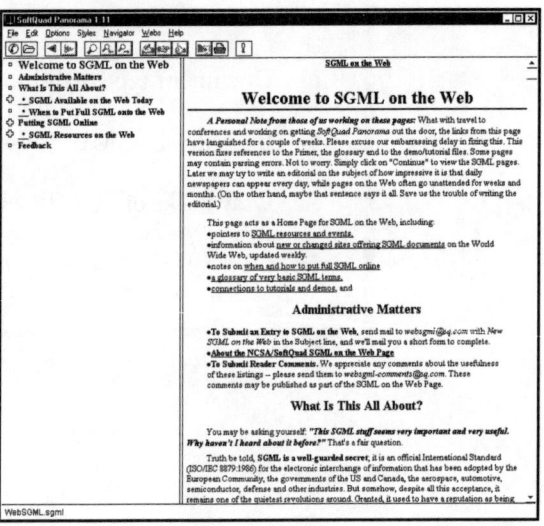

Content is the actual information, such as text and images, in the document. The format determines how the words and images appear on the screen or paper—for example, font, point size, italics, and bold. The structure of a document indicates the relationships among the various pieces of content, such as paragraphs, headings, subheadings, or lists. SGML is designed to preserve the structure and content of the document.

SGML Presentations
Chapter 24

FIGURE 24.2.
The SGML source code for the same document. Note the similarities to HTML code.

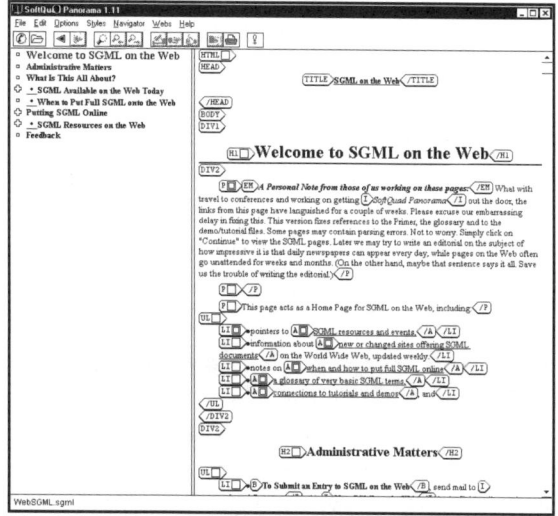

For example, in this book you know that you are now reading Chapter 24. From the Table of Contents and from the section heading you also know that Chapter 24 is in Part III. In the same way that the editors have organized this book into logical sections and subsections of information, SGML organizes and divides electronic documents into a recognizable and retrievable structure.

Because it is an international standard, all computer platforms can become capable of interpreting this code regardless of the document's source. The universality of SGML allows for the efficient and accurate transfer of all content and structural information from one computer system to another, while still allowing individual users to modify the format of a document to suit their needs and requirements. No matter how technology changes in the future, the SGML will make documents durable and exchangeable.

Using SGML to Preserve File Structure

The capability to preserve the structural integrity of a document is what makes SGML so revolutionary. For SGML to preserve the document structure, the document must contain discrete markers that identify the structural elements. These markers, called *tags*, are located at the beginning and end of each structural element. For example, suppose you have a paragraph such as the following:

> This is the first paragraph of my document.

You can tell any computer with SGML capabilities to preserve this information as a paragraph element by marking it like this:

```
<par>
This is the first paragraph of my document.
</par>
```

It's no coincidence that this looks a lot like HyperText Markup Language (HTML), the language used to create documents for the World Wide Web. HTML is simply an application of SGML. Thanks to the original SGML research, Web browsers from different formats can understand HTML files universally.

The specifics of the structural designations of HTML, and all other applications of SGML, are located in its Document Type Definition, or DTD.

Document Type Definition

If you regularly use documents that have an exact uniform structure, such as Web documents, time sheets, or product specification forms, you would want to use a template to ensure that these documents remained identical in structure as they pass from one computer system to another and as they are updated and re-created.

The template or framework for the various elements in an SGML application is the DTD. The DTD not only preserves the structure of a specific type of electronic file, but also enforces the rules of that structure. For example, if you had to submit a specific report, the DTD for that type of report could specify that the report must contain sections A, B, and C, and that each of these sections must contain at least one paragraph. In this way, the DTD helps ensure that documents have a uniform, logical structure. A document whose content has been tagged to conform to a particular DTD is called a *document instance*.

The best SGML software programs allow you to tag information by clicking on pull-down menus. When working within the confines of a particular DTD, the pull-down menus will list only those tags that are valid at the cursor's current position in the document. Therefore, you cannot diverge from the structure of the DTD even if you wanted to.

Different industries and companies obviously require different types of DTDs to facilitate and manage their information. Many SGML systems offer a set of preprogrammed DTDs that comes with the software. Relatively few people will want to write their own DTDs, because this process can be difficult. However, a high-quality SGML product allows users to create a variety of document types. This will give you the ability to create user-defined DTDs.

Benefits of SGML

The primary benefit of SGML is that it dramatically increases the ease with which people can access the information that your company creates. However, other benefits can be found in improved information collection, compilation, and dissemination, as well as in increased cost efficiency.

Increased Access

Using SGML for document creation allows universal access to needed information efficiently and accurately. At a time when different computers, operating systems, and applications abound, only a language that is hardware and software independent, like SGML, will allow all your users to exchange documents with ease. This way, if your art department creates a file on a Mac, your CEO, who uses a PC, can view and edit it before it goes to press.

Information Collection and Compilation

Structured guidelines for the creation of new documents will increase productivity by eliminating the time spent formatting new documents. It improves data integrity by reducing the need to filter data from one format to another and lengthens the period of time that stored information can be used by ensuring that the data will be retrievable regardless of future changes in hardware or software. Remember all those files you have on 5 1/4-inch floppies that are in some ancient DOS word processing format nobody uses anymore? With PDF, your files will have a much longer shelf life.

Information Dissemination

With electronic publishing sweeping the world, SGML enables you to translate information that was prepared for traditional printing methods into a wide variety of formats suitable for publishing on everything from CD-ROM to the World Wide Web. SGML also can improve information dissemination by allowing users to share whole documents or sections of documents without the need for wasteful hard copy reproduction and duplication.

Cost Efficiency

All the previously mentioned benefits of SGML can translate into direct and indirect cost savings by providing greater information accessibility, improved data integrity, increased life span of archival information, and a reduced need for printed products. Think about all the money your company spends on printing human resources documents, corporate directories, and internal memos every year. These costs can be all but eliminated by creating and duplicating your documents in electronic format using PDF. And any changes mean a few keystrokes, not thousands of dollars in printing and distribution costs.

Drawbacks of SGML

When using SGML, you might find the enforced structure of the DTD somewhat limiting. If you have a small number of DTDs available to you and do not have the ability to write new DTDs, working in SGML can be frustrating.

The universality of SGML is great, as long as your systems know the code. SGML translators are not native to most computer systems, so the ability to create and read documents with SGML tags requires an investment in systems and software.

Although SGML is an English-based language, it is not always intuitive and can be as complex as the documents you are trying to tag. Thorough knowledge of SGML does not come easily. For industries that are document intensive, the use of SGML must be considered part of an entire information management strategy. Although standardizing on SGML may require significant time and investment, the benefits (as explained in the preceding section) can make the transition worthwhile.

Does Your Company Need SGML?

When considering whether to standardize some of your company's information using SGML, several factors should be considered. The following questions can help you define your current information management needs:

- Do you need to exchange documents across different computer environments?
- Do you produce documents that follow a standard, uniform structure?
- Do many different departments or divisions use the same types of information?
- Does your information have a long life span? (That is, will it be useful for many years?)
- Does your information change frequently, and is it used often?
- Is keeping your information up-to-date expensive and time-consuming?
- Could a significant value be gained by distributing updated information electronically?
- Do you produce information that must comply with specific industry guidelines?

How you answer these questions will help you determine how SGML fits into your information management strategy. Remember that not all your documents will need to be standardized on SGML—only those that have a definable structure and need to last.

Summary

Over the years, the expansion and application of the SGML system has affected many areas of the digital information explosion. SGML and its execution are often complex and cryptic processes requiring well-trained and informed professionals who can best utilize and tailor SGML to specific needs. This chapter is only an introduction to SGML that should help you understand its uses and inspire a more in-depth investigation of this technology.

Audio Presentations

25

by Anne Marie Yerks

IN THIS CHAPTER

- Bandwidth and hardware **369**
- Audio formats **370**
- Audio server software **372**
- Recording audio **373**
- The future of online audio **376**

Think back to the last time you used a tape recorder not to play but to record a cassette. Maybe you taped your daughter's high school graduation ceremony or a company lecture. Perhaps you took a recorder with you to a family reunion to preserve some oral history. You might have even accidentally recorded a phone conversation on your answering machine. Most likely, though, it hasn't been all that long since you played a tape in a cassette player. Maybe you listened to an audio book driving to work this morning, or perhaps you carried a small portable cassette player with you on your daily walk. If you're a fan of music, you probably have a CD player on your stereo system. You also might have a CD player on your home or work computer. Both the tape recorder and CD player are familiar tools with which to play and create audio. But you can use another tool to make audio clips and import them into presentations, Web pages, and movies. This tool is the computer.

Your computer has the potential to be a microphone, mixer, and boom box all in one. The computer doesn't care what you are recording—your own voice, a telephone conversation off the speaker phone, a music CD, a bird call, a water fountain. You need only a microphone, speakers, an editor, and a sound card for your computer's motherboard. These days, many personal computers (and all Macintosh computers) are built with sound cards.

Creating audio files for an online (or offline) presentation is about as easy as tape-recording your grandfather's war stories—once you get the hang of it. The hardest part is determining your hardware needs and selecting suitable software.

This chapter explores the current options available for adding an audio segment to your computer system and discusses the future of computers and audio. To begin this discussion, let's look at what's happening to a fictional company called Nemosyne, Inc.

Nemosyne's main product is a series of foreign-language study packages. Each package contains a manual and two cassette tapes oriented to one of 30 different languages. Nemosyne's primary market is American executives who travel overseas on business. Although Nemosyne wants to expand its market to European and Asian executives, they have not yet reached that point. Currently, their biggest seller is the English-to-Japanese study package, with French running a close second.

Not too long ago, Nemosyne hired a Webmaster to create and maintain a corporate intranet because the board of directors wanted to capitalize on the advantages of a well-developed Web site. The new Webmaster set up a few employee bulletin boards, an online contact database, and CGI scripts that allow customers to order products via an electronic form. Nemosyne has already noticed an increase in sales.

The board of directors has big plans for expanding the public side of their Web site: They want to be the first to bring foreign language study to the Web. The company's Webmaster has told the board that by creating a large base of audio files (all of which can be extracted from their existing language tapes), they can make a site to which American travelers can refer when they need to know pronunciation for certain words or phrases.

A businessman on assignment in China, for example, needs to find a dry cleaner. If he's online, the businessman can go to the Nemosyne site where he can find a hotlink that looks something like this:

`DryCleaning.ra`

After he clicks the link, he is presented with a list of audio files for dry cleaning-related phrases such as "Where would I find a dry cleaner?" He selects this phrase, and within seconds a Chinese version of this phrase plays on his laptop. He can repeat the phrase as many times as he likes, until he can say it himself. (By this time, he might be so impressed that, before he looks for the dry cleaners, he'll take the time to order Nemosyne's Chinese language package electronically with his credit card.)

The board thinks the concept of online "instant phrases" is terrific, but they're still a bit hesitant. The Webmaster has been asked to create an online presentation that will give them a feel for how the proposed site would operate. The presentation needs to be posted on Nemosyne's intranet so that the CEO (who is spending the summer in Bermuda) can access it easily.

The Webmaster begins by browsing the Web, just to see what other users are doing with audio files. In one two-hour session, it becomes apparent that creating online audio is not a difficult task.

Bandwidth and Hardware

The biggest challenge for the Webmaster in developing the Nemosyne presentation is overcoming limited bandwidth. This is the challenge that all Web multimedia developers are facing currently. A 28.8 Kbps modem can move about 3.6 kilobytes (3.6K) per second, making it about 50 times slower than the 176K per second that is needed to play CD-quality audio.

To overcome the lack of bandwidth, you must compress all audio files for the Web. Otherwise, they would come out sounding like a tape recorder running on old batteries (or even worse). Although you can compress audio files in many different ways, you can offer audio on your Web site in only two ways.

The first option is to post files for users to download and save to their hard drives. The disadvantage of this method is that it asks a lot of the users. The users must know how to download, how to find and use an audio player, and they must sacrifice hard disk space—all just to listen to something that sounds merely okay. The second option, streaming audio, also sounds merely okay but is much less demanding. A streaming audio file plays just seconds after a user clicks its link—provided a plug-in player has been downloaded and stored in the proper directory.

Streaming audio works by creating an ultra-compressed version of a regular digital audio file, but by keeping the compression in an order that the computer (with the help of the player) can understand as the data comes in. Currently, streaming audio products are marketed by several different companies (more about them later in this chapter), but they all use coders and decoders, and have two components: a *compressor*, which compresses the audio stream; and a *decompresser*, which plays the audio stream. The compressor codes the original audio, and the decompresser reorders the data into a file that is similar to the original but not the same.

To hear some clips of presidential speeches that have been transformed into streaming audio files, visit Webcorp's audio archives at http://www.webcorp.com. To hear some streaming audio examples of presentation music, visit NetworkMusic's home page at http://www.networkmusic.com.

Opinions about the quality of streaming audio are varied. Although having a short download time is nice, many streaming audio clips—especially those that were originally created on old-fashioned tape players—sound rough. Don't expect even the most basic stereo sound from streaming audio; however, the quality should progress as bandwidth increases.

For the Nemosyne presentation, the Webmaster wants to use streaming audio. Using these files is quicker than making each user download the entire audio file before it is played. The Webmaster, however, anticipates that the proposed site will eventually include some audio files for downloading. If the Nemosyne company wants to offer a sample tape for downloading to potential customers, for example, streaming audio would not be the best choice. In this case, having a less-compressed higher-quality version is better. As it now stands, streaming audio is best for audio files that are meant to be played spontaneously online. Other formats might be used for longer audio files, especially ones in which sound quality is especially important.

As the quality of streaming audio improves, it might completely replace the other audio file formats (for online purposes). Streaming audio is easier to handle: the number of streams can be determined by the server software. A company that wants to have unlimited streams has the option. Likewise, having as few as five or six streams is possible. Streaming audio's flexibility is a new branch in the ways to distribute audio files over a network. But like most technology having to do with the Internet, its capabilities and protocols are always changing.

Audio Formats

Many times you'll be required to create your file in a sound editor and then transform it for real-time playback with a streaming audio encoder. For that reason, you should become familiar with the audio formats used to digitize sound for the Web. If you don't plan to stream your audio files, you can post any audio format on your Web site. Remember that your users will have to download the files and have the means to obtain a player. Including a compatible player along with your bank of audio files is usually a good idea. On the Web, the most frequent uses of nonstreaming audio are song samples (visit Geffen/DGC Records at http://www.geffen.com), audio greetings, stories, and clips from speeches.

Several different audio formats are available to Web developers. Each method has advantages and disadvantages, but all the methods are *lossy*, meaning the compression causes a decrease in sound quality. Remember that a particular sound format might support more than one way to encode the sound data.

For the Web, audio-MPEG, .WAV, .AIFF, and .AU—described next—are some of the most popular. Most likely, your sound editor will allow you to create files in one of these formats. However, you will occasionally run across sites that use other formats. Distinguishing between audio formats is a matter of testing them. You also should take into consideration what type of sound you want to post. Some formats work better with speech than with music and vice versa. The same holds true for sound editors and players, including the streaming variety.

The following are some descriptions of audio file formats:

- MPEG-Audio: A favorite of multimedia experts, audio-MPEG (Motion Pictures Experts Group) is a sound version of the digital video format MPEG. By executing a technique called *perceptual coding*, audio-MPEG compresses audio by removing extraneous data. This format produces small file sizes and good sound quality, probably the best of all the formats. You can choose between MPEG 1 (slower) or MPEG 2 (faster). You probably won't have to flip a coin to decide.
- .AU (also uLaw, NeXT, and Sun Audio): A common UNIX format, .AU is still popular for the Web. .AU is a versatile format used mainly for its capability to make a very small file rather than for its playback quality, which is usually rather poor.
- .WAV (MS Windows) and .AIFF (Macintosh): You can decide between 8- or 16-bit sound when using these formats. The advantage is the flexibility, but the disadvantage is a tendency to produce a "grainy" sound. These files have the potential to become very large, which means a long download time for the users.

Chances are good that you will be able to find a shareware program that produces audio-MPEG, .WAV, .AIFF, and .AU files. Go to Virtual Noise's Audio Help Desk at http://www.virtualnoise.com/audio1.html. You can find some hot links that lead you to some outstanding shareware sound-editing programs and players.

It's becoming more common for computer companies to pre-install sound editors, players, and other multimedia applications along with the system software. You can use the Sound Recorder that comes with Windows 95 or Macintosh's SoundMachine to make audio files and to play them. If you want to offer all your online audio files in .AU, audio-MPEG, .WAV, or .AIFF format, give your users instructions on what applications they need to play the files. You can be very general and say something like "You'll need a sound player on your machine to hear this file." To embed an audio file onto your site for download, use the following standard HTML reference tag:

```
<A HREF="example.wav">Example</A>
```

If you plan to make any part of your site dependent on audio files, and you anticipate that a shareware program will not meet your needs, you might want to look into some of the commercially available sound-editing packages, such as MacroMedia's SoundEdit Pro (for Macintosh only) or Cakewalk Music Software's Cakewalk Pro Audio (Windows). Expect to pay around $400 to $500.

Audio Server Software

One issue the Webmaster considers while developing the online Nemosyne presentation is whether to install an audio server. Think of the audio server as a supplement to the Web and mail servers: it gives you the capability to play audio streams from a given site. You should not confuse an audio server with sound-editing software. Think of sound editors as the "drawing programs" of audio: they are nonserver applications that provide tools for editing and manipulating sound.

A streaming audio server, available from the companies that are currently developing streaming audio products, allows a Web site to offer live, on-demand audio in real time. With one of the more expensive packages, at least a couple dozen users—and possibly many more—could therefore request the streaming audio files at any given time. No downloading is involved. Without the audio server, you would have to link streaming audio files to a site that does have audio server software.

The Webmaster decides on the most basic version of Progressive Network's RealAudio server software, which allows about five or six simultaneous users. Nemosyne will pay the $600 it costs to provide this service. The deluxe server would be quite pricey, as the capacity for unlimited audio streams runs about $5,000 to $6,000. The Webmaster plans to ask for the more deluxe server software during the Nemosyne final presentation.

Streaming Audio Packages

Most streaming audio packages come in three parts: the server, the encoder, and the player. Most likely, you can get some parts (if not all) of the package for free by downloading them from Web sites (URLs are listed next). Every package offers different features. Do some research to find the one that's best for you.

- RealAudio by Progressive Networks: RealAudio, developed by Progressive Networks—a pioneer in streaming audio technology—offers the most polished, most popular package. Most people find that RealAudio is easy to use, fully functional, and reasonably priced (as far as streaming packages go). RealAudio moves real-time audio over 14.4 Kbps and faster modems, and the player can be downloaded for free. Progressive Networks offers several packages especially for intranets. Each includes the server, the deluxe version of the encoder, license, and upgrades. Prices begin at $495. For more information, visit http://realaudio.com.

- StreamWorks by Xing: StreamWorks is a well-developed (although not particularly user-friendly) package. It's more expensive than some of the others but would work well for an intranet that maintains hundreds of simultaneous audio streams, like a broadcasting company. Like RealAudio, StreamWorks requires dedicated server software, whereas TrueSpeech and IWave (described in a moment) do not. Technical support for the free downloadable player costs $29. You might need the tech support considering that the Xing player is a bare-minimum MIME (Multipurpose Internet Mail Extensions) version operating from an embedded applet. Xing StreamWorks server software (platforms offered are SGI, Sun, HP, and Linux) starts at $3,500. For more information, visit http://www.xingtech.com.

- TrueSpeech by DSP: TrueSpeech, a freeware package, offers excellent—yet low-bandwidth—quality for both music and speech. Along with IWave (below), TrueSpeech requires no special server software, which makes both of them much less expensive than their competitors. The free TrueSpeech player, however, is a bit too basic for large files: users do not have the option of stopping and resuming the playback, or adjusting the volume. The TrueSpeech encoder is included with MS Windows 95 (it's integrated into the Sound Recorder). For more information, visit http://www.dspg.com.

- IWave by VocalTec: IWave (Internet Wave) offers high-quality—yet low-bandwidth—music, but it does not handle speech as well as other players. You can download IWave for free. You also can obtain a well-designed (but large) player by downloading the demo version of VocalTec's Internet phone. The IWave server is limited in its functionality, but if your streaming audio needs are for music, IWave is a good choice. For more information, visit http://www.vocaltec.com/.

- ToolVox by Voxware, Inc.: A freeware package, ToolVox is solely for speech. It lacks a fully functional player and does not have a server component. ToolVox audio files must be linked with standard HTML tags, which are then distributed in the same manner as GIF and JPEG files. IWave and TrueSpeech (above) also use the HTML method of distribution. The disadvantage of not having server software is that you lose the control and flexibility you might need for a high-volume commercial system. ToolVox is a good test run if you are thinking about developing streaming audio capabilities into your site. For more information, visit http://www.voxware.com.

Recording Audio

With a cassette from one of the foreign-language packages in hand, the Nemosyne Webmaster is ready to make a recording. She can record directly into the version of the RealAudio Encoder that came with the RealAudio server, but she wants to gain experience creating an audio file in a sound-editing program and then converting it to RealAudio format. For this reason, she must download the free version of the RealAudio Encoder from the RealAudio Web page. (The free version does not have the capability to record live; it can only convert an existing audio file into a RealAudio file). While the encoder is downloading, the Webmaster searches the Web for a good sound-editing program.

Choosing Sound-Editing Software

A sound editor's first purpose is to record a sound and transform it into a digital format (preferably one of the more popular ones). A good audio editor has the following functions:

- Operates with specialized sound cards
- Provides accurate input meters
- Allows a capacity to change bandwidth and format specifications
- Offers transitions between the RAM and the hard disk
- Creates more than one track
- Provides a variety of ways to mark time, such as in measures/beats and seconds/milliseconds

The Webmaster is going to use a Microsoft Windows-compatible program called GoldWave as a sound editor. The good thing about GoldWave is that it is a shareware program and can be downloaded from the Web for free. If you would like a copy of GoldWave, along with some good documentation, visit GoldWave's home page at

http://garfield.cs.mun.ca/%7Echris3/goldwave/goldwave.html

You also can download many other freeware audio editor packages (such as Cool Edit, Sonic Screwdriver, WAVany, and WHAM) from the Web.

After GoldWave is installed, the Webmaster creates a new file in which to record the first audio file, as shown in Figure 25.1.

FIGURE 25.1.
A new file is created in GoldWave.

Because the Webmaster is making a new audio file from an existing source (a cassette), she needs to route the computer to a tape player or stereo system. Most computers have audio ports that allow this routing. See Figure 25.2.

Using a sound-editing program, the Webmaster can extract a one-minute clip from the tape and adjust the bandwidth specifications. Once edited, the file is called "greeting" and is saved as a .WAV file, as shown in Figure 25.3.

FIGURE 25.2.
GoldWave's Device Controls panel allows you to play and record sound.

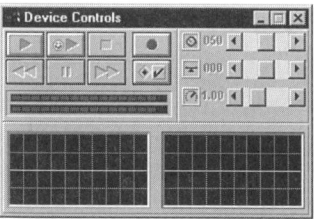

FIGURE 25.3.
The file is saved as greeting.WAV.

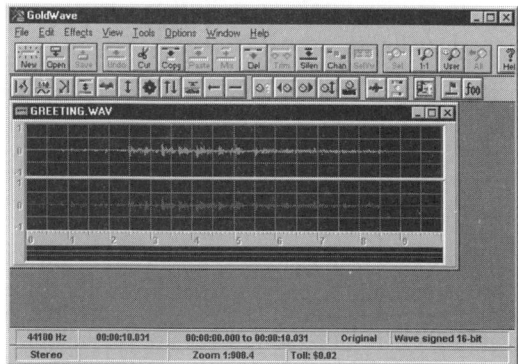

After an audio file is in .WAV (or another) format, it can be stored in the proper directory and linked into an HTML file. A user can then download the file and play it with a computer audio player.

.WAV files—like any that have to be downloaded—do not play in real-time, however. For this reason, the Webmaster pulls up the RealAudio Encoder, shown in Figure 25.4: It's already been decided that the Nemosyne presentation files will be streaming audio.

FIGURE 25.4.
The RealAudio Encoder can transform a variety of audio formats into streaming audio.

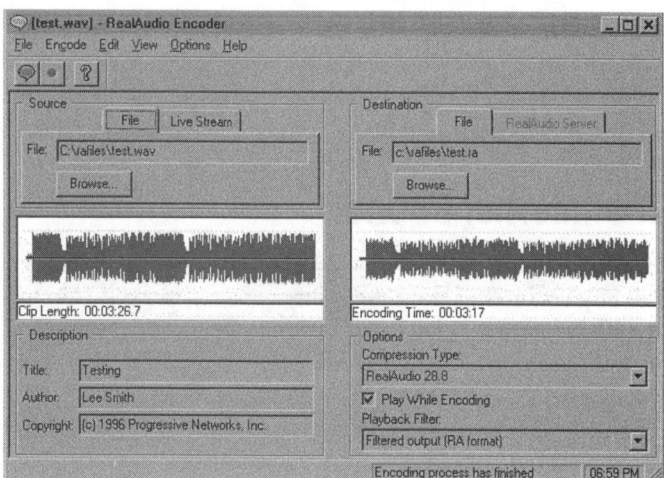

The RealAudio Encoder allows the Webmaster to transform the .WAV file into an .RA file (.RA is the extension used specifically for RealAudio files): greeting.RA.

Now that the file is in .RA format, the Webmaster wants to link it to the online presentation site. To do so, RealAudio requires that an additional document, called a *metafile*, be created and attached to the site. The metafile, which has the extension .RAM, is a text file that contains the URL of the RealAudio file. It provides a link between the Web server and the RealAudio server. The Webmaster also configures the Web server to recognize the .RA and .RAM MIME types. The RealAudio page (http://www.realaudio.com) gives specific instructions on creating the metafile and configuring the Web server.

The Webmaster creates the metafile (greeting.RAM), configures the Web server, and then links the audio file to the desired page. All that's needed to perform these steps is a simple HTML tag:

```
<A HREF="/greeting.RAM">Greeting</A>
```

Providing that the RealAudio Player is installed, the file should play on the computer in real time. This procedure can be repeated to make additional real-time audio files.

Streaming audio files are going to provide the Webmaster with what she needs to present her proposal effectively to Nemosyne's board of directors. But you should remember that the procedure described in this chapter is only one of many that you can use to make an audio file. You have to decide whether to purchase an audio server and what editing software you use. You also might decide that you don't want to use streaming audio. It's the trend of the future, but it's also expensive and a bit underdeveloped. Waiting for the streaming audio technology to progress also is an option.

The Future of Online Audio

Developments like streaming audio and other online multimedia are indicators that the Web is rapidly becoming a truly interactive environment. Real-time audio and video capabilities bring to the Web what satellite dishes brought to television. Conferences, court proceedings, talk shows, and celebrity chat hours eventually might be available online.

The Internet Phone

Internet Phone is more than a speaker phone and more than a chat room; VocalTec's Internet Phone gives Internet users the ability to talk to each other in their real voices. By connecting to the IRC (Internet Relay Chat) network, the Internet Phone software provides a list of online users and conversation topics. After you have a TCP\IP Internet connection, select a user from the list to call. The minimum connection is a modem SLIP\PPP connection of 14,400 baud. Internet Phone works best with at least a 486SX PC with 25MHz and 8MB of RAM. Versions for both Windows and Macintosh are available.

Internet Phone works by employing a voice compression algorithm that minimizes bandwidth consumption. Calls made from the Internet Phone cannot be traced, and the software allows for "private topics" that cannot be accessed by outsiders. Users of Internet Phone speak into a computer microphone.

A novel idea, the Phone's most obvious disadvantage is that you can make Internet phone calls only to people who also have the software. At this point, the Internet Phone is something like a very sophisticated chat room or BBS. But who knows, maybe someday everyone will be trashing touch-tones and buying high-tech microphones (with built-in answering machines, of course).

Besides the VocalTec phone, other audio-conferencing software is available. An excellent FAQ is available at http://www.gi.net/NET/PM-1995/95-04/95-04-28/0004.html. For more general information, visit VocalTec's home page at http://vocaltec.com.

Voice Recognition

Also in the future is the development of voice recognition computing. Imagine what it would be like to direct your computer to your favorite Web sites not with a mouse, but with your voice! Voice recognition often is used in word processing and other software as an aid to the visually impaired.

Just about any computer function that is performed with a keyboard and mouse has the potential to be performed with voice recognition. This is good news for people who get tired of moving the mouse around, or who were never that adept at dragging and clicking to begin with. Although it's doubtful that voice recognition would make the mouse and pad extinct (drawing programs are especially dependent on the trackball), you can count on the technology becoming integrated with more software packages.

The concept of machine-voice communication is older than you might think—about 60 years. It wasn't until the 1980s, however, that small vocabulary speech recognition software was developed to run on IBM PCs. The software has continued to progress and is greatly assisted by the Pentium and other powerful processors.

A twist on voice recognition is voice verification. You've probably seen science-fiction movies in which a fingerprint is used as a passkey; but because your voice is as unique as your fingerprint, anticipate the development of the "voiceprint," which might consist of a spoken password or phrase ("Open Sesame"?), or the repetition of certain words at the computer's request.

You can find an excellent directory of voice recognition resources at http://www.kurz-ai.com/gen-vr.html.

MCKEON & JEFFRIES

In the short term, McKeon & Jeffries has very little use or need for audio. Not only do most of their machines have audio capability, but the information that's most important to them is technical research and is important to be read and not heard. On the other hand, M&J hopes to use audio on a few applications in the future:

- Continuing education. Every CPA has to keep up with current tax law and accounting practices. To do so, many accountants attend seminars and talks given by experts. McKeon & Jeffries hopes to someday be able to broadcast these seminars through the intranet to their users to save time and money, as shown in Figure 25.5.

- Conference calls. In the distant future, M&J hopes to be able to hold online audio conferencing through its intranet. The next step would be to recognize the audio, save it to a file, and make it searchable for individuals who want to use it as a reference.

FIGURE 25.5.
Continuing education is much more convenient and efficient using an intranet.

THE SPORTING GOODS AND APPAREL ASSOCIATION

The SGAA plans to implement sound in several different areas of the intranet. As their users become more sophisticated and have the ability to not only listen to audio but also to create audio, the site will use more and more audio technology.

- What's new. The SGAA wants to be able to greet users as they visit the site every day with a list of the new things added to the site each day, as shown in Figure 25.6. However, they don't want to crowd the home page with a lot of text. Using the RealAudio server, the SGAA staff can record a new message every day so that when users log on, they can hear about new attractions on the site, fresh news, and any events scheduled for that day such as online chats or audio conferences.

- Advertising. Several of the manufacturers and distributors have product pages that contain information on specific products. For some of these products, radio advertising or the audio for television for advertising is captured and available on the server for resellers and distributors to hear.

- Audio conferencing. Several times a month, the SGAA's executive committee engages in a short conference call to discuss association business. Members are invited to listen in using RealAudio through the intranet.

FIGURE 25.6.
A different audio message greets users every day at the SGAA site.

Summary

You can use digital audio for online presentations and as a means to develop the resources of your intranet. Creating high-quality, functional audio is a matter of determining your needs (speech, music, or both) and scouting for software that will help you accomplish your goals. Deciding how to compress your audio is most important. Streaming audio packages enable you to play back in real time, so if you want to bring live conferences to your site, streaming audio is for you. On the other hand, if you are more interested in posting music files that do not have to be played simultaneously, and you want to preserve quality, you might want to post your files for downloading. You must then decide what format to use for posting your audio files. Audio-MPEG, .AIFF, .WAV, and .AU formats offer means of compression.

In both cases, take into consideration the software choices you have available: many servers, encoders, and players are available through shareware, so if audio will not be a large part of your presentation or intranet, they might be the best route. If you have plans to make audio an important part of your presentation or your intranet, look into one of the more sophisticated commercially available packages. Don't forget that online sources can answer questions that arise while you are in the process of creating audio.

Video Presentations

26

by Laura Sandage

IN THIS CHAPTER

- Producing your intranet video **383**
- Creating recorded video **383**
- Creating live video **385**
- VDOLive **387**
- Playback **388**

As more and more people are logging onto their computers, a dramatic change in the use of video has become apparent. Traditionally, video was used primarily in the television industry and in the homes of consumers in personal camcorders and VCRs. Video was stored and distributed on some sort of videotape whether the format was high-quality Beta or standard consumer preference, VHS. This format was fine for those needs. As computer technology advanced, however, the format of video for use on computers had to change. Not only has video been transformed from analog to digital, but storage methods also have changed. Videotape has certain limitations sometimes directly related to its physical characteristics, which deems it fragile and likely to damage by natural wear and tear. In the past few years, video has found a new home on CD-ROMs, which is a much sturdier form of storage. This format has increased the physical life of video, but it is an expensive method of distribution and currently is available only for viewing short clips. These limitations have contributed to the need for an inexpensive, immediate form of video, which has led to the most recent format: computer or server-based video.

Video on the Internet brings "on demand" access and increases interactivity from multiple client workstations. The same can be said for intranet users. Video is already a useful tool for training new employees, conducting presentations, and video-conferencing. Imagine the same tool used on a computer, in a form that's less expensive and more efficient. For example, if a company has offices throughout the country and is often hiring new employees, the use of a training video might be a necessity. Each time a company policy changes or executive offices change, however, the training video is not only re-edited but also redistributed, which is a costly task, considering that the tape purchases and dubbing fees can run into the thousands. This overhead can be eliminated with the use of video on an intranet. After the tape has been re-edited, the only cost is the time it takes to upload the video onto the server. The dubbing and distribution has been virtually eliminated. Time has not been wasted in the mailing process. The new video can be uploaded in one office and downloaded for viewing in another office across the country within the same hour. All offices or divisions have an up-to-date copy immediately.

The same advantages hold true for educational facilities that use video to give campus tours. Many universities have facilities branched off into different parts of the country or even the world, and in many cases, each campus has its own video tour. Then, for example, if a prospective student in the United States wants to tour the school's campus in Europe for study abroad, the video via the school's intranet allows the student to access up-to-date information.

Another major use of video is in presentations. Company employees are always presenting their ideas to potential clients, company executives, and board members. The use of video in their presentations is an efficient way of communicating complicated ideas and product changes to the audience. Video on an intranet could be easily accessed by several different presenters in different meetings. With video-conferencing, a company could also eliminate the need for travel among offices. In this instance, two people in two different offices could meet live, both seeing and hearing one another, and at the same time could have the option of recording the meeting so that anyone who was unable to be there could view the recording later. Many universities already use this method for long-distance learning, in which students gather in one classroom on one campus and the professor is in another on a different campus. The professor often is instructing several groups of students at the same time, allowing for interaction that otherwise would be impossible.

The intranet allows myriad video applications for both business and educational sectors of society. This new video technology can be stored on the same servers on which other software applications and files are kept. The tools for creating and playing video on intranets is the same as for the Internet.

Producing Your Intranet Video

Until recently, writing and producing video for distribution over the Internet, or the intranet, was different from creating video for regular distribution on VHS format. The current standard for transmission speeds on personal computers is the range from 1 fps (frame per second) to 10 fps. Compare this to real-time or actual video as viewed on TV programs or movie rentals, which are approximately 29.9 fps. Obviously, video is transmitted slower on computers than on television.

When video is transmitted, it is re-created on the client's workstation one pixel at a time. Pixels are dots of color information that can actually be seen if viewed at a close enough range. With a still image like a photograph, after the pixels are re-created, they remain intact until the user manipulates them in graphics packages such as Adobe Photoshop or Fractal Painter. With video, however, the pixels are constantly re-created because of the movement in the frames. Movement becomes a constant blur, defeating the purpose of using video. Until early 1996, when Starlight Networks announced its technology for downloading real-time video (30 fps) over intranets, the best way to produce a video for intranet use was to limit the use of zooms, pans, and color. Essentially, a "talking head" as often seen in documentaries, newscasts, and interviews would transmit better than most other video images. This is because the limited movement in video decreases the number of pixels that must be re-created during transmission, thus decreasing the chances of a blurred image. If you fear that the piece will be too boring to use, set up the production using two or three static shots: a close-up, a long-shot, and a medium shot. Cut between the three shots and work with what is available. Because the complete availability of real-time video tools from Starlight Networks is unknown, I advise using these tips while creating your intranet video.

Creating Recorded Video

After a piece is written and produced on standard video formats such as SVHS or Beta, it is time to convert it from analog to digital. Different software is available for the conversion and editing process, but the most popular is Adobe Premiere. This package is an editing system available on both PC and Mac platforms. It is ideal for corporations because it is an inexpensive way of combining video, graphics, and special effects in-house with the same professional quality as a post-production facility can produce. The following tables show the minimum system requirements for installing and using Premiere. To use this system, you must install a new type of video board with frame-capture capabilities on your computer.

Recommended Macintosh System Requirements

Macintosh 68020-68040	4 MB of application RAM
Power Macintosh	6 MB of RAM and an 80 MB hard drive; or, for full-screen video, 16 MB of RAM and a 500 MB hard drive
	Apple System Software version 7.0 or higher
	CD-ROM drive (for Deluxe CD-ROM)

Recommended Windows System Requirements

Pentium(TM) processor or i486 processor

DOS 5.0 or higher

Microsoft Windows 3.1 or higher with 8 MB of RAM with a 100 MB hard drive; or, for full-screen video, 16 MB of RAM and a 500 MB hard drive

CD-ROM drive (for Deluxe CD-ROM)

24-bit monitor

The following packages are compatible with either Macintosh or Windows for playback, manipulation of images, and creation of credits within the video:

Macintosh Compatibility

Images	Adobe Photoshop
	Adobe Illustrator
	PhotoCD
Sound	AIFF
	Audio CD
	Sound Designer
	SoundEdit files
Video	Adobe Premiere
	Targa
	QuickTime movie files
	QuickTime-compatible digital-video cards

Windows Compatibility

Images	Adobe Photoshop
Sound	WAV audio files
	AIFF audio files
Video	Microsoft Video for Windows (AVI)
	Apple QuickTime for Windows (MOV)
	Adobe Filmstrip, Autodesk Animator (FLC, FLI)
	Targa
	Digital-video cards compatible with Microsoft Video for Windows
	Adobe Premiere

Step-by-step tutorials and instructions are available for installation, conversion, and creation of your videos with each of these software packages.

QuickTime's current version for Mac is QuickTime 2.1; for Windows, it's QuickTime 2.0.3. This software has a third track, Sprite, that allows animation of any image in a movie file with the use of a basic editor like MoviePlayer. Previously, only two tracks were available for video and audio, but now four different tracks are designated for text, pictures, sounds, and time codes, all controllable by the user. Playback speed, image size, and the capability to have multiple movies playing in one window also are controllable. This software offers the user several other benefits, such as the ability to work with text in a word processor and bring it back into QuickTime without losing the video format. QuickTime claims that Sprite also provides the first level of interactivity within digital movies. And this version also offers better playback. As with Premiere, before using this package, you must convert your video from analog to digital format and then import it into QuickTime as either a movie or a PICT file.

An entirely different process is necessary if you want to create MPEG video from UNIX image files. First, analog video in Y, U, and V files must be converted. Pbmtoyuvsplit is a typical software package, available through the Netpbm toolkit, that performs this conversion for you. The next step is to encode the Y, U, and V files by using another software package, called MPEG. Another MPEG encoder, called mpeg_encode, also is available; this one does not require a pbmplus package, because all necessary libraries are included. The next step is to find an MPEG display program, such as Mpeg Play, which is another software package commonly used for this step. All this software can be downloaded via the Web.

Creating Live Video

Live video is now available through several software packages. Following is a brief description of the major players.

Xing StreamWorks

StreamWorks, developed by Xing Technology Corporation, is the first commercially available software for worldwide and local area network delivery of live and on-demand video. NBC uses StreamWorks to broadcast financial news programming to subscribers in the United States and Europe. Imagine the benefits to large companies and banks of having up-to-the-minute financial news running in a small window on employees' computers while they work in another package.

Unlike the current tightly coupled point-to-point client/server communication, StreamWorks "streams" its media, which allows the user to view and hear the data as it is being transmitted instead of waiting for it to download to the hard drive to be played back later. StreamWorks uses a client/server media distribution architecture that operates independently or complements existing WWW HTTP/HTML architectures on local area networks, private-data wide area networks, and public-data wide area networks.

StreamWorks uses the MPEG international standards for video and audio compression from UNIX and Windows NT servers. When used with the WWW, the software augments existing WWW architectures by providing CGI to existing WWW servers, and view extensions to popular Web browsers. In addition, it uses standard TCP/IP network protocols and "multicast IP" protocols for data delivery. This method allows multiple users to simultaneously view and hear the same data streams without duplication of data. Figure 26.1 shows a typical StreamWorks configuration.

FIGURE 26.1.
An example of a network using the Xing technology as drawn out by Xing Corporation and displayed on its Web site.

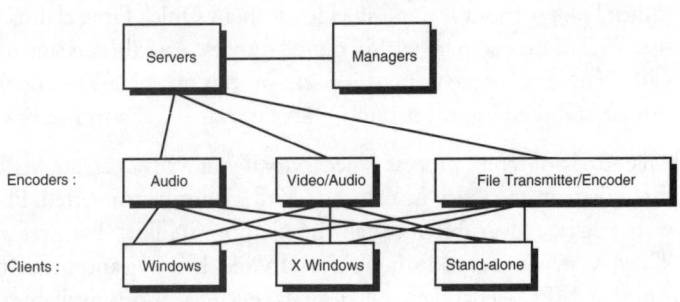

StreamWorks Network Manager

StreamWorks' benefits include compatibility with existing TCP/IP networks, including Ethernet, ATM, FDDI, ISDN, T1, and others. It adds live and on-demand video and audio services to private and public WANs and LANs without infrastructure changes, and it has low-overhead 3 percent to 5 percent video and audio streams that are fully routable. Network congestion is controlled by on-the fly birthrate reduction of video and audio streams. The streams are scalable from full-rate down to ISDN BRI (56 to 128 Kbps) and below (as low as 8.5 Kbps with LBR audio). Servers can be distributed for load balancing and stream caching. The client systems include software-only accelerated video and audio decoders. The compressed video and audio streams are compliant with MPEG-1 and MPEG-2 international standards.

Here are the URLs for two different galleries maintained by StreamWorks. For multimedia sites, surf to

`http://www.xingtech.com/streams/info/swSites.html`

which contains various sites using the StreamWorks technology in a multimedia fashion, and

`http://www.xingtech.com/streams/info/swLive.html`

which has sites using the technology live.

Pricing for StreamWorks depends on the system on which it will run and the package needed. StreamWorks ranges from $1800 for its file transmit system to $50,000 for its network servers.

VDOLive

VDOLive, shown in Figure 26.2, is a new technology developed by VDOnet Corporation to transmit video and audio over the Internet or any other TCP/IP network. It also uses client/server architecture in which the VDOLive Player is the client and the VDOLive Server is, well, the server. The current VDOLive Tools available with the VDOLive Server—to convert VHS/Beta videotape to a format compatible for use on VDOLive programs—must be used with VDOLive. The VDOLive Video Server allows users to capture, compress, and store audio and video to provide real-time playback.

FIGURE 26.2.
An example of VDOLive Player as used on VDOLive's Web site.

The following operating systems can run the VDOLive Video Server:

    MS Windows NT
    Sun Solaris 2.4 (or higher)
    SunOS 4.1.3
    SGI Irix 5.3 (or higher)
    FreeBSD 2.1
    Linux (a.out and ELF format)

The VDOLive Player allows users to receive and view the video clips while being transmitted. VDOLive Player transmits at 2 fps with a 14.4 Kbps modem, and a 28.8 modem transmits at up to 10 fps; an ISDN line transmits up to 20 fps. Currently, the VDOLive Player can run on any Power Mac. Following are the system requirements for using the VDOLive Player on a PC:

- 486 DX2 66 MHz or above
- MS Windows 3.1x with MS Video for Windows installed
- Windows 95 (video for Windows is built in)
- WWW browser capable of viewing graphics
- 8 MB RAM
- Sound card
- 14.4 Kbps or faster modem or LAN connection to the Internet

The benefits of using VDOLive Servers and Players include the capability to capture, digitize, compress, distribute, and view video over local and wide area networks using one system. Additionally, they play back at real time, and they need to store only one copy of each video. The VDOLive Video Server works with any Web server to add video to any Web site. Pricing for VDOLive products is based on either a one-time fee or yearly fees. Currently, the yearly fees include unlimited technical support via e-mail and phone, free access to VDOLive Products' WWW FAQ, and updates and patches for one year. For one-time purchase, the price ranges from $1,200 to $10,000, depending on the package. The VDOLive Player is free.

As I said, video must be compressed to be transmitted. A common package used for cross-platform, software-only, scalable compression-decompression video is Radius Cinepak. QuickTime, Microsoft Video for Windows, and several video-game companies, such as Atari and Sega, use Cinepak for their video compression.

Playback of Cinepak compressed video depends on the licensed platform. For example, QuickTime requires Apple Macintosh and MacOS systems, and a Windows OS platform requires Video for Windows or QuickTime for Windows. No additional hardware is necessary. Video can be decompressed on machines as low as LC III or a 20 MHz 386.

Cinepak plays back at a higher frame rate because it uses a vector quantization algorithm. It also uses very little processor bandwidth. Cinepak also offers online support for developers and is free to all content authors, developers, and users of any licensed computer platform.

Playback

Besides QuickTime, StreamWorks, and VDOLive, other video viewers exist. Xing Corporation offers the XingMPEG Player, which was the first software for adding MPEG playback capabilities to multimedia computers. Figure 26.3 shows an example of a Web site using the XingMPEG Player. The XingMPEG Driver is a high-performance Software MPEG Decoder capable of full-screen, full-motion, and full-color video playback with full-precision 16-bit 44 KHz stereo audio playback. It also offers support for VideoCD, CD-I movie, and KaraokeCD playback. For more specific information on using and configuring the XingMPEG Player, browse Xing's Web site at

```
http://www.xingtech.com/xingmpeg/index.html
```

FIGURE 26.3.

Access America's Web site requires MPEG Player to view its movie clips.

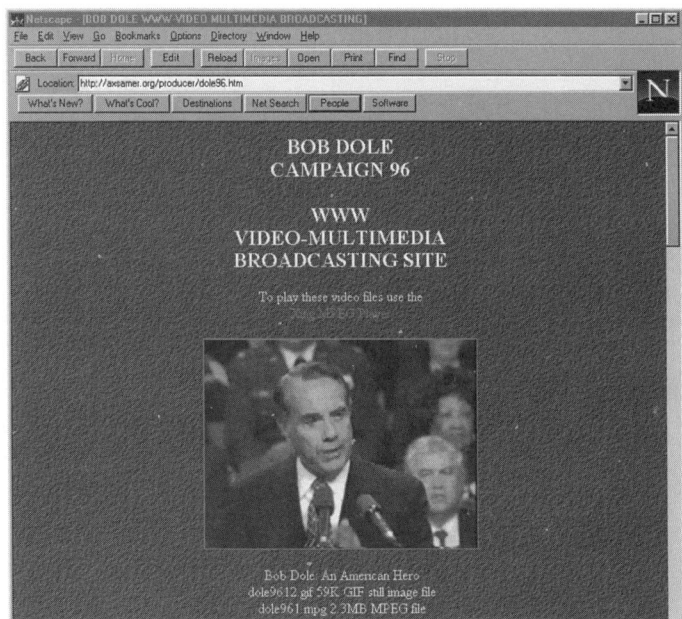

Following are the system requirements for using XingMPEG Player:

Minimum

386 CPU
4 MB RAM
Microsoft Windows 3.1 or higher version

Recommended

Pentium CPU
8 MB RAM
Microsoft Windows 3.1x
Video Accelerated VGA card with DCI driver
6-bit audio

Summary

The use of video on intranets opens up another dimension of communicating over intranets. Adding video applications to your intranet offers another avenue to support established organization programs, such as training, presentations, meetings, and conference calls. The packages mentioned here can get you started in creating and distributing video. The near future will bring the availability of packages developed by companies such as Starlight Networks that will allow you to distribute your video in television-like real-time transmission.

IN THIS PART

- FTP: Sharing Files **393**
- Using Databases **419**
- Telnet: Direct Access **437**

Using Your Intranet: Corporate Data

FTP: Sharing Files

27

by Art Klein

IN THIS CHAPTER

- A brief history of FTP **394**
- What does FTP do? **394**
- FTP clients versus FTP servers **396**
- FTP commands in detail **397**
- FTP: a complex example **402**
- Platform independence: why we use FTP **404**
- What is anonymous FTP? **405**
- FTP clients **408**
- FTP servers **411**
- What data should be shared via FTP? **413**
- Security (or how to share files smartly) **416**

In this chapter, you will explore the File Transfer Protocol (FTP). FTP is one of the cornerstones of the Internet, and it is an invaluable protocol for transferring files. FTP also is a useful protocol for sharing data, and using it wisely can help free up bandwidth on your local area network (LAN).

You will explore not only how FTP works, but also when it works best. You also look at the different implementations of FTP client and server software on different operating systems and examine their high and low points. The difference between FTP clients and servers also is addressed here. Over the course of this chapter, keep in mind that understanding the issues involved with logging into FTP and authenticating it are important. If any one issue stands out above all others, it would be this one, because a lax logon procedure to FTP can greatly compromise your entire LAN.

A Brief History of FTP

FTP is a component of the TCP/IP protocol stack. If you are familiar with the OSI seven-layer model, FTP functions at the application layer, at the same level as Telnet, the Simple Mail Transfer Protocol (SMTP), or any other TCP/IP application that interacts directly with the user. FTP specifications have been a key networking tool for more than two decades, and they have a proven track record in most major systems. The rise of the Internet as a tool for businesses and now the masses has greatly expanded use of FTP. Although once used only by systems experts and scientists, today FTP is popular among general users who have come to rely on it through their use of Web browsers and other similar programs.

What Does FTP Do?

Before I get into too much detail about FTP, an example describing how FTP works is in order. As I mentioned earlier, you use FTP to download and upload files across a local area network (LAN) or wide area network (WAN). As an example, imagine a user who wants to access a copy of a technical bulletin from a computer on her LAN and copy it to her own PC sitting at her desktop. Assume that this user's PC is running TCP/IP, and the system from which she wants to download the bulletin is on a UNIX file server named rocket. The file she wants is named bulletin.doc and is located in the directory /usr/docs. Following is an example of how the fictional user can download this file. Commands that appear in bold are those entered by the user.

```
C:\> cd temp
C:\TEMP>dir
 Volume in drive C is HAMSTRBRAIN
 Volume Serial Number is 1234-ABCD

 Directory of C:\temp

04/24/96  08:57a        <DIR>          .
04/24/96  08:57a        <DIR>          ..
```

FTP: Sharing Files

Chapter 27

```
            2 File(s)       0 bytes
                    300,638,720 bytes free

C>\TEMP> ftp rocket
Connected to rocket.
220 rocket FTP server (SunOS 4.1) ready.
user (rocket:(none)): suzanne
331 Password required for suzanne
Password: ******
230 User suzanne logged in.
ftp> cd /usr/docs
250 CWD command successful.
ftp> dir
200 PORT command successful.
150 ASCII data connection for /bin/ls (196.32.43.4,1945) (0 bytes).
-rw-r--r--   1     paul staff      2644     Mar  6   12:54    bulletin.doc
226 ASCII Transfer complete.
68 bytes received in 0.01 seconds (6.80 kbytes/sec)
ftp> ascii
200 Type set to A.
ftp> get bulletin.doc
200 PORT command successful.
150 ASCII data connection for bulletin.doc (196.32.43.4,1946) (2644 bytes)
226 ASCII Transfer complete.
2705 bytes received in 0.05 seconds (54.10 Kbytes/sec)
ftp> quit
C:\TEMP> dir
 Volume in drive C is HAMSTRBRAIN
 Volume Serial Number is 1234-ABCD

 Directory of C:\temp

04/24/96  08:57a    <DIR>           .
04/24/96  08:57a    <DIR>           ..
04/26/96  11:59a              2,644 bulletin.doc
              3 File(s)       2,644 bytes
                    300,134,912 bytes free
```

Let's review what happened on a line-by-line basis. First, the user, Suzanne, moves to the directory TEMP on the C drive on her PC and confirms that nothing is in it. Next, she uses the command `ftp rocket` to enter the FTP client program and open a connection with the server named rocket on her LAN. Rocket acknowledges that the connection is established and asks for a valid username and password. Note that Suzanne must have a valid login account on rocket to proceed with the FTP session. (FTP can be configured so that individuals without valid logons can gain access. This process is known as *anonymous FTP* and is addressed later in this chapter.) After the user successfully provides her logon name and password (I replaced her password with asterisks), rocket acknowledges that she has entered a correct name and password and passes control back to the FTP client program with a connection open between her system and rocket. Suzanne sees the FTP client program's prompt: `ftp>`.

Next, Suzanne uses the `cd` command from within FTP to change to the directory with the file she wants. Note that the `cd` command behaves within FTP much like `cd` does in UNIX or MS-DOS. The `cd` command moves Suzanne through the directory tree of the remote system. As far as FTP is concerned, the current working directory on her local machine is still C:\TEMP.

Suzanne then uses the `ls` command to get a listing of the files within her current working directory on the remote system, which is /usr/docs. She successfully identifies her target file, bulletin.doc, as being in this directory.

Suzanne, knowing that this is a flat ASCII text file and not a specially formatted file, such as an MS Word document, uses the `ascii` command to set the communication mode as `ascii` rather than `binary`. (The significance of the mode is addressed later in this chapter; see the sections "`ascii`" and "`binary`.") She next uses the `get` command to get the file from the client and place it in her current working directory on her local machine. The FTP program provides some statistics with regard to the data transfer and informs Suzanne that her transfer is complete. She then uses the `quit` command to close her session with rocket and exit the FTP client program. A quick type of the `dir` command confirms that the file exists on her local system, and Suzanne is done.

The heart of FTP is in the commands `get` and `put`. `get` requests files from the FTP server to which the connection is made and downloads them to a directory on the local machine. `put` sends files from the local directory and puts them in a specified directory on the FTP server. Figure 27.1 illustrates this process.

FIGURE 27.1.
A contrast of the `get` *and* `put` *commands.*

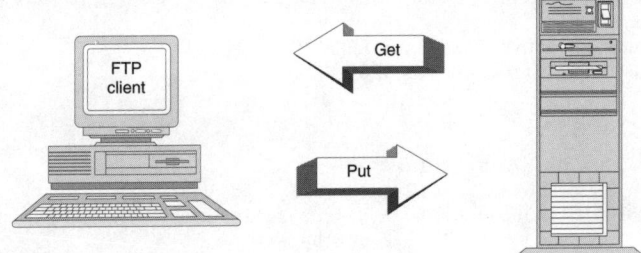

FTP Clients Versus FTP Servers

FTP is a protocol that involves two systems, one that requests a file transfer (the *client*) and one that then approves the request and does the sending or receiving (the *server*). These two systems have very different roles.

The client side of FTP is basically an interface to make FTP more usable for an end user. It provides an easy way for the end user to specify a transmission mode, from which directory to pull data, or other information pertinent to the FTP session. Every TCP/IP implementation comes with an FTP client program and is executable with the `ftp` command. Most PC and Macintosh-based TCP/IP packages have a graphical user interface (GUI) front end, so instead of typing the commands discussed earlier, you access FTP commands by using either pull-down menus or buttons the user clicks to invoke a particular FTP command. (An example later in this chapter shows an FTP client GUI and where commands typically may lie in a GUI.)

The server side of FTP does not run like the FTP client program. The FTP server functions in the background where it sleeps until an FTP client attaches to it. After an FTP client attaches to an FTP server program, the FTP server program wakes up, acknowledges that client, and handles the important task of authentication. The FTP server determines whether the username and password are correct and permits the client to proceed or denies access. (The "FTP Servers" section later in this chapter discusses how users and passwords are handled on a platform-by-platform basis.)

The FTP server program manifests itself in different ways on different systems, but it does not exist as an executable program. Rather, it is a process that exists on a server, as you can see in Table 27.1. What is important to remember here is that commands are executed from within the FTP client program and that the FTP server is not a program with which the end user deals directly.

Table 27.1. Different types of FTP server processes.

Platform	Implementation of FTP Server
UNIX	Daemon
MS-DOS	TSR that can be invoked as an executable
Windows NT	Service
Macintosh	Extension

FTP Commands in Detail

With the fundamentals of FTP clients and servers established, you're ready to examine some of the commands available within the FTP client program.

How to Enter FTP

To begin an FTP session, you must run the FTP client program. In the sample FTP session earlier in this chapter, this occurred when Suzanne typed `ftp rocket`. Typically, you enter FTP in one of two ways:

- By typing only the word `ftp` and then specifying which FTP server to open a connection to (see the section called "open" later in this chapter)
- By typing `ftp` followed by the name of the FTP server

It is clear that the FTP program has been entered when you see the prompt display (`ftp>`). GUIs to FTP are discussed later in this chapter.

Help from Within FTP

If you need help or a list of what commands are available from within FTP, at the FTP prompt, type the command help or a single question mark (?). Doing so generates a list of all commands available from within FTP, as shown in Figure 27.2. If you want information about a specific command, typing help [command] yields a one-sentence description of the command.

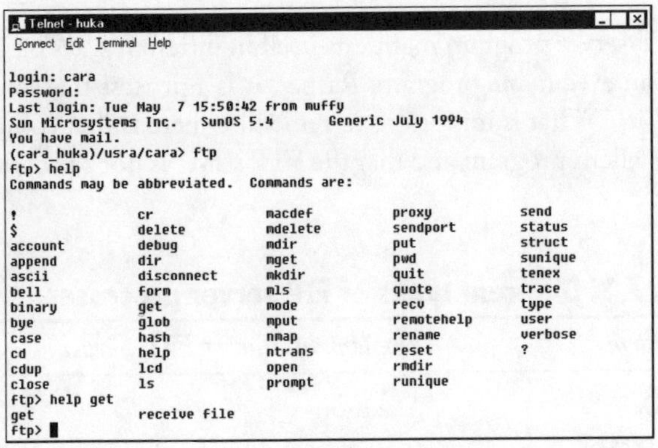

FIGURE 27.2.
Getting assistance for FTP commands.

```
login: cara
Password:
Last login: Tue May 7 15:50:42 from muffy
Sun Microsystems Inc.   SunOS 5.4     Generic July 1994
You have mail.
(cara_huka)/usra/cara> ftp
ftp> help
Commands may be abbreviated.  Commands are:

!           cr          macdef      proxy       send
$           delete      mdelete     sendport    status
account     debug       mdir        put         struct
append      dir         mget        pwd         sunique
ascii       disconnect  mkdir       quit        tenex
bell        form        mls         quote       trace
binary      get         mode        recv        type
bye         glob        mput        remotehelp  user
case        hash        nmap        rename      verbose
cd          help        ntrans      reset       ?
cdup        lcd         open        rmdir
close       ls          prompt      runique
ftp> help get
get         receive file
ftp>
```

ascii

As I mentioned earlier, you use the ascii command to set the transfer mode to ASCII data instead of binary. This mode for transfer of raw text or ASCII data is efficient and fast. It also is most often the default mode of FTP, because file transfers are much faster in ascii mode than in binary mode. Beware: Executable binary programs do not work when transmitted in ascii mode. If a program does not operate successfully after being sent or received via FTP, check to see if the program was transmitted in ascii mode. Users commonly make this mistake.

binary

The binary command is the partner to ascii. It sets the transmission mode as binary, meaning data will be transferred byte-by-byte as opposed to ASCII-character-by-ASCII-character. Although binary guarantees that a file transfer is complete and error free, it also is more time-consuming than ascii mode. Using binary, however, is the only way to transfer binary executable files.

bye

The bye command terminates an FTP session and exits from the FTP client program. It behaves identically to the quit command and exists to provide a set of commands familiar to users who have more exposure to mainframes than the PC or UNIX world.

cd

The FTP command `cd` permits movement through the directory tree on the remote system to which it is connected. The `cd` command functions much like the `cd` command does in UNIX or MS-DOS. The command `cd ..` moves you up a level in the directory tree, and a single dot (.) specifies the current working directory. Both a forward slash and backward slash are supported as delimiters to separate directory levels and to provide tools consistent for both PC and DOS users (that is, `cd /sales/files` and `cd \sales\files` changes to the same directory). From within FTP, I recommend using the absolute pathname rather than relative pathnames unless you are simply moving up or down the directory tree to avoid getting lost. Explicitly using the `cd` command helps keep you from getting lost in a large or complicated directory tree.

close

The `close` command ends an FTP session with the server without exiting the FTP program. This way, you can work with FTP files from two or more systems without having to fire up the FTP client program each time. See the section called "open" later in this chapter.

dir

The `dir` command functions exactly like the `dir` command in DOS. It permits you to see the contents of the current working directory on the remote system, providing the opportunity to confirm that a file is where you would expect it to be prior to downloading it.

get

The `get` command initiates an FTP `pull` command, which attempts to get a file from the current working directory on the remote system (directory movement controlled by `cd`) and pull it over to the current working directory on the local system (directory movement controlled by `lcd`). The `get` and the `put` commands are the heart and soul of FTP. The `get` command does not allow getting more than one file at a time. To transfer multiple files, refer to the `mget` and `mput` commands described later in this chapter.

hash

The `hash` command is convenient for transferring large files. Typing the command `hash` toggles on or off the printing of a hash mark (#) each time a full buffer of data is transferred. Thus, during a large file transfer, there is screen activity, reassuring the user that the system is not hung, but just in the midst of a large file transfer.

lcd

All commands discussed earlier in this chapter deal with movement within the directory tree related to the directories of the remote system. What about directory movement on the local system from within the FTP client program? Up until now, each time you entered the FTP program, you "got" and "put" in the local directory you were in when you fired up the FTP program. Just as the cd command moves through the remote directory tree, lcd (local change directory) moves you within the directory on the local system. Its syntax is exactly like the cd command. If you type lcd and press Enter, the lcd command will tell you what local directory you are in.

ls

The ls command lists the contents of a directory on the FTP server, much like the ls command within UNIX. It is redundant with the dir command discussed earlier. FTP was defined to be a usable system for people with exposure to many different operating systems. To ensure that a wide body of users find FTP usable, some commands are PC-based and UNIX-based, both yielding the same result. Although most PC users are familiar with the dir command and therefore don't need to use the ls command, it's there just in case.

mget

The mget (multiple get) command retrieves multiple files from a remote system with just one request. It interprets asterisks as wildcards and prompts you for a yes or no response for each file. It has no recursive features, meaning that although you can use mget to copy all the files in a given directory (mget *), you cannot use mget to get all the files in a given directory and *all directories beneath it*. You must use mget for each directory, one at a time. You also cannot deactivate the interactive nature of mget; you have to respond Y (yes) or N (no) for every file individually. A big advantage of a graphically based FTP client is that the interactive nature of both mget and mput (described next) is handled by the GUI, and multiple file transfers may be easier than in a text-based FTP session, contingent on how robust the GUI is.

mput

Just as mget gets multiple files, mput puts multiple files on the remote FTP system. Again, asterisks serve as wildcards, and mput is subject to the same limitations as mget is with regards to recursive directory trees and suppression of the interactive nature of the command. See the preceding section for more details.

open

Using the `open` command, you can open an FTP session from within the FTP client program. If you just completed a transfer session with a host named spanky, for example, and wanted to transfer some files from a different server named alfalfa, you could use the `close` command to close the session with spanky without quitting the FTP client program and type `open alfalfa` to open up an FTP session on the server named alfalfa.

put

`put` is the sister command to `get`. Just as `get` requests a file from an FTP server and transfers it to the current working directory on the client system, `put` sends a file from the current working directory on the local system and puts it in the current working directory on the remote system. It is a "push" type of operation as opposed to `get`, which is a "pull" operation. In other words, the command takes the file indicated on the local system and pushes it over the network to the current working directory on the FTP server.

pwd

The `pwd` command behaves exactly like the UNIX command `pwd`. It's also like typing the MS-DOS command `cd` with no arguments. It identifies the present (or current) working directory on the remote system.

> **TIP**
>
> To minimize confusion as far as the local current working directory, whenever you use the `lcd` command, use absolute paths instead of relative paths. Doing so makes it easier to keep track of the local present working directory.

quit

The `quit` command quits the FTP client program and closes any open sessions. It behaves identically to the `bye` command and again is there to provide commands familiar to a larger audience of users.

user

The `user` command permits you to send new user data to the remote FTP server in the middle of an open session. Assume, for example, you are logged in as user Mary, and you want to get a file that only user John has access to. If you know John's password, you can type the command `user John`, which prompts you for John's password. After you enter the correct password, you are logged in as user John and now can access the file.

FTP: A Complex Example

Now that you are more familiar with some of the key FTP commands, Listing 27.1 shows a more detailed sample FTP session that highlights many of the commands just discussed.

Listing 27.1. A complex FTP session.

```
ringo% cd tmp4
ringo% ftp paul
Connected to paul.
220 paul FTP server (SunOS 4.1) ready.
Name (paul:victor): victor
331 Password required for victor.
Password:******
530 Login incorrect.
Login failed.
ftp> user sales
331 Password required for sales.
Password:******
230 User sales logged in.
ftp> cd /sales/programs
250 CWD command successful.
ftp> binary
200 Type set to I.
ftp> hash
Hash mark printing on (8192 bytes/hash mark).
ftp> get forecast.exe
200 PORT command successful.
150 Binary data connection for forecast.exe (196.32.43.5,1398) (433599 bytes).
######################################################
226 Binary Transfer complete.
local: forecast.exe remote: forecast.exe
433599 bytes received in 2.5 seconds (1.7e+02 Kbytes/s)
ftp> close
221 Goodbye.
ftp> open george
Connected to george.
220 george FTP server (SunOS 4.1) ready.
Name (george:victor):[return]
331 Password required for victor.
Password:*****
230 User victor logged in.
ftp> cd /sales/files
250 CWD command successful.
ftp> lcd / myfiles
Local directory now /myfiles
ftp> ascii
200 Type set to A.
ftp> mget *
mget data1? y
200 PORT command successful.
150 ASCII data connection for data1 (196.32.43.6,1401) (216799bytes).
#
226 ASCII Transfer complete.
local: data1 remote: data1
216799 bytes received in 2.5 seconds (85 Kbytes/s)
```

```
mget data2? y
200 PORT command successful.
150 ASCII data connection for data2 (196.32.43.6,1402) (216799 bytes).
#
226 ASCII Transfer complete.
local: data2 remote: data2
216799 bytes received in 2.5 seconds (85 Kbytes/s)
mget data3? n
mget data4? y
200 PORT command successful.
150 ASCII data connection for data4 (196.32.43.6,1403) (216799 bytes).
#
226 ASCII Transfer complete.
local: data4 remote: data4
216799 bytes received in 2.5 seconds (85 Kbytes/s)
mget data5? y
200 PORT command successful.
150 ASCII data connection for data5 (196.32.43.6,1404) (216799 bytes).
#
226 ASCII Transfer complete.
 local: data5 remote: data5
216799 bytes received in 2.5 seconds (85 Kbytes/s)
ftp> close
221 Goodbye.
ftp> bye
ringo%
```

In this example, the user is Victor. Victor wants to download a sales forecasting program from the marketing department's FTP server, which is named Paul. He then wants to download some forecasting data files from the sales department's FTP server, which is named George. Victor starts by trying to open an FTP session to the marketing FTP server from his local machine, which is named Ringo. Victor does not have a valid login on system Paul, so his attempt fails. Although Victor remains within the FTP program, he is not connected to a server. Victor then remembers that there is a shared account on that system named sales for all the salesmen, like Victor, to access. Using the user command to resend data to Paul, he authenticates successfully. Victor then uses the cd command to change directories to where the forecasting program, named forecast.exe, is located.

Because this is a binary executable program, Victor sets the mode to binary and then toggles hash marks on so that he can see the transfer of the file progress. Next, he uses the get command to download the file and notes that the hash marks move across the screen as the file is transferred. Having downloaded the file from Paul, Victor uses the close command to disconnect from server Paul but remains in the FTP program.

He now uses the open command to open George, the sales department's server. Victor uses the lcd command to move to a different location on his local system before starting the download. He also use cd to change to the correct directory to get his raw data files and then uses the mget command to get all the files in this directory interactively. He then chooses on a file-by-file basis which ones to download. He enters close to close his connection with server George and exits the FTP program through the bye command.

With this information, you should feel comfortable using FTP to get and put files from and on systems to your LAN.

Platform Independence: Why We Use FTP

FTP is useful to an intranet because it provides a general protocol to permit movement of files between systems that have completely different architectures or operating systems.

As a component of the Transmission Control Protocol/Internet Protocol (TCP/IP) suite of protocols, any computer that supports TCP/IP has an implementation of FTP (or at least the client program, as some TCP/IP packages do not contain an FTP server program) and thus can communicate with any other computer running a TCP/IP stack. FTP is the easiest way to move files between UNIX, Macintosh, and PC systems, provided they all have a TCP/IP stack and at least one of them is configured as an FTP server. The systems that hold files for FTP need not understand or be able to run a file to make it viable for sharing or downloading via FTP, as long as it was placed on the said system by binary FTP transfer and not ASCII. One system with a large hard drive can serve as a repository for data. Programs that operate on a variety of platforms can be made available to a variety of different system types from a single FTP server. In Figure 27.3, a large UNIX system is storing files that run on HP-UX, SunOS, Windows 3.1, and Macintosh. Even though the system itself cannot run the SunOS, Windows, or MacOS programs, it still serves as a central repository for all these programs while making them available for downloading.

FIGURE 27.3.
A UNIX server sharing files that run on a wide variety of platforms via FTP.

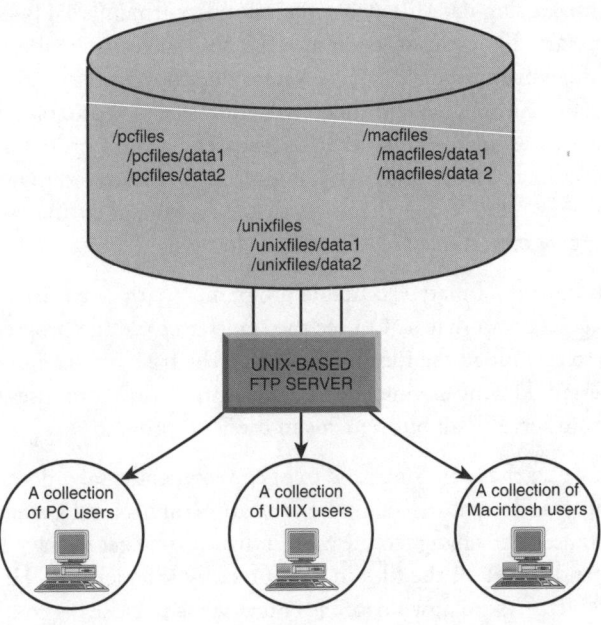

What Is Anonymous FTP?

FTP is the primary mode of transferring data over the Internet. Each time a file is downloaded over the Internet, FTP works "behind the scenes" performing the file transfer, which poses some interesting questions. Until now, you have seen examples of FTP where a user logs in to a system to use FTP by supplying a valid login name and a valid password. But how does a user download a file from an arbitrary Web page? How does a file get downloaded from Microsoft's home page to your system? Do you supply a password through your Web browser?

Because it is not possible for a systems administrator to maintain accounts for every person who may visit a public FTP server on the Internet, FTP functionality is provided for arbitrary users via *anonymous FTP*.

What Makes Anonymous FTP So Special?

Review the FTP commands at the beginning of this chapter again. Here are the most basic and fundamental commands used to transfer data via FTP. There are many more commands that were not discussed in detail, such as `delete`, `mkdir`, and `rename`. Remember, FTP is a powerful tool. From within it, the seasoned user can delete, rename, and move files fairly effortlessly. If a systems administrator is going to share files with the general public, he or she does not want to give the Internet community this level of power via FTP. For this reason, it is a bad idea to create a general account with a generic name and password (like "guest") for the general public to use for FTP transfer. Anonymous FTP is a special FTP account with access to a limited number of commands and access to a limited area on your FTP server. Anonymous FTP makes only a small portion of the FTP server's file system visible. It is impossible to use `cd` to change to the top level of the FTP server (for example, `cd /`) from within anonymous FTP.

When it is configured correctly, anyone can FTP to your system by supplying *anonymous* as their login name. Although the user still is asked to supply a password, any password (or none) is accepted, and the user is granted access. *Internet etiquette mandates that users should typically supply their e-mail addresses as passwords.* By doing so, the systems administrator at the remote system knows who has been visiting his or her system. After logging in, the anonymous FTPer does not have complete access to the entire directory tree on the FTP server. Instead, the user has limited access to a public area where files can be accessed and, if configured as such, a place where files can be placed via FTP.

Configuring Anonymous FTP

To illustrate how anonymous FTP operates and is administered, I will provide an example of how to configure a UNIX-based anonymous FTP server. If you're not familiar with UNIX, you may want to skip this section. PC and Macintosh systems are not configured from the command line; configuration usually is reduced to filling in dialog boxes, specifying information such as the anonymous user's home directory.

Building an Anonymous FTP Account

First, create a user logon named *ftp* that is a member of the group anonymous. Add a line to the /etc/group file specifying a new group with the name anonymous. Make sure that you assign it a unique Group ID (GID), one that is not used by any other accounts on the system. Next, add a user named ftp to the /etc/passwd file. It should have a unique User ID (UID) and should be a member of the group anonymous just created. The password entry for this account should consist of only a single asterisk (*), thus disabling the login. As a security precaution, you can set the login shell to /bin/false to make this account even harder to enter or break into. As an example, if you were going to reserve UID 50 and GID 60 for anonymous FTP, your group and password files would include the following lines:

/etc/group:

anonymous:*:60

/etc/passwd:

ftp:*:60:50::/home/ftp:/bin/false

Notice that I gave the account ftp a home directory of /home/ftp. Choose this home directory carefully! Only this home directory and the contents directly below it should be visible to those users who use the FTP site with the login of anonymous. When a user logs onto your system via anonymous FTP, a low-level system function named chroot is called. This command changes the root directory to whatever is referenced in the /etc/passwd file. In other words, the chroot call forces any reference to the top level of the directory tree ("/") to expand out to the home directory of the FTP account (/home/ftp, in this case), thereby sealing off all directories above this home directory, as shown in Figure 27.4.

Building Out the FTP Home Directory

After all directories above the FTP home directory are locked out, commands like ls are completely inaccessible. The ls command is used by the FTP client program to give directory listings with the dir and ls commands from within FTP, so somehow the system must access it. To do so, put a copy of this command and a few other files below the home directory of the FTP account. Make sure to place only a minimal number of commands and files at this level, reducing the number of potential tools available to break into the system. At a minimum, the program /bin/ls must be copied down to a subdirectory beneath the FTP home directory named bin (for example, ~ftp/bin). It must be set so that no one can read or write to it; in other words, it should only be executable, but executable by all groups. You can do this by setting the permissions on this file with the chmod command to 111.

FIGURE 27.4.
How the chroot *call changes the user's access and perspective of the file system.*

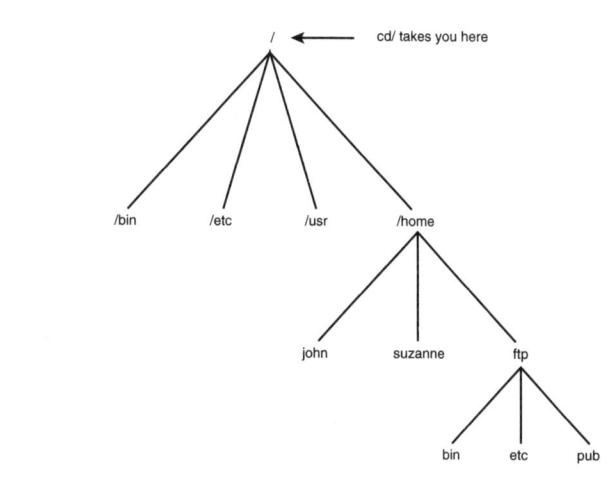

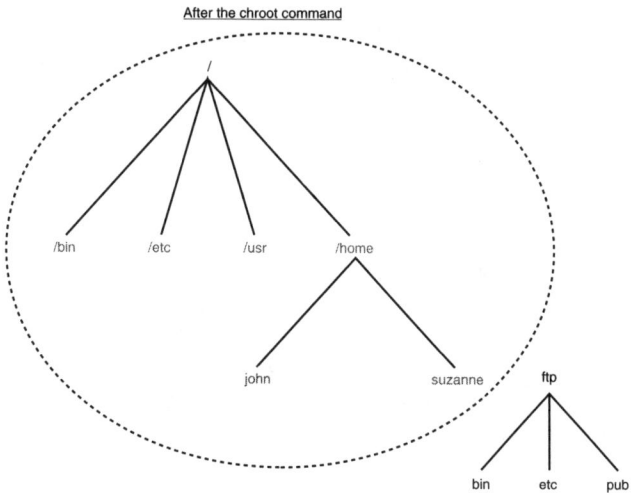

If you want the ls command to provide information about what users own what files, copies of the /etc/passwd and /etc/group files must be accessible so that the system can match the UIDs and GIDs of a file with a certain user and group. The copy of the password file should have the encrypted password field replaced with an asterisk, and if your site is very security conscious, you can eliminate all entries from the ~ftp/etc/passwd file except for those corresponding to root, daemon, uucp, and ftp. By eliminating the other entries, nosy browsers cannot get to see a list of all the local users in the local version of the passwd file. Using the chmod command, change the mode of these two files to 444.

If you want to permit users to put files on your anonymous FTP site, you should also create a public directory (a standard name for this directory is ~ftp/pub) directly below the ftp home directory and make it writable by changing the mode of the directory to 755 by using the chmod command.

If you are unfamiliar with the chmod command, it lets you control who can read, write (or remove!), and execute a program. The first number describes the privileges the owner of the file has. The second number describes the privileges of the members of the group the file belongs to. The third number indicates which privileges all other users have. Table 27.2 shows what numbers correspond to what permissions.

Table 27.2. Numbers used in the chmod command and the permissions associated with them.

Number	Permissions Granted
1	Executable
2	Writable
4	Readable
5	Readable and executable
7	Readable, writable, and executable

Testing Anonymous FTP

Before you can call your anonymous FTP site complete, give it a rigorous test to make sure that it operates as you expect. Try to get and put files both from places it should work and places it should fail. Try to break out of the FTP login, and make sure that the system is bulletproof before calling your job done.

FTP Clients

You will now look at some of the differences between FTP clients on different hardware and software platforms. After I briefly describe what you may expect to see in different types of FTP clients, I will address some of the important criteria used in selecting an FTP client to suit your needs.

UNIX/Linux

Typically, FTP from UNIX systems is handled at the command line. (Linux, an operating system freely available on the Internet, is functionally a derivative of UNIX. What works for UNIX works for Linux.) Although some decent GUIs may be available for UNIX, they rarely are used.

UNIX has always been a command-line-based language, and the use of FTP within UNIX is similar from platform to platform. FTP comes built into UNIX's TCP/IP implementation and is free with UNIX.

MS-DOS/Windows 3.x

To use FTP under MS-DOS and Windows 3.x, you need to purchase a TCP/IP package from a third party. Some of the more popular packages have been developed by FTP Systems (PC TCP), Spry, Inc. (AirConnect), and Wollengong Systems (Pathways).

Starting Up the FTP Client Program

Figure 27.5 shows what you see when you run the FTP Client GUI that is provided with the CuteFTP shareware package released by Alex Kunadze.

FIGURE 27.5.
CuteFTP running the FTP Client GUI.

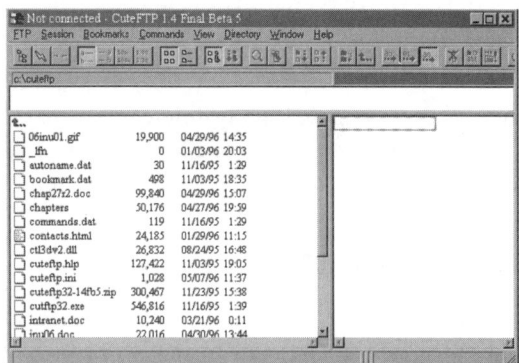

In Figure 27.5, notice that you have an icon-based image of the directory that you were in when you entered FTP. It is your local current working directory. You can reach most of your FTP commands through pull-down menus. To open a session with a system, choose FTP | Connection | Open. A dialog box appears, as shown in Figure 27.6, asking you what system to connect to, what username to log in as, and what password to supply.

FIGURE 27.6.
Connecting to a remote system.

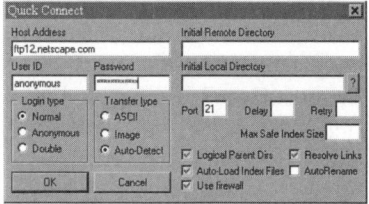

Upon correctly authenticating, you see a second icon-based directory tree, as shown in Figure 27.7. It is the current working directory on the remote system.

FIGURE 27.7.
Seeing the directory tree on both the local and remote systems.

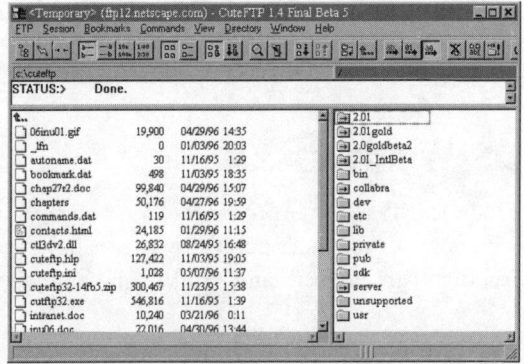

As far as getting and putting files, you do so in a drag-and-drop manner. Move through the different directory trees by clicking the icons, and when you want to transfer the file, hold down the mouse button as you select the file, and drag it to the directory to which you want to transfer it. You can find features such as binary and ASCII transfer, for example, under the Options menu.

Some client programs may have slightly different ways of transferring files, like buttons labeled get or put or two fixed subwindows, one for the local system and one for the remote system, with arrow buttons that transfer files in a given direction.

Windows NT/Windows 95

Windows NT and Windows 95 have a built-in TCP/IP stack, which has built-in FTP functionality much like UNIX. The implementation of FTP built into NT has no GUI; it has a command-line interface only. You can install third-party GUI-based FTP clients over NT's native TCP/IP stack, and this is done fairly often. This way, a GUI-based version of the FTP client is available. The example of the CuteFTP client shown in Figure 27.8 (shown later) is a good representation of the style of FTP graphically based clients you see in the NT world, along with the Windows 95 and Macintosh world.

MacOS

MacOS is much like Windows 3.1 in that you must purchase a third-party TCP/IP package that includes an implementation of FTP. Just like with MS-DOS and Windows, many firms like Wollengong Systems (MacPathways) and Intercom (TCP Connect II) provide TCP/IP packages. Like Windows 3.x and Windows NT, the Macintosh FTP clients are most often GUI-based, so the descriptions under MS-DOS/Windows 3.x apply.

Choosing the Right FTP Client Package

As far as choosing the right FTP client, ergonomics is really the only important feature of the client package. How usable is it? Are the features that you need to modify a lot (for example, ascii or binary mode) easily accessible? How easy will it be to train your users on this package given its look and feel?

A greater issue exists, however. Most FTP clients come bundled as part of a TCP/IP implementation. You must evaluate the entire TCP/IP package as a whole. To purchase a top-end FTP program that runs over a poor TCP/IP stack would be a big mistake. Look at the other features of the package, and evaluate it as a whole.

FTP Servers

Choosing the right FTP server for your needs is more important than choosing the FTP client software, because the FTP server actually deals with security. The FTP server handles security issues such as who can log into the server, who can download files from the server, and whether to enable anonymous FTP. Remember, any system that you want your users to connect to via FTP must have FTP server software running. In this section you will learn what differences to expect from FTP servers of different platforms and how they deal with security issues and anonymous FTP.

UNIX/Linux

UNIX and Linux's TCP/IP stack includes a built-in FTP server. It has an FTP daemon that is typically configured as part of the system's startup procedure. Its implementation of anonymous FTP is robust and well documented by many books; you also can access online manual pages by typing man ftp or man ftpd.

UNIX is probably the operating system best suited for acting as an FTP server because UNIX-based FTP is directly tied in with UNIX user accounts and passwords, so account management and password authentication are handled by UNIX. Furthermore, within UNIX, each file has a specific owner who can set the privileges on who can or cannot read a certain file. This feature adds another level of security to FTP from within UNIX. Not only is access to the file system controlled by logging in, access to certain files can be restricted by setting the read and write privileges of the files accordingly.

Of course, one of the biggest pluses of a UNIX-based FTP server is that UNIX implementations of TCP/IP and FTP have a two-decade history in the implementation of mission-critical systems. Twenty years is a track record unmatched by any other operating system.

MS-DOS/Windows 3.1/Windows 95

Just as MS-DOS and Windows have no built-in TCP/IP stack, they do not have a built-in FTP server either. When you're comparing FTP servers, pay close attention to how they handle validation of logins, anonymous FTP, and isolation of public areas of the file system. Because MS-DOS has no built-in user control, the only security in DOS-based FTP servers is what is built into the TCP/IP package.

I don't recommend using an MS-DOS system as an FTP server if the option on any UNIX system, such as a PC running Linux, is available because of these security issues. Although Windows 95 does have a built-in TCP/IP stack, it does not have a built-in FTP server service; thus, it behaves like a Windows NY FTP client and a Windows 3.1 FTP server.

Macintosh

Macintosh FTP servers are fairly few and far between but behave similarly to NT FTP servers. They are GUI based and typically enforce read and write privileges that exist on files and folders. These permissions are set through AppleTalk. Some access control from within the FTP extension is typically available if the Macintosh is running AppleTalk.

Windows NT

Although Windows NT has an FTP server built into its TCP/IP stack, and it provides most of the same functions as the UNIX FTP server, it is configured through a GUI rather than a command line. Windows NT is different from the UNIX implementation of FTP in a number of ways. Windows NT establishes only one directory, which is the default current working directory, upon connection for any user. Within UNIX, when a user connects to a server via FTP, the initial current working directory is set to the home entry in the user's entry in the /etc/passwd file.

Figure 27.8 shows the configuration screen for the FTP server on Windows NT. As you can see, through this dialog box you can control attributes like the maximum number of connections and the idle time-out time. Limiting the number of users connected to an FTP server can be very convenient so that the sheer volume of people attempting to perform file transfers does not generate unwieldy transfer times. As you also can see within the dialog box, the option to make the anonymous FTP login something other than anonymous is available also, but because the login of anonymous is an informal Internet standard, you probably should not change it if you anticipate strangers connecting to your FTP server. These features are not readily available within the UNIX implementation of an FTP server.

FTP: Sharing Files

Chapter 27

413

FIGURE 27.8.
Configuration of a Windows NT-based FTP server.

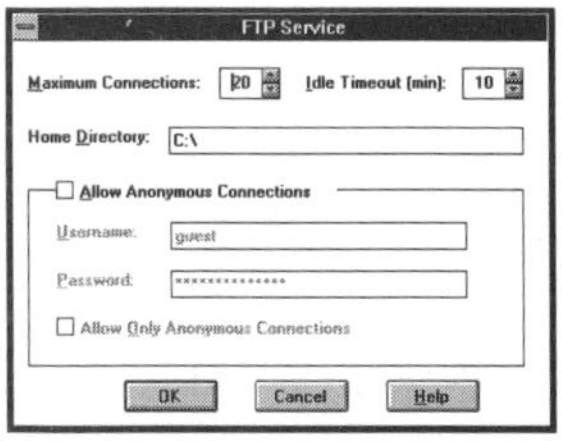

> **NOTE**
>
> Although FTP is a part of TCP/IP, the FTP server service for Windows NT is not automatically installed when you install the TCP/IP suite from the NT CDs. It is a separate package that you need to install; you can find it on the NT Server CDs.

On the flip side, the security of the NT FTP server is less robust. You can control read or write access on the partition level but not on the file-by-file level from within the FTP Server Security dialog box, as you can see in Figure 27.9. From within Windows NT, the user can set privileges of directories and files, but the procedure is not as straightforward as the chown or chmod commands within UNIX are. NT does have logging capabilities to track who is accessing the FTP server, both as "non-anonymous" standard users and as anonymous users.

FIGURE 27.9.
Configuring security on a Windows NT FTP server.

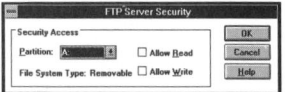

Several third-party FTP servers are available for Windows NT, for a variety of costs and with a variety of features. Most of these are new and might have unique features that you won't see in the standard FTP server prevalent in UNIX. Based on the sensitivity of the data on your LAN and the amount you want to spend on an FTP server, an NT FTP server might be an efficient and leading-edge solution to your file-sharing needs. UNIX FTP is very stable but not very exciting or visually straightforward.

What Data Should Be Shared Via FTP?

Now that the fundamentals of FTP have been addressed, the next question is, Why FTP? What should it be used for? Can you use some strategy to determine what should be shared and how? The answers to these questions depend on who your user community is and whether or not these users work within your firm. In the following sections, I answer these questions first from the standpoint of the Internet and then from the standpoint of your own intranet.

Over the Internet

When you address sharing files over the Internet, you are talking about making files public to the entire Internet community—that is, what to make available via anonymous FTP.

Inform Your Community

Making files available for public access is one thing, but letting potential users or viewers know that the anonymous FTP site is there and available is another. To alert potential users and viewers, I suggest a pre-computer notion: Advertise! Of course, you can advertise in many ways, both electronically and nonelectronically. A rather simple method is to set the logon banner of your system to display an advertisement making users aware of your FTP. If your organization has a Web page on the Internet, you can place information on accessing your FTP site on the Web page. If nothing else, place your organization's Internet address on the FTP site or any printed media targeted at general users.

What Type of Data?

Before selecting data to place, be aware that anyone can connect to this system. So, make sure that the only data or executable that is shared is ready for public consumption and is error free.

Any customer support documentation is a valued addition to an FTP site. Posting this type of "raw" data here provides an easy way for your customers to get immediate support, regardless of the time of day or the burdens of the support staff. Troubleshooting documents, how-to documents, and Frequently Asked Questions (FAQs) documents are popular with anonymous FTP sites. Also, if you're running a business, consider placing price lists, product information, nonconfidential sales and marketing data, and even biographies of prominent staff members. This way, you get free publicity and advertising. Anything your business or organization wants to publicize should be on the FTP site.

Now consider binary executables or other forms of data that are not "raw." If you have any public domain or internally developed programs you want to share with the public, you can place them on an anonymous FTP site. You also can put demos or evaluation software on an FTP site, as Netscape did with its 2.0 beta software, and you can place free upgrades or utilities on the anonymous FTP site also. Once again, remember that what you place on this site is available for all the Internet to access, so make sure that nothing confidential appears in this data. If you have an internal FTP site with sensitive data, make sure that the two FTP sites are isolated from one another.

Some Final Thoughts on Internet FTP

You should remember a few basic yet critical issues regarding anonymous FTP.

First, provide an index or table of contents. Make sure that one file named readme.txt, or TOC, carries an up-to-date index of what files are available via FTP and what they contain.

Second, unless you have a good reason, do not enable write privileges on your anonymous FTP site. Allowing write privileges is a sure way to have your system infected with a virus or Internet worm.

Also, ensure that the data you post is current. An outdated FTP site is a useless site and will not be visited frequently.

Finally, take a look at what files you can group (via Tar or PKZip) into one file and compress. Compressing files has two advantages. It reduces the space and bandwidth the file requires during downloading and on the FTP server. Additionally, grouped and compressed files allow a user retrieving a file to use the `get` command instead of the interactive and more cumbersome `mget` command.

Within an Intranet

Within an intranet, there is less concern about security because the site is not connected to the systems outside your local area network. Nevertheless, vigilance and awareness are mandatory when it comes to evaluating what data can be shared anonymously. You can post general internal toolkits or applications for users who want to download specific applications via FTP instead of installing new applications on individual systems. This approach is an efficient way to keep applications in an accessible location. Internal documentation, such as work standards, company policies, staff directories, and project notebooks can be made available. Be creative with the data you post.

As an example, at one large financial services firm, the Novell NetWare administrators loaded the all-important NetWare license and key executable file (SERVER.EXE) for each Novell server onto a UNIX-based FTP server, so any existing Novell server can be quickly regenerated in an emergency, even if the original installation media has disappeared.

Format Matters (and Does It Ever!)

Be aware of what format your data is in. If your user community is a group using UNIX, don't put Microsoft Word documents on your site. Make sure that any nonstandard data put on an FTP site is readable by the user community; if necessary, put the application needed to view the data on the FTP site also. Make sure that the file formats are well documented in your site's table of contents.

Also, the information you post is valuable only if it's accessible, so post with the least common denominator in mind. If your desktop system is a high-performance NT workstation, don't put 32-bit applications on a site to be shared by Windows 3.1 machines.

Security (or How to Share Files Smartly)

You should keep in mind a few issues regarding security and FTP. When you're thinking of setting up FTP, make certain that you understand all the issues behind system security before you enable it. As you've heard before, discretion is the better part of valor.

File System Structure

Look closely at the file system structure of your FTP server. Do you have the area reserved for anonymous FTP isolated correctly? Is it empty of any unnecessary files? Are you sure there are no symbolic links (which can be problematic for anonymous FTP because the chroot call may put the other side of the link in an area inaccessible to the FTPer) or NFS (Network File System) mounts below the home directory of the anonymous FTP account?

System Isolation

Is your system sufficiently isolated? If you have an FTP site connected to the Internet, is it sufficiently firewalled from the rest of your intranet? In general, try to minimize the number of points of intersection between your intranet and the Internet, as this will reduce the number of entry points a potential hacker can use to gain entry.

Controlling Access to the FTP Server

Controlling access to the FTP server has two sides: the physical and the digital. Physically, or geographically speaking, store the system in a secure place. Make sure that general members of your staff do not have access to the FTP server, reducing the chances that they might modify any system files or grant themselves a higher level of authority on the system. On the software side, do not put unnecessary accounts on the system. If only a handful of users are authorized to use FTP in your firm, do not put an account on there for every network user. You therefore should avoid distributing your account data to the FTP server by NIS, if you use NIS at your firm. NIS and NIS+ are services that permit many systems to share the same files—typically system files such as the password file—thus allowing the creation of a "master" password file that all systems can share. Watch log files carefully, and frequently audit who is connecting to your FTP server—from both the inside and the outside.

Also keep close tabs on who has access to what information. Check the permissions of all the systems files, and make sure that each user starts with read and write access only in the local and public area. If you permit your users to relax the access rights on their personal areas, make sure that they are aware of the risks and make sure that they cannot modify the privileges of the public area.

Using Inactivity Time-Outs

Whenever possible, configure your FTP server to time out after a period of inactivity. This reduces the risk of a user walking away from a system in the middle of an FTP session and leaving the system unattended and waiting to be compromised.

Anonymous FTP Revisited

I must reiterate that you must exercise caution with anonymous FTP. Remember that with anonymous FTP, you cannot control who accesses files. Any auditing of users accessing your anonymous FTP server is based entirely on their honor when it comes to supplying their e-mail addresses as their passwords. Test your anonymous FTP site thoroughly before opening it up to the public. Try to delete files from within it, and try to move above the home directory of the anonymous FTP account to make sure that the anonymous FTPer does not have more privileges than you allow.

Summary

FTP is an integral part of TCP/IP and almost all local area networks. Due to the nature of FTP, it requires user authentication—logging in with account names and passwords. This authentication directly affects the systems administrator in two ways. It is an extra application that needs to be maintained and kept aligned with the current user community, and it is an additional security issue.

In this chapter, you learned about the mechanics of how FTP works and the risks of providing FTP functionality. In all probability, at a bare minimum, you will want to permit bidirectional FTP within your LAN ("getting" and "putting" FTP out of your LAN so that your staff can get files from the Internet). You may not want to allow the external community into your LAN via FTP. Either way, you should address this issue early so that, as your file transfer needs expand, you know what tools you want to implement and on what type of platform.

Using Databases

28

by Frank Pappas

IN THIS CHAPTER

- Selecting tools **420**
- Evaluating database options **424**
- Advanced intranet database issues **429**
- Distributing your data across your intranet **429**
- Replicating your data across your intranet **430**
- Designing for growth **432**
- Implementation examples **433**

If knowledge is power, connecting a database to your intranet is probably one of the most empowering decisions that you can make to enhance and extend the functionality of your internal site. Throughout history—and especially in the fast-paced world of modern business communications—information (or lack thereof) has been the single most important factor in determining whether a particular company prospers or declines in the face of stiff competition. This being the case, it's extremely important that everyone supporting your company's business objectives—from the chief executive officer all the way down to the administrative assistant's assistant—be fully informed on every issue that will affect them in the performance of their duties. From product feature updates and revised production plans to customer contact lists or internal supply requisitions, an intranet database will help your employees to become more effective in their positions, increase customer satisfaction with your improved performance, and will, in general, make life a great deal easier for all involved in the day-to-day operation of your organization.

In this chapter, you will learn about some of the newest and most powerful database technologies that will be shaping the way both the Internet and your corporate intranet will evolve over the next few years, and how you can strategically develop your database "game plan" to maximize the benefits that these new technologies will provide. You also examine the important issues that you should take into account when including a database system as a major component of an intranet and look at how some of today's major intranet players have incorporated database systems into their individual sites.

This chapter is designed to guide you through the myriad options available to you in the database world—without all the hype generally associated with high-profile marketing plans that most often surround the really exciting and powerful intranet products. You'll be able to make educated decisions rather than seat-of-the-pants guesses, which means that you'll save yourself a good deal of research time and stress, and you'll (most likely) be able to deliver a much better product for your company. Remember that although a database system can ease any number of intranet tasks—from product distribution to scheduling to purchasing—you'll need to make sure that you don't misjudge your company's needs in the database arena, or you'll risk implementing either a low-end and ineffective database solution or an overly powerful and financially prohibitive debacle that can affect your company's communications efforts considerably. Keep in mind that although a database can effectively complement the balance of your intranet's resources, you must be extremely careful when utilizing this technology for sensitive or mission-critical data.

Selecting Tools

When you're evaluating your company's need for one or more of the many database systems available to you as core components for your intranet, you should realize that although each package is in its most pure sense a traditional database system, in reality the specific features that extend each particular program's functionality can be quite different, resulting in highly differentiated database systems. Familiarizing yourself with the various specialties presented by the different systems is therefore essential. Otherwise, you risk implementing a project that is doomed right from the start due to an inadequate or insufficient technological foundation. Although high-end database systems offered by Informix or Sybase are right for transaction-heavy or extremely data-laden intranets, you may find that more conservative packages such as Paradox or MS Access are both more affordable and practical in light of your particular intranet's needs.

If you've begun to consider whether the database route is the proper choice for your intranet, you've taken the first step in an important process that can ultimately influence how well your system is able to service the needs of your corporation. Generally, three central reasons or goals can serve as adequate justification for involving a database in your intranet design. The first is the ability to search quickly through large collections of data to find specific, relevant, and identifiable sections with ease, as you can see in the process shown in Figure 28.1. If your employees need to locate a customer's purchase order, find out about the status of an office supply requisition, or simply learn about the company's latest changes to the health plan, for example, a database is an excellent way to catalog such data, because important characteristics such as keywords, table fields, and other factors can easily be included in a Web- or intranet-based search system.

FIGURE 28.1.
Intranet databases allow for rapid and powerful searches of huge corporate information collections.

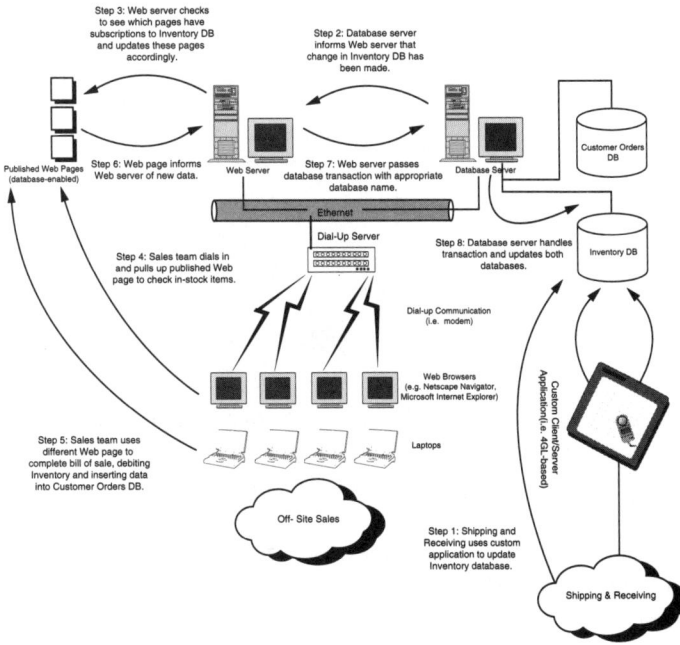

A second important goal that relies heavily on an effective database integration is the ability to change, add, or update an important company database from a number of locations, as shown in Figure 28.2. In this case, you are not dependent on having physical access to the machine that hosts the database. This capability is of tremendous importance if your business has a large number of sales or service representatives who need to update the company on sales, requests for parts to be shipped, or any other data that can affect how well your company is received in the business community. Using a database and the appropriate *gateway,* your employees can update sales records and projections, update customer contact information, and keep support and supply personnel informed of their every move, ensuring that everyone's needs are satisfied. In today's fast-paced and demanding business environment, presenting good news or bad news is acceptable, but surprises are no longer tolerated. With your employees able to update all your important records from their desks or their hotel rooms (or even that greasy spoon on I-70) via a Web browser, you'll be in the best position possible to serve your customers' every need.

FIGURE 28.2.
Intranet databases allow for the remote update of mission-critical information.

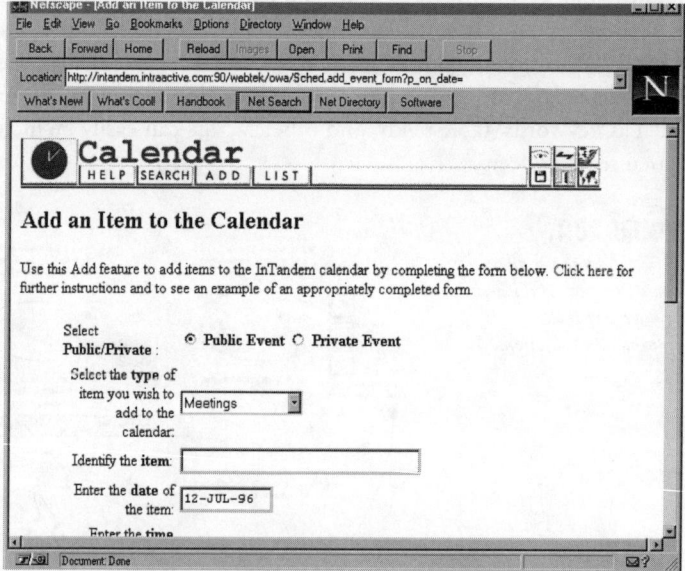

The third important need that a database system can service is an extension of what you've just covered, which is the need to provide timely, dynamic data to those employees who service your customers and in general facilitate the day-to-day operations of your organization, as shown in Figure 28.3. Just as a database can help your employees keep your records up-to-date, it is equally important that the information be made accessible in an easy, fast, and powerful fashion to those employees who depend on that data to make material decisions about purchasing needs, sales and repair requests, or scheduling issues. With this need taken care of, your entire corporate operation should, hopefully, proceed in a more fluid, reliable fashion because all employees have sufficient data (that's easily accessible) with which to do their jobs.

FIGURE 28.3.
Intranet databases provide employees timely access to the latest sales figures, inventories, or meeting schedules.

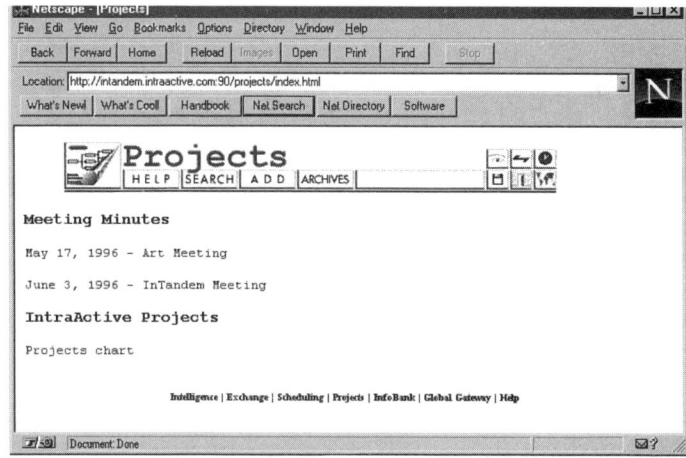

Now, just because I haven't mentioned the particular goal that your intranet database is anticipated to resolve, don't take that to mean it's not equally valid to the issues that I've presented. Because these applications of database technology are prevalent within modern intranets, however, taking a second look at your plans before you proceed may be a good idea.

Unlike some of the more exotic and nascent technologies that have come to the forefront of the intranet development scene, database systems have been around for some time. As a result, you've got a wealth of information available to you both in a variety of print publications as well as on any number of company-sponsored or third-party Web sites. Be sure to check these sites for up-to-the-minute developments, upgrades, and technical or implementation advice. Remember, although I can introduce you to some of the more popular and well-known systems that site and database administrators are using today for intranet development, you should put a good deal of thought and research into other options that may have surfaced since this book went to press. Or perhaps you should investigate other avenues that may be tailored more specifically to the particular needs of your organization. As always, you also should feel free to explore new and creative applications within your intranet for the emerging database technologies, and be sure to stretch the design limitations from time to time. With necessity being the mother of invention, you may be surprised at what your design challenges and a bit of inspiration provide!

As database systems have evolved and become more feature-laden and function-specific, your need to understand and appreciate the roles of each individual feature within the scope of your development efforts has become increasingly vital. The initial temptation of many intranet designers is to focus all their effort and energy on one primary (and trusted) database, say Borland's Paradox for Windows, and remain centered on that particular system throughout the life cycle of the internal site. This occurrence is common and understandable—database administrators like to work using the tools with which they are most familiar. Doing so, however, can cause huge headaches not only for your users (your employees) but also the people who depend on your employees for timely, accurate, and near-instant information (generally referred to in business terms as the *customer*). Depending on any number of factors—from the number of users accessing the system, to the type and amount of data included in the database, to your anticipated hardware or operating system combination, or any of a host of other factors—the database that you select to support your intranet may be the deciding factor in the success or failure of your corporate intranet experiment. Your particular needs may very well turn out to require a heterogeneous mixing of the available database tools and resources to implement your site successfully. Perhaps you need a high-end SQL server for the back-end tasks, working in concert with Web-based clients for general access and some PC-based clients for administration, upkeep, and so on. Make sure that you define the role of your database prior to deciding on your particular system, though, and spend enough time getting a feel for the anticipated usage patterns and your users' needs before you commit to any one technology. By thinking these issues through beforehand, you'll end up saving yourself a lot of time, energy, and frustration. At the same time, you'll end up with a much better intranet for your investment.

In the next few sections, I cover some of the key database resources you may want to consider for your intranet, including Informix, Sybase, Oracle, Microsoft SQL Server, and Paradox for Windows. I also discuss some of the more advanced issues that you need to take into account when providing access to any amount of data via the Web or an intranet. Finally, I showcase a number of powerful and emerging roles that companies have discovered for database systems when included as part of a corporate intranet, and hopefully stimulate your thinking for your own site.

Evaluating Database Options

When you're selecting a database system to integrate into your intranet, you should know a bit about the various options available to you. The following sections cover some of the more popular and powerful database systems available today, so you can be in the best position possible when you make your selection.

High End

Informix
Sybase
Oracle
Microsoft SQL Server

Middle

Paradox
Microsoft Access

Low End

Flat file

Informix

Informix's strategy revolves around an object-oriented database and program language. Informix rewrote all its base engine from scratch in 1991 following its purchase of Illustra, a company specializing in modeling and navigating complex data. Informix has always been a strong RDBMS vendor, and its latest move could lead to a breathtaking jump over the competition. The Illustra technology will be fundamental to Informix's new capabilities on the intranet. Specifically, Illustra adds support for complex objects, such as video, audio, and images. And, as I said before, they are critical pieces of the strength of the intranet.

Informix plans to expand the Dynamic Scaleable Architecture (DSA) of the Informix engine and merge it with Illustra's object-extensible architecture. The DSA-enabled engine specializes in parallel processing, enabling Informix to perform well in the face of increasing data loads. The database can create multiple threads on different processors to keep a consistent level of performance. This characteristic describes how *scaleable* a database is. Informix is providing the *relational* of the ORDBMS, whereas Illustra is providing the *object* component.

Lastly, through Illustra, Informix's Universal Server (available by the end of 1996) will have the ability to use DataBlades. *DataBlades* extend the functionality of the database by providing an object-oriented programming interface. The Web DataBlade, for example, allows users to create and maintain HTML-based Web pages that can be deployed against the Universal Server.

For more information about Informix's intranet strategy, visit their home page at www.informix.com.

Sybase

The Sybase family of intranet-applicable database products revolves around their System 11 suite of applications. When utilized in conjunction with other intranet technologies, Suite 11 can provide for an extremely powerful corporate communications resource. Sybase has gone to great lengths to ensure that the System 11 line is capable of handling the most rigorous intranet data-handling tasks, while simultaneously maintaining high degrees of scalability and performance that are essential in today's information-sharing world. System 11 encompasses all the Sybase database family, including SQL Server 11, Sybase IQ, Sybase MPP, and SQL Anywhere. Sybase's popularity and functionality are due to its core database-engine architecture, which is comprised of fully multithreaded, fully symmetric VSA engines that are capable of controlling and manipulating memory, I/O issues, and various other tasks that have traditionally amounted to bottlenecks for other systems, resulting in greater performance and fewer headaches for database or intranet administrators. Further, unlike other systems that require very specific combinations of hardware and software to achieve optimal performance, SQL Server 11 can function with great utility on any number of platforms with varying configurations, from 12MB single-processor systems to large-scale SMP systems with 12GB of RAM, which gives you great flexibility when integrating System 11 with your current system, as well as allowing you any number of options when considering future expansions.

SQL Server 11, the central component of the system, has been optimized for the sharing of data among a large number of concurrent users, which is an excellent benefit if you plan to implement your intranet in a large user environment. Traditionally, multiple users attempting to access the same areas of information within the database simultaneously had a great impact on system performance, resulting in slow access and frustrated users. Sybase engineers have spent countless hours analyzing hardware, software, and usability factors, however, to determine the most efficient methods of dealing with this problem. As a result, SQL Server 11 is a fully scaleable RDBMS that can take advantage of every aspect of your system, from CPU and RAM to other hardware resources to serve data at exceedingly fast rates.

For more information on the System 11 suite of applications, visit www.sybase.com.

> *Sybase SQL Server 11 System Requirements*
>
> Available for most major UNIX platforms
> Windows NT Server
> 15MB of RAM for SQL Server
> 48K of RAM per additional user
> 6MB of disk space to store system software

Oracle

Oracle, a company that has long been known for its superior database systems, has taken the data-serving needs of the Internet and intranet community into account when designing its latest product, the Oracle Universal Server Suite. The Oracle Universal Server Suite consists of an integrated server, client, and systems management package that have been specifically designed to lessen the design and development cycles that are usually involved in deploying such complex systems; these products are designed as installation-ready and are known to be compatible for almost any use. This is a tremendous advantage for your organization, in that your technical design team can focus its attention on designing functional, full-featured, and robust solutions to your particular needs rather than waste valuable time determining the constraints that your particular combination of software packages imposes on your systems.

Sporting an engine based on its popular Oracle7 Server, the Universal Server Suite has been specifically designed to provide for fast, effective, and powerful integration between your database services and the Oracle Web Server, which lets you get up and running without much hassle. Further, because your data is most likely going to be mission-critical to your organization, it is good to know that the Universal Server Suite has a host of recovery features that maintain and protect your data even in the face of some of the most damaging system failures.

For more information on Oracle's intranet database solutions, visit their home page at www.oracle.com.

Oracle Server System Requirements

Solaris or Microsoft Windows NT
100MHz Pentium processor
64MB of RAM
2GB hard disk space

Oracle Client System Requirements

Windows 95 or Windows NT graphical environment
16MB of RAM
500MB of disk space
Web-based tools require an HTML 2.0-compliant Web browser.

Microsoft SQL Server

As with almost every other product and service offered by Microsoft, their flavor of the SQL Server has been designed in part as a stand-alone application, but one that is immeasurably enhanced and extended by the functionality of other Microsoft-brand products. (Microsoft hopes that this move will ensure user loyalty and dependence on the software giant.) This means that if you've installed the MS-Internet Information Server (IIS), SQL, and other MS products, you're in a favorable position to design and implement complex intranet systems easily due to the inherent compatibility across the Microsoft suite of applications. Again, this capability is great if every legacy application you've installed was built by Microsoft. If, however, you're dealing with a mix of applications, services, and systems (as in most situations), you're not necessarily at a disadvantage. Microsoft—in trying to convince each and every IS manager to migrate to MS products—has developed a number of software packages to ease the integration of legacy database systems into Web-based intranets, using systems such as Microsoft TransAccess or Information Builders Inc.'s EDA/Open Database Gateway. These systems are fully compatible with MS-SQL and allow your design team to incorporate previously inaccessible data sources into your intranet.

The MS-SQL server is a powerful ally in your efforts to publish real-time information and provide interaction and customization for resources made available to your organization via an intranet. Microsoft's "Active Internet" strategy has evolved with corporate communications in mind. In conjunction with this "Active Internet" strategy, Microsoft has invested considerable time, effort, and financial resources into the development of their ActiveX technology, which is a robust and rather impressive mixing of technologies that will allow users to create and maintain interactive content using a number of software components, scripting languages (see Chapter 34, "Intranet Tools," for information on Microsoft's Visual Basic Script), and other currently available Microsoft applications by embedding them directly into either static or dynamically generated HTML pages. If you're familiar with OLE Controls, the ActiveX technology may seem somewhat familiar because a major component of the ActiveX resource is based on the data sharing that has previously been facilitated by OLE.

Organizations developing and deploying intranet applications will benefit from the same proven technologies that have historically provided MS-SQL with an important role in the corporate database arena—user and application security, data integrity and concurrency controls, data stream encryption, data replication, and transparent distributed transactions.

For more information on MS-SQL 6.5 and its potential for your corporate intranet, visit the Microsoft home page at www.microsoft.com/sql/.

Because some of the database systems that I've already covered may be out of your company's reach due either to technical or financial constraints, there remain some powerful yet somewhat more conservative routes for you to explore, which may be equally as acceptable as the "power" systems. In the following section, I talk about one of the "middleweights" in the database field, Borland's Paradox 7.0, and how it can play an important role in the development of your intranet database system.

Paradox 7.0

Borland's 32-bit Paradox 7.0 is a great improvement over earlier versions of their database package, which is impressive considering that Paradox has always been a multifunctional and useful addition to a corporation's suite of IS tools. Version 7 functionality is extended from earlier versions through a number of features intended to ease database creation, maintenance, and the eventual dissemination of your collected data. This is accomplished through the addition of many "experts," which are essentially automated processes that help you create tables, produce reports or data entry forms, perform mail merges, and import data from other sources. These capabilities can be helpful if your company deals with data from different vendors or currently utilizes multiple types of database technology within the office. Further, if you plan to migrate to a single, new database technology when you implement your intranet, Paradox can convert almost all your legacy database types into viable sources for continued use. Paradox also supports a variety of the major business application suites that are currently available (including Microsoft Office and Perfect Office) so you can easily share data among a host of applications. Additionally, with the new Paradox MS-Exchange/MAPI support, you'll also have the option of distributing some or all of your data via e-mail, which can serve as a fail-safe in the event of a Web server crash.

Paradox 7.0 System Requirements

Intel 386DX PC or higher
Microsoft Windows 95 or Windows NT 3.51
8MB of memory (12MB recommended) for Windows 95
12MB required (16MB recommended) for Windows NT

Hard disk drive with 13MB for compact installation; 30MB for typical installation
One floppy disk drive or CD-ROM drive
VGA or higher resolution monitor
Mouse or other Windows pointing device

For more information on Paradox 7.0 and other intranet solutions offered by Borland, visit their home page at www.borland.com.

Advanced Intranet Database Issues

For small- and medium-sized intranets, the issues of distribution and replication are not primary concerns. As the intranet grows, however, a new set of management demands will be placed on the organization, and distribution and replication can be implemented to help relieve intranet expansion woes. The question of data efficiency has been widely asked in the information community. Frequently asked questions are, "Where should data be stored?" and "How should we model the relationship between data and users?" The usual answer tells you that data should be close to the source and close to the users who need it. So, if a user in New York uses and updates a database daily, while a user in California uses the same database only once a month, it seems obvious that the physical data should reside in New York, "close" to both the primary user and the primary source (or maintainer). In the same way, database designers think about where data should be stored. Most often, they choose the techniques of distribution and replication to achieve this end.

Distributing Your Data Across Your Intranet

To distribute your data means to spread it out over more than one source. Distribution could be used to describe one database running on five machines or a table that is half on one database and half in another. In the former case, I mean to say that the five machines act as one virtual machine, so each is a vital component of the single database. In the latter case, the databases are the source of different data (rows) of the same table. A California database, for example, has only California-specific information, and a New York database has only New York-specific data. Note that the data is not duplicated; it exists on the source server alone. If you build a Web application on the intranet to display available items for purchase, the application would query the New York and California databases independently and display the resulting items side-by-side inside the browser.

Almost ironically, a basic premise of the intranet is its distributed architecture. Because the intranet works mainly through *pointers* (or *links*), the information inside the intranet is loosely connected by default. Distribution issues usually occur at the WAN level, where network or system bottlenecks between remote sites have a negative impact on overall performance of the intranet. The primary concern of keeping frequently updated data close to the source must be balanced with the need for users far from the source to access the data in a timely manner. The latter requirement brings replication into the picture.

Replicating Your Data Across Your Intranet

Replication is somewhat complementary to distribution because it simply aims to duplicate data strategically to improve query speed. Good replication strategies try to take advantage of the inherent nature of the type of data access. Replication can be done on a whole database (often called *mirroring*) or can be done table-by-table. Microsoft, for example, often mirrors its Web servers because of the sheer volume of connections it must contend with in a given day. A large intranet might face the same problem.

Replication is also used when remote users do not have acceptable access times to the source database. In this case, a user might want a summary of financial data from five different international regions. The time to connect to each region varies with amount of network traffic, and so the user might get information on three regions quickly but have to wait a long time to get the updates from the other two regions. One solution might be to collect all the regions' information at night and transmit a whole replicated snapshot of the five regions to a database server near the user.

The preceding solution works well if the user can accept only a one-day view of his or her financial summaries. If a more frequent update sequence is needed, the replication flow must be altered. Most replication-enabled DBMSs can also update dynamically, allowing the database administrator to set a "window" in which remote servers are updated. In the preceding example, the five regional servers could be told to send updated information every two hours to the database near the user. Ideally, this approach would solve the user's problem, but there is still a chance that two hours would not be enough time for one of the regions to update its data completely. In this case, the user would have the most updated view, but one region would be at least zero to two hours out-of-date.

Replication is tuned according to average network availability because it is bandwidth driven. High network availability allows for smaller replication "windows," so data can be transmitted more frequently. If a network is very crowded, replication speed must be slowed, or uncompleted requests might store in a queue for later delivery. In this latter case, the low network availability would cause a bottleneck of old data requests pending, forcing the user to wait longer for the update.

To help summarize and provide you with a few more examples, Table 28.1 summarizes the four basic types of data access.

Table 28.1. Management strategies for intranet database systems.

Data Type	Distance to Source	Need for Updates	Strategy
Type I	Close (or local)	High	Distribution/replication
Type II	Far (or remote)	High	Replication/distribution
Type III	Close	Low	Distribution
Type IV	Far	Low	Replication

Types of Data Usage

Type I data is categorized by a database close to the users who update it the most frequently. Most often, the data can stay in its current position because network speed is less of a factor when the data is close to the source. In certain situations, however, replication might be employed. Consider a group of users who are making updates to only a small section of a large database but need a short turnaround time to show the updated data quickly. Possibly, the large database server is slower because it must deal with requests for many different databases. In this scenario, you can replicate the parts of the database the user group needs and let them manipulate the data on another database server dedicated to them. This way, the group can make timely selects, inserts, or deletes and get results back quickly. Scheduled, batched transactions containing updates could be sent back to the central server. Because this group is also made up of the primary users, there is a smaller chance that other locations would send transactions that would have to be reconciled (possibly causing rollbacks).

Type II data is the most difficult to model because the data source is far away, but the update frequency is high. Often, you must employ a replication strategy to give remote (far) users good access time to the database. Replication ultimately incurs more overhead, but this type of situation leaves few options available, except possibly the installation of a very high-speed communications network (for example, thick fiber). The situation is much like that described for Type I data, except that the chance for out-of-sync data used by other clients is increased by the longer time the updated data needs to travel to the source. In some circumstances, data from the central server can be moved to the remote server, thereby redistributing the data to a new source. The central server then receives replicated "copies" of the data from the remote server.

Type III data is the simplest to address because it deals mostly with clients who want to perform read-only query operations. In other words, they call up information but do not update it often. Because they are close to the data source, access time is good and reconciliation (because of conflicting updates) is avoided. Data can be left distributed.

Type IV data is the same as Type III, except that the clients are remote. A replication technique is best used here because the clients want only read-only query access and do not update frequently. The only problem is a speed constraint (caused by being "far"), which is solved by replicating the portions of the database the clients need.

Designing for Growth

If you're planning an intranet, you need to consider where data should be stored. An obvious choice might be to take all the company's data and load it into a central Web server. This solution might work well if the organization is small or medium-sized, but one machine might not be able to hold the corporate directory profile if the employee count goes above 50,000. Or perhaps the company's accounting department is off-site and takes longer to upload its data to the central Web server. Managers might see a page with up-to-date project deliverables but out-of-date financial data. Deciding where to store data is a critical analysis phase of intranet database deployment. Designers should look at business needs first and then determine data size, *data longevity* (how long data is good before it needs to be updated), and *data availability* (what percent of the time data must be accessible). This equation is often not simple to estimate, and one point to consider is the miniature replication of data the intranet or Internet tends to lead users into.

Most users like to save a copy of the information that they are viewing when it interests them. Others download files for offline examination. Either way, information is being duplicated from the server to the local computer. This duplication might be okay for getting device drivers, recipes, or birth dates, but it is probably not okay for corporate directories or current price lists. The former data is more or less static in nature, and keeping a local copy, while using valuable disk space, is not completely critical to the accuracy of the data. However, dynamic data, like directories or price lists, should be retrieved from a Web server at the time of need, except for exceptional circumstances. The reason the dynamic data would be put on an intranet would be to keep it up-to-date. If users keep local copies to access instead of using the data contained on a Web page, they risk the chance of having "old" data whenever the Web page is updated. The need for proper training is highlighted in this example. The best system will fail if users cannot shift mental gears to adapt to a new environment. Intranet architects need to be aware of how users' occupy their local hard disk space, trying to keep dynamic data at the source, while encouraging users to be cautious about making multiple local copies of data that can be accessed almost any time.

Last, choosing a database vendor who is committed to efficient distribution and replication handling is a prudent choice when you're examining individual databases. Informix, Oracle, Sybase, and Microsoft are all committed to enhancing their product offerings as the economics demand. Although Sybase was first to get a stable replication technology to market in 1993, Informix might be better poised to take advantage of its object-oriented extensions to perform object-based replication. Microsoft bundles a mid-level replication service free with SQL Server 6.0 and 6.5. As OLTP (online transaction processing) moves to the Web, Web servers that rely on files or flat databases will not be able to perform adequately. Often people buy a product without ever examining all its features because they are not of use at the present time. Replication might be one those features, but be sure to evaluate it when selecting your database back end.

Implementation Examples

Now that you've had an opportunity to review some of the tools and other options that will enable you to integrate a database with your intranet, it's time to discuss some of the many different approaches that your company can embrace when searching for ways to enhance your site's functionality with a database. Granted, if you've come this far, you've probably got at least an inkling of an idea in mind for what you want to accomplish with your new system. Keeping tabs on what the competition is up to with their information systems design is always a good idea, mostly because you don't want to let them get ahead of you in the industry due to a superior corporate information-services infrastructure, but also because you can occasionally pick up a great idea or be inspired by what other companies are attempting to implement.

A number of great sources for information on intranet design are available; many of them deal (in varying degrees) with the topic of database integration and give examples of how real-world companies are utilizing the technologies. One of the best sites to visit is located at Netscape:

```
home.netscape.com/comprod/at_work/index.html
```

where you can learn a great deal about intranet database technology through intranet "white papers," demos of intranet technology, and examples of what is *en vogue* in the corporate intranet scene. (For information on implementing scheduling, see Chapter 36, "Group Scheduling.")

Contact or Employee Tracking

With companies growing, diversifying, and downsizing (often simultaneously these days)—all the while in need of excellent service and productivity—your employees must be able to locate valid and complete contact information that they can utilize to collaborate with colleagues or to touch base with important clients.

A great example of contact information enabled by an intranet database was developed by AT&T. As a huge corporate entity with an employee count in excess of 300,000, the days of utilizing paper-based or static HTML as a medium for distributing contact information throughout its various departments was rapidly drawing to a close. Taking advantage of new technology to save time, effort, and money, AT&T has implemented an intranet database with an HTML front end, allowing for fast searches of the entire company directory based on employee name, address, title, department, or other indexed information. And because the information is easily found within the system, it also has significantly eased the burden of updating more traditional systems, such as paging through any number of huge, static HTML files to find the proper record to update.

Online Inventory

In today's helter-skelter business environment, the salesperson who can satisfy a client's needs first (and most effectively) is the one who usually walks away with the sale. This is by no means a revelation that has occurred because of the integration of high-tech systems into the work force. With the introduction of these systems as integral parts of your business plan, however, you can make certain that you're always in a position to react instantaneously to the needs of your clients—any time, anywhere.

Consider John Deere, for example. To empower their employees, John Deere has implemented a parts database that contains not only images of the various mechanical parts that they offer for sale, but also provides specific data on each individual part, from dimensions to instructions for assembly and repair, and so on. This database enables purchasing, sales, and service representatives to access comprehensive information on John Deere products when seeking quotes from vendors, offering sales packages to customers, or verifying orders from the field for service requests, once again allowing for streamlined operations.

Time Reporting

Another area in which companies are turning to the Web, intranets, and database technology for assistance is in tracking employee assignments and the subsequent hours spent in servicing each particular task. Currently, companies use a dazzling array of technologies (or, perhaps, antitechnologies) to accomplish this goal: time clocks with punch cards, handwritten tables, Excel spreadsheets, phone reporting, and Lotus Notes interfaces. All of these technologies accomplish the basic task of recording hours but leave much to be desired in terms of data accessibility, flexibility, and overall use to the organization past the simple task of paying the employee.

An intranet-based time-tracking system holds a number of advantages for a company and its payroll office. First, as the information is stored within a database, users can handle it more easily than searching through dust-covered records from previous months, weeks, or even years, hoping to come across the appropriate file. This also means it's easier to store large numbers of past time data and will save quite a bit of space in the office storage area. Second, hours can be submitted and tracked on a daily basis rather than on a weekly or biweekly schedule, as a normal time-card submission would allow. This way, project managers, accountants, and other management personnel can have a more complete understanding of their employees' progress and the state of current projects; they also can more accurately target areas for improvement in their employees' development cycle.

Product Requisition or Purchasing

One of the most limiting factors to a successful business is not having the proper resources on hand with which to complete your duties. Whether employees are in need of an expensive computer platform, chemical solutions, or even a box of paper clips, an intranet database can play a vital role in ensuring that employees have near-instantaneous access to whatever item or service is needed. Using a Web interface, employees can browse through the inventory of in-house products and supplies, submit a request that certain items be sent to their location from the master supply room, or—if the company has run out of widgets—can request that the office manager order more.

Summary

Now that we've covered the basic—and not-so-basic—ideas, tips, strategies, and rules of thumb of intranet database systems, you've got a bit of work ahead of you. Even as this book goes to print, many of the companies responsible for some of today's most powerful and effective database solutions are developing and releasing new systems, updates, and options at a breakneck pace, which means that you'll have to use your own knowledge, understanding, and instinct if you want to move beyond the scope of what this chapter has covered. However, despite the introduction of newer, more powerful software and faster, more exotic hardware, the underlying concepts and issues involving the integration of database systems into corporate intranets remain basically the same.

From the various high- and middle-end database systems to the many creative ways in which various information systems professionals have melded such systems into highly effective resources for interoffice and intraoffice collaboration, it's clear that the role of the database in the workplace is no longer limited to a small set of complex, user-unfriendly tasks—nor is it solely the realm of your systems administrator. Rather, with the advent of the intranet, database systems are expanding into a new frontier in which they can flourish as centralized information-sharing tools.

Telnet: Direct Access

29

by Art Klein

IN THIS CHAPTER

- What does Telnet do? **438**
- How does Telnet work? **440**
- What is Telnet used for? **442**
- Server issues **444**
- Process control: ps and the process table **447**
- Connectivity issues **450**
- Security issues: transmissions over Ethernet **451**
- Commonsense issues **454**

The fundamental purpose of networking is to enable different computer systems to communicate with one another. This communication happens in different ways, ranging from a program accessing a database across a network to a person sitting at a workstation engaging in an interactive session with another computer by way of a direct network connection. This chapter focuses on the latter connection.

One of the most popular protocols that provides a direct interface for a remote system is the *Telnet* protocol. In this chapter, you learn about the Telnet protocol and how it works. This chapter compares Telnet to its partner remote logon protocol, *rlogin*. I explain Telnet's relationship to the intranet and discuss methods of monitoring resource utilization by way of Telnet. Additionally, I explore the all-important issues surrounding the security of data transmitted via Telnet.

Telnet is a well-established component of the TCP/IP protocol suite, and this is what makes it so relevant and useful to an intranet. The basic premise of an intranet is to offer universal access to an organization's public data and programs, and Telnet is the one universal cross-platform utility for directly accessing a host system. You don't have to worry too much about your client base—whether you have UNIX workstations, Macs, NT workstations, DOS/Windows machines with third-party TCP/IP stacks, or a mix of all of these—all will be able to interact with a system set up as a Telnet server. Telnet even lets your workstation run its own operating system, run programs on a remote host running some completely different operating system, and interactively display the results of that "incompatible" system's program back at your workstation! In short, Telnet's near-universal support across platforms makes it an ideal tool for enabling host access when you might not even know who will need to access your intranet or what machines they will be using.

What Does Telnet Do?

In a nutshell, Telnet provides the ability to perform remote logons. Telnet has both a client and a server component. When a user initiates a Telnet session through the Telnet client, the user sends a request to a remote system to supply the user with a *virtual* terminal session—in other words, a session that looks and behaves exactly as if the user were sitting in front of the remote computer. Figure 29.1 illustrates an example of a Telnet session. In the figure, a remote system named *varmint* is located on a local area network. At a different physical location is another system on the network named *vittle*. Assume that a user is sitting in front of vittle, and he or she must look at a file that resides on varmint. The user initiates a Telnet session with varmint from within a window on vittle; the window then responds exactly as a session would respond if the user were actually sitting at varmint.

Now look at an actual initiation of a Telnet session. In this example, a user named Anna is sitting at the vittle system just described. In Listing 29.1, Anna types the command `telnet varmint`. This command executes the Telnet client program with the argument varmint, which tells her system to initiate a Telnet session with a system named varmint. Her local system maps the name varmint to an IP address, 194.5.30.68. The Telnet client program then informs Anna that it is trying to connect to that IP address via Telnet.

FIGURE 29.1.

A Telnet session between varmint and vittle.

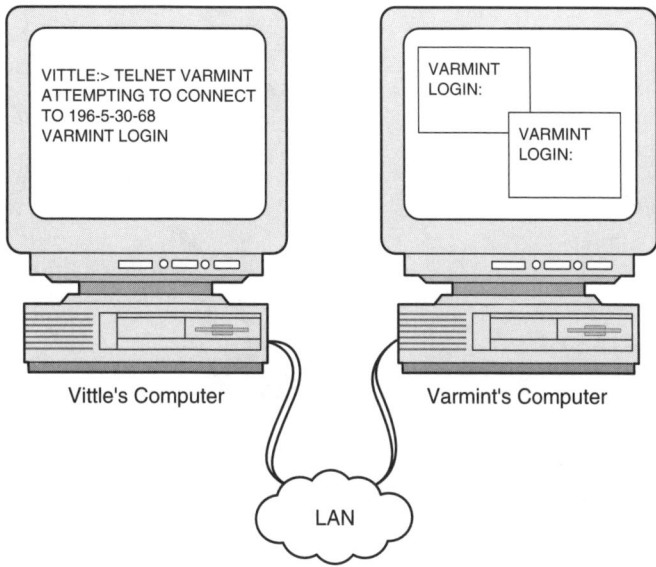

Listing 29.1. Initiating a Telnet session.

```
Vittle% telnet varmint
Trying 194.5.30.68 ...
Connected to varmint.
Escape character is '^]'.

SunOS UNIX (varmint)

login: anna
Password:

varmint%
```

Vittle begins sending packets of data addressed to the IP address 194.5.30.68 and requests a response from the Telnet server. If the Telnet server process is running on the system addressed to 194.5.30.68, the server responds and a connection between the two systems is established. The Telnet client announces it has connected successfully and surrenders control of the window to system varmint. At this point, Anna sees in her window exactly what she would see if she were sitting in front of system varmint. All the commands Anna executes from within this Telnet session are executed on the remote system varmint, not on her local machine vittle. If she prints a file to the local printer, as illustrated in Figure 29.2, the file is printed on the local printer connected to varmint, not vittle.

FIGURE 29.2.
Printing to the local printer from within Telnet.

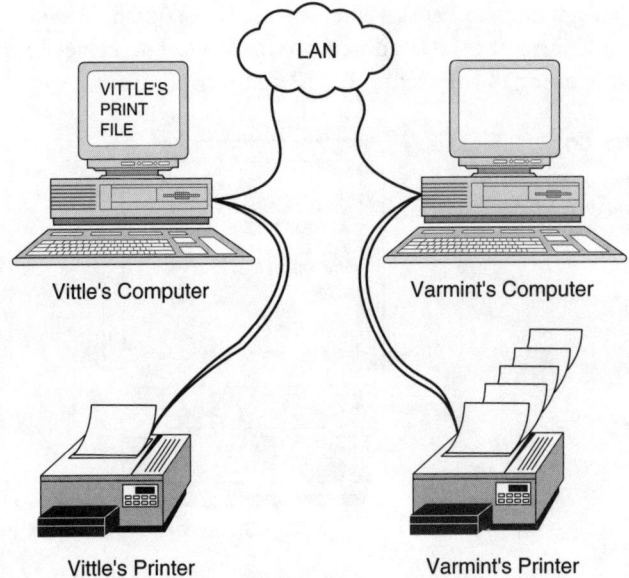

When Anna is finished working on system varmint, she ends her Telnet session by logging out or exiting her session in the same way she would if she were in front of varmint and wanted to log off and go home for the weekend. The control of the window is then returned to her local system vittle.

How Does Telnet Work?

Now that you've witnessed a brief example of a Telnet session, you'll look more closely at how Telnet works in the following sections.

Telnet Clients Versus Telnet Servers

Telnet is a client/server-based program. The client side of Telnet is a program that a user runs to request an interactive session. The server side of Telnet is a process that is in a dormant or sleeping state until it hears a request from a Telnet client. The server side grants the client's request and passes the keystrokes entered from the Telnet client session on to the operating system of the server.

As a part of the TCP/IP protocol suite, Telnet is provided with most TCP/IP packages, and clients behave much the same across the board. On the server side of Telnet, however, are some limitations. Telnet operates on the principle of *multitasking*; in other words, the system can divide its attention among multiple functions and perform them all at the same time, although slower than if performing only one function at a time. Multitasking lets Anna Telnet to the system varmint while another user is actually at the system's console doing something else. Multitasking permits the server to divide its attention between the person at the local machine and Anna, who is at a remote location. If varmint were not a multitasking system and if Anna were granted access via Telnet, the local user would be unable to perform any functions.

If your system does not multitask, it can't serve as a Telnet server. Because MS-DOS systems lack multitasking capabilities, they cannot serve as Telnet servers. PCs do have multitasking capabilities, however, as the ability to multitask is tied to the operating system, not the type of hardware. Linux (a PC-based implementation of UNIX), for example, is a multitasking operating system and can serve as a Telnet server. Windows NT also is a multitasking operating system, but Telnet servers for this operating system just recently hit the market. For these reasons, I focus on the UNIX implementation of Telnet, which is more stable and more prevalent than Windows NT Telnet services.

Telnet as a Part of TCP/IP

Although this section gets somewhat technical, you need to understand how Telnet works at the TCP/IP level from a security standpoint. TCP/IP is a set of protocols that use the concept of *ports* and *sockets*. Within TCP/IP networks, many types of transactions move from machine to machine across the network, including Telnet requests and commands; FTP transactions, such as "getting" a file; and network routing data. TCP/IP uses the port/socket model to distinguish the data being received and to sort the different types of transactions coming into a system through a single network connection.

Each type of transaction is assigned a certain *port* number. Think of your computer as a popular delicatessen with a large menu of sandwiches. Instead of ordering sandwiches by name, you order by a corresponding number that appears next to each sandwich on the menu. If you want pastrami on rye, you order "number 42." In this analogy, different network transactions are the same as different types of sandwiches. Whenever a chunk of data (a "packet") is transmitted, a header appears before it, identifying a certain port number. This way, the system can handle multiple network sessions concurrently. As the data from the different transactions is received by the network interface, it is passed up to different applications by the port number in the header. If you want a portion of the TCP/IP "menu" identifying certain services with certain port numbers, look at the /etc/services file on any UNIX system. Port number 23 is typically reserved as the port number for outgoing Telnet data. I come back to the port/socket model later in this chapter; see "Security Issues: Transmissions Over Ethernet."

Telnet Versus rlogin

Telnet has a similar "sister" remote login protocol called *rlogin*. It also is a part of TCP/IP, and most UNIX systems with a TCP/IP stack provide both Telnet and rlogin as connectivity services. Why two different protocols? What is the difference? First, from the user standpoint, rlogin automatically assumes that when a user tries to connect to another system, the username will be consistent from system to system. If user Bill utilizes rlogin to connect to another server, the remote system assumes that it is user Bill trying to connect and asks immediately for a password, not permitting Bill to use a different login name.

rlogin also can be configured to allow *trusted hosts*. This way, a user can connect directly to another system via rlogin without even typing a password. rlogin may seem like a tremendous time-saver, bypassing the inconvenience of typing in usernames and passwords when connecting to another system. Keep in mind, however, the security issues that arise. Walking away from your desk for a half hour does not merely compromise the security of your local machine, but also any other systems on your LAN that permit rlogin and regard your system as a trusted host.

From a technical standpoint, Telnet is not only more secure, but it also is more stable than rlogin. The Telnet protocol allows both the client and server systems to negotiate the flow control and duplex, letting the systems make adjustments for slow network links, which rlogin does not.

What Is Telnet Used For?

Now that you know what Telnet does, look at how it is used in most local area networks.

The System Administrator's Best Friend

Telnet is one of the most coveted tools of the system administrator. Usually the first step in troubleshooting a system's problem is to Telnet to the problem system. Many system administrators set up the system on their desktop with a large number of windows, each one connected to another system via a Telnet session. If a system goes down unexpectedly, the Telnet session ends abruptly. Thus, by looking at the screen and seeing that all the Telnet sessions are running, the system administrator can see that all the systems appear to be up. Of course, this method is not foolproof because in many situations a system "freezes," leaving the system administrator in the dark until he or she tries to execute a command and then learns that the system is hung. So, consider the Telnet a fundamental troubleshooting tool but not the end-all and be-all of the system administrator's tools.

Command-Line Uses

Any command that you can enter from the command line on a system works via Telnet. These commands include any command that is not in a graphics window, that is not comprised of a "point and click," or that does not elicit a graphical response (like a dialog box opening up or displaying a new window). All other commands function as expected through Telnet. Graphic applications are addressed in the next section.

The following are some examples of command-line uses of Telnet:

- A person wants to run a program on her machine, but she is far from her office, so she logs into her system via Telnet and runs her job.
- An application developer wants to test his program on a faster machine, so he Telnets to a high performance system, copies over his program, and runs it on the remote system.

- A bitter coworker Telnets to your machine, reads whatever files he has access to, and then deletes them.
- A hacker wants to break into your system, knowing that your system's name is varmint. She uses Telnet to attempt to log in as root (the administrative account) and tries each time to guess the correct password.

These examples run from the very appropriate to the sneaky to the illegal. I included them to prove that Telnet is more than just a powerful tool; it is a powerful tool that can be used to elude authority. Keep your eyes open, and be aware of what activities can occur during a Telnet session. In fact, in the last example, the Telnet session was not even established, and there was a substantial security risk. I address using Telnet to keep tabs on all the users on your system in the section called "The who Command." Right now, just be aware of the breadth of ways individuals can use Telnet, and don't underestimate the resourcefulness of the wicked.

Graphic Applications: The X Window System

In the preceding section, I alluded to the complexities surrounding a graphical application. Let me show you why this is a sticking point. Imagine that user Anna is still sitting in front of vittle and connected to varmint via Telnet. She's had a long day, and she needs a break. She knows that varmint has a graphic blackjack program on it, and Anna feels she's due to relax for a few minutes. She runs the blackjack program.

Now when she runs the blackjack program, the system runs it exactly as though she is sitting at the console. The program therefore displays a window on the console with a deck of cards spread out waiting for Anna to click the Shuffle button. The problem is that Anna is not at the console; another user, Bill, is. Bill is surprised when a window with a deck of cards appears on his screen. If Telnet behaves exactly as if you were sitting at the console, applications that are run from within it don't know that you are at a remote location. This means that you can't simply run a graphical program over a Telnet session by just running the program as if you were on the system. You must take certain steps prior to running the program in order to direct the application to send graphical images and tools to your "remote" screen. In a moment, I will describe these steps for a system running the X Window windowing system.

One of the most popular graphic windowing systems under TCP/IP is the X Window windowing system. The X Window system has a way to designate another system running X Window as the system to display any new graphics. Anna can log into varmint via Telnet, for example, tell it to send any graphic displays executed from within this session to vittle, and then run the blackjack program and have it display on the system at which she is sitting. Two steps make this process possible. First, on the local system, you can enable the display of remote graphics. This option typically is disabled because enabling remote displays results in other security issues. Anna can turn on the display by typing xhosts varmint to allow varmint to display graphics on her system or xhosts + if she wants to allow applications from any system to display graphics on her system. This command is entered on the system vittle, but not on varmint. After logging into varmint, Anna tells varmint to display data to vittle. She can do so by setting an *environmental variable* named `DISPLAY` (note that it is all in caps) to her local machine, followed by a colon and the number 0 (`:0`). If you're using the C-shell to run UNIX, you set it with the command `setenv DISPLAY vittle:0.0` and then press Return. If you're running the Bourne Shell, you use the command `DISPLAY=vittle:0.0; export DISPLAY`. Following these two steps, all graphics spawned from the window in which the `DISPLAY` variable was set should display on the local system.

Remember, to change the display successfully, you must have a version of X Window running on the client system. If you have a PC with a Telnet client and TCP/IP stack, this is not enough. Make sure that you have a PC-based X Window emulation program, such as Hummingbird System's Exceed, to handle the local side of the graphics displays.

Server Issues

In the following sections, I explore the issues behind the effects of enabling Telnet from the server, with emphasis on user control and process control. I address the following questions:

> What affects its performance?
> How can you troubleshoot a Telnet server effectively?
> How can you administer it better?

I wrote this chapter from a UNIX standpoint, because when this book was published there were limited Windows NT-based Telnet server capabilities.

The Number of Users

Because running Telnet services opens up an individual host machine to an entire LAN, when that system becomes overworked, you must look beyond the console for the culprit. Here I address how to track who is logged into a system and how to monitor who logs into it.

When Telnet is used within a LAN, the user community of a given computer is extended beyond the physical system. As a result, any interruption of service, maintenance, or general system administration tasks may affect people outside the LAN. You must keep in mind that you cannot simply reboot a system without first asking, "Who is this reboot affecting that I *can't* see?"

Application resources also may be affected by the number of users. If you have purchased a database application with three concurrent licenses, all the users may be staff members accessing the application via Telnet, and the person at the system console may be unable to run the application. You may get a call from a frustrated user telling you that the database program is not working when, in essence, the database program is almost working too well.

Basically, enabling a system to be a Telnet server mandates a different philosophy of ownership. The computer on your desk is no longer yours and yours alone. You must keep this fact in mind in all circumstances, whether you're using a system's resources or interrupting its availability.

The who Command

Using the UNIX command who, you can quickly discover who is logged into a system. Listing 29.2 shows the output of the who command.

Listing 29.2. The who command.

```
Varmint% who
anna     ttyp0    May 29 12:35    (vittle...
anna     ttyp0    May 29 12:38    (vittle...
varmint%
```

One entry exists for every unique login session. Listing 29.2 shows that Anna has two different Telnet sessions into the local system, and for that reason, two different entries correspond to her. Each line also displays the device that the user is using to connect to the system, the date and time the user logged in, if the session is a remote session, and from where the session originated. When prompted, the who command immediately gives you a quick snapshot of the system's user community.

The last Command

If you want to review more detailed data on who has been logging in and accessing your system, the last command may fill your needs. Each time a user logs into a UNIX system, the system adds an entry to two files, one named /etc/utmp and another named /usr/adm/wtmp (or /var/adm/wtmp in some systems). When a user logs out, the entry in the utmp file is removed, and another entry is added to the wtmp file. As time passes, the wtmp file keeps a running history of who logs into the system, how long they were logged onto the system, and from where they logged in. At the same time, the utmp keeps track of who is logged into the system currently.

As you may guess, the who command parses data from the utmp file to provide the list of who is logged into the system. Likewise, the last command parses data from the wtmp file and presents a history of all the previous logins back to the time of creation of the wtmp file. Of course, for a system with a lot of activity, the output of this command can be unwieldy, but some command-line arguments can make it more reasonable. You can supply as an argument a certain username and gain as output only the time that that certain user logged into the system. You also can supply a number as an argument and get only the last *n* entries instead of the whole list. The command last -40, for example, generates only the last 40 sessions recorded in the wtmp file.

Listing 29.3 shows the output of the command last -5 Anna, which outputs data corresponding to the last five times user Anna logged into the system.

Listing 29.3. The `last` command.

```
varmint% last -5 anna
anna     ttyp0      varmint      Wed July 17 02:34
anna     ttyp0      varmint      Wed July 17 15:21
anna     ttyp0      varmint      Fri July 19 06:54
anna     ttyp0      varmint      Fri July 19 12:01
anna     ttyp0      varmint      Sat July 20 03:15
varmint%
```

The output of the `last` command contains fields that display the user's login name, an entry corresponding to the type of connection, the IP address or remote host name of the remote host system, the time of login and logout, and the total network time for which the connection was open. A plethora of information is available through the `last` command to aid the system administrator in determining who was logged into the system at certain times or to develop some trending data. This data helps track use of a given system.

The ac Command

You can use the command `ac` for connect-time accounting. It formats the data in the wtmp file in total login time in minutes. This command is available only in BSD-style (Berkeley Standard Distribution) UNIX implementations such as SunOS or Digital's OSF. The command `ac` with no output generates the total hours of connect time since the start of the wtmp file. The command `ac -p` shows each user who has logged in and the total number of connect hours each user has expended. The command `ac -d` provides a profile of total connection hours by date, as shown in Listing 29.4. Keep in mind that these commands monitor connections established not only by Telnet, but also by rlogin, along with any connections established at the console or any other terminals directly connected to the system. Interpret the data carefully.

Listing 29.4. The `ac -d` command.

```
varmint% /usr/etc/ac -d
Jul 10   total       6.06
Jul 11   total      25.36
Jul 12   total      23.91
Jul 13   total      24.00
Jul 17   total      96.06
```

Some Final Thoughts on User Accounting

Do not try to edit the utmp or wtmp files directly. They are not standard ASCII files, and you should access the data within them only with the commands designed to extract data from them. Also remember that these files contain all your historical data. Anyone can delete these files and erase his or her tracks. Of course, other tools to track down rogue users or hackers are at your disposal, but you should keep in mind that your data is only as reliable as the stability of these files. On the flip side, if your system is up and running for, say, 18 months, your wtmp file may get quite large, and you may want to "prune" this file. The best way to prune is to remove the file by using the rm command and re-create it empty with the touch command by typing touch /usr/adm/wtmp. By doing so, you lose the accounting data from the previous period. But if you want to keep that data, just print it out and store it in a folder before removing the file. Plan to prune monthly or at least at regular intervals.

Also, remember that you are looking at connection time by account, and not necessarily by person, so train your staff to log off or lock their systems when they leave their desks or go home for the weekend. Also, advise staff to keep their passwords to themselves so that the activity of their accounts is directly attributed to their own work and tasks. The significance of logging out at night is twofold. Not only does it ensure that no one else will sit at a person's desk and start working with the system assuming the identity of the original user, it also helps yield relevant accounting data. The person who stays logged in for the weekend logs at least 50 extra hours of connect time if you examine data from the ac command.

Keep in mind, too, that so far you have looked at the users logged into a system, not the processes running on the system. A single user can tie up a system's CPU with just one process, just as 50 users can have two Telnet sessions each open to a system and use very little CPU time. The latter might occur if a majority of sessions are inactive or the users are just performing non-CPU-intensive tasks. The greatest skill a system administrator has is the ability to interpret data wisely. You need to understand not only what data implies, but also what it does not imply.

Process Control: ps and the Process Table

Now that you have explored how to monitor who is accessing a system via Telnet, you're ready to look at how to understand what these remote users are doing on a system. As I mentioned previously, the number of users logged onto a system don't necessarily have the most effect on system performance, rather the jobs and tasks the users are performing are likely to have the most impact. In this section, you explore how to monitor processes, how to determine how demanding certain processes are, and how to match specific processes with a specific user.

All multitasking operating systems have internal methods to track the different processes running concurrently on a system and the various attributes associated with them. These attributes typically are kept in a *process table*. If you're a systems administrator, your ability to look at this process table and draw sound conclusions from it is perhaps the most important troubleshooting skill you can possess.

One of the main tools for process control under UNIX is the ps command. Because this command has many different options that vary from system to system, you should read your system's online man page or systems manual to utilize ps fully. (*Man pages* are a UNIX-based form of online help. If you type the command man followed by a UNIX command, an online "systems manual" page for the command you entered is displayed.) Here, I briefly cover the basics of the command and differentiate only between the BSD style of UNIX (for example, SunOS and DEC OSF) and the AT&T SVR4-style of UNIX (for example, Solaris and HP-UX). I focus on the BSD implementation of ps in this section.

The ps command unadorned lists the processes created by the current user from the same controlling terminal, as you can see in Listing 29.5. Each line corresponds to a unique process. The first field on each line is a *process ID* (PID). The PID is a unique number assigned to each process by the operating system kernel. The next two fields describe the processes controlling the terminal's ID and the current process status. The status field can be extremely useful in determining whether a process is behaving properly. Status codes may tell if the process is running (R), sleeping (I), or stopped (S) among other states. The next field tells how much CPU time has been utilized, and the last field shows exactly what the program or command tied to the process is.

Listing 29.5. The ps command.

```
vittle% ps
  PID TT STAT    TIME COMMAND
26312 p3 IW     0:00 -sh (csh)
26431 p3 IW     0:00 telnet varmint
26503 p4 S      0:00 -csh (csh)
26579 p4 R      0:00 ps
```

If you are addressing performance problems systems-wide, looking at the process you own only gives you part of the picture. If you supply the argument -aux (or the argument -elf, if you're using SVR4 UNIX), you get more extensive data on all processes running on the system, as shown in Listing 29.6.

Listing 29.6. Partial output from the ps -aux command.

```
vittle% ps -aux
USER      PID %CPU %MEM   SZ  RSS TT STAT START    TIME COMMAND
root        1  0.0  0.0   52    0  ? IW   Jul 23   0:13 /sbin/init -
root       55  0.0  0.0   68    0  ? IW   Jul 23   0:07 portmap
root       98  0.0  0.0   64    0  ? IW   Jul 23   0:32 syslogd
root      105  0.0  0.0  108    0  ? IW   Jul 23   0:04 /usr/lib/sendmail -bd -q
root      140  0.0  0.0  128    0  ? IW   Jul 23   1:36 /usr/etc/snmpd -c /etc/s
root      261  0.0  0.0   52    0  ? IW   Jul 23   0:00 /usr/lib/lpd
root      582  0.0  0.2   32   44  ? S    12:24    0:00 in.telnetd
.
.
.
anna    27536  0.0  0.0   88    0 p0 IW   Aug 1    0:01 -csh (csh)
john    27540  0.0  0.0   90    0 p0 IW   Aug 1    0:01 -csh (csh)
anna    27555  0.0  0.0  500    0 p0 IW   Aug 1    0:24 vi myfile
ron     27554  0.0  1.1  164  296 p0 S    Aug 1    1:28 -csh (csh)
```

```
craig    27535  0.2  0.0  312     0 ?   IW   Aug  1  0:20 -csh (csh)
john     28720 12.7  0.0 6268     0 p1  IW   Aug  1  8:12 netscape
vittle%
```

The output from the ps -aux command tells exactly who is doing what on your system. You not only get a list of how many users are on your system, but also what, if any, programs they are running. In Listing 29.6, you can see that user Anna is running an interactive shell program (csh), and she is using the *vi* text editing program to edit a file. You also can see that two users named Ron and Craig are running interactive shell programs, and a user named John is running the Web browser Netscape as well as an interactive shell session. If I were contacted because this system was running sluggishly, given the above user information, I would start with John. I would ask John to exit his Netscape application to see whether the performance improves. Undoubtedly, I would probably learn that Netscape had used more of the CPU than any other user processes.

Again, interpretation of the results is important. A process that has been up and running for weeks may have, over the course of these weeks, logged a great deal of CPU time but may not be the culprit of a sudden drop in performance. Take careful note of the %CPU field. It tells exactly what percent of the system resources are expended by each process. Many more sophisticated commands and tools are available, but they vary dramatically from system to system. I recommend that you refer to a book that focuses on your specific operating system (AIX, Solaris, and so on).

Before leaving the arena of process control, I want to touch briefly on an attribute of processes called Parent Process ID. If you execute the command ps -alx instead of ps -aux, a different set of process attributes will be listed, much of it advanced data regarding process control. The one field I want to focus on in this data is the Parent Process ID, which is under the heading PPID. Listing 29.7 shows the output of the ps -alx command for the exact set of processes shown in Listing 29.6.

Listing 29.7. Partial output from the ps -alx command.

```
vittle% ps -alx
F       UID  PID PPID CP PRI NI SZ  RSS WCHAN    STAT TT TIME COMMAND
20088000   1    0   0   0   5   0  52    0 child    IW   ?  0:13 /sbin/init -
   88000  55    1   1   0   1   0  68    0 select   IW   ?  0:07 portmap
   88001  98    1   1   0   1   0  64  148 select   S    ?  0:32 syslogd
   88000 105    1   1   0   1   0 108    0 socket   IW   ?  0:04 /usr/lib/sen
80488000 140    1   1   0   1   0 128    0 socket   IW   ?  1:36 /usr/etc/snm
   88000 261    1   1   0   1   0  52    0 select   IW   ?  0:00 /usr/lib/lpd
20088001 582    1 258   0   1   0  32   44 select   S    ?  0:00 in.telnetd
.
.
.
a048800010368 27536    1   0   3   0  88    0 Sysbase  IW  p0  0:01 -csh (csh)
a04880001037- 27540  582   0   3   0  88    0 Sysbase  IW  p0  0:01 -csh (csh)
```

continues

Listing 29.7. continued

```
2008800010368 27555 27536  0  1  0 500    0 select   IW   p0  0:24 vi myfile
2008800110368 27554        582 0  1  0 164  296 select   S    p0  1:28 -csh (csh)
2008800010368 27535        582 0  1  0 312    0 select   IW   ?   0:20 -csh (csh)
2000800010370 28720 27540  1  1    06268    0 select   IW   p1  8:12 netscape
vittle%
```

Every process is fired off by another process—its *parent*. If you look at the `ps -alx` output, you can trace John's Netscape process to its parent by way of its parent's ID, which is the program `csh`. In turn, you can trace the `csh` process to its parent, the process `in.telnetd`, the Telnet server program. You can effectively trace back the potential system overload to a program executed by a user over a Telnet session. Through the PPID, you can learn a great deal about the origin of a process.

Connectivity Issues

When users are connecting to a system remotely via Telnet, there are more points of failure than if they are not remote. To the Telnet users, any problem with the network or either the local or remote system yields the same unhappy responses from users—"The system is down! I can't do my work!" Understanding the connectivity issues is as important as understanding the issues regarding system availability. In the following sections, I troubleshoot connectivity problems, first by looking at the remote system (which appears down since it is unreachable) and then by working into the local system.

Problems with the Remote System

When a connectivity problem occurs, most often the first assumption is that the remote system is down. Is it really down? Can you reach it with a `ping`? `ping` is a TCP/IP-based command that sends a signal to a remote system and expects a reply. It is named after the term used for sending sonar signals. Even if you cannot `ping` it, that does not mean that the problem lies within the remote system.

Assume that you can physically reach the system and confirm that it is up and running. A good first test is to try to Telnet to the machine from itself. This approach may seem confusing or recursive, but because a system that can serve Telnet commands must be able to multitask, it should be able to assume both the role of the client and the server. If you are in front of a system that is unreachable from other systems, for example, and its name is vittle, type `telnet vittle` and try to establish a Telnet session without moving over your LAN.

If you cannot connect, make sure that you are using the right hostname by executing a command such as `hostname` on the local system. Make note of the system's IP address. Make sure that the process `in.telnetd` is running by looking at the process table. Try to rlogin into the system instead of Telnet. One of these commands should give you a connection. If you can rlogin to the system, try restarting the Telnet daemon. Also, try to bring down and then back up the network interface by using the `ifconfig` command. If all these efforts fail, try to reboot the system. These symptoms probably indicate a fundamental problem with this remote system at the operating system level.

Problems Getting to the Host

If, upon visiting the remote system, you find that all is well, look at the network running between the two systems. Can you Telnet to the system from a third system that is independent of the other two? If not, try to Telnet to the IP address instead of the hostname. In other words, if system vittle has the IP address 10.23.5.30, instead of typing `telnet vittle`, try typing `telnet 10.23.5.30` and see what happens. If Telnetting via IP address is successful, look at how your systems translate hostnames into IP addresses. This translation is typically performed through either a local file named /etc/hosts, the Network Information Service (NIS) protocols, or Domain Name Services (DNSs). Make sure that whichever of these your LAN uses, it resolves the names correctly.

Try to Telnet to another system on the same network segment. Try to Telnet to another system on a different network segment. Are the problems limited to the one system in question, a single network segment, or is it LAN-wide? Check both the network segment on which the local system resides and the segment of the remote client in the same manner. If you can confine the problem to occurring over an entire network segment and duplicate the problem when two entirely different systems are involved, you should probably get a network specialist involved.

Furthermore, if the problem is poor response time, determine if it is isolated to communication between the two systems or if poor performance occurs across a larger collection of systems. Examine the process that is trying to run over the network through the Telnet session. Your network is only as fast as the slowest device that your data is passing through. Even if a system is powerful, if it is receiving data over an Ethernet interface that yields a throughput of 10 megabits/second, the system can respond only as fast as it can receive data on which to operate. Be aware of these network limitations and where bottlenecks are likely to occur on your LAN data.

Security Issues: Transmissions Over Ethernet

I want to focus on Ethernet-based networks in our discussion about security. Most LANs in industry are built with at least some Ethernet networks, so the issues surrounding these networks are pertinent to almost all readers. Ethernet, as a network protocol, differs dramatically from Token Ring (often considered the second most popular network protocol) in one significant way: Ethernet is a broadcast-based protocol. This means that data packets are not sent in an exclusive channel from host A to host B. Instead, when system A wants to pass a data packet to system B, it broadcasts the data packet over the network. Every host on the LAN gets the packet addressed to system B, and all systems disregard the packet, because it's not addressed to them, except for system B, which receives the packet. System B then passes the packet up the TCP/IP stack, which looks at the port number and so on and then processes the data. Because every computer receives the packet, the data passes through every wire in the LAN, as illustrated in Figure 29.3. With all this data flowing, you should begin to understand why physically securing your network is so important. Can someone actually list data off the wire? Would the data even be readable? Yes and Yes. A common tool of network specialists is even engineered to "sniff" out such data. Not surprisingly, this tool is called a *sniffer*.

FIGURE 29.3.
Data broadcast over Ethernet.

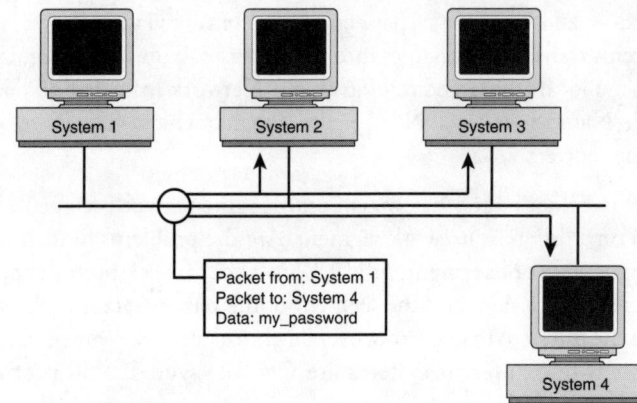

Think of a sniffer as a nosy networked computer. Most systems ignore any data packet that is not specifically addressed to them. A sniffer is a computer with a network interface configured to keep and store every data packet passing through the wire for later analysis. A network specialist may use this type of tool to determine what is causing excessive network traffic or to collect some statistical data to get a baseline on a network. A *baseline* is a profile of what standard network activity looks like on a specific LAN.

Consider a Telnet session. When you Telnet to a system, a connection is opened between the two systems. The remote system asks for your login and password. In other words, it sends a packet to your system, addressed to port number 23 (the Telnet port) with the text string `Password:` in it. You respond by typing in your password. Even though you do not see it when you type it, that password is passed across the network in data packets addressed to port number 23 on the remote system. A malicious person with a sniffer can simply plug the sniffer into your network, instruct it to listen specifically for any data targeted to port number 23 on any system, and in time can probably lift more than a few users' login names and passwords off your LAN.

The creative technologist can configure almost any system to behave like a sniffer, although doing so is very difficult. Ironically, rlogin, with its *trusted host* issues, gets around this problem. Because passwords are not necessary, they are never typed in and never sent out on the wire. Remember, though, that trusted hosts open up another Pandora's box of issues. With rlogin, if one system is compromised, so are all those that trust it. For this reason, in the most secure networks, the actual wires and network ports are physically secure, perhaps even sealed in conduit tubes.

Another solution for securing data that is gaining popularity is to encrypt all data passed over the wire. In other words, system A encrypts the data and broadcasts it scrambled. System B accepts the data, decodes it, and then uses it. Of course, the flip side is that because every piece of data transmitted must be encrypted on the way out and decrypted on the way in, data moves slower. You also may get complaints about shoddy network performance.

Raw Data Passed Via Telnet

The risks that apply to passwords transmitted across the network apply to any ASCII data transmitted over the network. If payroll data is sent unencrypted from one system to another, this data too is broadcast with the possibility of getting picked up by a sniffer.

Packet Filtering

One way to protect portions of your LAN is to implement packet filtering. *Packet filtering* is a standard feature with most routers. Through packet filtering, a user can tell a router to permit or forbid data to pass through it onto a portion of the LAN by either IP address or by TCP/IP port number. With packet filtering, for example, you can tell a router to forbid any data addressed to port 23 to pass through a router, thereby disabling Telnet between two systems on different sides of the routers. You also can then enable port 23 only on a system with the IP address w.x.y.z, thereby permitting only Telnet access through the router from that one system. This is an example of basic and simple network security. The method of configuring packet filtering may vary from router model to router model, so you should consult the user's guide for your router for specific information on how to configure it.

Another Look at the Process Table

I want to discuss briefly the process table from the standpoint of security to underscore the amount of data visible to a user looking at the process table and use this section as a segue to a discussion of common sense and security.

Assume that you write a program that performs a task and requires a password. Perhaps it is a password of another account on the system, or maybe it is a password that is used by a specific application. Being a clever programmer, you write the program so that it takes a password as an input argument and then uses whatever is typed on the command line as the password. Assume that the program is named special_program and the password is booboo. To run this program, you can type special_program booboo. Listing 29.8 shows part of the output of the ps -aux command while this program is running.

Listing 29.8. A look at the program `special_program` from `ps -aux`.

```
USR         PID   %CPU %MEM   SZ TT  STAT START TIME COMMAND
root          1   0.0  0.1   52 ?   S    May 1 0:36 /sbin/init -
root          2   0.0  0.0    0 ?   D    May 1 0:06 pagedaemon
root        159   0.0  0.0  108 ?   IW   May 1 0:31 cron
.
.
.
root        159   0.0  0.0  108 ?   IW   May 1 0:31 cron
anna      26479   0.0  0.0   40 p0  IW   11:36 0:31 telnet varmint
anna      25926   0.0  0.0  220 ?   IW   09:53 0:06 special_program booboo
```

Remember that any user can execute the `ps -aux` command. Any user, therefore, can see that the password passed through the program is booboo. You are obviously compromising the account's security by basically publishing the password in the process table. (Not to mention opening yourself to personal embarrassment with the password booboo!)

This example underscores the need for system administrators and programmers to expand their concepts of security and heighten their awareness of the many places that may seem harmless and reasonable but could be substantial breaches of security. You could do everything right technically and still have a potential disaster on your hands. At this point, you move away from the technical issues and more to the commonsense issues.

Commonsense Issues

At one time, a potential hacker trying to guess passwords could log into a system via a modem, try to guess a password, fail, get disconnected, and try again, each attempt necessitating another phone call. Today, with the rise of the Internet and the greater implementation of TCP/IP over it, a hacker can repeatedly Telnet into a system and guess passwords without having to redial into a system via a phone modem. This means that today a hacker can move faster, guess more passwords, and have a better chance of finding weaknesses in your LAN than in previous times. This example further underscores the need to set strict rules regarding passwords and security in your LAN. Before you even worry about a hacker sniffing passwords out of your network traffic, worry about the dreaded account named guest with a password guest. Accounts like this (with the same password and login names) are called "joe" accounts—any old Joe can guess the password!—and are probably the first place that a hacker will look to break into your system.

Always practice the following commonsense recommendations:

- Don't allow users to develop easy passwords.
- Don't publicize any confidential data.
- Be aware any time you send or receive sensitive data over the wire.

- Don't let your staff plug modems into your systems so that they can dial directly into systems from their homes.
- Remember, as the systems administrator, you are the keeper of the key to the kingdom. Use it accordingly.

Summary

Telnet is an often-used and powerful tool. As with most powerful tools, understanding its limitations is as important as understanding its benefits. Telnet and similar remote access protocols force you, as a system or network administrator, to look beyond the physical workstation when you consider the user community. This is true from both a user standpoint and a resource-utilization standpoint. Retaining this broader vision is important when it comes to making decisions regarding remote access. Do you permit unlimited access? Do you enforce different passwords on different systems? How much protection do the physical lines your network is composed of need? The answers are important, but asking the right questions is absolutely essential.

IN THIS PART

- E-Mail: The Basic Model 459
- Internet Chat Tools: An Intermediate Model 477
- Internet Phones: The Advanced Model 487
- CU-SeeMe: The Next Wave 501

Using Your Intranet: Communication

PART

V

E-Mail: The Basic Model

30

by David Garrett

IN THIS CHAPTER

- A brief history of e-mail **460**
- Making e-mail work **460**
- Features, functions, and freedom: the benefits of e-mail **463**
- Mail server issues **469**
- Client tools **472**

As one of the first applications to find a widespread acceptance on the Internet, electronic mail (e-mail) has gained popularity and maintained its functionality based on one central factor: simplicity. Unlike many tools and resources that have made their way into the inner sanctum of the corporate office—only to be underutilized (or ignored altogether) due to 11 1/2-inch-thick, hieroglyph-illustrated manuals—e-mail has been embraced as a godsend for both management and employees for three reasons: first, it saves time (instantaneous distribution of news); second, it saves money (fewer photocopied memos, briefs, and so on); third, it is completely easy to master, even for nontechnical people. Now, if you don't believe that the "simplicity factor" holds true for your office, try this simple test: Corner an employee and ask him or her to perform one of the following tasks.

1. Make a double-sided, auto-stapled, sorted, and 90 percent reduced copy of today's sales report.
2. Send an e-mail message.

Chances are that your employee will jump at option 2. E-mail is a fast, affordable, and effective means of communication and group collaboration—one that the developing world of corporate communication must not fail to integrate into the heart of the corporate intranet.

A Brief History of E-Mail

Once there was a time when e-mail resided in "The Dark Place," the term sometimes used to refer to the UNIX (and occasionally DOS) operating systems, due to their lack of attractive interfaces and cold, dark, command-line screens. E-mail clients were almost always UNIX-based, and they consisted entirely of text commands and ASCII characters—not very exciting. If you can remember what computers (and users) were like in the '70s and '80s, you'll understand perfectly that e-mail was developed to facilitate communication across a wide geographical region at a reasonable price and speed—not to provide online entertainment to government workers and scientists. Fortunately for everyone involved, e-mail servers and clients have evolved quite a bit in the past few years. And although you'll find that today's e-mail systems include many more exciting and useful features to enhance your company's communications, at heart the e-mail process is even easier than before, thanks to rich graphical interfaces and the ease of point-and-click technology.

Making E-Mail Work

The underlying functionality of e-mail rests on a protocol called the Standard Mail Transfer Protocol, or SMTP. If you're familiar either technically or casually with some of the other prevailing protocols such as HTTP, FTP, SNMP, TCP/IP, or a host of others, SMTP is simply another acronym to add to your lexicon of computer jargon. Boiled down to the essentials, a mail server accepts your outbound e-mail message, translates the text of your message into a standard character string, and routes it to the desired destination based on the address that you provided. Assuming the process goes as planned, the message arrives at another mail server at the destination, is unscrambled, and is delivered to the recipient. Voilà! What could be easier?

E-Mail Addressing

Now that you know how an e-mail message is transmitted from the sender to the recipient, how do you tell the computer where the message should go? Well, that's easy! All you need to direct a message successfully is the recipient's e-mail address. The e-mail address is akin to the standard address that you have been writing for years on bills, wedding announcements, and so on. In place of name, street, city, and state, though, the e-mail address is composed of something different. For those of you unfamiliar with e-mail addresses, here's how a typical address might appear:

`Beavis@vandriessen.highland.edu`

For starters, anything to the left of the `@` (at) sign should be the name of the account that the recipient uses to receive e-mail—in this case, your friend Beavis. To the right of the `@`, you find the *host name* (the server on the recipient's end) `vandriessen` plus the *domain name*, which in the example is `highland.edu`. This address tells your computer to "Send this message to the user `Beavis` who has an account on the machine `vandriessen` that is part of the `highland.edu` domain." With all this information, your message will almost always get through.

More on Domain Names

If your company or organization wants to have a unique domain name (such as `fruitbat.com` or `flyingmonkey.org`) and not simply an Internet Protocol (IP) address (for example, `206.55.46.10`) to denote your presence on the Internet, you need to apply for one from InterNIC (`www.internic.net`), a company with a mandate from the U.S. Government to manage and regulate Internet addressing issues. This process takes about 30 minutes (you must complete a form) and costs about $100. Unfortunately, the craze to be online, especially on the World Wide Web, has prompted everyone and his uncle to register everything from `dink.com` to `sausage.com`, and everything in between. And if you're thinking about basing your domain name on the `cyber`, `inter`, or other such computer roots, you can pretty much forget it (unless you're extremely creative)—they're mostly all gone. If you do a little research ahead of time to determine what is and isn't already taken, you can save yourself time, money, and a lot of headaches.

> **TIP**
>
> An easy way to find out if a domain name is taken is to use the UNIX command whois. Simply log onto a UNIX machine that is connected to the Internet and type whois *domain name*. The InterNIC database is then queried to look up information on the domain name specified. For example, if you do a whois search on intraactive.com, InterNIC replies with the following:
>
> ```
> (dave_huka)/usra/dave> whois intraactive.com
> IntraActive, Inc. (INTRAACTIVE-DOM)
>    888 17th Street, NW Suite 1200
>    Washington, DC 20006
>
>    Domain Name: INTRAACTIVE.COM
>
>    Administrative Contact:
>       Garrett, David   (DG215)  dave@ID1.COM
>       202-667-7048
>    Technical Contact, Zone Contact:
>       Simon, Richard   (RS2599) simon@INTRAACTIVE.COM
>       202-667-7048 (FAX) 202-667-7055
>    Billing Contact:
>       Majersik, Cliff  (CM235)  cliff@ID1.COM
>       202-331-8495
>
>    Record last updated on 09-Jul-96.
>    Record created on 21-Apr-96.
>
>    Domain servers in listed order:
>
>    NS.INTRAACTIVE.COM           206.55.46.10
>    NS2.INTRAACTIVE.COM          206.55.46.103
> ```
>
> ```
> The InterNIC Registration Services Host contains ONLY Internet Information
> (Networks, ASN's, Domains, and POC's).
> Please use the whois server at nic.ddn.mil for MILNET Information.
> (dave_huka)/usra/dave>
> ```
>
> However, if you were to type whois matzohballs.com, you would see the following:
>
> ```
> (dave_huka)/usra/dave> whois matzohballs.com
> No match for "MATZOHBALLS.COM".
> The InterNIC Registration Services Host contains ONLY Internet Information
> (Networks, ASN's, Domains, and POC's).
> Please use the whois server at nic.ddn.mil for MILNET Information.
> ```
>
> As you can see, this particular domain name has not been taken.
>
> You can even do a whois on people. Typing whois garrett produces a list of several hundred Garretts on the Internet.

You may be wondering what the .com, .org, and other extensions mean on e-mail or Web addresses. To keep track of everything and provide enough unique addressing possibilities, addresses are subdivided based on the type of the organization that maintains the address. Called the "top-level" domain, the letters (in the United States) indicate the following:

.com	For-profit company
.org	Nonprofit organization
.gov	Government institution
.net	Site with computers used to maintain the Internet
.edu	Four-year educational institution
.mil	U.S. military site

As I've mentioned, domain names are used in place of the unfriendly and difficult-to-remember IP addresses, which took the form of four sets of up to three-digit numbers, such as 204.157.203.11. Originally, to send me e-mail, you would have had to send mail to dave@206.55.46.10. This manner of dealing with e-mail certainly would be cumbersome (remember, the keyword is simplicity), so the wonderful designers came up with the easy-to-use and catchy domain name option to help users remember addresses quickly and efficiently. These days, you can send my e-mail to dave@intraactive.com, no fuss, no muss!

Features, Functions, and Freedom: The Benefits of E-Mail

In the corporate environment, the ability to send messages quickly and easily to any of a number of users, clients, and managers is a fantastic benefit, but it is an extremely broad and unimaginative application of the technology. I'm not saying that it is not a perfectly valid one, but with just a little more imagination and forethought, the integration of advanced e-mail messaging functionality can bring extraordinary gains to the richness and productivity of your system.

Aliasing

Suppose that your company has a technical support office with a number of highly skilled employees. Generally, the nontechnical employees either befriend a particular person in the support department and rely exclusively on that individual for support, or they randomly e-mail people in the corporate directory whose names happen to fall under the "tech support" category. This approach is both counterproductive and frustrating for both the user and the support personnel.

Using *aliasing* (not the same as the UNIX command), you can create a "virtual" account—for example, support@fojfo.com—that can be used as the standard tech support address, collecting all messages and directing them to a specific user, say david@fojfo.com, until such time that he is on vacation or leaves the company. This method saves a good deal of hassle in that you don't have to publish new contact information for the department. It also maintains the flow of work requests, questions, and so on, and generally enhances corporate productivity.

Remote Messaging

With companies and their employees constantly on the move—dealing with clients, closing million-dollar deals, updating documents on remote machines—ensuring that employees are never out of touch with their support staff, managers, and clients is more important than ever. E-mail can facilitate this communication, especially when coupled with two other high-tech solutions: namely cellular phones and alphanumeric pagers. When e-mail is coupled with software that can forward incoming e-mail to appropriate services (gateways), companies can enable their employees to send mail to pagefrank@fruitbat.com, for example, and have those messages appear on a PCS handset, cellular phone, or pager screen. These messages inform technical support people of malfunctioning servers, allow dispatch centers to schedule service calls more efficiently, and so on.

Photographic Memory: The E-Mail Transcriber

When was the last time you had a telephone conversation (especially since the advent of conference calling) that you hung up with the feeling that you had a thorough grasp of every detail that was covered during the course of your discussion? If you answered "never," give yourself a point for being honest—or at least not overstating your capabilities. With e-mail, every employee can keep an exact record of important as well as trivial correspondence for later review, allowing employees "total recall" and (theoretically) the ability to never overlook minor details for lack of not having a particular memo on hand.

Bigger Ain't Better: Powerful Tool, Small Bandwidth

Unlike some of the other popular features on the Internet, such as the graphical and lively World Wide Web, e-mail is not a "pipe-hog," that is, a resource that is bandwidth-intensive. *Bandwidth* is simply the amount of data that a particular *pipe* (the cable connecting you to the Internet) can transport. If you want to connect a large company to the Net and give each employee desktop access to the Web, FTP, and so on, you'll most certainly need a large pipe, say a T-1, unless you want your users to lay siege to your IS department because of the slow, frustrating access times that would result from a smaller line.

E-mail is a great feature because it requires only a minimal amount of bandwidth to work at an optimal rate. If you work in a small office, say up to five people, a 28.8 Kbps modem or ISDN may suffice. A larger company, however, can also rely on ISDN or perhaps a fractional T-1 if e-mail is the only service you want. This benefit is fantastic because it is a goal that can be accomplished with minor financial investments and can be altered to accommodate high growth or more conservative trends.

Office Uses for E-Mail

Of all the technological revolutions that have occurred in the office environment over the past 15 years, e-mail has had the most significant impact on the daily functions of office life. Radically changing many of the most basic and traditional tasks of the corporate machine, perhaps the biggest change has taken place within the realm of the office "memo." In the past, to circulate an announcement, policy change, and so on, a manager had to go through a number of steps to make sure that all relevant employees were informed. From drafting and editing to copying and circulation, the creation of the memo involved a number of time-consuming, labor-intensive, and costly steps. Today, a manager needs simply to write the memo in his or her e-mail client, quickly spell-check it (to avoid looking like a buffoon in front of employees), and fire it off. This whole process greatly facilitates information distribution.

Sending memos, however, is not the only manner in which e-mail can facilitate interoffice communication. By examining your company's day-to-day activities and needs, you can probably identify many more. For better or for worse, e-mail has dramatically decreased the number of phone calls, voice mail messages, watercooler meetings, and sticky-notes on keyboards. Companies today have implemented intranet e-mail systems to conduct multiparty conversations, schedule meetings, order office equipment or other supplies, or to submit time sheets and sales reports. E-mail allows your company to have an almost paperless office, with much less need to spend valuable time filing volumes of paper in space-hogging file cabinets.

E-mail is an ideal method for coordinating among an entire staff or department. With e-mail, you can be assured that everyone receives the original message firsthand and that the content of the message is not distorted by office scuttlebutt. E-mail lets employees forward information to colleagues, delegate tasks to subordinates, or quickly respond to a directive and request further information. As shown in Figures 30.1 and 30.2, telephones and "While you were out" message slips seem almost archaic when compared to the wonders of modern e-mail, such as the Eudora e-mail client.

FIGURE 30.1.
The old...

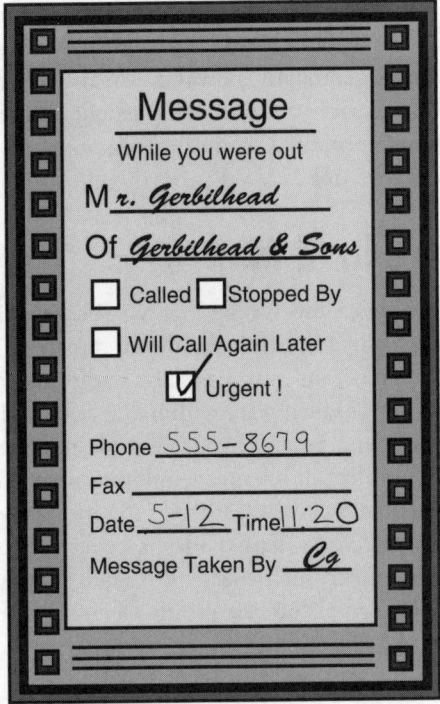

FIGURE 30.2.
...and the new.

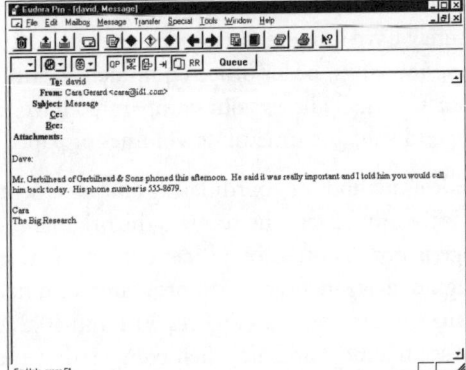

File Sharing

Along with the ability to transfer text messages, users can utilize e-mail as a means to share files between one another, including word processing documents, programs, or any other type of computer file. Instead of making multiple floppy-disk copies of the particular file—or more recently making such a file publicly available on a file server—an employee can attach a file to an e-mail message, address it to the appropriate people, and send it off almost immediately. Using collaborative editing tools such as MS Word for Windows, many people can edit or review a single document either simultaneously or in succession. Press releases, newsletters, proposals, logos—anything that requires input and approval from a team—are all excellent candidates for e-mail collaboration.

You can also exchange documents using e-mail with people outside your organization's particular local area network (LAN) or wide area network (WAN). Even though any documents attached to e-mail messages must be encoded by your e-mail client prior to transmission, most e-mail clients can code and decode any document, so compatibility is not an issue.

Mailbots

If you've ever received the unofficial title of "office expert" on anything having to do with your organization's mission (or anything, for that matter), you're bound to appreciate the functionality that mailbots provide. A *mailbot* is an automatic response site; it provides a way to disseminate simple answers to simple questions (such as setting up Netscape on a desktop computer or requesting vacation time). You can compile a FAQ (frequently asked questions) sheet with step-by-step instructions on any subject and put it in your mailbot. If a staffer at the White House needs information on setting up Netscape, for example, she could send e-mail to netscape-setup@whitehouse.gov. The server would then automatically return the FAQ to her.

What's more, you can create mailbots for a wide range of questions, including everything from standard templates for press releases to health insurance plan options. You can even link a mailbot to a database to provide current prices and other information that changes frequently. The mailbot can search the database automatically and return the requested data, with no human interaction required.

Mailing Lists or Listservs

Mailing lists (also known as *listservs*) are programs that sit on a server and take and broker requests. Mailing lists are commonly used to carry on a conversation among a large number of people, but they also are useful in the corporate environment for disseminating information.

A listserv consists of two addresses: an actual mailing list address and an administrative address. Any individual can send a message to the administrative address and ask to subscribe to the mailing list. Any message that is sent to the mailing list address automatically gets sent to all subscribers.

In addition to subscribing, you also can unsubscribe or perform other functions such as requesting the last nine messages, the first three messages, or any message that has a particular word in it. If you are on a mailing list that gets a lot of messages, you can make a digest of the list so that it sends you all the messages at once (daily or weekly) rather than as they come in.

There are two kinds of mailing lists: moderated and unmoderated. David Letterman's Top Ten List, for example, is a popular moderated mailing list. Only one person, the moderator, can send information out to the mailing list. In unmoderated lists, anyone can send mail to the list, and the mail goes out to everyone.

Companies use mailing lists to keep employees abreast of frequently changing information—price changes, for example. A database could keep this information, but then employees would need to check in periodically to verify prices. A mailing list immediately alerts employees to changes and new information.

Businesses also subscribe to mailing lists for news and information from outside organizations. You can find a mailing list for just about any topic imaginable. The University of North Carolina's Edupage is a "summary of news items on information technology and is provided three times each week as a service by Educom—a consortium of leading colleges and universities seeking to transform education through the use of information technology." Edupage is one of the most widely read mailing lists on the Internet. To subscribe to Edupage, send e-mail to `listproc@educom.unc.edu` and enter the message `subscribe edupage` *your name*.

Mailing lists don't have to be large to be useful, however. You can set up a mailing list for a single department, allowing mail to be sent to everyone in the department quickly and easily. Mail sent to `art@intraactive.com`, for example, would be received by everyone in the art department at IntraActive, Inc.

Wide Area Network Communication

For companies with offices in different locations, e-mail has become practically a necessity. Before e-mail, if you had a document that someone in another location needed to review, you had four choices: postal mail, express mail, facsimile, or if local, courier. Postal mail takes three to four days with the possibility of getting misrouted or even destroyed while en route. A fax is quick but incurs long distance charges and is often printed on paper that fades in a few days or can't be easily manipulated. Express mail offers overnight delivery but at a premium cost. If the document is just headed across town, a courier is an option, but this choice also has its price.

With a WAN, you can attach a file to an e-mail and send it to another office in minutes. The organization saves on long distance telephone charges, postage, and delivery fees, which is sure to be a help in today's budget-conscious office environment. E-mail is fast and free, and if the recipient prints it out, the quality is better than that of a fax. Table 30.1 shows cost and time comparisons of these different methods.

Table 30.1. Cost and time comparisons of typical mail delivery methods.

Method	Cost	Time
U.S. Mail ("snail mail")	$.32 or more	2 to 3 days
Federal Express	$12 to $20	1 day
E-mail	Free	10 minutes

Chapter 30

Global Communication

With an Internet gateway running on the organization's computer system, you can send e-mail to virtually anyone with an e-mail address—associates, customers, vendors, suppliers, accountants, lawyers—outside the organization's WAN or LAN. E-mail eliminates the frustration of "phone tag" or waiting for a fax or package to show up. And because e-mail is free, employees can send as many personal e-mail messages as they want without racking up the company's long distance phone bills. (Not that I'm condoning personal e-mail while on the clock!)

Mail Server Issues

Running a mail server is certainly not the most difficult task that you will encounter when you design and implement your intranet. If you've never dealt with e-mail services before, however, you need to understand some basic concepts, terms, and features so that you can be in the best position possible when evaluating your company's needs in relation to the resources available to you during your design stage.

If you are able to send and receive e-mail either across the Internet or simply through a company's internal communication network, you most certainly have an e-mail account on a server somewhere within your organization. Whether it's on a LAN, a WAN, or the Internet, a machine somewhere maintains a list of your name, aliases, and other pertinent information to be able to broker your requests to send e-mail, as well as receive and process incoming messages and files. Several types of mail servers are available. For a corporate LAN or WAN environment, you can use commercially available servers such as GroupWise, Microsoft Mail, and AppleTalk. GroupWise is available for most PCs and Macs. But because these servers don't use open standards, they cannot communicate with e-mail servers on the Internet. LAN and WAN servers use their own protocols instead of SMTP or POP3 (Post Office Protocol 3) for sending and receiving mail. LAN servers such as Microsoft Mail or GroupWise can be integrated into Internet e-mail by upgrading the software.

POP3 is the standard for receiving mail. Using this protocol, the server talks to your e-mail client software. If you have a mail account on a server, your mail sits in your account on that server until you sign on and retrieve it. Although POP3 is the most widely used protocol, it does have one serious drawback. POP3 functions well only from the client side. Your mail goes to your client machine and can be saved and manipulated only on that machine. If you're traveling, or your computer goes down and you need to use another computer, you're out of luck. You can't retrieve your mail.

With Interactive Mail Access Protocol (IMAP), however, you would be in luck. IMAP is a new post office protocol for receiving mail; it functions from the server side. With IMAP, you can log on to your mail account and review your mail from any machine, at any location.

SMTP is the standard for sending mail. Every mail host has an SMTP server, whether the server for receiving mail is POP3 or IMAP. An SMTP server sorts mail and routes it to the proper address. If you use a server-side client such as Pine or Elm, you usually log in to your SMTP server rather than your POP or IMAP server to get your mail. Because POP3, IMAP, and SMTP are open standards, they are available for any kind of platform.

Server Options

Although literally hundreds of options are available when you're searching for new e-mail client applications, the arena for e-mail (SMTP) servers is not quite as populated. A number of excellent choices are available for a variety of platforms, though. Just remember to do your homework before committing to a particular server.

Post.Office

Post.Office, a powerful new e-mail server available for the Windows NT and UNIX environments, has been developed based on the open standards and protocols of the Internet community. The designers had a couple of very important goals in mind when they built the system: efficiency and reliability. Of course, Post.Office has been designed to accommodate the ever-increasing demands of e-mail messaging that exist in the corporate messaging sphere. To alleviate any problems, Post.Office includes excellent administration and security features.

Post.Office does a lot of things right, and not many wrong. It includes a number of tools that make it an excellent choice as the facilitation tool for office communications. Specifically, Post.Office includes new utilities such as remote configuration, auto-reply, and integrated POP3, SMTP, and Finger servers, which should allow you a lot of latitude when configuring and enhancing your intranet's communications capability. Probably the best feature of Post.Office is the Web-based remote administration tools, which allow you to change each and every aspect of the server's functionality—from forwarding to signature files to security, queues, and processor intervals—from any location that provides Web access.

You can find more information on Post.Office and can even download a fully functional 45-day trial copy by visiting www.software.com.

Netscape Mail Server

The Netscape mail server is, according to Netscape Communications, "...a native SMTP/IMAP/MIME messaging solution that interoperates with other SMTP compliant messaging systems, providing faster, higher-quality message delivery. It offers enterprise customers a robust, high-performance corporate messaging backbone they can rely on." And, boy, they're not kidding.

While not scheduled to be available to the general public until mid-to-late 1996, this UNIX and Win NT/Alpha-based server will support Internet Mail Access Protocol (IMAP4) and will also feature extensive server management and centralized network administration to make the

IS department's life much easier than has traditionally been the norm. This mail package will also integrate with Netscape's SuiteSpot, which means that it will support the Java and JavaScript programming languages for creating, managing, and deploying enterprise applications on corporate systems, adding yet another level of functionality to your services.

For more information on features and availability for Netscape's mail server software, visit

http://home.netscape.com/newsref/pr/newsrelease124.html

Microsoft Exchange Server

Microsoft's strength in the Internet/intranet business is twofold: their first strategy is to make top-flight, exciting software packages to entice IS managers and Joe User to adopt their software as standard. The second is a little more exciting: they tend to give it away. Now, although this isn't the case with Microsoft's Exchange 4.0 mail server, the power and flexibility that this system offers is quite compelling. Because Exchange supports a variety of standards, including X.400, SMTP, MIME, MAPI, TCP/IP, PPP, SLIP, and X.509, it's a safe bet that you'll be able to integrate Exchange 4.0 into any system that you currently have installed within your corporate intranet or will be able to replace current systems completely in favor of an all-Exchange system, should you so desire.

You may have noticed a lack of support for some of the more popular features such as POP3, HTTP, NNTP, and LDAP. According to Microsoft representatives, support for these services is currently in the works and is scheduled to become available in versions sometime later in the year. Although this lack of support is somewhat of a stumbling block if your goal is to enable POP3 service in the immediate future, waiting for a later version (assuming it is on schedule) may be a good idea, especially if you can maintain an all-Microsoft platform, which eases administration and support burdens immeasurably.

For more information and technical data on the Exchange server, visit

http://www.microsoft.com/Exchange/InetExch.htm

An ideal choice if your company is very small or is hesitant to invest large amounts of cash at the start, Seattle Lab's Windows 95-based SMTP/POP3 server is an affordable and popular solution that offers lots of functionality for a small investment of around $180. With a somewhat snappy interface, Slmail95 allows you to create mailing lists, establish auto-responding bots, maintain aliases for user accounts, forward mail, use finger user accounts, and even work with gateways and from behind security firewalls—which means that you don't have to sacrifice security in the name of enhanced communication.

For more information on this 32-bit Windows 95 mail server, visit

http://www.cloud-nine.co.uk/slmail95.htm

Client Tools

Hundreds of different kinds of e-mail clients are available, including freeware and shareware. You could spend years trying them all. Fortunately, most of them do basically the same job, so the following sections give a rundown on five of the most popular but distinct client tools.

Pine

Pine, an e-mail client, was developed at the University of Washington in Seattle in 1989. It is used mostly by people who have direct access to a server (Pine is popular among programmers). Although Pine does not provide a graphical interface, it is a feature-rich client. It's also relatively easy to use. With Pine, shown in Figure 30.3, you can reply to mail; forward mail; send copies to, or "cc," other addressees; create custom mailing lists; create nicknames; and set up as many folders as you want. And because Pine operates on the server, you can retrieve your mail from anywhere. Pine does not use POP3.

FIGURE 30.3.

A closer look at the Pine interface. It's not pretty, but it does a great job.

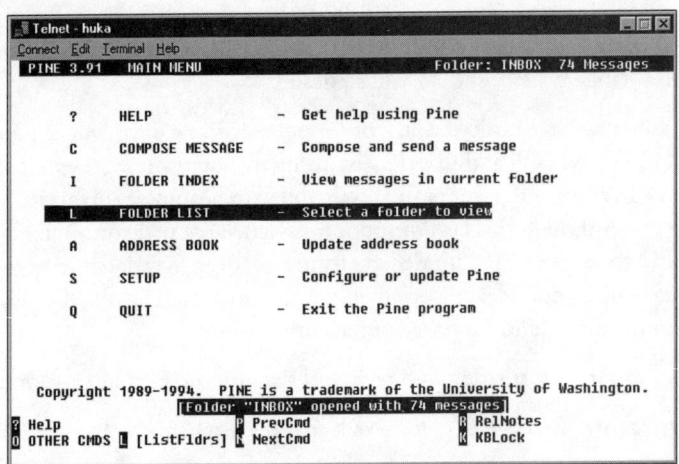

Eudora

Eudora, which also is loaded with features, comes in both PC and Macintosh versions. Eudora, shown in Figure 30.4, is an easy-to-use, intuitive mail client. It is available in commercial, freeware, and shareware versions, with the commercially available version providing extra features such as spell-check. The downside to Eudora is that it is client-side mail, meaning you can manipulate your mail only after you've downloaded it. You can't access your mail from any machine other than your own.

E-Mail: The Basic Model
Chapter 30

FIGURE 30.4.
The Eudora e-mail client.

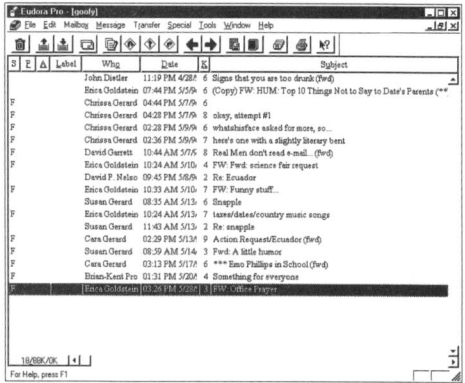

SPRYMail

SPRYMail has one nifty feature that deserves a mention. With SPRYMail, you can read the messages in your mailbox before downloading them from the server. This feature lets you delete any messages you don't want to read, or you can reply immediately to a message. You can also leave messages on the server so that you can retrieve them from another location. Other mail clients can perform this function, but none as cleanly as SPRYMail, which is shown in Figure 30.5. SPRYMail, however, does not have the flexibility of Pine or the intuitive design of Eudora.

FIGURE 30.5.
The SPRYMail e-mail client.

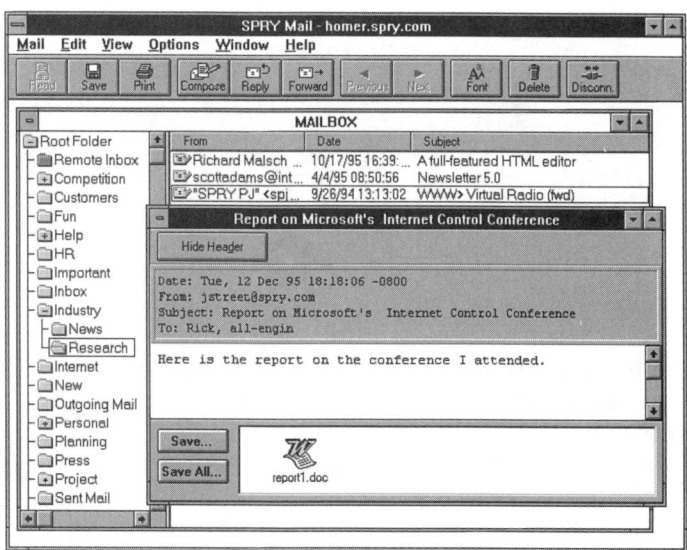

GroupWise

GroupWise is an e-mail client that is commonly used in LAN environments, but it can be easily upgraded to Internet mail compatibility. GroupWise is not as feature-rich as Eudora. It also lacks some features that Internet users prefer. For example, Eudora allows you to change your mail password, a task that Internet users are encouraged to do frequently. With GroupWise, your mail password is the password to your computer.

Netscape Mail

Netscape Mail, shown in Figure 30.6, is a cutting-edge client that can imbed multimedia into your e-mail messages. It's not perfect, but it is as close to perfect as anything that has been released in a number of years. Plus, because Netscape Mail is integrated into the galaxy's most popular Web browser package, it's fairly certain to have a wide install-base quite soon, which will make it easy to troubleshoot, train, and so on.

FIGURE 30.6.
Netscape's top-notch e-mail client.

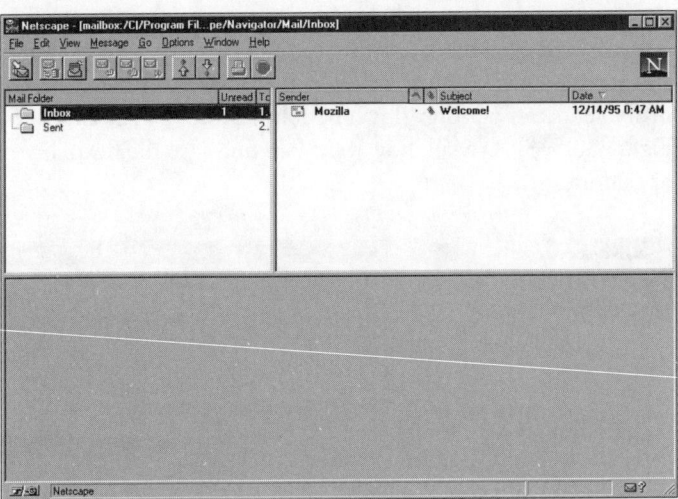

The one feature of Netscape's mail client that is so wonderful is that you can embed sound, video, text—anything that you can normally place within an HTML document—right within the mail message. If you're marveling at this bit of technology, it's not really that big a deal, though the idea was a great one on Netscape's part. Basically, they took the same technology that enables their Web client to dominate their market and extended it into their mail system. So, all you need to do is create a mail message that includes either standard (or Netscape) compliant HTML tags, and you'll be well on your way to reaching new heights of creativity in your electronic communication.

E-Mail: The Basic Model
Chapter 30

To find the mail program that's best for your company, you should first decide what you plan to use e-mail for and then try out these five "biggies." If you anticipate a need to include sound or images in your e-mail in the future, you might want to go with Netscape Mail. If you prefer a solid, easy-to-use client, Eudora may be your best bet. Table 30.2 gives you an easy comparison of features for these five clients.

Table 30.2. Comparing mail clients and their functions.

Feature	Pine	Eudora	SPRYMail	GroupWise	Netscape
POP3	No	Yes	Yes	Limited	Yes
IMAP	No	No	No	No	Limited
Nicknames	Yes	Yes	Yes	Yes	Yes
Folders	Yes	No	No	No	No
Filters	Limited	Yes	No	Yes	No
Remote access	Yes	No	Yes	No	No
Spell-Check	Yes	Yes	No	Yes	No
Offline use	No	Yes	Yes	Yes	Yes
Searching	Yes	Yes	Yes	No	Yes
Sorting	No	Yes	No	No	Yes
Attachments	Limited	Yes	Yes	Yes	Yes

MCKEON & JEFFRIES

McKeon & Jeffries has been using interoffice e-mail for several years through Novell's Groupwise software and a special patch obtained on the Internet that allowed Groupwise to talk to other SMTP servers on the Internet. The accounting firm's employees can not only send mail to users on their WAN, but they also can send to anyone on the Internet. Although Groupwise might not be the most robust e-mail client for M&J, it is an easy solution because users were already familiar with it. Also, by using Groupwise, the firm didn't have to purchase, install, or configure a new mail server.

> ### THE SPORTING GOODS AND APPAREL ASSOCIATION
>
> The SGAA decided on Eudora Pro for its employees and recommended Eudora to its members who didn't already have a mail client. The SGAA picked Eudora because of its many features and because it is available for all versions of Windows and MacOS. Eudora also has a freeware version that was bundled with the software package sent out to members.
>
> The SGAA also purchased Netscape mail server to serve mail for the group. They picked Netscape because it was easy to install and configure and because the association didn't expect a large volume of mail. Also, the only machine on which the mail server could be installed was the Sun server. Netscape mail is available on the Internet for the Solaris platform.

Summary

Because e-mail is one of the most useful, functional, and easy-to-master services offered on the Information Superhighway, you should embrace wholeheartedly some level of e-mail connectivity for your developing intranet. Whether you administer your own in-house SMPT server or have remote accounts that you access either through a Telnet or POP3 client, the benefits that can be reaped by office communication demand that you explore all the possibilities.

Although to date most e-mail consists almost entirely of standard, somewhat boring ASCII text—lacking the whiz-bang features that have made WYSIWYG applications and the World Wide Web so famous, such as boldface, italicized text, underlining, and graphics—the future of e-mail communication is certainly a bright and prosperous one. With the beginning of a trend toward embedded multimedia features within e-mail messages, including sounds, video clips, .jpegs and .gifs, and so on, you can be sure that you'll be in for a wild, exciting ride in the world of corporate communication.

Internet Chat Tools: An Intermediate Model

31

by Nikki Goth and Paul Itoi

IN THIS CHAPTER

- Origins: Internet Relay Chat (IRC) **478**
- How Chat works **479**
- Applications **480**
- Server issues **481**
- Client tools **483**
- Comparing Chat to Internet Phone and video-conferencing **484**

Now that you are familiar with how e-mail can enhance business communications on the Internet, you'll want to consider the options for providing synchronous communications tools on your intranet. Synchronous methods of communicating allow two or more users to maintain an open channel through which information can be sent and received in real-time; that is, with no significant time delay. Talking on the telephone, for example, is a synchronous means of communication. Writing, listening, or interacting with others in real-time adds a valuable dimension to business communication. Users can save time, reduce travel expenses, and better communicate complicated ideas in real-time. While information can be easily misunderstood when it is sent over e-mail, real-time communication enables users to provide context for the information they are transmitting and answer questions as they arise.

Several alternatives will be presented in the next three chapters: WebChat, Internet phones, and video-conferencing over the Internet. Chat is the simplest of the three tools. Although it originated as a text-only means of communicating, Chat tools now support graphics and hypertext links. Applications for making phone calls or conducting video conferences via the Internet enable audio and video in real-time; however, they also consume enormous amounts of bandwidth. Because of its relatively low bandwidth requirements, consider Chat a practical intermediate tool for facilitating synchronous communication among groups of employees and customers.

Origins: Internet Relay Chat (IRC)

On the Internet, the two most popular chat tools are Multiuser Dungeons (MUDs) and Internet Relay Chat (IRC). While MUDs often add game components in addition to Chat, IRC is a pure chat system. IRC's main network often has more than 10,000 users online at any given time. On average, there are about 18,000 users and 5,000 channels on IRC worldwide. IRC was designed as a replacement for the rudimentary UNIX `talk` function, which enabled two people to converse in text in real-time over the Internet. As `talk`'s successor, IRC made it possible for multiple users to converse in text using a shared channel on the Internet.

Chat, as the name implies, originated as a playful means of communicating with other users around the world in real-time over the Internet. It first gained international recognition during the Persian Gulf War, when updates from around the world were sent over the wire to individuals who had tuned in to one channel on the Internet Relay Network. This ability to communicate real-time news feeds also was used in the following global events:

- The 1994 California Earthquake
- The 1993 Russian Revolt
- The 1992 Russian Revolution
- The 1992 USA Presidential Election
- The 1991 Gulf War

The excerpts below are from a log of a chat that took place on IRC during the Gulf War (source: `http://urth.acsu.buffalo.edu/irc/WWW/ircdocs.html#logs`):

```
This is IRC CHANNEL +peace
( till ca. Jan 17 02:22 )
( jnweiger@immd4.informatik.uni-erlangen.de )
IRC Log started Thu Jan 17 01:03
<umfonta6> bombs are droppiong in baghdad
<hstanley> jeesh
<spamgod> am i getting through?
<CaptainJ> CNN HAS THE SCOOP!
<umfonta6> cbc
<Lipstick> Wow! why is everyone leaving?
...
<Goofa> Operation desert storm{_ has started.
<CaptainJ> OPERATION DESERT STORM
<Anipa> operation Thunderstorm!!!
<tsh> liberation...hah...
<MistDrake> Announcement from the president of US: The liberation of
Kuwait has begun
<Arkie> i'm listening to nbc radio....
<Starhawk> "Desert Storm"
<Lipstick> Operation desert storm has begun as of 7pm!
<Mark> we knew an hour ago.
```

After IRC began to gain popularity, a group of commercial IRC client products emerged and helped standardize the slash commands used to communicate on IRC. Consumer online services, such as America Online, also began offering chat groups to subscribers. By some estimates, chat services account for approximately 30 percent of the revenues earned by these services.

More recently, Chat has become a feasible business communication tool as companies such as Netscape and Microsoft integrate the chat feature directly into their Web browsers. This new relationship between the browser and the chat client allows casual Web users to take advantage of Chat without leaving the Web environment. As Java-enabled browsers become more prevalent, applet-based chat services will become more common. 3D chat enabled by VRML (Virtual Reality Markup Language) may appeal to some businesses as a means of enhancing the customer's shopping experience by providing 3D views of their products. In 3D chat, channels become virtual spaces that the user can explore. Users can personalize an avatar to represent themselves in this virtual space. The avatar can communicate basic chat expressions such as a grin with simple animations. Because of the bandwidth required to simulate 3D space, the high-speed intranet environment provides a fertile proving ground for this emerging technology.

How Chat Works

To use Chat, the user runs a client program, which connects to either the IRC network or the company's own server. Servers then pass messages from user to user over the Chat network. The IRC servers can have hundreds of channels. Once connected, the user lists all the channels, scrolls through the list to find a topic of interest, and joins that channel. Once the user joins a channel, anything the user types can be read by the other channel members. It is possible to page other users who are in different channels, and to talk to a user privately by using the `/msg` command. Other IRC slash commands allow users to express behaviors, for example hug and smile. Business users will most likely begin using one of the graphical user interfaces to IRC and therefore will not need to learn the commands; however, typing `/HELP` will usually assist in finding information about specific commands.

Today's chat tools simplify the chat process just described into a graphical interface that makes the underlying commands transparent to the user.

Applications

Until very recently, Chat has been presented as a feature primarily for enhancing consumer entertainment on the Internet. Few businesses actually depend on a chat system in the intranet environment. Nevertheless, WebChat does lend itself to a variety of business communication applications. The first example of a business application for WebChat serves as a bridge between the consumer environment and the internal business environment. On the most basic level, companies can build the chat function into their corporate Web site to allow public visitors to join a chat group in which particular product information from the company is being discussed. A sales representative from the company moderates the chat room to answer questions and direct users to other relevant Web pages. Chat is practical for handling customer questions because it allows a sales representative to provide information to customers in real-time and to stimulate discussion among customers. As moderator of the chat session, the sales rep will have a significant, new opportunity to measure and influence customer satisfaction.

Within the corporation, WebChat is a particularly useful tool for group settings that require discussion, answers, or feedback in real-time. Companies might choose to use intranet Chat to hold text-based conference calls with remote employees, or to conduct employee training sessions. A remote sales representative can routinely brief the employers located at the company's headquarters on meetings with clients. The ability to transmit and respond to competitive information in real-time can play an important role in winning new accounts or keeping existing clients. Chat would also be good for brainstorming among design engineers or problem solving between people who have experience with similar equipment. Unlike video-conferencing or an Internet phone conference call, WebChat provides an open channel for group communication in real-time without consuming excess bandwidth that might be needed for other network applications.

In another scenario, customer support agents might use Chat to communicate questions and answers to other agents in real-time, while they are talking with customers on the telephone. Because Chat is text-based, customers will not even need to know that the agent with whom they are speaking is typing questions and receiving answers in real-time. The process of answering customer questions can go more smoothly, and the chat system can save considerable amounts of time for both the customer and the help desk.

Consider these additional examples of how Quarterdeck's Global Stage customers are applying chat functions (the scenarios were found on Quarterdeck's chat product Web site—`http://www.qdeck.com/chat/`):

- Special interest community discussion groups. Several large organizations are building community by sponsoring live events at which members are able to share personal home pages including photographs and sound clips with peers while they interact.
- Sales staff can assist customers in real time and "sell" Web merchandise in a prominent Web-based retail store.
- Real-time technical support for a software company to answer customer questions immediately and guide users to technical documentation contained on the company's Web site.

These examples can be extrapolated to apply to business scenarios in which users facilitate business discussion groups, sales support, technical support, and slide presentations by using WebChat. A Human Resources department could open a chat room to discuss employee ideas regarding the formation of a new policy, take questions regarding health care changes, or take queries about the company's policy on sexual harassment, smoking, benefits, or hiring practices. The applications just described suggest that WebChat is a useful tool for saving time, reducing travel expenses for on-site visits, and enhancing employee training methods. Currently, Chat is probably the most practical tool for implementing real-time communications functionality within the intranet.

Server Issues

Businesses that plan to use Chat extensively may want to provide a server internally for Chat. In contrast to the IRC network, commercial chat servers are normally stand-alone. This means that when you want to chat on a certain channel, you connect directly to the server that carries that channel, as opposed to joining a server and then listing all of the channels on that server. Currently, few companies offer commercial WebChat products for the business environment. However, as the chat functions are increasingly supported by the most popular Web browsers, the availability of chat functionality should increase. Chat provides the real-time interactivity that static Web pages traditionally lack.

To meet the needs of commercial organizations that want to manage their own chat events, a company called Prospero (now Quarterdeck) developed the Global Stage IRC chat server (`http://www.globalchat.com/`). This server extends the basic IRC functionality to include these features:

- Password authentication linked to member databases of sponsoring organizations
- Optional payment capabilities through First Virtual
- Advanced production and moderator tools to create entertaining, content-rich events
- Simulcast capabilities for graphics, sound, and links to Web sites
- Expandable code for easy customization and user-specific features

Quarterdeck offers several different versions of its chat servers. The Café version is provided free of charge for small sites and not-for-profit sites. The company recommends using this version to learn more about chat before purchasing one of the more enhanced versions. The Theater version is intended for sites that have a limited budget and plan to conduct infrequent or occasional chat sessions with a relatively small user base. The Stadium is the company's high-end version intended for sites that have a large user base and are seeking to attract up to hundreds of users to special chat events. Businesses that want to hold members-only chat or offer real-time multimedia advertising during the chat should look into this product. Quarterdeck provides the following summary of its specific chat server features:

The Café Version

- User-created channels
- Restricted channels
- Moderated and unmoderated channels
- Easy to administer
- Unlimited number of simultaneous channels
- Ability to record transcripts
- Up to 50 simultaneous users
- Free text link from the Internet Chat Guide to your chat site
- Available for free use

The Theater Version

Everything the Café offers, plus

- Up to 100 simultaneous users
- Support, maintenance, and upgrades are available
- Basic (DBM) member database (in the near future)
- Graphical and descriptive links from the Internet Chat Guide to your chat site

The Stadium

Everything the Theater offers, plus

- Up to 1,000 simultaneous users today, support for 10,000+ users in the near future
- Ability to send real-time advertisements to users in Chat
- Integration with broad range of Web-based member databases
- Custom enhancements are available
- Branded versions of Global Chat client software are available

More recently, a company called iChat has introduced its ROOMS (Real-time Object-Oriented Multimedia Server) component that works with standard Web servers to link specific text within a chat to a particular Web page. A plug-in also is available for Windows 95 and Windows NT, and iChat has a stand-alone product for Windows 3.1, Windows 95, or Windows NT. The price range depends on the number of users. A 20-user license for iChat begins at around $495, while a 100-user license is approximately $2,995; a 5,000-user license runs about $19,995. For an additional 25 percent charge, customers can get free server upgrades for a year. For connectivity, the iChat server uses the Telnet protocol; for integration with the Web, it uses HTML.

Client Tools

Users need to have IRC clients to connect to the IRC network of chat groups. Clients are available for both the PC and Macintosh platforms. These client applications can have graphical or command-based user interfaces. Most of the IRC clients use slash commands, such as /JOIN #chatzone to join, /LEAVE to leave, /QUIT to quit, and /HELP to ask for help. However, as mentioned previously, in the Web environment, most of these commands have been replaced by a graphical interface.

Ircle is one application for using IRC on the Macintosh. Ircle is a small but full-featured IRC client that recognizes most of the common IRC commands. Ircle also has some extra functions not found in clients on other platforms. For example, it implements pictures of people online and speech, if Apple Speech Manager is installed. It is capable of transferring files to other IRC users, even if the other users are on other hardware platforms. Ircle is a relatively stable program that requires little memory to run. It is compatible with all Macintoshes and requires System 7.0 or higher with MacTCP installed. Ircle will work with black-and-white monitors, but the company recommends a color monitor. Ircle currently needs only 450KB of RAM.

In June 1995, Prospero Systems released the Global Chat client as the first software to add live interaction to the Web. The product was designed to offer the Internet the same types of social chat and live special events that users find appealing on commercial online services. Global Chat works automatically and continuously like a radio or television receiver. It can also add graphics and sound to the text-only chats available to commercial online subscribers. After the user downloads the client, clicking on a link from a Web page will enable the user to enter a chat channel. The software opens a new window containing the ongoing chat, along with any graphics and sounds being transmitted. The Global Chat program is compatible with existing IRC servers, as well as the company's own Global Stage servers.

iChat is another of the few companies offering chat products that are completely integrated with the Web. As mentioned earlier, its plug-ins for Netscape and Internet Explorer enable users to structure chat rooms that correspond with Web pages. The company's client combines a basic Telnet client with enhanced features to support MUDs and IRC. The IRC and MUD components of iChat's client provide graphical user interfaces to these two chat systems, which help new users to learn and use these existing Internet resources. The iChat client also provides in-line HTML parsing. This allows hyperlinks and other HTML tags to be added into IRC, MUDs, and other Telnet sessions. The iChat client calls Netscape or Mosaic to launch the hyperlinked URLs automatically. Basically, iChat's products enable users to combine the graphical features of the Web with the real-time features of Chat. Suppose your intranet needs to involve real-time chat about images or text. A Web page could be created with the content in question provided, as well as a link to a chat room. Now users of the intranet can look at a Web page and discuss it in real time with other users.

Comparing Chat to Internet Phone and Video-Conferencing

Because it is text-based, Chat may be the most realistic near-term solution for providing real-time communication capabilities over your intranet. Its lower bandwidth requirements make it infinitely more scalable than audio or video, so you can support many more users on one chat channel than on an Internet phone conference call or a video conference. You don't need any additional hardware to support Chat. Chat does have its own technological limitations, however. It is possible, for example, to interrupt a conversation by flooding the channel with text. If one user attempts to send too much text to another chat participant with a slow modem, the session can be terminated by the overflow of data.

Another problem with intranet chat is its potential to put extremely sensitive information at risk to outsiders. If someone unknowingly enters a chat session, he or she will have easy access to all the information that is "spoken" by the authenticated chat room members. Therefore, it's important to establish a secure protocol and procedure for your intranet's chat users. At this point, it's best that users not discuss top-secret projects during a Web chat session. All users should know this, and those who break the rules of confidentiality should have chat privileges revoked.

One alternative to establishing hard-handed protocols is to develop a means of encrypting chat data as it travels from one machine to another. A standard encryption procedure would work, because intranet chat data is the same as any other data that traverses an intranet, and it can be manipulated in the same way you would manipulate, say, a more static message board. What all this boils down to is that intranet chat can be considered a security risk—but not any more so than other applications you might choose to run. If you've taken the necessary precautions in developing your intranet, data from chat areas will be as safe as data from any other application.

Summary

WebChat enables employees to explore a text-based method of real-time communication, while reserving excess bandwidth for other intranet applications. In choosing a chat product, intranet architects should evaluate whether the product is easy to navigate for the user and whether it supports open systems for the system administrator. The chat functions bundled by server software companies, such as Netscape and Microsoft, meet these criteria. Although Internet phones and video-conferencing will be positioned as more sophisticated Internet communications tools, Chat is a valuable means that can be used now to facilitate synchronous communication within a corporation.

Internet Phones: The Advanced Model

32

by Steven Greenberg and Josh Becker

IN THIS CHAPTER

- What is an Internet telephone, and what can it do? **488**
- System resource usage **490**
- Privacy **491**
- A brief history and barriers to proliferation **491**
- How does an Internet phone work on an intranet? **493**
- Internet phone uses for intranets **494**
- Server issues **496**
- Legal and regulatory issues **497**
- Client tools **498**

Internet telephones have the potential to change the rules for long-distance telephone companies, open the way to increased electronic commerce, and make corporate intranets more useful and productive. This is because Internet telephones can improve communication while cutting travel and long-distance costs. These benefits have already led more than 500,000 people to use Internet phones daily.

This is all possible thanks to simultaneous voice and data links between two parties who are connected by the inexpensive computer network links of today, not the expensive long-distance lines of yesterday. This means two things. First, it means that two people can talk through their computers at the same time—and on the same "line"—as they work on a shared electronic document or "whiteboard." Second, it means that Internet phone users save money because the computers they use to transmit their voices back and forth are hooked together using inexpensive local calls to Internet Service Providers (ISPs), not high-priced long-distance calls.

Recent developments in firewall software have opened the world of intranet phones to intranet users. It is thus important for intranet users and managers to understand how Internet phones work, what their costs and benefits are, and how they can improve corporate productivity.

What Is an Internet Telephone, and What Can It Do?

In a nutshell, an Internet telephone is a computer software program that converts voice into data for transmission over the Internet, compresses that data for faster transmission, transmits the data in small "packets," and then reassembles those packets, decompresses the data, and converts it back into voice at the other end. Thus, the current Internet phone technology requires two users, with two computers and two copies of Internet phone software.

The minimum recommended hardware configuration for using Internet telephony products is a 486 PC operating at 25 MHz with 8MB RAM, a 14.4 Kbps modem, a sound card, a microphone, and speakers (these plug into the sound card). The minimum supporting software required is Windows 3.1 and a Winsock 1.1-compatible TCP/IP Internet connection.

Currently, to complete an Internet phone call, both users must be running the same Internet phone software program. Additionally, both users must be logged onto the Internet concurrently to initiate a "call."

The reasons for these requirements are twofold. First, each Internet phone software program uses its own protocol, so if the users' protocols don't match, they cannot communicate with each other. Second, even when the two users are able communicate with each other, they must be able to find each other on the Internet—and it's not as simple as knowing each user's e-mail address or telephone number. This is because most users do not have dedicated IP (Internet Protocol) addresses; rather they are assigned a new address each time they log on to their ISP's server. To solve this problem, the popular Internet phone software packages have each user call an "operator." This operator then posts each user's address to an online "phone book," which other users can utilize to find the addresses. This system is referred to as IRC (Internet Relay Chat).

Given the limitations that these requirements place on widespread Internet phone use, computer companies are cooperating in new ways to eliminate them. For example, 10 of the major Internet phone software providers, including VocalTec, Netscape, Intel, and IBM, intend to adopt RTP (Real Time Protocol) as a "standard" protocol for Internet phone software. This standard is expected to promote communication not only between Internet phone users, but also between audio/video-on-demand systems and video-conferencing software. (Video-conferencing software already has its own standard, called "H.320.")

Similarly, both private and public organizations are working to connect conventional telephones with Internet telephones. In the public arena, a nonprofit organization called Free World Dialup (FWD) has volunteers around the world who have set up their computers to serve as "gateways" to connect incoming Internet calls with outgoing conventional calls in their local calling area (that is, it's a free local call for the volunteer). In the private arena, VocalTec's new Internet Phone Telephony Gateway software can be coupled with a special card from Dialogic and a 28.8 Kbps modem to accomplish the same result. It calls a VocalTec server on the Internet, which acts as the gateway.

The following figures show how the path that a phone call takes will change with the advent of Internet phones. In "Today's System," shown in Figure 32.1, the caller uses a conventional phone. Regardless of whether the caller dials a local or long-distance number, the call is routed to the switch of the local phone company (the RBOC—Regional Bell Operating Company). If the caller is making a local call, the switch routes the call to the person being called. If the caller is placing a long-distance call, the switch hands the call over to the network of the long-distance carrier, which routes the call to the local phone company serving the person being called. That company's local switch then routes the call to the ultimate location for completion.

In "Tomorrow's System," however, shown in Figure 32.2, you will notice that the Internet essentially replaces the long-distance company. The local switch serving the dialing party routes the call to the dialer's ISP (usually a local call). The ISP, in turn, puts the call on the Internet. The IP address of the receiving party is used to locate that person's ISP, and then the receiving ISP routes the data to the recipient's local RBOC switch, which completes the connection.

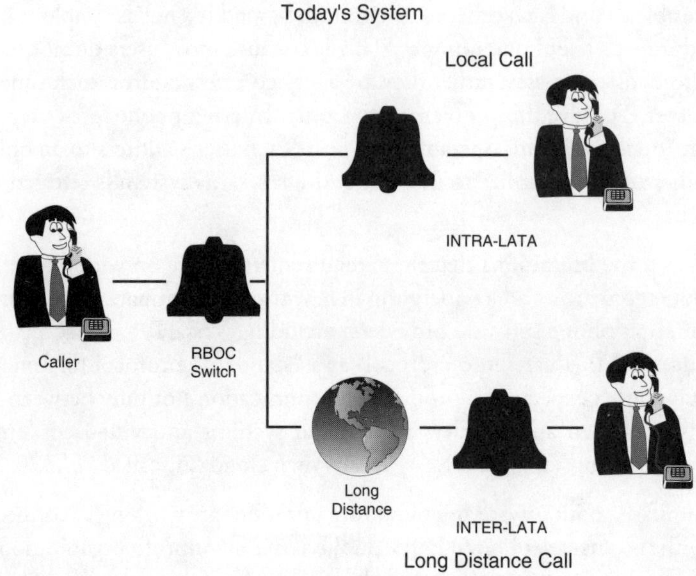

Using Your Intranet: Communication
Part V

FIGURE 32.1.
Today's system.

FIGURE 32.2.
The path that a phone call takes will change with the advent of Internet phones.

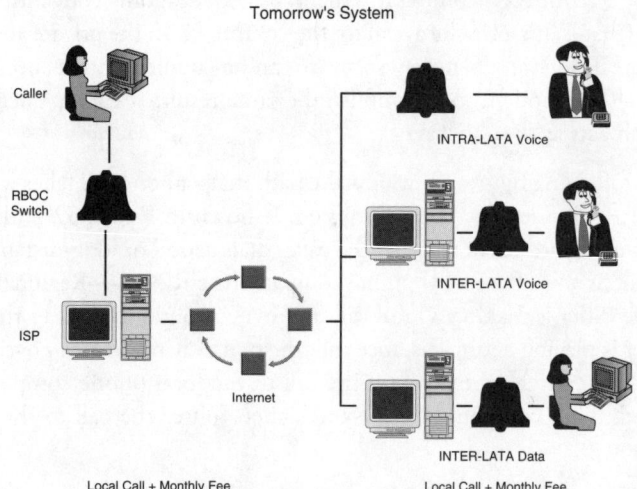

System Resource Usage

The amount of system bandwidth used by Internet telephony conversations varies directly and proportionally with the number of simultaneous conversations, and inversely with the amount of data compression used. Unfortunately, the tradeoff for additional compression is compromised audio quality.

Bandwidth consumption with Internet phones runs as little as 6720 bps per conversation, meaning that even 9600 baud modems can support Internet telephony. This level of consumption is efficient for standalone desktops using a dedicated telephone line, but for intranets that are local area network (LAN) based and wide area network (WAN) based, multiple conversations can quickly eat up bandwidth capacity. This problem is exacerbated by the fact that Internet telephony software is designed to run in the background to allow multitasking, meaning that the same user can transmit other data to the network at the same time.

For example, on a network with 100 users, 50 concurrent Internet phone conversations can eat up 350 Kbps or more of bandwidth, in addition to the current load on the network. Because many networks do not operate well with sustained loads over 30 to 50 percent of capacity, this level of consumption can be significant. Indeed, it equates to almost 25 percent of a WAN T1 connection.

Techniques are available for managing this increased traffic, however. One such technique is called buffering. In buffering, data is pretransmitted by a brief amount of time to allow the system to maintain transmission during peak periods by delivering data from the buffer rather than in real time while the network performs its normal tasks. Such a technique is usually acceptable for data transmission but is not acceptable for voice transmission, which is time-sensitive. A second technique for traffic management is called prioritization. This involves prioritizing the type of data packet that will be transmitted first. Like buffering, prioritization can interfere with time-sensitive voice communications.

Privacy

Most Internet phone software sends and receives audio directly between the users without going through a central server, although the server might track who is online. This means that Internet phone calls are very hard to trace or listen in on.

A Brief History and Barriers to Proliferation

The basic Internet telephone software has been around since the early 1990s, when VocalTec introduced a program called VocalChat. The initial version of VocalChat allowed LAN users to conduct real-time audio conferences over the network. VocalTec then introduced VocalChat WAN, providing the same service to larger organizations with decentralized offices. Then, in early 1995, VocalTec introduced its first Internet Phone package, which provided the same service at slower speeds, permitting connections over the Internet. Although the initial version of Internet Phone was more like a CB radio than a telephone, because it didn't permit simultaneous talking and listening, this feature was quickly added.

Since Internet Phone hit the market, other vendors have jumped on the bandwagon, adapting digital audio software to the task of real-time voice communication. Most recently, the big boys in the computer world have made it clear that they too will be getting involved. By March of 1996, in fact, IBM, Netscape, and CompuServe all announced that they would distribute Internet phone software to all of their users at no additional charge.

Although the precise number of Internet users (currently about 8 percent of Americans) and the future growth rate (as much as 100 percent per year) are widely debated in the industry, it is generally accepted that use is growing fast and continues to grow. The Telecommunications Act of 1996 helped spur this growth by getting big phone companies such as AT&T, Bell Atlantic, and Pacific Bell into the ISP business, as did the recent creation of the Microsoft Network. Further, all this new competition is bringing down the price of Internet access, which in turn leads to more users. Also, the growth in use leads to growth in advertising and content, which gives even more incentive for new users to sign up.

The increased number of users, as well as the advent of industry software standards that allow a user of one vendor's software to talk to a user of a different vendor's software, increases the likelihood that Internet phone software can be used to connect users who want to talk to each other. This makes the Internet phone a useful tool rather than a toy or an experiment. New applications such as Internet fax (using the Internet to send long-distance faxes), Web page voice links, and video-conferencing further increase the number of interested users.

Also leading to the popularity of Internet phone software is the improvement in sound quality since its initial introduction. Early Internet phone software had the sound quality of an AM radio, not a telephone. This was the result of three factors: slow modem speeds, no audio compression, and no provision for simultaneous transmission and reception, also known as talking and listening or "full-duplex audio." Today's software overcomes all three of these factors and is comparable in sound quality to cellular phones. Despite these gains, the sound quality of Internet phones remains inferior to that of conventional phones. Therefore, the major software companies are continuing to develop improvements to the technology to make Internet phones more competitive. "You have the best minds out there working on Internet calling. They will make it work," says U.S. West's chief strategist Catherine Hapka (*Business Week,* 4/22/96). Other areas for improvement include the replacement of microphones and speakers with telephone handsets, particularly the ones people already own.

Larry Darby, a former chief economist for the Federal Communications Commission (FCC), said in a 1996 report that he doesn't think that the Baby Bells will pay for expanding the Internet as traffic grows without finding a better way to be compensated. Indeed, he argues that data transfer rates are now the primary barrier to the growth of Internet use and will remain so until technology finds a solution. One potential solution GM Hughes is working on is a satellite-based Internet service.

Another potential solution is moving the Internet to the cable system, which has far greater bandwidth than the telephone system. Cable companies are quite aware of this advantage but are equally aware of its main disadvantage: cable systems were designed to send data in only one direction (to you), not two directions as is required for interactive data or voice communications. The hurdles to switching over to a cable system are technical, because two-way traffic flow on coaxial cable is susceptible to interference, and the amplifiers and routers required to permit two way pre-addressed traffic would cost billions of dollars to install. Nevertheless, cable companies know that they have the ability take both data and voice communication away from the telephone companies as soon as these problems are solved.

How Does an Internet Phone Work on an Intranet?

Several differences between intranets and the Internet are relevant to a discussion of Internet phones. These differences include the speeds at which they operate, the communication protocols both support, and the bandwidth available.

Speed Differences

Internet connections usually operate at modem speeds of 9.6, 14.4, or 28.8 Kbps. Intranets, by comparison, often operate at much higher speeds. They can involve LANs and WANs linked at speeds of 10 Mbps to 100 Mbps internally, and operating in real time over leased lines with remote offices. This speed range is fast enough to support Internet telephony, because uncompressed voice communication consumes only about 7 Kbps of bandwidth per conversation. Faster speeds, of course, are recommended for better performance.

Protocol Differences

The Internet supports two communication protocols, whereas most intranets support only one. These protocols are TCP/IP (Transmission Control Protocol/Internet Protocol) and UDP (User Datagram Protocol). TCP/IP uses relatively large "packets" of data, guarantees that each packet will arrive at its destination, and controls packet traffic. Because it guarantees delivery, TCP/IP resends lost data packets, resulting in transmission delays that interfere with time-sensitive voice communication. Nevertheless, for more common data transmission, TCP/IP is the most commonly used protocol.

UDP, in contrast, uses smaller data packets, doesn't guarantee delivery, and doesn't control its packet traffic. This "best efforts" delivery approach is better suited to Internet telephony applications than TCP/IP because it avoids the delay that results when a missed packet must be resent, while minimizing the loss by using smaller packets.

Unfortunately for intranet users, most firewall software, and therefore most intranets, do not support UDP. Hence, UDP-based Internet telephony software cannot be used on most intranets. Recently, however, CheckPoint Software Technologies, a leading firewall software provider, announced that it has added UDP support to its latest release. Thus, intranet use of Internet telephony is expected to grow as the new UDP support software proliferates.

Bandwidth Differences

As mentioned earlier, UDP lacks the traffic control mechanism that TCP incorporates. This means that UDP traffic can get out of hand if large amounts of data are being transmitted, absorbing excessive amounts of bandwidth. Whereas Internet bandwidth problems are the responsibility of phone companies and ISPs, intranet administrators must deal with such problems as they arise. Luckily, Internet telephony involves short bursts of data, and it should not overload a TCP/IP-controlled system, such as an intranet, unless used for a large number of simultaneous conversations.

Internet Phone Uses for Intranets

The uses of Internet phone software for intranets will include all the benefits of Internet phones available to general users, plus the added benefits that arise from the use of this technology in a commercial environment. This is because the commercial environment that supports an intranet has already recognized the need for greater internal communication by setting up the intranet in the first place. The addition of voice and real-time video capabilities will only increase the benefits that the intranet brings to the organization.

Long-Distance Savings

Currently, the main benefit to using an Internet phone is the avoidance of long-distance charges. Indeed, because long-distance charges are time- and distance-based, whereas Internet access charges are usually fixed per month, the marginal cost of an Internet call is negligible, versus the $.25 or more per daytime minute charged by long-distance companies. Therefore, the more intranet calls displace conventional long-distance calls, the greater the monetary savings to the organization. Because international calls traditionally carry the highest long-distance rates, especially when initiated from outside the United States, firms with international offices connected to their intranet stand to save the most by rerouting this traffic to the Internet or to the company intranet.

> **NOTE**
>
> The discrepancy in rates is due, in part, to subsidies and other fees included in the long-distance rate structure that do not really relate to the cost of service. These include local access fees, which pay the local phone company for handing off a long-distance call to long-distance providers, and universal service subsidies, which require customers who can be served at a low cost to help pay for service to customers who can be served only at higher costs. The FCC is in the process of reviewing these rate structures and subsidies in light of the increasing use of local ISPs to handle what are essentially long-distance communications.

Web-Page Voice Links

A second way to benefit from Internet phones is to link them to Web pages. To a visitor, the page would appear as it always does, but one (or more) of the hypertext links would include an Internet phone link to the page owner's designated agent. For example, a Christmas home page could have a link that would call Santa Claus. Further, because the Internet phone "packet" approach supports simultaneous voice and data, the Christmas Web page would continue to be displayed on-screen while you and Santa converse.

This application of Internet phone technology is expected to be particularly useful for online commerce. Indeed, a browsing customer could place a call for assistance, or to order, while sharing the same "catalog" page as the sales rep answering the phone. Or a bank customer could ask about his statement or loan application while he and the bank officer both look at it.

For intranet users, these external applications available through Internet links are but a small part of the fun. Internal help desk applications are another example of intranet phone applications, as are internal legal, finance, or engineering discussions. The possibilities are endless, limited only by what the company needs to accomplish. A whiteboard even can be substituted for the shared document or Web page, thus enabling inter-office brainstorming and internal education sessions.

Video-Phone Use on Intranets

A third application of Internet phone technology is in the area of real-time video transmission. In 1995, Cornell University developed the CU-SeeMe program, the first real-time video-conferencing link that ran on the Internet. (For more details on CU-SeeMe, read Chapter 33, "CU-SeeMe: The Next Wave.") This software requires slightly more computing power than an Internet phone does, as well as a small video camera that costs about a hundred bucks. Also, like Internet phone software, it requires a platform that supports UDP.

White Pine Software licensed the CU-SeeMe technology from Cornell and added some improvements. These improvements make the technology even better suited to intranets. Indeed, White Pine introduced a "traffic cop" to make sure that the bandwidth requirements of CU-SeeMe don't take over the network. (Some ISPs banned the original version of CU-SeeMe because it lacked such traffic controls and required large amounts of bandwidth.)

White Pine calls this traffic cop "reflector" technology. Reflector technology involves software that resides on network servers and provides the data addressing management function that is already incorporated into TCP/IP. Reflector software also minimizes the amount of bandwidth required for video "broadcasting"—transmitting video over a network for viewing by multiple users—by eliminating the need to send redundant packets of data to each viewer.

The applications of video-conferencing by intranet are numerous. The technology can be used to facilitate inter-office meetings, to reduce travel costs, to improve internal communication between workers, and to enhance employee education programs.

Server Issues

Any intranet operator is concerned not only that system users enjoy as many benefits as they can, but also that the system continues to operate smoothly so that one application or user doesn't degrade system performance to the detriment of other applications or users. The system operator utilizing Internet phone applications has two concerns: server bandwidth allocation and server software application.

As indicated previously, Internet phone or video-conferencing software does not present a bandwidth consumption problem unless multiple sessions are occurring simultaneously. If this becomes a problem, the cure can be either managerial or technical. The managerial solutions are to instruct users to reserve video-conferencing times or to designate times when Internet phone applications can be used. The technical solutions are to assign data priorities or to implement a data buffer.

Two types of server software may be needed to provide effective Internet phone services to intranet system users while maintaining bandwidth control. The first of these is the "operator" or IRC software. The IRC software acts as an address book that Internet phone callers use to find the network address of the party they want to call. If, however, the intranet is set up so that each terminal is always online or always has the same network address, this type of software is unnecessary. Instead, network users could keep a local file with a list of all addresses and simply enter the desired address into an IP-based Internet software package called DCT (Direct Connection Telephone).

The second type of software that might need to reside on the server is the "traffic control" software. This software ensures that numerous packets of phone data do not consume an excess amount of bandwidth. It does not require significant server space or resources.

Finally, the administrator must select firewall software. Firewall software connects the intranet to the Internet, but it has a security function that permits unauthorized users to access only designated files. Thus, an employee at home, for example, could call the company's Web site on the Internet and then enter a password to get the same degree of access she would have at her office terminal. A customer, in contrast, could have access only to public information, such as a product catalog. Because there are benefits to having an Internet gateway to an intranet, firewall software is common. Unfortunately, most firewall software today does not support UDP and thus is incompatible with Internet phone and video-conferencing software. One firewall maker, CheckPoint Software Technologies, however, has released a version that supports UDP. Other firewall vendors are sure to follow as Internet phone software gains wide acceptance in the marketplace.

Legal and Regulatory Issues

In response to the competition presented by Internet phones, some long-distance companies, primarily resellers (companies that buy large blocks of time from true long-distance providers and then resell that time to individual customers), have petitioned the FCC to make new rules subjecting Internet phone software companies to regulation as telephone companies.

The big three long-distance companies, AT&T, MCI and Sprint, have sat out this battle on the sidelines, yet the telecommunications giants actually see Internet phones as big future business. MCI's head of data architecture, Vint Cerf, says, "We are very interested in real-time services—telephony and video—over the Net" (*U.S. News & World Report,* 4/15/96).

Will the FCC regulate Internet phones? Several Washington lawyers don't think so. They believe that the Telecommunications Act of 1996 was designed to spur competition, not hinder it. They also believe that software providers are not subject to FCC jurisdiction because they don't own or operate any communication lines (*InfoWorld,* 3/18/96). Finally, the lawyers say that the FCC is reluctant to regulate Internet service based on the data content—that is, whether it is voice data or non-voice data—because this would open the door to a plethora of other issues, including privacy.

The FCC's unofficial response is that "[It] is not interested in refereeing between technologies" (*U.S. News & World Report,* 4/15/96). However, the FCC has taken actions which indicate that it will not regulate Internet phone software providers, but will instead change the universal service subsidy structure to require ISPs or local telephone companies to charge universal service fees for ISP access. The FCC also has indicated support for permitting free broadband (24 Mbps) wireless access over a broadcasting spectrum frequency range provided that use is for a limited range (distance), such as within factory complexes or college campuses. This shows that the FCC is in support of expanding, not restricting, low-cost information and multimedia access.

Client Tools

After the basic hardware requirements previously outlined have been met, each intranet client will want to lay hold of several tools. The first tool is the Internet phone software itself, and the first thing to know about choosing between vendors is whether the particular intranet is set up with permanent network addresses, thus permitting the use of DCT-based software, or whether a central operator will be required to keep track of each user's address while online, thus necessitating the use of IRC-based software. Table 32.1 lists the major phone vendors.

Table 32.1. The major Internet phone software vendors.

Company	Product	Type	Price and Availability
ITEL	WebPhone	DCT	Retail stores, about $50
VocalTec	Internet Phone	IRC	Retail software, about $50
Quarterdeck	WebTalk	IRC	Free trial download from http://www.qdeck.com
Freetel	Freetel	IRC	Free download online at http://www.freetel.com

In addition to these dedicated software packages, Internet phone software soon will be available from major vendors such as IBM and Netscape. IBM has announced that its product, IC Phone, will be incorporated into all new IBM personal computers starting in mid-1996. Netscape plans to incorporate Internet phone software into version 3.0 of its Netscape Navigator software, based in part on its acquisition of InSoft, an Internet video-phone company. Both IBM and Netscape are expected to make the basic program versions available for free download on the Internet. Additionally, CompuServe has announced that it will provide free copies of VocalTec's Internet Phone software to all of its members.

The second client tool to consider is video-conferencing software. The use of video-conferencing also requires a digital video camera, such as the Connectix. Both Connectix and White Pine offer video-conferencing software. A company called VDOLive also puts out a video product that is useful for intranet users, but it provides video broadcasting, not video-conferencing.

The third client tool is the appropriate firewall software. As of May 1996, the only major firewall software vendor that supports Internet telephony applications is CheckPoint Software Technologies.

The fourth client tool is bandwidth management software. This software will be dictated by the type of network being run, such as Ethernet, FDDI, or token ring. For systems running on Cisco equipment, the operating system can be programmed to manage the traffic. For other types of systems, White Pine's reflector software might do the trick.

Of course, if you're still wondering where the sound comes out of your old PC, there are a few tools you will need before all others: a sound card, speakers, and a microphone. Kingston Technology Corp. has announced a new sound card that will include a modular telephone jack that will permit Internet or intranet users to use a stand-alone modular telephone in place of a microphone and speakers. This will make Internet phone conversations feel more like conventional ones and will offer more user privacy than speakers.

Summary

Internet telephony and video-conferencing are great tools for businesses and consumers, whether run on intranets or over the Internet. Although low-cost long-distance telephone service might or might not happen, depending on how long-distance rates are set in the future, improved commerce, education, and worker productivity *are* certain.

Companies not yet familiar with the benefits of these applications should begin becoming familiar immediately or prepare to be outsold and outperformed by their competitors. As Internet usage greatly increases among the consuming public, companies that don't provide Web-based voice links will be seen as less customer friendly, with less customer information and with less time and fewer resources with which to make sales. Internally, companies that don't hop on the Internet phone bandwagon might find a lack of communication between geographically separate offices or divisions rather than an emerging national or international team of workers. Finally, increased business efficiencies, as well as the attendant cost and time savings of those efficiencies, will come easier and quicker to companies that master the multimedia applications of their computer networks.

Use caution when implementing and distributing Internet phone and video-conferencing software to a large number of employees. The novel level of interactivity permitted by this software might make it prone to abuse by employees (in terms of time), resulting in unnecessary bandwidth consumption. Therefore, we suggest seriously considering traffic management through both consultations with the software provider and internal usage regulations. With a few simple rules and precautions, the transition to real-time multimedia communication will prove a terrific investment.

CU-SeeMe: The Next Wave

33

by Nikki Goth and Paul Itoi

IN THIS CHAPTER

- What is real-time video-conferencing? **502**
- Real-world applications **503**
- Server issues **504**
- Bandwidth and video compression **505**
- Client hardware and software packages **507**
- First steps **508**
- Serving video-conferences on an intranet **509**
- Implications of video-conferencing over the Internet **509**

In the preceding chapters, you have seen how you can set up your corporate intranet to facilitate business communications using e-mail, chat, and Internet phones. By now, you might be wondering whether you need to take the leap to support video-conferencing applications as well. Video-conferencing, although certainly not an essential part of every intranet, can offer a practical means of providing cost-effective, in-person communications among employees and customers. To evaluate the pros and cons of video-conferencing over the Internet and intranet, you will want to consider bandwidth constraints, hardware and software requirements on the server and client sides, and the cost incurred for each desktop you want to equip with video-conferencing capabilities. The information provided in this chapter is intended to help you decide whether video-conferencing is a realistic, practical communications tool for your corporate intranet.

What Is Real-Time Video-Conferencing?

Once symbolic of the space age, communicating both voice and video in real time has become a realistic option for many clients. Whereas early "room based" models required participants to gather in a conference room equipped with cameras and look at monitors displaying similar rooms at remote sites, the desktop model works more like a telephone call, allowing participants to call up the other participants from their own PCs. Vendors, such as PictureTel and Intel, introduced desktop video-conferencing systems that use regular phone lines about five years ago; however, these proprietary systems can be extremely cost-prohibitive to set up and maintain. By comparison, the use of TCP/IP over Ethernet LANs provides a favorable environment for applications that require the simultaneous transmission of audio and video. The intranet environment offers more bandwidth than solutions that run over regular phone lines. Unlike with the Internet, the network operator of a corporate intranet can control the type of connection between desktops using video-conferencing applications, which makes performance levels more manageable and predictable.

This wave of Internet communications began to attract attention when Cornell University released the CU-SeeMe program as freeware for the Macintosh in 1993. The program allows users to conduct point-to-point communications, group conferencing, and broadcasting with audio and video over the Internet. Since its release, more than a half million individual users have downloaded CU-SeeMe for recreational and educational purposes. More recently, commercialized versions of CU-SeeMe, such as the enhanced version offered by a company called White Pine, are making it a viable means of business communication. Now, the corporate intranet provides a fertile territory for real-world business applications of video-conferencing over both local and wide area networks.

The basic parts of a video-conferencing system include video, audio, a whiteboard, a running application, and encoding software. Video requires a camera and video capture board; audio requires a microphone and speakers or headphones. Almost all commercial software offers a "whiteboard" function to display graphs, images, text, and documents, or to write on shared applications. Finally, software encodes and compresses the signal and then transmits the signal to remote sites.

The key limiting factor in video-conferencing is bandwidth consumption. Bandwidth is the amount of information per unit of time that a particular transmission medium can handle. Sending audio and video through any communications channel requires an enormous amount of bandwidth. To avoid a bottleneck, system administrators need to consider carefully the issues raised later in this chapter that relate to compression standards, server hardware and software requirements, and client packages.

Real-World Applications

Video-conferences facilitate cost-effective face-to-face contact among employees, clients, and other business contacts who might be scattered throughout the world, as shown in Figure 33.1. The early adopters of video-conferencing technologies that run over the Internet include professionals in the education and scientific communities, who in 1993 and 1994 began discovering the opportunity for conducting in-person communications via video-conferencing applications.

FIGURE 33.1.
A multicast video-conference.

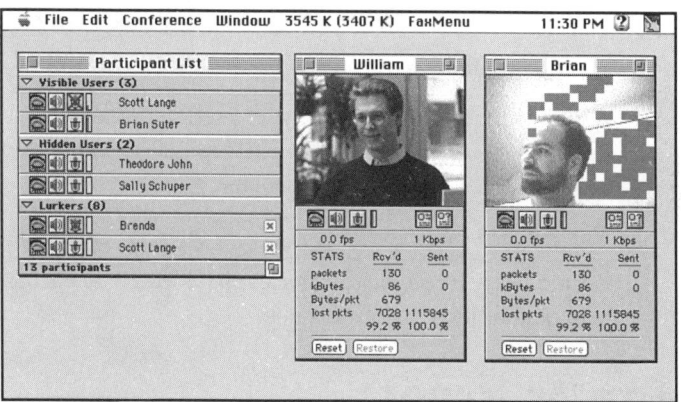

For the corporate intranet, the applications for video-conferencing include connecting distributed work teams, enabling learning or training from remote locations, and providing entertainment broadcasts. Currently, corporate usage of TCP/IP-based video-conferencing is progressing from testing among small groups and pilot projects into an established communication medium for select groups of users. Widespread adoption of desktop video-conferencing is an increasingly viable option as the latest browsers with integrated video and audio capabilities become available. Currently, Netscape is beta testing its Atlas browser, which includes full support of the LiveMedia framework, which integrates real-time audio and video into the browser itself.

Following are a few examples of how companies across different industries are using desktop video-conferencing to reduce travel costs, facilitate quick communication of time-sensitive information, and provide enhanced customer service.

Sales and Marketing

Ameritech uses a video-conferencing application to communicate between sales offices and headquarters. This lets the company save on travel costs and improve the distribution of competitive information between the field and headquarters.

Technical Customer Service

SAP AMERICA uses video-conferencing to offer customers real-time, in-person support without the expense of on-site customer visits.

Portfolio Management

Chase Manhattan Bank has improved consultations between portfolio managers and institutional accounts by providing video-conferencing capabilities.

College Recruiting

At the Georgia Tech Institute of Technology, video-conferencing lets employers screen candidates in real time without incurring travel expenses.

Medical Applications

A radiological services company is lowering the costs of patient consultations by using desktop video-conferencing. Medical specialists in remote locations have immediate access to X rays and surgery videotape.

Real Estate Applications

Loan officers at real estate agencies use video-conferencing to contact home buyers for loan qualification and processing.

Server Issues

Video-conferencing applications use the UDP (User Datagram Protocol) for sending streams of information, rather than packets of information. This protocol passes the responsibility of ensuring packet reliability to the application.

Therefore, the protocol is better able to manage the dynamic data feeds required for video-conferencing. The UDP Protocol also ensures that new information has precedence over confirming what was already sent; instead of checking to see that every packet has been received, the protocol places a higher priority on maintaining a steady flow of new information. This method of operation is important because lost packets of video will not interrupt the user's understanding of the information being transmitted in the way that lost packets of text or audio will. In the case of video, it is crucial to keep new information flowing and less important to allocate resources for error-checking applications.

Reflector Technology

The UDP Protocol made possible the development of a video server, called a reflector, that intelligently routes multiple streams of data during a conference. Reflectors act as intelligent broadcast stations for the participants in group video-conferences. They improve bandwidth capabilities by transmitting streams of managed video and audio broadcasting. By chaining reflectors together in a distributed network, companies can improve scalability and expand coverage by supporting different networking setups. The network operator is able both to adjust a video-conferencing setup as the number of users grows and to accommodate a network that uses several different platforms. Reflectors also can serve as effective agents for bandwidth-management, as discussed later.

Video-Conferencing Without Reflectors

To understand what a difference reflectors make in facilitating video-conferencing over the Internet, it is helpful to consider how group conferences operate without reflectors. Some products use the unicast method, whereby individual data streams are transmitted, and dedicated bandwidth is set aside for each participant in the conference. This method consumes excessive bandwidth because multiple copies of the video and audio data stream are transmitted to every attendee.

Alternative products use the Internet's MBONE (Internet Multicast Backbone) capabilities designed for multicast techniques. Multicasting involves sending information from one computer to a group of computers that are not necessarily on the same network. The earliest MBONE-based conferences began in the late 1980s, and by 1994, the system had grown to include more than 1,200 individual networks. Currently, more than 2,000 sites support MBONE, and the number continues to grow rapidly. Unfortunately, these products lack some essential broadcasting features—for example, they transmit data only when people are watching. Network administrators who need to minimize unnecessary bandwidth consumption will not want a video-conferencing application to transmit data when no one is watching. Additionally, these products require dedicated routers and software configured to take advantage of multicasting. Considerable effort is required to configure an MBONE router (mrouter), but after it is installed, relatively little daily maintenance is involved.

Bandwidth and Video Compression

For system administrators, the basic dilemma in adding manageable video-conferencing to an intranet is balancing the speed and quality of video and sound with taxing bandwidth requirements. Although it is extremely difficult to measure the bandwidth needed to transmit audio and video on the Internet, the amount is recognized as being high. To alleviate bandwidth constraints, network administrators can increase bandwidth or improve compression methods.

The higher bandwidth communications channels, such as ISDN (Integrated Switched Digital Network), Ethernet, Fast Ethernet, or ATM (Asynchronous Transfer Mode) are ideal for supporting video-conferencing. The most important consideration is selecting a circuit switch setup, which will accommodate the continuous stream of data necessary for video-conferencing applications.

The way in which specific compression algorithms are actually performed should be of little interest to the intranet architect. What is crucial, however, is understanding how well the compression performs, how well it inter-operates with products from other companies, and how well it handles operating on a heavily loaded network. Most products available today use the H.261 compression standard for video. When combined with a standard audio compression algorithm, the two components form the H.320 standard. These standards, originally established for video telephones, are capable of supporting two frame sizes, neither of which takes up an entire screen. QCIF is the standard frame size, with 176×144 pixels, and CIF is a larger frame size yielding 352×288 pixels. The number of pictures shown per second, called the frame rate, varies depending on CPU speed and bandwidth. For example, bandwidths of about 128 Kbps (video) and 64 Kbps (audio) could result in about five frames per second. This rate is adequate for video-conferencing, but not equivalent to a VCR-quality playback rate of 30 frames per bandwidth for audio. This might be desirable because audio is transmitted on the Internet in packets, which have to be synchronized with the stream of video. A delay, however, usually results in lost packets, which is more problematic than sacrificing some of the video quality to preserve the quality of the speech.

System administrators interested in supporting video-conferencing over the Internet without the compromise of excessive bandwidth have several tools at their disposal. As mentioned previously, reflectors also can serve as effective managers of bandwidth. The servers from White Pine are able to adjust transmission rates of individual users on-the-fly during times of heavy network traffic. Also, reflectors can manage data for supporting applications such as whiteboards or chat windows. System administrators can set minimum transmission rates that will adjust to different speeds of connections to the network. Thus, bandwidth can be optimized for ISDN, ATM, or modem lines. The bandwidth management capabilities of reflectors are essential to Internet Service Providers that have to balance the requirements of their non-video-conferencing network with the bandwidth consumed by their video-conferencing users during peak times of the day.

Finally, system administrators should turn some of the responsibility for bandwidth management over to individual users themselves. Courteous desktop video-conferencing etiquette alleviates bandwidth crises significantly. Users should not leave video windows transmitting empty offices or conference rooms open. Also, users should be reminded to conserve bandwidth by avoiding unnecessary transmissions.

CU-SeeMe: The Next Wave

Chapter 33

Client Hardware and Software Packages

Various packages of hardware and software for video-conferencing over the Internet are available from vendors including White Pine, Automated Management Systems, Connetix, Insoft (Netscape), and BBN Systems and Technologies. Table 33.1 summarizes many of these products.

Table 33.1. Video-conferencing products.

Product	Mac	PC	UNIX	Company	Phone	Web	Notes	Price
CU-SeeMe	Y	Y	N	White Pine	(603) 886-9050	www.cu-seeme.com		$69.95
CoolView*	N	Y	N	Netscape (Insoft)	(415) 327-2655	www.home.netscape.com or www.insoft.com		
Picture-Window	N	N	Y	BBN	(800) 422-2359	www.bbn.com		$495
CineVideo	N	Y	N	Cinecom	(703) 680-4733	www.cinecom.com		$39.95
FreeVue	N	Y	N	N/A	N/A	www.freevue.com		Free
Video-Phone	Y	Y	N	VIC Hi-Tech	(310) 643-5193	www.connectix.com	Not TCP/IP	$249

*Will be bundled with Netscape Navigator.

White Pine offers its enhanced CU-SeeMe software for Windows, Windows 95, Macintosh, and Power Macintosh. Users can have up to eight participant windows and an unlimited number for audio and talk windows. The caller ID feature is a message alert box for incoming connections. It provides a whiteboard for collaboration during conferences and supports multiple users. White Pine offers Mosaic browser support for direct launch of CU-SeeMe from its Web page. It also allows for selectable audio compression algorithms with 100 ms and 50 ms sampling settings: 2.4 Kbps and 8.5 Kbps audio codecs to support 14.4 Kbps and 28.8 Kbps modem connections; and 16 Kbps and 32 Kbps codecs for higher bandwidth connections. Additional features include support of 24-bit true color and 4-bit gray scale; a phone book for saving, adding, and editing participant addresses and reflector sites; standard and high-resolution settings for video compression; and password, caller ID, and other conference and inbound call security. Installation is relatively simple and user-friendly with TCP/IP network software.

Another vendor, Connectix, initially produced only computer-mounted cameras for the Mac and PCs; however, it now bundles video-conferencing software with the cameras. Insoft (now owned by Netscape) offers CoolTalk and CoolView software products designed for Windows 95. These products have been designed right into that Netscape browser so that users do not need to leave the browser to use the video-conferencing client. The disadvantage of using these products is that all participants in the call must have the company's software installed. At this time, Insoft has no plans to release similar products for the Mac.

BBN Systems and Technologies recently released PictureWindow, a software package that allows workstation users to hold video conferences over existing IP networks. The product uses Sun's VideoPix frame-capture board and a video camera to bring video-conferencing to a color or gray-scale SPARCstation. The software retails for about $495 per workstation; a PictureWindow package, including software, a frame grabber, and a color camera, is available for $1,495. For the first release, the company offers a receive-only version of the software at no cost. The software can be used in either point-to-point or multicast mode. The multicast option allows for an unlimited number of receive-only stations, which could be ideal for some training courses or company-wide presentations. The frame rate is generally about three to six frames per second, depending on the system and the network. The product functions best with network paths of at least 256 Kbps, but it can be used with bandwidths as low as 56 Kbps by accepting a lower frame rate and quality.

In addition to these vendors, some of the leaders in the market for desktop video-conferencing over regular phone lines, for example Intel and PictureTel, might offer products for the Internet soon. As these bigger players bring products to market, the prices for video-conferencing applications should come down significantly.

Additional factors to consider in selecting a client package include security demands for the video-conferences your employees will hold, reliability of product support, and the quality of broadcasting you will require.

First Steps

Do you need a video-conferencing component built into your intranet? Probably not; however, it could save considerable time and money to provide for video-conferencing while you are planning your intranet strategy. As the technology improves, you might decide that video-conferencing is an essential tool, and you won't want to change your entire hardware setup to support it. Fortunately, the latest generation of browsers and server software is bundling support of live media. Netscape Navigator already provides its LiveMedia structure to send audio and video from within the browser.

If you have decided to implement video-conferencing over your corporate intranet, you should consider these initial steps for setting it up. First, you should start with a very small test group. Try beginning with no more than 10 clients for the first pilot project. Second, refer to the table provided to get an idea of the products that work on PCs and Macs. Third, be sure that each pilot desktop has the following components:

Minimum System Requirements for Macintosh

System 7.x with 8 MB (16 MB recommended)
Connectix QuickCam or Video card with Video Camera
Microphone and speaker

Minimum System Requirements for Windows

486DX/66 8 MB RAM
Connectix QuickCam with serial port digitizer
Microphone and Speaker
Sound card with 8-bit sound (SoundBlaster 16 recommended)
8-bit video with 640-480 resolution

Install the client software on each system, and test the software configuration by using one of the public reflectors. When connecting to a public reflector, keep in mind that most reflectors do not allow connections at rates greater than 80 Kbps.

Serving Video-Conferences on an Intranet

After the clients are configured and tested, it's time to tackle the server side of the operation. CU-SeeMe's reflector software is written in C code and can be compiled and installed on various UNIX platforms, including, among others, Solaris, SGI, BSD, FreeBSD, and OSF-1. This software is also available for Windows NT and Windows 95. The reflector can be configured quickly in UNICAST mode, which allows for point-to-point conferencing. More time and experience, however, are required to set up the reflector in MULTICAST mode.

Implications of Video-Conferencing Over the Internet

Although the video phone has been around for many years, only recently has this method of communication been seriously entertained by system administrators for business communications. Proponents of video-conferencing over the Internet think that it could ultimately replace the telephone as the primary means of business communication; however, compression and bandwidth issues are still stumbling blocks for successful implementation of the technology in corporate intranets. Video-conferencing technologies are likely to improve along the same timeline as technologies for increasing bandwidth are developed and implemented.

Summary

Is video-conferencing a viable business communication tool that should be included in the corporate intranet? The answer depends on the specific goals and configuration of individual networks. Video-conferencing affords corporations the sophistication of in-person communications in a model that can be incorporated into a cost-effective intranet strategy; however, bandwidth concerns still create challenges for the system administrator.

As practical solutions to these issues are developed, video-conferencing over the Internet might ultimately become a de facto standard for business communications. In the meantime, most businesses will continue to rely on e-mail, chat, and even Internet phones to handle the bulk of communications traffic over their intranets.

IN THIS PART

- Intranet Tools **513**
- Creating Real-World Applications **535**
- Group Scheduling **549**
- Message Boards **561**
- Contact Databases **575**
- Alert Messaging and Real-Time Chat **587**
- News Feeds **599**
- Group Document Creation and Editing **619**
- Private Messaging Areas **633**
- Document Submission **649**
- Search Functions **659**
- Help Desk **673**
- Reference Desk **687**

PART VI

Developing Intranet Applications

Intranet Tools

34

by Frank Pappas

IN THIS CHAPTER

- Choosing your tools **514**
- Languages **521**
- Interface tools: Perl **529**
- Prewritten TCP/IP applications **530**
- Wayfarer QuickServer **532**

Now that you've examined some of the content and aesthetic concerns relating to intranet design, the next step is to become familiar with the various tools and resources that you and your staff will use to construct an intranet. Remember that although these tools offer powerful, enticing solutions to your design problems and challenges, you need to make careful and informed decisions when selecting the technologies that will support your intranet. Remember, the right tools and the right design plan will do wonders for your company, its productivity, and your reputation as an IS miracle worker. If you have a great intranet design but attempt to complete it with incorrect or inadequate intranet technology, you may soon be staring a pink slip straight in the face.

In this chapter, you will learn about some of the new technology that is available to make your intranet functional and efficient. You also will examine the steadfast technologies that have helped the Net emerge as the fastest growing and most powerful communications medium in history. After you finish this chapter, you should be familiar with many of the tools available to you as you build your intranet.

Choosing Your Tools

When you're evaluating your company's need for one or more of the many tools and resources available to you as intranet building blocks, you should realize that none of these languages, suites, or applications has been around very long on the intranet scene. In the development world, they're pretty much the new kids on the block, and although people may tout themselves as "Intranet Experts," "Java Gurus," or claim to have installed their first Web server on a Western Union telegraph wire, keep in mind that you're sailing in more or less uncharted waters. Webmasters, IS managers, and CIOs alike are all still learning the benefits and limitations of these new resources and are busily finding the most efficient and appropriate ways to integrate them into current and future intranet systems. Although you do need to put a good deal of thought into the design and development of your intranet, you also should feel free to explore new and creative applications for the emerging technologies and stretch the design limitations from time to time.

One thing that many people forget when they begin to develop an intranet architecture is that "intranet" does not equal "HTML." Although HTML is on many levels an integral part of a successful intranet, it is only one of a growing number of technologies that your development team will ultimately use. Nontechnical managers and end users may often ask why anything more than HTML (and the requisite HTTP server) is necessary for the successful implementation of a full-featured internal site; after all, they simply want to share information, and HTML does that just fine. You can explain that although HTML is indeed a useful tool for distributing text-based information, it isn't necessarily the answer for every information-distribution system. HTML, as a document-development language, is quite adept at simple markup and the presentation of reasonable amounts of static (unchanging) data. HTML, however, is limited in that it cannot (and was never intended to) provide any degree of interactivity whatsoever between the client and the server. The variety of tools that you will undoubtedly encounter during your research have been developed and have proliferated because of the widespread need to extend the basic capabilities of HTML to allow for data manipulation, advanced and dynamic generation of Web pages, and high-level interactivity.

You should address the following five central issues when selecting the tools and applications that you will include within the scope of your intranet:

- Portability: How well your intranet's technology will function across a range of hardware and software platforms (extremely important in a large, heterogeneous environment)
- Scalability: Your system's capacity to expand easily and incorporate large-scale installations
- Robustness: The stability of your software and hardware
- Ease-of-use: How easily both the designers and end users will be able to work with and understand the system
- Complexity: The extent to which your system is capable of handling a wide, ever-changing set of responsibilities or simply a few routine tasks

These factors are integral aspects that you must account for both in the definition of your intranet's functionality as well as in the selection of the tools with which you will build your intranet. By thinking these issues through beforehand, you'll end up saving yourself a lot of time, energy, and frustration. You'll also end up with a much better intranet for your organization.

In the next few sections, I cover some of the key resources you need to construct your intranet, including Server-Side Includes (SSI), the Common Gateway Interface (CGI), the Application Programming Interface (API), prevailing languages used for Web development, and some of the more popular third-party tools and applications used to build corporate and organizational intranets.

Server-Side Includes (SSI)

Using Server-Side Includes (SSI), one of the easiest methods for incorporating semi-dynamic HTML creation into your intranet, is an excellent way to introduce short-term or small-scale functionality into your system. Table 34.1 illustrates the ease with which you can add SSI. SSI is a great tool—especially if you're not a programmer—because it allows you to specify, via HTML-like tags, various points within a Web page that should be generated on-the-fly (such as date/time, the inclusion of standard header/footer files, or HTTP environment variables) when a specific page is requested by the client. It's also great for "quick fixes," intended to be remedied later by full-featured CGIs, because little development time is required to implement SSI. Open your HTML file, specify the type and location of the included information, and off you go.

Table 34.1. A closer look at Server-Side Includes, HTML, and the results.

	Low	Medium	High
Functionality	■		
Technical requirements	■		
Development cycle	■		
Danger	■		
CPU load			■

If you've ever written your own Web page or worked on a Web site, you should feel confident in using SSI after only a brief review of the steps involved. Because SSI is so simple, however, its functionality also is limited to basic, straightforward tasks, and utilizing it for anything other than the most routine, simple operations is usually beyond the scope of what SSI was intended to facilitate. This is mildly compensated by the fact that due to its inherent simplicity, you can easily update and modify your SSI tags to account for changes in your intranet's information delivery requirement.

A good example of SSI would be to include a standard header and footer file reference tag for each page of HTML on your site. If for any reason your header or footer needs to change, you have one point of contact to make a global change instead of changing every page of HTML individually.

Finally, you should note that because of the manner in which Web servers deal with SSI functionality, you experience moderate delays when serving SSI-enabled documents because the server must first read in the HTML file, find the locations within the document requiring SSI data, and then complete the client request by building the full HTML page and transmitting it back to the client. If your data-serving needs are conservative, using SSIs can be a great way to increase your intranet's value. If, however, you need to serve more than small amounts of data, you should seriously consider one of the options discussed in the following sections.

Application Programming Interface (API)

The Application Programming Interface, or API for short, is another of the primary ways to extend a Web site's (or, more specifically, a Web server's) functionality. Table 34.2 illustrates the benefits of using APIs. By loading extension code (offered by many companies such as O'Reilly, Netscape, Microsoft, and so on) onto a machine equipped with an HTTP server that has a defined API, you can extend that particular server's capacity to deal with information, requests, and so on, based entirely on what that particular API has been designed to accomplish. As powerful as standard CGI programs and much more so than SSI, APIs allow your design team to increase your intranet's capabilities significantly.

Table 34.2. A closer look at APIs.

	Low	Medium	High	Very High
Functionality			■	
Technical requirements			■	
Development cycle			■	
Danger				■
CPU load	■			

Because APIs run in the same process as the server and are preloaded at runtime, they are faster than the CGI. Here are some popular APIs and their corresponding HTTP servers:

NSAPI (Netscape API) from Netscape
`http://home.netscape.com/comprod/server_central/server_add_ons.html`

ISAPI (Internet Server API) from Microsoft
`http://www.microsoft.com/win32dev/apiext/isaphome.htm`

WSAPI (WebSite API) from O'Reilly and Associates
`http://software.ora.com/wspro/wsapi/html/`

It should be noted that APIs are not for everyone. Some HTTP servers don't support any API. Generally, APIs are very server-specific. There are no current standards, so don't expect to bring API code with you if you change server platforms. Microsoft implemented the Internet Server API (ISAPI), which they hope will become the industry standard.

The benefits gained from using APIs, however, do not come without a significant cost, in this case an increased risk of having your server die as a result of inappropriate or poorly designed API code. Additionally, the level of technical know-how required to implement an API is well beyond the realm of most system administrators and most likely outside the skills held by many in-house programmers. Therefore, you probably will need to contract with an outside company or programmer to develop, test, and integrate a specific API that will address your needs and concerns.

As with CGI technology, APIs are implemented using standard programming languages such as C or C++ and as such offer a significant level of server-extension capabilities that should not be ignored. Due to the complexity involved in using APIs, however, and the fact that your intranet may be dependent on a high-priced, external source for its API development and troubleshooting, you'll want to consider carefully how strongly you want to embrace this option.

Plug-Ins

If your company currently uses (or plans to use) Netscape Communication's browser as a client for your information services, you'll be more than pleased to learn about *plug-ins*, a new family of software products that will enable your users to accomplish any number of tasks more easily than you ever imagined. Microsoft's Internet Explorer plans to support the Netscape Navigator Plug-In format. From playing any number of different audio formats to viewing hundreds of different formats of word processing documents, plug-ins provide for an ever-increasing array of possibilities. By virtue of how they work, a plug-in could be written to handle any file type the user could ever dream of. The HTTP server handles requests for files, and files have types. Plug-ins are just extension code that handles new or nonstandard file types.

Using Netscape Navigator as the foundation, the plug-in is installed on the client machine and resides in a directory that the browser knows to look in for plug-ins. Functioning whenever it is called upon (based on requests for a file type it has been written to handle—called MIME in Internet lingo), the plug-in software processes a given set of information and then presents it to the user in-line. This resource is fabulous whether you're considering the in-house creation of specialty software to enhance your intranet or would prefer to purchase prebuilt systems that are ready to go. A great example of this functionality is the Real Audio plug-in (http://www.realaudio.com). Netscape Navigator can't handle a Real Audio MIME type (.RAM) straight out of the box, so the user must install the Real Audio plug-in. Then, when the user requests a Real Audio clip (http://www.realaudio.com/products/server/hpeval/overview.ram), the Real Audio plug-in says, "Hey—I can handle that!" and takes over.

Additionally, as these plug-ins are built by a variety of companies all competing for market share, you will see no end (assuming no huge shifts in browser preference) for the short- to mid-term of publicly available and affordable third-party solutions for your intranet needs. For a list of plug-ins that you can use to extend the capabilities of the Netscape Navigator browser, visit

http://home.netscape.com/comprod/products/navigator/version_2.0/plugins/index.html

The Common Gateway Interface (CGI)

The Common Gateway Interface is a standard for connecting client-based forms with HTTP servers and other tools on the server side. Table 34.3 illustrates the benefits of using CGIs. Unlike standard HTML documents, which are static (unchanging) in nature and content, a CGI-compliant application is executed in real time, allowing for the dynamic generation of complete HTML files, the manipulation of data within a database, or any number of other complex tasks.

Table 34.3. A closer look at CGIs.

	Low	Medium	High
Functionality			■
Technical requirements			■
Development cycle		■	
Danger			■
CPU load			■

One of the most beneficial uses of the CGI, for example, is to create dynamic, or "on-the-fly," Web pages in response to user queries. The CGI receives the query from the client and passes it to the database engine or other specific application, which then completes the requested action. After the request has been processed, the CGI receives the answer from the server-side application and transmits the resulting data back to the client for display. This is a prime example of a CGI database-gateway.

Although CGI seems like a straightforward concept, implementing CGIs on anything more than a basic scale is often extremely difficult, due to the fact that databases, Web servers, and back-end programs often have complex and divergent needs that must be thoroughly addressed. CGIs are also difficult to debug. Additionally, enabling a CGI program on your system is equivalent to allowing a total stranger to run an application on your hardware without your supervision, which has some rather serious security ramifications if your CGIs are sloppy or are designed by inexperienced programmers not familiar with possible security issues. When and if you decide that CGIs are essential to your intranet, keep in mind the following points to create winning CGIs:

- ■ Remember that all CGIs must reside in special CGI directories.
- ■ Be sure to limit access to these directories so that only authorized personnel can write and enable CGIs. (This way, a hacker or inexperienced programmer cannot severely injure your site.)
- ■ Craft your code with speed in mind. If users have to wait, they'll often just leave, never to return.
- ■ Test, test, test. Make absolutely certain that your programs do what they are supposed to do—no more, no less.

Your team can build CGIs for your intranet in a number of different ways. You can select from among C/C++, Perl, UNIX Shells, Visual Basic, FORTRAN, TCL, REXX, and others, which gives you a good deal of flexibility in your design strategy and allows you to benefit from your employees' skills in the particular languages. Keep in mind, however, that each of these tools is different from the next in complexity as well as function, so be sure to evaluate them in the context of your specific project. You would be wise to invest some time researching the specifics of the environments prior to embracing a particular language, especially considering that the platform-language combination that you choose will have an enormous impact on the quality of your intranet. (For more background on programming, see Chapter 22, "Creating a Functional Site.")

Before finalizing your system's development needs, you have to make many choices. To help you get a handle on some of them, review the following sections in relation to what you anticipate as your system's central requirements.

Text Manipulation

In recent years, if your site depended heavily on text searches and large-scale text manipulation, UNIX would have been your first (and probably only) choice. As Windows NT has expanded into a widely-embraced and versatile server platform, however, the power, speed, and graphical interface sported by Windows NT seem to have reduced the UNIX lead, except in the most demanding of environments.

Nontextual Data Handling

Another area in which the Windows platform excels is in dealing with word processing, spreadsheet, and database manipulation. Because of the built-in capacity for Windows applications to share data by virtue of OLE and DDE, writing CGI scripts for this platform provides for a comprehensive and extremely versatile information-processing system.

Database Interaction

Here's a short list of preferred tools for database connectivity—in no particular order:

    C++
    C
    PL/SQL
    Perl
    Visual Basic
    Java

Although a number of competing database systems run under UNIX or Windows, UNIX is the preeminent choice when you're using an extremely high-end data system such as Oracle, Sybase, or Informix because many different gateways have already been created to facilitate their connection to your system. If your data-handling needs are less than legendary, however, you'll probably find the Windows options to your liking, as you can utilize tools like Visual Basic to write interfaces to ODBC-compliant data sources—for example, Microsoft Access, SQL Server, and so on.

The Relative Power of Popular Database Options

High

Oracle
Sybase

Medium

Microsoft SQL Server
Microsoft Access
Paradox

Low

Flat file

Languages

When designing customized software for your intranet, you can utilize a number of different languages. As with any aspect of information systems design, you need to have a thorough grasp of the features each product offers as well as the relative benefits and drawbacks of implementing a particular language. In the following sections, I cover the more popular languages that are prevalent on current intranets. I also cover a few emerging technologies that will soon offer your intranet some exciting options for new and improved data-serving roles.

Content Tools

Some of the easiest and relatively simple languages to work with for intranet design (aside from HTML), content tools work as enhancements to the base functionality inherent to HTML. Generally, you use them to provide error checking for data input through forms (masks), to change various features of the browser, or to perform other easily definable tasks for which the higher-level languages are ill-suited. Working hand-in-hand with the technology underlying HTML and HTTP, content tools are essentially useless without these complementary technologies because the instructions that are created with these content tools reside within the HTML of a particular page and depend on the HTTP server to transmit them to the client.

JavaScript

JavaScript, a compact, object-based scripting language, is one of the latest and increasingly popular ways to create "smarter" HTML pages for your intranet as well as the Internet. Currently, various browser and operating system platforms support different degrees of JavaScript functionality. So, if you decide that JavaScript is the answer to your needs, be sure to find out whether your client workstations are equipped to process your JavaScript code. In general, you'll find that newer versions of Netscape Navigator (and forthcoming browsers from America Online, Microsoft, and Spry) will be ready to take on the task of enabling JavaScript on your intranet.

As a content tool, JavaScript is an excellent choice to make "dumb" Web pages into data-processing geniuses. Well, maybe not geniuses, but by combining JavaScript with standard HTML forms, you can do a good deal of preprocessing to save time, bandwidth, and frustration when your intranet goes online. Because JavaScript statements are included directly (embedded) within an HTML document and are interpreted directly from a browser (requiring no compiler or other traditional programming tools), JavaScript is fairly simple to implement and maintain. It is readable to humans, can be changed almost instantly by an administrator, and requires no supporting software other than the client's browser. One of the most valuable features of JavaScript is its ability to "sense" a user's actions (such as mouse clicks, form input [masks], or page navigation) on the client side and respond to them via a predetermined script.

You can develop a JavaScript function, for example, to verify that users have entered appropriate information within a form field, such as a telephone, Social Security number, or zip code. Without any outbound transmission from the client once the Web page has been loaded into memory, the embedded JavaScript can evaluate the user-provided text and alert the user through an alert dialog box if the input is invalid or otherwise unacceptable for processing. This capability is extremely important if you are considering a database-to-intranet connectivity plan, as you'll want to reduce processing overhead on the server as much as possible and keep bandwidth usage to a minimum so that priority traffic can get through.

You also can use JavaScript to perform certain actions (such as play an audio file, execute an applet, or communicate with a plug-in) in response to a user's actions. Depending on your intranet's needs, or perhaps to enable additional resources for the hearing or visually impaired, JavaScript's sensing capabilities may prove useful.

Resembling Java in many ways, JavaScript lacks Java's static typing and strong type checking, which can be an important consideration if your system needs to perform complex mathematical calculations. JavaScript supports most of Java's expression syntax and basic flow constructs, so if you've got some in-house talent in Java, using JavaScript shouldn't be much of a stretch for you. In contrast to the compile-time system of classes built by declarations that is employed by both Java and C++, however, JavaScript has implemented a runtime system based on a small number of data types representing numeric, Boolean, and string values, which ease development burdens significantly but decrease flexibility. JavaScript also provides a relatively straightforward instance-based object model that still provides significant capabilities despite the fact that it is quite limited in comparison to Java.

As a descendant of smaller, dynamically typed languages, such as HyperTalk and dBASE, JavaScript is accessible to a wider audience than its big-brother counterpart (Java) because of its easier syntax, specialized built-in functionality, and minimal requirements for object creation. Although not a replacement for Java as a Web development tool, JavaScript serves a complementary role by allowing script authors to include limited amounts of Java functionality, including changing the properties and performance of applets, plug-ins, or even certain aspects of the browser itself, including shape, color, and orientation. Table 34.4 outlines some of the more technical differences between Java and JavaScript. These differences are commonly questioned on Internet newsgroups.

Table 34.4. Important differences between JavaScript and Java.

JavaScript	*Java*
Interpreted by client (browser, plug-in, and so on)	Compiled on server before client execution
Code integrated and embedded in HTML	Code is distinct but accessed through HTML
Object-based code that uses built-in, extensible objects but no classes or inheritance	Object-oriented; applets consist of classes with inheritance
Loose typing	Strong typing
Dynamic binding; object references checked at runtime	Static binding; object references must exist at compile time
No access to HD	No access to HD, although the browser can run native applications

You can embed JavaScript in HTML in one of two ways, and depending on how you plan to utilize JavaScript, you should examine both possibilities. Your first option is to include JavaScript statements and functions within your HTML using the <SCRIPT> tag, using the following format:

```
<SCRIPT LANGUAGE="JavaScript">
Your Wonderful JavaScript Code Functions
</SCRIPT>
```

Call the functions from within the HTML based on browser actions such as clicking on a link and so on.

> **TIP**
>
> JavaScript code is case-sensitive, so be sure to keep that fact in mind when writing your code.

One of the nice things about JavaScript is that because it is embedded within the HTML document, you can examine it by viewing the document source. Most browsers support the ability to view the underlying HTML. I recommend that you view the source of the JavaScript examples offered by Netscape at

```
http://home.netscape.com/comprod/products/navigator/version_2.0/script/script
➥info/index.html
```

This choice is ideal if you plan to develop extensive systems with a great deal of JavaScript. If, however, you are interested in more direct and targeted uses of JavaScript, your second option is to embed the JavaScript within your HTML not as <SCRIPT>-separated commands, but rather as event handlers using HTML tags. Recall that JavaScript applications are almost wholly event-driven—they respond to the actions of the person using the client browser. When you're working with a browser such as Netscape Navigator, it is prepared to recognize a series of predefined events and deal with them in various ways. An excellent example of an event is when a user clicks a button or perhaps points at a particular link on a Web page. Because the browser can recognize when each event occurs, your JavaScript application can use the browser as its virtual "eyes" and therefore respond to the event instantaneously. It accomplishes this through the use of event handlers, which are essentially scripts that are automatically executed when an event is initiated. If you're familiar with C, you should be well on your way to understanding JavaScript's event handlers, because much of JavaScript's form is modeled on C. Event handlers take the form

```
<TAG eventHandler="command1;command2;command3">
```

where *TAG* is an HTML tag and *eventHandler* is the name of a particular event handler.

> **TIP**
>
> Currently, you cannot print output created by JavaScript, so be sure to include a standard text-based option if you anticipate that your users will require hard copies.

If you're even basically familiar with any type of functional programming, you should have little problem picking up the fundamentals of JavaScript. Novice programmers (or dedicated users), however, shouldn't necessarily shy away from JavaScript either, as a small investment in time and effort can yield surprising results.

VBScript

A new and promising technology, the Microsoft Visual Basic Scripting Edition (VBScript) is actually a subset of the traditional MS Visual Basic language that has simplified the development of Windows-based applications in recent years. Although VBScript just recently made its appearance on the intranet development scene and has yet to become widely available, the benefits to be gained from the use of VBScript are many and are sure to cause a good deal of industry confusion and turmoil as developers decide whether to embrace VBScript or its Sun Microsystems counterpart, JavaScript. Microsoft has gone to great lengths to develop and make available an enticing alternative to JavaScript, and in the coming months the battles between Microsoft and the Sun/Netscape alliance should prove entertaining, and will hopefully result in even better products for developers as the companies vie for market dominance.

As a mainstream and powerful development language, Visual Basic had to undergo a number of nip-and-tuck procedures before making its debut as an Internet development tool. The most important of these changes is the revamping and restriction of the more security-sensitive commands and functions (those most likely to allow a hacker to injure your system), which means that although VBScript still offers powerful functionality, you can feel safe in knowing that your system will not be highly susceptible to the whims of hackers. Remember, though, no system is hacker-proof, so be sure to consider other options for securing your intranet as well, especially if you are hosting proprietary or otherwise confidential corporate data.

VBScript, the Internet-targeted flavor of Visual Basic, has been designed to provide a fully functional suite of enhancements to intranet designers, ranging from scripting and automation to the complete customization of various properties of Web browsers (initially to be incorporated into Internet Explorer 3.0).

Like JavaScript, VBScript is an interpreted language that is read into memory when the Web page containing it is transferred to the client browser. Its code is embedded directly into the HTML file. VBScript lets developers write VB code to be included directly in the file and work in conjunction with ActiveX. VBScript is included in the following manner:

```
<SCRIPT LANGUAGE="VBS">
Sub BtnAlert_OnClick
MsgBox "I no need hall pass!!!"
End Sub
</SCRIPT>
```

When the browser reads the initial `<SCRIPT>` tag, it calls upon the VBScript language engine to perform a runtime compile of the VBScript code and then makes that particular piece of compiled code available to the system (assuming the client browser is VBScript-enabled; check with your system administrator or check the original documentation that came with your system).

One of the most impressive features of the forthcoming VBScript is the arrival of OLE automation to intranet design. With this capability, VBScript will be able to manipulate both the browser and other client-side applications based on predetermined events, user input, or any of a host of other variables. Additionally, VBScript will have the capacity to set both properties and methods on ActiveX controls (.OCXs) and Java applets, which will extend the overall functionality of your intranet even further.

Although VBScript is far from being an industry standard (or even a released product), it will most likely be a powerful tool that will have a tremendous impact on the intranet design process. Microsoft is (as usual) muscling its way into the Internet game, playing catch-up with Sun and Netscape. In this instance, Microsoft is offering free licensing of the VBScript source code to developers. Although there are certain drawbacks to embracing a nonstandard technology that is still in its infancy—including compatibility with existing and evolving systems, cross-platform security and portability, and so on—as Microsoft refines VBScript in response to user needs and industry trends, it will find a definitive niche in which to flourish. To examine more information on VBScript, visit Microsoft's home page at `http://www.microsoft.com/intdev/vbs/`.

The following table compares Visual Basic, Visual Basic for Applications, and VBScript:

Visual Basic

Ideal for large-scale distributed client/server systems.

Extremely powerful, robust, and readily scalable.

Visual Basic for Applications (VBA)

A specialized subset of Visual Basic for Office applications.

Geared toward high-end users.

Great for integration with existing systems.

VBScript

Optimized for Internet and intranet applications.

Small command set.

Extremely fast.

Low overhead.

VRML

At the first World Wide Web Conference held in Geneva, Switzerland, in the spring of 1994, Tim Berners-Lee and Dave Raggett spearheaded a focus group to discuss the future and direction of three-dimensional modeling using the Internet as a transmission medium. During these discussions, the term "Virtual Reality Modeling Language" was adopted and the technical development of VRML began shortly thereafter. Existing as a subset of the Silicon Graphics, Inc., Open Inventor ASCII File Format, which provides an excellent environment for the specification of polygons and three-dimensional landscapes, VRML has become one of the major tools for delivering interactive, three-dimensional online content, despite the fact that it is somewhat difficult to work with. Version 1.0 of the language had three simple goals that have served to speed its acceptance into the development cycle: first, as with HTML and other Net technologies, it is platform-independent; second, it is extensible; and third, it is optimized for transmission over low-bandwidth connections, which is important if you plan to transfer VRML data to more than a few workstations on your intranet.

As VRML evolves and incorporates support for high-end graphics, simple and rapid integration and interaction with data sources, and is able to optimize both its speed and memory requirements, VRML (or an equivalent tool) will become the *de facto* standard for presenting graphical information online. Although the technology is not quite at a level acceptable for widespread integration with functional corporate intranets, the concept of three-dimensional presentations of large data sets is one that has circulated in the academic, scientific, technical, and business worlds for many years, as humans are able to comprehend complex data sets more easily when rendered graphically. Because the technology was (until mid-1995) nonexistent, however, the concept remained just that. Now that "interactivity" is the buzz word and key feature when dealing with most online systems—and because the majority of client hardware and software now can support such tasks—many third-party utilities, applications, and design suites have been released to facilitate the development and utilization of VRML-based worlds for log analysis, database access, or any similar tasks.

If you want to consider the benefits that VRML can bring to your intranet project, visit http://www.sdsc.edu/SDSC/Partners/vrml/examples.html. You can read up on the technical specifications, catch up on VRML development, and see some interesting demonstrations that may help you in the design process.

Java

Of the many application languages used to build systems for the Internet or intranet, Java is perhaps the most revolutionary. An object-oriented (OO) development environment, Java enables you to create fully-functional applications that are served either across the Web via an HTTP server or locally on your client machines, which gives you added flexibility in deciding how and when people will have access to intranet resources.

The early years of Web development found a marked lack of tools to facilitate the development of interactive, multimedia-based systems. Responding to this need for high-end functionality, developers at Sun Microsystems assembled the Java language, an object-oriented, platform-independent environment that allows you to build robust, secure, high-performance intranet applications and systems. Java allows you to develop two distinct types of software. The first, referred to as an *applet*, is served over the Web and is distributed through the client browser. The second type of software that Java supports is stand-alone applications. Either way, the usefulness of your intranet will increase tremendously with the incorporation of Java technology.

Originally conceived as the backbone of so-called "smart" appliances and interactive TV, one of the most remarkable features of Java is its platform-independent nature, which is the key to its acceptance as an Internet/intranet standard. This means that the programs applets that you develop for your intranet using the Java language will function on any platform that has its own version of a Java interpreter (generally built in to your browser, plug-in, or third-party application). Today, Java interpreters are available for all major platforms and operating systems, so if you poke around on the Net, you'll be certain to find one quickly.

Another important feature of Java is its robust nature. Essentially, in the search for a technology that would be able to work on many platforms using many operating systems, Sun took special care to ensure that the environment was sufficiently stable so that it would avoid disastrous effects—such as crashes or lost data—when Java applets were downloaded and executed on client machines. If you want your Java tools to handle secure or sensitive information, you can be somewhat reassured by the fact that your development environment can accommodate you.

Additionally, Sun Microsystems decided hands-down to include a number of important benefits within the new environment to position Java as the unchallenged middle- to high-end development tool for your intranet. First, unlike Perl, shell scripts, or JavaScript, Java is a full-featured, object-oriented language that allows for the inheritance and reuse of code both dynamically and in a more traditional static fashion. Further, as a high-performance tool, Java supports features such as multithreading and native code usage. This capability is especially useful now that many businesses are preparing roll-outs of Windows 95 and Windows NT machines as their in-house client workstations. Finally, to ease the burden of C or C++ development, Java assumes more responsibility for the final disposition of the code itself, taking on the task of memory management and pointers, traditionally the unenvied work of programmers.

The following is an example of Java source code:

```
//(Copyright Notice: This source code is (c) Copyright 1995-96, EarthWeb LLC.)
package eweb.awt;
import java.awt.*;
public class Thingy extends Canvas
{int mx, my;
public Thingy()
{mx = my = 50;}
public void paint(Graphics g)
{for (int i=0;
i<size().width-1; i+=8)
{g.drawLine( mx, my, i, 0 );
{g.drawLine( mx, my, i, size().width-1 );
{for (int i=0; i<size().height-1; i+=8)
{g.drawLine( mx, my, 0, i );}
g.drawLine( mx, my, size().width-1, i );}
g.drawRect(0, 0, size().width-1, size().height-1);}
public void Action( int x, int y )
{mx = x; my = y;
repaint();}
public boolean mouseDown(java.awt.Event evt, int x, int y)
{Action( x, y );
return true;}
public boolean mouseDrag(java.awt.Event evt, int x, int y)
{Action( x, y );
return true;}}
```

You can license, purchase, or simply take a host of existing applications into account when you're using Java as a platform for your intranet. To get some interesting ideas about how to include Java applets within your site, visit

```
http://www.gamelan.com
```

For a good overview of the Java language and some great examples, visit

http://www.sun.com/sunsoft/Products/Developer-products/java/Workshop/index.html

Interface Tools: Perl

Unlike content tools, which offer front-end extensions to the capabilities of HTML, interface tools take on the extremely technical and demanding job of facilitating back-end tasks, such as the transmission of data from an HTML form or the execution of an application on the server side of the connection to perform specific functions, including the processing of a request for information or storing a user's address. I already covered CGI in an earlier section, but another important interface tool that you should be aware of is Perl, the Practical Extraction and Reporting Language.

Perl is a widely available, extremely useful, and fairly simple language to learn and incorporate into your intranet. It is also free, which, by the way, has never been known to hurt the appeal of a great product. An ideal choice for low- to mid-complexity projects, Perl combines many of the most desirable features that are found both in the UNIX shells and the higher-level languages such as C++.

Unlike shell scripts, Perl exists as a runtime-compiled language, which means that it exists as human-readable coding until the program is executed. It then is compiled into code that the computer can understand and performs its function. Although this is a definite performance killer, if used wisely and sparingly, Perl can increase the functionality of your site without significant drawbacks.

The most popular Perl library for writing CGIs is cgi-lib.pl by Steven Brenner. You can find it at http://www.bio.cam.ac.uk/cgi-lib/.

The following is an example of a simple Perl program:

```perl
$CRLF = "\n";
$method=$ENV{"REQUEST_METHOD"};
print "Content-type: text/plain",$CRLF,$CRLF;
print "CGI/1.2 report:",$CRLF;
print "                ^^^^^^^^^^", $CRLF;
if($#ARGV eq '-1')
{
print "No command args";
} else
{
print "ARGC=",($#ARGV+1),", ARGV: ";
for (@ARGV) { print; print " "; };
}
print $CRLF,$CRLF;
print "Environment variables:",$CRLF;
print "REQUEST_METHOD:   ",$method,$CRLF;
print "SCRIPT_NAME:      ",$ENV{"SCRIPT_NAME"},$CRLF;
print "QUERY_STRING:     ",$ENV{"QUERY_STRING"},$CRLF;
print "PATH_INFO:        ",$ENV{"PATH_INFO"},$CRLF;
```

```
print "PATH_TRANSLATED:  ",$ENV{"PATH_TRANSLATED"},$CRLF;
if($method eq "POST")
{
$cfile= $ENV{"CONTENT_FILE"};
print "CONTENT_TYPE:     ",$ENV{"CONTENT_TYPE"},$CRLF;
print "CONTENT_FILE:     ",$cfile,$CRLF;
print "CONTENT_LENGTH:   ",$ENV{"CONTENT_LENGTH"},$CRLF;
print "---- begin content ----",$CRLF;
print while <STDIN>;
print $CRLF,"---- end content ----",$CRLF;
}
print $CRLF,"end of report",$CRLF;
```

Originally developed for UNIX-based systems, Perl has been ported to work on a variety of popular operating systems, including DOS, OS/2, Macintosh, and Windows NT, so virtually any server you have installed should take advantage of some form of Perl when and if you decide to embrace it.

Prewritten TCP/IP Applications

If you decide that designing all your own applications from the bottom up is not the best avenue for your intranet, you should consider evaluating some of the many intranet-enhancing tools that you can purchase and integrate into the rest of your system, and utilize your computer's TCP/IP stack rather than your browser package. Software companies have spent a great deal of time creating well-planned, useful, and affordable solutions to many of your needs, including real-time collaboration (audio, graphics, and text), messaging, file sharing, and data processing. But before you delve into what could be many weeks of research, here are some pointers that will make your job quite a bit easier.

PCN, shown in Figure 34.1, is a TCP/IP-based client that allows users to obtain and access news and information that is broadcast from a PointCast Server. Their PointCast-I Server, which retails for less than $1,000 per server CPU, resides on a company's internal network and can facilitate the transmission of corporate stock data, human resources reports, production updates—virtually any text or graphical information that you choose to deliver. One of the greatest benefits of PCN is that you don't need to familiarize yourself with a new and confusing language because the text-based portion of the system relies on HTML for its format and even provides a number of built-in forms to facilitate the creation of online content. Unlike standard HTTP servers that are not optimized for the large-scale transmission of information, however, PCN has been designed especially to reduce traffic across the network, and you'll enjoy fantastic benefits if your company has Internet firewalls included in your network. Currently only available for the Windows NT platform (supporting up to 500 clients with a 75MHz 32MB NT server), PointCast plans on expanding their coverage to include other popular systems, including UNIX and Macintosh. For more information on PCN, visit http://www.pointcast.com.

Intranet Tools
Chapter 34

FIGURE 34.1.
The PCN interface.

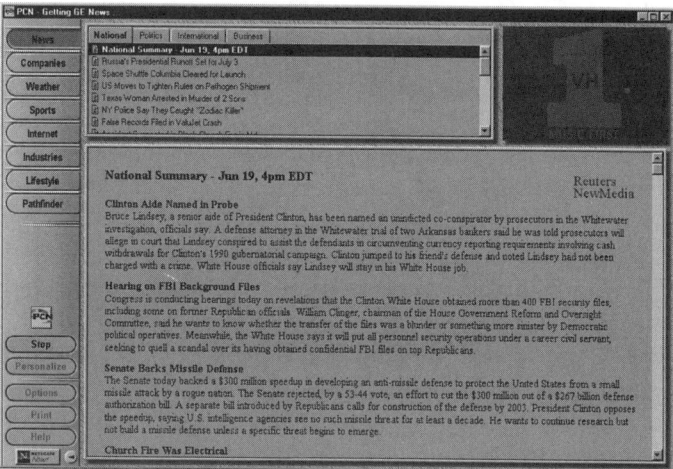

Marketed as a "real-time audio and data collaboration tool specifically designed for the Internet," CoolTalk, shown in Figure 34.2, allows your employees to work together and become more productive—without having to pick up the telephone or visit a remote company site. CoolTalk provides full-duplex audio-conferencing capabilities, which means that, like a telephone, both participants can speak and be heard simultaneously—a fantastic improvement over the earlier, half-duplex applications that have made their rounds on the Net. What's more, CoolTalk functions as a virtual answering machine for TCP/IP-based audio messages, allowing your employees to recall messages received during meetings, lunch breaks, or even the night before. Functioning over a 14.4 or 28.8Kbps connection, CoolTalk also supports a chat tool for text-based conferences, a whiteboard collaboration tool that allows users to draw images and transmit them to their associates, and many other features to improve your organization's communications. For more information on CoolTalk, visit http://www.netscape.com.

FIGURE 34.2.
CoolTalk.

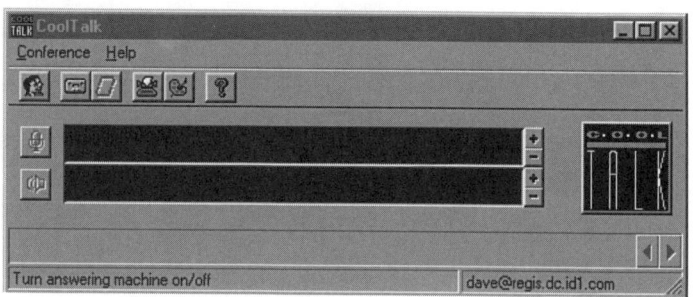

Wayfarer QuickServer

If you decide that your intranet will require more than the basic data sharing that is easily accomplished with HTTP services but would instead like to make available full-featured applications to client machines across the Net with real-time data delivery, you should take a serious look at QuickServer from Wayfarer. The QuickServer product from Wayfarer brings true client/server real-time computing to the World Wide Web. As a development tool that provides important primitives for developing the client and server sides of any application, QuickServer manages connections, access control, and encryption while providing a reliable low-bandwidth connection across the Internet or your intranet. The product allows programmers to handle only basic issues when developing networked applications and allows information to be sent in a form called a *Wayfarer Value Object*, which can be customized by the developer. QuickServer supports clients written in Java, C++, and Visual Basic. Wayfarer promises more cross-platform and language support in the near future. You can embed any application developed in Java and Visual Basic in the Netscape browser as a Java applet or plug-in, respectively, and the user can operate the client as part of an HTML document. Figure 34.3 shows one example.

FIGURE 34.3.

StockWatcher was developed in Visual Basic and is being displayed in the Netscape browser as a plug-in. This application utilizes Wayfarer's client/server development technologies.

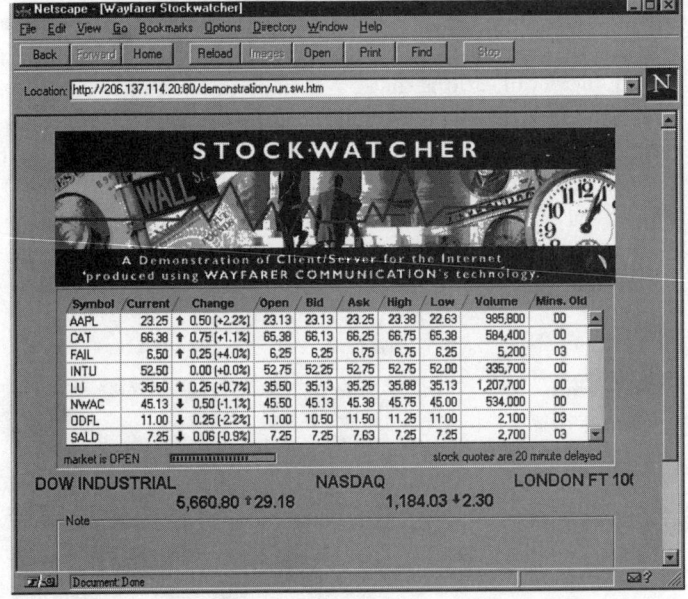

The performance of the server is excellent, and the optimized communication between the client and server is very efficient. A modest Windows NT server can support 1,500 simultaneous connections. This product will grow in popularity and will likely become the basis for many internal corporate and mass market products. For more information about Wayfarer technology, visit `http://www.wayfarer.com/`. Be sure to check out `http://www.wayfarer.com/demonstration/index.htm` for an excellent demonstration of the system's power.

Although I've described only a few of the many TCP/IP-based third-party applications that you can utilize when constructing your intranet, this chapter should give you not only a good understanding of the currently available offerings, but also should give you a good base with which to begin construction of full-featured, company-ready intranets to enable your organization to reach new levels of productivity and profit.

Summary

In this chapter, you looked at a number of different tools and technologies that will enable you—if used properly—to build an effective, powerful, and well-received intranet for your company or organization. From the server-enabling options of Server-Side Includes (SSI), Application Programming Interface (API), and the Common Gateway Interface (CGI) to the many languages that facilitate intranet-based software development, the environment in which both Internet and intranet systems evolve has never seemed brighter. Far from the sterile, text-based world that online, Internet-based, and in-house systems used to exemplify, these high-tech features will allow you to build "smarter" and more appealing systems that will help your company to maximize the potential of today's intranet applications.

Remember, as important as it is to have a fantastic intranet architecture on paper, without the right tools and support, the system is doomed to fail. Be sure to consider thoughtfully the needs of your users (and designers) prior to the construction of your intranet, and then select from the many and varied options that are emerging nonstop in the development world. With some careful planning, a lot of hard work, and a little bit of luck, your intranet will be an incredible resource that your colleagues will embrace as the backbone of modern office communication.

Creating Real-World Applications

35

by David Garrett

IN THIS CHAPTER

- The need for needs assessment 536
- Involving users: why, when, and how 540
- A user survey example 543

The key to effective intranet usage is practical application. Intranet value is a function of utility, not of bells and whistles. To capture the value of the intranet, an organization must focus on specific needs, conduct in-depth research, and consider organizational values and requirements just as it would before making any other significant change or addition—such as moving its corporate headquarters, changing its internal structure, or completely revamping its mission and vision.

An organization wants to build an intranet that reflects its real world and that can be assimilated into its real world as an effective tool. This medium offers a range of opportunity for effecting positive change, because it encourages new ways of interacting within the organization. It can rid barriers, expedite communication, and link users who are geographically removed. The challenge of the intranet is to strike a balance: to work within the real world without foreclosing opportunities for innovation.

Creating real-world applications begins with defining the real world—in this case, the organization that is considering building an intranet. A clear understanding of the organization's strengths, weaknesses, goals, and resources, and of the context in which it does business, provides an essential foundation. Such an understanding keeps the intranet development process focused and grounded and helps ensure that the result properly reflects the sponsor's character and requirements—in other words, that the intranet does what it is intended to do.

This chapter discusses the process of defining organizational requirements and preferences as they relate to a range of intranet capabilities, which are discussed in further detail in Chapters 36 through 46.

The Need for Needs Assessment

Like any other significant initiative, constructing an intranet requires front-end analysis and planning and extensive involvement of the user. Too often, organizations fall in love with a technological capability without giving adequate thought to how it furthers a business objective, what its impact is likely to be, and how to manage the implementation process. As a result, such organizations might end up with a system that doesn't meet their needs or one that doesn't maximize the benefits of intranet capabilities. In the process, organizations also can waste time and money.

Therefore, discipline in the preliminary stages pays off in efficiency and user satisfaction. This involves assessing the needs and setting the goals that the intranet will be designed to address and achieve. At the most basic level, an organization should define:

- Where—and what—it is today
- Where—and what—it wants to be
- How an intranet can help it get there

A lot of these macro decisions must be made at a high level of the organization by people who understand and recognize the potential of the strategic impact. The manager of information systems probably doesn't have a good overall grasp of the company and therefore is probably not the person with the authority to make these macro, long-term decisions.

An intranet needs assessment should encompass three levels of inquiry:

- Broad organizational priorities
- Specific internal communications needs
- Technical capacity and requirements

Organizational Priorities

Defining priorities often involves an organization's strategic planning process. For organizations that do not have a formal strategic planning function, intranet design can provide a focal point for this activity and, in fact, can be used to jump-start it. This process alone is a very helpful one because it begins to bring people in with the focus—the medium is the message. Getting employees' input and getting employees involved in understanding users' needs lays the groundwork for effective usage.

Because some organization offices and staffers do not talk to each other daily, the intranet provides a focal point for getting those discussions started. As the site is launched, it offers an opportunity to maintain this newly established communication.

The organization's priorities are the management specifications for which you are designing the intranet. You want an intranet that achieves the goals of the employees who will be utilizing it. Broad priorities include competitive, cultural, or philosophical issues that affect the entire company and that are often expressed as goals. For example:

- "We need to become more customer-oriented."
- "We need to instill safety-consciousness at every level of our company."
- "We need to encourage and reward innovation."
- "We need to attract and retain name-brand R&D talent."
- "We need to flatten and simplify our organization."
- "We need to get our products out faster."
- "We need to manage growth."
- "We need to get a better handle on our financial goals."
- "We need to share a common vision."

After priorities have been defined, the next step is to identify barriers to the goals and possible solutions to the barriers. Obviously, achieving complex goals requires multifaceted efforts, and an intranet isn't the silver bullet. Each of these examples, however, suggests a potential shift in how business gets conducted and in how people interact—and internal communications has a role to play. Defining that role takes the intranet needs assessment to the next level.

Internal Communications

Virtually every analysis of barriers to organizational goals yields some discussion of information exchange. The underlying problem might be timeliness, content, or access, and the issue might be mechanical, structural, or philosophical. Some organizations (for example, within the defense industry) have traditionally operated strictly on a "need to know" basis and are only now beginning to expand their internal communications channels. In other organizations, such as high-tech companies enjoying rapid growth, the challenge is very different; last year's hallway meetings are no longer adequate now that there are five regional offices in three time zones.

On the principle that knowledge is indeed power, organizations that seek to empower their employees (or members) do so in part by disseminating information and providing meaningful channels for response and feedback. For these kinds of organizations, a highly interactive intranet can provide an ideal forum.

Take the example of a trade association. The association is responsible for collecting information, processing it, and disseminating it to their members. By creating a dynamic site that allows users not only to view information, but also to update it and add new content, the value of the intranet increases for the members, and the cost savings increase for the association. Let's say that one of the functions of the association is to collect news items and share them with the members. By allowing users to add news items in an interactive way, the intranet becomes a useful real-time tool and is expanded through the efforts of employees who add their own information.

Another example is an intranet for a sales force. It might be essential that inventory information be completely up-to-date all the time. In this situation, both the company and the individual salespeople can keep inventory updated if the salespeople can input their sales information as soon as they have it.

On the other hand, companies that, for whatever reason, stringently control information flow will likely design a very different sort of intranet, intended primarily to display the results of a deliberation (for example, a corporate policy) rather than to elicit participation in it.

The internal communications dimension should be addressed as part of a needs assessment process, and the organization should define specific gaps and rank them by priority. For example:

- "Our sales force doesn't get new product specs on time."
- "Our divisional R&D people should be talking to each other."
- "The finance department needs monthly budget and head-count reports."
- "Our regional managers should get together more often."

- "We have to speed up our orientation program for new employees."
- "The grapevine is a lot faster than Corporate Communications."
- "Our environmental people need to stay on top of state regulations."
- "Our facility managers need guidance from the law department."
- "We really should get more input from the field on these new procedures."

Although no intranet can effectively address every item on a wish list, compiling such a list provides a clear sense of the high-priority gaps that system design must address.

Technical Requirements

No intranet can be designed in a technological vacuum. The third level of needs assessment therefore evaluates the technical underpinnings that already exist in terms of their adaptability to intranet applications. Undertaking such an evaluation early in the process helps avoid costly mistakes and helps suggest solutions that leverage existing investments in technology.

While establishing broad priorities, the organization also must establish what the technical realities currently are and how the intranet can fit in with them. For example, if the goal is to bring people together from different geographic offices for video-conferencing and the headquarters has excellent technological capabilities but the field locations don't, the intranet won't fulfill the goal unless the organization is willing to upgrade the technology in the field offices.

Don't aim for the lowest common denominator in the technical requirements; aim for an average one. If it's a matter of upgrading only 2 of 40 offices to meet the technical requirements for an application, the upgrade is worth investing in.

If video-conferencing is a priority but some users work from their homes and have only 14.4 Kbps modems, those users need to be upgraded to faster, direct connections, such as ISDN, frame-relay, or cable—or the organization should reevaluate its needs and the importance of video-conferencing.

This again comes back to organizational priorities. Is the intranet supposed to enhance what people do in their individual functions or bring people together?

If you're trying to automate things for the marketing team, it's OK to supply the technical capability for only this team. But if the intranet priority is focused on R&D and the marketing members work closely with R&D on trends, the R&D team needs the same technical capacity as the marketing team.

A thorough review of current resident technology provides the basis for means testing for various intranet capabilities before they are incorporated into the intranet's design, as shown in Figure 35.1. For example, if most people in an organization don't have video cards or if they work on 10-year-old 386 PCs, it makes no sense to design an elaborate video-conferencing function.

FIGURE 35.1.
Matching workstation capabilities with intranet applications.

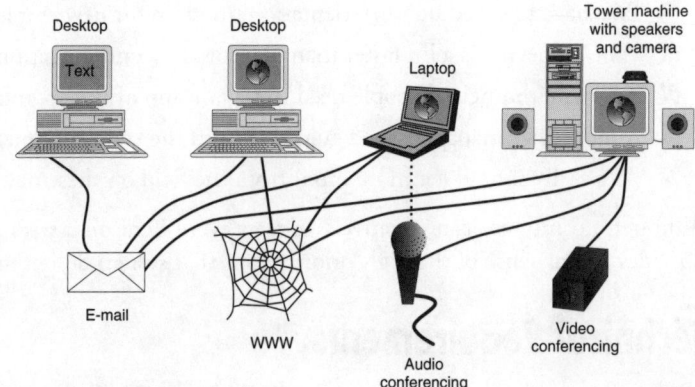

A needs assessment is the discipline applied to understanding the context from which an intranet can add value. It requires compiling and analyzing available information on organizational needs, technical capacity, and intended usage.

Involving Users: Why, When, and How

Intranets, at their most powerful, are user-driven. For this reason, experience shows that involving potential users early in the development process produces better results. The intranet is intended to be used by people inside the organization, so employees must be involved in the front-end design and the decision process; otherwise, they will not use it. Just as product-related research and development increasingly engages customer participation, so should intranet developers engage prospective "customers" for their "product" from the beginning.

After the priorities are established, you need to decide who your intranet will affect. This is the user universe, the people who are going to use your intranet. The group might comprise every employee, every member of a trade association, the heads of trade groups, upper management, or any other segment that makes sense for your organization. These people should be involved in the decision process with the priorities in mind.

Here, the difference between the Internet and the intranet becomes important. The Internet can be an anonymous corporate presence that's established without involving many users. But the intranet belongs to the organization and the user universe. Those in the user universe have to feel ownership and must feel that the intranet is accomplishing their needs; otherwise, the intranet won't function optimally. An intranet has individual ownership. It is private; it is "our" office. Within that office can be many different conference rooms, some labeled by profession, some labeled by task, others labeled by other distinguishing common agendas. Depending on how the intranet is organized, users within an organization can have individual identities, making the presence of user "buy-in" vital.

Assume that Kristi is a scientist at the High Times Coffee Company. She has her user name and she has her own password. At High Times, a goal in establishing the intranet is for top executives and the public relations team to be aware of the latest developments in bean roasting. As Kristi works on the intranet, she leaves footprints. Those who have access can stay up-to-date on the very latest developments. The top executives benefit from being "in the know," as they should be, despite the demands of their positions, and the public relations team is armed with the latest news—good, bad, or otherwise.

User Input

The sponsoring organization should involve the user universe by soliciting user input during the needs assessment phase. Doing so achieves two goals: supplementing, validating, or challenging project management's understanding of what is needed, and initiating the process of gaining the user buy-in that will be critical to successful implementation. Because a goal of the intranet is to effect change inside an organization, the user must be involved.

User research can take many forms. Two of the most common and useful are surveys and focus groups. Depending on the size of the user universe, surveys can be conducted in person, by telephone, through electronic mail, or on the Web—or in some combination of these methods.

User surveys, like the needs assessment framework discussed previously, should be structured to elicit three levels of information: general needs, specific requirements, and technical capacity. Surveys also should define the user group's familiarity and competence with computer technology, which must be factored into any questions of system design.

To reach a broad group of potential user universe, a paper survey might be the best form. If you want to see who is capable of using the survey, it is better to carry it out on the Web or through e-mail.

At the end of this chapter is an example of a user survey designed to be administered in person, including multiple-choice, yes/no, and open-ended questions.

Also consider focus groups, because these take user research to a deeper level and probe for underlying opinions and attitudes. Properly facilitated and with appropriate participants, an internal focus group on intranets can do double duty as a brainstorming session that can yield extremely useful insights and ideas.

User Participation

Before launching a new intranet or adding significant new functions to an existing one, many organizations select a small group of users to participate in beta testing. This method can be highly effective and can greatly improve the intranet's functionality while helping to generate users' enthusiasm and sense of investment.

User input at the beta level is important because it offers a reality check to the intranet. Beta is the second letter in the Greek alphabet, and beta testing is, in essence, the second test. After the programmers and designers think that they have a functioning prototype (the first test), they open an application, program, or system to a limited group of pilot users—or beta testers—to see how well the prototype really works. The beta test is interactive; it tests both technical capacity and user interface, which are equally important at the beta level.

The beta testing should be conducted when the intranet is still open to changes and modifications. Feedback and analysis from users will result in another series of improvements and enhancements in the features and functions—the interface—of the intranet. This beta testing allows the organization to find out what the intranet is currently doing compared to the organizational expectations for its design. It tests whether the intranet had the desired effect. It exposes needs that weren't anticipated at the beginning, because users will change the way they do things with a new system or technology, and additional, unplanned-for needs are sure to surface.

At this point, the organization will want to note what changes to make to ensure that the intranet is in line with expectations and user suggestions. Adjustments are made accordingly before the software in question goes into production use.

Beta testing might reveal interesting, and often not-thought-of, results. For example, a business might want to provide an intranet to achieve better communication between accounts payable and vendors. After beta testing, the business might discover that instead of using the intranet to improve factual exchange of information and follow-up, users were using the intranet only as a cyber water cooler to swap jokes.

In another case, one priority of the intranet might be to bring 20 news and information sources together in a manageable format so that information is easily retrievable in an organized manner. The beta group might easily access the 20 sources with the intranet but might find there are 20 more news sources they want the finished intranet to include.

Beta testing is best conducted as a hands-on interactive group session, with no more than 15 user-participants. Part training, part focus group, these sessions should be led by an intranet project manager, with adequate programming support to enable on-the-spot modifications.

The specific selection of beta testers varies, depending on the individual organization and the priorities established for the intranet. It is generally useful, however, to choose pilot users who fulfill these requirements:

- Represent a cross-section of the user universe
- Have a relatively high level of technical competency
- Actively support the overall project

If a priority of the intranet is to flatten the hierarchical nature of the organization, the beta group should have members from every level represented. In general, the techno-experts should not be included in the beta group.

Aiming for a cross-section of users is primarily to ensure a "functional" cross-section (that is, ensuring that people from different parts of the organization, at differing levels of seniority, and so on are included in the user group). The "relatively high level of technical competency" issue means you want to be sure they know enough and have the right equipment to actually participate in the beta test. Of course, if 95 percent of the people in your organization have never logged on to the Internet before, the whole beta group should be skewed downward in terms of technical competency. On the other hand, if everyone is a UNIX wizard except for the one mailroom clerk, the technical competency level among the beta group should be skewed upward.

A User Survey Example

If you are interested in participating as a pilot user in the development of the intranet, please complete the following survey:

CONTACT INFORMATION

Name:

Title:

Organization:

Mailing Address:

City:

State:

Country:

Postal Code:

Telephone:

Fax:

AREAS OF ORGANIZATIONAL RESPONSIBILITY

1. Circle the choice that best describes your areas of responsibility in your organization:

   Scientific/Technical/Engineering

   Marketing/Sales

   Legal/Regulatory

   MIS

   Corporate/Managerial

   Accounting/Financial

   Communications/Public Affairs

   Operations/Production

   Other

2. Circle the choice that best describes your primary work location:

   Production/Manufacturing facility

   Research & Development facility

   Corporate headquarters

   Association headquarters

   Other facility work patterns

3. Circle the choice that best describes the frequency with which you personally use a personal computer:

   Frequently throughout the day

   At least once a day

   Almost every day

   Weekly

   Occasionally

   Rarely

4. Circle the choice that best describes the frequency with which one or more support staff members who report directly to you use a personal computer:

   Frequently throughout the day

   At least once a day

   Almost every day

   Weekly

   Occasionally

   Rarely

5. Circle the choice that best describes the frequency with which your work requires you to travel:

    Almost every day

    Weekly

    Monthly

    Quarterly

    Rarely

6. Circle the choice that best describes the frequency with which your work requires you to meet with, telephone, fax, or otherwise contact individuals who work at other locations within your organization:

    Frequently throughout the day

    At least once every day

    Almost every day

    Weekly

    Occasionally

    Rarely

7. Circle the choice that best describes the frequency with which your work requires you to meet with, telephone, fax, or otherwise contact individuals who work within your industry, but outside of your own organization:

    Frequently throughout the day

    At least once every day

    Almost every day

    Weekly

    Occasionally

    Rarely

8. Are you comfortable working in English?

    Yes

    No

9. Next to each of the potential features of the intranet listed below, indicate the degree to which you would find each of them useful in the course of your work (1 = Very useful, 2 = Somewhat useful, 3 = Not at all useful):

    Access to a database of scientific and technical information relevant to our industry:

         1   2   3

    Access to a database of news and public affairs information relevant to our industry:

         1   2   3

Access to a database of financial information relevant to our industry:

    1   2   3

The ability to navigate quickly and easily to other, nonproprietary Internet-based information relevant to our industry:

    1   2   3

The ability to exchange e-mail with colleagues in like member organizations:

    1   2   3

The ability to exchange formatted documents with colleagues in other like member organizations:

    1   2   3

The ability to post and read public messages regarding developments in our industry:

    1   2   3

The ability to collaborate with colleagues in similar member organizations online, in real time:

    1   2   3

A central scheduling calendar of relevant industry meetings and events:

    1   2   3

Other:

    1   2   3

COMPUTER RESOURCES

10. Do you have routine access to a personal computer?

    Yes

    No

11. The personal computer you most frequently use is:

    A PC

    A Macintosh

    Other _____

12. The personal computer you use most frequently has:

    A single-user modem

    Dial-out capability through LAN, WAN, or some other network

    No dial-out capability

13. If you use a laptop or another portable computer, is it:

    A PC

    A Macintosh

    Other

    Don't use a portable

14. If you use a laptop or another portable computer, does it have:

    A single-user modem

    No dial-out capability

15. If you have one or more e-mail accounts, please provide them:

    Primary e-mail address:

    Secondary e-mail address:

16. Circle each of the following services to which you have access:

    America OnLine

    Prodigy

    CompuServe

    Internet

    SLIP/PPP

    Other

SYSTEM REQUIREMENTS

If you use a personal computer with a high-speed modem, color graphics, at least 8 megabytes of RAM, and a 486 or better processor (PC) or System 7.1 or higher (Macintosh), you will be able to participate in the pilot user group without making any significant enhancements or upgrades to your system.

If you use a personal computer that doesn't have the features listed above, you will need to make enhancements and upgrades that cost between approximately $250 and $1,000 U.S. dollars.

If you do not have access to a personal computer, you will need to purchase and configure equipment that costs between approximately $2,000 and $3,500 U.S. dollars.

17. Based on this information, circle the appropriate choice below:

    The personal computer I use meets system requirements, and no significant upgrades or enhancements are required.

    I am willing and able, either personally or through my organization, to procure the system I need. I will get technical assistance through my organization.

    I am willing and able, either personally or through my organization, to procure the system I need, but I request technical assistance from the intranet development team.

Thank you for completing this survey.

Summary

By now you should be convinced that the most important person to consider when creating real-world applications is the user. The organization that from the onset includes the user in the decision-making process and testing ultimately will get the most from its intranet. Don't leave out the all-important and often-revealing needs assessment. The results will put you in step with the organization's priorities, internal communications network, and technical capacity, leaving you with the most appropriate blueprint for your intranet. When the time arrives to make application decisions for your intranet, fully explore three key questions—What does the intranet as a medium offer? What does my organization need? and What is the mix between the medium and the organization's needs?—and your intranet will begin to build itself.

The next 11 chapters further examine the specific core functions offered with intranets.

Group Scheduling

36

by Anne Marie Yerks

IN THIS CHAPTER

- Scheduling for intranets **551**
- Online scheduling applied **553**
- Scheduling applications **555**

In a more orderly world, everyone in your company would eat lunch at the same time—not only at the same time, but in the same place. If this were the case, the jobs of the scheduling secretaries would be much easier, because then they could communicate with everyone all at once. Meetings and projects could be organized, vacation days established, conferences planned, sales calls set. After lunch, the secretaries could write up a company schedule and send it out before the work day ended.

However, we do not live in an orderly world—not everyone eats lunch at the same time. In fact, very little that is done in a company happens concurrently. Each member of a sales team has individual calls to make. Each department has different conferences to attend. Meetings sometimes happen spontaneously. Sometimes a prearranged schedule is abandoned altogether, and sometimes a schedule is lost.

If you've ever joined coworkers for an out-of-town conference, participated in a bus day trip, or taken your kids to Disney World, you know how difficult coordinating a group schedule can be. No matter what the occasion, everyone seems to have a private agenda—an agenda that can't be compromised. Working around personal agendas to achieve a time for a group meeting can be next to impossible.

Many tools and techniques are used to keep track of everyone in the office. Wall-sized calendars are one favorite. This technique requires employees with strong biceps, as much erasing and rewriting is required. Another tool is the In/Out magnet board. With this implement, each employee is signified by a circular (sometimes rectangular) magnet. The idea is that each employee moves the magnet to "in" when arriving at work and moves it to "out" when leaving. The success of the In/Out board is questionable. Most often, the magnets wind up on the refrigerator in the lounge.

The most popular way to manage group scheduling is to require all employees to tell the secretary where they are going every time they leave the office. Additionally, employees must plan their work schedules ahead of time so that secretaries know when they are going to be out of town, at a conference, or even in another part of the office building. This technique leads to a sure bottleneck. Even a team of secretaries can't keep up with the comings and goings of employees at a good-sized company, especially when the employees themselves often forget to pass out their schedules.

To get a grasp on group scheduling, many companies have put their group schedules onto a computer system. With LANs, the first group scheduling programs have taken hold. These scheduling applications are more successful than the In/Out board for a variety of reasons. First, they give employees the means to enter their schedules whenever doing so is convenient. In this sense, a scheduling application is something like an old-fashioned date book. Meetings and events can be entered when the scheduler is first learning about them.

The second way in which scheduling applications are useful is that they provide a clean interface for arranging appointments. Instead of the employees scratching dates on paper and having to erase them later, the computer can do all the work and keep the calendar looking nice.

With a group scheduling program, employees also can view the schedule of a coworker or workers (this capability can be very helpful if your boss is known to take off to Europe at the last minute). In short, a scheduling application can provide what was previously impossible: a schedule for a group of people that can be viewed in one piece and that isn't pasted on the wall in the reception room. Instead, this schedule is available from the computer desktop of whoever needs it.

A third way in which scheduling applications are handy is that they usually can integrate with other computer applications, such as e-mail. In these applications, e-mail messages can be sent out automatically as reminders or updates. Having a scheduling application integrated into a personal or company contact list is also helpful; this way, appointments can be linked to addresses and phone numbers. Some LAN scheduling applications take integration to the extreme, providing complicated features like the ability to send a fax from a calendar or automatic phone dialing.

All these features are nice, but no software application can add hours to the day. Likewise, no software application can convince people to compromise their personal agendas. What a group scheduling application can do is make life easier for everyone by offering an organized and efficient way to coordinate and view a multiple-person schedule.

More than likely, your company already has some sort of scheduling application installed on the computer network. This application might be part of a groupware package, such as Novell's Groupwise, or it might be stand-alone software, such as On Incorporated's Meeting Maker. Or maybe your company has not yet developed an electronic scheduling system. (Is the In/Out board working for you?) However your group scheduling is being done, you can undoubtedly find room for improvement.

In this chapter, you look into the future of group scheduling. The Web brings new possibilities to the well-developed LAN scheduling applications. These possibilities are the focus here, as online scheduling is an online application that has not yet been widely used. Because the potential benefits of online scheduling are tremendous (I describe those benefits later in this chapter), you can anticipate that online scheduling will eventually be a common intranet application.

Scheduling for Intranets

The topic of online scheduling brings to mind the old proverb that in order to take one step forward, you sometimes have to take two steps back. Such is the case with online scheduling and with the Web in general. Many of the features in the LAN scheduling applications simply have not yet been made available for intranets. This does not mean that you'll have to paste yet another wall-sized calendar above the reception room sofa. In fact, online scheduling can offer more in the way of convenience than the most sophisticated LAN scheduling application.

The advantage that online scheduling applications have over their LAN ancestors is that they allow you to view your schedule inside a Web browser. If you need to check out your meeting list late Sunday night, you therefore can do it from your home computer and modem. LAN scheduling applications are beginning to offer plug-ins that will give you some means of using the application though an intranet. Novell's Groupwise, shown in Figure 36.1, has recently developed tools for integrating Groupwise functions into a Web browser.

FIGURE 36.1.
You can register for a Novell Groupwise WebAccess trial at http://www.novell.com/groupwise *to see how Groupwise scheduling can be integrated into a Web browser.*

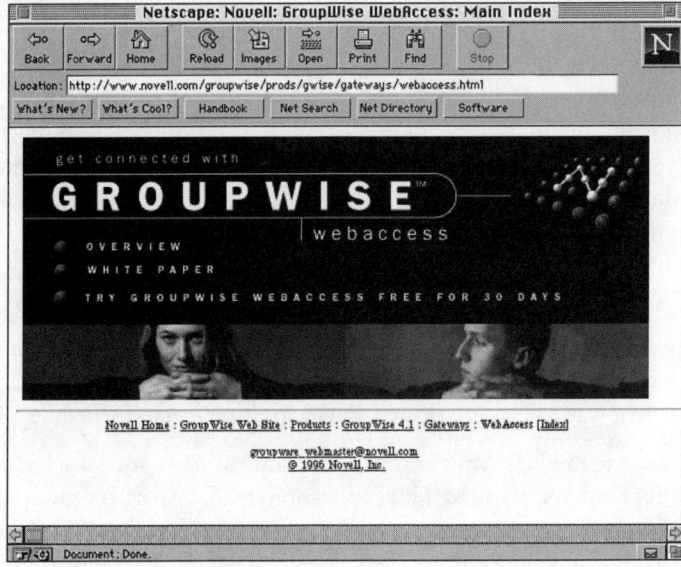

If your company is working from a groupware product that already offers scheduling, and the scheduling is well-developed, check with the application's home office to see what they are offering for intranets. If the options are not adequate, one of the intranet suites might be a good option.

I've already pointed out the advantages of using a suite of applications for online scheduling. The easy integration with messaging and contact records makes scheduling less of a chore. Add online functionality to an already convenient package, and you can toss the In/Out board in the trash. An online schedule is there when you need it, even when you're on the road. You're less likely to be late to a meeting when you can easily look up an address straight from your schedule. And if you are running behind, you'll appreciate being able to bring up a phone number you need with a simple point-and-click in your computer's day planner.

The advantages are clear, but are they possible? For the most part, yes. The future for group scheduling is bright. Besides the LAN schedulers that are building Web tools, a few intranet applications provide group scheduling functions.

Online Scheduling Applied

How are the online scheduling applications to be used? To answer that question, consider how a fictional company, called LifeLine, Inc., used an online scheduling application to organize a group of employees for a conference in Las Vegas, Nevada.

LifeLine distributes vitamins to health food stores throughout the southwest. They are sending employees to the Las Vegas conference as a way to check out their competition and get some leads on new vitamin science. Fourteen employees are attending the conference, and all of them will be spending three nights at the Radcliffe Hotel in downtown Las Vegas.

The conference begins on Saturday, but the employees will arrive at the hotel on late Friday afternoon. A secretary has the job of getting the whole group from the office to the airport and setting up a group schedule for the length of the conference. The schedule will be a tight one.

Almost everyone who is going to the conference has meetings with people from other vitamin companies. The boss wants the LifeLine group to meet at least three times as a group during the conference for brainstorming sessions. Three big conference events—the welcome speech, a dinner party, and a lecture given by a vitamin industry bigwig—are required events for all LifeLine conference attendees. A three-session workshop series about hybrid herbs is of special interest to about half the LifeLine employees, and they don't want to miss a minute of it. At least one employee must attend to a LifeLine booth in the main ballroom from nine to five on Saturday and Sunday.

To complicate matters further, three of the attendees can't leave with the group because they will be out on calls late into the afternoon. They will be arriving later than everyone else, and special arrangements are made for getting them to the airport. The boss's wife, two kids, and Aunt Martha are arriving on Saturday, and a few of the employees have requested that Saturday night be open for "a night on the town," and want to coordinate a starting point.

The secretary originally making the group conference schedule will not be going to Las Vegas. He plans to have a quiet weekend at home. But because he created the schedule using the online scheduling application, all the attendees can adjust their agendas accordingly after they arrive. They can view the schedule from the laptops that most of them are taking along, as well as from the workstation that will be set up at the LifeLine booth. Before the group leaves, the secretary sets up the system to send reminder e-mail messages to everyone who needs one and a general reminder to check the schedule for last-minute changes.

The first group of employees arrives at Las Vegas according to plan. But it doesn't take long before things go awry. The clerk at the Radcliffe doesn't have space for everyone and doesn't seem to have a record of the reservation the secretary made so carefully three weeks before, even though the secretary confirmed the reservation before the group left town. As a result, six employees are moved to a hotel called Star Palace down the street. Late Friday night, someone meets the second group of employees at the airport, and they are taken to Star Palace as well.

The next problem arises early Saturday morning, when the boss is detained at the airport, waiting for his family's flight to come in (late). A group brainstorming meeting ends early, and a few attendees abandon the conference in favor of shopping. The person scheduled to attend to the LifeLine booth is sick from allergies (no vitamin seems to help), and another person takes her place instead of attending the first workshop. Because the computer is set up at the booth, these changes are easily entered into the group schedule as the attendant checks her e-mail.

Now everyone is back on track again, and it's a good thing. The boss needs someone to get him and his family at the airport. He has left his wallet at the hotel and doesn't have money for a cab. His wife has only travelers' checks, and no cabby will take them. After the booth attendant is alerted by a phone call, she is able to contact the second in command, who is attending a lecture as scheduled. After the boss's wallet is retrieved, two employees leave the conference to take a bus to the airport. A second brainstorming meeting is canceled, but when the boss and company arrive back at the hotel, it is rescheduled for early that evening. The booth attendant enters these changes, and it seems something of a miracle when everyone shows up on time.

Online group scheduling, when applied, is indeed something of a miracle. Out-of-town conferences, which are notoriously subject to Murphy's Law, are just one example of how online scheduling applications can be useful. For day-to-day operations, a company like LifeLine might use online scheduling to keep track of employees who are out on sales calls and to enable all employees to make scheduling changes from their desks, at their homes, or on the road.

MCKEON & JEFFRIES

Due to the relatively static nature of M&J's intranet, it has little opportunity for a scheduling application. Typically, such an application would require fairly advanced CGI or database programming. The firm does use the intranet, however, to announce meetings and events for the firm. Each office has its own page that is regularly updated with new items by the administrator. This way, with minimum effort, the employees of the firm can have an updated schedule of items at their fingertips at any time. On the calendar page is an e-mail link to the administrator who updates the page, so if a scheduling conflict occurs, or if someone wants to add an event, making the change is as easy as clicking the mouse and sending a message to the correct person.

THE SPORTING GOODS AND APPAREL ASSOCIATION

The SGAA has a more advanced and dynamic scheduling system. On this system, users can get information on trade shows, press releases, deadlines, new product releases, or any other type of event. Some users can even post events to the calendar by using an interactive form. This function is available to both SGAA staff and members. Users can easily post events and relevant materials relating to the events. If a manufacturer posts a press release or a new product release, for example, the text of the press release or the specification sheet for the new product can be posted and linked from the event itself. Along the same lines, SGAA staff can post events regarding a convention or meeting and link the event to a sign-up form or an agenda.

This scheduling function is built using a back-end database, and all the event information is stored in the database. The information is pulled from the database by CGI scripts, and the event pages are created on-the-fly by the Web server. In this manner, events can be posted, modified, or deleted immediately without using HTML. The scheduling function is useful to the association because having up-to-date event information makes avoiding conflicts easy when scheduling for dozens or hundreds of individuals.

Scheduling Applications

Online scheduling applications are likely to be a part of most of the up-and-coming intranet suites. A few suites already offer scheduling applications. The advantage here is that you can integrate the scheduling with the other suite applications. Intranet group scheduling is different from LAN scheduling in that group and personal schedules can be updated without the limits of geography. The applications reviewed in the following sections are featured for a simple reason: they are the only ones available at this time. But because more and more pop up every day, you might do some research on your own.

InTandem by IntraACTIVE

The central scheduling calendar in InTandem, shown in Figure 36.2, can be viewed by day, week, or month. Events also can be displayed or printed out on a single chronologically ordered list. The calendar gives organizations the opportunity to maintain a complete list of important events, including everything from upcoming meetings to employee vacations. All authorized users can add new events to the calendar and modify the events that they have added.

You can add events to the calendar by simply typing information into an online form. Using this form, you can upload document files or images and link them to events, as shown in Figure 36.3. Similarly, you can embed images and hypertext links to information elsewhere on the intranet or on the Internet itself within the specific event information, allowing participants to have instant access to agendas, maps, online registration forms, and other relevant information.

FIGURE 36.2.
InTandem's add-an-item form allows you to designate an appointment as public or private.

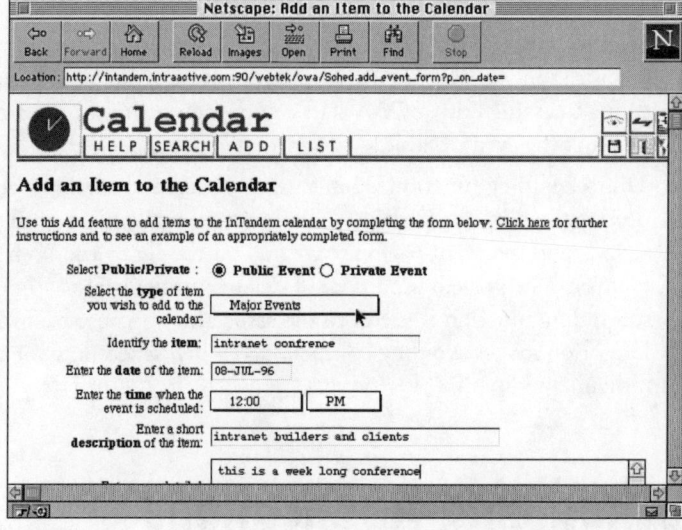

FIGURE 36.3.
InTandem offers a hyperlinked event list. Colored buttons designate event categories.

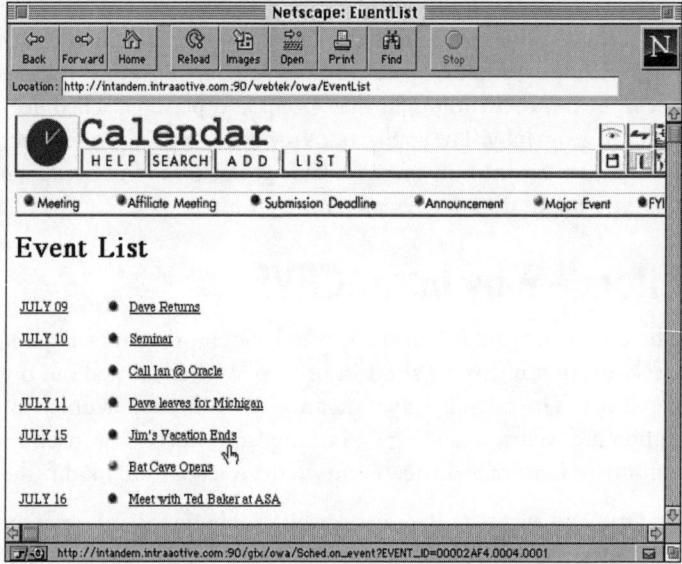

Each time an event is added, InTandem's calendar is instantly revised, providing all authorized users with accurate, continuously updated information. Events are shown listed by title on the given date and can be viewed in detail with the click of a mouse. Users have the option of entering public, private, and group events into the calendar. This flexibility ensures that only items of interest to everyone are posted in the public area. Obviously, not everyone in the office needs to know that Joe's daughter Suzy has a dentist appointment on Wednesday, September 3, at 12:00.

Public events are visible to all authorized users, and private events are visible only to the user who created them. Group events are visible to all the members of a group—for example, the budget committee. Group events are used to post information that is confidential or not of interest to all users. As an aid in scheduling meetings, the schedules of an entire group can be automatically superimposed on a single calendar to determine times at which the entire group is available to meet. A contact address is automatically included in every calendar event for those people who need further information. By simply clicking the name of the person who posted the event, users can send an RSVP or ask questions by way of an automatically generated e-mail message. As with all of InTandem's features, the scheduling software is completely customizable and can be searched using a powerful search engine.

WebShare by Radnet

The WebShare Calendar, shown in Figure 36.4, is part of the WebShare intranet suite and is a hearty tool for group and individual scheduling. A demo on the Radnet home site (http://www.radnet.com) provides a sense of the WebShare Calendar's basic functions. You can pull up a daily, two-week, or monthly view of a group or individual calendar. An additional feature enables you to group and view appointments in specific categories.

FIGURE 36.4.

The WebShare starter calendar offers multiple views and a calendar overview.

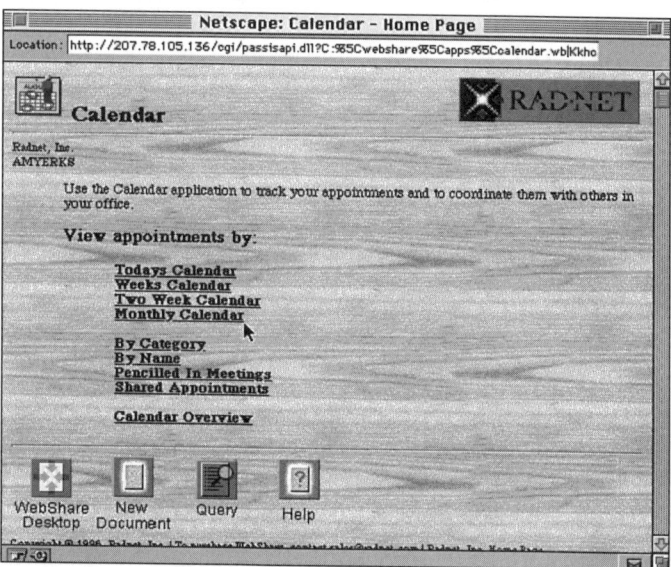

WebShare users can purchase the WebShare Designer (for Windows NT) and customize the WebShare Calendar to their liking, as shown in Figure 36.5. The interface can be redesigned for more detailed views. Integration with the other WebShare applications (Calendar, Problem Tracking, Resources & Reservations, Discussion, Moderated Discussion, Employee Record, Newsletter, and Contacts) is well-constructed and can be taken further with the WebShare Designer.

FIGURE 36.5.
You add appointments to WebShare by filling out an online form.

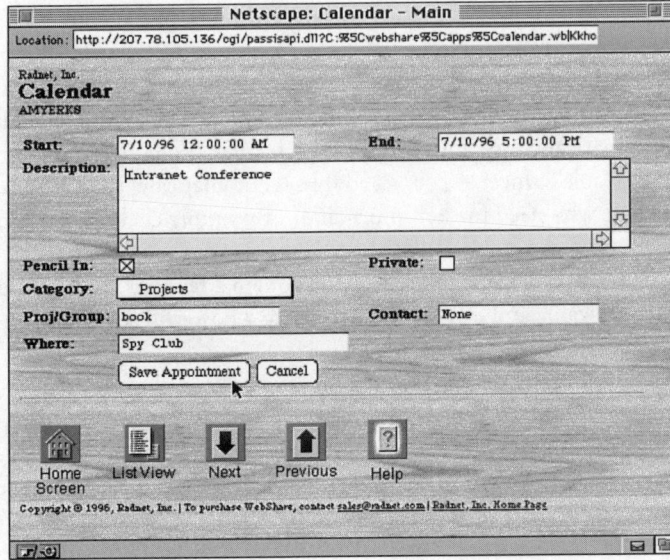

In WebShare, you add appointments to the calendar by using a form. Fields for descriptions, categories, and start and end dates are provided. You can add customized fields with the WebShare Designer. The original WebShare developers were once employed by Lotus Notes, and when they created WebShare, their goal was to create "Lotus Notes for the Web." You decide whether they achieved their goal.

Crew by Thuridion

Crew Calendar, shown in Figure 36.6, is an online scheduling application that comes with Thuridion's Crew intranet suite. Integrated with the other applications (Locker, Messenger, Cardfile, and Office), the Crew Calendar features a handy and well-constructed calendar that can be used for group and individual agendas. The highlight of Crew Calendar is the ability to search for free blocks of time. You also can share your schedule with others, including those people who do not have Crew accounts.

Another Crew Calendar highlight is the way it integrates with the Crew Office application. It works so that a user logging in can go to the Crew Office and retrieve a page with the day's plans outlined on-screen, as shown in Figure 36.7.

Never short on hyperlinks, Crew Calendar allows users to stock their day planners with contacts, documents, and any other item that might come in handy.

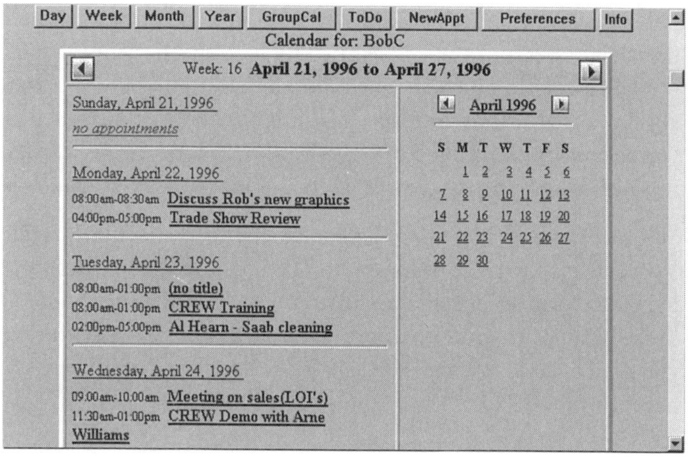

Group Scheduling
Chapter 36

FIGURE 36.6.
The Crew Calendar provides a week view and a month view on the same screen. Both views are supplemented with hyperlinks.

FIGURE 36.7.
Crew Office integrates with Calendar so that information about scheduled appointments is accessible from either application.

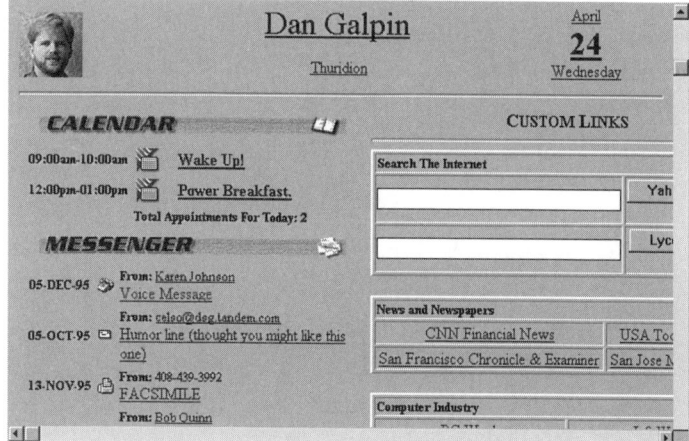

Summary

Online group scheduling can't add hours to the day or eliminate Murphy's Law, but it can be a tool for decreasing the chances that unexpected emergencies and last-minute changes will hamper your company's productivity. A fluid, easily updated group schedule is a resource that can benefit everyone from interns to CEOs. What's more, a group schedule brings a sense of unity to a team of people who might not see each other all that often.

When you're looking for an online scheduling application, you'll find that most of them are part of intranet suites or redeveloped LAN applications. Which of the two will serve your needs the best depends on what scheduling application you are currently working with. If a LAN application is already in place, you might want to supplement it with tools for the Web. If you're unhappy with the LAN application, or if no means of computer scheduling is currently in place, an intranet suite with a scheduling application would be a good choice.

Whatever you decide, pay special attention to a scheduling application's capability to provide a comprehensive array of functions. The best online scheduling application allows you to add hyperlinks and send e-mail right from your calendar. It should also provide a streamlined interface that looks good when printed onto paper. All these features will be the miracle workers you need to keep on top of a group and to keep track of your personal agenda, which you should never compromise.

Message Boards

37

by Anne Marie Yerks

IN THIS CHAPTER

- Message boards on the Web   **563**
- Why use message boards?   **566**
- Using internal message boards   **566**
- Message boards for intranets   **567**
- Group conversation   **571**

Message boards are a form of online conferencing but are different from real-time chat because the group discussion takes place over a period of days, months, or even years. Chapter 39, "Alert Messaging and Real-Time Chat," covers real-time chat, which is the term for conversations that appear (as text) in the browser as they are taking place.

The first online message boards (and still the most active) were those that comprised Usenet, which is the Internet's "hub" of Net conversation. Intranet bulletin boards are different from Usenet boards because they are not available to the Internet public. Even though a message board might be "public" to the intranet, it isn't, in most cases, accessible to anyone outside the company.

Message boards on the Web are rather new. "Threads," a Web conferencing project by *HotWired* magazine (http://www.wired.com), was one of the first sites to offer message boards inside a browser window. "Threads" was different from the text-only Usenet message boards because the messages were appended with small inline graphics, such as icons that identified one thread from another. The name "Threads" caught on and became the euphemism for the format of online conversation.

A *thread* is a conversation chain. When one person makes a post and someone else replies, the chain is started. Each subsequent post adds another link. Chains of posts and replies grow in whatever direction the message board participants take them. Just like a spoken conversation, the topic at hand can evolve and change. This system of reply-upon-reply can be confusing when you enter an ongoing conversation for the first time.

Group conversation on a message board is possible because new and returning members can scroll through the list of postings to see what conversation threads are active. (Old threads are deleted or archived by the site administrator according to a specific schedule.) Newcomers to the message board can read the FAQ (frequently asked questions) to learn board protocol and to find general information about how to post and reply.

How the board's conversation threads look depends on the software application being used and on the capabilities of your browser. Until Web conferencing becomes more developed (with sound and graphics), you would be wise to keep things simple. Most successful Web conferences are conducted in an easy-to-use and easy-to-read environment. For example, look at the Web group conference administered by The Intranet Journal, shown in Figure 37.1.

Whatever your topic, you will find a message board about it (if not, you can start one). This chapter focuses on group message boards for intranets. Private message boards—boards for specific users—are covered in Chapter 42, "Private Messaging Areas."

Message Boards
Chapter 37

FIGURE 37.1.
The Intranet Journal offers a group conference about intranets.

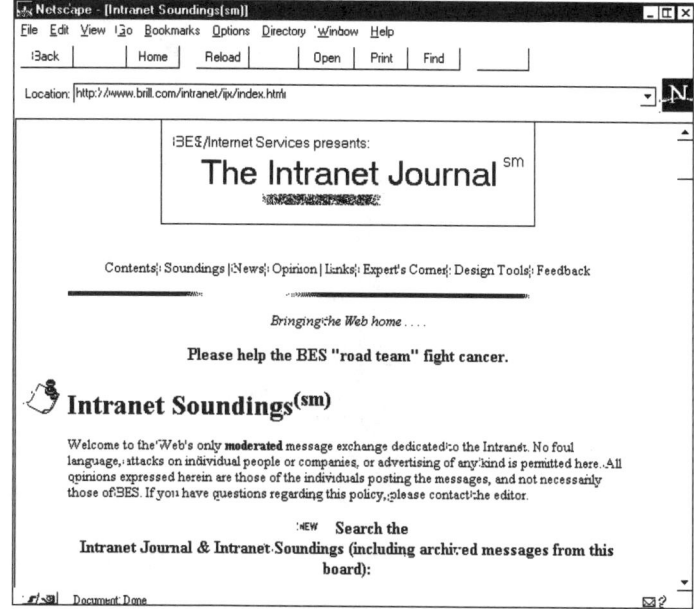

Message Boards on the Web

Even though the text-based Usenet is still the most frequently visited message board site, Web message boards are the future of online group discussion. You can already view Usenet message boards through Web browsers such as Navigator. Web message boards are popping up all over, and some of them are spruced-up versions of their text-only ancestors. One example is The Well, shown in Figure 37.2, a Web conference and news site born of a text-only Gopher. The Well is over 10 years old, and its Web conferences are some of the most haunted in cyberspace.

To participate in The Well, you must register and pay a fee, all of which can be done through an online form. Because of its good reputation and large following, The Well's sponsors are able to charge for access. Most message board sites on the Web, however, are free. One example is Apple's Table Talk.

Table Talk is similar to The Well in that the group discussions revolve around popular topics like movies and sports, as shown in Figures 37.3 and 37.4. Apple uses Web Crossing, a Web message board software application, to run Table Talk. Web Crossing is reviewed later in this chapter.

FIGURE 37.2.
The Well (http://www.well.com) was one of the first Web conferencing sites, and it continues to be one of the most active.

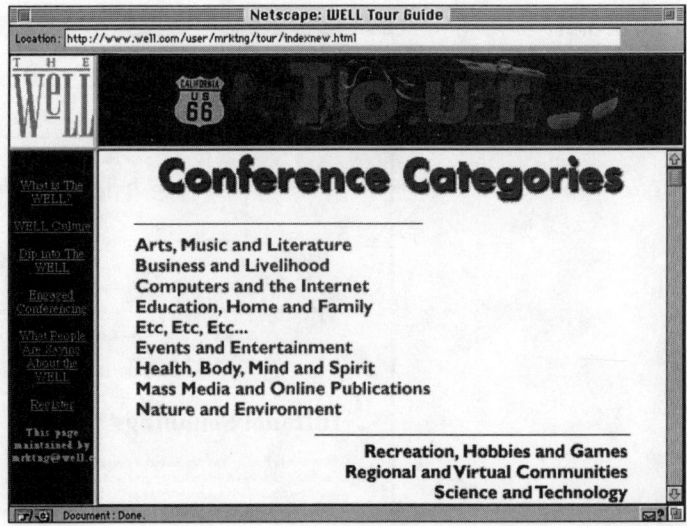

FIGURE 37.3.
Apple provides general topic areas on Table Talk's main menu.

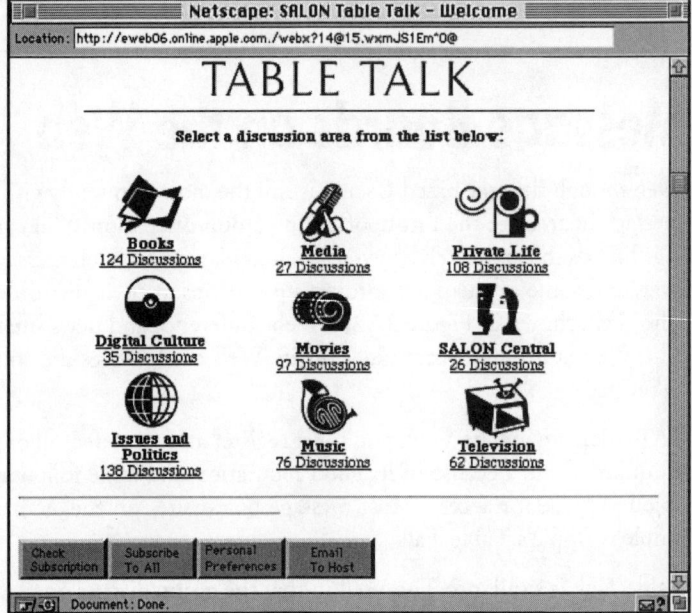

The Well and Table Talk are only two of the many group conferences on the Web. Online discussions, which are not limited by geography, are one example of how the Internet and the Web can serve the world. A few people such as Web guru David Wooley have theorized about the potential of online discussion. Wooley's Web site, shown in Figure 37.5, offers an array of resource links that can be a helpful aid to anyone who is building Web message boards. You can find it at `http://freenet.msp.mn.us/people/drwool/Webconf.html`.

FIGURE 37.4.
Table Talk lists participants' messages under the topic heading.

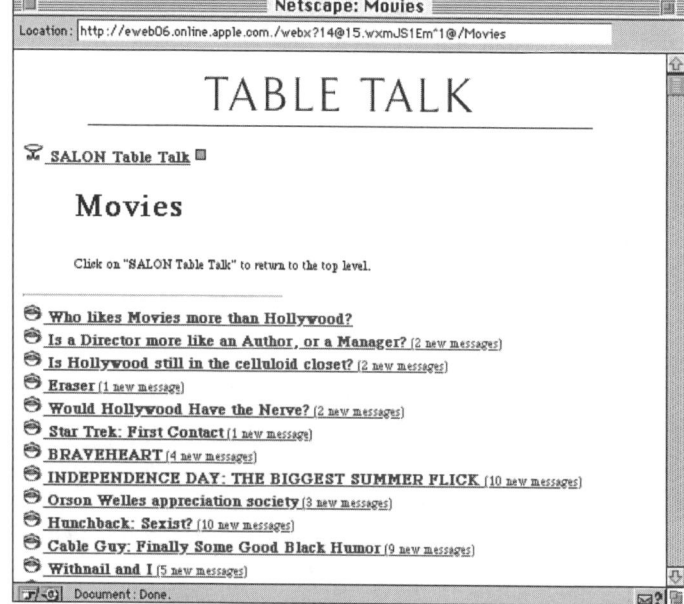

FIGURE 37.5.
David Wooley's Web Conferencing Page gives links to online message board vendors and other related resources.

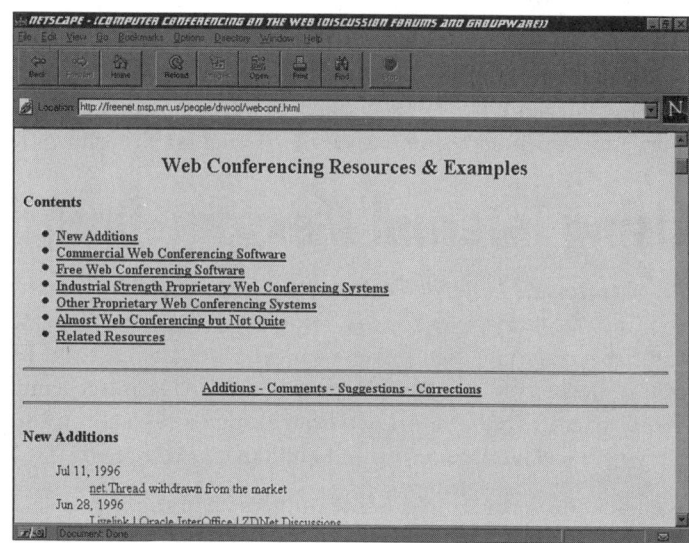

Why Use Message Boards?

Message boards offer more than random discussion. Besides queries and responses, users can (and do) post FAQs, proposals, treatises, and memos. Message boards can take the place of conference calls and other laborious meetings, and open up the time it takes to schedule them. When you're in a conference call or a meeting, you sometimes cannot do the thinking or the research you need to respond to a particular question or query or to propose a theory or proposition. On a message board, you have time to answer intelligently. Also, setting up a technical support message board can be handy so that customers and clients can ask questions to people inside the company. Or you might have a message board for the comments of those people who visit your public site. In these cases, the boards can be both internal and external.

To create intranet message boards, you need to either find a software application that will provide a bulletin board function or create it yourself by writing a CGI script. If you're not a programming whiz, you'll likely be shopping around for an application that will provide your intranet with message boards. Many of these applications are already on the market; I review a few of them later in this chapter.

One advantage of setting up internal message boards is that you can put your boards into the Web browser and enhance them with graphics. Other Web tools, like forms and frames, provide the means for quick and easy posting. Forms are the best way to manage the data generated from a Web bulletin board. They are easy to make (with CGI scripts or your software application) and easy to use. You can use forms to establish accounts, create new boards, post queries and replies, conduct searches, and set preferences (like font size).

For an example of CGI-based message boards, visit Time-Warner's Pathfinder site at http://www.pathfinder.com. The Pathfinder message boards are oriented toward providing users with information about the Time-Warner companies, such as Geffen Records. Also on the site are a few topic-oriented boards such as the Virtual Garden, shown in Figure 37.6.

Using Internal Message Boards

Fancy forms and complex CGI scripts will get you nowhere until you determine what needs your internal message boards will fulfill and what will be done with the data they produce. To make this determination, first evaluate your resources. If you have a small intranet running from a small server, you should keep your message boards to a minimum to save some space. If the intranet's administrators don't have much experience maintaining message boards, start out with a few message boards and build that area later on.

Well-attended boards can produce volumes upon volumes of data. This data consists of all the text that the users have entered into the CGI forms. One method of handling this data is to make it an archive. That way, if a user wants to search it, he or she can do so. Eventually, all that data can take up lots of valuable space, so figuring out a way to compress it and store it less expensively, like on a tape drive, might be to your advantage. (Then again, there's always the Delete key.)

FIGURE 37.6.

From the Virtual Garden, one of Pathfinder's CGI-based message boards, users can post new messages by using a form.

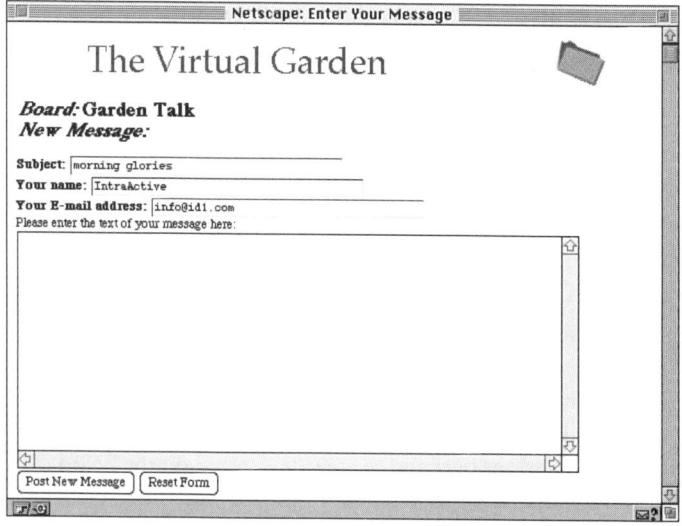

If you already have a search engine installed on your server, you can probably configure it to search not only the message board archive, but also the message board's active posts. Searches through a message board work much the same as they work in other intranet applications. The engine crawls through the data, retrieves matching words, and generates an HTML page to display the search results.

Message board searches are most efficient when users are able to set some search controls. For example, one user might want to search through posts that were added to the board on a specific day. Another user might want to search through a message board thread and collect all the results in a file to be opened later in a word processor.

Message Boards for Intranets

Some companies stock their intranets with work-related Usenet newsgroups or create Usenet groups that revolve around their products. But because Usenet is such a high-traffic area, the most efficient message board system for an intranet is internal, specific only to the employees, administrators, and associates of a company. An internal message board system, modeled on Usenet, could develop into the hot spot of the intranet.

To bring the benefits of message boards to an intranet, you must first find a software application that will help you work toward your goals. If you are a programmer or know a programmer, you might even develop your own message board software. In this section, I discuss some features of good message board software. Even if you aren't going to develop your own software, you'll want to choose an application that allows you to customize according to the needs of the intranet.

First, look for an application that will allow users to send a post or a thread to themselves (or someone else) as e-mail. Most of the time, you can perform this action in the browser. In Netscape's Navigator, for example, you can click a Quote button in the mail window toolbar, and the text of the page you're on is copied directly into your message. In this case, the message board application isn't doing the work; the browser is. But you want your message board application to have this same capability. In instances where a browser other than Navigator is being used, or when the user doesn't know about the Quote feature, having a Mail Article or Mail Thread button right on the message board is handy.

Along the same lines, message board software should offer the means to embed hyperlinks within a post. Assume, for example, that an accounting firm has a technical support message board on its intranet. This board's main purpose is to answer employees' questions about the accounting software application that is used by everyone in the office. The board is moderated by the network administrator, who finds the board to be very helpful: No longer does he have to answer the same questions over and over again. Posted on the board is a FAQ (frequently asked questions) that serves as a supplement to the software's reference manual, as well as a guide for using the message board for technical support. All new employees are required to read this FAQ.

When a new version of the accounting application is released, the administrator installs it on the machines, only to find—a few minutes later—that the new version has a nasty bug. Fortunately, the developers have created a patch for the bug, and the administrator downloads it from the Web. By this time, the administrator is tired of going around from machine to machine (it is a very big company), and because of the intranet message board, he doesn't have to. Instead, he uploads the patch to the server and announces its availability on the message board. Moreover, he creates a hyperlink to the specific file in the FTP site so that the employees can download the patch directly from the board. At the same time, they can read the administrator's post on how to install it.

Good message board software should be a time-saver not only for intranet administrators, but also for employees. Another feature to look for when selecting software is an application's capacity for password control. With passwords, specific messaging areas can be available only to predetermined users. This way, employees can have private space for discussing matters that might not be pertinent to all members of the intranet. For a more detailed examination of private message boards, read Chapter 42.

I've included reviews of four message board systems: InTandem, WebBoard, NetNotes, and Web Crossing. They are featured because of their easy installation processes and their user-friendly interfaces. Additionally, they allow for user-defined message boards and password protection.

IntraActive's InTandem, shown in Figure 37.7, contains powerful messaging software that allows users to post, download, review, and search messages quickly and easily. This integrated suite of intranet applications can be licensed separately or as a package. In a section called "Forum," users can read through all the message boards that have been established and have the opportunity to create new message boards of their own choosing.

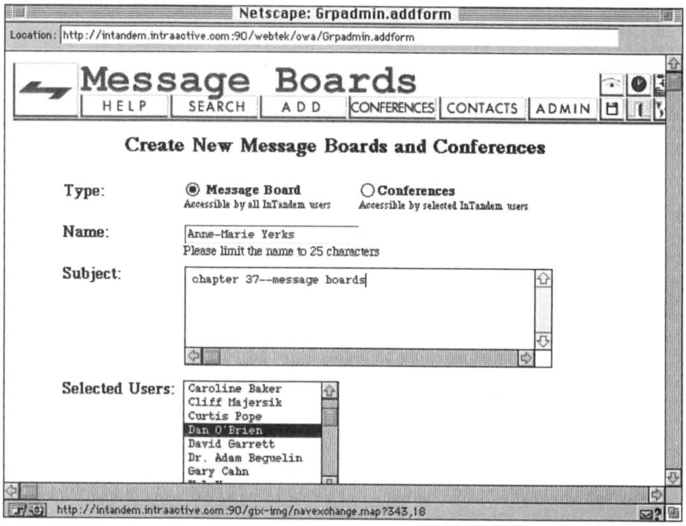

Message Boards
Chapter 37

FIGURE 37.7.
IntraActive's InTandem allows users to create a message board.

After a message board is established, users can post new messages to the board or can reply to messages that have already been posted. Replies are linked to the original message, enabling users to immediately get the answers they are seeking. All authorized InTandem users have access to the Forum, allowing complete organization-wide collaboration and information sharing. Select users also can modify and delete messages and message boards.

The Forum is presented in an easy-to-use, completely interactive format. Users click the name of the message board to review the subjects of the posted messages. They then simply click the subject itself to see the complete message. Users also can click the name of the person who posted the message to get that person's contact information and send him or her an e-mail message.

InTandem also offers its users the option of embedding images and hypertext links within the content of a message. Users can create a link, for example, to a project under development to get feedback, a report that needs approval, or a document needed by a number of employees. In all these cases, the hyperlink saves time—by providing the information instantly—and money—by bypassing the printing and distribution process.

Most Web message board applications allow some means for establishing password control. O'Reilly's WebBoard, shown in Figure 37.8, is one of many that offer this feature.

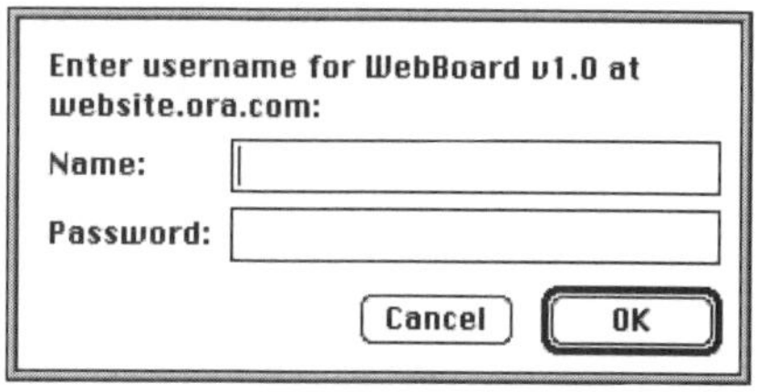

FIGURE 37.8.
You can configure O'Reilly's WebBoard to require a username and password.

Developing Intranet Applications

Part VI

WebBoard works on any CGI-compliant server and can accommodate as many as 255 boards, each of which can be divided into subconferences. The boards share a common user database, so users don't have to repeat the logon process when moving among conferences. Users also have the means to check profiles of other users, see who has logged on to particular conferences on any given day, and search any number of conferences for a specified word or phrase.

The NetNotes (recently purchased by SpyGlass) home site, shown in Figures 37.9 and 37.10, has a demonstration that gives a good sense of how group message boards work.

FIGURE 37.9.

The NetNotes topic list is presented below a browser-style menu bar.

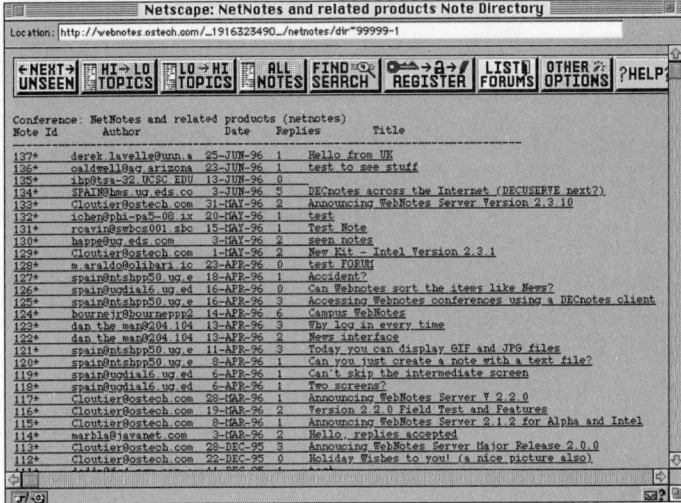

FIGURE 37.10.

All NetNotes users are identified by hyperlinked e-mail addresses.

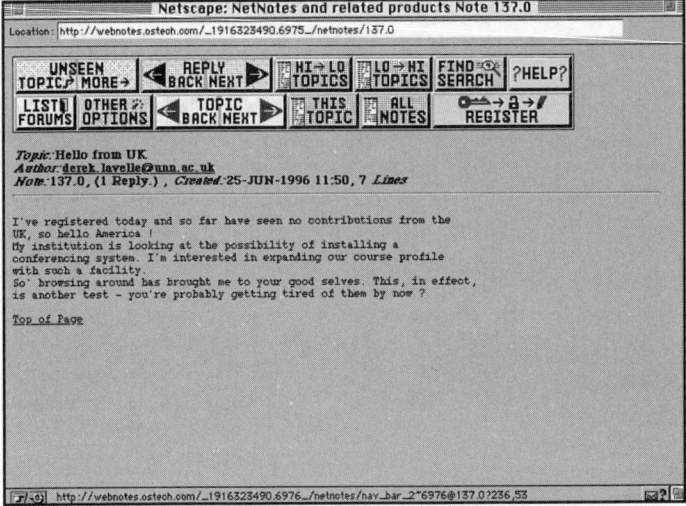

NetNotes is a self-contained server deployed on Windows NT. Aside from the server, no other software is required because NetNotes is not implemented as a CGI script; the server does all the work. Security issues were foremost in the thoughts of NetNotes' developers. Each level of conferencing can be password-protected. A special Conference Manager controls the security options. Future versions of NetNotes will include the ability to encrypt postings.

With Web Crossing, shown in Figure 37.11, a server and CGI are the means of establishing the conference boards. Web Crossing puts a new spin on traditional conversation threading by enforcing a linear conversation flow, which eliminates an entire layer of user interface. A response-to-a-response is started as a new discussion in the same folder and simply refers to the original post.

FIGURE 37.11.
Web Crossing offers visitors to their home site (http://lundeen.com) the opportunity to participate in a demo discussion.

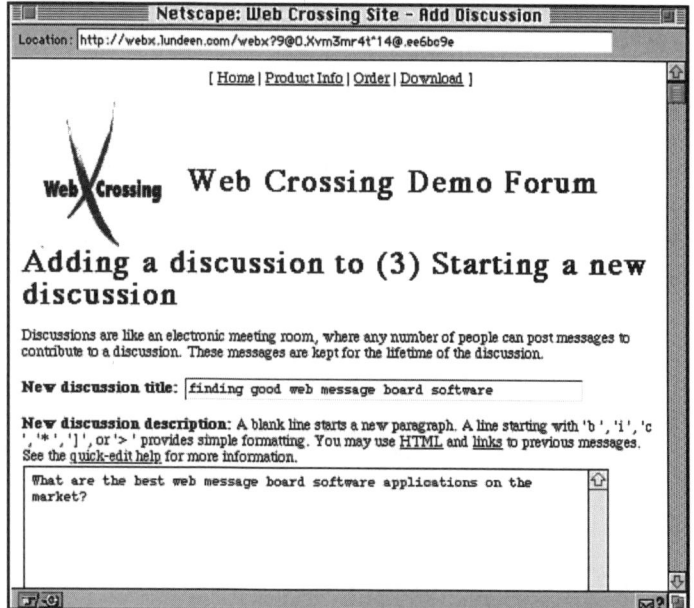

Web Crossing is easy to customize, offering templates for banner, footer, and background colors. The layout for headings, folders, and message items is also easy to change. Web Crossing is available for Windows NT, Macintosh, the DEC Alpha NT, and UNIX.

Group Conversation

The right messaging software is only your first tool. Online conversations are most successful when someone behind that fancy interface is helping the discussion thrive. For that reason, every message board should have a moderator. A moderator's job is to observe the group conversation and sometimes participate in it. Some groups go as far as having the moderator screen every post before it appears on the board. The reason for screening is that sometimes people on a board get overly excited about communicating online and post their views and opinions regardless of how they might be perceived to the other patrons of the board. These "flames" are often the first source of arguments that could cause the conversation to drift away from the original topic.

On an intranet, the members work with each other in the same office and are united toward a common goal (their bread and butter) and are more likely to release their frustration in the employee gym rather than on the company message boards. A list moderator on an intranet might have an easier job than that of a moderator on a public board. An intranet board moderator might keep the FAQ posted and spur the conversation when it falls quiet.

The moderator should have a sense of the dynamics of group conversation and how it is affected by the electronic environment. Online conversation is different from face-to-face conversation for many different reasons. First, people are writing rather than speaking. Although the day of audio message boards is not too far ahead, right now text is the primary means for posting and replying on a message board. Small details like grammar and spelling errors can lead to miscommunication, but that's only the beginning. Many people do not consider themselves to be good writers and therefore do not want to express themselves through writing, whereas other people enjoy writing and can write overly detailed descriptions.

These discrepancies can hamper the balance required for productive conversation. If you've ever taken an active part in any of the Usenet groups, you might have noticed that a few people sometimes monopolize the conversation. On the Internet, these "board hounds" sometimes become gurus of sorts, and might be considered as experts of the topic at hand. On the other hand, the group could have a negative reaction to the idea of having a board guru, leaving the list moderator with the problem of how to get particular individuals to be less active in the discussion.

A moderator might also have the job of creating and maintaining message board archives. The best way to develop a message board archive is to make sure your message board application is operating from a back-end database. That way, your data will be archived automatically. Message board archives can provide useful data for compiling reports and proposals, as well as for record-keeping. The way in which you maintain your message board archive will depend on the structure of your intranet. A message board moderator should let board members know the ins and outs of accessing the board archives.

A skillful moderator works to bring every member of the list into the conversation forum. Although frequent posts are always appreciated, the whole point of group conversation is to hear from everyone in the group. An online group conversation has the potential to be more productive than a face-to-face conversation because many obstacles are removed. Participants don't have to worry about interrupting each other, and they have time to express their thoughts.

People who don't contribute to the board (called *lurkers* in Net lingo) might be encouraged to write in if the moderator specifically (and casually) asks for their input. Other ways for a list moderator to spark interesting conversation are to post articles, bring in a post from someone outside the intranet who has something to add to the group conversation, or to post polite challenges to messages that could be expanded upon. Using these approaches might bring even the most reticent of lurkers out of their shells.

MCKEON & JEFFRIES

McKeon & Jeffries wanted a simple message board system to exchange messages about specific topics, such as administration and management issues within the firm, as well as issues regarding their core business, taxes, and audits. With this in mind, the system administrator purchased NetNotes, a message board system that runs on its Windows NT server. The simple format allows users to post and reply to messages. Because the site is authenticated by just a few user IDs and passwords (not everyone has his or her own user ID, remember), each time a user posts or replies to a message, that user must type his or her name and e-mail address.

The firm created a group of message boards to discuss administrative issues, one for taxes, one for audits, and one for technical support. If a user wants to create a new message board, he or she can send e-mail to the system administrator, who can then create a board. The message boards are functional for the firm's needs, although a little clunky for most users who are familiar with Usenet.

THE SPORTING GOODS AND APPAREL ASSOCIATION

The SGAA decided to make its message boards one of the central attractions of its intranet. After all, communications and networking with industry colleagues are membership draws. The message boards serve as a place for users to get online and talk about issues from association policies to manufacturing problems to new packaging and distribution methods. On these boards, members of the association can congregate to share ideas and engage in meaningful debate. Manufacturers, distributors, and resellers also can pass information to one another. All the while, these boards offer the opportunity for feedback—whether it be the discussion of the popularity of a particular product or the latest media interest in sporting goods and apparel. They provide a way for the free flow of information among interested parties from all corners of the industry. Of course, some issues are not for public consumption, such as membership fees that are based on company sales or maybe a pending lawsuit against one company. These issues are discussed in the private messaging areas, which you will learn about in Chapter 42.

The message board system, which was written by the consultants who SGAA hired to build the intranet, is complex. It takes aspects of the user database and implements them with CGI scripts. The code was written in Perl. Users do not have to enter their

> user IDs or e-mail addresses when posting a message. Because each user has an individual user ID, the script takes the ID from the environment variables (when users enter their user IDs and passwords to gain access to the site, they follow the users around as environment variables) and goes to the user database and looks up the user's name and e-mail address from its records. The script then enters the information automatically when a user posts or replies to a message.

Summary

Message boards just might become the hot spot of your intranet. Encourage their use by choosing a message board software application that allows features such as password protection, embedded hyperlinks, and customized searching.

Intranet administrators should benefit from message boards just as much as the users. Setting up a technical support message board is a great way to save the time and trouble of answering the same questions repeatedly. A tech support message board should have a FAQ posted at all times.

In addition to your internal boards, give users the ability to access Usenet groups that revolve around company-related topics. Although Usenet groups are public, they are a good source of information. Data from Usenet and from your internal boards can be transported into a word processor. With so much easily attainable information, your intranet will thrive.

Contact Databases

38

by Anne Marie Yerks

IN THIS CHAPTER

- Shared resources **576**
- Software for contact management **578**

If you go into any office supply store, you can find numerous items to help you organize your client or vendor list. A real traditionalist can find a little black book. A more stationary person might prefer a weighty Rolodex. For the pack rat, there's the business card portfolio (with plastic sheets to be added as required).

In the electronics department, you can find a few personal digital assistants (PDAs). They are handy in looking up numbers when you're on the road. The electronics department might also stock a few software applications that promise to be your little black book, Rolodex, business card file, and PDA all rolled into one. These software applications are often called *contact managers* or *contact management systems*, and are threatening to eliminate their paper-dependent ancestors.

The Web is the next frontier for contact management systems. The convenience of having customized contact information online is so compelling that many software developers are working furiously to make it happen. Online contact managers have an advantage over PDAs because they can separate and organize public and personal contacts. For companies that want to streamline the contact records of their employees and clients, this capability can be a big advantage.

This chapter focuses on establishing a contact management system on an intranet. To do so, most companies take one of two approaches. The first approach, but not necessarily the easiest, is to search for and purchase a software application to hold all the employee and client contact information. The other approach, which is more intimidating, is to create a customized system for contact management using CGI scripts and a database. Here, I address both of these approaches and help you choose a contact software application. If you have your heart set on creating your own contact management system, you might read Chapter 48, "Maintaining a User Database," for more information about managing databases. You might also look at Chapter 21, "Creating a Dynamic Site," for guidance on developing dynamic HTML pages.

Shared Resources

The main advantage of a central contact database is that employees can share information. Instead of everyone having separate Rolodexes and instead of having an annual directory, employees can access contacts and information through the intranet. If the basic contact information like name, address, and phone number is supplemented with comments, the advantages of shared contacts increase.

The best contact databases allow input for both private and public comments. Only named individuals can see the private comments; everyone can see the public comments. A sports equipment sales team's contact comments, for example, are viewed only by those employees who go out on calls, their supervisors, and of course, the database administrator. Contact database software programs should supply fields for assigning public and private factors.

If shared resources are the main advantage of computer contact database systems, why go to all the trouble of putting the information online when that same information could be shared over an already-existing LAN? And if you need contact information from the road, why not use a PDA?

The answer to these questions has to do with the whole idea of the "virtual community." It's no secret that the Web is growing. Bringing a contact database into an intranet means that many employees can access it from their home computers. Very simply, such a database makes work easier. This answer might not sound like a very good reason, but consider all the times you have needed a number at home, only to remember that it is stored in your office computer or published in the corporate directory, which you would never consider carrying home. These logistics are often the source of great frustration, and many of them will be eliminated as the virtual community is built.

A contact database can serve not only as a point of reference, but also as a tool for more efficient workflow. Like the other communication resources on an intranet, such as message boards and real-time chat, a contact database links the members of the virtual community without the limits of geography or paper.

Corporate Directories

One of the first ways a company can save a great deal of money with an intranet is by putting the corporate directory online. The cost of preparing and publishing a paperback directory (especially in these days of increasing paper prices) can run thousands of dollars. Although the Web might at first seem like too public of an environment for contact listing, remember that you can employ passwords and firewalls for security.

Not only are printed directories expensive and cumbersome to search through, they also are limited to names, addresses, and phone numbers. An online contact database can go far beyond names and addresses. Photos, audio greetings, and hyperlinks to personal URLs are just a few of the features you can incorporate into an online directory.

An online corporate directory can be updated daily, whereas a paper directory loses accuracy as soon as it goes to press. Another advantage is that employees can enter in the contact information themselves with an online form, which means that the site administrator or department head doesn't get bogged down with keeping track of new contacts as they come in.

Contact Databases for Intranets

Deciding to put contact information and directories online is only the first step. After that comes the decision how, exactly, to get all the required information into the intranet.

If your company has a LAN contact database, you might be able to use that same database for the intranet. How you do so depends on the type of database the LAN is using and on how the intranet contact database will be established. Most contact databases, such as those built in management systems like FoxPro and Act, can be exported into a pipe or comma-delimited standard format. This means that your database places each record on a separate line and separates the fields with a special character, such as a pipe or comma. If the fields were last name, first name, company, and e-mail address, and you were using commas to mark the fields, the delimited database would come out looking something like this:

>   Eldredge, Marcia, IntraActive, marcia@intraactive.com
>   Garrett, Dave, IntraActive, dave@intraactive.com
>   Yerks, Anne-Marie, IntraActive, anne-marie@intraactive.com

If pipes were the special character, it would look like this:

>   Eldredge| Marcia| IntraActive| marcia@intraactive.com
>   Garrett| Dave| IntraActive| dave@intraactive.com
>   Yerks| Anne-Marie| IntraActive| anne-marie@intraactive.com

After the information has been delimited, you can transfer it into the intranet, as long as your contact management software allows you to do so. If you're creating your own contact management system, you can build it around your delimited database.

As the heart of the contact management system, the database must be implemented and managed properly. Here, a contact management software application can be a great resource. A few browser-compatible contact managers have begun to spring up on the market, but most of them—if not all—are part of an intranet suite. This is not a disadvantage. Using a suite (software packages that contain more than one related application) often means that the various applications can be integrated with one another.

Software for Contact Management

Although the number of intranet products on the market increases daily, online contact management applications are hard to find. This availability will no doubt change in the near future as more and more applications currently in development make their big debuts. Two intranet suites, IntraActive's InTandem and Thuridion's Crew, have contact management capabilities. I review them later in this chapter, along with a popular LAN contact management program, GoldMine, which is rapidly incorporating itself into the intranet stream.

When you're looking for a contact management application for an intranet, several factors are key, as you learn in the following sections.

Customized Fields

A contact record is no doubt going to include a name. It will probably include an address of some sort (either home or office or both). It will almost certainly include a phone number and maybe an e-mail address. This information fills the basic information field for contact records, but in many cases more information is needed.

Members of a sales force might want a field that gives the name of the person who originally entered information for a specific contact. Employees who are not involved in the sales force might not care about having this field. Therefore, they should have the option to remove fields, even ones that were established by other users. By removing fields, these employees can avoid having to view extraneous information. This capability may not seem important, but it can be a way to save paper and ink when printing the list on an expensive-to-use laser printer.

In short, look for an application that gives the option for customized fields so that users can specify what contact information they want to see on the screen when they pull up records.

Customized Phone Lists

Once again, customization is the key element for developing and maintaining an efficient contact management system. The best contact managers offer the means for creating customized phone lists. This way, users can create and distribute contact lists especially for special projects.

If the customized contact list contains information that should be kept private (for example, the CEO's beeper number), you need an application with password protection for customized lists.

Support for Large Volumes of Data

If your company employs many hundreds of people and keeps records on associates and clients, you need a contact database application that can support as many records as you need. It should give you room to add more as new associates and clients come along.

The size of your contact database is limited by how much room you have on your server, but the management application should give you the liberty to include as many records as you like.

Public and Private Comments

When viewing or creating contact records, users should be given the means to make either public or private comments along with the records' basic information. These comments might give some additional information specific to the records that is not common enough to require the addition of a field. Someone working with a client who always brings his dog with him to meetings, for example, might put out a warning to other employees ("Watch out—The dog's a biter!").

Public comments should most likely be viewable to every user who has access to the contact list in question. Private comments might be viewable only to the user or to a specified user group. This feature can be especially handy for sales teams or for anyone who deals with a particular client more than once.

Hyperlinked Records

In most circumstances, e-mail addresses and URLs are a standard part of contact records and should be presented in the window as hyperlinks.

Hyperlinked fields allow users to communicate with the contacts without leaving the contact management application. For times when you have many messages to return, this capability can be a tremendous convenience.

A Search Engine with Controls

When you need to find all the contact records that contain a specific word or field, you'll want the information in the contact database to be searchable.

Some contact management applications might have their own engines or a "find" command. You might also use the engine that's installed on your Web server. In either case, it's best if you can set some controls for your search.

Profiles

The users of the contact management application will have their own contact information stored in the database. The application therefore should have the means to develop specified records into detailed profiles.

An employee profile might include a photo, a biography, and even an audio greeting. Other features such as hyperlinks to other parts of the intranet are also advantageous. The best contact management application should offer the capability to create a detailed user profile and keep that information secure from the outside world.

Other factors to consider are how easy the application is to use. Entering a contact record should not be a frustrating or confusing experience. Right now, electronic forms are the best way for employees to enter and update contact records. They might look like the one provided by IntraActive's InTandem, shown in Figure 38.1.

InTandem provides users with highly developed software for storing, retrieving, and searching important contact information. This integrated suite of intranet applications can be licensed separately or as a package.

InTandem's flexible contact list software offers users numerous options for maintaining public and private information, as shown in Figure 38.2. All authorized users can add new entries to the main contact list and modify the entries that they have added. All these functions are performed quickly and easily using only a Web browser.

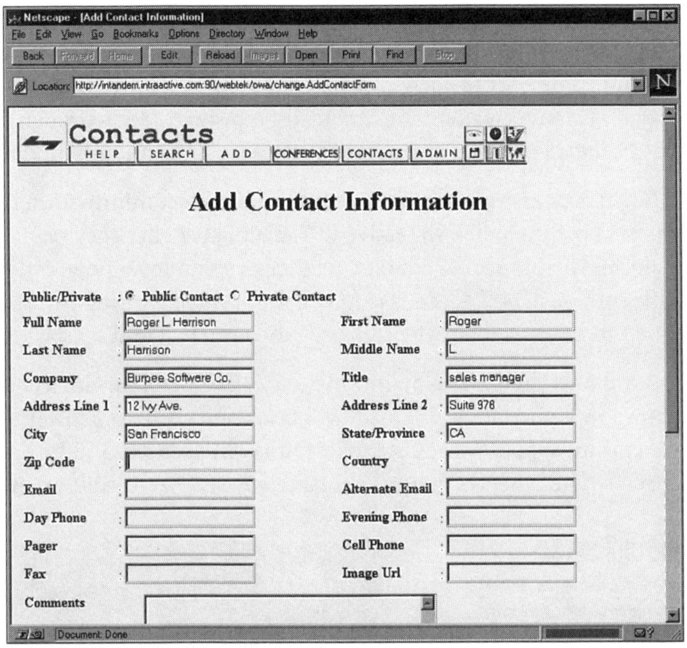

Contact Databases

Chapter 38 581

FIGURE 38.1.
IntraActive's InTandem provides a form for entering contact information into the database.

FIGURE 38.2.
InTandem's contact information is generated into an HTML page.

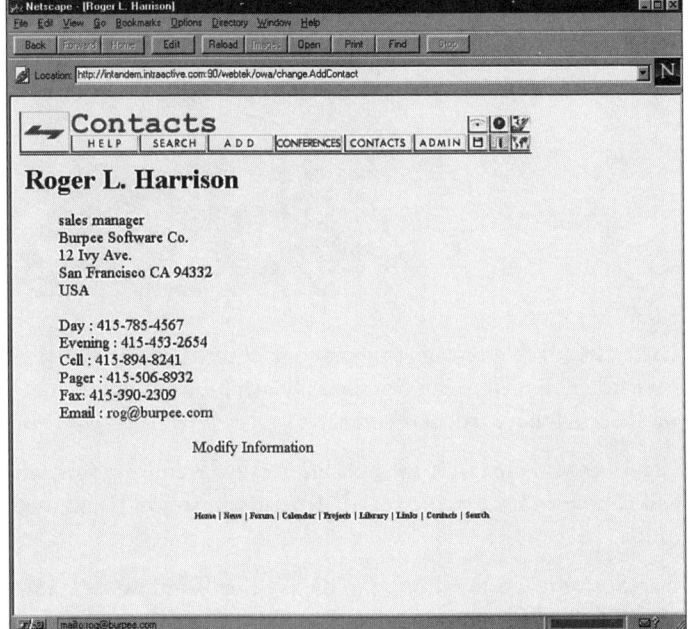

Users can add new contacts by typing information into a computerized form and then submitting this new information into the system. Users have the option of adding both public and private comments to each entry they create. In addition, users can add comments to entries that others have created. The contact list is instantly revised when new data is submitted, thereby providing all authorized users with accurate, continuously updated information.

The list is as easy to use as it is to update. Contact information is stored in alphabetical order. Users can either click the letter of the alphabet that they want to review and then click the name of the individual contact, or they can employ a powerful search engine to locate a specific entry instantly. Users also have the option of creating personal contact lists. This information can be viewed only by the user who creates it and by the system administrator.

Thuridion's Crew also is an intranet suite. Crew comes with a contact manager called Cardfile, shown in Figure 38.3. As an address book and group organizer, Cardfile is integrated into the other suite applications: Calendar, Office, Messenger, and Locker (for keeping track of documents). The other sections of the suite are easily accessible from the Cardfile window.

FIGURE 38.3.
Cardfile users can add an image to a contact record.

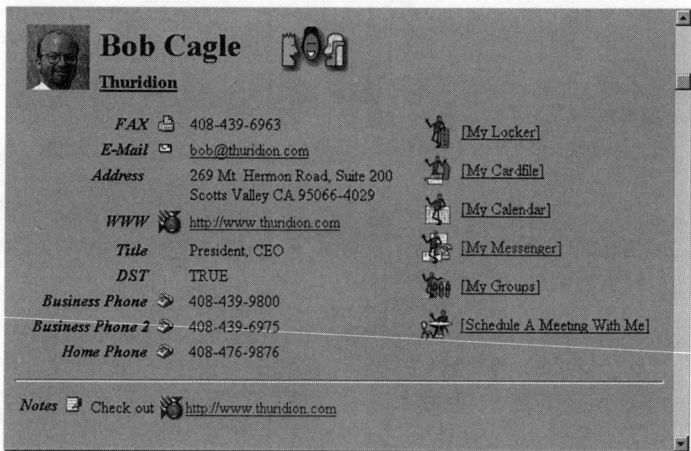

Users can attach an image to their contact cards, and cards within cards are linked to the parent card. This feature can be especially helpful if the user wants to keep track of how he or she was referred to a particular contact.

Crew is maintained with an application called Administrator, which provides the means to add and remove contact records as needed. Administrator is also used to customize the other applications in the suite.

Elan Software Corporation's GoldMine (for Windows NT and Windows 95), shown in Figure 38.4, has long been known as an easy-to-use contact manager for LANs.

FIGURE 38.4.
GoldMine's contacts screen looks something like an address book.

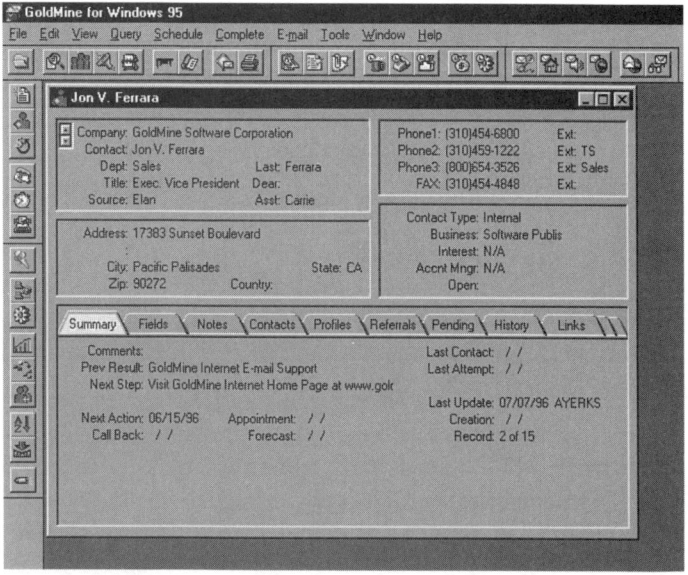

The new version includes the GoldMine information center, through which you can link photos and sounds to contact records. Personal URLs are linkable from the contact record screen. Folders, text, graphics, and other multimedia files can be structured hierarchically. A tabbed format on the contact record screen serves as a way to create a customized contact database. A new form especially for network administrators makes it easy to download new contact information as it comes in.

One helpful feature places specified contact records on automatic tracks. This way, users can create custom and personalized internal or external e-mail lists. This feature is especially helpful in keeping key clients aware of company news. Another key feature is the ability to create a private contact list, as shown in Figure 38.5.

FIGURE 38.5.
In addition to the main contact list, GoldMine users can organize a private contact list.

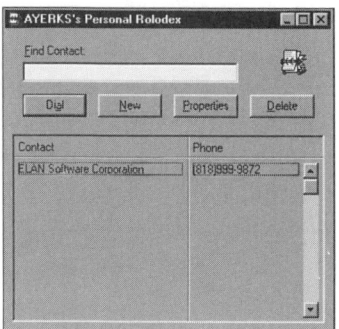

Many of the LAN contact managers, like GoldMine and Symantec's Act, are integrating into the Web. You can expect that more and more contact managers for the Web will be on the market in the near future. Intranet suites such as InTandem and Crew are good options if you want applications that are easy to integrate with one another. They are also good options if you're building an intranet from a paper-based system.

Companies with LANs should check to see whether the developers of their current contact managers are creating new versions that will allow users to view contact information from browsers. If not, an intranet suite would be a good option.

MCKEON & JEFFRIES

McKeon & Jeffries implements a contact database on the site in much the same way it does the scheduling function. Instead of each user being able to dynamically update the database, the administrator updates a static page on a regular basis. The database is merely an alphabetical list of contacts and their information. Integrated into this page is the accounting firm's client directory, which makes the list a centralized place to go for any phone number, address, or other information. Contacts and e-mail addresses also can be included on the page with a link that allows users to e-mail them directly from the page with the click of a mouse.

Users can go to the page and search for contacts using the Find function on their Netscape browsers. Using this type of contact list is inexpensive for M&J and is functional for their users. This way, if a phone number, address, or reference number changes for a client, vendor, prospect, or other contact, the administrator updates it once, instead of by each employee individually. When updates are made, users can e-mail the administrator directly from the page. This system is economical but hardly efficient, and it is not quite as useful as a fully dynamic database.

THE SPORTING GOODS AND APPAREL ASSOCIATION

The SGAA has built a more sophisticated contact database. Pages are generated dynamically so that users see only the information they request. Users can add or update contacts through a Web form. Users can modify only contacts they have submitted, so if an update must be made, other users can click and e-mail the person who posted the contact. The purpose of this list is to inspire networking throughout the SGAA. The database is completely searchable via another Web form.

Summary

An intranet can be the storage box for multitudes of contact records. It can be the little black book that can be accessed anywhere yet still remain secure. How you create your contact database depends on what kind of contact record system you're currently using, how many users you anticipate having, and whether you want to purchase an application or create your own.

Moving contact records from a LAN to an intranet is a chore but might not be as difficult as you would expect. Already-existing contact databases can be transported into many of the intranet suites. Also, your current LAN contact manager might be developing tools for the Web.

An intranet's contact management system can offer more than phone numbers. Photo-enhanced user profiles and detailed public and private comments go far beyond what a printed directory can provide. As you work to bring contact management to your intranet, be creative with the possibilities.

Alert Messaging and Real-Time Chat

39

by Anne Marie Yerks

IN THIS CHAPTER

- Why real time? **588**
- Alert messaging for intranets **589**
- Real-time chat **591**
- Chat for intranets? **594**

The '90s have blossomed into the decade of the beeper. Everyone from company CEOs to department interns are accessible to anyone at anytime. With a beeper on your belt or purse strap, you have the liberty to go where you want, when you want (until you get beeped, that is). Now that the '90s are spiraling into a new millennium, the beeper's quick-alert capability is being adopted by the Internet. It's now possible to send an alert message directly to the desktop or Web browser of another user, and to do so without the cost or geographic limitations of a beeper.

An alert message is one that travels from sender to recipient in real time, meaning that, unlike e-mail, an alert message does not go to a recipient's mailbox. Instead, it flashes on the screen, no matter what intranet application the recipient is working in. An alert message is usually short and brief, something like an electronic telegram. You might send an alert message when you can't afford to let the message sit in a mailbox.

If you've ever worked on a UNIX or VAX system, you've probably sent or received an alert message. These messages are usually sent straight from the command line (the main prompt of your system), and pop up on the screen, usually accompanied by a beep. Replying to the message is optional. There's no difference between the way alert messages and real-time messages are sent or received; the only difference is content.

An alert message is one that is sent to "alert" the recipient of something important. For example, a systems administrator (known as "Sysop" for short) might send an alert message to all system users to let them know that everyone must get off the network for a while. This way, the Sysop can do maintenance without having to wait for everyone to check their e-mail, and the users can be informed immediately of what is going on with the network.

A real-time message is delivered in exactly the same way as an alert message but is not an urgent message. A Sysop might send a real-time message to let users know that a new version of an often-requested software application has just been added to the FTP site. Any message that is short enough and meaningful enough to send in real time can be sent as an alert.

It's now possible, using the Java programming language, to send an alert message into a Web browser. Java is the programming language of choice because alert messaging and similar functions, like real-time chat, require an open connection between the server and the client so that communications are not interrupted. You don't have to know any Java to send or receive an alert or real-time message (this chapter uses these terms interchangeably); you need to know Java only if you want to write a custom application for sending and receiving real-time messages.

Why Real Time?

Think of real-time messaging as an intercom system for a computer network. Devices like intercoms and walkie-talkies have been used to relay urgent messages for years, but these devices have the disadvantage of being expensive to maintain, awkward, and loud. An alert message on a computer will allow you to send an urgent message to someone privately, whereas a message sent over intercom or walkie-talkie will be heard by everyone in the immediate proximity of the recipient.

Alert messaging could also be called broadcast messaging. Immediate information meant for many people, like schedule changes, can be distributed through the intranet in real time and appear in the browser window or an open application. Sending multiple-party messages can be assigned to administrators or to anyone who has the need. For example, let's assume that a (fictional) bottling company runs an ongoing training class for new employees. Each group of trainees spends their first week in the class learning company ins and outs. Real-time messaging is used as a way to communicate with the trainees about where they should go for their instruction. This method is used because the company's manufacturing schedule is always fluctuating, and the administrators never know when a particular event is going to occur. When something is happening on the floor that the trainees should witness, such as a new bottling technique, the network administrators send an alert message to the computers in the training room. This way, the new employees know where to go and also get a chance to see the company intranet at work.

This chapter focuses on using real-time messaging, including real-time chat, as a tool for intranets. As of now, real-time messaging for the Web is still under development. Even the intranet suites do not yet offer this tool. Likewise, Web browsers that do not support Java are not always capable of sending alert messages to individual users. As the technology required for real-time messaging develops, and as Java and similar programming languages pick up speed, you can expect that real-time messages and chat boards will become commonplace on the Web.

Until then, start thinking about how real-time communication can aid the productivity of your intranet. This chapter gives an overview of how alert messaging and real-time chat techniques are being incorporated into the Web. A few examples of Web real-time messaging are featured.

Alert Messaging for Intranets

When employed creatively, an alert messaging system can be beneficial to an intranet in a variety of ways. First, any message or warning can be delivered to a predetermined group of users (or a single user) within seconds. There's no waiting for e-mail checks.

The form in which the message arrives depends on the software application you choose or how the JavaScript or program is functioning. The LAN software programs that currently offer alert messaging features send the message directly to the recipient's screen in text, no matter what part of the intranet the recipient is working from. With Java, it will eventually be possible to send a message as a sound file.

You might not like the idea of your computer talking to you, but you might appreciate other benefits of real-time messaging. It can be a terrific method for keeping up-to-date with stock quotes. Real-time stock updates are already available to those who subscribe to stock-oriented news services like Quote.com, as shown in Figure 39.1.

FIGURE 39.1.

Quote.com's real-time capacities provide members with charts based on information gleaned five minutes before the request.

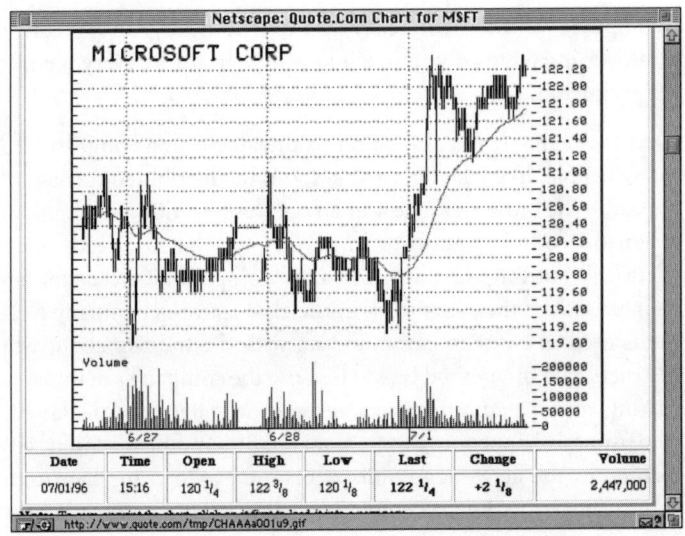

You can use real-time messaging not only to obtain stock quotes but also to communicate with others about new economic developments. For example, let's say that two (fictional) investors at two different companies are friends, and both hold stock in an auto parts manufacturing company. Investor #1 subscribes to a stock market news service. On her computer desktop is a Java applet (an applet is a Java application that can appear on a browser window on a computer desktop and that runs at all times) that serves as an alert console. Each time news pertaining to a specified stock comes in, the applet flashes. This alert is a signal for Investor #1 to check the stock news service for an update. If she finds that the news is something that her friend (Investor #2, who does not subscribe to the stock market news service) would be interested in, she might send her friend an alert message about the stock update.

The form in which the alert message arrives to Investor #2 will depend on the application she uses for her real-time messages. If she is logged in and has a Web browser on her screen, the message might scroll in the bar at the bottom of the browser window. There are quite a few Web sites that already use these scrolling messages as a way to welcome visitors to the site. Scrolling messages are written with a JavaScript (easier to learn than the programming language Java) and look something like the LED (lighted electronic display) signs used by department stores and other businesses.

Another way to receive an alert message is with a Java applet. An applet can also be created with JavaScript. An applet will sit on your desktop or in your Web browser and perform some specified function when a real-time message comes in. In most cases, the applet will blink or perform an animation to let you know that you have a message, and then the message itself will appear inside the applet window or in the browser window. Applets can give you real-time updates because they are always in communication with a client or clients you have previously specified.

Mailing an alert message to someone else can also be done with an applet. Because Web real-time messaging is so new, there aren't any working examples of sending a real-time message into a browser. For now, anticipate that sending and receiving real-time messages in a Web browser or on a desktop will be done with various Java applications.

The advantages that real-time messaging can bring to an intranet are numerous, but what are some disadvantages? If you've ever gotten "instant messages" on a UNIX or VAX system, you know that they are sometimes more intrusive than helpful. The same is true for Web-based alert messages. However, the more organized your intranet, the less likely that alert messages will be sent unnecessarily. You might also be concerned about alert messaging software interfering with other intranet functions. If so, you'll want your alert messaging features to integrate with other intranet applications. For example, it would be useful to have an alert message feature in an e-mail program, or as an option on the browser toolbar (then you don't have to worry as much about software conflicts). Although neither of these features is currently available, it's likely that they will emerge as the demand for them becomes strong.

Real-Time Chat

Along the same idea as real-time messaging is real-time chat. Chat forums are nothing new. Internet Relay Chat (IRC) is enormously popular. IRC works in real time but is limited by the text-only UNIX and VAX environments. The next wave of chat is operated from a Web browser and will allow "chatters" to post photos of themselves onto the chat board. Also in the future is audio chat, in which members of the chat board can communicate in real time with their own voices. This is already possible to some extent with tools like the Internet Phone (see Chapter 32, "Internet Phones: The Advanced Model") but will not require that all the parties be using the same software application.

Real-time chat is similar to group message boards (see Chapter 37, "Message Boards") in that it most often revolves around a particular topic and responses are posted as text in a messaging arena, like a window or applet. Real-time chat is different from group message boards in that the conversation appears on the screen as the users are typing into their home computers. The text input by each user appears after the user's name or "handle." Until recently, chat was limited to text-based systems. Now that limitation has been overcome. With a tool like the plug-in provided by a Web development company called WBS (Web Broadcasting Service), chat can be orchestrated inside a browser window.

Web chat boards, such as those found on WBS's WebChat site (http://wbs.net), are different from Web message boards in that the group conversation is ongoing rather than intermittent, as shown in Figure 39.2. To understand this difference, consider the discrepancies between a phone conversation and a written correspondence sent through the postal service.

FIGURE 39.2.
WebChat, at http://wbs.net, *is one of the first browser-based chat forums. It operates as a plug-in that you can download from the Web.*

MOOs, MUDs, and WOOs

Similar to chat boards are MUDs (multiuser dimensions) and MOOs (MUDs: object-oriented), which are chat boards that go beyond text-only conversation. Members of MUDs and MOOs are asked to visualize the chat board as a real place. MOOs are object-oriented versions of MUDs, and because they are more sophisticated, they are a bit more popular than their MUD ancestors.

One example of a traditional MOO is Hero Village, a UNIX community sponsored by the University of Virginia's department of Post-Modern Culture. In Hero Village, users assume a character name of their choice, and then write a description of their characters in a text editor (like PINE or ELM). When one user encounters another, he or she can enter a command to read the other's profile. Other operations allow users to read and write descriptions of rooms, acquire tools, page other users, and create mini-MOOs of their own. Discussion among users occurs in real time and appears on each user's screen as text, distinguished from user to user by username or handle. For example:

```
Pinky: How is everyone today?
LuLu: Doing pretty well--now that I'm typing in real time
```

MOOs like Hero Village serve as educational games rather than work forums, but it's entirely possible to build an Intranet MOO to educate employees about some facet of the company. For example, the training class I used as an example earlier in this chapter might use a MOO or MUD as a way for students to learn their way around the factory floor.

It's already possible to build a MOO or MUD inside a Web browser. For an example of a Web MOO (increasingly known as a WOO), visit SenseMedia's The Sprawl (http://sensemedia.net/sprawl), shown in Figure 39.3.

FIGURE 39.3.
The Sprawl, sponsored by SenseMedia, is one of the first WOOs.

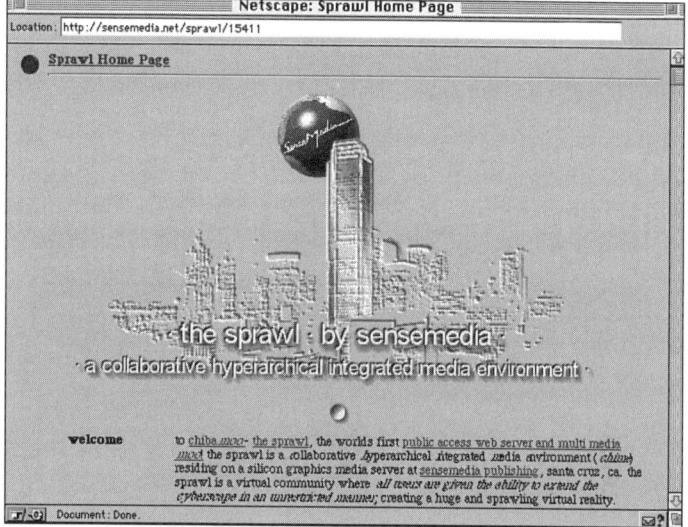

Members of The Sprawl navigate themselves to the chat forum of choice by clicking a series of image maps. These maps provide a graphic environment for The Sprawl, which makes it seem more like a real place than a text-based MOO could. Sprawl members can do most of the things possible in text MOOs, such as check to see what users they've joined online, as shown in Figure 39.4.

FIGURE 39.4.
The Sprawl/Chiba Who listing gives handles, connect time, and location of all logged-in users.

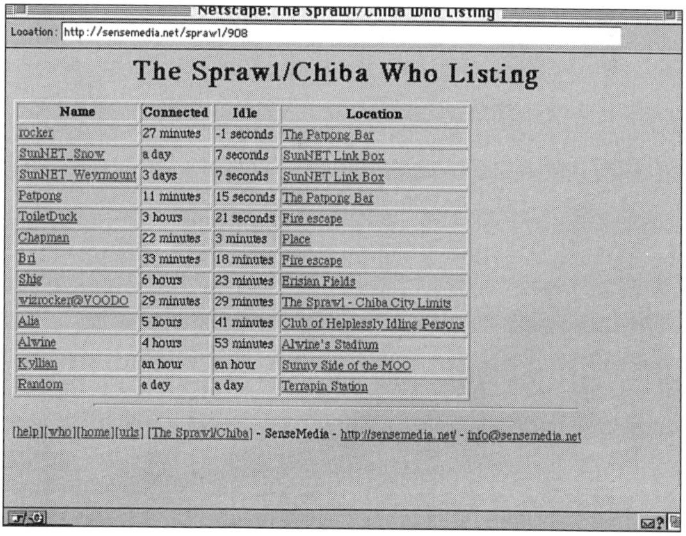

The Sprawl is available to anyone with a Web browser. At this time, you can still get an account for free.

Besides Web-browser WOOs, you can download special software to run a graphic MOO independently. One example is AlphaWorld (see Figure 39.5), sponsored by Worlds Inc. AlphaWorld (http://www.worlds.net/alphaworld) was developed with VRML (virtual reality modeling language) and allows users to communicate with text in real time. The difference between the browser-compatible AlphaWorld and the text-based Hero Village is that AlphaWorld provides a graphical interface, and users can see animated figures that represent all the characters that are currently logged in. These figures move about the browser window according to instructions typed in by the user and are visible to all the participants.

FIGURE 39.5.
Worlds Inc.'s AlphaWorld is a graphic environment for real-time interaction.

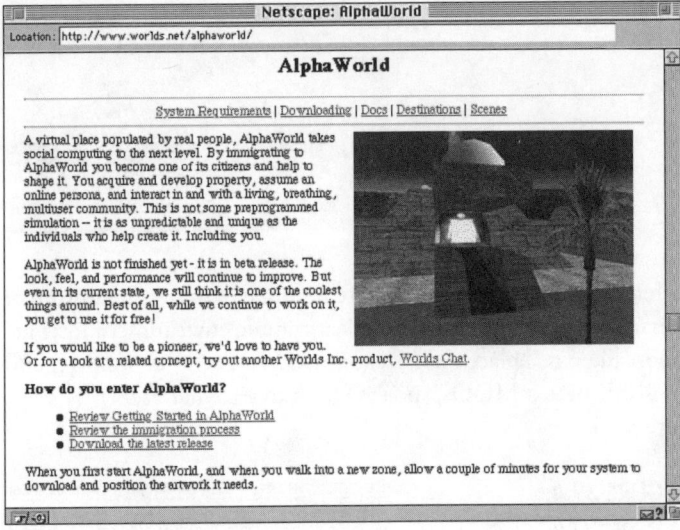

AlphaWorld users work together to contribute to the virtual community by building chat rooms and creating new tools. Although AlphaWorld exists primarily as a game, it also serves as an example of the potential of combining VRML and real-time chat.

Universities have been involved with the creation of MOOs and MUDs since their text-only beginnings. The MOO has already served as a model for online educational tools. For example, an archeology department might use a MOO structure to build a "virtual dig," which would allow archeology students to hunt for and uncover artifacts with a computer. A medical school might develop a human-body MOO for an anatomy class. The possibilities can be applied to almost any discipline. In all cases, a MOO provides users the means to communicate with one another with real-time messages; users are not limited by geographic bounds.

Chat for Intranets?

You might have heard stories or watched talk shows about chat "addicts" who have developed complicated relationships with other people in their chat forums. This type of chat is essentially entertainment and is not the kind of chat forum you will want to incorporate into your intranet. Indeed, "chat" is usually considered to be light, simple conversation. Why would you want to offer employee chat for your intranet? After all, people are supposed to be working, not chatting.

The truth is that chat has gotten a bad name; it is no less likely that the people on your intranet would abuse chat any more than they would abuse e-mail. Chat forums can be beneficial to intranets, as long as they are organized and focused around a specific topic. You might want to go so far as to have someone moderating chat sessions, so that people don't get off track.

Real-time chat forums can be used for interviews, online meetings, "ask-an-expert" instructional discussions, and maybe as intranet kiosks. Imagine how helpful it would be to have a central point where users could go whenever they had a question and needed a real person to answer it. This need could be served through a real-time chat information room.

Chat can be integrated into other intranet applications. Let's say that you put up a new logo on the Web and would like some input. You could configure your chat software to give you a chat window right below the logo and then invite other users to view the image and offer their opinions.

The look of your chat forums will depend on the software you choose. At this point, there aren't any real-time chat applications especially for intranets; but that doesn't mean that they aren't on their way. For an example of how an intranet chat might work, go to the EarthWeb Gamelan Page at http://www.ew.com, shown in Figure 39.6.

FIGURE 39.6.

Gamelan's Java chat provides a message-board applet that operates in real time.

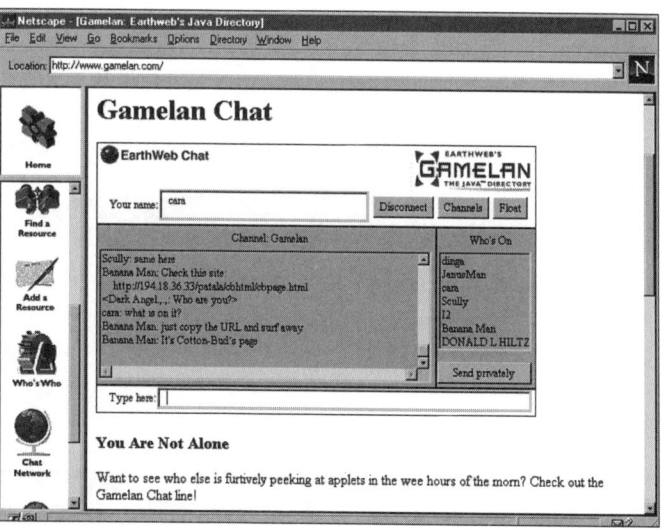

Streaming audio is another tool for Web chat. RealAudio, shown in Figure 39.7, already offers the means to hold live broadcasts on the Web.

Part VI — Developing Intranet Applications

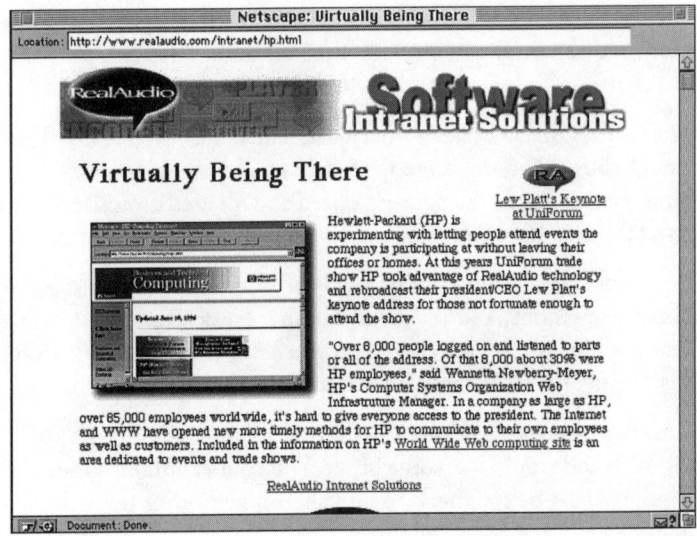

FIGURE 39.7.
Progressive Network's RealAudio is host for many companies that use real-time audioconferencing on their intranets.

Information generated in group chats can be saved, archived, and used as "minutes" for future reference. This is a great way to save a secretary's time. A search engine can hunt through the archive for a specified word or phrase.

Whatever your business, real-time messaging and real-time chat can be handy and effective ways for intranet users to communicate with one another instantly. The way you put real-time messaging to use will depend on the applications you use. As more real-time tools become available, read reviews and do some research to find the ones that will suit your needs. If you are a programmer and know some Java, you might be able to write a script, applet, or full-fledged application that will provide the real-time functions you desire.

MCKEON & JEFFRIES

When McKeon & Jeffries has a need for alerting users to a particular message, it uses the easy solution of changing text on the home page. As the administrators become more sophisticated, they will start using Java and JavaScript to make the text scroll across the page catch the user's eye in some other way.

THE SPORTING GOODS AND APPAREL ASSOCIATION

The SGAA implements two ways to alert their users with up-to-the-minute messages. The first is a Java applet coded by the consultants who put the intranet together for the association. It sits on the desktop of many users (some do not have Java-compliant browsers) and flashes messages to the users as soon as they are sent by the administrators.

The second uses a RealAudio server to send audio messages to those users equipped with a RealAudio player. The audio messages can be played as soon as the user executes the "play" button on the player.

Summary

Online real-time messages are in the near future, so think now about how to use them to your advantage. The immediate distribution of announcements to the employees of your intranet is just one possibility. Unlike the telephone, online alert messages are not limited by geography. If you want to send a message about a stock status update to someone in Japan, you will be able to do so. Also under development is real-time chat, a message forum similar to group bulletin boards, but that is conducted online in a graphical interface. Anticipate that both real-time chat and real-time messaging will eventually be enhanced with sound.

Real-time messages are one feature you can use in a larger-scale online forum, such as a MOO or MUD. If you don't want to get that complicated, you could establish a simple chat applet, such as that which appears on EarthWeb's Gamelan Page. When determining your intranet's needs for real-time chat, consider how your company is currently using intercoms and beepers. Real-time messaging can replace expensive intercoms or supplement them, and give everyone a chance to remove their beepers (at least while in the office!).

The software that will give you the ability to create and distribute real-time alert messaging and group broadcast messaging is still being developed. Some products, like RealAudio, are already on the market. As more real-time applications join the market, look for a product that is flexible with configuration settings and that can be integrated into other intranet applications.

News Feeds

40

by Anne Marie Yerks

IN THIS CHAPTER

- Just the facts **600**
- Getting online news **602**
- News that fits **604**
- Signing up for news **604**
- News clips **606**

One of the simplest ways for you to get the news is to open the front door and pick up a newspaper off the front walk. You don't have to worry about how the newspaper got there, what was involved with putting it together, or the trials the carrier went through (broken bike, barking dogs) to get it onto your porch by the time you woke up. You can select what you want to read, clip out pertinent sections for future reference, rip out a humorous cartoon to share with colleagues at the office, or pass the paper on to a friend.

The advantages of the home-delivered newspaper (plus more) can be offered to every user of a corporate intranet. As a new form of media, the Internet is fertile ground for the news wires and news services around the globe. The Internet's capability to provide news has the potential to be more convenient than newspapers and faster than television. The advantage of using the Internet as a news vessel is that the ocean of news coming in from the wires can be filtered, organized, and delivered to customized news boxes on a computer desktop, and—if desired—through a Web browser.

The first thing to know about getting news on an intranet is that the choices and options are already overwhelming. Even though the Web is less than five years old, news providers have taken root en masse. Businesses are looking to provide customized online news for their employees not only for the major news wires, but also for Internet news services and news link sites.

The second thing to know about getting news on an intranet is that it can be a very expensive endeavor. Satellite dishes, proprietary software, servers, and publisher royalties do not come cheaply. Businesses that need up-to-date, specialized news that's accessible to the entire intranet can expect to pay about $40,000 per year, and that's the low end of the scale. Before you hide your face behind that newspaper, rest assured that if you are aware of all the options, there's a good chance of getting the news service you need at a price you can afford. The truth of the matter (and this is the third thing to know) is that online news is an Internet boom, and if you familiarize yourself with the heart of the explosion, you will no doubt come out ahead.

In this chapter, I discuss the ways in which you can bring news to intranets. I also review some news providers, such as electronic clipping services and national news wires.

Just the Facts

Online news feeds and news services should be distinguished from topic-oriented, discussion-based newsgroups (such as those on Usenet). The two are different entities. Providing Internet newsgroups to an intranet requires that you install news server software on your intranet server and that you also install a news reader on your client machines. Chapter 37, "Message Boards," goes into more detail about getting access to newsgroups.

Online news is nothing more than the same news you would find in newspapers, on TV, or in hard-copy trade and association journals. The key difference is that you access this news through the Internet. Unlike newsgroups, online news is not participatory. You won't find many online news services or news wires that offer group chat or topic discussion boards (except for technical support). The point of online news is to keep companies up-to-date with the news that might affect them and to bring that news right to the computer desktop.

At first, the idea of online news might not seem to be very advantageous. Online news is expensive and requires technical expertise. Why bother when you can just flick on the TV or pick up a newspaper? The answer lies with the way in which online news is fed into the Internet and—in turn—distributed to users.

News from TV, newspapers, and periodicals is limited in one very important way: It must appeal to a common audience. The audience might be enormous, small, or very specific, but it is always more than one person. This means that the newspaper you receive on your doorstop is a compilation designed to suit the reading needs of (depending on the size of your city) quite a few people. The news that you might be most interested in reading may not make the cut. This is especially true if you have any peculiar hobbies (like collecting bottle caps) or work in a specialized business (like frozen yogurt). Another limitation of print and broadcast media is that you—as the consumer—can read only one newspaper or watch one news program at a time.

Online news is—when dissected—the same news you would find in the mass media, and each story is still addressed to more than one person. But now you have the option of custom-designing news to suit your needs and those of your workplace. Thanks to a few software developers, you can make your own newspaper, your own television news program, your own trade journal, or your own newsletter; roll it all into one package; and have it arrive at your desktop quicker than the carrier can toss a paper to the porch. You can also receive news simultaneously from more than one source. Yet another advantage to online news is that it is possible—if your intranet is properly stocked—to have your news arrive in real time, as it's being reported to the wires.

All these capabilities are possible because no "Internet central" really exists. Although you see references to "cyberspace," the truth is that there is no one space. This idea might at first seem alien, but it means that the boundaries that have been limiting news services since time began are no longer there. The Internet is unlimited in the number of news wires it can support and in the number of stories it can transmit. News sent through the Internet can be retrieved or denied according to the needs of an individual user or to an intranet collective.

The advantages of a customized news service can easily be applied to companies with interdisciplinary departments. An accounting department's need for financial news like up-to-the-minute stock quotes, for example, is much different from the educational and psychology-related news needed by a human resources department. Online news services and Web-accessible news wires can provide for these specific needs. Likewise, each user can read news customized for his or her specific job.

With online news, people can get the information they need for reports, proposals, and other company literature through the intranet as it is coming in. Other needs you might have for real-time news are also served. With ease, you can retrieve up-to-the-minute stock quotes, press releases, and economic data that are specifically oriented toward your company's interests through the Internet. Depending on what sort of news system you establish, all the news that fits will be there when you need it.

Getting Online News

You can bring online news to your intranet in a couple of different ways. You can bring in some good news without any special software or equipment if you simply link all the browsers to some of the free "newslink" sites. Most of the searching services such as Yahoo! and Lycos are fed news by many of the major wires, and they are pretty good about keeping the news up-to-date. Internet providers such as America Online and CompuServe even offer "executive" news, in which you can customize your own news page, for a charge above the regular subscription rate. Figure 40.1 shows the Executive News Service on CompuServe.

FIGURE 40.1.
The Executive News Service is available to CompuServe members at an additional charge.

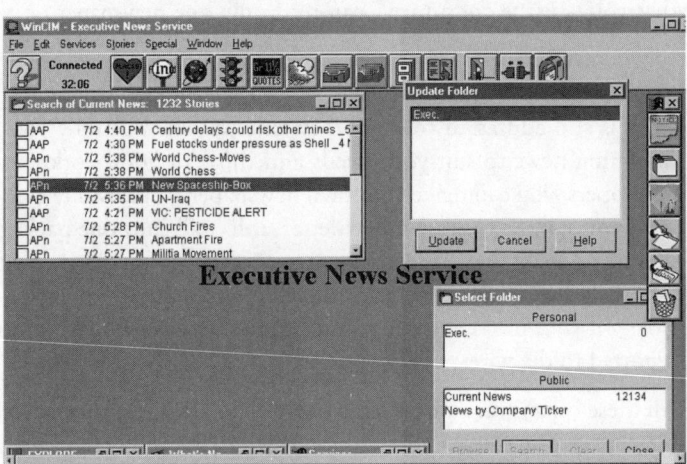

With CompuServe, customized news is an additional charge per user (usually about $15 per hour). The disadvantages, besides the price per hour and mandatory CompuServe membership, are that customized news can be arranged from only three topics (technology, business, and sports). The advantages are that you can read the news on the Web browser after logging onto CompuServe and that it's an inexpensive way to access news just coming in from the wires. For intranets with a minimum need for news—but a real need for up-to-date news—CompuServe could be a good way to go.

Another well-developed free news service is offered by PointCast, Inc. This service, which works with server software, is free because PointCast makes money from the big companies that place ads on their news service (such as 20th Century Fox). Beta copies of the software you need to run PointCast through a Web browser are available for download from the home page at http://www.pointcast.com. The PointCast Network is a combination of client and server software, backed up by the hardware at PointCast Inc. Users can "pointcast" the news that they want. This individualized news is delivered directly to user desktops during idle periods.

PointCast news is gathered from national, international, business, industry, entertainment, and company news, as well as stock quotes, sports scores, weather reports, and other key sources, including major newswires like Reuters. Another good thing about PointCast is that you can use it on Windows 3.1, Windows 95, Windows for Workgroups, Windows NT, and Macintosh.

Free news and low-cost (as in pennies per story) news can be brought from independent (or university-sponsored) sites such as the Clickshare Corporation, shown in Figure 40.2, or New Century News. These companies are linked into Internet news and arrange it according to topic. Participants can use a form to design a customized news page from the links that are most interesting to them. Usually, some sort of user account is required, but right now accounts can be obtained for the asking. You can access Clickshare at http://clickshare.com.

FIGURE 40.2.
The Clickshare Try It Page gives information about the news retrieval service.

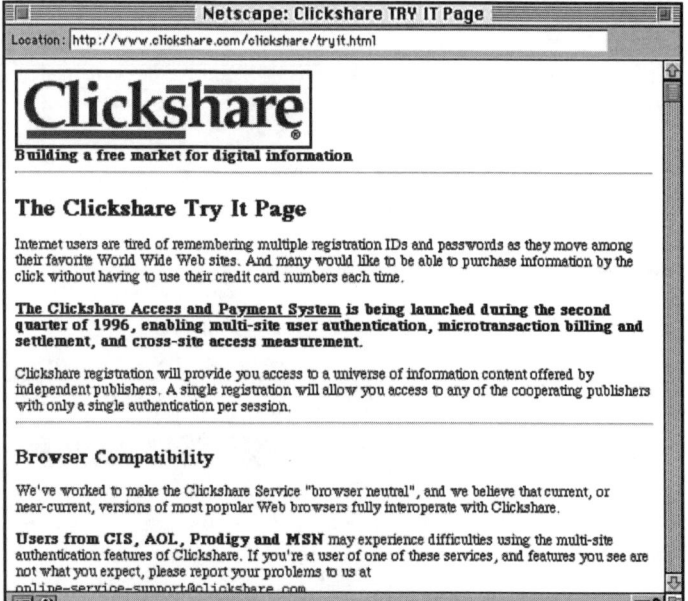

Although these low-cost news links are helpful and might work for parts of your intranet that don't need ready access to news, they aren't going to be quick enough or developed enough to bring a new level of efficiency to a workplace.

To have online news make a difference in the workplace, to depend on it for accurate information, it's best to subscribe to some type of news feed, electronic clipping service, or to install a separate news server that stands alone from the Web server. Which of these three options is best for your intranet depends on the kind of news you need, how much of it you need, and in what form you want it presented.

News That Fits

Intranets function best when users can use a Web browser to access everything they need. For that reason, many clipping services and news feeds that have been part of the Internet for quite a while are beginning to send their news to the Web as well as to the e-mail boxes of their subscribers. Other services have sprouted from the growth of news on the Web and are entirely browser-based.

Companies moving to an intranet from a more traditional LAN might already be subscribed to some type of news service or might be working from groupware such as Lotus Notes. If so, you can—in many cases—integrate news into the already-existing structure. Bringing forth the transition for the news depends on what your current news service offers or how flexible your groupware is. Desktop Data's NewsEDGE and IAC/SandPoint's Hoover, Individual's First! Intranet, and Lexis-Nexis Trackers are all compatible with Lotus Notes. Figure 40.3 shows the Hoover service. Many more groupware packages are likely to begin to address the need for online news.

FIGURE 40.3.
Hoover is an information agent technology for monitoring, searching, integrating, and organizing external information within a groupware environment.

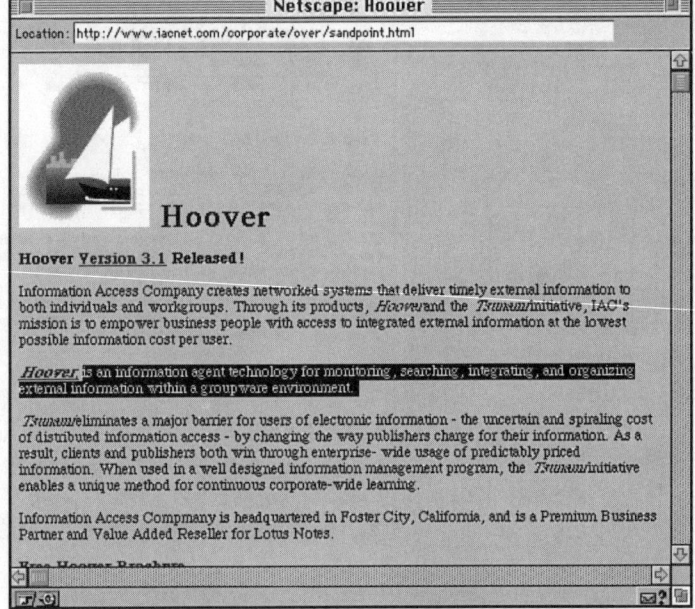

Signing Up for News

Just as subscribing to the daily newspaper is necessary, so is it necessary for an intranet to subscribe to a news feed or an electronic clipping service. Investing in the news is not a matter to take lightly. Subscriptions to news feeds and services can be a huge expense, so choosing them well is important.

Connecting an intranet directly to one of the more well-known national or international news feeds, such as the Associated Press (AP), United Press International (UPI), or Reuters, shown in Figure 40.4, might at first seem most logical. All three of these well-known wires are linked to the Internet and offer subscriptions to interested companies. You can obtain information from any of the three wires through a Web browser such as Navigator or Explorer. The Reuters Business Alert, located at `http://bizinfo.reuters.com`, allows users to read the news through Lotus Notes, and it also creates Notes databases. Reuters Business Alert costs $950 per person per month for 10 users.

FIGURE 40.4.

Long a major news wire and reputable news source, Reuters offers subscribers the opportunity to access news from the wire with a Web browser.

The Reuters Web site offers its subscribers news not only from the Reuters wire, but also from other specialty wires, such as Le Figaro. This variety of news keeps the site competitive with other sites and online news services that are connected to more than one wire. Such is the trend, and many sites offer a cornucopia of news links and feeds, and categorize them for their clients. For example, Bloomberg, also a reputable news wire, has created Bloomberg Personal, shown in Figure 40.5. It is an online news subscriber service that divides news into specialty categories.

The major drawback of subscribing to a major news wire is the expense. Because most of the news is coming straight from the first source, you pay a higher price. Another disadvantage is that many of the news wires are still in the process of making the move to the Web, and they don't offer the variety of news you can get from some of the Internet-originated services.

If your company needs news about a specific trade or industry, specialized news wires such as Business Wire, PR Newswire, or US Newswire offer subscriptions. Specialty wires bring in news from the small press and from lesser-known sources that are not as likely to be part of major news wires. Business Wire focuses on keeping subscribers up-to-date with the stock and other economic news. PR Newswire brings its subscribers a steady stream of press releases from companies around the globe, as well as other corporate information. You can find specialty news wires on just about any topic. They are usually less expensive than the major news wires.

FIGURE 40.5.
Now available to subscribers on the Web, Bloomberg Personal offers news in multiple areas.

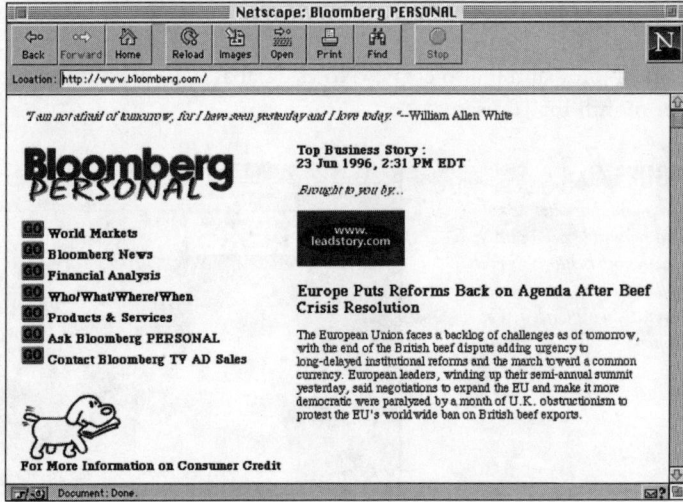

For intranets that need quick access to accurate stock and economic information, Dow Jones offers an online service called DowVision, shown in Figures 40.6 and 40.7. The service is built on the Dow Jones' international news service, the Capital Markets Report, the Professional Investor Report, and the *Wall Street Journal*. In addition, the service provides full text of articles from publications such as *Barron's* and *The New York Times*.

News Clips

In the true sense of the word, a "clipping service" is a company that combs through newspapers and magazines, cutting out articles that pertain to the business of specific clients. The articles are then taped to paper, bundled up, and sent out through the postal service to arrive by a specified deadline.

Electronic clipping services work the same way but without as much paper. For online news, "clipping" means filtering out specified news from the barrage of news coming in from the wires. Clipping services work with specific clients to provide news from trade journals, specialty wires, mainwires, even newsletters. The form in which the news arrives depends on the agency. More and more of them are appealing to the intranet market by making the news available through a Web browser such as Navigator or Explorer. Some services provide news to the desktop of every employee for one price; others charge according to the number of users. Almost all of them allow some customization of the news.

News Feeds
Chapter 40

FIGURE 40.6.
DowVision can be integrated directly into client servers.

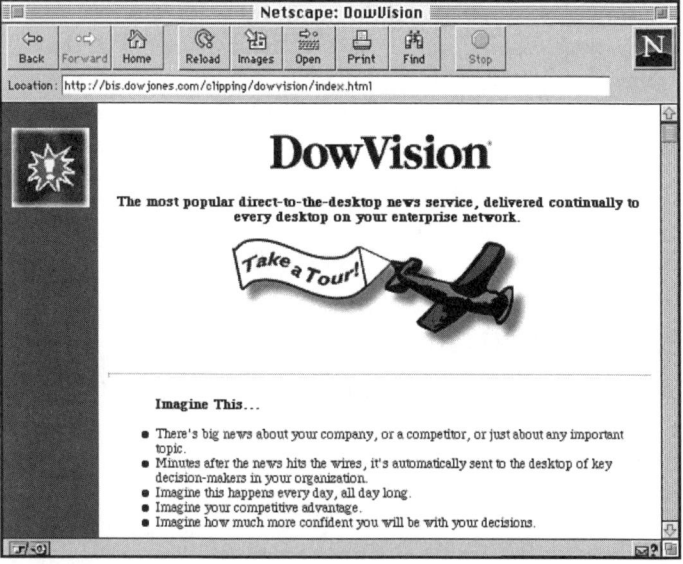

FIGURE 40.7.
DowVision's desktop menu is based on user-specified profiles.

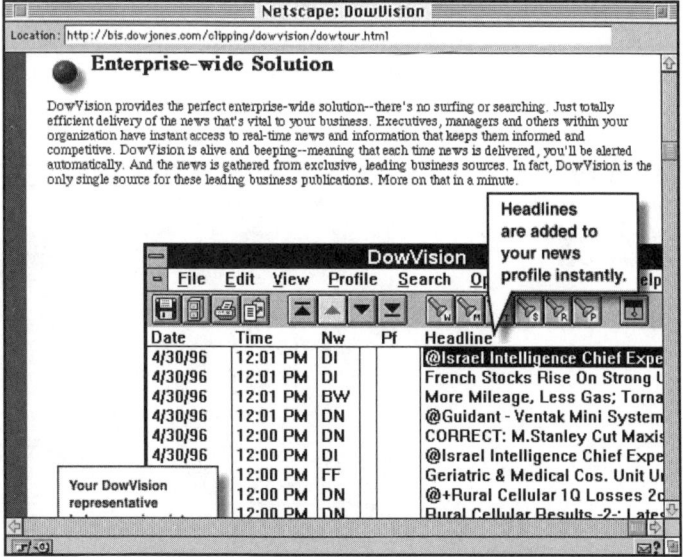

For trade-specific news gleaned from small-press sources, like trade journals and association newsletters, many clipping services offer e-mail digests to be distributed as often as mandated. The digest probably arrives as e-mail, but increasingly, as the Web becomes more mainstream, that will change.

The sort of news you need and the amount of it is determined during the subscription process. The various clipping services have different ways of handling their customers. The prices vary tremendously, as does the type of service. If you need very customized news, you will pay more than a company that can work with more general news. Some of the clipping services, however, are good about offering news that comes from small press sources.

The reviews in the following sections will give you a sense of what is offered by various Internet news clipping services. They are featured here because the of the variety of news they offer and because they customize the news for individual clients.

Information, Inc.

Employees at Information, Inc., in Bethesda, Maryland, arrive at their office at 5 a.m.; spend a few hours going through newspapers, press releases, and periodicals; and then sit down to compress all that news into customized mail and Web digests that are mailed to their clients by 8 a.m.

Information, Inc., considers itself a "business intelligence service" because they work closely with specific clients (see Figure 40.8). Association and trade news is supplemented with articles from national and specialty news wires to create unique bundles that are assigned to one of eleven categories: banking, corporate security, electric power, food service, information technology, insurance and benefits, microcomputers, natural gas, pharmaceutical, real estate, and telecommunications.

FIGURE 40.8.
Information, Inc., works with specific clients to customize news.

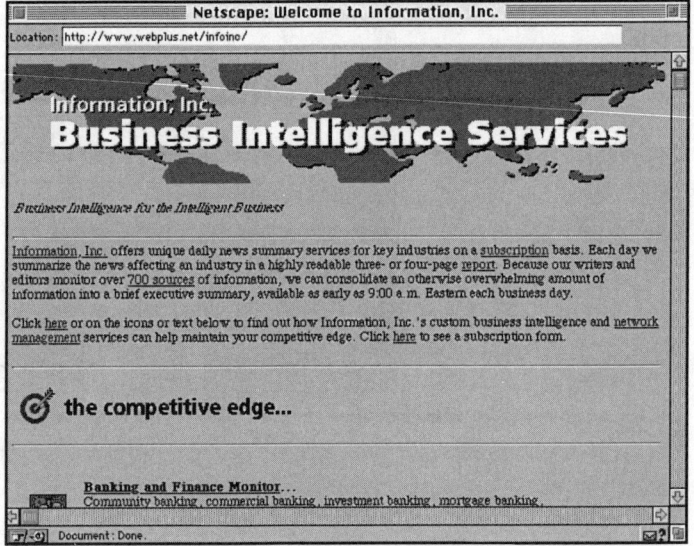

Subscriptions to the service are offered on a monthly or yearly basis, the average price running about $1,500 per month. News about banking, insurance and benefits, and telecommunications is more expensive (see Figure 40.9). If this price sounds steep, consider that a subscription to Information, Inc., includes a site license, which means that the news can be distributed to as many users as necessary.

FIGURE 40.9.

Information, Inc., charges businesses according to the type of news to be delivered.

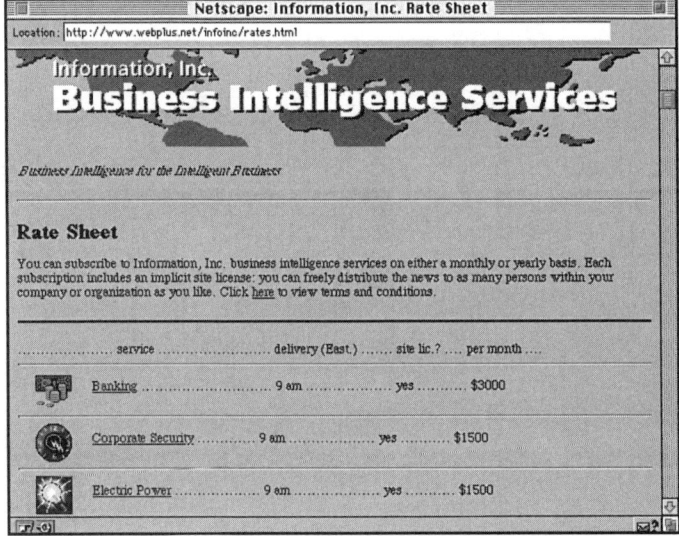

Most electronic clipping services differ from Information, Inc., in that they charge per user or group of users. You might consider this type of service if you don't need customized news for all the users on the intranet, but for only a few people.

MCKEON & JEFFRIES

McKeon & Jeffries decided not to get a newsfeed pumped into the site every day. They have managed, however, to keep their users informed using plain HTML. Each day, a site administrator skims some of the online newspapers like http://www.wsj.com and http://www.washingtonpost.com and news pages like http://www.cnet.com and collects links to relevant articles. He then creates a daily page of links to these articles so that users can quickly and easily get news from the Web. Certainly, this page will never replace the morning newspaper, but it can help to keep users abreast of news from several different sources, and it provides a way for users to skim through news items quickly if they are pressed for time.

Developing Intranet Applications
Part VI

Individual, Inc.'s First! Intranet

In cases where each intranet user could benefit from a customized news page, a subscription to a service such as Individual Inc.'s First! Intranet 2.0 might be in order. For UNIX and Windows NT, First! Intranet is one of the first news feed services specifically for corporate intranets. Users can customize their views so that they receive the stories that are most interesting to them and pertinent to their work, as shown in Figure 40.10. The stories are downloaded from the FTP server at Individual and delivered to the Web servers of their subscribers. Users can view story headlines through a Web browser (or through Notes and Folio Views) and can retrieve full text as needed.

FIGURE 40.10.
With First! Intranet, news stories are categorized according to industry.

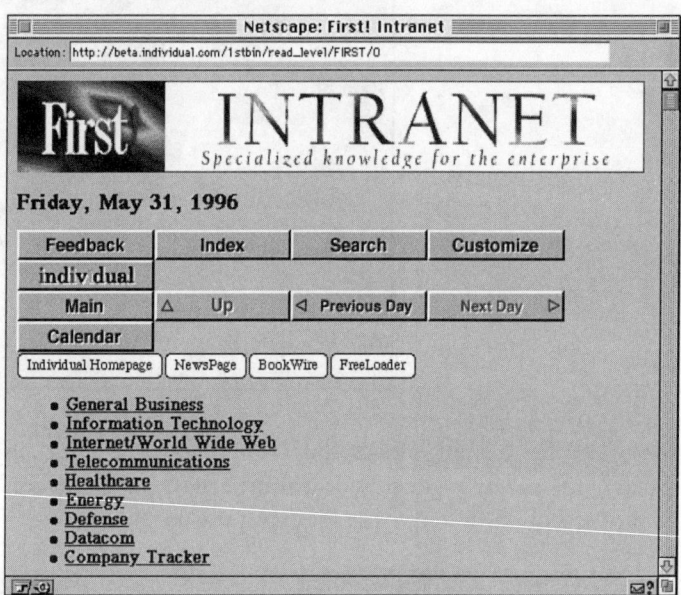

Users of First! Intranet are notified of news updates through e-mail messages. These messages might contain headlines and abstracts of the articles and, in some cases, hyperlinks to the full text. The news can be searched with a Verity Search engine. With news coming from 650 different sources, Individual sorts through about 20,000 stories a day, dividing them into 2,500 topics. All the news sent into an intranet can be archived to create a database of news for future reference, which can be searched with an integrated Verity Search engine. Other features include e-mail briefs, alert messages, and an easy-install mechanism. Figure 40.11 shows a demo of First! Intranet, which is available at http://www.individual.com.

FIGURE 40.11.
A demo of First! Intranet.

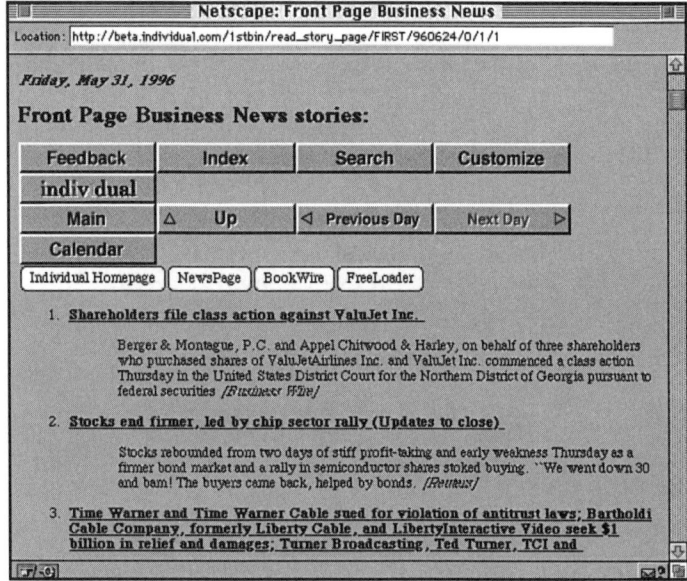

Grayfire

Grayfire's strongest area is business, and they provide a number of investment services and tools. For example, subscribers can build an individualized online stock portfolio. By specifying company names through a form, you can receive the latest stock prices and a listing of headlines from all the sources relating to those companies, including the latest press releases. This news is updated on a real-time basis, as shown in Figure 40.12. Stock quotes are on a 15-minute delay (the standard for the Web).

Grayfire gets their news from well-known providers such as PR Newswire, Business Wire, CNP Publications, Knight Ridder, and Reuters. They also work with the exclusive Market Scope (a special service for brokers and dealers) disseminating the information into more than 60 specialized reports, which you can retrieve through a hypertext menu.

The news is divided according to industry, with at least 30 categories, including auto, health care, pharmaceutical, and other industry-by-industry reports. About 15 different categories cover Internet issues such as online security. Search capabilities will be available soon.

By clicking the appropriate icon, users are provided with the means to redistribute a story through fax or e-mail. Along the same lines, subscribers can receive their information (such as a list of industry-specific headlines) by fax. This capability is helpful in cases where it's not possible to log in.

FIGURE 40.12.

Real-time news for intranets.

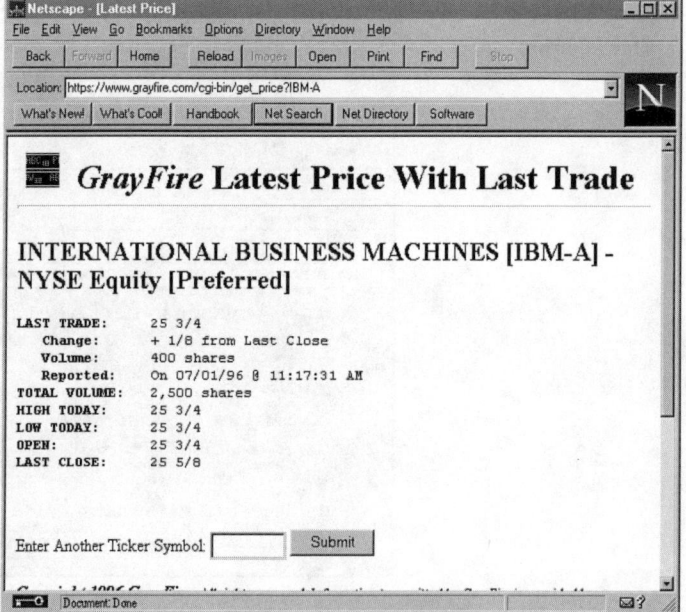

You can obtain a lot on the Grayfire Web site for free. You can look up any stock price and view a 90-day graph of high-low pricing. Subscriptions are $10 a month per 10 stories (full text) and include the custom stock portfolio. Every story after 10 is $1 apiece. Subscriptions are on an individual basis, but site licenses can be arranged. You can also run a private, custom-designed intranet information service from Grayfire.

It seems that "real-time" is the catchphrase for intranets. Web browsers with appropriate plug-ins provide the capabilities for real-time audio, video, messaging, and chat. Some companies such as Desktop Data and Wave Systems are taking things a step further by developing real-time news. Both anticipate that the Web browser will become the primary vehicle for delivering news to intranets and are developing their servers with that forecast in mind.

With the servers, news will come into the intranet as it's being reported to the news wires and as the news service companies update their information. The method of distributing the news to intranets depends on the provider. The ones reviewed here have similar structures but use different means for bringing the news to the computer desktop. In most cases, users will be able to configure the settings to suit their needs throughout the workday.

Network News Corporation by Wave Systems Corporation

The Reston, Virginia-based Network News Corporation works with national and specialty news wires to bring their subscribers news as it's being reported, as shown in Figure 40.13. The stories—obtained from 25 different wires, culminating in about 8,000 pieces per day—are sold individually and are selected from an ever-changing list of headlines. With a metering technology termed by Wave Systems as "WaveMeter," the stories are decrypted and fed into the users' machines by a special server that is a requirement of the system.

FIGURE 40.13.

Network News provides real-time news. Individual users can select specific articles from the desktop.

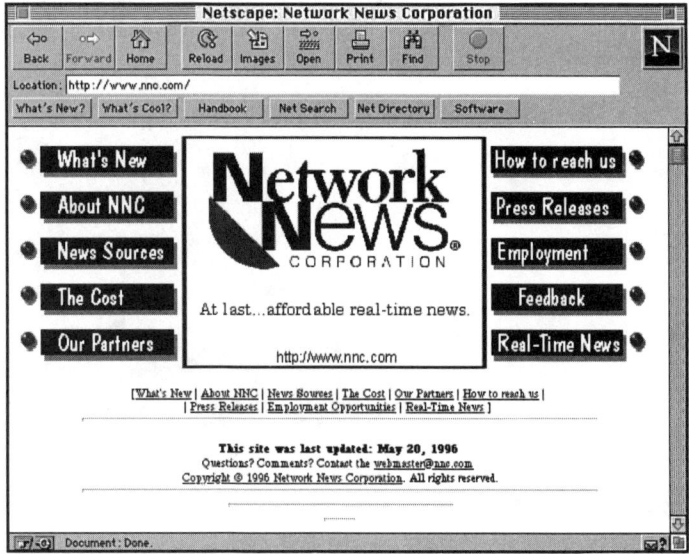

The server, a Pentium PC, is connected to a 24-inch rooftop satellite dish. If you think this system sounds a bit pricey, you're right: The initial setup charge is $11,000 for 25 users. Of this amount, $5,000 is for the Pentium, and the rest is for the dish, the software, and the licensing charges. After the setup, you pay for the stories retrieved from the service; the prices are determined by story length and from what source they were obtained.

NewsEDGE/Web by Desktop Data Corporation

Desktop Data's NewsEDGE server has been supplemented with a module for the Web, so information from 500 news wires and publications can be viewed from the Web browsers of NewsEDGE subscribers, as shown in Figure 40.14. Charges are based on the number of users and the amount of material delivered. For 100 users, businesses can expect to pay about $55,000 per year. With NewsEDGE/Web, users view headlines and the full text of their selected articles through a page they customize themselves. NewsEDGE is available for Windows NT, UNIX, Macintosh, and OS/2.

Developing Intranet Applications

Part VI

FIGURE 40.14.
NewsEDGE/Web by Desktop Data offers real-time news and customized news desks.

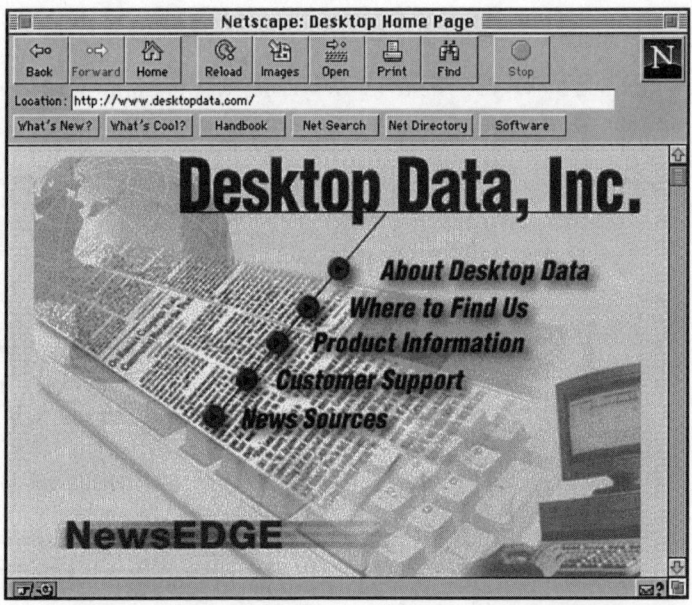

NewsAlert

As a UNIX-based system, NewsAlert is designed to collect, update, and distribute business news according to the needs of individual subscribers. Intranets can use TCP/IP to access the service, which is fully accessible (to subscribers) from the Web. Figures 40.15, 40.16, and 40.17 show how the NewsAlert service works.

FIGURE 40.15.
NewsAlert offers a demo on its Web page.

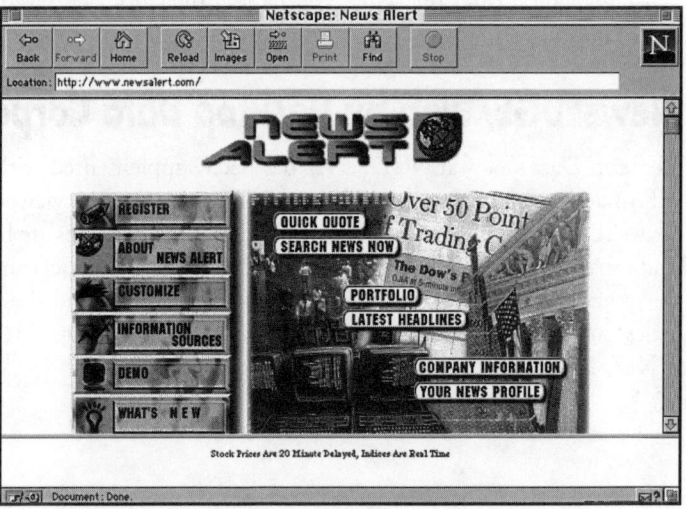

FIGURE 40.16.
To access NewsAlert through the Web, you must first be authenticated by entering a username and password.

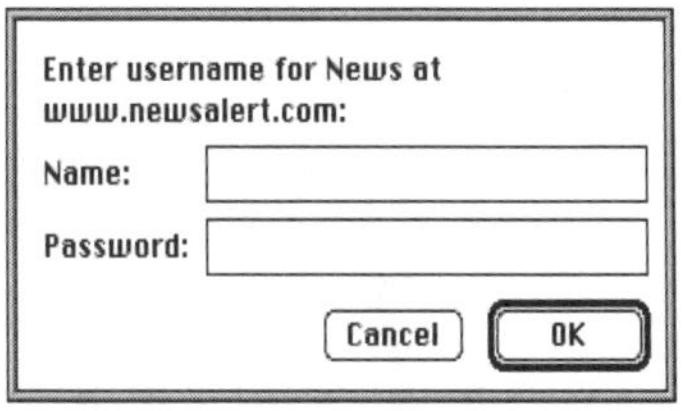

FIGURE 40.17.
NewsAlert lists story headlines. Full text is available to subscribers who click the hyperlink.

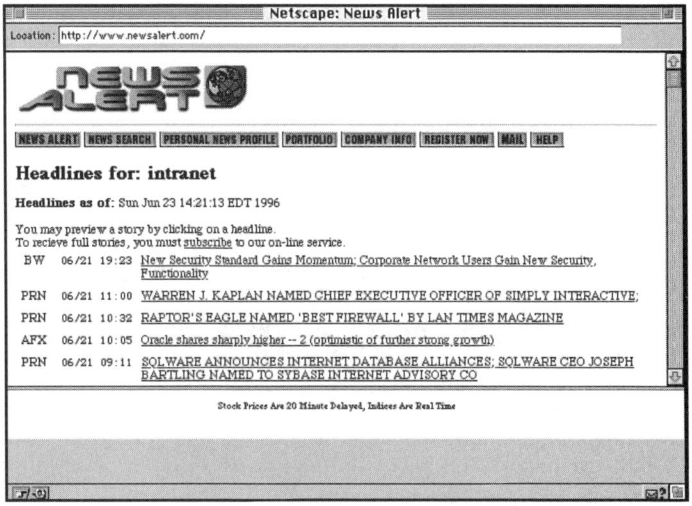

Maintaining a real-time stream for news is an expensive undertaking but can be well worth the price. Providing an intranet with up-to-date information will increase the quality of work produced. Real-time news is not necessary for every intranet, but it does give an extra edge over companies that don't have it. If the extra edge is going to bring your intranet to life, go for the real-time news. You can anticipate that real-time news will be the future of news on the Web.

AUDIO NEWS

Progressive Network is true to their name by bringing online news into the audio stream. RealAudio, the most well-known audio provider to the Web and the most widely used streaming audio application, recently released Timecast: The RealAudio Guide. Timecast, shown in Figure 40.18, makes it possible to navigate your Web browser into custom-designed "narrowcasts" of multimedia news.

With Timecast, you can choose audio clips from dozens of reputable news organizations. What's more, you can access any of the dozens of radio stations that broadcast in real time over the Internet. You can also search through audio databases.

Running Timecast on an intranet requires the RealAudio Player 2.0, which you can download from the RealAudio Web site at `http://realaudio.com`. A beta version of Timecast is available for download at `http://www.timecast.com`.

FIGURE 40.18.
Timecast is Progressive Network's premier online broadcasting tool.

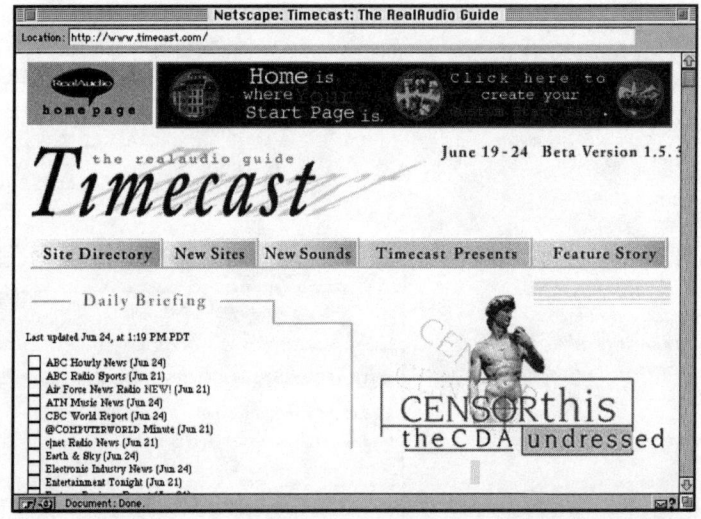

THE SPORTING GOODS AND APPAREL ASSOCIATION

The SGAA provides news to users in a few different ways. The first is through the Reuters online news service. This method gives users news from a first source (Reuters) but also gives them news from the specialty wires and periodicals that Reuters offers. Specific kinds of news items, specifically economic news and financial news, are automatically sent to the site by a contracted electronic clipping service. When these news items reach the site, they are converted by CGI scripts into HTML pages and are served by the Web server when users click on the news page, which is then dynamically generated. This way, users always get the latest news.

In addition to getting news feeds for its members and staff associates, the SGAA staff associates also write news stories that are of interest to association members. These items either appear on a separate page that is created by an administrator and that users can go to at their leisure, or if the news is more timely, the text of the article is fed through the CGI script in the same way the news feeds are and then appears on the news page with all the other news.

Summary

Lifting a home-delivered newspaper from the porch might be the easiest way to get the news, but for an intranet, news is best delivered straight into the Web browser. With real time being the trend of the Web, many companies buy the software and servers required to access news by the minute. If real-time news is too much of an expense, you can turn to one of the numerous electronic clipping services for custom news and quick delivery. Remember that many of the services are focused on offering news from particular disciplines, such as business, and can offer news from a multitude of sources. Major news wires are also offering subscriptions and are developing their own online services. When you're deciding how to bring news into an intranet, you need to consider a few key questions.

First, do you want news from small presses and from hard-copy trade journals? If so, clipping services are the way to go. Many of them have editorial staffs who skim specific periodicals. Another option is to check out the specialty news wires and subscribe to one that shares your focus.

Do you need a wide variety of news? Or do you need news in only one or two disciplines, such as business and technology? If you need news from one general category, and timeliness is not really a factor, you can access the news you need without spending very much money. Consider using one of the free services that allows individualized news pages. Or else subscribe to a news link such as CompuServe's Executive News Service, which allows each user to view up-to-date news from three of any of the offered categories.

Do you need to customize the news access of each of your company's departments? Each employee? Look for an online news service that offers a long list of news sources and also offers the means to customize news pages and desktops. If your company employs hundreds of people, look for a news service that offers one site license rather than a pay-per-user service.

In what electronic form do you need the news presented? Can some of the news arrive in e-mail digests? Or is a Web browser the only form acceptable? Make sure that your subscriptions are to services and wires that bring your news to you in a convenient form. For intranets, it's best if the news can be viewed from the Web browser. Many news services that have not been Web-accessible in the past are beginning to develop browser modules.

Is your company dependent on up-to-the-minute knowledge about economic fluctuations? Real-time news brings in news updates as they are being reported, but you have to pay the price. For real-time news, you need a special server or a wire feed to the subscriber's server.

You can fill the news needs of your intranet in as many different ways as you like. Customization is the key, and it is the element that will change the way news is delivered and received.

Group Document Creation and Editing

41

by David Garrett and Anne Marie Yerks

IN THIS CHAPTER

- Collaborative documents **620**
- Online document collaboration **622**
- Document collaboration for intranets **623**
- Document collaboration applications **627**

In the electronic age, managing group documents on a computer makes sense. The problem is that computers can make the document creation and editing process more confusing than a paper-based system. At least when everything is on paper, you can see it right there in front of you. Little details like paper color, coffee rings, highlighter marks, and handwriting can be helpful clues as to who did what when. On a computer, all those little details are lost when the file is saved and the author trashes the only printout.

The logical solution, of course, is to develop a computerized system for keeping track of document changes. These types of document management systems are already used with success on LANs. Programs such as Lotus Notes offer a sophisticated array of features for tracking changes to documents. Document tracking lets you know what sorts of changes were made to a document, who made them, and when. These little details can keep file shuffling to a minimum and prevent the need for "just-in-case" printouts.

Establishing the means for creating and editing online documents not only changes how you think of desktop publishing, it also changes how your intranet's users will exchange written information. Most likely, it will be a change for the better. You've probably experienced the frustration of having to send paperwork over fax machines or having to wait for a colleague to turn in a report. The stress of paper shuffling can be eliminated if you establish your intranet with the means to create and edit documents straight from the Web browser.

This chapter focuses on how to manage and track group documents on an intranet, using the Web browser as a common interface. Many LAN document management programs (like Lotus Notes) are building tools for the Web. A few Web development software companies are also creating groupware document managers. Toward the end of the chapter, a few of them are reviewed. All these applications allow you to manage documents online.

Collaborative Documents

A *collaborative document* is any file that is created or updated by more than one person. The file might be straight text from a word processor (such as a project proposal written in Microsoft Word), an HTML file, or even an art file (like a JPEG or GIF). Group documents might include daily records, ad copy, memos, meeting minutes, fundraising letters, and press releases.

In the days of paper, collaborative documents were shuffled back and forth among the authors and the person who was to approve (or not approve) a final draft. Then computers came along, and it seemed that a lot of paper shuffling could be eliminated with a simple software application. Thus, document managers were integrated into the workplace.

Ideally, document managers work by tracking the changes made to group documents. Details such as time, date, notes, and authors' names can be obtained by viewing the track record for a particular document. They usually have some sort of "check-in" and "check-out" system so that contributors can save a particular document to a personal computer and work on it off the network. Almost all document managers allow documents to be edited by more than one person at a time (not always simultaneously). Other features allow old versions to be revived and mistakes to be pinpointed. Access to documents can be determined by the head of a user group, by the network administrator, or by a document's original author.

HTML pages that make up internal and external company Web sites are usually collaborative documents. Perhaps one person writes the HTML coding, another person might write the copy, another person makes the art, and yet another person contributes some related text files for links. Updating the site means changing the HTML file, and often the Webmaster or the site administrator must call upon the individuals who originally contributed to the site and ask them to once again add their input. In this case, a Web-based document manager is needed.

Likewise, you can move the entire process of creating and editing collaborative documents from the LAN to the Web, or from paper to the Web. When you're making the transition, you would be wise to determine and weed out the problems that resulted from your old document management system so that the move to the Web will increase efficiency as well as convenience.

The Exquisite Corpse

A party game called The Exquisite Corpse exemplifies the difficulties of creating and maintaining multiple-author documents. The game works like this: One person in a group takes the lead by writing a phrase on a sheet of paper and passes it on. The second person adds a line to the first line and then folds the paper so that only the new line is visible to the next person. This process is repeated until the last person has added a line. The result is a fragmented (yet often hilarious) piece of writing. This piece of collaborative writing is called an Exquisite Corpse because it is truly unique—but, like a corpse, not worth much in the long run.

To avoid afflicting group documents with the Exquisite Corpse syndrome, an online document manager should offer a well-developed method of version control. Poor tracking of a document's changes is the primary reason that group document collaboration doesn't always work efficiently. Problems such as lost old (and needed) versions, misplaced updates, multiple overwrites, and incomplete histories cause workgroup members to lose confidence in the management system. This lack of faith culminates in the need to save a copy of a group document onto a hard drive or floppy "just in case," thereby creating yet another version of a document that has already been saved in more than enough places.

If your documents are breeding like flies, the move to an intranet is a golden opportunity to revamp your company's or department's document collaboration system. Working online can be an advantage in this regard. For one thing, all users will be using the Web browser as their only interface. Using the Web server as the main storage space for a document database brings you the capability to generate dynamic HTML pages from excerpts from collaborative documents and information input through CGI forms. Version control systems are going to vary according to what software application you choose.

With version control, your document goes through a course of states. If you have a document that is created and maintained online, for example, all the departments that are participating in the intranet—regardless of location—can access the document at the same time and edit at their convenience. Each version that is created and uploaded can be stored separately, so no information is ever lost, and users can easily refer to prior versions of the document without deciphering confusing color schemes or engaging in costly and unproductive conference calls or group meetings. Each version is available at each user's fingertips.

Another advantage of group document collaboration is faster communication. The waiting period between revisions and reviews is quicker simply because the document is available on demand from the site. Additionally, holdups like misdirected faxes, overnight delivery, or courier calls are eliminated if the document in question is online.

> **NOTE**
>
> David Rowley, Vice President of Business Development for Mortice Kern Systems, an Ontario-based software development and marketing company, has developed seven criteria to follow when choosing or developing a document collaboration system. According to Rowley, a document collaboration tool should enable you to do the following:
>
> - Retrieve any specific copy of a file from the file repository, no matter how many new versions have been developed
> - Lock the file so that others can't change it while you edit
> - Put the file back into the archive
> - Unlock or lock the archive
> - Identify the different versions with a number or a name
> - Provide an index or list of changes made
> - Allow simultaneous changes on files that are not locked
>
> Rowley's criteria are based on the years he has spent manipulating document databases for Mortice Kern.

Online Document Collaboration

Online document management systems are not limited by geography. Workgroup members can join their skills and talents together to create a group document, no matter what part of the world they are coming from. Assume, for example, XYZ Incorporated, with offices in New York, Chicago, and Seattle, decides to use its intranet to put together its year-end report.

Because the central accounting is done by the CFO in New York, the Chicago and Seattle accountants can upload their statements to the New York office, which crunches the numbers and puts the document on the intranet so that the other offices can download the file and check it for accuracy.

Next, the writer in the Seattle office writes the surrounding text and sends it back to the legal department in Chicago, which downloads it to make sure the wording is appropriate. The lawyers, of course, have to send the document back to the writer who has to make 467 changes. When the lawyer re-reads the edited version, she wants to check it against the original version, which is still there on the intranet. Then the art department in New York downloads the file, adds the art, and uploads it so that the CEO, who is vacationing in Ecuador, can give the final okay—no FedEx, no faxes, no losing a version between one office and another.

Document Collaboration for Intranets

One easy way to start group document collaboration on an intranet is to use forms to create descriptive Web pages for each document you upload to the server. Figure 41.1 shows an example. The pages can contain information about the document and a link to the document itself (for viewing or for downloading). If the pages are HTML, they are searchable by a standard search engine and can be tracked with version control.

FIGURE 41.1.

A searchable Web page describes a document and provides a link to it.

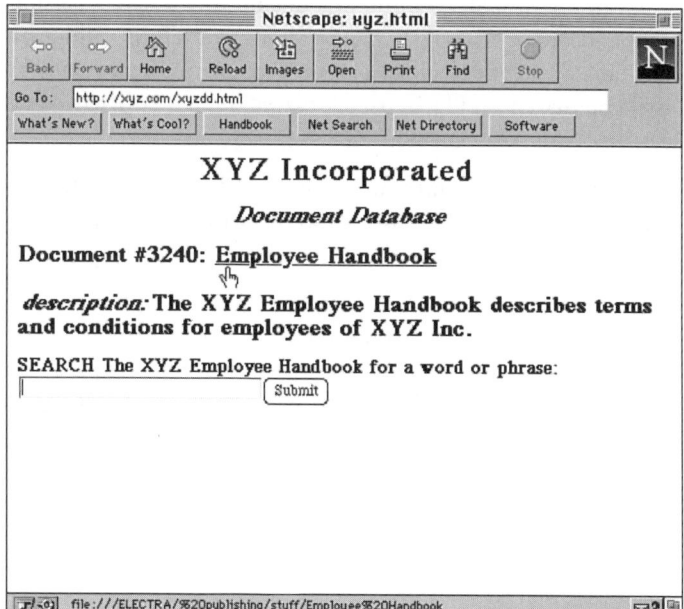

The forms you use for document descriptions can be custom-designed according to your needs. If the document collaboration process at your company or department is already sophisticated enough to be running from a LAN document manager, or if you want to develop a sound online collaboration process, then one of the intranet suites, or an intranet application development tool, is in order.

Most of the intranet-specific applications on today's market are not specifically focused on document collaboration and management, and there is a good reason for that. The applications within intranet suites (packages that combine intranet applications) are designed to integrate with one another. Such integration is especially useful when you're dealing with group documents. If you want to be able to mail a document to someone outside the workgroup, for example, a document manager that is fully integrated with an e-mail program allows for easy transport. Along the same lines, having a document manager that is integrated into a contact database makes it easy to create a list for sending the document out to more than one person at a time. These are just a few examples of what's possible with an integrated document collaboration system.

Besides the intranet suites, you always have the option of developing a customized document collaboration system. To do so, you might use an intranet development tool such as WebShare by Radnet. WebShare, shown in Figure 41.2, is one of the first commercially available development tools designed especially for intranets. A demo is available at http://www.radnet.com.

You can use WebShare to build a document database. Version control fields (such as time, date, and author of changes) can be arranged in a form. Filling out the form could be a requirement to upload or download a group document from the database. The documents themselves could be viewed as HTML pages or saved to a hard drive in whatever format is available on the database.

WebShare allows administrators a great deal of liberty in designing applications for group collaboration on documents, as well as other intranet functions. You can fine-tune the controls according to your needs.

A development product like WebShare works best if a programmer is around to create the applications as needed. If you want a document collaboration program that is already intact, one of the suite applications or a workflow product would be more suitable. The following sidebar gives you some factors for consideration when choosing a document collaboration application.

Group Document Creation and Editing
Chapter 41

FIGURE 41.2.
WebShare is a development tool for intranets.

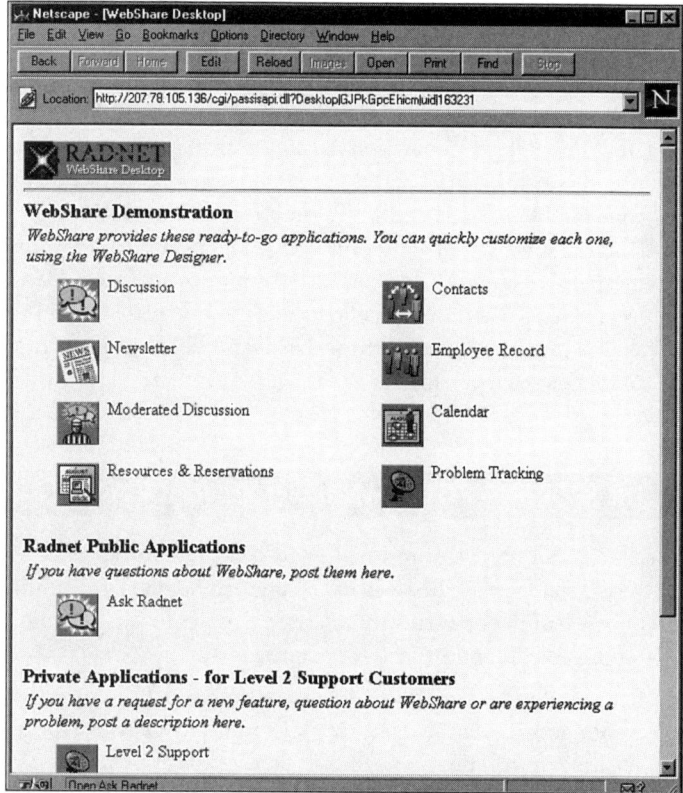

MCKEON & JEFFRIES

One of the primary uses for McKeon & Jeffries' new intranet is to provide an easy way for various employees in different locations to facilitate the creation and editing of documents. Because of the cost constraints, real-time group editing was not an option. The software was either not available or too expensive. The accounting firm devised a simple strategy, however, using its FTP server and simple HTML to better manage the editing of documents by different employees.

The plan consists of creating an area called "Documents" on the Web site. In this area, each individual document on the site is given its own Web page. Users access this page to find out information on each version of the document, such as who created it, who edited each version and when, as well as the links to download it.

Using this interface, getting information on a document and downloading any version are simple. Uploading new versions, on the other hand, is a little more difficult. One employee was given the responsibility for managing and maintaining the documents area. To "upload" a new version to the area, a user merely has to click on the administrator's name and e-mail the latest version as an attachment. Then the administrator edits the HTML file and FTPs the new document to the server. Although not the most efficient way of managing documents and group editing, this strategy allows for a very inexpensive way for McKeon & Jeffries to control documents and versioning, as well as have an easy interface that allows their simple search engine to find documents on the site. Because each document has its own HTML page, it can be found easily using its simple search mechanism.

THE SPORTING GOODS AND APPAREL ASSOCIATION

The SGAA had plans to invoke much the same strategy as McKeon & Jeffries but in a very different way. Because of the powerful database running behind its server, the SGAA had the opportunity to create a much more dynamic way for individuals and groups to edit and maintain documents.

Instead of maintaining the documents on an FTP server, the association stores the documents inside the database. This not only provides for more efficient means of version control, but also provides an extra layer of security. Because the documents are not sitting on an FTP server on the Internet, they are not available for download by just anyone. Using the database also provides a way for each user to be authenticated before downloading or uploading a file.

The interface built by the SGAA is similar to that built by McKeon & Jeffries, with two important distinctions. Unlike at M&J, the page is not created manually in HTML by an administrator. Instead, it is created dynamically through online forms filled out by the user. The data from these forms is used to modify the information on the document page. The other important distinction is the method for uploading documents to the server. Uploading is accomplished using the browser feature and an FTP script written by the consultants who helped SGAA build the site. Users can merely click a button, find the file on their hard drive, and submit the file to their server. It is automatically stored on the database, and the document page is updated. This system allows for more sophisticated version control and more efficient document management.

Document Collaboration Applications

Now you're ready to look at some applications created by companies who are in the process of developing document collaboration applications. At this point, not many exist. Online document collaboration is still being tested and developed. The three reviewed here are featured because they are focused toward group collaboration—not just with writing documents but also with other types of work. Anticipate that group-oriented document software will be at the heart of many intranet suites in the future.

IntraActive's InTandem

IntraActive's InTandem, shown in Figure 41.3, is a complete server-side intranet software package. Its features include integrated document management and version control. Accessing InTandem using only a Web browser, users can upload and download documents, programs, or any other types of files to and from the server. InTandem automatically displays the author who uploaded a file and checks out files when they've been downloaded to prevent others from editing them. Authors also are given the opportunity to create searchable summaries of their documents. Version control identifies the most recent version and provides access to older versions.

InTandem allows users to share files in their native format. One user therefore can upload a Microsoft Word document to the server, for example, and then another user can download, edit, and re-upload the document without ever converting it from a Microsoft Word file. In this way, InTandem users can edit documents with their favorite word processing application without having those documents' layout garbled by reformatting.

Thuridion Crew: Locker

Like InTandem, all applications in the Thuridion Crew Intranet Suite are used inside a Web browser. For document management, Crew members use the Locker application, which is shown in Figure 41.4. You can think of Locker as an Internet file cabinet, a repository set up in a hierarchical environment. You can upload and download text files, graphics, and audio clips by opening and closing the locker door. Access to group lockers can be set by the creator of an original document or document set, or by the site administrator.

After opening a locker, you click the document you want to download. If you save it as HTML, you can then view it right in browser. You also have the option of saving the document in another format (such as Microsoft Word) and saving it to your hard drive.

Crew's Locker version control is minimal right now. It requires that users change the name of a document each time they make changes. Future versions will offer a more sophisticated means of version control. Despite the minimal version control features, Locker can be a good choice if you are especially interested in fully integrating all your intranet applications. Locker integrates with other Crew applications (such as CardFile, Calendar, and Messenger) seamlessly.

Developing Intranet Applications

Part VI

You can put a group of documents in a crew locker and link an e-mail message to the locker so that recipients of the message have instant access. Locker documents can contain hyperlinks to other documents in other lockers or to a specified date on a group calendar.

FIGURE 41.3.
InTandem features integrated document management and version control.

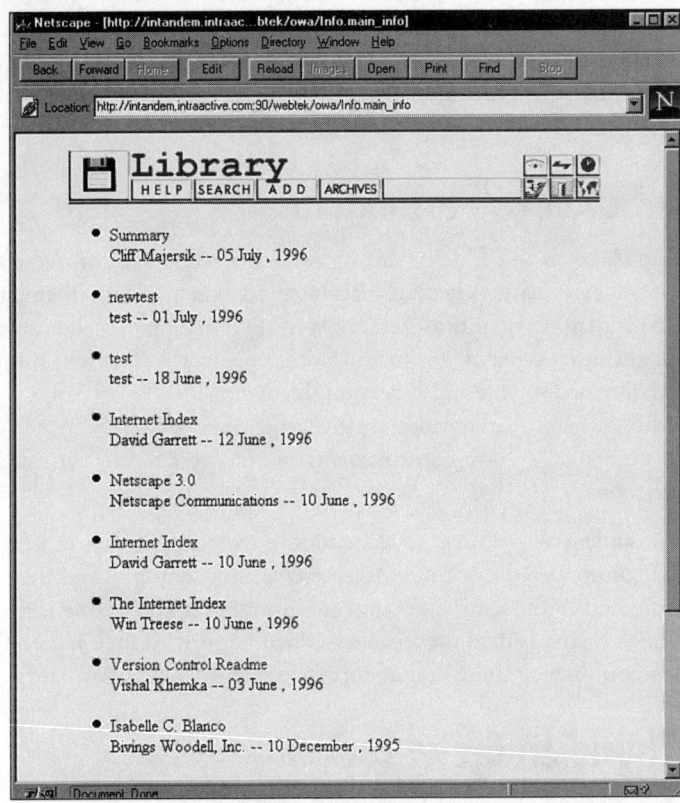

FIGURE 41.4.
Each Crew member has a locker for file sharing.

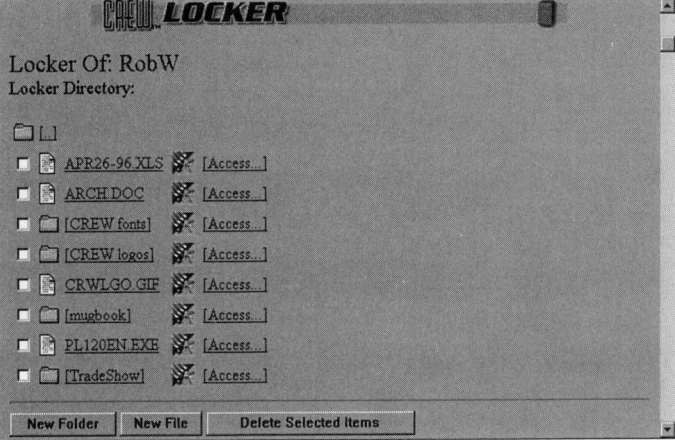

WebFlow Corporation's SamePage Intranet Work Processor

SamePage, by the California-based WebFlow corporation, differs from suites like InTandem and Crew in that it is designed for a small workgroup (10 to 15 people) and in that its focus is to provide "work processing." Rather than delegate specific intranet functions to individual applications, SamePage is one application with many different functions, all of which contribute to the general work flow.

For document management, SamePage works with the idea that a document as viewed on an HTML page is not really a document but merely a representation of a document. SamePage plays on this idea by letting users make comments directly in a document rather than as attachments. SamePage calls these collaborative documents "live documents."

To create a SamePage live document in a word processor, you save or convert it to HTML, put it on the network drive, and import it into SamePage. A copy of the file is then part of the work flow. It is open for comments by other workgroup members (or by whomever you specify), and the document can be updated directly from the SamePage application. A history marker shows why and when changes were made. (See Figures 41.5 and 41.6.)

FIGURE 41.5.

You can open a SamePage work folder into a Web browser.

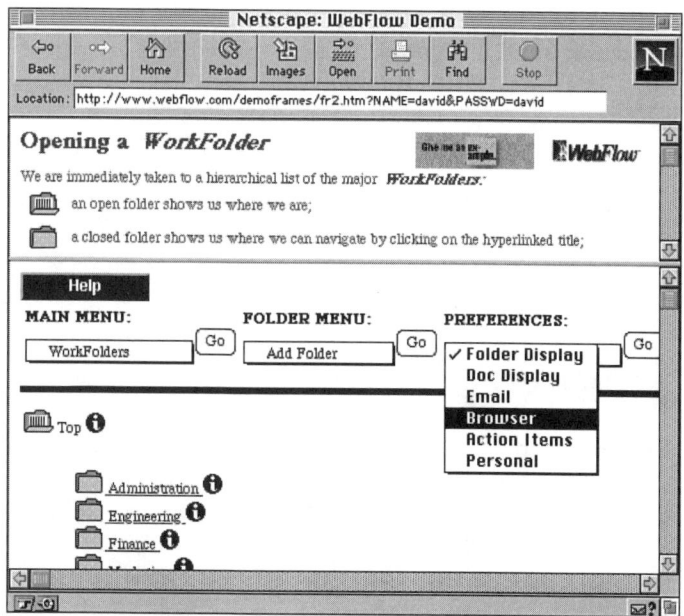

SamePage gives you the means to declare other workgroup members "mandatory" or "optional." Mandatory members get e-mail messages as reminders to look and comment on specified SamePage documents. The administrator can determine a length of time for which a particular document is up for review.

FIGURE 41.6.
A SamePage folder contains documents pertaining to specified projects.

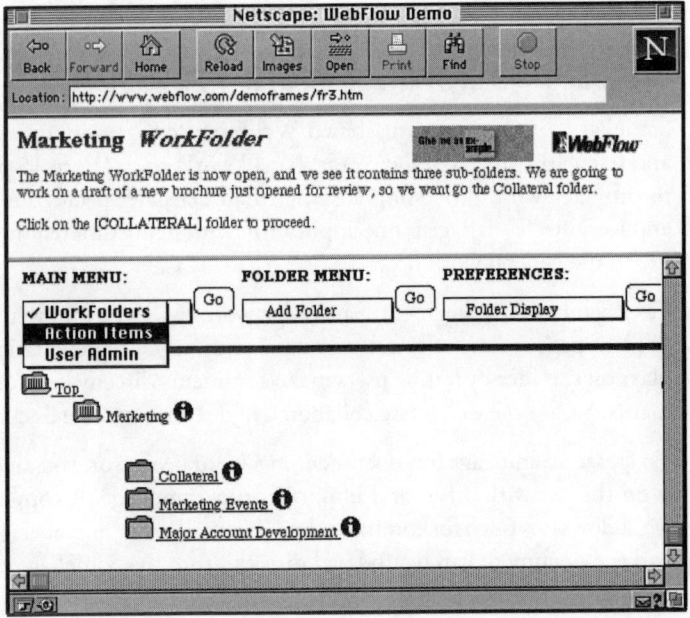

Another feature allows members to assign activities to other members and to make those assignments right inside a SamePage document. Members also can supplement a document with hyperlinks and images. A special voting feature can establish a topic on which all workgroup members can cast a vote. The document or page can be redrawn according to votes received.

A SamePage document looks like a document but is really a representation of the power of database information systems. You can reconfigure, update, add, and subtract as much as you like. If your intranet documents are often generated from a small workgroup, an application like SamePage would serve you well.

Summary

Collaborative online documents have the advantage of being a product of the knowledge, skills, and talents of many different people. When contributing to a process is simple and convenient, people will do so. Online group document creation and editing applications can be a low-cost alternative to paper shuffling and miscommunication. If your company has any sort of ongoing documentation, the intranet can become its new home. The prepress expense of publishing manuals, directories, and marketing materials will decrease significantly when all parties work together in a common text.

Software applications that provide a document collaboration function should be flexible, user-friendly, and should be easily integrated into database, scheduling, and other intranet applications.

Creating custom group document applications is a matter of minding the online environment. Use a language that is suited for the functions you want to establish. If you keep yourself open to the potential of group document development, you are likely to come out on top of the paper heap.

Private Messaging Areas

42

by Anne Marie Yerks

IN THIS CHAPTER

- Private message boards for intranets **634**
- Customizing message board software for privacy **635**
- Conference software for the Web **638**
- Privacy issues **646**

The Internet's resources are as wonderful as they are because of the public environment, but most creative acts require peace, quiet, and privacy. Could Michelangelo have painted the Sistine Chapel with thousands of people watching him? Probably not. More than likely, he closed those chapel doors behind him every morning when he went to work. And many of us do the same.

One reason that many companies build intranets is to create a private—but online—working environment for their employees. When company projects are in their early stages, too vulnerable to be exposed to the entire world, privacy is integral to their success.

Intranets, unlike the Internet, are not open to the public—unless you want them to be. Most companies have a public site and a private site; the two might be linked to some degree, but for the most part, the private site is off-limits to outsiders. Within that private site are private areas, which means that they are not accessible to all members of the intranet. This chapter discusses why and how to set up one of those private areas: the private message board. Chapter 37, "Message Boards," details searching for message board software. This chapter focuses on uses of a private message board and what software lets you customize message boards for privacy.

Any password-protected board could be considered a private message board, but for an intranet, you want the means for creating message boards that can be accessed only by specific users. For example, a company's art department might have an independent messaging area that is not accessible by users in other departments. An online message board open only to specific intranet members is sometimes called an *online private conference*. In this chapter, the terms "private conference" and "private message board" are used interchangeably.

Private Message Boards for Intranets

When you're out of town on a business trip and you need a private place to work, it's easy enough to hang the "do not disturb" sign on your hotel room door. Likewise, when you're in the office, special project meetings with colleagues can be held in a locked conference room, and your calls can be forwarded to voice mail.

This same ease of privacy is possible on an intranet with private message boards. In a sense, they can serve as electronic versions of the "do not disturb" sign and the locked conference room door. To get a better sense of how they work, consider the example of an intranet operated by a fictional hospital called Border General.

Border General Hospital in Seattle is developing both a private and a public Web site. What's unique about the internal site (the intranet) is that parts of it are open to the patients and their families. When walking into the main lobby of Border, visitors can use a computer to enter an online welcome booth. Directions to the wards, cafeterias, and the gift shop; a contact list; and FAQs for various health questions are contained in the information center. For the most part, this is as public as Border's intranet will get. Anyone walking in the door can access the welcome booth, but patients and their families can be authorized to access other parts of the intranet. This is where private message boards come in.

The hospice nurses thought of the idea. After developing their skills on the intranet, they wanted to create a message board specifically for each patient in the oncology ward. The problem was that all information about patients must be kept confidential. Not only is this rule of confidentiality a tradition, it's also required by the hospital's insurance company.

Thanks to the intranet's administrative team, the patient message boards became a reality. They configured the message board software so that a password is required for access. To get a password, a user must first be authorized by the hospital. The nurses and the doctors are automatically authorized to access the message boards of the patients they care for. The patient can allow family members and—in some cases—close friends access to the message board.

By using the board, doctors and nurses can update family members about a patient's condition and post documents to the board. It also allows family members to have easy communication with the hospital while they are at work. Because the message board is online, it can be accessed from anywhere. Family members who live long distances away from the hospital can check the message board—as long as they have been appropriately authorized.

Other posts to the message board include instructions on administering medicines (helpful for patients who go home from time to time), journal articles relating to the patient's condition, and letters of support. Again, all the data generated from the board must remain confidential. When the patient is released, the board must be deleted from the server by the intranet administrator.

Maintaining patient confidentiality is a matter of first concern for Border General, and with the private message board system, the hospital truly comes out ahead. Not only do the private message boards provide easy access to Internet resources, but they also keep patient records private.

Customizing Message Board Software for Privacy

Group conferencing is part of the Internet's public tradition. Usenet, the popular message board forum, is entirely public and free of charge. Because no one is restricted or banned from Usenet, it has become something like the "downtown" of cyberspace: It's rich with culture but not so private.

Private conferences are more likely to be found on the World Wide Web, because the conferencing software for browsers is more sophisticated than the text-only system that makes up Usenet. On the Web, visitors register for a private conference by entering their names, addresses, business affiliations, and other personal information into an online form (see Figure 42.1). After obtaining a username and password, users are eligible to participate in the Web conferencing forums.

Developing Intranet Applications

Part VI

FIGURE 42.1.
Visitors to The Well are required to fill out an online form before they can fully access the conference area.

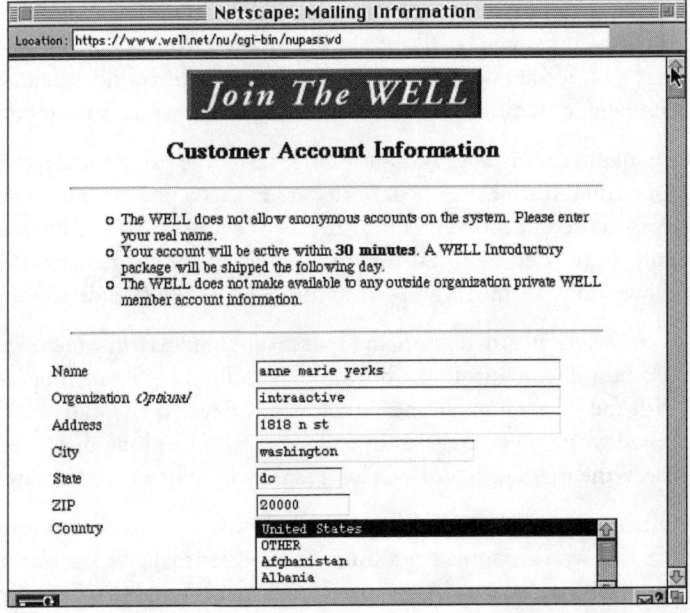

Having the ability to restrict access to Web conferences means that companies that want to make money from their external sites can do so. Users enter a credit card account number into the form for immediate payment. Another developing trend is "cybermoney," such as that offered by companies like Cybercash (see Figure 42.2). The Cybercash home site is located at http://www.cybercash.com.

On an intranet, it's not likely you would be charging employees for access to conferences, but you still might use a form with pull-down menus to have users register. The fields included in such a form will depend on what type of information you want to obtain from the conference members. Most likely, you'll have fields for name and username. A password field might be included if you want the members to choose their own passwords. Other fields might include social security number, address, mail stop number, department affiliation, and comments.

If users are given the ability to create their own private conferences, another form should be used. In addition to asking for basic personal information, this form would also require the conference initiator to determine a topic for the conference. Topic fields might be predetermined (such as business, art, accounting) and the user could set a subcategory. The user might also have the option of choosing other conference members. This selection process could be accomplished through the form.

FIGURE 42.2.
Cybercash-secured "wallets" can be purchased through the Cybercash home site.

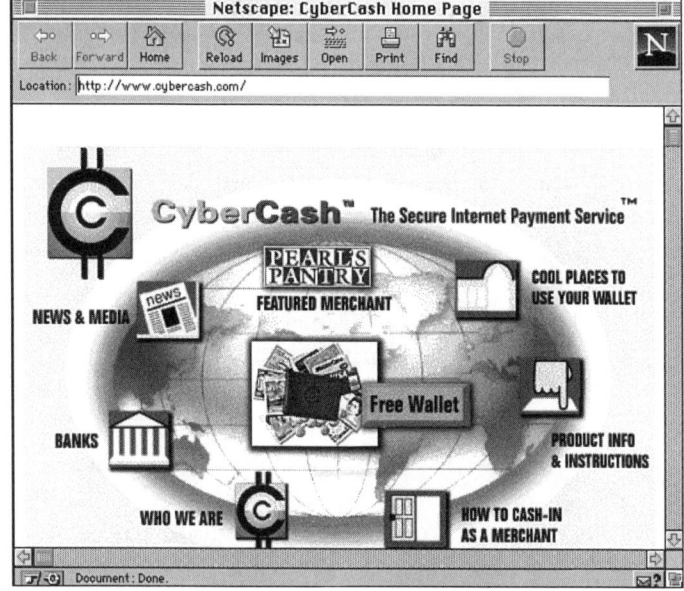

Removing private conferences might be a task for the site administrator, or it could be an option for the user who originally set up the conference. No matter how the conference itself is removed, the issue of what to do with the data generated from the conference comes to light. In many cases, you will want to preserve the postings from private conferences. They could be useful at later times, for a variety of reasons. It's best to have a tightly secured archive for this data. Security for the archive should be handled by a trusted expert.

In some cases, the private message board data can be deleted when the board expires. This prevents hackers from finding and reading it. The problem with completely deleting the data is that it's possible that the postings from message boards, private ones in particular, will be needed at some later time. For example, Border General (the hospital profiled in the preceding section) encrypts the data from the private boards, stores it on tape, and then locks it in a safe. This might seem like a lot of trouble, but it is well worth it. In case of a lawsuit, the data is there and can be easily retrieved and presented as evidence in a courtroom. Details like the time and date that particular postings were made can make all the difference to a jury.

How you store your data, and if you store it, will be one of the many decisions to make as you build your intranet. Whatever you choose to do, play it safe.

MCKEON & JEFFRIES

M&J had a relatively limited need for private messaging areas. They really just wanted to create an area where a few partners could discuss sensitive issues without the entire firm seeing the conversation. The accounting firm created a "Budget," a "Steering," and a "Human Resources Managing" private message board, where the executive committee and the board could talk about those issues, using the same software that it did for the public message boards: WebNotes. WebNotes is a simple message board system that runs on the firm's Windows NT server.

To make it a private area, McKeon & Jeffries put these new message boards in a special directory on the server, which was given a special authentication. For simplicity's sake, this area had one username and password given to each user who was granted access. In this manner, only those selected users could access the private messaging area.

Authentication was handled through the user database. One of the most interesting features of M&J's private message board system was the method of showing users only the private message boards to which they had access. Thus, there were no closed doors.

THE SPORTING GOODS AND APPAREL ASSOCIATION

The SGAA, on the other hand, decided to use its sophisticated message board system to create private messaging areas as well. Using its system, any user could create a new, private message board and select the users to whom he or she wanted to give access. To that end, if a particular sector of the association wanted to talk about issues in private, it could do so. For example, a group of resellers wanting to discuss sales techniques could keep that information private from other resellers and distributors. In the same manner, the budget or new member committee of the association could form a private messaging area to discuss private issues.

Conference Software for the Web

To create private messaging areas, you must configure your software to authenticate users who want to log into the private areas. If you are a programmer, you could write your own software for password protection. Some of the messaging board software on the market allows administrators to protect specified message boards. For example, InTandem, by IntraActive, allows conferences that are open to the entire intranet, as well as conferences for specific users. InTandem provides users with the option of creating private virtual meeting rooms or conferences for communicating with a select group of people. Following the same format used for message boards (see Chapter 37), conferences are presented in an easy-to-use, completely interactive format (see Figures 42.3 through 42.5).

Private Messaging Areas

Chapter 42

FIGURE 42.3.

The messaging areas on InTandem can be viewed according to conference topic.

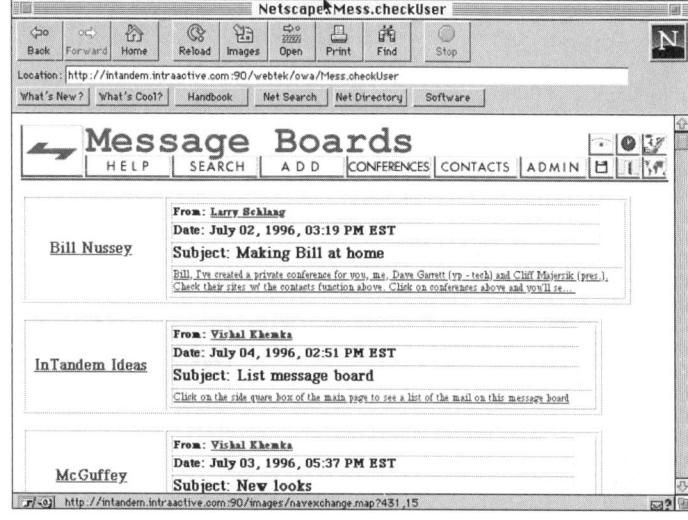

FIGURE 42.4.

InTandem users can enter a command to see in which conferences they have membership.

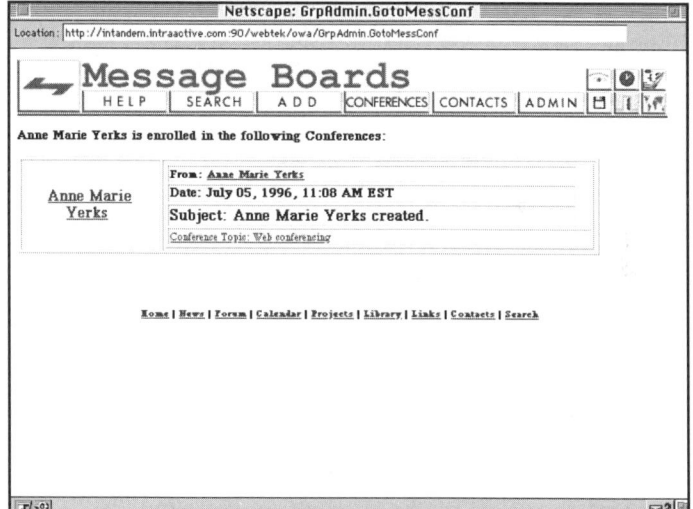

IntraActive's software allows individual users to create their own private discussion areas to which only a limited number of people can gain access. Creating a conference is simple; users type information into a form that specifies the subject of the conference and then select which intranet users should be included in the discussion. Using just a Web browser, authorized individuals can instantly delete or modify a conference by adding or removing participants from the discussion.

Part VI *Developing Intranet Applications*

FIGURE 42.5.
InTandem allows users to determine conference participants upon creating the conference.

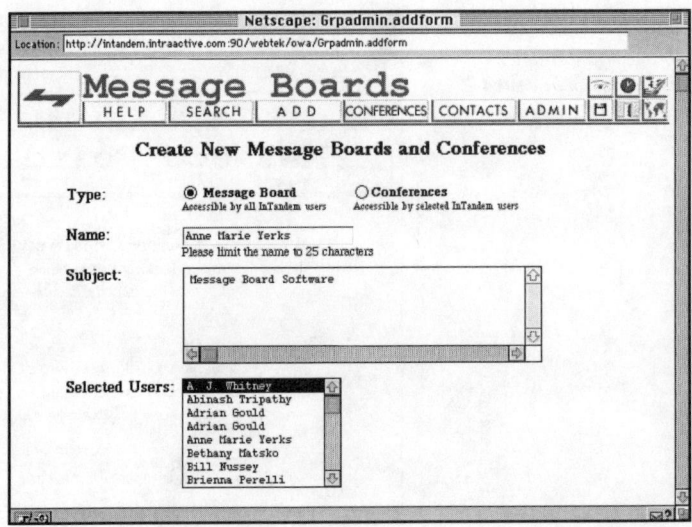

When a user enters the conference area, he or she immediately sees all the conferences to which he or she is enrolled. Users only become aware of the existence of a particular conference when they are enrolled in it.

Authorized users can post new messages to a conference or reply to messages that have already been posted. As in the main message board area, replies are linked (or threaded) with the original message, and users can toggle between chronologically and threaded-subject–sorted views. Users have the option of embedding hypertext links or images in messages.

Other Web messaging software applications work similar to InTandem. The ones reviewed here were chosen because their private message board features were specifically developed, in contrast with other message board software applications.

Forums.com by the Media Machine, LLC

The highlight of Forums.com, by the Media Machine, LLC, is the user-customizable interface. Threaded discussions can be mapped or sorted according to time posted. A choice between a graphic or text navigational bar is also provided. Forums.com runs on a SQL (simple query language) backend database. Customized versions are available.

Unlike InTandem, Forums.com is not part of an intranet suite. It is stand-alone Web conferencing software. If you do not plan to purchase an intranet suite but still want to have well-developed online conferences, Forums.com would be a good choice. Figures 42.6 through 42.8 show several aspects of Forums.com.

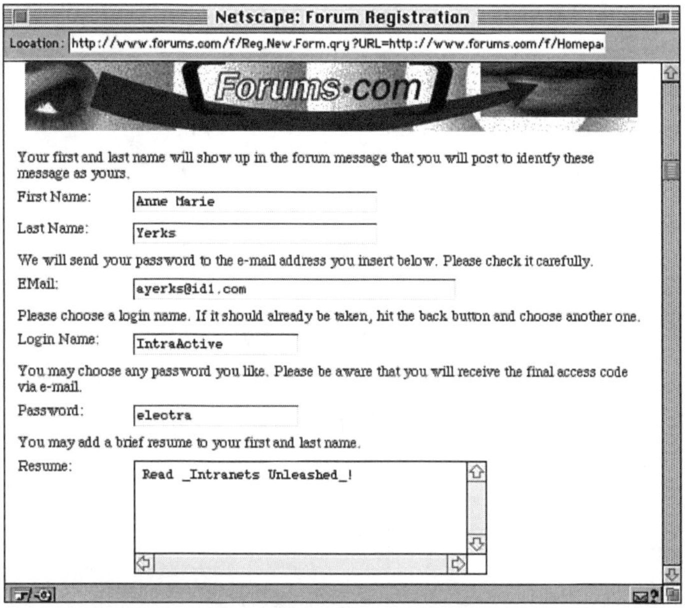

Private Messaging Areas
Chapter 42 641

FIGURE 42.6.
Users are required to fill out a registration form before participating in Forums.com conferences.

FIGURE 42.7.
A form is used to post a message to a Forums.com conference.

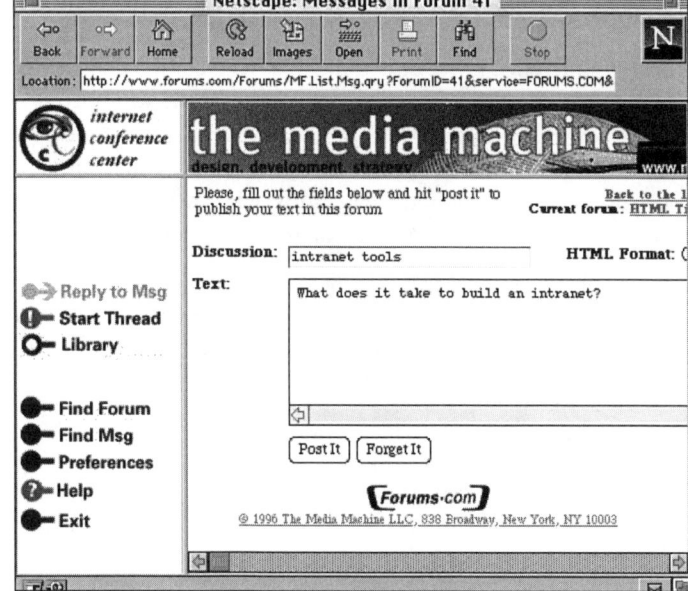

FIGURE 42.8.
Discussions are listed alongside abstracts. Forums.com users can click a link to view a discussion thread.

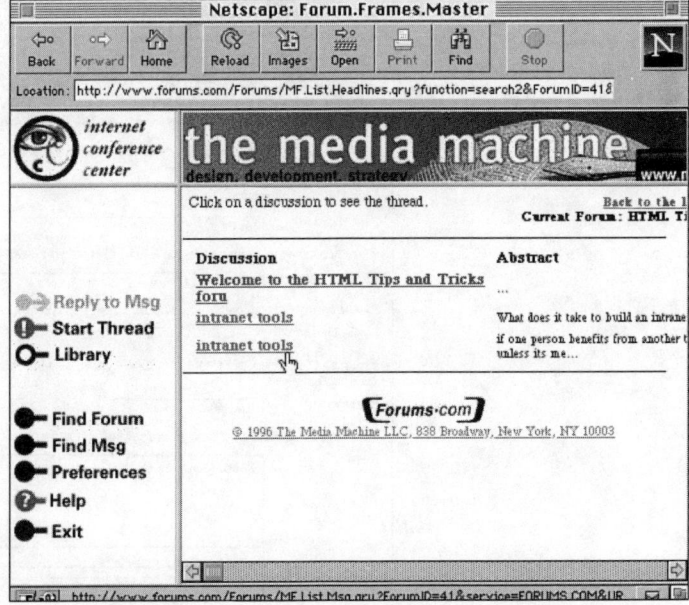

Motet Conferencing by Motet

Motet Conferencing was one of the first Web conferencing software applications and continues to progress, offering many features to serve the administrators and users of intranets. Like Forums.com, Motet Conferencing is stand-alone conferencing software and is not part of an intranet suite. In Motet Conferencing, conference topics are set by the site administrator. Private conferences are moderated by hosts, who are supplied with tools for maintaining the conferences' privacy. Figures 42.9 through 42.11 show several aspects of Motet Conferencing.

Motet runs from a backend suite of programs written in CGI. Web pages are generated on the fly. Motet runs on UNIX platforms and will with almost all Web servers. The data generated from Motet conferences is stored in ordinary UNIX files. This means that conferencing data can be easily secured during scheduled system backups.

Businesses will appreciate Motet's usage tracking feature, which monitors user visits to specific conferences and topics. Statistics about number of users, hits, and postings provide worthwhile information and make site maintenance a snap.

Private Messaging Areas
Chapter 42

FIGURE 42.9.
Motet Conferencing users must fill out an online form before entering conferences.

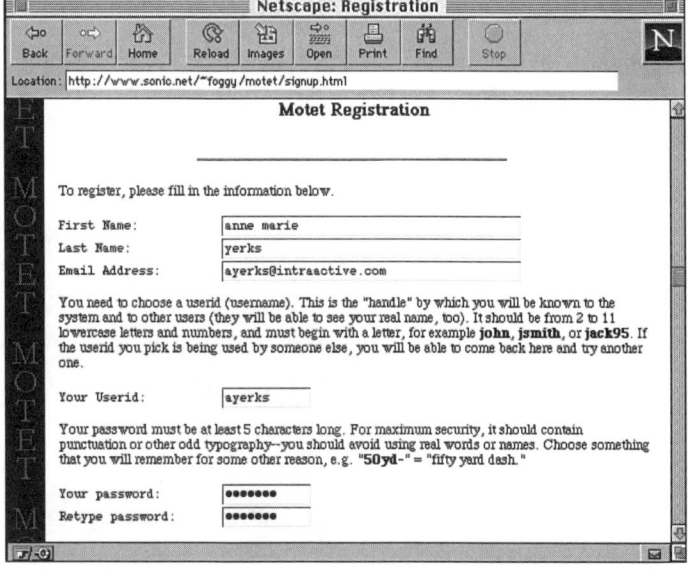

FIGURE 42.10.
After being authenticated, a Motet Conferencing user can enter the conference forum.

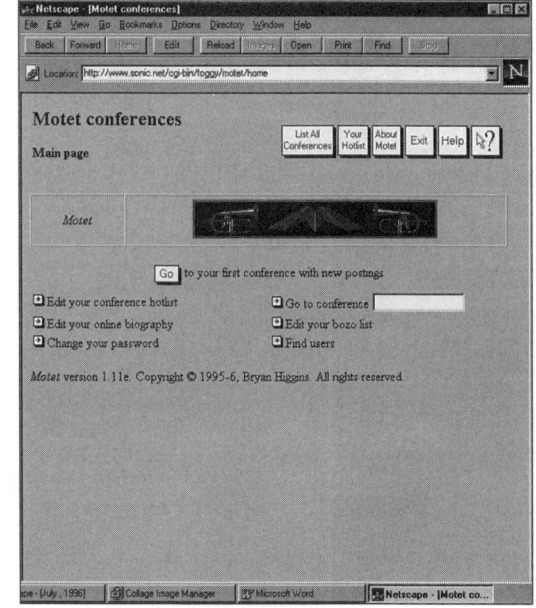

Part VI — *Developing Intranet Applications*

FIGURE 42.11.
In a Motet conference, you can "dog-ear" a post you want to read again later.

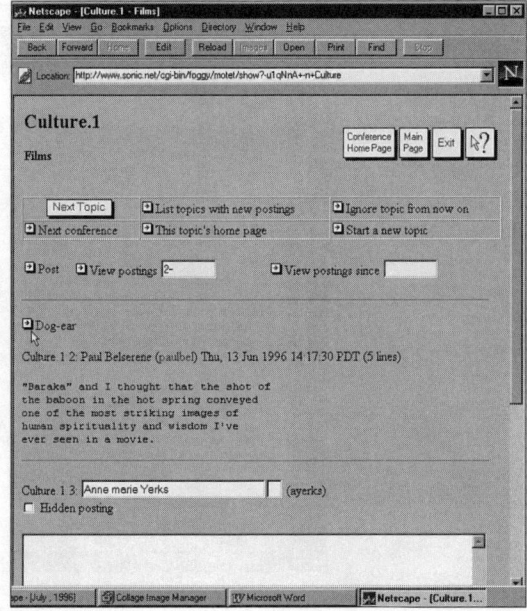

WebShare by Radnet

The conferencing application in Radnet's WebShare, an intranet suite, is worth mentioning here not only because it has a terrific demo on its Web site, but also because it is designed as an online groupware application. Figures 42.12 through 42.14 demonstrate WebShare conferencing.

FIGURE 42.12.
In WebShare conferencing, threads can be viewed according to date, author, or items submitted.

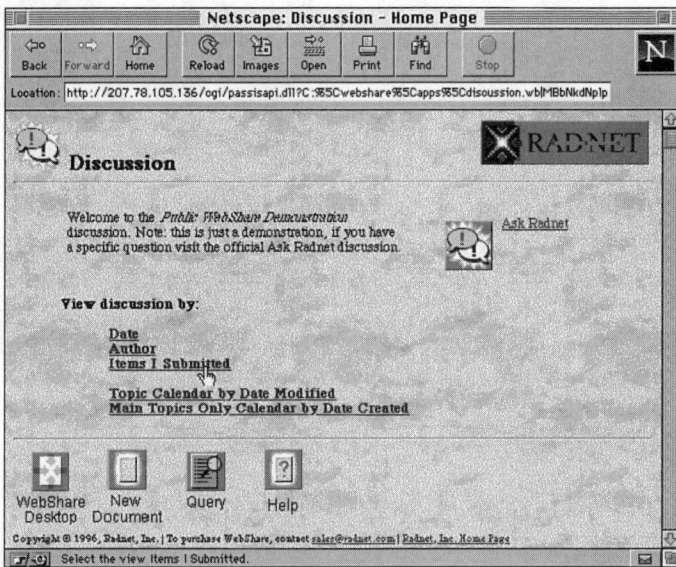

FIGURE 42.13.
With WebShare's moderated conferences, all posts are screened by the conference moderator.

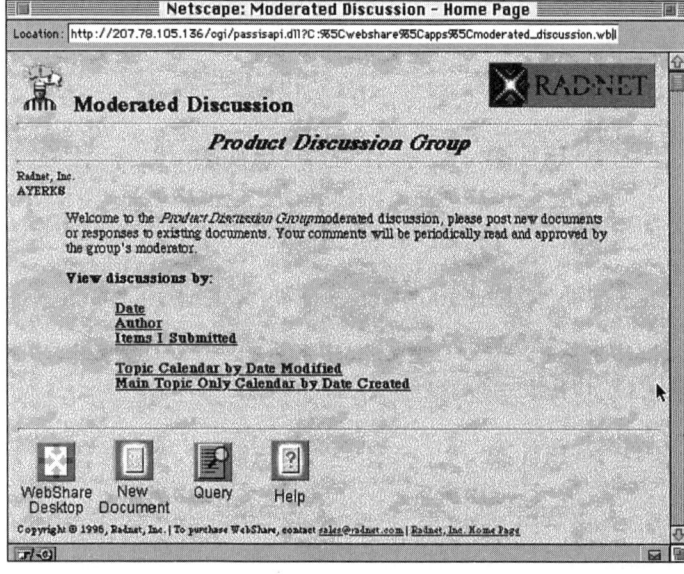

FIGURE 42.14.
WebShare users can attach files to their postings.

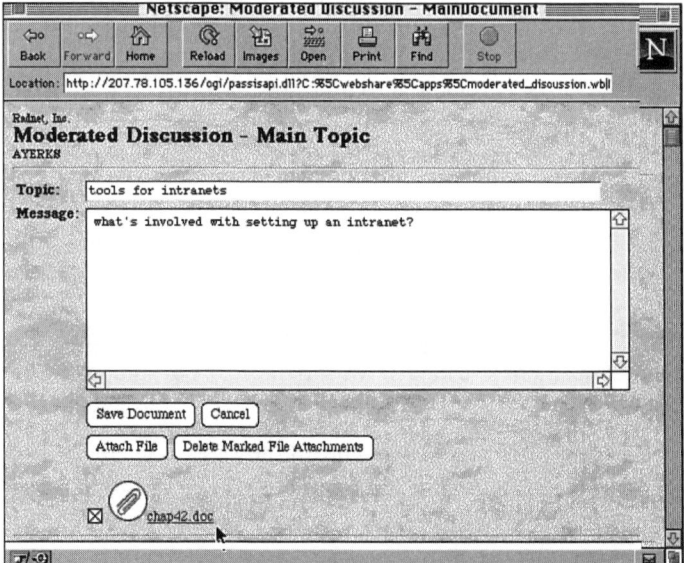

WebShare divides conferences into two categories: public and moderated. Moderated conferences are private and all posts are screened. Another handy feature of WebShare conferencing is the ease with which the user can attach a file to a post. When filling out the "post message" form, users can click a paper clip icon and browse through their files for an attachment.

WebShare runs on Windows NT and stores all data through SQL. Server software is required.

With an application like the ones reviewed here, you can offer private message areas on your intranet. These private areas will bring some breathing room to the very public atmosphere of most online environments. Use them for special projects, meetings, interviews, and so on. But remember that any time you digitize sensitive information, you take the chance that someone, somewhere, might be able to hack into it. The chances are low, but the possibility still exists. Any information that would devastate your organization if broken into should not be stored on a message board. Along the same lines, intranet administrators should take special care about how the data generated from private message boards is archived.

Privacy Issues

This need for privacy while online is one of the main reasons many corporations are building intranets rather than simply offering Internet access. Having the best of both worlds is possible, but restricting access to a site, or even to a message board, brings up some complicated issues.

First, restricted access causes logistical problems. For example, users must remember the password for every conference to which they belong. This can be practically impossible for people like department managers, who belong to large numbers of conferences. This problem can be eased if the users are allowed to pick their own passwords or have the option of changing their password after it has been assigned. This way, people who belong to multiple conferences can use the same password for all of them.

Adding new users to already existing conferences and removing users who no longer have an interest in the conference (or who are disturbing a conference's quality) are other issues to consider. Look for messaging board software that will handle these sorts of problems with a minimum of difficulty. In some cases, the users themselves will be able to add and delete members from the conference. Sometimes this is the best way to keep the conferences up-to-date. If the site administrator is loaded down with the chore of adding and deleting members, a bottleneck could result.

There's a lot of Web messaging board software on the market, so you'll have the opportunity to pick and choose. Another important consideration is how users view the private conferencing forum. There might be times when people want to have a private conference without anyone's knowledge. In this case, they want their private-private conference off the main private conferencing screen, so that users who do not belong to the conference won't even have to know that it exists. Many messaging applications have this feature. Most often the private-private conferences are only listed on the screens of the users who are actually members, not on the screens of those who aren't.

Keeping things private isn't always the easiest task. It's possible that problems not even mentioned here could arise. It's best to remind all users that, on an intranet, one can't completely close the door; there's always a chance of electronic eavesdroppers. But for the most part, private conferences can be closed off enough to help you get the job done.

Administering and maintaining private conferences is a task that usually can be done with Web conferencing software or through a central point in an intranet application suite. Figures 42.15 and 42.16 show how conference administration is done in Radnet's WebShare.

FIGURE 42.15.
WebShare's administration is done online in a hyperlinked environment. The administrator can click a link to add new groups.

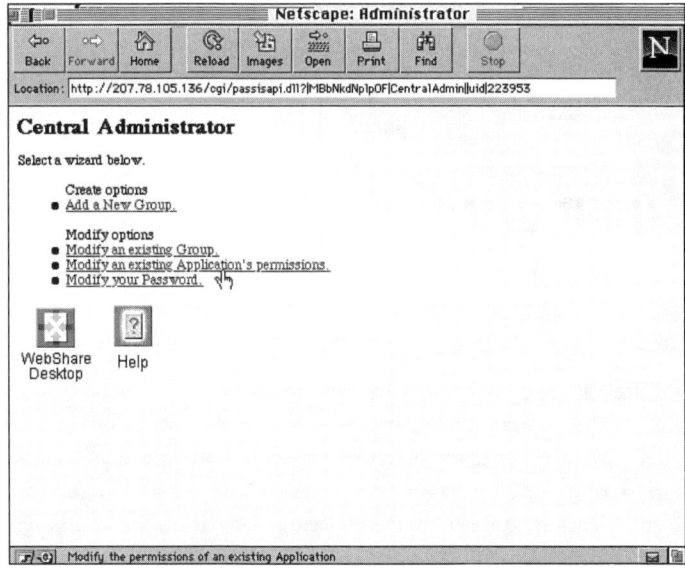

Online administration like that provided by WebShare makes the job of keeping conferences private easy and quick. It's still important, however, to ensure that only the administrator has the means to enter the administrative windows. If it seems too easy, it probably is. Check the software out completely before you purchase it.

FIGURE 42.16.
The WebShare administrator can establish members to a new group with an online form.

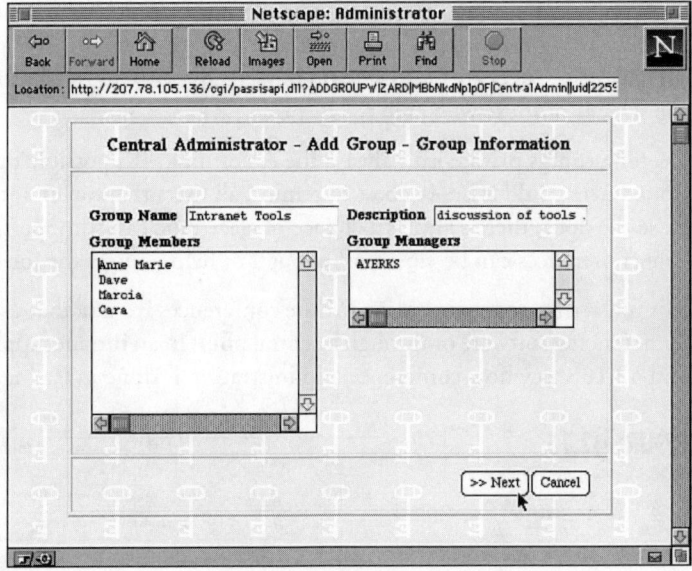

Summary

The best intranets provide space for private discussion. A password-protected message board can serve as an online version of a conference room. By determining a method for authenticating users, you can assign access to private message boards accordingly.

Private message boards can be used in any number of ways—project meetings, conferences, and product updates, to name a few. Many commercially available message board applications offer a private messaging area capacity. The software application you choose should provide a variety of private messaging features, such as the ability to have multiple private areas, user authentication, and the means to delete data quickly and efficiently.

Data from the private message areas, if archived, should be encrypted and stored in a safe; otherwise, you are leaving your sensitive information vulnerable to break-ins. Although any digitized data is vulnerable, especially while online, the chances of exposure are low if you care for the data properly. With enough attention to privacy issues, you can provide a locked door to your intranet's private messaging areas.

Document Submission

43

by Anne Marie Yerks

IN THIS CHAPTER

- Document submission with FTP **650**
- Submitting documents to a database **651**
- Document database software **652**

Back in high school, when you turned in your term papers to the teacher, it was unlikely that anyone else would see your papers or grades. In the corporate world, you've no doubt learned that this is not the case. Computer network systems, such as LANs, allow many people to have access to the same document. Although this is different from high school, you've probably realized that file sharing has many advantages.

You also might have realized the one big disadvantage of working on a LAN: File sharing is limited to the files on the network. Transferring documents or data to people outside the network requires extra steps that can take up valuable time.

File sharing on an intranet can eliminate the hassle of sending paperwork through a courier or the postal service. Company-related literature, such as white papers, guidebooks, guidelines, job descriptions, press releases, and other documents, can be uploaded and made available to the individuals who need it. An intranet file-sharing system allows you to make your corporate documents available through a Web browser, so that employees can access them from home or on the road.

This chapter discusses how to use your intranet as a detailed and convenient document submission system. A few commercially available applications, like IntraACTIVE's InTandem and Livelink's Intranet Suite, can help you establish an online file sharing system. In most cases, you'll store your documents in an online library. How this library is created and maintained is a decision to be made when building the intranet.

Document Submission with FTP

The first way to set up a file-sharing system on an intranet is to build an FTP (file transfer protocol) server. (For details on creating FTP servers, see Chapter 27, "FTP: Sharing Files.") The advantage of storing common documents on an FTP server is that when you need the documents, you can use FTP from any computer—not just the computers in the network. This is especially convenient for users who frequently travel, as files can be downloaded to their laptops with a modem. It also means that individuals outside your company, such as clients and customers, can utilize your files, as long as you give them access.

Another advantage of FTP is that many FTP servers allow you to write file descriptions, which then appear next to the filenames in the main listing. For example, assume an advertising firm wants to store the text of all its product advertisements on an FTP server so that the information is available when an art agency is hired to do the packaging design. The FTP server makes things convenient for both the ad agency and the artists. Although the ad agency and the art agency do not share a computer network or a LAN, the common information that they need to exchange is readily available on the ad agency's intranet—at any time from any location.

Submitting Documents to a Database

Databases have become so popular and functional that users now store files and documents rather than just simple information. (For more details on relational databases, see Chapter 28, "Using Databases.") A document database allows you to store more information about your files than would an FTP site. If you use customized software applications like those offered by OpenText and IntraACTIVE, users can submit documents to a database using an online form. What's more, users can describe the document and its contents, and give other information, like the date of creation, the author, and the number of times the document has been revised. Any information that might be helpful to those who will download the document can be entered into the database form.

For example, assume that a national residential real-estate agency based in Phoenix has set up a corporate intranet. The agency administrators plan to use the intranet to foster communication among employees in various offices. They also want to put all housing lists online, so that potential clients moving from one state to another can be helped out by a local agency, and the sale can be closed at the office in the city to which the clients are moving.

To do this, the agents submit house descriptions, prices, and contacts to the appropriate document database. To make things easier, the intranet administrator has created a custom online form. In most cases, the housing description is short enough to be contained in its entirety in the form; longer documents—like leases and reference materials—can be described in the form with a short abstract. The document file is then uploaded to the FTP server, so that users who want the entire file can download it. A software application provides a user-friendly graphical interface and server settings, so maintenance of the site is minimal.

The result of the system is that both employees and clients can download housing information. The agency meets its goal in appealing to a national market, and the agency's employees appreciate the convenience. One advantage of the system is that it offers version control. Whenever changes are made to a particular listing, an agent can update the file and mark the time and date of the change, but both versions can still be downloaded if such a need arises. Yet another advantage to the system is that agents can be notified as changes come in. For example, an agent in Los Angeles is promoting a house in Philadelphia to a couple who plans to move there. When the agency in Philadelphia sells the house locally, that information is entered into the intranet, and the house is marked "sold."

The information added to files as they are submitted to the database can be displayed in any format. You can write a program that will suit your needs and the specifications of your Web server. For example, if your company's FTP server contains many long documents, some medium-sized documents, and some very small documents, you could configure the server to display the documents in order of size, as well as to display the approximate download time of each.

Another plus for databases is that they are searchable. Assume there are a thousand documents on your file server. With this many documents, it is hard to find the one you want unless you have a well-defined and thorough document tree that everybody uses correctly; such a tree is not needed if you are using a database.

A database allows users to store descriptions and details about documents and employ the means to search the information. You could write a program that would allow you to look through the descriptions with keyword or Boolean searches of that information. A Boolean search is a "concept" search rather than a search for specific words. With a Boolean search, it's possible to join two or more words into a phrase. This control is helpful when looking in a long document for something very specific.

One of the biggest advantages of using an intranet to manage your documents is that handling very large documents becomes easier and less expensive. For example, a small agency in Washington is responsible for counseling substance abusers about their rights to rehabilitation and their rights while in rehabilitation centers. This agency deals not only with the substance abusers, but also with rehabilitation center administrators.

The agency has a lengthy document that covers all the laws related to substance abuse and the rights of those afflicted. The document, which has many chapters, is printed yearly at a cost of about $100,000. When someone requests the document, it is mailed through the post office. The agency's administrators are frustrated with the costs of printing and distributing the document, especially because the person requesting the document typically needs only one or two chapters. However, a law requires that they be given access to the entire document upon request. An easy solution for the agency—one that will dramatically reduce costs and labor—is to store the document in a database. Key information about each chapter—including excerpts and a detailed abstract—can be listed next to the filename. Now, when someone requests the document, he can be referred first to the FTP site. The person requesting the document can do a search on his topic and will likely get the information needed simply by reading the document description; the person might download the chapters needed. In either case, the agency's problem is solved: The entire document is accessible to whomever requests it, but it no longer must be printed. This saves a great deal of money, as well as paper!

A document database will store files in whatever format you choose. The file descriptions will be entered into a form, so you won't need to worry about crossing platforms.

Document Database Software

Now let's look at some software applications and browser features that will help you develop a document database. The applications featured here are some of the best you'll find for creating an online document submission system. As online documents are incorporated more into daily business, more applications like these will join the market.

If you are thinking about purchasing an intranet suite in the immediate future, you should visit the home pages of the companies featured here to get a feel for their products and the support they offer. Both Livelink's Intranet and InTandem have online demonstrations. Participating in such demos will give you a sense of the product, and you can send an e-mail to a representative with any questions you might have.

If you are going to create a database for files yourself, keep in mind a few considerations. First, does your database support capturing files? Oracle and many other high-end databases do, but even if your database doesn't, don't worry. You can store the location of the file in the database, which is almost as good. First figure out what kind of information you want to collect and store in the files, keeping in mind two things: how you want to store and display the information and how you want to be able to find it later with a search engine. A typical database structure for a file database might look like this:

Title of File	Budget Analysis for Fiscal 1996
Name of File	budget.doc
File Type	Microsoft Word
Date Submitted	February 15, 1996
Author/Source	Beth Johnson
Comments	This is the first crack at a budget analysis for fiscal 1996. Not yet included are the final projections for the fourth quarter. The final document should be ready by March 1st.

If you are going to add version control or you want to sort or search by subject or other controls, you must make your database that much more complex. If you have a Web server and database that can talk to one another, it should be relatively simple to write a gateway that will display the contents of the database any way you wish. In this manner, you can provide much more information about your files to your users.

The market is small right now, but be assured that online groupware will progress right along with other new Web applications and programming languages.

IntraACTIVE's InTandem

InTandem, by IntraACTIVE, is an intranet suite that offers file-sharing capabilities in each of its five main workgroup functions (messaging, library, contacts, calendar, and news). The InTandem Library provides a space for posting and responding to work-related documents. The Library works in a message-board style, and each document can be described in an abstract. Administrators can assign users the ability to modify documents online.

Developing Intranet Applications
Part VI

All Library documents can be downloaded to a hard drive or viewed in a Web browser. An InTandem search can be narrowed to the Library, the archives, or even a specific document. Documents in the Library can be linked to other InTandem Boards, such as InTandem News or Forum (see Figure 43.1).

FIGURE 43.1.
Each document in the InTandem Library is submitted with an on-line form.

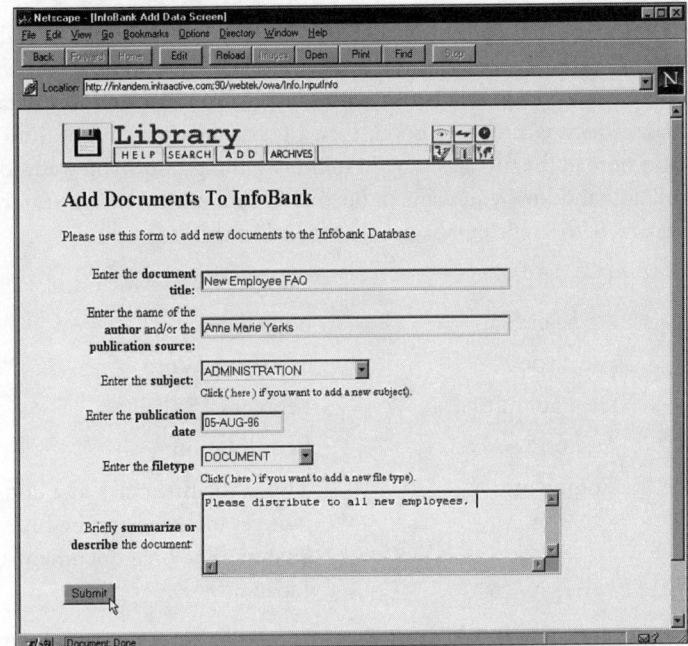

Livelink Intranet's Library

Besides a remarkable search engine that will search through document collections of any size and retrieve documents in one of 40 file formats, OpenText offers the Livelink Library—a tool for group document sharing (see Figure 43.2).

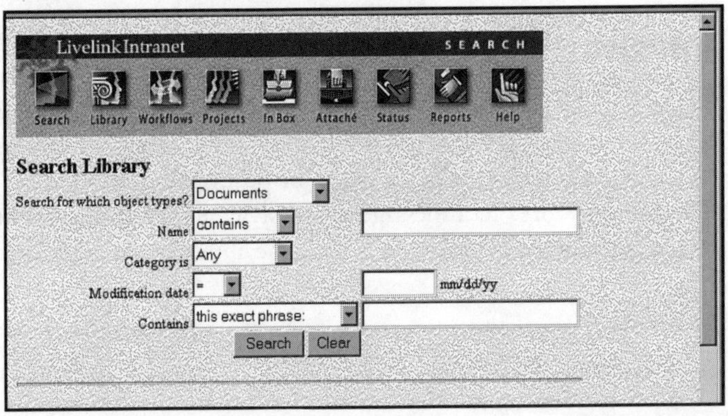

FIGURE 43.2.
The Livelink Library is especially useful for document submissions.

Livelink's library consists of documents posted by users and administrators. The Livelink Library works like a traditional library: You can check out or copy documents, attach documents to discussions, and keep a record of revised versions. You can make dynamic links to the library with an alias. Site managers and predetermined users can set permissions for multiple users and set document attributes.

Automatic version control will manage documents submitted to the library. Also, users can configure their documents' attributes and build multipart documents that can be linked to one another.

Lotus InterNotes

InterNotes, from Lotus Corporation, is a variation of the popular Lotus Notes groupware. What makes InterNotes different from the original Lotus Notes is that users can store Web pages into a common bank and create "doclinks" to them. Information retrieved from the Web is converted to Notes database format. The pages are viewed through the InterNotes Web Navigator, a Lotus browser that retains the pages' original links and graphics, as shown in Figure 43.3. Another feature of InterNotes is that users can create Internet links in non-Web documents.

FIGURE 43.3.

The Lotus InterNotes Web Navigator works in a browser window.

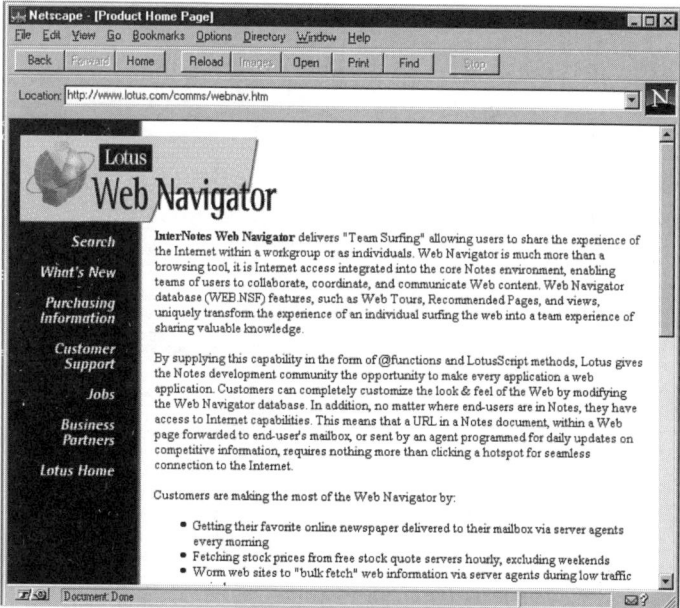

Netscape Navigator

Netscape's Navigator helps intranet developers build document databases by offering its own users the ability to upload a document. With a simple drag-and-drop mechanism, files are easily uploaded to the intranet (or Internet) for exchange with others. This feature works with any platform except UNIX; but users can upload using a pull-down menu. Figures 43.4 and 43.5 outline the FTP process for Netscape users on UNIX.

FIGURE 43.4.
An FTP site called "doorstop" as it appears in the browser window.

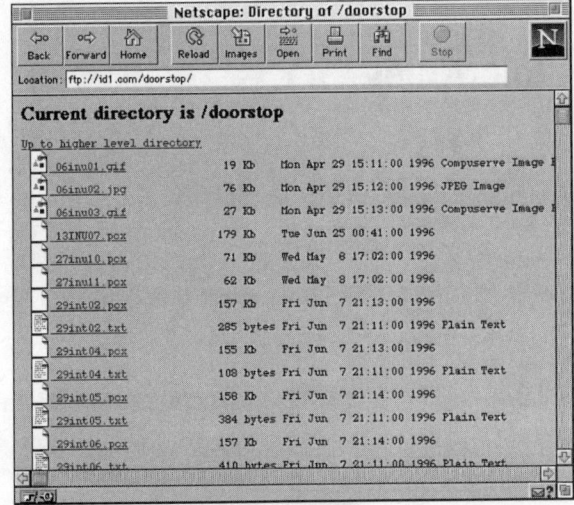

FIGURE 43.5.
Choose a file from a disk to upload to the FTP site.

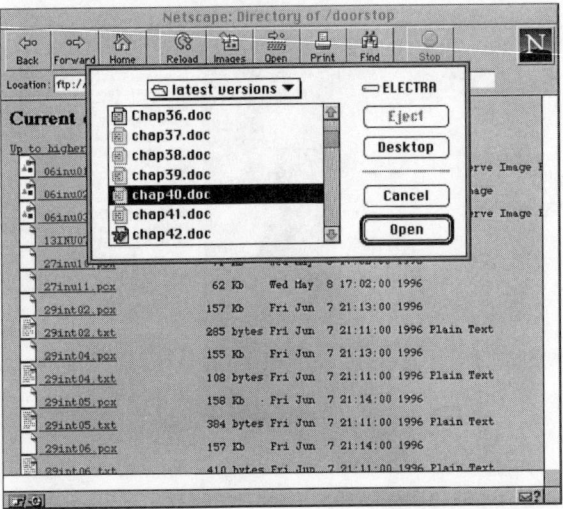

This upload feature in Navigator is yet another way in which a Web browser can serve as a generic interface for a majority of intranet functions.

MCKEON & JEFFRIES

McKeon & Jeffries had two ways of submitting documents to the server. When submitting a document to make it accessible for others to download and edit, users could use the "documents form" to e-mail documents to the administrator, who would then place them on the site. For simple document exchange, however, this was not an efficient method. Users needed to place a file in an area where others could have access immediately. Using the FTP server, this was relatively simple; the administrator merely set up an anonymous FTP site. Of course, because it was behind the firewall, this FTP site was only available to users on the WAN. For organization purposes, the administrator set up the FTP server with a directory tree that would make it easy for users to find what they were looking for. This directory included areas for user space, software, corporate documents, and each of the practice areas. Users had the authority to upload files to their own space or to space in their own practice area, and any user could download any file on the site; but only the administrator had the authority to upload and delete files anywhere.

THE SPORTING GOODS AND APPAREL ASSOCIATION

For security reasons, it was important that the SGAA only allow documents to be uploaded onto the database. Therefore, the document submission and document creation and editing areas were one and the same. The SGAA could do this because of the security allowed by the database and because of the instant availability allowed by its custom software. When submitting a document, users could decide which other users or groups of users they wished to grant access to the document, so every document had its own individual authentication procedure.

Summary

Intranets with document databases offer employees and clients a wealth of resources. Think of a document database as an electronic clearinghouse in which all company-related literature can be stored for easy exchange. Such a clearinghouse is possible only if the document submission process is quick and simple. No one will put information into the clearinghouse if the doorway is blocked. Likewise, no one will visit the clearinghouse if it's a hassle to find information inside. A search engine should be a part of a document database so that users can easily find what they're looking for. Establishing a convenient and complete document-submission process will aid you and your intranet in the long run. Version control, the means to keep track of revisions, is especially helpful for companies that work with ever-changing documents. Along with version control, a well-established document submittal process allows users to describe a document's contents (and other pertinent information) using an online form.

Setting up document submission is a matter of checking out the commercially available packages that offer such functions. Right now only a few exist, but you'll probably find that one or more will suit your needs. You should be able to customize your software for your own specifications.

If you anticipate that your intranet will be the home of many company-related documents, you should start thinking now about how to take advantage of the resources a document database provides. What can you do with all the information that will be offered and shared? No doubt you'll find that employees and clients both will benefit from the electronic clearinghouse.

Search Functions

44

by David Garrett and Anne Marie Yerks

IN THIS CHAPTER

- How search engines work **660**
- Setting up your search mechanisms **663**

Search engines are proof that technology can make your work faster and easier. Remember the days of library card catalogs? Seeking out a single article or book could take hours. Cards, microfiche, and hard-bound indexes are put to shame when compared to the speed and efficiency of an electronic search engine.

More than likely, an original goal in building your intranet was to put your corporate documents online. Digitizing such documents makes sense both time- and money-wise because online documents are easily updated and distributed. But the best thing about having your documents online is that you then can search them in a variety of ways. Companies such as AltaVista and Verity—known for their sophisticated search engines—have developed some search mechanisms especially for intranets. You will look at what they have to offer later in this chapter. First, you will examine the technicalities of search engines and explore the different ways to utilize them on your intranet.

How Search Engines Work

Electronic searches can be accomplished in a number of ways, but they all start the same way. A person requests some information, referred to in electronic terms as a *query*. Typically, when a search engine is activated with a query, it crawls through your site and looks at the contents of your files. Increasingly, those documents are HTML pages, but search engines can incorporate a variety of file formats. If the search engine finds a match, it lists all items that correspond to the information you requested. This function is especially helpful for searching through documents for a specific word or term.

The speed of search engines can vary dramatically. Sometimes this difference is a result of the search software, but often it reflects the kind of information that you provide. Search engines can examine text files in different ways. A direct, brute-force method examines every word in a document and then provides a list of matches for the query word or phrase. You can configure other engines to comb through pages every night—or whenever you like—to form a database of the text and arrange it into predetermined categories. When a search is activated, the computer searches through the database and returns the matching results. So instead of going out and searching your pages every time you start a search, the search engine does it only once a day. Some of the new search engines, such as Livelink Search by Open Text, keep the database up-to-date in real time. They repeatedly update themselves, incorporating any changes in the data they will be required to search.

Both types of searches can work very well. The type of intranet you create will dictate how you establish your search mechanisms. For example, if your intranet uses a back-end database, your information isn't necessarily stored in HTML pages, so your search engine isn't going to find that information. Later in this chapter, you learn more about how to search through information in a back-end database. For more information on databases in general, see Chapter 28, "Using Databases."

Chapter 44

The Range and Complexity of Search Engines

At the same time that many computer developers are struggling to create systems that can understand one another, certain basic distinctions remain. Unlike HTML and SGML, which use files written in universal text that any computer can understand, multimedia applications and word processing programs create items with a programming language specific to those particular applications. Search engines handle these differences in a variety of ways. Some are simply limited to searching ASCII text documents. Others can search a range of file formats.

The most effective Web-based search engines work with SGML. The federal government created SGML (Standard Generalized Markup Language) as a way to mark off text in meaningful ways that would enable different computers to communicate with one another. HTML was, in fact, developed from SGML, and it uses the same concept of tags typed into the text document. Web browsers use HTML to format documents. SGML provides far more information, like keywords, document divisions, and specific page references. These tags usually do not appear on the browser screen, but search engines use SGML to operate more efficiently or to conduct more sophisticated searches. A relational database obviously could not conduct a search for a house by looking at a bunch of images. The computer cannot attach significance to images, nor can it recognize how the combination of lines and colors in an image relate to objects in the real world. But if you provide a brief list of subjects to an image, the computer can place the image within a broader context. In this case, if you search for "house," the computer produces a list of every file where that word appears, plus a list of other items where the word "house" appears as a keyword or as a part of the title.

Most Web-based search engines are limited to text documents. A number of companies have begun to develop systems for indexing relational databases. Relational databases are large collections of material incorporating different types of data. These search engines analyze information at various levels. First, they are capable of searching through the text of HTML, SGML, and word processing files. Second, they utilize file information and keyword indexes for other items like images or sound.

Other engines can search the document descriptions on your FTP server. Say, for example, you have a Microsoft Word file available for FTP. The engine can't search the file directly, but it can search the information submitted with the document when it was originally uploaded to the server. If your engine searches through the document descriptions, users can find both HTML pages that relate to their query and downloadable documents. (For more information on how to set up your documents with searchable descriptions, read Chapter 43, "Document Submission.")

You can use search engines with just about every application on an intranet. Contact lists, message boards, and calendars are all potentially searchable. If you're looking for a particular topic discussed on the message board, for example, a search engine can help you find it. Not only does this search application help with research, but it also increases the efficiency of the message board system. Topics that come up frequently can be supplemented with text from previous but related discussion threads.

Search engines allow users to search through any information on an intranet site. When information and resources are easily and smoothly searchable, users get the most from their intranet. Try to set up search engines to be as simple and helpful as possible. Avoid setting too many controls; although controls can help narrow a search, they also can be a point of confusion.

Types of Searches

You can perform two basic types of searches: keyword searches and Boolean searches. Other types of searches are a combination of keyword and Boolean. You've probably heard combined searches described with a variety of terms, such as *fuzzy logic*.

A keyword search looks for a certain word or phrase. If you type monkey, for example, the computer searches for any document containing the word "monkey." If you type spider monkey, it searches for documents containing both words.

A Boolean search is the opposite. The word "Boolean" refers to George Boole, the nineteenth-century mathematician who created the method by which electronic searches are conducted. In a Boolean search, certain words such as "and" are used as the controls. For instance, you could type spider and monkey. Using these controls, your search is narrowed to documents that contain both "spider" and "monkey." Now assume that you want every document that has the word "spider" but not the documents with the words "spider monkey." You can search for "spider not monkey," and that search returns all the pages with "spider" that don't include "monkey."

All these searches have to begin with an interface, something that appears on the screen and allows people to enter their search queries. For most search engines, the interface is the place where you have the greatest control over the form and content of an individual search. The interface defines the complexity of the search and establishes the limitations within which users must work. Many basic search engines simply provide a blank line or a window where users enter a query. They are quite similar to the Find function on the Netscape viewer.

Using Web-based forms has become a common way to provide an elaborate but comprehensible interface. Instead of entering text, users can utilize a form to control what they're looking for. Some engines, for example, provide users with pull-down menus to search the whole Web or to search only parts of the Web. Figure 44.1 shows this type of form on the search engine developed by a company called Lycos. By making similar controls, you can decide what areas of your intranet the users can search. Creating forms involves several steps. First, your search engine must be able to conduct complicated searches. Second, your interface must be able to convert the information requested by a form into a language that your search engine can understand. Third, you must construct the forms for the interface itself. Some search engines help you create the forms; most Web-based engines do not. Instead, you need to create an HTML page that inserts a form and use a programming device called a CGI script to submit that information to the search engine.

FIGURE 44.1.
Users can configure search and display options from the Lycos page.

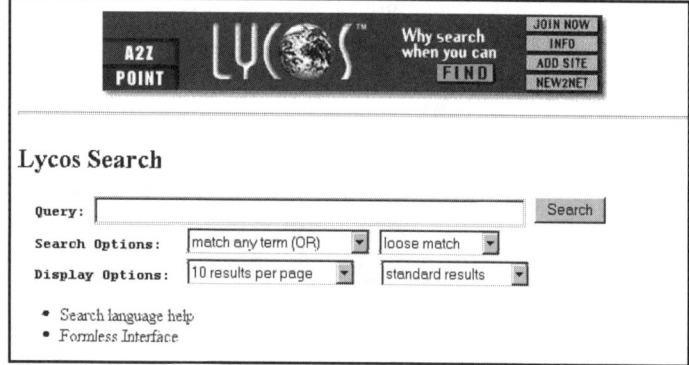

You could create a form that limits your search to particular categories within your database. All the categories correspond to defined elements within a database. The computer can search for people of a certain age because the database designates what number refers to a person's age. Remember that a computer can only understand the significance of information if you tell it to do so. As a result, a search interface with highly specific forms is not enough. Your database should include a degree of specificity that is appropriate to the type of searches you need to conduct.

Users can also combine search features. If someone types in a keyword, for instance, a keyword search is activated. If someone types in two words connected with a Boolean control word, a Boolean search is activated. And if someone types in a keyword, uses another keyword plus a Boolean control word and one of the other predetermined controls (like a pull-down menu), it becomes a controlled search.

After you know what kinds of searches you want to offer on your intranet, you need to start thinking about finding a search engine that satisfies your requirements. What's most important here is making sure that the product will meet your needs and not conflict with other applications. In addition, the search engine must fall within the technical support of your company. Some of the most sophisticated search engines can indeed accomplish remarkable things, but they require a level of technical support that may be unrealistic in certain circumstances. Before you get to the review of some search engines later in this chapter, the following sections discuss potential difficulties with them.

Setting Up Your Search Mechanisms

The main problem with commercially available search engines is that they cannot search a back-end database. Most of them can search individual pages quite well, however. The reason goes back to what you learned at the beginning of the chapter, which is how search engines work. Remember that when a user requests a search, the engine does one of two things: it goes through, looks at all the pages, and then returns the matching information to the Web server (and subsequently the user); or it examines the database created from the text HTML pages of the previous night, searches through them, and then returns matching information to the Web server and then to the user. The problem is that a back-end database is not included in this chain of events. Figure 44.2 shows the events of a search.

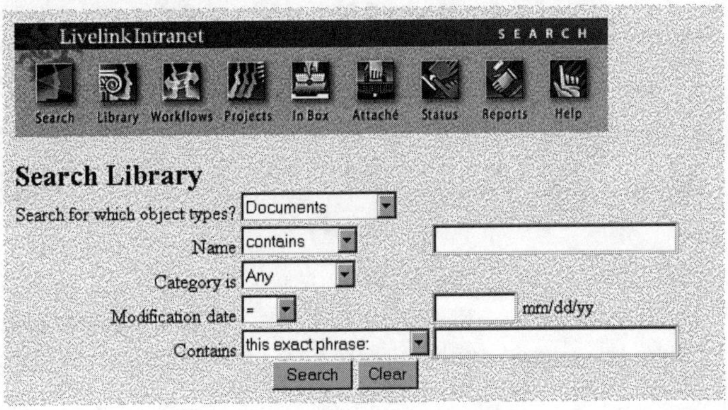

FIGURE 44.2.
The Livelink search engine "searching" a database.

The good thing is that your back-end database usually has a little search engine of its own. Most of them do. So if you want to search for information on your database, you can use the home search engine.

If you do use a back-end database on your intranet, you'll want to use both types of search engines: one engine that searches the back-end database (it is the engine that's included with your database) and one that searches the static HTML pages. Another option is to put all your intranet's information into a database. That way, you don't have to worry about installing a search engine for the static pages.

In the following sections, you examine a few commercially available search engines. These search engines offer special packages especially for intranets. Before you purchase an engine, determine what sorts of searches your users will want to execute. Another factor to consider is what type of Web server you're running (engines are platform-specific) and if the engine product is flexible enough to grow with your intranet.

AltaVista

Digital's AltaVista, shown in Figure 44.3, is a search engine that runs on UNIX or Windows NT. The company offers a package for each. The UNIX package, called AltaVista Enterprise, is a 64-bit text retrieval tool. The Windows NT version, called AltaVista Team, is a 32-bit tool designed for workgroups. Both engines search through an intranet, private networks, user groups, or single hard disks for HTML pages.

FIGURE 44.3.
A sample AltaVista search, including a partial list of hits.

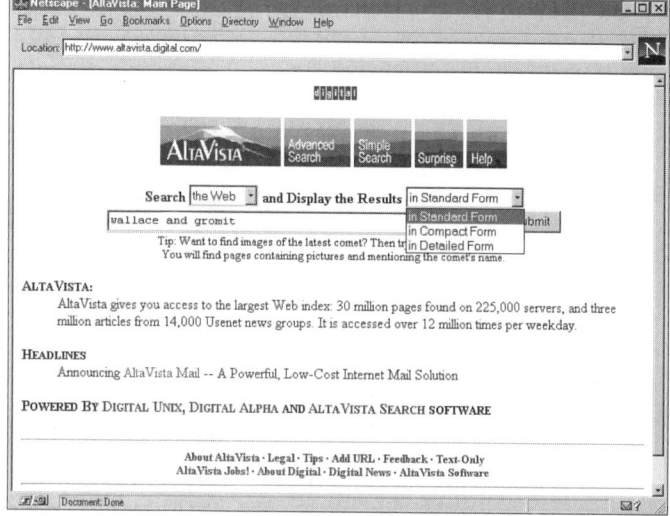

AltaVista created its database with a rather ambitious goal in mind: to search all HTML pages and produce a massive list of hits. The company has already applied this function to the World Wide Web. The Web search engine is available at http://www.altavista.com. It conducts Boolean searches, and it can be applied to all Web pages or can be restricted to particular intranets. The engine has become extremely popular because its indexing system provides access to just about everything on the Web, as opposed to systems with databases that are limited to the specific references that have to be added manually.

Not only does this search engine conduct an extensive search, but it also provides a surprisingly fast return, arranged according to the likelihood that the response will correspond to what you requested. As a result, if you search for "John Doe," AltaVista searches for all Web pages where those two words appear next to one another, followed by pages where both words appear separated from one another, and finally ending with a list of every page including either word by itself.

This sort of search has the obvious strength of producing a large number of hits, but it is also something of a blunt instrument. A search can easily produce thousands of hits, the vast majority of which may have nothing to do with what you want to know. AltaVista is particularly effective if you need to conduct quick searches for a simple string of words. It is less effective as a means to retrieve highly specific types of information.

Excite

Excite's search engine, shown in Figure 44.4, is highly stylized yet charmingly simple. Users are not asked to control their searches narrowly. Instead, Excite takes on the responsibility, bringing forth results in a subject-ordered format. Users can sort the results and read short summaries about the retrieved documents.

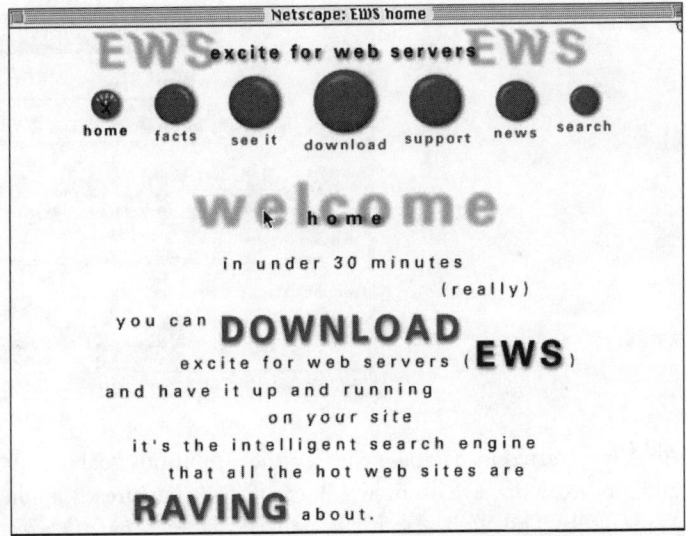

FIGURE 44.4.
Download a demo of Excite from their Web page at http://www.excite.com.

Excite backs up its claims that it's faster than most engines. Excite's engine creates a lot of extra-small indexes (rather than a few big ones), which are easier to crawl through. As a result, it is less effective at crunching large requests because these queries force it to pick through numerous subindexes. Likewise, Excite has a limited range of search options. At the same time, it remains faster than most other commercial search engines. In addition, it runs on a broader variety of machines and systems than most other search engines. New content is added with an automatic update feature. Excite runs on SunOS, Solaris, SGI, HP-UX, IBM AIX, BSDI, and Windows NT.

Livelink and Pat Search

Open Text Corporation is working hard for their intranet clientele. Their intranet suite's search engine, Livelink Search, is considered by some Web developers to be one of the best search engines on the market. Livelink Search is noted for its ability to comb through document collections of any size. It can index more than 40 different file formats, such as HTML, PDF, and SGML. What's more, the engine translates any supported file format into browser-viewable HTML. You can find a Java-enhanced tutorial at http://www.opentext.com.

Livelink emerged from another Open Text application called Pat. Now almost five years old, Pat remains an extremely effective search mechanism. Open Text created these search systems for one of the earliest commercial applications of the Internet: searchable online texts. Both Pat and Livelink are sophisticated SGML search engines that involve a two-step process. First, they construct an index from a large database. This process, which can take hours, creates a list of all the words used in the database and also incorporates the full range of SGML tags. After the index is complete, Pat and Livelink can conduct sophisticated, complex searches. All searches are case sensitive, and if you enter a combination of words, Pat conducts a standard keyword search. But you can conduct searches for word pairs that appear near each other, and you can designate the proximity. Other search functions include limiting the search to a given section of the database (a particular document or documents by a certain author) or to particular document types (books, technical reports, poems). All these documents must be in SGML-encoded ASCII text, with tags that designate document types.

After Livelink or Pat conducts a search, it displays an abbreviated list of results. This list is linked to a series of documents, which in turn can be displayed in a variety of ways. If SGML tagging includes chapter, section, or other divisions, Pat can display a particular division. Likewise, you can see the keyword or keyword combination plus a given number of words in either direction.

Pat runs only on UNIX machines. In addition to its own particular programming requirements, it works best with heavily encoded SGML documents. Because Pat uses a hierarchical index to know what text appears where, SGML tagging enables it to restrict its effort to a particular part of a document. As a result, it can search documents with minimal tags, but these searches take considerably more time.

Although the Open Text search device offers impressive and flexible searching capabilities, it has never come with a similarly sophisticated interface. Instead, users have developed their own Web-based forms. Figure 44.5 shows a sample form, and Figure 44.6 shows the result of a search using that form. Although Pat does not require the same sort of programming experiences as other search engines, it does require extensive familiarity with SGML formatting and HTML forms.

Part VI — *Developing Intranet Applications*

FIGURE 44.5.
This example shows a Web search form for a version of the Oxford English Dictionary searchable through Pat.

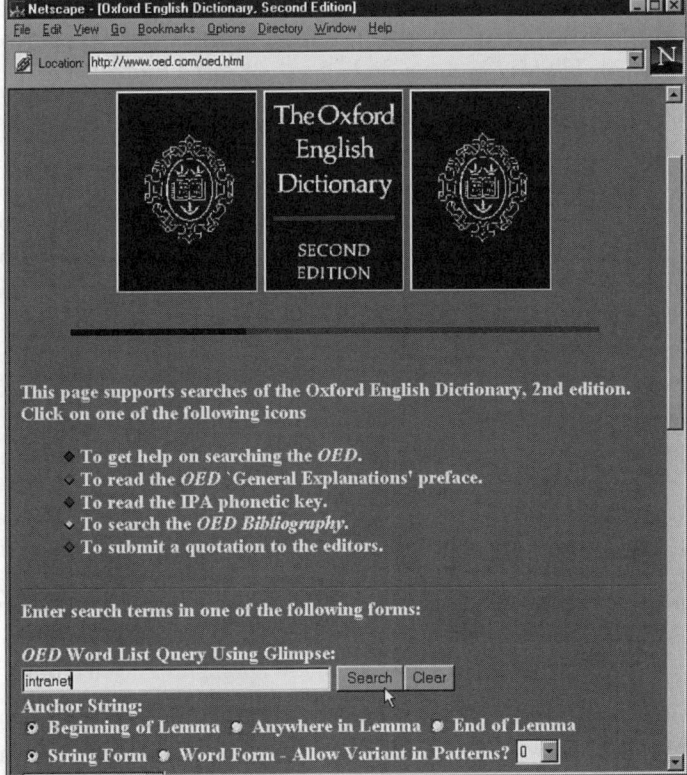

Oracle Relational Database

At a time when some software companies have become cultural icons (Microsoft and Netscape, to name a couple), a number of others remain relatively anonymous despite their size. This has been the case with Oracle, which is one of the largest software venders in the United States. Because Oracle makes few applications for the home market, however, it remains relatively unknown outside the corporate environment.

Oracle has developed one of the most sophisticated relational databases currently available. The company seems intent on applying the technical goals of a relational database (searching items from various formats) to the conceptual framework for their software package. Not only can the database create indexes for a variety of media formats, but it also can run on numerous computer platforms. Oracle works on UNIX, Novell network servers, and most LAN configurations. These computer systems can in turn be connected so that one database can connect numerous formats stored on entirely different computer systems.

FIGURE 44.6.
The Pat search for "fractal" produces this response.

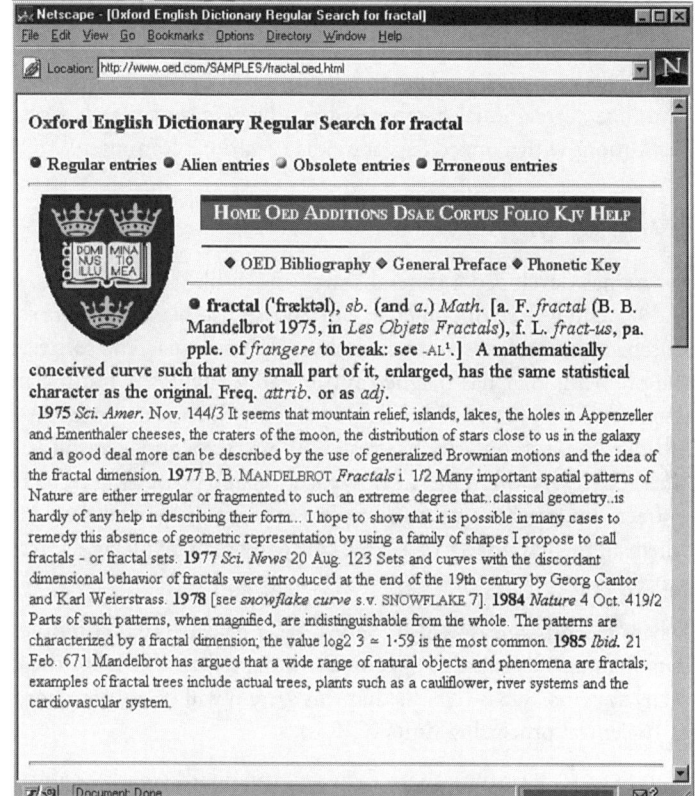

As this potential suggests, Oracle's system is not simple—nor is it cheap. Maintaining an Oracle relational database requires considerable in-house computer support. This support begins at the planning stage, where the complexity of such an all-encompassing system requires considerable forethought, and continues through the process of adding new material or fixing problems. In addition to the cost of maintaining the system, the software itself is more expensive than most standard search engines.

Oracle has attempted to respond to these costs by establishing a considerable user-support infrastructure. Unlike other search engines, which are the products of recent companies that have emerged along with the World Wide Web, Oracle's relational database evolved from various other database packages stretching back over a decade. In the short life of the computer software industry, Oracle is something of an elder statesman. Oracle employs a large number of technical support personnel and maintains a 24-hour phone line for questions. The company has also begun something of a promotional road show. It regularly dispatches customer service representatives to provide demonstrations of Oracle's various packages.

Both the Oracle Corporation and its relational database enjoy a breadth that many of the newer Internet search systems have difficulty matching. The costs that go along with these advantages have limited the system to large companies with appropriate financial resources. In addition, like all relational databases, the advantages of Oracle's system become evident only in institutions with a mixed bag of media or various computer systems that have to be integrated.

Sybase SQL

Sybase has developed a general search much like other engines, working on UNIX machines and searching Web documents. But Sybase also plans to create something between a standard search engine and a relational database. In particular, the software is designed to tackle one of the problems that has plagued most search engines: handling multiple servers with a heavy demand. The World Wide Web—let alone Web search engines—may be a recent invention, but the Web's popularity has resulted in a tremendous amount of activity on search devices. This activity has often meant slow reaction and processing time, or the tendency for a machine to freeze up, crash, or fail to complete a query. These problems can occur on intranets as well, where all the employees of a large company may be placing search requests on the same set of processors.

Sybase recently released SQL Server 11, a package that combines a search engine with a new data management system specifically designed to eliminate the demand problems placed on many systems. Sybase claims that this system will be able to coordinate the activity of as many as 16 central processing units (CPUs).

SQL Server 11 is somewhere between a standard search engine and relational database. It is instead a document organization and retrieval system. Sybase has aimed this product at the high activity market, hoping that potential clients will want a system that can kill two birds with one stone.

Verity

With a client list that includes names like Netscape, Adobe, and Lotus, it's not surprising that Verity's Topic search engine products are gobbling up a big portion of the intranet software market.

Verity's Topic Product list is long, offering about 20 specialized packages, including those with a Web and news server. Intranets that need a powerful engine to search through voluminous relational databases would benefit from TopicTools, a comprehensive software development toolkit. TopicTools provides the means to integrate searching, indexing, and retrieval capabilities into already existing intranet applications. By using a simple application programming interface (APT), you can build features such as real-time index updates, shared document libraries, and document configuration panels.

Topic products are available for practically every platform. Because Verity offers its clients so many options, you're likely to find what you need. If you anticipate that searching and indexing will be a main function of your intranet, Verity should be at the top of your list of considerations.

Choosing a Search Engine

The brief reviews in the preceding sections indicate the range of search engines that are currently available. Choosing a search engine, however, is not as simple as selecting the one with the most features. The critical factor in selecting a search engine is to define exactly what you need to search and how you want people to be able to use that information. If you have a strictly textual database, than you do not need to consider relational databases. But then you must decide whether you want people to conduct simple word searches (whether keyword or Boolean) or more complicated topic and category searches.

For textual databases, the complicated searches can be accomplished only with databases that can be structured to interpret SGML or some other form of tagging. These searches can be extremely helpful when you want people to be able to limit searches in a variety of ways. For example, you can easily create a search engine that searches a mailing list for everyone who lives in a certain state or falls within a certain age range. A word search could turn up much of the same information, but it would take longer (because it would look through an entire database rather than just the particular categories) and would produce numerous extraneous answers. In the case of an age search, for example, a basic search would also turn up addresses that include a particular age.

Relational databases can accommodate a much broader range of information, but they have their own limitations. They are usually the most expensive search engines. In addition, their very sophistication means that they require considerable technical support and computer expertise. Although most companies provide assistance, you will need someone on-site who is fully capable of maintaining the search engine.

Finally, people often have a tendency to see the capabilities of search engines and plan according to the greatest possible range of options. Although this kind of planning is a good way to allow for future developments, it may not always be an adequate reflection of the sort of information you will actually be running through the search engine. If your database includes simply text without any complicated categories or tagging, even the most sophisticated search engine can do little more than an inexpensive engine. Complex searches will only be possible if you are willing to retrofit your databases in such a way that the search engine can do its magic. This obviously is not a problem if you are constructing the database at the same time that you are purchasing the search engine, but it is an important consideration if you intend to attach a search engine to an existing database.

> ### MCKEON & JEFFRIES
>
> McKeon & Jeffries decided to use the OpenText commercial search engine because most of its site was static HTML. Installing and setting up the search engine on its site was simple. It provided clear and efficient search results and allowed users to instantly find any information on the site that they were looking for.

> ### THE SPORTING GOODS AND APPAREL ASSOCIATION
>
> The SGAA wrote a search engine of its own to search through all the information stored on the database. It chose this route because the Oracle database built-in scripting language contains the elements of a powerful search engine, which made it easy for the association to create custom searches. Using PLSQL tools and Oracle's Textserver, its search engine can search not only the information stored in the database, but also any word processing or desktop publishing document stored there as well. Because of the large amount of information stored on the server, the search results page was carefully crafted to include the context surrounding key words and phrases. The search interface was created in such a way to allow users to search any one of several areas of the site, including the message boards, interactive calendar, documents, and the reference area. For example, if a user wants to find a specific contact, she can just search the contact database. On the other hand, if she wants the contact's phone number and all the messages posted to a message board, she can search both those areas. The search interface also allows users to search information by date using Boolean controls such as AND, OR, and NOT.

Summary

Although searches are not the only function of your intranet, they are the means by which you can build efficiency. A search can be implemented with a keyword or with a keyword plus controls. Boolean searches—the type with controls—help users to narrow a query.

Many popular Web-search companies, such as Lycos and AltaVista, have created search engines especially for intranets. You should set up your search engine according to your needs. If you have a back-end database, you need to configure the database search engine so that users can search the database's information and the HTML pages. Specially formatted documents, like those created in word processing programs, are not searchable directly, but you can include those descriptions on the searchable FTP server.

Intranet administrators have control over determining what parts of the intranet are searchable. It's best that users search through all the applications, including message boards, calendars, and contact lists. The more information that can be retrieved through a search, the more your users can benefit from the intranet.

Help Desk

45

*by Anne
Marie Yerks*

IN THIS CHAPTER

- Organizing help **674**
- Writing the help text **678**
- Developing help **680**
- Images **680**
- Managing help and questions **681**
- Buying help **684**

If you've ever changed a flat tire, assembled a bicycle, raised a crop of tomatoes, or done any type of home improvement or mechanical work, it's likely that you referred to a book or manual for help. You probably agree that how-to instructions should be helpful, simple, and clear. The same is true for the help pages on your intranet. The help text you offer your users is a first line of defense against potential problems. It's also a convenient way to offer online assistance for simple questions.

Creating and maintaining a help desk is unlike other areas of electronic management. Technical issues do not occupy center stage the way they do with other hardware and software considerations like word processors, storage systems, and search engines. Help desks are very much a personnel consideration. Your help desk must provide effective assistance to everyone in a company and organization. Achieving that goal involves a lot more than choosing the right applications. It requires familiarity with the knowledge and attitudes of your colleagues. It means thinking exclusively in terms of how to best deliver services to the people within your organization. Unlike many of the other elements of an intranet, which are designed to support your contact with the outside world (inventory, advertising, and so on), the help desk is entirely insular. You will need to plan accordingly.

This chapter covers the basics of setting up your intranet's help functions. We talk about ways to write and organize help text, examine the help features of a few software applications, and discuss how you can develop your help features for the maximum benefit of your users.

Organizing Help

Help has always been a part of software programs, and for that reason, just about everything has been done with it. Help functions often include balloons, bookmarks, scrollbars, buttons and icons, command lists, even audio files. Some programs and commercial software manuals include "help CDs" with digital movie tutorials. Everything short of a house call is available for people who want to learn.

Because your users will expect to have support and it will save you time and money to offer support, think carefully about how you will incorporate help into your intranet. Consider your help functions to be not just "yes or no" answers to common problems, but more as a guide to getting the most out of the intranet's applications.

How you initially organize your help will make a difference in both the short and long run. Because your intranet contains many functions, like message boards and calendars, you will need to provide help for every area. Therefore, you must determine how you will assign help categories and where to put them on the site.

Some of the applications on your intranet will already have help pages. In this case, you'll need to decide if you are going to supplement the existing help with your own help. Sometimes it is easy to direct people toward supplementary information. You could offer users some links to additional sources, like a related newsgroup or the application's home page. Figures 45.1, 45.2, and 45.3 show some examples of help windows.

FIGURE 45.1.
Microsoft Office has an elaborate help function that includes balloons and an "Answer Wizard."

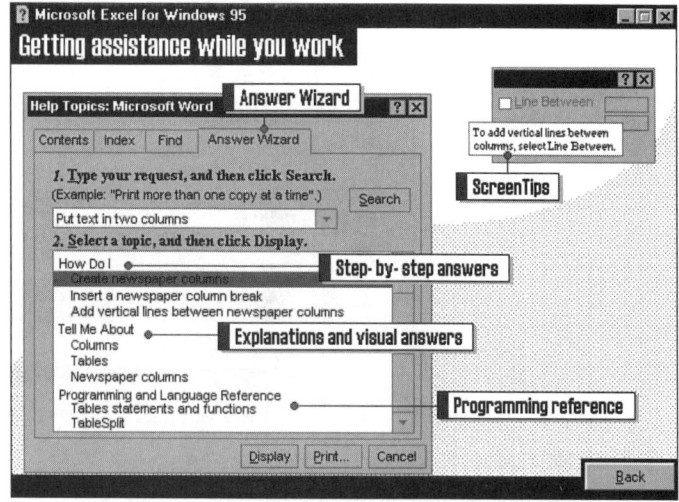

FIGURE 45.2.
NicoMak Computing's WinZip offers a help tutor.

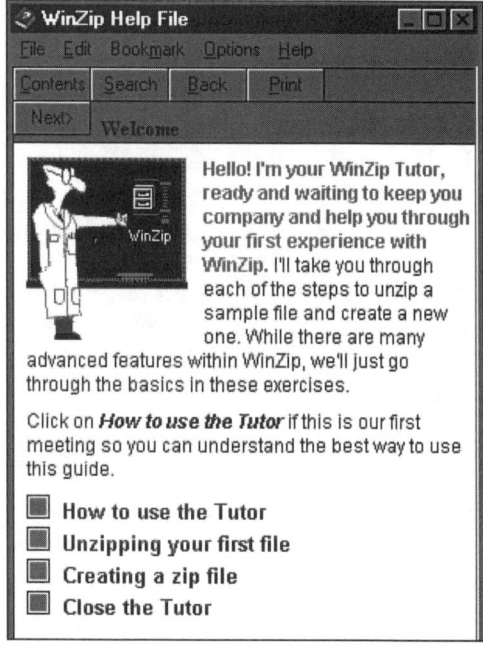

FIGURE 45.3.

Progressive Network's RealAudio Player help offers a table of contents, index, and search engine.

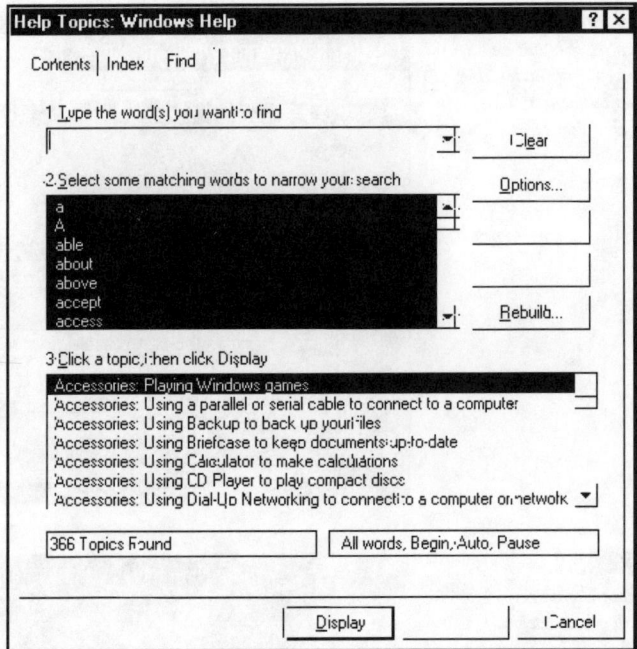

These examples, like many of the scenarios discussed here, are founded in hypertext. Hypertext formats have emerged as the best way to organize help information. If you know anything about HTML and how links work, you'll know that it is easy to construct flexible, uncluttered help pages with hypertext. The help functions on most word-processing, spreadsheet, desktop publishing, and officeware programs—whether they are for Windows, Macintosh, or other operating systems like Solaris and SGI—use SGML, the forebear of HTML. Because of this relationship, you can model the help functions of your intranet on the help functions of programs that are especially appealing to you.

If any of your intranet's applications have insufficient help mechanisms, you can do a Web search, and, more than likely, you'll find that someone has written a FAQ (frequently asked questions) about the application or operating system in question (see Figure 45.4). You can use this FAQ as a help reference: Simply link your users to the site, or ask the author if you can use it on your own site.

But even if your software comes with thorough documentation, there are links to other help resources, or you can find a FAQ sheet, you will probably need to produce some help documentation yourself. Every organization makes some distinctive use of software that will not be covered by the original software help. More importantly, however, software help is usually written by software programmers, people whose familiarity with computers and with specific applications usually exceed the knowledge of most users. As a result, software help is consistently loaded with jargon that many readers do not understand. Although these help documents—

whether printed or electronic—may be "complete," they may nonetheless be unhelpful. You should plan on writing supplementary help documentation that users can understand. In addition, you should consider a variety of ways for making this material accessible to others.

FIGURE 45.4.
Microsoft Windows NT's FAQ can be found on the Internet.

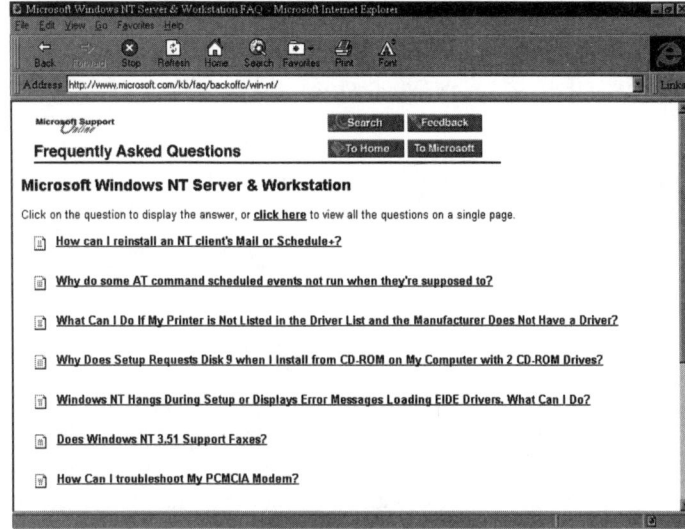

When organizing help functions, be especially sensitive to possible problems. It's important to look at the application in a new way. Try to get yourself in a bind and then write some step-by-step instructions on how to get out of it. Also, remember to put help links, a hypertext link to an HTML page with help text, in spots where users are likely to need them. For example, put a help link in or near the document upload window on every application, as this is an area that perplexes many users.

Using HTML rather than various help extensions for each particular application also is a good way to centralize and standardize your documentation. Some of the most effective help resources bring together material on a variety of applications. This kind of setup allows people to know exactly where they should go for help. It also will enable you to make all of your help searchable. If you have purchased a search engine for databases, records, and so on, you should be able to apply that engine to your help material. This too will make people more comfortable with help resources, because they should already be familiar with the search engine.

Keep your users foremost in your thoughts as you organize your help functions. Not only do you want to maintain peace, but you also want to avoid having to hire a phone staff to answer questions and go out on calls. With a fully developed help function, you'll keep everyone happy—most of the time.

> ### MCKEON & JEFFRIES
>
> M&J chose a simple and user-friendly interface for users to get help on the site. Using text from the commercial product's readme files, as well as text created by M&J's staff, a large help page was created with internal links to specific areas. Each page on the site had a link to the help page, where users could go to find out how to use specific applications or to answer specific questions.

> ### THE SPORTING GOODS AND APPAREL ASSOCIATION
>
> The SGAA, because of its many users and the lack of in-person training and help that could be provided, created a much more sophisticated help function. For each area or application of the site, the SGAA created two separate help areas, the first providing basic help, the second offering more in-depth help.
>
> When users first click help from any application on the site, a frame appears on the right side of the screen with help information to guide the user through performing that particular function. From here, users can link to a more sophisticated help feature that includes screen shots and slide shows taking users step by step through how specific functions are accomplished.

Writing the Help Text

At some point, you might find yourself sitting in front of a blank word processing screen. Your assignment: to explain, in a written form, the complicated operations of a particular intranet function. When writing help text, say things simply and clearly. Pretend you are talking to a young child (or better yet, your mother; young children probably have a better handle on this stuff than your mother does). Remember that not everyone is a computer expert.

If you wanted, you could include help for the entire intranet in one long document and give users the ability to link to specific areas as needed. However, it would probably be more convenient to create a help function for each application on the intranet, so that you can customize it to suit the questions you think are likely to arise. In addition to placing this material online, you also can run it through any search engine or indexing system that you may be using for the rest of your intranet material.

Although hypertext allows you to move around from one document to another, you should still organize your help documentation in a hierarchical fashion. Like any other complicated written document, your documentation must open with a table of contents. You might want to put special words in boldface (they could evolve into hyper-links later on). You can save the more complicated things for last, so that readers are warmed up by the time they get to the end and won't be as intimidated. A hypertext format will allow more experienced users to skip straight to those advanced instructions.

If you are writing a FAQ, you'll need to think of some questions for yourself to answer. You might want to ask around the office or make an online "suggestion box." Don't forget that your viewpoint—as something of an expert—is much different than that of someone who is using a program for the first time. The questions that you think of could very well be a bit too complex for a beginner. Likewise, you might regard beginning questions as elementary. However, you can't let yourself forget that your audience probably doesn't know as much as you do.

The critical consideration for any help text is the language you choose. The goal of any help text writer should be to avoid any terms that people do not use in everyday conversation. There will be times when you will have to use technical terms, but these should be limited to specific and necessary occasions. For example, multimedia applications increasingly refer to "authoring a project," which is just unusual enough that many people would not know that it actually means "creating a project." In this case, the technical term is completely unnecessary, and another term is just as precise and infinitely more familiar.

In other cases, however, you will not be able to avoid technical phrases. Words like "upload," "tag," and "hypertext," for example, are unavoidable. They refer to highly specific activities, and there is no simple way to replace them without going into lengthy descriptions. At the same time, however, never use a technical term without immediately providing a definition in everyday terms. In this case, for example, you might have a sheet that says, "You should now upload the document. 'Uploading' refers to copying a document from a personal or desktop computer onto a shared computer system."

As these issues should indicate, help documents most likely will not be limited to only those applications that did not come with their own help documentation. You should be prepared to write help information to reinforce and clarify any documents that are difficult for novices to understand.

You will have to aim all computer documents for the lowest common denominator of computer knowledge; every help text must make sense to people with limited computer knowledge. Yet you also will need to plan around the computer training of your particular organization. This means meeting with the people who handle training and orientation. You should learn exactly what your colleagues know about computers. Get a sense of how comfortable they are with computers and what areas seem to cause the most persistent problems. If your organization has just installed an intranet, for example, you will need to write extensive, detailed help documents. However, if everyone has familiarity and comfort with computers, your help documents should explain sophisticated options that the basic help that came with your software may not get into. Finally, if you have a large number of employees with a broad range of computer skills, you will need to write more help documents explaining basic activities.

Every help document needs to pass a simple test: Can somebody who does not work regularly with computers understand it? Proofreading is helpful with any document, but it is particularly important with computer information. You should give every help document to a computer novice, and make certain that he or she can understand what you have written before putting it online.

Developing Help

Keep an eye out at all times for new ways to help your users. One thing you can do right away is build a "search help" mechanism. We've already discussed the mechanisms and applications of search engines. There's no reason you can't apply your search engine to your help documents. You should be able to customize your engine to search specifically through the help documents. Your "search help" function should be easy to use and available from every intranet application. Keyword, Boolean, and controlled searches all will be useful for your help files. These search functions should exist alongside a simpler hypertext version. Many of the most effective help documents begin with a linked index of topics, followed by a search form that enables people to locate specific subjects or terms.

Another thing you can do while looking for ways to improve your help is to develop *tutorials*, documents that provide introduction and practice for applications. They are an effective way to bolster your training system. Tutorials enable people to develop their proficiency on their own time. As the technical sophistication of users continues to increase, so does the use of tutorials. Many programs are best learned in a hands-on environment. Users appreciate the chance to learn and do simultaneously. Tutorials should provide increasingly challenging scenarios. Instead of telling people how to do things (the logic of standard help documentation), effective tutorials include tasks and assignments that people can use to practice their skills.

Images

Although it is important to be sure that your help text is clear and concise, it also could be helpful to include screenshots of the pages where users are likely to run into trouble. It might even be helpful to annotate those screenshots with comments, arrows, and drawings to further explain the operation. Some intranet developers use Java and/or animation to show actual mouse movements and keystrokes to give the users an even better idea of how to use the software. Another useful way to take advantage of the multimedia aspect of the Web is to include a drawing or diagram that shows users how this particular operation fits in with the intranet as a whole. In time it may even be practical to include audio and video clips as part of your help function.

Check to see if any tutorials that would suit your needs are commercially available, or consider creating a tutorial on your own. You can use one of the many commercially available multimedia-development applications to produce tutorials and other educational presentations. Look at other online tutorials for models. Sun Microsystems has one on creating Java applets (see Figure 45.5). View it at http://www.sun.com.

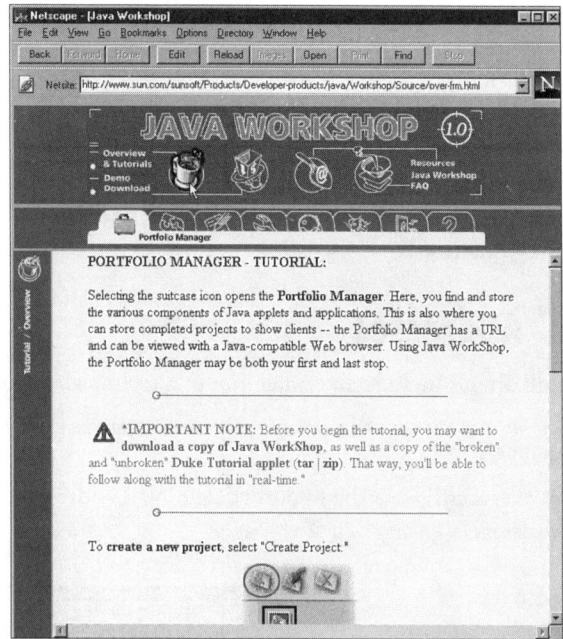

FIGURE 45.5.
Sun Microsystems Java Workshop is an online tutorial.

In addition to all the fancy features you will have for your help, you should include two simple bits of information: a phone number and an e-mail address. When users are in a real bind they need to communicate with someone who knows the ropes. You should give an in-house technical support contact for every intranet application. If you've developed a good system for help, the users won't need to ask for guidance all that often.

Managing Help and Questions

The success of help desks eventually turns on the communication skills of the people offering help. Some of the most intelligent programmers are disastrous help desk personnel, because they do not know how to communicate in a language that other people can understand. The size of your help desk will vary according to the number of people in your organization, but you should make certain that someone is always available to answer questions or fix problems. Few things are more frustrating for computer users than sending a question off by e-mail to some nameless help desk and then waiting for a reply. Online help material should never be a permanent replacement for individual assistance. Not only do people feel depersonalized, but they often cannot find exactly the solution they need in help documentation. Even the best documents for the oldest applications, developed and refined over many years, do not answer every question. In addition, there also will be people who have difficulty interpreting online help, even when it has been written clearly and without computer jargon.

A successful technical support division will provide a variety of ways to solve problems. Online help information can handle the most basic and common situation, in which someone has forgotten (or never learned) how to conduct a particular computer activity. At the opposite end of the spectrum are situations in which people need someone to coach them over the phone. In between these poles are wide areas of possibilities in which people have specific questions that are not addressed in help documents but do not require personalized assistance. Most of these questions will arrive in the form of e-mail, and there are several ways to handle the flow of incoming questions.

E-Mail Addresses

You should always include an e-mail link to a technical person who can offer help:

```
<p>Please write the <a href="mailto:help@organization.com">help desk</a> with any
➥questions.</p>
```

help@organization.com is the hypothetical e-mail address for a help desk. Figure 45.6 shows how this passage appears on a Web page.

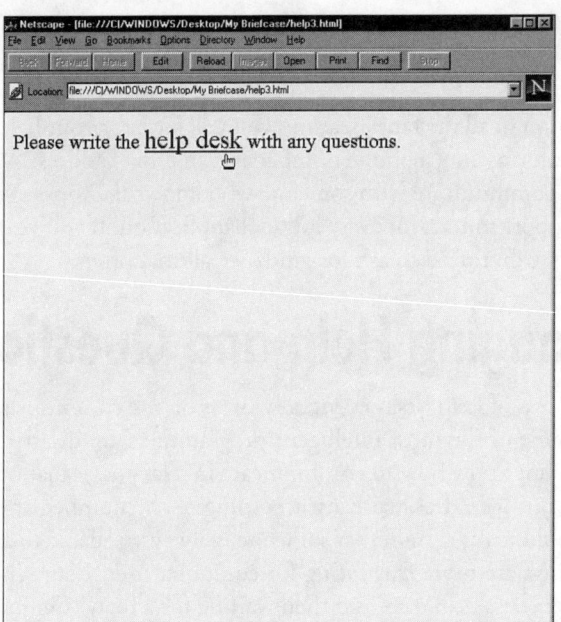

FIGURE 45.6.
Creating a link to mail a document is an easy and effective way for users to send questions.

When a user clicks that link, he or she will see a screen like the one shown in Figure 45.7.

The mailto system automatically calls up a separate screen in the Web browser. These screens are easy to use, but the person sending the mail must designate his or her e-mail address and other information in the browser's general configuration. Not only is it a nuisance to do this with each message, but many Web novices have difficulty providing the right information. Another option that produces a more elegant and simpler outcome is to insert a form on the Web page on which the user can write questions as well as provide his or her e-mail address, as shown in Figure 45.8.

FIGURE 45.7.

Almost all browsers have built-in mailing screens. They are often similar to this one, from Netscape 2.0, although they can vary slightly.

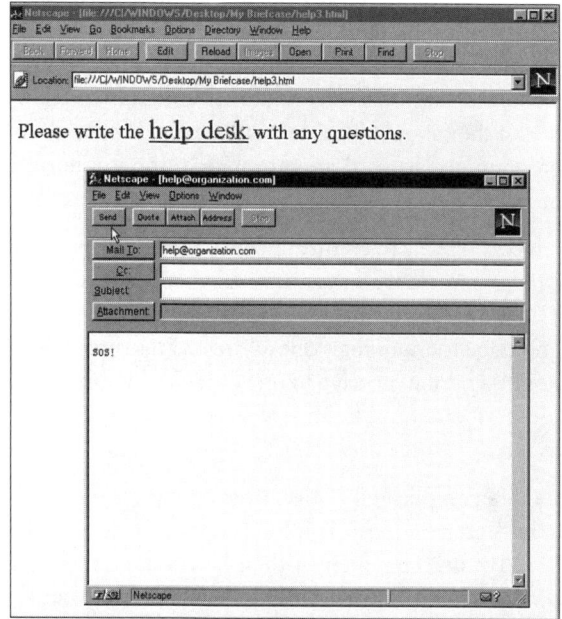

FIGURE 45.8.

The Excite search engine uses this form to solicit questions and comments.

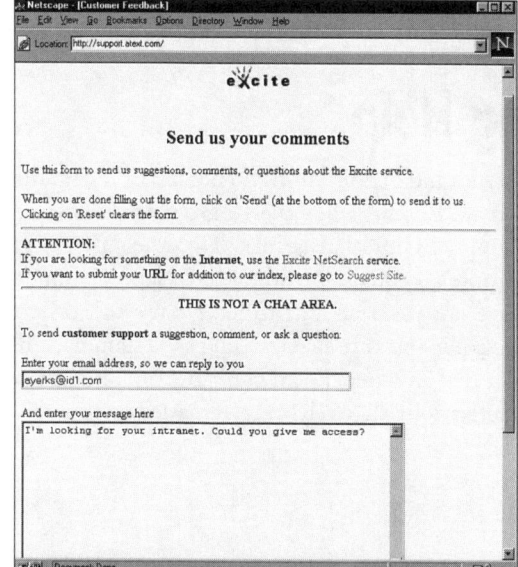

Mail Routers and Chat Lines

It is one thing to solicit questions or problems; it is another to answer those questions. There are several ways to manage incoming help requests. The easiest is in cases in which a single person is responsible for answering questions: The mailto tag will send e-mail directly to that person. Another option is to have an automatic mail router that will randomly send the message to any one of a number of consultants. Because e-mail systems vary so dramatically, commercial software companies rarely create mail routing programs. A more reliable solution is to ask the people who administer your e-mail system to develop a router. Mail routers are simple programs, and they should be able to create one for you. You also should have your help desk address programmed to send an automatic response, informing the person at the other end that his or her question has been received by the help desk.

E-mail is the easiest way to connect people with questions to help desk personnel, but you may also want to keep track of all the questions that reach your help desk. There are several ways to do this. The simplest solution is to create an e-mail address for the help desk that actually delivers the message to more than one address. This sort of setup, usually called an alias or mailing list, would send the message to one of the randomly selected help desk personnel as well as the help desk supervisor. The supervisor thus would be able to keep tabs on what problems users encounter.

A slightly more complicated option in Web-style intranets is to create a grep file for the help desk address. A grep file extracts information from an e-mail message and automatically places it in an HTML file. This file can then be made publicly available or restricted to help desk personnel. Grep files are an easy way to keep tabs on what sort of questions people have been asking. This can be a vital component of a successful help desk. Your help documents and help desk staff must be aware of the technical skills of the people within your organization, so you should be asking constantly what applications are creating problems.

Buying Help

Some companies and organizations do not have the resources to produce help information and staff a help desk. Recently, however, a growing number of companies have been created specifically to supply technical assistance. These help desk organizations offer a wide range of services and require an equally broad range of fees. Commercial help desk suppliers are so new that they have not yet been able to receive the sort of scrutiny that software companies undergo. These companies are also treading on unfamiliar turf. They are banking their future on the novel idea that an independent company can understand the requirements and likely problems of organizations that rely on a remarkably vast array of software and network applications.

These companies tend to offer similar services. Rarely do they provide actual telephone contact between customers and an actual help desk. Instead, they have focused on developing software that can answer common questions about software and system management. Most of their systems have been designed for organizations using a Windows or LAN setup, but systems for Mac, UNIX, Windows NT, and, increasingly, Windows 95 are available. Atrium, Quintus, Vycor, and Vantive are among the first organizations to develop integrated help desk systems. More recently, the Molloy Group has won considerable praise in computer trade journals for the cognitive processor at the core of its help desk apparatus. This programming structure is designed to interpret questions. Although it uses keywords like any other search function, it is designed to associate words and phrases. Ideally, it should return answers to complicated requests, regardless of how those questions are submitted.

The Molloy cognitive processor encompasses the strengths and limitations of help desk vendors. This can be a cost-effective way to provide substantive technical assistance. These companies are growing quickly. Many can deliver a level of technical detail and expertise that is rarely possible with the staff of the technical assistance departments at most small- and mid-size organizations. At the same time, however, many of these companies are providing automated help, whether through electronic responses or prerecorded phone help. This approach constitutes a fundamental difference from the traditional organization of help desks, which have enabled people to describe their computer problems and receive human assistance.

Deciding whether to use a separate help organization depends on the size and the technical requirements of your organization. It bears repeating that these commercial vendors can offer considerable advantages to small businesses that do not have people who can provide constant technical assistance and cannot afford to hire an entirely new staff for the help desk. Help desk companies also can prove useful to organizations whose members already have considerable computer training. These people know how to ask the kind of questions that an automated system can understand. Likewise, they are less likely to be intimidated by changes or corrections that they will be required to make on their own.

Summary

An intranet is only as strong as its users. You want your users to have readily available guidance for all your intranet's functions and applications. Develop your help pages with HTML links to make the help documents easy to move around in. You can use the help files that came with your software or write your own.

When organizing help, keep your users in mind. The quirks that are no doubt in some of your intranet's applications are points to focus on. If you are writing help instructions or a FAQ, do so in simple and clear language; this is not the time to try your hand at poetics. But it is the time to write clearly. The greatest problem with computer documentation remains the absence of language that many people can understand. Help, whether provided by documents or a dedicated help desk staff, must function as a translator, explaining intranets and computers to people without relying on the cryptic, confusing language of computer specialists.

You should never stop developing your intranet's help features. Be aware of new resources. Likewise, sharpen your own skills and consider producing a custom tutorial. And don't forget that—when all else fails—users should be able to contact a support person for in-house guidance.

Reference Desk

46

by Anne Marie Yerks and David Garrett

IN THIS CHAPTER

- Listing resources **688**
- Linking your resources **690**
- Guiding your users **693**
- Deep sea fishing: six rules of online research **694**

Just for a moment, pretend you are a contestant on a game show and have been asked to describe your dream office. Maybe you'd want the shelves lined with specialty encyclopedias, law books, atlases, trade journals, and manuals. In the center of the office, adjacent to the bay windows, a foot-thick dictionary would rest on a wooden podium. To the left would be a lighted globe, phone books for every city in the world, hard-bound volumes of your favorite magazines, and a newspaper rack that's updated daily. To the right is the most important item of all: A top-of-the-line copy machine that never breaks down or runs of out paper.

With such a resource array, imagine the incredible reports you could churn out, the techniques you would learn, the theories you'd invent. But alas, the expense of such a dream office is unfathomable. Not only for you, but for every one else as well (unless you're the CEO). It's true that fancy dictionaries and gold-embossed encyclopedias are going to cost. But if the information inside these expensive resources is what's closest to your heart, I'm happy to tell you it all can be yours.

The Internet isn't called "the information superhighway" undeservedly. Every minute of every hour, somebody somewhere adds yet another resource to the pile. The only problem is that finding what you want, when you want it, is a task comparable to digging a five-mile hole into a mountain. Well, you might chuckle, on an intranet, we don't have that sort of problem. On an intranet, everything is organized.

True, but is that organization going to hold when someone jumps the nest? It will depend on the resources linked to the intranet's reference area. You can't expect that the intranet is always going to be the only place users will turn when they need information. Give them a well-developed launching pad so that their excursions into the Internet will be less frustrating and more likely to reap rewards.

Listing Resources

You can begin your resource list by looking around you. What sorts of materials are people in your company using? All those materials should eventually be put online, including dictionaries, encyclopedias, journals, catalogs, and maps. A quick Net search for "dictionaries" will bring up about 12,500 responses. Thumb through them and you will find about 50 complete dictionaries available to use for free. Write some of those URLs on your resource list. Encyclopedias are harder to find, but you can purchase your favorite in an online version. For an example, visit the Encyclopædia Brittanica's Web site (shown in Figures 46.1 and 46.2) at http://www.eb.com.

However helpful they are, traditional reference materials should be at the bottom of your stack. Keep building your resource list with documents specific to your intranet (such as that shown in Figure 46.3). No doubt you'll want to include the employee handbook and perhaps make a link to the home page of the company health provider. Other items on your list might be training manuals, links to trade and association journals, and a zip code directory.

FIGURE 46.1.
The Encyclopædia Brittanica Company charges for their online reference, but you might find it's worth it.

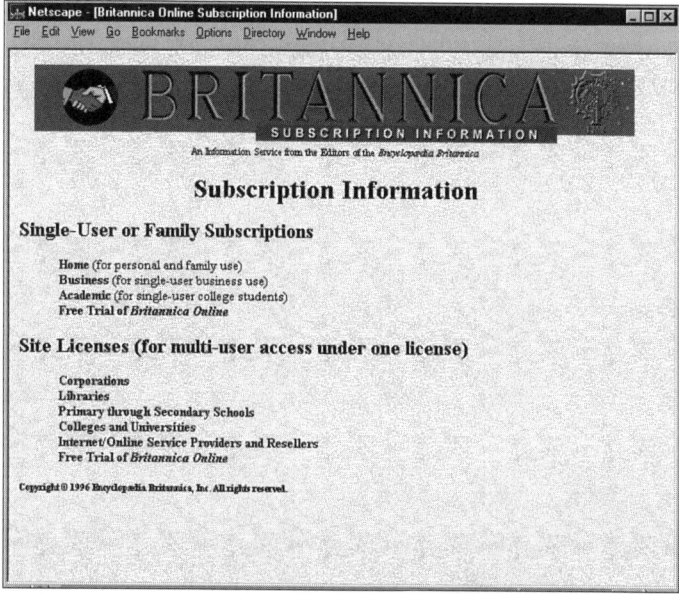

FIGURE 46.2.
By setting up a free trial, users can access the online version of Encyclopædia Brittanica.

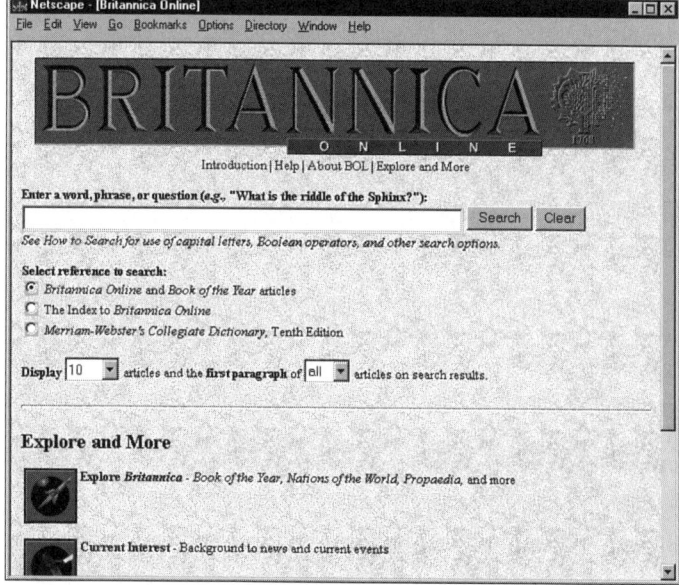

FIGURE 46.3.
Periodicals like the Investor's Business Daily might be a helpful addition to your reference desk.

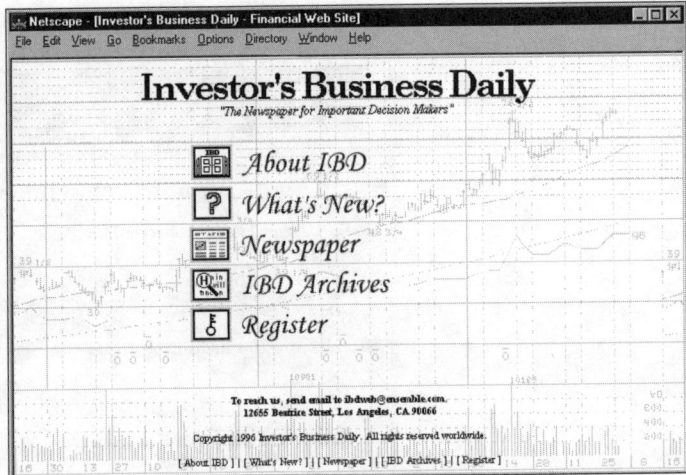

If your company has a periodical as a product, such as a special directory or journal, you should create an online version and an archive. How much of the periodical to put online is an issue worth some thought. If your company makes money from selling the hard copy, obviously you don't want to make the electronic version available for free downloading. However, you do want to assist the employees who are working on the periodical. Ask them what they would like to see online. You can secure it with passwords if it's more than you'd like to make available to the public. Your resource list can be as long as you like, and you can keep adding to it.

Of course, the free reference tools will be the easiest to include, but don't forget the commercial tools or specialized sites, such as Electric Library, shown in Figure 46.4. It's a collection of articles taken from newspapers, magazines, trade journals, and other periodicals that users can search and from which they can pull articles. With a price of about $10 a year, it can be well worth the cost. To see for yourself, visit the Electric Library at http://elibrary.com.

Linking your intranet to library sites is a good idea. Many Universities, such as Carnegie Mellon (see Figure 46.5), are working to develop sophisticated "virtual" libraries.

Linking Your Resources

If you find online libraries are helpful when building your resource list, check out one of the biggest ones around—the Library of Congress, shown in Figure 46.6.

As your resource list grows, so will your need to organize. Your users will want to know what's available, and you want them to access it easily from the home site. All the applications of your intranet can be supplemented with reference resources. For example, link the employee handbook to the training manuals, and vice versa.

FIGURE 46.4.
Infomatic's Electric Library is a low-cost, subscriber-only reference site, but you can get a free trial.

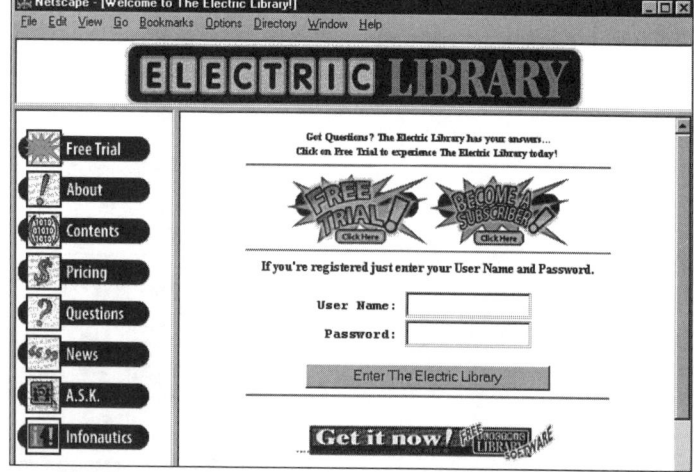

FIGURE 46.5.
Carnegie Mellon's Informedia is an online multimedia library.

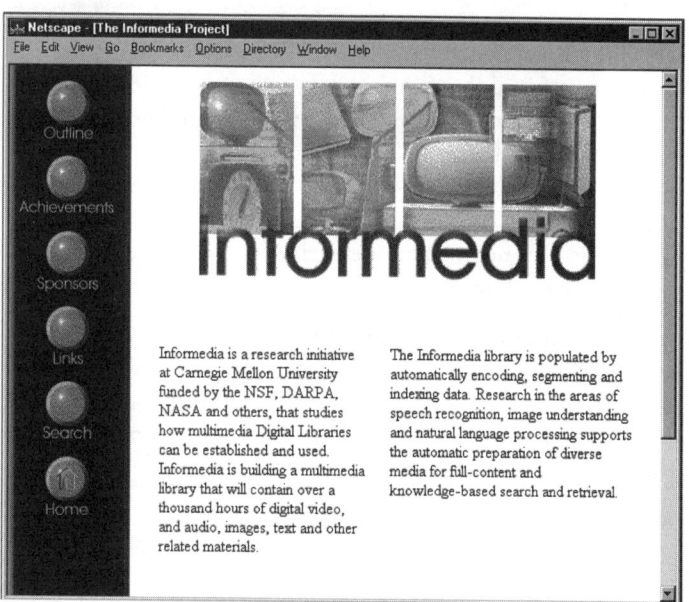

At this time, also consider the technicalities of developing digital reference materials from prewritten documents. For example, let's say that you want to make online versions of all the company newsletters from the past year. Fortunately, you were able to obtain the PageMaker file from the publicity department. It's easy enough to move all the text into Microsoft Word, but then what? To put the text online, you will need to add HTML code.

FIGURE 46.6.
The Library of Congress home site provides many reference links.

This is true for all the documents you put online. If you've ever had the frustration of reformatting a document for the Web, you will appreciate that some software companies are trying to make the feat less troublesome. Future versions of popular Web browsers will support the PDF (portable document format), which means that files from publishing programs like PageMaker and Quark Xpress will be viewable as they are, making HTML formatting unnecessary. Also, more programs are beginning to include HTML editors so text can be converted without so much trouble.

If you want to make an online resource from a document that has never been digitized, there are two options: type the document into the computer—simple enough if you know a fast typist, or scan the document and use an OCR (optical character recognition) software program to transform the image into real text. Again, simple enough if your document is on crisp clean paper for the scanner to photograph.

After you have your resources in digital format, it's only a matter of arranging the files in the proper directories and getting the permissions. Now you have the job of setting up the interface of your reference desk. Perhaps you will want to use frames, image maps, and button bars as a means of encouraging users to visit key sites. For example, you might include a link to the online yellow pages: http://s12.bigyellow.com/home_excite.html (see Figure 46.7).

The reference desk is the main hub of your online reference resources, but you should sprinkle every site on your intranet with applicable links. For example, if you know that your boss and the board of directors are discussing copyright laws on an intranet message board, you might earn a few brownie points by linking that message board to Cornell University's Law Library. The URL is http://www.law.cornell.edu/library/default.

Reference Desk
Chapter 46 693

FIGURE 46.7.
The online yellow pages can help you find both postal and electronic addresses.

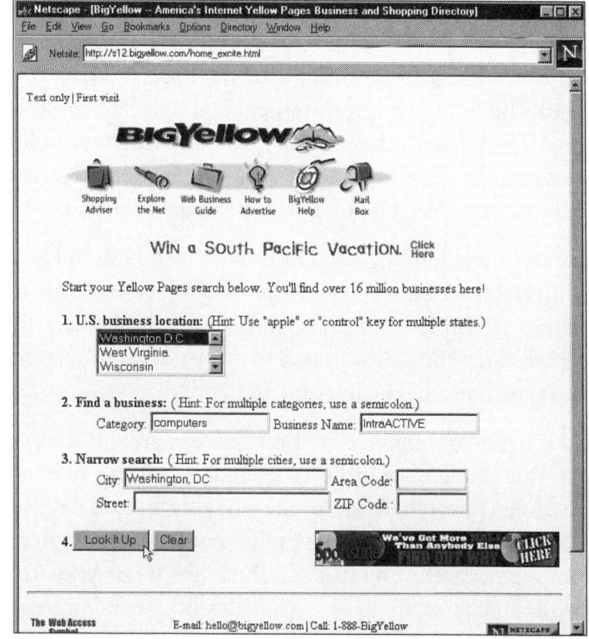

> **TIP**
>
> Speaking of copyrights, you should get permission for every document you put online. The same holds true for photographs and illustrations.

Guiding Your Users

The "librarian" of the reference desk is the person who maintains the links and software applications. This person should be available by e-mail and phone should users have questions or suggestions about using the intranet as a research tool. Questions about the content of the resources should be referred to the creators. Therefore, you might want to make a link from the company newsletter page to the press department, the scheduling board to the secretarial pool, and each message board to the e-mail box of its moderator. Your reference desk also might contain a map of the intranet itself and a guide on how to use it. Link these documents to the home page. Review Chapter 44, "Search Functions," for advice on setting up search engines, as you will probably want to make your reference resources searchable. The logistics of configuring the engines will depend on the resources you are using and your engine. Many sites already have their own search mechanisms, so make sure you really need to make your own. It could work out that the intranet-wide search engine will suffice.

Online Research

What is there to know about doing research online? Many things. First, know that just about anything can be found on the Internet. You just have to know where to look, which is not always easy. The URL for the exact site you need might be so long and complex that you would never guess it in a million years. Search engines are helpful, but you might have to wade through 20 screenfuls of unrelated hits before you find one that is even close to your query.

To find what you're looking for on the Web, you have to know the Web pretty well. If you're not looking at a few new sites every day, when it comes time to do research, your hunt for the needle in the electronic haystack is going to be a long one. One of the roles of an intranet can be to make research simple for people who are not on the external Web every day. This is where the intranet reference desk can come in handy.

Besides the basic company-related reference materials and the traditional materials already covered in this chapter, an intranet reference desk can offer a collection of linked sources for employees doing research. It will be the job of the person developing the reference desk to collect those links. And to do that, some online research will be necessary. This section offers some tips for online research. You can use these tips when you are building the intranet reference area, or you might pass them on to others who are doing research.

Deep Sea Fishing: Six Rules of Online Research

As a sample topic, we'll use "deep sea fishing." Now it's time to buckle down and plunge into the deep dark ocean we call the Internet and World Wide Web. The most tempting strategy is to immediately type in the URL for a favorite Web search site and enter deep sea fishing into the query box. This is not a bad strategy, provided that the first rule for online research is at play.

Research Rule #1: Know Your Search Sites

Although all the high-profile search sites (Lycos, Yahoo, AltaVista, Excite, Netscape Search, and Web Crawler) seem to work pretty much the same way, the truth is that they differ widely in how their engines retrieve information. Even if all six sites contained identical information, a query for "deep sea fishing" would retrieve different hits, because the engines are not looking for information in the same way. (To learn the technical details of how search engines work, read Chapter 44.)

You don't have to be an expert on the technicalities of all the search sites to do research, however; you simply should be aware of how each site allows you to set controls for your query. Before entering a search term or phrase, look for a nearby hyperlink that says something like "advanced search" or "controlled search." Even though you might not want to have to wait for yet another page to load, clicking these links and setting controls for your search can help you in the long run.

A controlled query will get you better results, but if your query is weak to begin with, no engine will retrieve what you need. Therefore, heed the second rule of online research.

Research Rule #2: Know What You Want, and You Just Might Get It

For example, assume that instead of typing `deep sea fishing`, I typed `sea`, or even something more detailed, like `sea life`. In this case, I would get some awful results. In computer lingo, "sea" is an abbreviation for a file compressed in the Macintosh self-extracting archive format. Any Web search with "sea" is going to pull up the zillions of compressed "sea" files from FTP sites around the globe, none of which are likely to have anything to do with fishing. On the other hand, a controlled search with "deep sea fishing" stands a good chance of bringing up something useful. The search engine used will have a particular way for setting controls. In the Excite search, shown in Figure 46.8, the + entered between the terms brings them all together, so that the engine looks for documents that contain all three words, rather than for documents that contain only one or two out of the three.

FIGURE 46.8.

The Excite search engine has pull-down menus for control configuration. The + between words helps narrow the search.

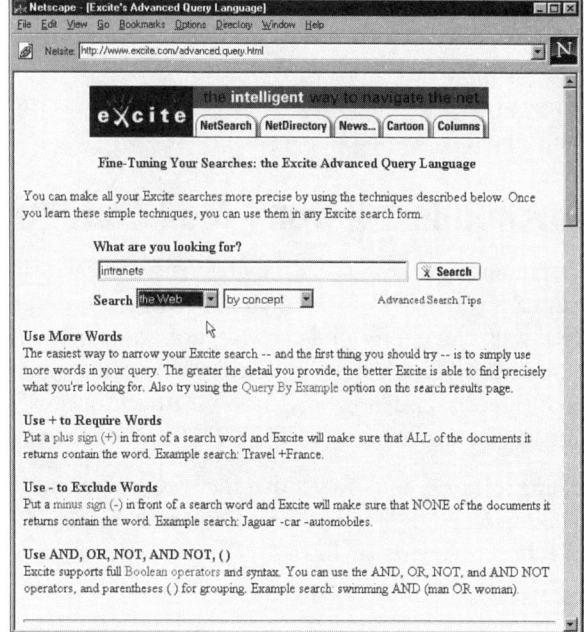

Besides search engines, there are other ways to find good sources of information. One way is simply to guess. For example, information about deep sea fishing might be found on the home site of a fishing or wildlife organization, like the World Wildlife Fund (WWF). Rather than employing a search site to find the right URL, use common sense and type `http://www.wwf.org` in the browser location window and see what happens. In this case, `http://www.wwf.org` goes right to the home page for the World Wildlife Fund. From there, the challenge is to find some good information about deep sea fishing.

When hunting through a home site for a high-profile company, it's helpful to employ the third rule of online research.

Research Rule #3: Break the Maze

Unless you want to spend a good hour or two navigating through screens of publicity and product information, get savvy about how those button bars work. Innocently clicking a "demo" button can result in five minutes' worth of flashy frame-enhanced screens and animated GIFs, none of which have anything to do with deep sea fishing. Remember why you came. Look for a button that could take you to the right place. Avoid getting lost in a "site within a site." These mini-sites often have button bars that look exactly like those on the home page, but really just take you deeper into a place you don't want to be to begin with.

If you break the maze early in your visit, and you're lucky, you'll find something to take home with you. For example, assume that the World Wildlife Fund's site contains a detailed article about deep sea fishing. In Netscape's Navigator, you can use the `mail document` command. With such an option available, you can mail yourself documents right and left. The trick is to make sure you mail it in a form that will be easy to read later. In other words, adhere to the fourth rule of online research.

Research Rule #4: Don't Mail Code (Unless You Want To)

Before beginning your search, set the preferences in the mail option of your browser so that any documents you mail from the Web will arrive to you as text, not text embedded in HTML code. That way, you can read it later without having the aggravation of parsing out the bracketed abbreviations. Here's how it works in Navigator. Choose File | Mail Document. In the Message Composition dialog box, click the Attach button, as shown in Figure 46.9. In the Attachments dialog, choose either Plain Text or Source (code), as shown in Figure 46.10.

When doing research, don't forget that the Web browser can assist you. Besides setting preferences, make bookmarks for sites that are especially helpful. Do this, and you will be following the fifth rule of online research.

Reference Desk
Chapter 46
697

FIGURE 46.9.
Click the Attach button.

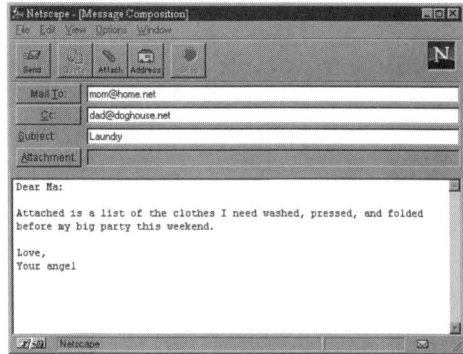

FIGURE 46.10.
Choose either plain text or code.

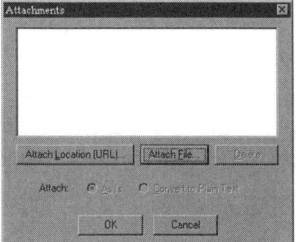

Research Rule #5: Build Your Bookmark List

Most people don't use browser bookmarks for all they're worth. Most browsers offer an option for categorizing bookmarks and for saving the bookmark list to a file that can be imported, exported, or mailed to other people. To access your bookmark list, select Window | Bookmarks. Figure 46.11 shows what a categorized bookmark list looks like.

Arranging your bookmark list in categories will keep things neat, but too many categories can be worse than none at all. Also, don't forget to make a bookmark for your favorite search site. Keep it at the top—outside your category list—so that it's easily accessible. Go through the bookmark list from time to time and delete bookmarks you no longer need.

There's a bit of an art to making bookmarks. The biggest mistake is marking a site too quickly after arriving at it. Don't do it until you are on the page that contains the information you're most interested in. If you mark a site's home page but really care only about the information you get three pages later, every time you use that bookmark you'll have to move forward three pages. It may seem trivial, but it will save you and your users valuable time.

Although the Web as we know it has been around only about three years, it's likely that you will sooner or later (sooner rather than later) come across a page that has some good information but is hopelessly out of date. The chances of finding old information on the Web are very high. It seems to be something of a tradition to leave Web pages up even after new ones take their place. So, the most important rule of online research is last but certainly not least.

FIGURE 46.11.
Bookmarks can be arranged by category or user.

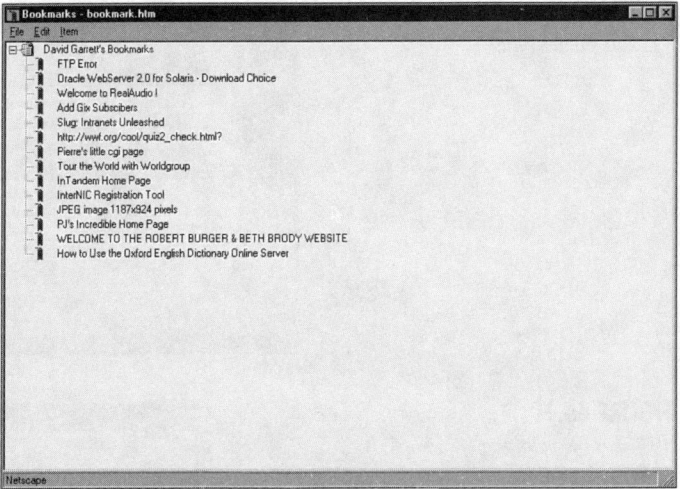

Research Rule #6: Old News Is Not Good News

The bottom line is that it's not a good idea to use information from the Web without knowing how old it is. Imagine how stupid you would feel going into a board meeting and declaring that a beta version of software product X is going to be released in the fall, only to have the CEO inform you that you're about four seasons behind.

Another worry for Web researchers is accuracy. You might find a great FAQ about deep sea fishing on a sports page, but who wrote it? If the author has only been deep sea fishing in the Atlantic, and you are focused on the Pacific, you might not want to take that advice to heart. The rule here is check the facts behind the FAQ before you make them your own.

Summary

One goal of any intranet always should be to make it as valuable as possible to its users. Stock your reference desk with company-generated and related resources. Begin the creation of your reference desk by listing what books and journal your organization's employees are using.

Digitizing prewritten documents can be a chore, but scanners and some new software features will help you along (however, a fast typist is always an asset). Take advantage of the Web sites that offer dictionaries and other reference tools for free. Also, consider buying corporate accounts at sites that store valuable information.

Assign responsibilities for reference desk maintenance to the individuals who are the most qualified. The reference desk should have a page of its own, but the resources it contains should be distributed throughout the intranet accordingly. Be creative with your links, and your intranet will be well served.

IN THIS PART

- Integrating Existing Applications **701**
- Maintaining a User Database **717**
- Designing a Successful File Structure **727**
- Maintaining Security **739**
- Hardware and Software Upgrades **747**

PART
VII

Administering Your Intranet

Integrating Existing Applications

47

by Edmund Landgraf

IN THIS CHAPTER

- A brief history of modern applications **702**
- Goals of integration **703**
- The current state of the application environment **707**
- Integration with the intranet **711**
- Intranet- and Internet-enabled applications **714**

With the intranet comes yet another opportunity to evaluate your organization's computing infrastructure. Applications are at the core of the business as they are the final interface presented to both the employee and the customer. If your applications are built around a closed architecture, the benefits of open databases and highly connected networks are limited. In other words, if your application can't support TCP/IP or medium-resolution graphics, integrating into the intranet is going to be very difficult.

To weigh the cost versus the benefit of moving into the intranet, your organization needs to take an honest look at both your critical and peripheral support programs and attempt to itemize, categorize, and assign usefulness in each core area. You should pay special attention to the amount of time and resources to add necessary intranet functionality, total life of the application, and specific goals the intranet integration is meant to achieve. Because application development is one of the fastest changing markets in the industry, the task of creating a strategy to manage the intranet interface of each application can be daunting, if not seemingly impossible. This chapter tries to provide a basic structure so that you can examine the intranet's impact on current and future applications.

A Brief History of Modern Applications

Applications have traditionally relied on proprietary mechanisms to share information between them. When the industry was dominated by a few key companies, commercial applications were focused on integrating themselves only with other programs, databases, or networks made within the same company. All-In-One was a product made by Digital Equipment in the late '80s; it attempted to pull together word processing, e-mail, database access, and PIM capability into one package. Although the applications worked fairly well with each other, the program was required to run on a VAX/VMS platform, had no significant import or export capability, and took no advantage of the suite of TCP/IP support the VAX had to offer, such as Telnet and FTP.

The next generation of applications stressed openness, and each vendor struggled to obtain market dominance. Companies attempted to create standards more through marketing at times than on technical merit. During this time, cross-platform communication was greatly improved, as users successfully lobbied for better import and export filters (for example, dBASE to Paradox, Excel to Lotus, and so on). Even more seamless integration could take place, but the strain to both the hardware and network began to show. Many technologies that are rich in functionality, like OLE and OpenDoc, take up a fair amount of systems resources. This additional overhead can at times actually decrease the overall productivity of a user, achieving exactly the opposite of the intended effect. Using the initial release of OLE (version 1.0), for example, a Microsoft Word user could link an Excel worksheet inside an open Word document. On a 486 computer with 4MB of memory, opening the Excel file while in Word would cause Excel to load. Loading both these applications into 4MB of memory is nearly impossible, and the time it took the computer to swap information back and forth to disk was much longer than if the user had kept the documents separate. This is a classic example of the technology being good but the real-world situation demanding a more robust technology with less overhead.

Lastly, the intranet takes cues from both the previous generations of applications and provides openness without excessive complexity. It takes advantage of industry standards like TCP/IP; provides for audio, video, and text via HTTP; and provides a standard set of security functions through SST or S-HTTP (secure HTTP). Ironically, the intranet supports the same concepts as originally set by the proprietary suites but does so in the flexible and extensible way the legacy applications could never achieve.

Goals of Integration

All applications, by their very nature, lose their value over time. Some commercial applications age gracefully, as either a combination of customer or company enthusiasm and application sales feeds capital into upgrades and extensions that keep pace with the changing computing environment. Other 4GL-based custom applications fall quickly behind the edge of new technology. Any Visual Basic, PowerBuilder, or other GUI programmer can explain the usually extensive modification needed to change an application when trying to add new technology that was never considered at design time. Modifying a VB application to use OLE servers to communicate with ActiveX objects on a Web server sounds like a great idea, but often this modification produces a mediocre solution at a premium cost. With this in mind, one of the most useful ways to look at integration goals is in terms of time—specifically, short-term, loosely defined as three to six months, and long-term, six months or longer.

Short-Term

For the short term, look at what internal applications would benefit most. Commercial applications are often out of the control of the individual, with the exception of possibly being able to buy add-ins that extend functionality to existing applications (for example, a Web authoring assistant for WordPerfect).

Internal applications whose main functions are to provide rudimentary, fairly static data to a user group are an easy first target for integration or elimination. The merits of discarding the application versus building an interface to the intranet are largely dependent on the breadth of the program. Some might be highly customized to provide organization-level detail that would not be trivial to duplicate on a Web server, whereas others might be no more than small programs that look up phone numbers of employees, a task much better suited to an intranet.

Short-term goals should be clearly defined, have a limited scope, and can be implemented in parallel with other development efforts. The success of the short-term integration is most often based on how well the target application is "suited" for modification.

One sample opportunity involves broadcasting information contained in weekly or monthly status reports over an intranet. Most companies include documented reports of employees' progress in various work areas, often taking the form of written minutes of a regularly scheduled meeting. Too often, however, these valuable minutes are confined to the distribution list of the immediate members of the project or department group. The minutes are not available to higher management or marketing, and no one outside this selected group knows the week-to-week developments. This communication omission can lead to duplication of effort and waste of resources. One system that you could create to solve this problem involves extending the power of the word processor and combining it with Web server publishing technology.

First, you would need to fit the word processor with an HTML converter. This fairly simple task is offered (or soon to be offered) in the major suites (for example, MS Word, WordPerfect, and WordPro). If no HTML converter is built into your word processor, many free or off-shelf options exist. (For a good list of HTML converters, check out

http://www.ncsa.uiuc.edu/SDG/Software/Mosaic/Docs/faq-software.html

For a free Microsoft Word extension, see http://www.microsoft.com/msword/fs_wd.htm).

The next step is to move the newly created HTML version of the minutes to the Web server. But it would be best if there were some way to categorize the minutes so that you could have a Web page with a complete index. Ideally, you would just want to submit the information and give the additional project description and date details. But this information is most likely already contained in the document itself, in a title or heading, indicated using a special style (for example, department name, week number, project code, and so on). To accomplish this task, you can write a Perl script that executes whenever a new minutes submission is made. The script can scan the HTML for the special styles mentioned previously and place this text into temporary fields for further use. The fields are then used to update the Web page that contains the index information. If styles aren't available, you can create a page to query a user with summary information via CGI. Either way, the index Web page makes it simple for anyone in the organization to pull up the status of any project in any department. The index automatically inserts new documents as they are submitted. Note that an entire enterprise could add minutes by this manner because there are no inherent physical restrictions and no need to manage the logical organization. A sample intranet Web page for this hypothetical project might appear as shown in Table 47.1.

Table 47.1. Main weekly minutes index page (`http://www.org/intranet/weekly_status/mainidx`).

Document Name	Week Ending	Link
IS: Project A	10/15/96	`//www.org/intranet/weekly_status/IS/project_a/101596`
IS: Project C	10/15/96	`//www.org/intranet/weekly_status/IS/project_c/101596`
Support: Project D	10/15/96	`//www.org/intranet/weekly_status/Support/project_d/101596`
IS: Project A	11/1/96	`/www.org/intranet/weekly_status/IS/project_a/110196`

Even though this example is text-based, there are other ways to add functionality. Icons, letter bars (A B C...Z), and graphic timelines are just a few alternative or additional features that could be added.

Realistically, you must allow for some management. The Webmaster would be responsible for archiving or deleting old weekly minutes. You also could extend this solution to create a cross-reference page that lists projects by employee name. Employees could be searched, and their appropriate projects (and links to their status reports) could be displayed.

Short-term projects are the best way for an organization to "get its feet wet" developing intranet applications. Although the preceding example is probably not mission-critical for most organizations, it brings together a world of related information into a concise reference tool, further enabling workers to make better decisions with better data.

Long-Term

The long-term goals of integration are clear, but the implementation is much more subtle. Users should be able to access internal data through a single point of contact. The contact interface should mask the complexities of the underlying database technologies, so a grid that can be pulled up on a Web browser can draw its data from either a flat file (for example, a Comma-Separated Variable, or CSV) or an RDBMS (for example, Oracle or Sybase) without the user's ever needing to know the source. This seamless integration increases power to the support infrastructure of the organization by reducing the cost of maintenance and leveraging data to its maximum. A phased implementation plan is best, allowing your organization to examine its goals carefully and concentrate on the simplest or redundant applications first.

A long-term intranet example has many similarities to a long-term client-server project. Both have the same goal of either breaking up large, high-maintenance, inflexible applications into more precise components or building new systems in which the workload is spread evenly (or almost evenly) across all pieces of the architecture. One long-term intranet strategy might be to adapt slightly nonmainstream technology to utilize many applications' capability to use ODBC. Using products such as Nomad Developments Corp.'s WebDBC or Allaire Corp.'s Cold Fusion, developers can build pages that send and retrieve data using ODBC instead of building SQL inside CGI, Perl, or Embedded SQL-C scripts.

Another long-term goal might be to provide a universal client for every PC or workstation. The Web browser serves as the universal client and must be able to access and display data from virtually anywhere. UNIX-based and NT systems have an edge as a data source, because they support intranet standards. However, mainframes and midrange computers are not as fortunate. Not only do you have to convert networking protocols, you also must concern yourself with different text standards (ASCII versus EPSDIC) and the nuisances of terminal-based communication. One way of handling this problem is straightforward: You convert terminal-based forms into Web pages, creating CGI fields mimicking the source screen. This process is often called *wrapping* (or *screen scraping*), because you are simply adding a translation layer between the terminal-based application and the Web-based application. The following step is a bit more complicated because the data must be repackaged and sent off to the mainframe with the proper credentials. While the data rearranging can be handled, the authentication procedure generally requires a proxy server, which acts as a processing server between the user and the Web or the request's intended destination.

MCKEON & JEFFRIES

McKeon & Jeffries integrated several existing applications into its intranet. Because they had used Groupwise mail for several years, they merely installed a patch and could use it with their Internet mail as well as their LAN and WAN mail. They also had used Microsoft Word as a word processing application. So by using the Microsoft add-on for Word, the intranet administrator could easily convert documents into HTML.

THE SPORTING GOODS AND APPAREL ASSOCIATION

The SGAA integrated its existing database into the intranet. By importing its database into Oracle, the group hit the ground running with a full data structure.

The Current State of the Application Environment

The first step in preparing your applications for the intranet is to examine the characteristics of your current application environment. Drawing a model of your application structure builds a solid foundation for your intranet integration strategy. Four basic divisions—purpose, application range, frequency of use, and functionality—aid in characterizing your applications' suitability for the intranet.

Purpose

The purpose of your applications generally focuses on the central business function of your organization. You should look at purpose without regard to any specific technology. Depending on whether your organization's ultimate goal is to sell a product, provide information services, or simply establish office communication, the purpose sets the background for how an intranet will emerge.

The purpose of a custom application might be to provide management with real-time data of a given production process. It also may hold addresses of customers who are recipients of the goods produced. This second function may or may not be part of the original purpose; it may have just worked out that this information is stored here. You should look for applications that might have this kind of all-encompassing functionality and see whether this noncritical information is already held in another database.

Applications that have redundant purposes are red flags, and you should investigate them further as potential candidates for the intranet. You need to evaluate the purpose for each individual application because it will assist you in ranking the relative priorities of integration into the intranet.

Application Ranges

Application range refers to the different types of software that permeate an organization, such as spreadsheets, databases, and word processors. Some companies emphasize word processing and order management, whereas others are more concerned about spreadsheets and statistics. In many larger environments, the full range of applications exists. Planning for the intranet is difficult when the range of applications is broad because each application could require its own intranet strategy. Often with newer PC software such as suites, however, the applications share at least one common communications technique, so intranet integration can focus more on providing a service to bridge this technology instead of attempting to create custom solutions for each application.

Frequency of Use

Frequency of use is fairly self-explanatory: You examine the overall use of applications. Frequency can vary greatly in an application environment that has a large range, from one database package used by all the employees to three graphics programs that are used by one person. Low-frequency applications are often better suited to short-term intranet integration because they affect fewer people and tend to occupy a small niche of functionality. Low-frequency applications uncover places in the organization where technology is understood by only a few.

The inherent nature of the intranet to provide seemingly ubiquitous information access unlocks the knowledge trapped in the infrequently used applications. For example, a company might have a sole graphics designer using a complicated set of graphics tools to provide users with images; that setup might be replaced with the same designer having a graphics "pool" with a Web browser on users' desks to scan through all the available graphics before making a selection. The low-frequency applications could still be used, but the image files could be placed in a universal area readable by a browser that supports viewing standard graphics formats (for example, TIFF, EPS, or GIF).

Functionality

Functionality is a heavily weighted factor when you're examining the effort to integrate existing applications into the intranet. Each application has a level of technical prowess by default. Some applications are built more on Internet-like standards, with open standards and hooks for other applications to communicate with. *Hooks* are small application interfaces that developers try to build into their products in anticipation of future enhancement or integration with other products. If someone writes a word processing program, for example, but doesn't have time to write a speller, he or she could leave a "hook" in the program to access a speller if one is provided in the future. The program would not have to change; it could check the interface to see whether another speller is trying to communicate and, if so, enable the speller in the word processor. These applications obviously require less work to integrate than programs that function in a closed environment.

Functionality is often defined by the architecture of the application. Two common choices made by software designers are either to enable an application to communicate over a network or not, meaning an application is network-enabled or stand-alone, respectively.

Network-Enabled Applications

The communication infrastructure of an application describes its ability to access data outside its immediate realm. Network-enabled applications have an infrastructure to support some type of a network protocol. The most common protocols are NetBIOS, NetBEUI (Named Pipes), IPX/SPX, and TCP/IP on Intel-based machines. These applications make use of the network in two common ways; to access a file server or to access a peer computer. Accessing a file server could be for tasks as simple as copying a Word document or more complex actions such as updating a local database program from a server-based RDBMS.

Peer networking most commonly looks to share files or printers. This networking scheme also most closely resembles an intranet. Intranets use addresses on Web pages to mark locations of files, much like peer-to-peer networking uses shared drives and directories. Both structures enable universal naming conventions, but only the intranet standard allows standardization, as each vendor often has its own scheme for locating resources distributed in a network (for example, Novell works differently than Microsoft, which works differently than Banyan). To access a file called `index.doc`, for example, you would use the following for HTTP (intranet or Internet):

```
http://my_organization/my_computer/folders/editor_group/index.doc
```

With UNC (Universal Naming Convention), you would use the following :

```
\\my_computer\folders\editor_group\index.doc
```

With HTTP, the URL needs to exist and point to a valid file. With UNC, a "share" must be created on the folder that contains `index.doc` (that is, `editor_group`). Note that UNC does not inherently support more than one organization. If a new department is brought online and has a duplicate computer name, the connection fails. You can avoid this problem through careful domain planning and design. The final analysis reveals that UNC was designed for organizations, whereas the Internet was designed for global access.

Domains are part of the Microsoft network architecture model that create logical "units" to which computers are assigned.

Stand-Alone Applications

Although most people believe that today's applications can take advantage of a network, some programs today are meant to "stand alone." Often they are database-type applications that might come on a CD. They allow users to interface with the database via an application on the same computer. Some actually prohibit network access due to licensing concerns. Stand-alone applications generally have a specific scope and function. Most DOS games are good examples; they are meant to be played on a single computer with one user, and they do not need to interface with any other programs. Other examples are proprietary databases that are often subscribed to on a monthly or quarterly basis. A market research firm might publish their findings on a CD once every month with the intention that only one machine can use the information at any given time.

As I mentioned earlier in this chapter, programs that exist to solely provide access to data are good candidates for the intranet, because the intranet is a more natural medium to share data. More vendors will begin to integrate their stand-alone applications into the intranet, possibly as Java applets, and licensing issues will ease with the increased use of metering software. Metering software limits the number of "copies" the server allows to be checked out at one time.

If you buy a 10-user pack, for example, you can install one copy of the software on the network and have the metering software ensure that no more than 10 people are using the program at any one time.

Application Integration (OLE, COM, OpenDoc)

Application integration is the final component of functionality, addressing the inter-application communications. Application integration applies to both stand-alone and network-enabled applications, as two applications that can communicate with each other may not necessarily communicate over a network. Other mechanisms designed by software companies or nonprofit standards organizations help create vendor-independent applications that share a common protocol. Dynamic Data Exchange (DDE), Object Linking and Embedding (OLE), Common Object Model (COM), and OpenDoc support such interapplication communication. Existing applications that use one of these or other technologies can still benefit from an intranet. Consider, for example, publisher whose editors use OLE or OpenDoc to create compound documents and distribute them within the group. A possible integration project would be to establish a gateway for a group of machines to connect to the intranet. Although only one gateway would exist, it would appear to the group of publishers that they are directly connected to the intranet and could send files to the group of editors in another workgroup (for example, via FTP). Figure 47.1 illustrates a possible scenario.

FIGURE 47.1.
Bridging the gap: nonintranet applications.

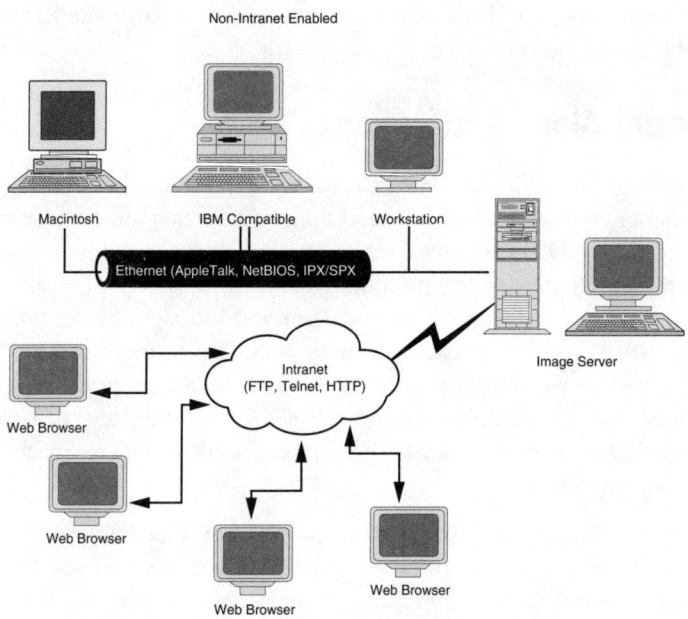

Non-intranet machines can continue to use and distribute images to a server. This machine in turn can implement a Web server component to provide universal image access to any other computer running a Web browser.

Although many commercial products will become more and more intranet-enabled, the internally developed applications will require the most planning. Many client-server systems with front ends developed in Visual Basic, PowerBuilder, or SQL Windows were built without the intranet or Internet in mind.

Integration with the Intranet

Eventually, most organizations will want to take a proactive approach to integrating their applications into the intranet. Creating an appropriate timeline for integration can prove difficult and evasive. Because the intranet is still a relatively young concept, there is danger in moving too quickly in an attempt to revolutionize an entire information system environment. A better approach, as this chapter has alluded to, is to break down the IS structure into definitive, manageable, functional components. You can incorporate each broken-out component into well-constructed intranet integration timelines that have distinctive milestones, where time is allocated to both reflect and evaluate past and current progress, as well as make minor changes to future tasks as needed. Three such breakdowns are inventory, focus and implementation, and feedback and evaluation.

Inventory

An accurate inventory is critical in any intranet integration project. Although it might sound incredible, many mid-level IS managers do not have a realistic picture of their application environment. This occurs most in organizations that do not have strict standards for what applications are used. Colleges and universities, for example, often have supported applications from which faculty and students can draw. Too often, however, freedom is granted to use other applications that might be too specific to support at a departmental or school level. When an intranet plan is introduced, users likely will be perplexed by two different standards: one in which their applications can use the intranet, and another in which they cannot. The central problem is users' conceptions of the intranet model, and they won't adapt as easily as users who are presented with a consistent view of application services.

The following list provides tips and techniques to help ensure an accurate inventory:

- Develop a complete list of all applications.
- List the characteristics of each application, including purpose, range, functionality, and frequency of use.
- List standard non-intranet communications mechanisms (for example, OLE, COM, CORBA, DDE, and NetBIOS).
- List standard intranet communication mechanisms (for example, SMTP, TCP/IP, FTP, Telnet, and HTTP).

An example might look like Table 47.2.

Table 47.2. A sample inventory.

Application	Purpose	Range	Functionality	Frequency of Use	Non-Intranet Communication	Intranet Communication
Microsoft Office	Office automation	Enterprise	Network-enabled	High	DDE, OLE, MAPI	SMTP, HTML
PowerBuilder Oracle C/S delivery system	Product delivery	Product group	Network-enabled, proprietary Oracle SQL Net	Low for enterprise; high for product group	Proprietary database language; custom non-intranet post office	TCP/IP, Perl scripts
Peoplesoft Human Resources System	Human Resource management	Human Resources, executive	Stand-alone (Peoplesoft peers only)	High for HR; low for executive	Multiple	Optional

Focus and Implementation

The next stage takes the organization through its first and successive intranet integration projects. For commercial applications, you can concentrate your focus on third-party software that gets the most out of an existing environment. Older commercial applications that look like they will never embrace the intranet might now have enough momentum to justify their replacement. With custom applications, you need a more thorough strategy because they likely are not as unified in their construction. Deciding on a standard intranet tool set is a good choice to provide a standard way of delivering intranet functionality to custom applications in the future, while providing a framework to revisit older programs that have been selected for enhancement. Three such visual tools are Jamba by Aimtech, Symantec's Café, and Distinct's Visual Internet Toolkit. All give you a development environment supporting HTML, dynamic controls (that is, CGI objects), and Java support.

Training, focus groups, and milestones cannot be understated here. Users must understand how the intranet addition will help them with their responsibilities, and users must be involved in the implementation of any integration project. Also, milestones help create linear breakpoints where software can be tested during construction.

The following are tips and techniques for the focus and implementation stage:

- Target applications that are "closest" to being intranet-enabled. Examine functionality.
- Examine applications that are most conducive to becoming an intranet-enabled application (for example, the electronic phone book) by purpose, range, and frequency of use.

- Create focus groups of users familiar with the applications being selected for integration.
- Look for a standard set of TCP/IP-based tools that allow custom applications to be modified to add intranet functionality (for example, Distinct's TCP/IP suite for Visual Basic and PowerBuilder or NetManage's Chameleon visual TCP/IP suite).
- Consider "dual-path" integration. Allow the applications to work as they would normally, and add intranet integration. Create a side-by-side list showing equivalent functionality using two different methods (that is, intranet and non-intranet).
- Construct solid timelines for short-term projects. Use short-term successes to guide long-term strategies.

One focus project underway at a large consulting firm addressed a situation in which employees had developed small applications written in Visual Basic, C++, or Uniface for the PC. They were available through a cc:Mail/Notes bulletin board system, and many copies were downloaded. One application was an electronic phone book that came with a 4MB directory file of every employee in the company. Another was a skill searcher, which used previously created employee profiles with a small front end to gather needed project skills. Yet another was a program to guide users through all available training courses. Each application was created with a need, but the proliferation of tiny programs became hard to organize and difficult for individual users or groups to maintain. A focus group sat down and created the basic inventory document (as described previously) and decided what type of tools it would use. They decided that no program was worth saving individually. Eventually, the group lobbied for WebData from Corel Corporation as an easy way to create Web pages that do not need to update a database. Additionally, the group verified that the phone directory, employee profiles, and training courses existed in the corporate database (if not, they could have created a data warehouse of information available to the Web server). By keeping the data in the database, each responsible area would maintain its piece of information (for example, Human Resources maintains skill profiles, and Telecommunications maintains phone directories). Lastly, accuracy of the data would be higher as the browser requests always return any changes in a source HTML page.

Feedback and Evaluation

No process is complete without feedback and evaluation. Feedback and evaluation are gathered in phases and can help further shape intranet integration efforts. Sometimes projects that do not serve the organizations' goals are attempted solely to prove the technology can work. Although this approach might be fine in a laboratory setting where proof-of-concept studies are done, it is not appropriate for large-scale integration efforts. History has shown that many times this becomes evident during this stage of the project life cycle. Evaluation goes most smoothly if you develop all the essential components within the same time frame. An application modified to use the intranet can hardly be evaluated if no internal Web server is in place.

The following are tips to help your feedback and evaluation go smoothly:

- Build in milestones that return both technical and usability information about the integration project.
- Examine the impact of each integration project. Specifically, attempt to show that the original goals of the project were fulfilled or not fulfilled and the reasons why.
- Build a business case that justifies the use of more intranet integration or replacement based on feedback from intranet project users.
- Continually refine the vision. Think incrementally. Keep asking the questions "For what business reason am I doing this?" and "How does intranet integration add value to my organization?"

Intranet- and Internet-Enabled Applications

As the intranet is the logical extension of the Internet, the computing industry will begin to embrace the intranet-Internet cross-communication paradigm. One of the main drivers for intranet evolution is the native accessibility to the Internet. Applications that can use the intranet also can use the Internet, provided the communications structure is in place (that is, a gateway to the Internet). Users will be blinded to whether data is coming from inside the company or from outside. Managers can screen content of their organizations' Web pages and add links to the outside world where appropriate.

A Commercial Application

Delivering support to developers and end users has been a neverending cost in most software and hardware vendors' bottom line. The days of free support dwindle by the day, and pay-as-you-go or fixed-contract support policies are being spread throughout the industry. As vendors claim that it's their time to finally charge for these previous gratis services, irate users might cast permanent stigmas on companies they feel are doing them a disservice. Some companies, however, are trying to take a more proactive approach. Microsoft and Novell have long recognized the need to keep the advanced technical users yearning for new technology while learning how to support the old.

One offering from Microsoft is the Microsoft Developer Network, a CD subscription service with both applications and product documentation presented to the developers or other computing professionals. The main information CD allows queries on keywords and brings back related articles, white papers, or sample code. Recently, Microsoft has bolstered their offerings with links back to their own headquarters, as well as links to third-party developers that they feature in the CD subscription service.

Because the amount of information a CD can store is limited (approximately 660MB), Microsoft has recognized the need to look structurally at how they distribute data. For the same reasons that a dictionary that comes on 12 CDs would not be very convenient for most people (because most people have only one CD drive, and swapping CDs is neither fast nor convenient), bundling every software patch or hardware compatibility document to be sent out every month could get very unwieldy.

In addition, many things change over time, and nothing changes faster than the information industry. Information stored on CDs can get out of date very quickly. Consider the same informational requirements but with a different approach. The CDs contain links to Web pages or FTP sites that can be accessed through Microsoft's Internet Explorer. For example, the CD might contain information on SQL Server, a popular RDBMS. It could have many articles and performance statistics contained in files on the CD itself. But for communication drivers, where by nature most companies need only one or two, having a link to a central communication driver FTP site that could be accessed from the CD would be more efficient. This keeps the drivers up-to-date because Microsoft can maintain the FTP files, and the user can be assured that he or she is getting the latest release of the software.

At this time, only Microsoft's browser works here. Due to market competition and a lack of written standards in the browser arena, Netscape's offerings currently do not work. However, users can expect more integration and less application dependence in the future.

An In-House Application

As organizations look to get the most out of their in-house applications, they recognize that the line between the intranet and the Internet is disappearing. You can spend a lot of time in the WWW searching for places that you found days or hours before. Although bookmarks help greatly in this situation, it makes sense to take the internal information on the one side of the firewall and link it with information on the Internet. These maintained links ensure that employees have at least a consistent view of what the organization deems related to its business and can be arranged by category or by name (for example, Software vendors…, Search engines…, Sales contacts by region…, and so on).

For example, a small- to medium-sized company with an in-house Web server linked via an intranet (dedicated to provide internal information to employees) decided to add outside links into their Web page. The company chose to put very logical information into their page, such as the home page of the database vendor they use, multiple links to support organizations that have similar goals as the company, and links to competitors' home pages to assist marketing personnel in selling their products. In addition, they are connected to an in-house FTP server with the latest software patches, UNIX, Perl, and Informix scripts, and historical documents employees had completed. Of course, all users had Web browsers on their desktops and had some training in how to use the intranet. The next step is to begin to integrate the internal, custom-built applications to use this internal Web server.

Both examples illustrate how two different sized companies are adjusting and attempting to engage the intranet proactively to create applications that better serve their users.

Summary

Application integration requires careful planning when you're considering both the advantages and difficulties of building an intranet. You must evaluate each application and give thought to solutions that provide access, allowing existing applications to leverage the intranet right now.

Although you must evaluate each networked application individually, these types of programs are better viewed in the long-term plan of the intranet. The key consideration is to examine the reasons that an intranet-enabled application would be superior to a networked application in terms of actual functionality. Focus a solution on providing a gateway between the intranet and to the applications that provide the best cost/benefit ratio.

You shouldn't "push" applications into the intranet; each should have a valid business reason to be considered. Commercial applications will continue to evolve and become more intranet-enabled. The custom applications, however, will yield the most formidable challenge as your IS department chooses between retrofitting old programs to make the intranet leap or accepting the heavy financial burden of rebuilding an application from scratch, this time making it intranet-enabled.

Maintaining a User Database

48

by David Garrett

IN THIS CHAPTER

- Creating a sustainable user model 718
- Implementing a user database 721

If you were designing your own home, you might spend a great deal of time planning and designing the room where you and your family will spend much of your time. Perhaps this is the family room or the living room, or maybe even the kitchen. Whatever the room, it's an important choice and, most of you would probably agree, well worth the extra time spent in the planning process. As you begin to build your intranet, you'll want to take the extra time to consider the setup of where your users will continually "congregate"—the user database.

Early in this chapter I'll discuss what to consider when creating a database and later how to maintain that database. The user databases covered are appropriate for UNIX, Windows 3.x, Windows 95, Windows NT, and Mac networks. Although the technical specifics of how the user databases are actually implemented vary slightly from platform to platform, the concept remains the same. The important and sometimes complex issue of running a database for all users, but with limitations for some of those users, is addressed. In addition, I discuss integrating user databases on mail servers, file servers, Web servers, and other servers into a common database so users are required to remember only one user ID and password. Finally, I talk about maintaining a secure user database while making it user-friendly for all.

Creating a Sustainable User Model

While building the infrastructure of your intranet, one of the most important issues to consider is how to keep track of who's using the system and the system's limitations. The first step is to make a list of all the users who will have access to the intranet and then to make a second list of the functions you intend to provide these users. It is likely that you will want to provide different levels of access to different users or groups of users. For example, you might have a Web site or portion of one that has sensitive financial information. You may want your financial administrators to access that information, while keeping it private from the majority of the users. Similarly, you might want to have a group of users who are allowed to post content, either in the form of Web pages, files, or new applications, while other users are merely allowed to view and download the files.

Building a successful and sustainable user database is a complex project. Be sure to set aside enough time up front to devote to the building of a solid and thorough database. A few hours spent developing the plan will save days or possibly weeks of retooling should you later decide that your database doesn't have the functionality you need.

In an intranet setting, especially if there are multiple types of servers, several different user databases must be maintained. Web servers, FTP servers, and database servers all have different methods for authenticating users. Many organizations find it easiest to designate different user databases as subsets of one large database. Especially on an internal network, like a LAN or a WAN with no connectivity to the Internet and thus reduced need for exorbitant security measures, it might be more important to create an easy interface for your users who must adhere to strict security standards. Where this is applicable, the intranet developer can create a common user database in which all the other individual databases can be built. Some organizations keep these lists separate to enhance security. That way, if a single user's ID and password are compromised or cracked, the security hole is limited. Remember, though, the more separate user databases you run, the more passwords users must remember. Multiple databases can be detrimental to security, however, as users are more likely to write down their passwords in insecure locations.

User Groups

The largest group of users to consider when developing a database is the basic user. Ask yourself what the least common denominator is as far as what functions you want accessible to everyone and at what level. For example, if you keep a comprehensive contact database on your intranet, you may want everyone to access it so they can look up names, phone numbers, addresses, and so on. However, you might want to deny access to some of the information on that database, such as a comments area, to some users, while allowing all users access to general information.

To begin establishing levels of access, consider developing a list of functions that will be available to all the users. Next, make a list of the functions that will require both public and private areas. A simple way to do this is to make a chart of sets and subsets. You may find that many of your subsets will include many of the same users. If this is the case, consider if there are distinct user groups in the organization that fall into similar categories. For example, a company has a sales group that has access to pricing information, a development/production group with access to research and development information, and an administration group that can access human resources information. Taking the subsets one step further, there is a supervisor group with access to all the subsets. Following this example, Table 48.1 is a potential listing of individuals, their titles, and subsets into which they might fall.

Table 48.1. A list of individuals and their titles and the subsets into which they fall.

Name	Title	Subset
Paul	Administrative Assistant	General
Nancy	Sales Associate	Sales
Pat	Engineer	Development
Steve	Human Resources Manager	Administration
Sheila	Vice President/Operations	Supervisor

Using this structure, the sales, development, and administration subset groups are all members of the general group. Thus, anyone who is a member of these three groups is also a member of the general group, and therefore can access general information. Similarly, the supervisor subset includes membership in the administration, sales, and development groups, whose members are also members of the general subset group. To that end, Paul, in the general group, has the most limited access. Nancy, Pat, and Steve can access everything that Paul can in addition to their specific areas. Sheila, as a member of all the groups, can access everything.

From this example, you can begin to appreciate the importance of developing a thorough and reasonable database from the onset. Remember, though, for each user database, each user can only be a member of one group, but an entire group can be a member of another group.

Administrative Groups

Depending on the size of your organization and the size and complexity of your intranet, an intranet administrator may be necessary. An intranet administrator is responsible for maintaining the intranet—adding users, adding content, editing content, and performing all other functions necessary to maintain a useful intranet. Administrators need special access to the intranet. Not only must they install and operate all applications, but they must also access the server with more privileges and permissions than other intranet users.

The intranet developer should construct an administrative Web site with the intranet administrator in mind, meaning that the system should be designed to perform all the functions the administrator needs. Most administrators will need a suite of Common Gateway Interface (CGI) scripts running behind the Web site to perform the tasks of maintaining an intranet. With such tools, administrators do not need special technical knowledge or UNIX training. For example, an administrative Web site could perform functions like creating new message boards, adding contacts, or even adding a new user to the site.

Some other important administrator tasks include uploading files to the server for user availability and creating HTML pages for use on the Web servers. In these cases, the administrative users who are maintaining the infrastructure of the site (such as adding users, editing passwords and group tables) or content providers who are adding files, HTML pages and images, audio, and other information to the site need permission to manipulate the file structure and add new files to the server.

In a UNIX operating system environment, this is relatively simple. One of the first things a UNIX administrator learns is the UNIX file permission structure. Each file and directory is accessible in three ways: read, write, and execute; and by three types of users: the owner (the person who created the file), the group (any user in the same group as the owner), and the user. Any file or directory can give any combination of these permissions to any of these classifications of users. For example, a typical HTML file on a Web server is readable by everyone, but only the owner, or the owner and the group, are given write privileges. (HTML files are not executable, so there is no need to set the execute permissions.) This means that everyone can read the file, whether they are surfing the site with their Web server or looking at the file in a UNIX environment directly on the server. However, only the owner of the file, or in some cases any user who is in the owner's group, can write over the file.

When assembling these user groups, it is important to consider what operations the administrator must perform in order to administer the intranet properly. There might be configuration files that need to be edited or informational files that the administrator must access. For example, if the administrator wants to configure image maps for the Web site, he or she must edit the image map configuration files.

Superusers

In every intranet, there should be at least one user with the ability to access and edit all areas. This user should be a member of every group and have the knowledge and training to perform most of the functions of the administrator, if needed. The "superuser" is key in emergency situations, or if there is a problem with the group configurations.

Implementing a User Database

When your user model is set up, it is ready to implement into your intranet. Different servers use different methods for authentication. The way you build the file structure of your intranet might be influenced by the permissions structure. For instance, you might want to put all the configuration files in a common area, while all the files for different groups might be in an area accessible only by administrators for that group. Consider also that different servers may be unable to use a common user database. In these instances, a master user database should be constructed and referred to if any changes are made to any of the individual databases.

FTP Servers

An FTP server is the area on the server where files are stored to be downloaded by users. FTP servers are set up using a file structure that is the same as on any Windows, Mac, or UNIX hard drive. To limit access of certain files in the server, there are two options: You can set up a single server with restricted access to certain directories by certain users; or you can set up multiple servers with full access to a limited number of users. Both have their advantages and disadvantages. In the single server scenario, the advantage is that a single server uses less server capacity than do multiple servers. Also, if there are several files everyone must access, those files can be placed in a common directory. On the other hand, users will see directories to which they typically may not have access. The multiple-server model allows users to see only files they can access. Along with increased resource utilization, however, the major drawback to multiple servers is the possible redundancy of providing common files to both servers, which can cost time and energy for your administrators.

Web Servers

Web servers handle permissions somewhat differently. Different Web server software packages provide authentication in different ways, but basically they all do the same thing: provide access to all the files and subdirectories in a directory according to a password file. Some Web servers can even set security on single files. Traditional National Center for Supercomputing (NCSA) servers and Netscape servers use htaccess, a freeware authentication program, to limit access to a particular file structure. The htaccess file accesses a user database (usually the htpasswd file) and allows access to the directory and all its subdirectories to a user with the correct user ID and password. htaccess allows for multiple users.

On a different note, the Oracle Web server, along with several other commercial Web servers, has authentication based on the individual file. With this kind of authentication, every file on the server can have a distinct and unique authentication table if the administrator so desires. For example, if a confidential financial document is posted on the server, access to that document could be limited to one or two users, regardless of where the file is placed on the server. With this method, each user would have to authenticate only once, rather than several times for different secure areas as they would with some older versions of htaccess. If you plan on having many separate areas with separate authentication and you need nontechnical administrators to maintain the password tables, it might make sense for you to purchase a Web server with individual file authentication options. If your administrators have some knowledge of UNIX and your password tables will not be complex, you can get away with a much less expensive Web server using htaccess.

Maintaining Security

After the user database is set up and implemented, it must be securely maintained. A reliable model for changing passwords on a regular basis should be adopted. (See Chapter 14, "Security: Keeping Hackers Out.") In addition, you should decide whether users will have the same password for each of the different interfaces they use in the intranet. For example, will their user ID and password be the same on the Web site as it is for their mail or the file server? If you've read Chapters 14 through 16, you probably have considered how you will maintain a secure system. If you haven't read these chapters, I suggest you do so before implementing a security model.

Keeping Records

It's important to keep track of your users and their passwords. Rebuilding accounts and changing passwords in many locations is time-consuming. In situations in which constantly changing passwords are inevitable, it is possible for the organization to write an application for password management that would allow administrators to change passwords of users from a Web form. The Oracle Web server has a built-in administration form and supporting scripts that allow administrators to add or delete users and change passwords. A similar application can be built on an NCSA or Netscape server as well. A developer who knows basic CGI and HTML could design and implement such an interface in a relatively short amount of time. It is important to keep a hard copy of your user information and group structure, as shown in Figure 48.1. Not only will a flow chart or physical construction of your user model help you expand and add users correctly, but it will also help you rebuild the model in an emergency.

FIGURE 48.1.
A flow chart of users.

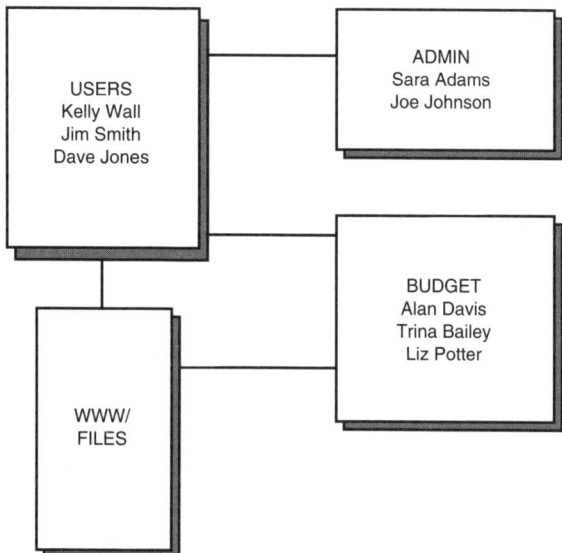

The first step in creating a flow chart is to make a list of all your users and all the files or directories. Then start matching them up by drawing a line from the user to the directories or files you want to give that person access to. It might help to use a different color of pen for each user. The different colors should help you easily identify what groups need to be created. Then you will be able to develop a sustainable user group.

MCKEON & JEFFRIES

M&J's user database was a fairly simple one. Because the interactivity on the site was relatively limited and there was very little need to limit access to specific parts of the site, it wasn't necessary to create user names and passwords for each user; it was sufficient to create a single user name and password for an entire group of users. This required much less time and effort of the systems administrator to keep all that information organized. M&J divided their user database in the following manner:

1. Mail. Mail service on intranet stayed almost exactly the same as it was using the traditional Legacy system already in place. No changes needed to be made; no special records needed to be kept.

2. FTP server. The FTP server needed to have just a few special areas. The first was an anonymous area where any user could upload and download a file. The second was an administrative area, where users could gain access to the document route of the Web server. Only administrators and content providers, and of course the systems administrator, had the user name and password to access these files. That user group consisted of the human resources manager, the newsletter editor, and a few administrative personnel. Another area was set aside specifically for the executive staff or the partners to be able to exchange files that were private from the rest of M&J's employees. Only partners of the firm had a user name and password to that area. These two user names and passwords were kept by the systems administrator in a safe.

3. Web server. Because the majority of the information available on the intranet was meant to be accessible to all employees, one user name and password sufficed for the main document route of the Web server. The private messaging areas were located within a special folder on that document route and were protected by a separate password door that, again, had only one user name and password used by each user allowed to access that area.

Each password on the site is changed once per month. M&J decided on a simple strategy to replace the passwords: Every month, on the first day of the month, the high and low temperatures are taken from the front page of the *Philadelphia Inquirer*. Separated by the three-letter abbreviation for the day of the week, it becomes a simple password that anyone who knows the secret can find at any time. It is not the most secure method, but it serves M&J's purposes. The password for the restricted area is changed once a month to a random number and letter combination and told to the partners directly by the systems administrator.

Monitoring Users

After the user model is in place, the intranet administrator should monitor its use. Constant monitoring will help organizations discern which software and hardware need upgrades to increase performance or functionality. There are several ways to monitor users. Most FTP and WWW servers keep logs of each transaction as it happens. Each time a user requests a file, the server logs the file, who requested the file, and when the file was requested. The server tracks this information by the PI address of the user's machine. By matching PI addresses with users on the database, the server can determine which user accessed what and at what time. Another way to log users is to write CGI scripts that create logs by user ID. When a user enters his or her user ID into a Web server or FTP server, that user ID is carried around as an environment variable, which means that every time he or she requests a page, the server logs it.

This information can help the intranet administrator, and ultimately the organization, determine which functions are popular, what services are being used, and who is and isn't using the system, among other things.

> ### THE SPORTING GOODS AND APPAREL ASSOCIATION
>
> Because of the great number of users, and because the SGAA intranet requires separate and distinct authentications for each user, the user database for the SGAA intranet is much more complex. Because of the nature of the Oracle Web server and the authentication process, two separate databases had to be kept—one had just a user name and password, the other contained contact information and data for each user. There were several types of users of the SGAA intranet. Some are merely users: They can access information, they can even update information using online forms, but they cannot add images or new types of content to the site. For example, an average user can log on, view news, participate in a message board, check out the interactive calendar, and find a contact on the contact list. They can also participate in real-time chats, view an update, view the contact database, and add relevant URLs to the hierarchical links page.
>
> The next group is the administrative group. Administrators can add news items, create new message boards, add new users, and perform general maintenance on the site. Some administrative users also have Telnet and FTP access to the site, which allows them to upload and edit files.
>
> The last category of users is the "superuser." The superuser can delete users, message boards, and contacts and moderate message boards or online chat.
>
> Because of the online commerce model of the SGAA intranet, several other user groups must be maintained. For example, most distributors have different price lists for different sized resellers. A large sporting goods store buys in such a large quantity that its prices are much lower than department stores that carry only selected items. For some distributors, there are several tiers. The tier to which each reseller is ascribed must be carefully maintained by the system administrator. Obviously it is important to the distributor that the right prices be shown to the right resellers.
>
> All the permissions and the tier structure are individual elements of the user database. Consider it a different field in a database.
>
> The password database for the SGAA site was at once easy and difficult to maintain, because no database existed. Each password, once created, is encrypted on the site, so it is impossible for even the administrators to access. If a password is forgotten, a new password must take its place. Only the system administrator can perform this task. So, on the one hand, no records are kept, but on the other, when a password is forgotten, or a new account must be made, only one individual can do it. This may not be the most efficient method, but it is one of the most secure.

Summary

At this point, you should have a solid idea of how to create a workable plan for creating and implementing a user database. The key attribute to your database is that it be workable. By beginning with the end in mind, the building of your database will go smoothly. Along the way, don't neglect the important security issues discussed here and in other chapters. And, remember, a well-organized database goes hand-in-hand with an efficient intranet.

Designing a Successful File Structure

49

by David Garrett

IN THIS CHAPTER

- The file structure game plan 729
- Hardware issues and disaster planning 730
- Platform issues 732

Assume that, for one reason or another, you've been stuck with the job of designing, implementing, and maintaining the file structure for your company's collection of intranet servers. You therefore must find a viable method to support not only your corporate intranet Web (HTTP) server, but other services such as e-mail, file transfer (FTP), Gopher, and anything else under the sun that your boss can find to throw at you. (After all, what could possibly be more exciting than running every available information server on your machines "just because"?) Take heart, though, because with a little bit of effort, a familiarity with the issues covered in this chapter, and just a bit of luck, you'll be able to come up with a plan that will serve your intranet's needs with amazing success.

Because you don't really have much hope of escaping the technology whims of your boss, it's best to spend a good deal of time prior to setting up your intranet evaluating your specific file structure needs, establishing an overall "game plan" to guide the future development of the particular file structure, and generally making sure that your plan is sustainable and extensible from the beginning. (If you've ever had to perform a major restructure of a file system on a "live" server, you know what a pain it can be.)

Here are a few things to keep in mind beforehand so that you don't lose control in the design and planning phases. First, the file structure that you eventually implement will, more so than any other factor, be dependent on the particular operating system and other services that you have running on your machines. Although they are not entirely disparate, you'll find various intricacies and "sweet spots" that exist on certain platforms, but to really exploit them takes time, effort, and dedication.

Second, realize that despite your best efforts to stick to a predetermined set of rules for expansion and adaptation, your file structure will, from time to time, develop in ways that are out of your control. This development usually is the result of a new server or application that has special requirements, such as special directories or partitions, particular security concerns, and so on. The trick of the trade is to be flexible enough to incorporate these virtual road-bumps into your intranet file structure without being subservient to them. This kind of creativity and resourcefulness should win you lots of points with the boss—if the boss knows what you're doing. Remember, your job is to make the intricacies of the file system as transparent to the user as possible.

Third, and perhaps most important, (strictly speaking) there's no textbook answer to building a good, workable file structure. Sometimes they work, sometimes not. But it is important to always be on top of the situation and constantly strive to improve the system based on the intranet's evolving needs. Don't be too upset if your first plan doesn't survive very long; just make sure that the second round is much better.

Chapter 49

The File Structure Game Plan

When you sit down to plan your file structure, you need to take a few steps to ensure that you have the best possible understanding of your intranet's requirements and a good grasp of the reality of what you can and cannot accomplish given the particulars of your situation. You can begin on a simple note by making as comprehensive a list as possible of all the machines, servers, and components that you plan to have running as part of your intranet. A small- to medium-sized company, for example, may have sufficient resources (financial support and so on) for only one physical computer to function as an information server but needs to run a Web server for both internal and external access, an e-mail server for corporate communication, a streaming-audio server to support an in-house product, an FTP site for sharing corporate files, and requires space for users to store their personal files. Thinking ahead of time about each service's requirements will keep each one running smoothly and effectively for years to come.

The most important thing you can do during the planning phase (after identifying these requirements) is to make an initial estimate as to the amount of storage space that will be required by each particular feature. This step is so important that I cannot stress it enough. The fastest route to service failure is to run out of disk space with no plan for recovery. Servers can crash, e-mail can go down, and essential information-distribution channels can come to a halt if, for example, your hard drive fills up and it downs your server. You can be sure that no one in your company—especially management—will be pleased if this situation happens. The best way to avoid this situation (always think proactively) is to have incredible amounts of drive space on hand. With the recent and continuing trend toward more affordable mass-storage solutions, this option is fast becoming a "no-brainer" for many companies, and one that you should not hesitate to explore if you have the financial resources. You also need to do a little fancy footwork to arrange your services on your drives in such a way that the dynamic, space-intensive services will have more than sufficient room to grow, say 20 percent over your estimates. All the disk space in the world is useless if, for example, your Web files are on a 240MB drive and are hard-coded to absolute paths.

Going outside your usual design team is also a good idea when you're evaluating the demands that will be placed on your intranet. Although your users might not seem well informed, you might be surprised how much insight they have about their needs, wants, and expectations for the corporate intranet. By soliciting feedback from your user base, you can further clarify design requirements, possibly get some ideas for future functionality, and can provide a significantly better system than you would have been able to otherwise.

Assume that your company's intranet will be centered around a minimal Web server that stores an employee handbook and some other basic corporate information. On your FTP server, you want to place a wide array of applications, templates, documents, and other files. Your RealAudio server will hold some common audio files and will be used for broadcast announcements. In addition, your users will have space on the server to store files, host Web pages, and store mail.

Administering Your Intranet
Part VII

To meet these four needs, you should create four new areas on the hard drive or four new drives on your server. Your Web server will probably not take up a lot of space if it is being used only to store basic information. Many organizations can get away with having just 300 to 400MB of disk space available for their Web servers. Depending on how many audio files you will be using, allotting at least the same amount of space to the RealAudio server might be a good idea. Current compression methods (the way audio sounds are turned into digital data and compressed) for audio are not nearly as effective as they will be in the near future. For now, you may need to purge your RealAudio server of old files on a regular basis (300MB can be eaten up by just a few hundred audio files). You should also reserve a significant amount of disk space for your users. If they want to host Web pages in their accounts on the server or store files for access from a remote location, users easily can consume 10MB. To be safe, you should allot at least 20MB per user account. Figure 49.1 illustrates a sample file structure.

FIGURE 49.1.
A beginning file structure.

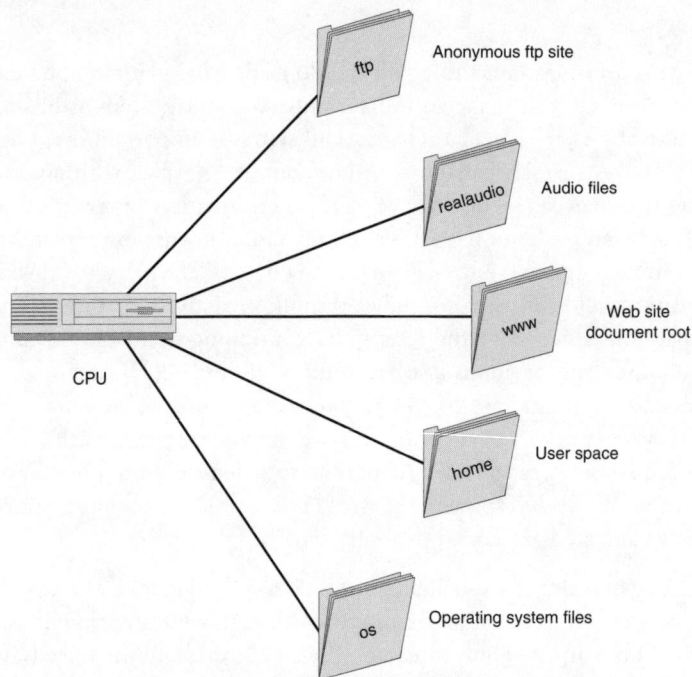

Hardware Issues and Disaster Planning

As you certainly recognize from what you've learned so far, the storage requirements of your intranet are anything but trivial in scope, either financially or in terms of management. Depending on the size, extent, and nature of your intranet data (that is, is it mission-critical?), you may want to invest in anything from a simple multiple-gigabyte internal SCSI hard drive to a full-blown external RAID array. Doing so will certainly make disaster-recovery much easier, as will an excellent DAT backup solution. If you have the money, which is always an issue these days, you would be wise to invest in a top-of-the-line external SCSI DAT drive, with a capacity of at least 4GB. This solution is perfect because the DAT drive is portable (you can back up other machines or move it if a machine dies), fast (SCSI and its variants are about as fast as possible), and easy to use.

> **TIP**
>
> If you're running a UNIX server and suddenly find yourself on the verge of running out of disk space, the ALIAS directive can rescue you from the edge. If you've been using the standard document path, and your corporation's intranet features directories for both Human Resources and Marketing, your directory tree may look something like this: %ls /usr/local/etc/httpd/htdocsHumRes/Marketing/.
>
> To restructure your physical disk setup to allow Human Resources to post the new benefits manual, you can move Marketing to its own drive, mounted as /CorporateHQ/Master by following these simple steps:
>
> 1. Create a Marketing directory on /CorporateHQ/Master.
> 2. Copy the contents of the current Marketing/ tree to /CorporateHQ/Master/Marketing.
> 3. Add an alias to your srm.conf configuration file:
>   Alias/Marketing/CorporateHQ/Master/Marketing/
> 4. Reboot so that changes take effect.
> 5. Free up the extra space on the original drive by deleting the old /Marketing directory.

When you create your system, try not to split file structures between disks. Don't have part of your Web server on one hard drive, for instance, and part of it on another. With UNIX, splitting structures is easy. The operating system includes a simple way to link certain directory structures with one another. Doing so, however, is not advisable. If a disk fails, getting your system up and running again is much more difficult if a file system is split between two disks.

On the other hand, if you need only minimal hard drive space, don't have the physical space for multiple drives, or can't afford to install multiple drives, one solution is to create physical partitions on your single drive. Depending on your operating system, creating partitions can range from simple to moderately difficult. With Windows, creating partitions is just a matter of following a few basic instructions. But remember that, in most operating systems, once you create a partition, you cannot modify it without erasing the entire drive. So be sure to create partitions that are large enough to accommodate your servers as they grow.

Platform Issues

Although Web and mail servers (as well as a host of other servers, services, and applications) are available for most of the popular as well as high-end platforms, trying to implement a full-featured, heavily used intranet using a Mac, PowerMac, Windows 3.11, or Windows 95 platform won't get you very far. In fact, you may even be laughed right out of your IS department for even suggesting such a thing, so be careful where and when you make such recommendations. In today's market, the best avenues to explore for intranet building are either the Windows NT (especially the forthcoming 4.0) or UNIX operating systems, running either on the Intel or Alpha processors. I'm not saying that you might not be able to come up with something impressive outside this limited arena. If you can, fantastic; go with it. But, as with every other decision that you make when designing and implementing your corporate intranet, the operating system that you adopt as the intranet's foundation will be a major factor in both the file system requirements as well as the success of the overall endeavor.

UNIX

Of all the major operating systems, UNIX has the most flexibility regarding file structure. In UNIX, each drive, or partition of a drive, has a distinct and permanent name (whereas in Windows or DOS drives are identified by letters). This naming system provides for a much simpler and succinct way to create a file structure from several different sized partitions on several different sized drives. This way, you can add a drive or partition within a file structure. Distinct names also make it easier to store files in a meaningful way.

Creating symbolic links between one directory and another is also easy in UNIX. With symbolic links, the same directory can appear to be in multiple places. For example, the cgi-bin directory of the Web server, where all the cgi scripts are stored, must be in a specific place so that the Web server can recognize it. If several users want to put the cgi directory within their own Web pages, however, you might consider creating a symbolic link between the cgi-bin and the users' directories, as in the following example: /usr/local/etc/httpd/cgi-bin/ is the real directory, but /usr/dave/public_html/cgi-bin/ could be a pointer to the same directory. This way, your users can access the cgi directory from within their own user space.

UNIX directory structure is based on a number of conventions. The following are a few examples:

bin: Contains standard UNIX distribution programs, available to all users. Some examples are ls, cd, and mv.

etc: Contains files such as the group, named, and password files that are required for system administration. Both data files and programs may be kept in this directory.

dev: Contains files corresponding to external devices such as drives and printers.

home: Usually contains files belonging to users.

lib: Contains libraries of compiled C subprograms that can only be called by and linked with C programs.

tmp: Contains temporary files created by various programs as they run. In some systems, files in tmp are lost when the system is shut down.

usr: (substitute for home) Usually contains files belonging to individual users.

var: Used in some UNIX systems to store files that change in size, like spool files and log files.

Windows NT

Microsoft's Windows NT operating system has come a long way from the top-heavy, unwieldy system that it once was. Although it's still probably not the ideal choice if you are planning on handling more than about 10,000 user sessions in a single day, that may very well change with the release of version 4.0 later in the year. With the highly rated Windows 95-style interface, faster response times, and the robust and powerful Internet Information Server (IIS) system, NT may grow by leaps and bounds if UNIX isn't careful.

The file system that you'll encounter if you implement a Windows NT solution has a couple of distinct drawbacks, but you'll also find some great flexibility and excellent ease-of-use that certainly counter—if not negate—the negative aspects that the operating system features. Topping the list of drawbacks is the lack of the symbolic-linking feature that is offered by UNIX. Although the file structure in and of itself lacks this functionality, however, you'll often find that third-party applications such as Web servers provide shortcuts or workarounds that accomplish the same task.

The second unfortunate aspect is that many software designers don't necessarily take the IS manager and established file structures into account when designing the directories and other resources that their individual packages will require. As a result, your well-planned systems—that up until now had plenty of drive space to spare—will suddenly be dashed against the rocks as your new search engine software builds a 200MB index file that must reside in the root of the HTDOCS directory. This problem generally is a result of shoddy planning and programming, although sometimes there are technical motivations for certain placements. Fortunately for the NT administrator, many software options are available to you, so you're never committed to one server's eccentricities and mandates. If you're not pleased with how a particular package integrates with your system—especially if it will have a serious impact on your storage structure—keep looking for a software solution that more closely matches your needs.

Dueling Servers

You can easily be overwhelmed by the myriad of servers that run on the host machine. The relatively simple system described at the beginning of this chapter can have a Web server with public areas and either mappings to user sites or additional Web servers for each user. It also can have an FTP server to point anonymous or public logins toward a common file service area and point individual users to their own directories. Finally, it can have a RealAudio server that is pointed to the Web server and that needs to be part of the FTP structure as well. In all, several servers are required, many of them serving files from several different areas of the host machine's hard disk space. It is crucial that you map out these connections on paper, as shown in Figure 49.2, before you implement them.

FIGURE 49.2.
An advanced file system.

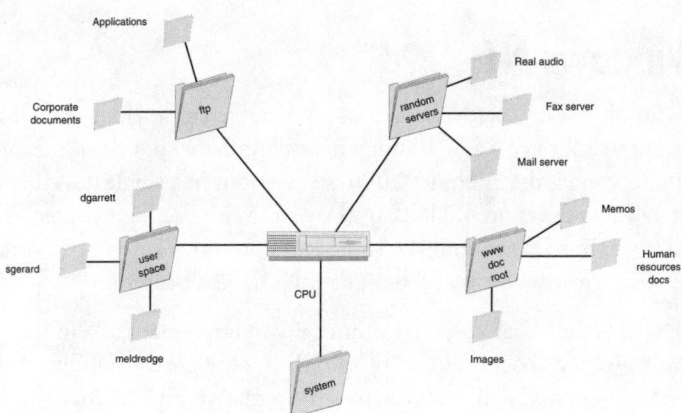

Web Space

A Web server serves documents in a particular fashion. Within the Web server configuration, you designate a directory as the document root. This directory is usually called WWW or public_html and, on UNIX hosts, it is generally located in the usr or home directory. On Windows or Mac systems, the document root is usually right off the root directory. The document root allows the Web server to serve files in the following manner: http://www.intraactive.com/home.html serves the file /usr/public_html/home.html when /usr/public_html is the document root. For most Web servers, the default file for any directory is index.html. Therefore, http://www.intraactive.com serves the file /usr/public_html/index.html.

With some Web servers, like NCSA (National Center for Supercomputing) and Netscape Web server, you need to put any cgi scripts into a cgi-bin directory. Usually, that directory is located within the Web server tree. In these cases, the server itself maps the cgi-bin directory for you, which means that http://www.intraactive.com/cgi-bin/test.cgi runs the script /usr/local/etc/httpd/cgi-bin/test.cgi.

Several other servers allow different kinds of directory mappings. NCSA servers, for example, typically have automatic mappings to user accounts. Some servers are preconfigured so that without any additional setup http://www.intraactive.com/~dave serves the file /usr/dave/public_html/index.html and http://www.intraactive.com/~cara serves the file /usr/cara/public_html/index.html.

Of course, this is in the UNIX environment. Setting up a similar system with Windows is somewhat different and generally differs in methodology based on the server software that you implement. Note, however, that regardless of the server software, you'll generally find that maintaining separate subdirectories or multiple Web sites on one NT-based server is extremely easy. Refer to Chapter 8, "Server Software," for a more thorough discussion of the various Web servers available for the Windows, Mac, and UNIX platforms.

FTP Space

For all intents and purposes, the entire file structure of your server, be it a Mac, a Windows, or especially a UNIX environment, is FTP space. This means that with the correct settings on the FTP daemon, a user with the right permissions can copy, delete, or create any file on the server, in addition to uploading new files. Typically, FTP space is used for three functions:

- Making files available in a centralized, easily accessible area so that they can be shared among colleagues, clients, and so on
- Storing files within your user account, whether they are Web documents or images, or files you want to make available to remote sites
- Uploading and downloading of files by the administrator

The first two functions are relatively simple. For the public file server, you want to arrange the files in a directory structure much like you would on any file server on a LAN. Decide on conventions, and be diligent about organization. Try to begin with fewer than 10 files per directory. If you have more than 10 files per directory, be more specific in your directory structure. Individual users should practice the same, although they might want to create a slightly different structure if they are going to serve HTML files or images.

Very few people (preferably only one person) should have permission to read, write, or execute documents outside their own home directories. The typical user should have read and write access to his or her own account. For example, Dave should have access to usr/dave/ and all the subdirectories. Also, Dave and other typical users should have read and write access to the public FTP area—in this case, /usr/ftp/. Users who provide content for the Web server, however, also should have read and write access to /usr/public_html/.

The Web server administrator should have read and write access to /usr/local/etc/httpd/. Finally, the system administrator should have read and write access to the entire file structure of the server.

User Space

Allowing users to have their own space on the server is one of the most useful things you can do with your intranets. This capability gives users the opportunity to store files on the server, serve Web pages, and even keep their mail on the server.

Users may want to store files on the server for several reasons. A user who works on several different client machines may want to access the same files from all the machines. Additionally, if a user wants to retrieve a file from home or another remote location, having an area on the server where the user can store files and download them using any FTP client is convenient.

Serving Web pages also is an important option to provide your users. You can set up each user account to have a document root as a subdirectory from the users' home directories. This way, users can easily publish documents on the intranet for other users to see—for example, /usr/dave/public_html.

As you learned in Chapter 30, "E-Mail: The Basic Model," the current standard for Internet mail servers is POP3. Using POP3, mail sits in the users' inboxes on the server until it is deleted. Unless users use a mail reader that resides on the server mail client like Pine, it is difficult for users to leave mail on the server. However, that is about to change. The new standard for mail servers is IMAP, which will allow users to move mail on the server into folders. Using this method, users easily can leave all their mail on the server, which will allow them to access it from any client machine.

The key to creating user accounts is to allow users to perform work from any machine with network connectivity. The accounts give users greater flexibility through increased mobility. This system also makes backup easier; if all the important information is on the server, you can centralize your backup procedures on a single machine.

MCKEON & JEFFRIES

McKeon & Jeffries came up with a simple file structure for its server. The accounting firm didn't have to worry about having area for users, or even mail, because all that was handled on another server. The firm merely had to create two directory structures and map them to the software servers. The first was for the Web server. Within the document root directory for the Web server, the intranet administrator created an images directory, a CGI directory, and directories for all the major areas of the site. Within the Web directory structure was also a private directory where the private message boards were stored. A new directory was created for that use because access is limited to just a few users. Additionally, an FTP directory was created with directories for all the major files that needed to be filed.

> **THE SPORTING GOODS AND APPAREL ASSOCIATION**
>
> The SGAA had a slightly more complex file structure setup than the accounting firm, but because it was set up on a UNIX server, many of the decisions were already made. Within the /home directory, each user on the server was set up with a directory. Within that directory, each user has an area for mail, and each has a /public_html directory for user Web space. The anonymous FTP site is located in /home/ftp, and from there a directory structure was created to store the many types of different files that are available to the users. The Web server's document root is located in /usr/local/etc/public_html, but really only images and a few basic documents are stored here. Most of the data for the Web site is stored in the database, which is in /export/oracle. All the data, uploaded files, and software are stored in the predetermined areas within the Oracle area.

Summary

By incorporating the specific examples given in this chapter, you should be on the road to building a sustainable file structure for your server. A stable and efficient file structure is one that benefits your users, is easy to administer, and will sustain future growth. Also, plan to save time later by taking the time now to map out the most appropriate connections for all the servers on your intranet. If you had a 2,500-piece jigsaw puzzle to assemble, you would probably begin by separating the edge pieces from the inside pieces, and then you'd sort these two groups by colors. This process would take time, but in the long run, you would cut hours or possibly days off your completion time. The same idea holds true for file structure development—indeed, for any aspect of intranet design.

Remember, as important as it is to have a fantastic intranet architecture on paper, without the right tools and support, the system is doomed to fail. Be sure to consider thoughtfully the needs of your users (and designers) prior to the construction of your intranet, and then select from the many and varied options—both hardware and software—that are emerging nonstop in the development world. With some careful planning, a lot of hard work, and a little bit of luck, your intranet's file structure can be an incredible, transparent resource that will serve the needs of your intranet, your IS staff, and your corporation with flying colors.

Maintaining Security

50

by David Garrett

IN THIS CHAPTER

- Physical security **740**
- Passwords **741**
- Web server security **743**
- Securing applications and functions **744**
- Crack! Crack! Crack! **745**

The easiest way to keep your data and information secure from the outside world is to avoid connecting to the Internet. If everything done inside your intranet is local, the outside world can't see what's going on and can't get to it. In other words, if you aren't connected to the Internet, there is very little chance that anyone can hack into your system. But that means that your intranet is slightly less functional and slightly less valuable. If you can't communicate with the outside world as well as you can with the people inside your network, and if you can't take advantage of the bevy of resources on the Internet, you're not fully taking advantage of technology. However, it's possible to keep your information relatively secure even if you're connected to the Internet. To maintain a secure network, you must take a number of precautions and consider a number of options.

Physical Security

When developing a secure intranet, your first concern should be physical security. How do you make sure that no one tampers with the actual machines? Make sure your server is located in a locked, climate-controlled room where no unauthorized person can get to it. Your server is your most valuable piece of hardware and usually contains all your data and therefore should be as secure as possible. Limit access to the room in which it's kept to your system administrator and maybe one other technical person. Give access to as few people as possible.

Many companies sell carts or cabinets in which you can store your server. Storing the server in a locked cabinet in a locked room makes it difficult for someone to physically touch it. And that's not just for cases of industrial espionage or someone trying to steal information; this also prevents accidents. Sometimes, when people see a sophisticated computer or an intriguing piece of equipment, they want to play around with it. It's extremely easy to lose information and vital data if these people don't know what they're doing.

Besides maintaining security for your server, it is also important that user workstations be kept physically secure. If any of your users have access to highly sensitive information, such as financial data or proprietary pricing information, or if your intranet contains any sensitive information, make sure that the computers of the individuals who can access this information also are in locked rooms or offices. In a similar manner, you can make groups of computers secure by limiting access to certain parts of the server to just those machines. That way, if you have a group of unsecure or relatively unsecure machines—in a cubicle environment or a large, open work area, for example—your data can remain secure.

The computers of your CEO or CFO (and of people who have access to private information) should be locked in offices so that someone wandering through the building can't log on to them. Also, I can't tell you how many people write passwords on sticky notes and stick them to their monitors. This practice defeats the general purpose of passwords. If you store passwords in a ledger, make sure it is kept in a safe.

Safes also are good for storing backup tapes. Any intranet should be backed up regularly onto some sort of magnetic tape. Make sure that the tapes are stored in a safe or a locked area. Someone who can't log on the server may access vital or private information through backup tapes.

Passwords

Typically, if you are running an intranet, each of its users will have passwords that allow them to log into the system. Passwords are not only for security reasons (because you want to make sure you authenticate your users so you know that the people who log on are who they say they are). Passwords can also supply the server with a host of other information about the user. A userid and password can identify a user to the server. For much of the software run on an intranet, you'll need to identify incoming users for many different reasons, including environment variables—such as preferences—and communication purposes, such as identifying the user on message boards. When the server knows who the user is, many tedious aspects of communications functions can be automated. For example, when users participate on a message board, it might be useful for them to not have to type in their e-mail address every time they submit or reply to a message. Userids also allow for tracking users around the site.

Again, if your network is on a LAN or WAN that is not connected to the Internet, you don't need to be quite as paranoid as you do if you are connected to the Internet. If you are running a system where some users can access sensitive information and other users can't (such as financial data), ensure that user passwords are at least difficult to guess, if not impossible. Regardless of the system, however, I recommend that a password have at least eight characters, including a mixture of upper- and lowercase letters, at least one number, and one special character. Your password shouldn't be or contain any word that can be found in the dictionary, because these passwords are the easiest to crack. The idea is to have a password that is random enough so that guessing it would be impossible. This is especially true for remote-access users. If you are dialing into the system, you want to have a password that is even harder to crack. If a stranger is wandering around your office, he probably will be seen before he does much damage. However, this is not true with hackers. They have all the time in the world to try to crack your password. So make it tough.

For an internal network, you might change your passwords only every once in a while. Base your changes on need, or develop a regular schedule. Perhaps you'll change passwords every time you upgrade your hardware or software, or whenever it's convenient. Again, if some users are privy to particularly sensitive information, you might want to change their passwords more often, but on an internal network, you don't need to change your passwords too often. Passwords are more of a first means of defense. In a local network, users are in the same physical location as the machines, and it would probably be easier to break into the room that has the password file in it than to guess the passwords. This is not true if you are connected to the Internet or if your LAN has remote-access capability.

If your network is connected to the Internet, you want to change the passwords at least once a quarter. And certainly you'll want to change all your passwords immediately if you find any evidence that someone has been trying to break into your network or *has* broken into your network. Various commercially available software packages offer you a password-changing system. Depending on the software, hardware, or platform you're using on your server, you'll find software packages that require users to change their passwords on a regular basis. When you update information on your server, pay close attention to your procedures. It doesn't matter if you're using scripts or how you choose to update, but make sure to carefully examine your methods and watch out for any potential security holes, such as programs that blank out a user's password instead of prompting for a change when it expires. Some older password-changing programs just delete the old password, whether or not a new one has been specified. Unfortunately, this nullifies the password, and anyone can get onto the system. Make sure your password-changing script is up-to-date and secure.

Various password programs that require users to enter passwords in an acceptable form are also available. You can insert whatever parameters you choose. For instance, if you want to require a capital letter, a lowercase letter, a number, and a special character, the password program will check the password to make sure it has all those parameters. If it doesn't, the program kicks it back and makes the user type in a new one.

Another way to improve security is to make sure each branch of the network is accessed by a different password. For instance, the mail password (often determined by the user) should be different than the one for the network database. Although you shouldn't create too many passwords (and thus create a temptation for users to write them down), you also should not risk an insecure intranet. Develop the passwords in a systematic way. Keep your list of users in alphabetical or some other order. Allow for plenty of room for updates and additions.

TIP

When you're issuing new passwords to users, it's best not to send them via e-mail, one of the least secure methods of communication on the Internet. It's quite easy for someone to pick out a password from an e-mail message. One of the very best times to use the phone instead of your intranet is when you're issuing new passwords to your users.

MCKEON & JEFFRIES

Maintaining security for McKeon & Jeffries' intranet was a relatively simple undertaking at first, but it grew more complex as more interesting applications were added. In the beginning, there were just two user names and passwords—one for the executive committee, and one for the rest of the users. These passwords were kept in a safe place and changed every few weeks. The information kept on the site wasn't terribly valuable to anyone.

As the site grew more functional, and especially when M&J started giving passwords to clients so that they could take advantage of the site's communications and file-sharing aspects, the security safeguards grew more complex. Instead of having one password for all the users, M&J issued separate passwords for each user. Although the site still wasn't accessible from the Internet, with nonemployees dialing up and exchanging information with the server, McKeon & Jeffries also spent plenty of time tracking users and potential security holes.

THE SPORTING GOODS AND APPAREL ASSOCIATION

The SGAA knew from the start that security was going to be a big issue, and they hit it hard from the beginning. Users are required to change their passwords every month. Each password must contain a capital letter, a lowercase letter, a number, and a special character—combinations that are not in the dictionary. The systems administrator runs SATAN (discussed later) and Cracker (a password-cracking program) every month to check security.

Physical security wasn't too much of a problem for the SGAA. Its only server was in a locked room, and the SGAA paid careful attention to the log files. Local users connected through the same password door as Internet users. If it looked as though a user were connecting consistently from more than one IP address, that user was contacted to make sure that he or she did indeed have two different accounts.

Web Server Security

It is as important to have a secure Web server as it is to maintain a secure mail and database system. As discussed in Chapter 14, "Security: Keeping Hackers Out," one method of Web server security is .htaccess, which causes the server to recognize that a directory tree is or should be authenticated. One problem with .htaccess is that it's often easy to accidentally place the password file in an inappropriate directory. (There are two files: One is .htaccess, which tells the Web server that the files in that directory tree should be authenticated, and the other file, .htpasswd, actually stores the user ID and password.)

It often happens that whoever creates the authentication puts the .htpasswd file in the same directory as the .htaccess file. For example, suppose the document root for your Web server is /home/dave/www, and you put the file .htaccess in /home/dave/www, and you put the password file in /home/dave/www. Then you want to look at a Web page within that directory tree, so you go to `http://dave.intraactive.com`. You'll get an authentication page that asks for your username and password. When your username and password are authenticated, you'll get the index.html page—/home/dave/www/index.html. However, once you're beyond the password protection, you could type `http://dave.intraactive.com/.htpasswd` to bring up the file containing the user IDs and the passwords.

Therefore, any user who could get onto your system could immediately get all the usernames and passwords he wanted. It's very important to keep your .htpasswd file outside the document root of your Web server. There are various other ways to keep your Web server secure. Read the security section of your Web server documentation and be sure to follow those instructions.

Even though on a typical Web server you can give access to certain pages to certain users, the information that gets sent from the server to the users' browsers is sent through the Internet unencrypted, or as plain text. I recommend that you avoid sending information unencrypted, especially if it is confidential.

Again, remember that millions of terabytes of information traverses through the Internet every day. The chances of your data actually being intercepted and read are small. However, if you are concerned that your data is being intercepted and read, consider getting a Secure Socket Layer (SSL) server. Examples of SSL servers include the Netscape Secure Server and the Oracle Secure Server. SSL servers encrypt data before sending it, which makes it almost impossible for anyone to intercept and read the communication going back and forth between your server and the client on the other end.

Any browser that can accept SSL will decrypt your information as it is sent back. Your server has a public key and a private key, and your browser has a public key and a private key, and when the browser makes a connection with a server, the two exchanges keys. In this sense, your browser and your server mesh by talking to one another cryptically.

You can do something similar with mail. PGP (Pretty Good Privacy) was developed for Internet mail by Phil Zimmerman a few years ago and is another option for maintaining security on an intranet. It can be used for any text transmission over the Internet. PGP functions in much the same way as browsers do in that PGP exchanges keys with an individual or a site on the Internet. The information is encrypted before it is sent and is then decrypted on the receiving end. Should someone intercept it in transmission, the information wouldn't be useful—it would be gibberish.

Securing Applications and Functions

In checking off the security list, don't overlook the security of functions and software. Whichever way you choose to build your software—through commercial applications or through developing your own applications using a back-end database or CGI scripts—one of the most important things you can do with those software applications is pay careful attention to potential security holes. For example, on most Internet forms, information is passed via a URL or from the HTML on a page back to the server. Sometimes you might be tempted to pass information such as user IDs or other various pieces of information important to the security of your intranet through one of these pages. However, suppose, for example, that you have a message board. While users are talking or exchanging messages on the board, a user ID gets passed through an HTML file. If you are passing that information, it's easy for one of your users (or even for someone on the outside) to recreate that HTML file, change the variables, and pass the information back to your server. You want to make sure that no vital information passes through HTML files.

> **TIP**
>
> One way to prevent information from being passed via HTML files is to tie it to a user ID via a database. A user ID can always be taken from an environment variable. No matter what kind of server you're using, whether it's Netscape, NCSA, or Oracle, the user ID that you type in for authentication is always kept as an environment variable. So if you can tie important information—information that could be misused—to the environment variable user ID, you prevent the possibility that the information would be passed via an HTML form back to the server.

Crack! Crack! Crack!

Finally, you should try to defeat crackers—users who intentionally try to "crack" secure zones. It isn't easy. The bottom line is this: Any information that is 100 percent vital—information that would devastate your company should it be made public—should not be stored in digital form on the Internet or on your intranet. No matter how much time or money is spent on securing information, it is always possible for someone to break into your network. Even sites such as Netscape get broken into, and Netscape employs extensive security methods. The possibility of a cracker gaining access to your files always exists, and the risks increase for high-profile companies. But regardless of your company's size, profile, or mission, if people think they can gain something by breaking into your system, expect that they will try.

> **SATAN TO THE RESCUE**
>
> To eliminate security holes in your computer system, I recommend that you turn to SATAN. That's right, SATAN—Security Administrator Tool for Analyzing Networks. Practically any TCP/IP network with a UNIX server can benefit from using SATAN to investigate potential security holes. Even if you are on a local network with no fear of intrusion, SATAN can help protect against accidents by your own users. SATAN's

main function is to evaluate the security of your system. The security program gathers information about specific hosts and networks by examining network services—including FTP, NIS, and NFS—as well as the current hardware and software being used. SATAN then reports its findings or investigates potential security risks. For example, if one of your users has a password that is easy to crack, or if a particular directory has a permission structure that allows anyone to upload and execute a binary on the server, SATAN will tell you.

One interesting aspect of SATAN is that when it's finished analyzing your system, it will poke around other systems looking for security holes as well. You can set up SATAN to comb the entire Internet, looking for security problems, if you desire. Although that information might not be useful to you directly, learning about how other systems are set up and what problems they face can help you make your network stronger.

The program was designed by San Francisco security expert Dan Farmer and a security programmer at the Netherlands University of Eindhoven, Wietse Venema. It is free and available for download at the following address:

`http://www.cs.ruu.nl/cert-uu/satan.html`

For documentation on SATAN, visit this site:

`ftp://ftp.win.tue.nl/pub/security/satan_doc.tar.Z`

Summary

From server and software to passwords and the physical location of equipment, you'll have several security holes to patch. But remember, your best offense is a good defense. An understanding of the always-vulnerable transmission route, a careful examination of your system's physical surroundings, an educated user base, and a commonsense approach to all security issues all add up to a secure environment. But don't stop here. Stay on top of evolving security technology and keep in step with crackers.

Hardware and Software Upgrades

51

by David Garrett

IN THIS CHAPTER

- Maintaining compatibility **748**
- Keeping up with technology **748**
- Upgrading servers **749**

To keep a system sustainable, it is important to ensure that the infrastructure is easily and swiftly upgradable and that neither time nor money is wasted on hardware or software that has little to offer except a short life span. Although it's anyone's best guess what's around the corner for the computer industry, it's still important to stay on the leading edge and prepare for the next surge of technology. While waiting, however, I recommend approaching upgrades cautiously whenever possible. Upgrades across a multiplatform or geographically diverse network can be very time-consuming and expensive.

For example, if eventually you want to add video-conferencing, you might want to start with audio-conferencing and add the video component later. Testing audio-conferencing is much less expensive without the video component and might be a good way to test your upgrade procedure and the effectiveness of real-time conferencing on your network without the additional expense and time involved in setting up a video-conferencing function.

Maintaining Compatibility

Compatibility begins with selecting hardware, software, and peripherals that are prime for expansion. Spending more up front for a machine with many expansion slots is sure to save you money down the road than if you have to replace a machine with a lower price but with fewer expansion slots. Although some in the industry swear by OS/2 software rather than Windows 95, I'd think twice before settling for this operating system. It is difficult to find support, software, and other products and services for OS/2.

A dearth of products may leave the user settling for cheap software that is unlikely to come with upgrades. For example, I bought a cheap financial program, and when I upgraded my operating system to Windows 95, the program didn't work. It took me weeks to figure out how to get it to run on the new operating system. The same is true of peripherals. I recommend SCSI (Small Computer Standard Interface) devices, because several devices can be added in a chain but require only one slot on the computer.

Keeping Up with Technology

Advances in computer technology keep the masses scrambling to computer stores and flipping through product catalogs. Along with keeping up with and acquiring the latest software and computer products, configuring new technology into a network presents another challenge. New products arrive in the stores and catalogs daily, and some are practically outdated before hitting the shelves. To stay ahead, you must know what is available and which products will add real value to your intranet, while also considering the cost.

One of the best ways to stay on top of technology is by using the Internet itself. There are several online news sources and mailing lists. A few to pay special attention to are Edupage (educom@educom.unc.edu), c|net (http://www.cnet.com), and Innovation (http://www.newsscan.com). Before making new purchases, take time to figure out the total cost of an upgrade. For example, an upgrade from Windows 3.1 to Windows 95 may cost just $89 per workstation for the software and $50 per workstation for installation and training. However, adding the required additional memory to each workstation may run an additional $150 per workstation.

Testing

First things first: When you find a new technology for your system, test it yourself. Regardless of the new technology—an operating system, hardware, software, or client applications—it absolutely must be tested by a user or group of users. Test it for compatibility with the rest of the intranet and other software, for ease of installation, for use and maintenance, and for ongoing compatibility with your system. Most TCP/IP applications are available on the Internet for testing purposes. Your systems administrator can download a preview version of the server and client software and test it before incorporating it into the rest of the intranet. That way, serious problems can be avoided.

Ready for Prime Time?

After you have tested the software adequately (preferably with a group of users that represents a good cross section of your users), you must assess whether the technology is ready for prime time. This involves asking a few questions:

- Will it run on this system?
- Will it be compatible with the system?
- What are the users or the organization trying to accomplish?
- Is there a less expensive or easier route?
- What is the total cost?
- Will the users use it?
- Will it accomplish the goals of the users and the organization?
- Is it worth the cost and downtime for installation and training?

After you have thoroughly considered these aspects, you are ready to make an informed decision.

Upgrading Servers

Depending on the number of users (and their abilities) who are using the intranet and the type of server you have, upgrading the server might prove much easier than upgrading the clients. With the server, you are typically upgrading a single machine—and one that you should know very well. When upgrading clients, you are always talking about multiple machines—sometimes cross-platform—that are always in various states of functionality. At the same time, it is important to monitor the status of the server so you know when an upgrade is necessary. If the server goes down, the whole network is down; whereas if a client goes down, all other clients continue to run uninterrupted.

Plan to spend significant time and resources monitoring the connectivity (bandwidth), the processor speed, the memory, and the available hard drive space on the server. The surest way to kill a client/server network is to have the server down, or slowed, for any amount of time. Be kind to the network and your users: Try to perform upgrades and maintenance on the server during off-hours.

Upgrading Server Hardware

Because upgrading server hardware usually requires turning the machine off at some point, plan to do as much upgrading at one time as possible. When upgrading hardware, it is absolutely necessary to turn the machines off and unplug them. When installing a new hard drive, for example, if you know you soon will need new memory, schedule both installations for the same downtime. That way, you subject the users to as little interruption as possible.

Because servers run continuously, they need more maintenance than a typical client machine. When you do perform hardware upgrades, take the opportunity to have the machine cleaned.

If you are upgrading the machine itself, it sometimes makes sense (if feasible) to run both the new machine and the old machine simultaneously for a few weeks or a month. Sometimes the quirks of new machines don't show up right away, so a backup system will cover problems if the new machine fails. Even if you have to disconnect the old machine from the network or rename or configure it so as not to interfere with the new server, it can be saved as a backup measure.

Upgrading Server Software

Upgrading the server software is a little less tricky but still should be treated delicately. You don't want to lose months, or possibly years, of work because the new server you install is incompatible with the present functionality of the intranet. Follow the same precautions when upgrading the operating system as you would for upgrading the hardware. If it's feasible to install a new host machine with your new operating system or operating system upgrade, that's all the better. That way, you can keep the old server up while configuring the new server, and you can keep the old server around as a backup for a few weeks while testing your new server.

Upgrading Workstations

Upgrading workstations should be a normal part of routine workstation maintenance, as shown in Figure 51.1. This process should include upgrading memory and freeing hard drive space. Create a comprehensive checklist plan before upgrading the operating system or adding new client software. The plan will differ if your users are on a self-contained LAN than if all your users are remote. For example, if the cost of the upgrades are borne by the company or organization, the timetable may be more rigorously defined. Also, if a systems administrator is responsible for upgrading the workstations on a self-contained LAN, the plan does not have to take into account user participation or delays caused by incompatibilities or upgrade problems. In either case, you should write a detailed instruction and information sheet that shows all the upgrade's details, including these considerations:

- Cost
- Timeframe
- New functions
- Changes in functions
- Obsolete functions
- How-to information on new functions

FIGURE 51.1.
Routine workstation maintenance.

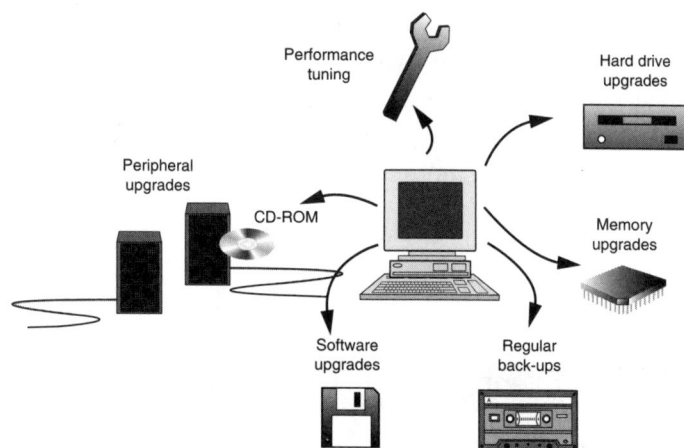

For example, let's say you want to add audio-conferencing functionality to your intranet using a RealAudio server on your internal Web site. You might create a checklist like the following:

- How much does the server cost?
- What kind of configuration do I need on the host machine to run RealAudio?
- How much memory, hard disk space, and computational capacity does it require?
- How much does the client software cost?
- What kind of client configuration do I need in order to run it?
- How much memory/hard disk space do I need in order to run it?
- How many of my clients have audio capabilities?

- How much is it going to cost to upgrade those that don't?
- Do I have any other use for client-side audio, and will the upgrade be compatible with current and future needs?
- Do I need to upgrade connectivity for the server or for clients to use the technology effectively?
- Will the users take advantage of this new technology?

If remote users are connecting to the system via clients for which you are not responsible for maintaining, consider putting together an information sheet that explains changes and new features to these users. Also do this when you install new hardware or software. When Windows 95 came out, much of the client software with which users had been connecting to the Internet either didn't work or didn't work properly. If users had been informed of exactly what they needed to do to make their connections with Windows 95 *before* it came out, and everybody upgraded, the transition to Windows 95 might have been much smoother for many users. Do yourself and your system a favor: Keep all your users in the know.

MCKEON & JEFFRIES

McKeon & Jeffries performed several low-level upgrades in their first year of operation. The first was to upgrade the Web browsers on each client. The next was to upgrade each client platform to Windows 95. Because most of the client machines were self-contained on the WAN, the upgrades went relatively smoothly. The few users who connect from home were given an instruction sheet explaining how to upgrade their own machines.

THE SPORTING GOODS AND APPAREL ASSOCIATION

The SGAA also performed several upgrades on their intranet. Keeping up with technology, the administrators added new software as it became available. By providing instructions right on the intranet itself, the SGAA helped its members download and install the new software they needed to use the new technology. By providing phone and e-mail technical support for its members, the SGAA made the process much easier.

Summary

The job of an intranet administrator is never done. You must be ever vigilant in finding out about new technologies and keeping your network as efficient as possible. The good part is that you get to play with new toys; the bad part is that you have to exercise considerable restraint and thoughtfulness (a trait only *good* sys admins have) in upgrading the network. The administrator needs to develop a good plan and stick to it. Heady zealousness about the latest newfangled toy has led to the collapse of many networks due to compatibility problems. Remember, the network is only as strong as its weakest link. Just because you can install and figure out how to use new software and hardware doesn't mean your users can. The careful balance between a geek playing with new toys and a careful, practical businessperson who looks out for the health of the network as a whole is the perfect administrator.

PART

IN THIS PART

- Managing and Planning for Large Web Projects 757
- The Future of Intranets 781

Advanced Topics

Managing and Planning for Large Web Projects

52

by Nova Spivack

IN THIS CHAPTER

- Initial plans for the Web   758
- Choosing a production team   758
- Formulating a business plan   763
- Developing a site specification   767
- Defining operating procedures   770
- Creating a marketing plan   772
- Defining a long-term plan   774
- Emerging technologies   775
- Outsourcing   778

In this chapter, I discuss EarthWeb's model for managing and planning large Web projects. EarthWeb has consulted on various such projects for major clients including The Metropolitan Museum of Art, The New York Stock Exchange, Morgan Stanley, BMG Music Service, AT&T Business Network, Reuters New Media, and many others. In the course of our work, a model has emerged that might be helpful to others. As well as discussing the model, I will provide helpful guidance on the complex issues that might arise during such projects.

EarthWeb considers a Web project to be "large" if the following criteria are met:

- It has a first-year budget of at least $250,000
- It involves at least 10 team members, two of which are full-time on the project
- It involves multiple departments or subcontractors
- It involves between 100 and 10,000 pages of information
- It utilizes a database, groupware, or a publishing system
- It has an initial development timeline of from 3 to 12 months to launch

Initial Plans for the Web

I will step through the process of developing a project plan for a large Web project, illustrating the thinking that goes into this process along the way. I then will conclude with a discussion of special topics, including outsourcing and emerging technologies.

To develop a large Web site, EarthWeb usually follows a series of logical steps:

1. Choose a production team.
2. Formulate a business plan.
3. Develop a site specification.
4. Define the operating procedures of the site.
5. Define the next steps for the project.

These steps will be explored in more detail in the following sections.

Choosing a Production Team

Large Web projects are orders of magnitude more challenging than smaller projects. Not only do large Web projects require a firm grasp of dozens of emerging technologies, advanced graphics design techniques, and systems integration, but they also require experienced planning and management. When you are embarking on such a project, it is important to make sure that appropriate vision, resources, and management are in place. It is almost impossible to "bootstrap" a large Web project successfully.

In the first few years of the Web, large Web projects were usually initiated by marketing departments to extend the organization's marketing reach to a global Internet audience. Today, however, the new trend is to develop large intranet projects as well. It is projected that most large Web projects will focus on intranet services in the future.

Intranet Web projects are often quite different from Internet Web projects because they involve different parts of the enterprise. Whereas the typical marketing-oriented site for the Internet might involve the marketing and sales departments, an intranet site usually must involve feedback from almost every department and level of the enterprise. This tends to make intranet projects much harder to manage than Internet projects. Furthermore, intranet audiences, due to their extensive knowledge of their own organization, are often harder to please than the general public. In either case, however, it is important to provide a project with a qualified management team to lead it. I suggest the following roles:

- Executive producer
- Product manager
- Program manager
- Production manager
- Design manager
- Editorial manager

Executive Producer

The executive producer is responsible for the vision, business relations, management, and resources of the project. As well as facilitating the project definition process, the executive producer is responsible for managing the team and its operations, ensuring that appropriate resources are in place, and managing these resources over time. The executive producer should have significant experience with project management and a realistic understanding of how creative or technology projects proceed. For large projects, I suggest that the executive producer be an internal, full-time employee of the host organization (the organization that will own the resulting Web site). An internal executive producer is preferable to an external (consulting) executive producer because an internal person will have a better understanding of the organization, the personalities involved, and the goals of the project. It is important that the leader of a large Web project be able to navigate it through the organization effectively.

Product Manager

The product manager is responsible for the marketing and/or communications goals of the project. This person's role is to determine what the marketing and communications needs are and to formulate goals that meet them. The product manager is in charge of ensuring that project vision and features are defined and are in accord with these goals. He also interfaces between the project and the users or partners in the project. The product manager also should be internal to the host organization.

Program Manager

The program manager is responsible for the technical aspects of the project. It is her responsibility to deliver solutions for the project that meet the stated goals and any limitations that might apply. The program manager must be consulted as to the feasibility of various concepts and is in charge of determining the technical timeline for the project. Unless very Internet-centric technologists exist within the host organization, it is often beneficial to hire external experts to fulfill this role on large projects. The program manager should have an advanced understanding of HTML, Java, CGI programming, relational databases, Internet standards, ActiveX, security, and the hardware platforms and operating systems the project will use.

Production Manager

The production manager is in charge of leading the production of the site. This person works within the timeline, managing designers and programmers to implement the project. He works directly under the executive producer and is parallel to the product manager and program manager. The production manager should be experienced with the production of large Web sites. The production manager should know basic HTML and should have a general understanding of Java, CGI programming, databases, and networking.

Design Manager

The design manager is the creative lead on the project. His role is to create a "look and feel" for the site and lead other designers in implementing it on each page of the site. The art director, who should have extensive experience designing state-of-the-art Web pages, is generally best found in an external consultant. The design manager should be experienced with HTML, Adobe Illustrator, and Photoshop, at the very least. A good Internet art director can usually hire freelancers for specialized work such as 3D rendering and animation, VRML, and illustration. It is important to ask any potential design manager about his access to freelancers.

Editorial Manager

The editorial manager is responsible for the content of the site. She is in charge of content creation, approval, and management. For large projects, the editorial manager might function more like a librarian than a copy editor. Often, editorial managers serve as a good resource in providing freelance writers for particular aspects of the site. The editorial manager should define and police an editorial process that ensures the quality of information on the site. The best editorial managers come from the publishing world, not the Internet world, although one with experience in both areas is preferable.

These are the key management roles on a well-managed large Web project. For particular types of projects, however, other managers might be needed in areas such as sales, business development, systems integration, and finance.

Besides managers, the project also will need a production team to implement the site. A Web production team usually consists of the following types of roles:

- Internet software developers
- Internet multimedia designers
- Internet systems administrators

Internet Software Developers

Internet software developers are necessary if a project involves the creation of any site that needs custom scripting, software components, management systems, or database back-ends. Expert Internet software developers are very hard to acquire because most of them have good jobs with high salaries and often potentially lucrative stock options. The best Internet software developers are treated like "stars" by the industry and are generally impossible to hire full-time, although many will consult for high fees. However, thousands of highly experienced Internet software developers are available for those organizations that can afford to compete for them.

Salaries range from $40,000 for a recent college grad to $65,000 for a programmer with four years of Internet programming experience to $125,000 or more for a seasoned 10-year programmer/manager. Superstar programmers might cost about $200,000, if you can get them at all. Generally speaking, most programmers are motivated by their interest more than by money; however, money is important too. Full-time positions usually require stock options and generous benefits to retain hires. It also is recommended that all programmers be given "flex time" so that they can program until late at night without having to come into the office early in the morning. Internet software developers must have the following skills to be considered qualified:

- Java: At least one year of experience writing actual code
- ActiveX: Not required yet, but becoming an increasingly important topic
- C/C++: At least three years of experience
- CGI programming: At least one year of experience
- Database design: Familiarity with relational databases and SQL
- Scripting: Experience with at least one language such as Perl, JavaScript, or Visual Basic Script
- Environments: Fluency in UNIX and Windows environments
- Servers: Familiarity with Netscape and Microsoft Web servers
- Internet: Fluency in HTML, understanding of security, and understanding of key protocols

Internet Multimedia Designers

Internet multimedia designers lay out and design Web pages. Huge numbers of people claim to be Internet multimedia designers, but relatively few of them are truly qualified experts. Still, a good Internet multimedia designer is becoming increasingly easy to acquire because many art schools are teaching Internet-related skills to their students. The best Internet multimedia designers can be found in New York City ("Silicon Alley" area), San Francisco ("South of Market" area), Boston, and Chicago. There are also a number of ways to locate designers on the Internet, such as Usenet groups and e-mail lists that designers utilize. Consult your present designers; they will be able to tell you which groups and lists are current and may even be able to help you post your job announcements there. In addition, many regions have new media associations that can provide leads to freelancers and subcontractors, as well as designers looking for work. For example, in New York, the New York New Media Association provides many useful resources. Salaries for Internet multimedia designers range from $30,000 for a recent art-school graduate to $50,000 for a designer with four years of Internet experience to $65,000 or more for a seasoned career designer with Internet expertise. Required skills include the following:

- Markup: Latest version of HTML, as well as dialects of HTML for Netscape Navigator and Microsoft Internet Explorer browsers. Experience with VRML optional.
- Scripting: Basic Perl and JavaScript skills
- Animation: Gif89 animation is required, 3D rendering and animation is optional
- Design: Mastery of Adobe Photoshop and Illustrator required, experience with Macromedia Director and Shockwave optional.
- Environments: Fluency in Macintosh and Windows environments, some UNIX experience
- Internet: Extensive experience surfing and designing for the Web

Internet Systems Administrators

Internet systems administrators are different from traditional systems administrators. They are not "LAN administrators," nor are "network administrators" necessarily Internet systems administrators. Internet systems administrators are able to design, implement, optimize, and maintain hardware and software servers connected to the public Internet. In other words, they ensure that your site has a back-end, and they keep it running. Generally, Internet systems administrators are best found in universities, Internet companies, high-tech companies, and large financial institutions. Every large Web site should be under the watchful eye of at least one professional Internet systems administrator. Salaries range from $40,000 for a recent college graduate to $65,000 for a person with four years of professional experience to $90,000 for a seasoned professional manager. Required skills include the following:

- Environments: Mastery of UNIX and NT platforms required, ability to purchase and configure machines with these operating systems
- Networking: Ability to configure Internet routers and high-bandwidth leased lines
- Internet services: Ability to configure HTTP, e-mail, Usenet, and IRC
- Databases: Ability to configure relational database servers
- Systems design: Experience planning and implementing complex Internet systems
- Systems administration: Experience maintaining, optimizing, and scaling complex, mission-critical Internet systems
- Protocols: TCP/IP, HTTP, SSL, SMTP, NFS
- Security: Experience configuring firewalls and monitoring systems

Formulating a Business Plan

After the project management is done, business planning can begin. EarthWeb usually takes clients through the following steps:

1. Definition of goals
2. Brainstorming for concepts
3. Critique of concepts
4. Mission statement
5. Budget, projections, and timeline
6. Reality check
7. Project planning

Definition of Goals

Before a project can begin, a clear set of goals must be defined. This should involve suggestions from the various stakeholders related to the project. The stakeholders usually comprise the key managers of the project as well as representatives from other departments, contractors, or teams on the project. I have found that both group discussions and private interviews are necessary to really understand the goals and potential conflicts that might exist. The end result of this phase of the project is a prioritized list of potential goals for the project.

Brainstorming for Concepts

In this stage, the team produces various alternative visions for how the project will proceed and what the deliverables will be. I have found that it is most efficient to do this brainstorming in a three-phase process. First, hold a meeting to present the current situation and any necessary limitations of the project. Discuss the business goals, technological environment, and marketing goals of the project. Be sure to address the following questions to stimulate the team's thinking:

- Who is your market?
- What can you offer that market?
- What competitive services are already in place?
- What advantages might you offer over the competition?
- What limitations apply to this project?

It also is helpful to be aware of the four archetypal business models for the Internet:

- **Communications model:** No revenues are generated directly by the site, but the site fulfills other goals such as marketing, internal communications, or project management and collaboration.
- **Advertising model:** Revenues are directly generated by advertisements that run on the site.
- **Subscription model:** Revenues are generated by subscriptions from users.
- **Merchandising model:** Revenues are generated by transactions done via the site.

Some sites combine all four business models, whereas others focus on just one or two. It is important for the executive producer of the project to determine which of these business models will be appropriate for the project and to communicate this information clearly to the team.

The next step is to ask all the stakeholders to spend a week independently generating alternative concepts for the project. Ask the stakeholders to write up the concepts in a standard format to be presented to the group. I usually suggest a simple "Idea Template." Each stakeholder can fill out as many Idea Templates as he wants. The Template ensures that each vision will be thought out in a standardized manner so that all ideas can be compared by the team. The final step, after everyone has done some thinking, is to bring the team together to review the concepts and critique them. A sample Idea Template might include fields such as these:

- Name of concept
- Goal of concept
- Intended audience
- Brief description
- Technologies
- Advantages of concept
- Disadvantages of concept
- Timeline
- Required skills
- Required resources
- Budget
- How realistic is this concept?

After a suitable number of concepts have been defined, they should be distributed to the team and analyzed.

Critique of Concepts

To select a direction for moving forward, the team must critique the various concepts generated by the individuals. The critique should proceed along three dimensions: business, market, and technology. Each concept should be evaluated as to its capability to meet the business goals of the organization as well as the feasibility of its method of doing so. Each concept should be tested relative to the market in which it must exist. Each concept must be evaluated according to its technological requirements and feasibility. In each of these areas, it might be necessary for the project team to consult with experts from other parts of the enterprise, as well as with external expert consultants if necessary. It should be relatively easy to narrow the field of concepts down to three options. Getting from three to one is often quite hard, however. Be prepared to spend at least a week choosing the final direction.

Mission Statement

After a concept is chosen, it should be expressed in a mission statement. A mission statement is helpful in defining the concept and building consensus around it from the outset. A clear mission statement also prevents conflicting goals from arising after the project gets underway. The mission statement should be concise and specific. For example, "The mission of this Web project is to create a project collaboration and information exchange for the consultants in the enterprise" is much more useful than "The mission of this Web project is to create a site that will go online throughout the enterprise within four months," which in turn is better than "We will create the most advanced intranet on the planet."

Budget, Projections, and Timeline

With a project direction and mission in hand, the team is now in a position to evaluate the resources and time needed for the project. Usually this involves an exploration of the existing people, content, funds, and infrastructure that are already in place. Will these be sufficient, or will the project require additional resources? It is the role of the executive producer to ensure that this question is answered by consulting with the various managers and related departments, contractors, and partners. It is helpful to make a table of resources required by the project that indicates which resources exist and which need to be acquired.

An understanding of resources enables the formulation of a budget. The budget should be realistic—you get what you pay for. Competitive Internet sites are developed with *annual* budgets ranging from $100,000 to more than $30 million. EarthWeb believes that state-of-the-art "high end" sites can be realistically developed for between $300,000 and $4 million annually.

If the goal of the project is to make money on the Web, it is valuable also to develop a set of financial projections for the site. Generally, projections should start with an "Assumptions" sheet, which lists market size, market penetration, and growth of market assumptions. The Assumptions section also might include the costs of raw materials and prices for products or services. Following this sheet are some scenarios, including Expenses, Sales, and Revenues. It usually is a good idea to develop worst-case, conservative-case, and best-case scenarios. This exercise often reveals potential problems, or unrecognized opportunities, in a Web project.

Also note that it costs money to make money. At EarthWeb, we have an adage that we often convey to clients who want to make money on the Web: The "#1 Site Killer" is underfunding. The "#2 Site Killer" is understaffing. No matter how good your content, no matter how advanced your technology, if you don't adequately fund and staff your project, it will fail. And if your project fails, it won't make money.

Closely tied to the budget is a timeline. Time must be allocated for the organization of existing resources as well as the acquisition of new ones. Furthermore, time needs to be allocated for the design and implementation of the project. It is EarthWeb's experience that after a complete final specification is developed, most large Web projects take a minimum of 3 months and a maximum of 12 months for the site's first live launch. It is unrealistic to expect a large Web project to proceed more quickly than three months. Generally, I advise that you multiply the time your CEO thinks the project will take by 3 to arrive at a realistic estimate.

Web project timelines proceed in several phases:

- Design: The initial planning and experimentation before actual development
- Implementation: The actual development of the site pages and functionality
- Alpha: Specification of the complete feature set (no new features are added)
- Beta: Testing and bug fixing of the site
- Launch: Opening of the site to live audiences
- Intensive care: Close monitoring of the site under actual usage conditions
- Stabilization: Optimization of the site to handle actual usage patterns reliably
- Evolution: Addition of new features and content to the site

Reality Check

Just as the team critiqued concepts in a previous phase, now the team critiques the feasibility of the proposed concept. During this phase, the team should examine the entire concept, resource table, timeline, and budget to determine whether it is realistic for the organization to undertake the project. Often this is the phase where an organization realizes that external contractors and increased budgets and extended timelines are needed, and in which the team discovers how committed to the project the organization really is.

Project Planning

Finally, a realistic, well-defined project exists, and it is time to create a project plan. A project plan is a "living document" that changes as the project advances. Even so, it is absolutely vital to have some sort of a project plan at all times to ensure that the project proceeds in a coordinated manner. For a large team, it might be helpful to put this plan up on the Web for easy access. The plan should be a document that team members can refer to, and it should eventually include the following:

- Mission statement
- Business plan
- Production team
- Timeline
- Budget
- Site specification:
    - Site architecture and features
    - Site content
    - User interface
    - Site technology
- Operating procedures
- Marketing plan
- Long-term plan

I already have fleshed out the first five sections of the project plan. In the remainder of this chapter, I will flesh out the rest of the plan.

Developing a Site Specification

Designing a Web site involves four key considerations:

- Site architecture and features
- Site content
- User interface
- Site technology

Site Architecture and Features

The structure of your information space is called a *site architecture*. A typical site architecture is either a hierarchical outline that lists each page of the site and the elements and links on that page, or a graph of the structure of the site that shows each page and how it links to the other pages on the site. The functionality found within the site is called its "feature set." The feature set of a site is defined as a list of key features or functions and a description of what each feature does and in which part of the site it is available. EarthWeb uses Microsoft Word's outliner to outline site architectures feature sets, and a program called VISIO to graph site architectures. The outline of a site architecture should look something like this partial example:

1. Home page
   Home icon and logo banner
   Animation
   Graphical background
   Announcements
   Opening message
   Button bar
      About
      Products

2. About page
   About icon and logo banner
   Graphical background
   About text (four paragraphs)
   Button bar
      Home
      Products

3. Products page
   Products icon and logo banner
   Graphical background
   Intro text
   Links to products
      Acme Rocket
      Acme Scooter
   Button bar
      Home
      About

Much more sophisticated graphs can be made to illustrate relations and choices among the pages or functions of a site. Usually the executive producer and the product manager spearhead the site architecture outline, and the program manager develops the site architecture graph and feature set.

EarthWeb suggests that you keep two principles in mind when building your site:

- The Law of Links: The number of people who click a link on a Web page decreases as the number of links that compete for attention on that Web page increases.
- The Law of Clicks: The number of people who visit a Web page decreases as the number of links it takes to get to that page from the home page increases.

If you manage to strike a balance between these two laws, it is likely that your site architecture will be effective and easy to navigate.

Site Content

Site content specification consists of choosing or creating the content for the site. This includes choosing or creating text, graphics, or other forms of content. The editorial manager is in charge of this task, in association with the product manager and executive producer. A content specification is usually a list of the content in the site—something like this:

- Home page intro text—two paragraphs
- Home page background image
- Home page illustration
- Large corporate logo
- Small corporate logo
- Home icon
- About icon
- Products icon
- Product Line icon
- Generic Banner art
- About page text—four paragraphs
- About page illustration
- Photo of headquarters
- Product page text—three paragraphs
- Large photo of Acme Rocket
- Small photo of Acme Rocket
- Large photo of Acme Scooter
- Small photo of Acme Scooter
- Acme Rocket product information—three pages
- Acme Scooter product information—three pages

User Interface

The user interface of a site consists of the look-and-feel of the site and its various applications, such as button bars, Java applets, and ActiveX components. The user interface is designed by the design manager and the designers, in association with any programmers who might implement particular interface applications. Generally, the user interface is specified in the form of sketches or diagrams that illustrate the interface guidelines and standards for the project.

Advanced Topics
Part VIII

Site Technology

The site technology specification consists of a list of necessary technologies for the site. This is prepared by the program manager and the systems administrator, based on the previously listed specifications. The site technology specification is usually a list like this:

- Netscape Commerce Server
- Four Sparc Ultra 170 servers
- 1 gigabyte storage
- 2 gigabyte backup storage
- Uninterruptible power supply
- Solaris
- Java Development Kit
- Perl
- C++
- Informix database
- T1 leased line
- Web site to database scripts
- Credit-card authorization system
- I/Pro usage auditing
- EarthWeb Chat server
- EarthWeb Chat applet
- Excalibur search engine

Defining Operating Procedures

Most large Web sites must provide a consistent, quality service 24 hours a day, seven days a week. Defining operating procedures for a Web site involves two aspects: planning for problems and planning for normal operations.

On the Internet, a certain number of technical difficulties should be expected and must be planned for, even if they cannot be entirely avoided due to the nature of the medium itself. As well as these difficulties, various problems might arise on a management level.

Following is a list of technical difficulties that will almost inevitably take place on any large Web site project:

- Server goes down
- Data is accidentally erased
- Local network connection goes down

- Remote network connection goes down
- Routing table gets corrupted or address changes
- Bugs occur in software applications
- Content is not updated on time
- Errors in content occur
- Hardware and software incompatibilities occur
- Conflicts between engineering and marketing teams arise
- Conflicts between engineering and design teams arise
- Conflicts between design and engineering teams arise
- Conflicts between management and production teams arise
- Management changes specification midway through project
- Management changes timeline midway through project
- Emerging technologies change specification midway through project
- Competitive sites or products emerge during project
- Personnel turnover occurs
- Budget becomes insufficient

It is important to expect these difficulties and to plan for them appropriately. It can be helpful to discuss them openly with the team at the outset of the project. With enough time, the Internet systems administrator and program manager can prepare for or prevent most of the purely technical setbacks previously listed. Management, on the other hand, can only prepare for, but probably not prevent, the management setbacks that are likely to occur. Generally, EarthWeb advises clients to allow for delays, to manage the project as inclusively as possible, to allocate a realistic budget, and to have redundancy in key engineering, production, and design positions in case of turnover during the project.

It is a good idea to create a backup server that mirrors the live server so that the site can be quickly switched if the primary server goes down. It also is very important to make sure that updates and changes to the site are first developed and tested on a "staging server" before being copied over to the live site.

As well as planning for problems, it also is important to plan for normal operations. In general, EarthWeb suggests that a large Web site always have at least one person "on watch." The person on watch is responsible for checking the site periodically to detect problems and to alert the appropriate parties if problems arise. It is a good idea to equip all engineers, producers, and designers with national alphanumeric pagers in case they need to be reached. It also is helpful to create a script that periodically pings the server to ensure that it is up and that it automatically pages the Internet systems administrator if the server goes down.

Another aspect of normal operating procedures is the definition of access to the content and a procedure for managing and approving content before it is posted onto the live site. This task is usually carried out by the editorial manager. Some larger organizations use groupware products like Lotus Notes, or Internet content management products like the Netscape Publishing System, to help in this process. Generally, it has been our observation that content should be approved by a qualified copy editor and a marketing representative before being posted to the live site, unless it is pre-approved content of a certain type, such as a wire feed.

The team also should define an updated schedule for modifying the site regularly. It also is important to define a testing procedure whenever a significant update of the site is generated:

- Spell-check the content before giving it the HTML markup team
- Test every link and application/applet in the site by hand
- Test the site on Windows 95, UNIX, and Macintosh platforms
- Test the site on a 28.8 dial-up modem as well as a high-bandwidth connection
- Document bugs in a standardized manner
- Carry out all these actions on both Netscape and Internet Explorer; no other browser matters anymore

Finally, during both production and post-launch, it is important to have regular team meetings to discuss status and the next steps for the project. During initial production, meetings should be held every day. At launch, meetings should be held every week. After the site has stabilized, meetings should be held every two weeks or monthly.

Creating a Marketing Plan

Before a site is created, significant thought should go into marketing considerations. Primarily, the team should consider the intended audience. It is often useful to construct a user profile of the intended user and then examine Internet demographics to determine whether such users actually exist on the Internet. If you feel that you already have a good understanding of the typical Internet user, the next step is to develop a set of special features that your audience will appreciate. Next, conduct a competitive analysis by using the major search engines to look at related and competing sites. This might need to be done multiple times during the project to keep up with breaking developments. After evaluating competitors, modify your own design and marketing goals to differentiate your site significantly.

Whether a site is intended for intranet use or public Internet use, some thought should go into how the site will be tested for and promoted to its intended audience. If the audience is internal to the enterprise, the site should be tested in user focus groups early in the design phases to evaluate user-interface alternatives. After the site is launched, it should be promoted to employees through training sessions and in printed corporate communications.

If a Web site is intended for public Internet use, market testing and promotions become much more complex. Generally, EarthWeb recommends that a site be tested by a pre-launch Beta audience. If necessary, have them sign confidentiality agreements first, although this agreement is generally hard to enforce over the Internet. Users should provide feedback via e-mail or, better, on an online survey form via the Web.

Active promotion for a Web site should begin at least two months before launch. During this initial period, seed interest at trade shows and in discussions with potential users and partners. Never give away anything proprietary until you are ready for publicity. During this period, prepare printed marketing collateral, advertising, and promotional programs.

One week before launch, seed the press with an embargoed press release or a media alert for a press conference on the launch date. This is best done through a public relations agency. It is important to target the Internet trade publications as well as the key wire services and at least two national business or entertainment newspapers. At the same time, register the site with the major Internet directories and search engines, and create a live "Coming Soon" page in place of your home page so that users who hear about your site will see something enticing if they visit your URL before the opening. When the site opens, replace the Coming Soon page with the home page.

It is best to time any new site opening to coincide with a major trade show such as Internet World; however, it is often hard to get noticed by reporters during such events even though more interest is focused on the Internet from the press. At a trade show, be sure to create a media kit and seed the press room with it. Also try to hold a press conference and make sure that you have reporters committed to attending before the event. Press releases with strategic partners can often help create a buzz around a launch as well.

During the first week of opening, announce the site in the appropriate Usenet directories. Be careful not to alienate potential visitors by posting inappropriately. For guidelines on posting to particular groups, see the FAQ for those groups, which is usually available in the groups themselves. If you cannot find the FAQ, you can usually post anyway as long as your posting relates to the topic of the group, does not try to sell something shamelessly, and does not repeat numerous times in a single group or set of related groups. Under no circumstances should you send unsolicited e-mail to mass audiences of potential visitors as a form of site promotion, because this will create a severe backlash that would not further your marketing goals.

Following the opening, solicit links from the webmasters of related sites by sending them e-mail. It sometimes helps to offer "reciprocal links" to their sites in return. Also consider advertising online—the surest way to reach actual Internet users. EarthWeb suggests advertising through an Internet advertising network, such as DoubleClick, or by contacting the advertising sales representatives for key sites that relate to your target audience.

EarthWeb has found that online banner advertising on major sites and offline print advertising are the two key direct drivers of Web site traffic. Registering in directories and search engines, Usenet postings, press releases, press conferences, and promotional events are far less effective but should be done anyway to ensure a complete marketing presence.

Part VIII

Defining a Long-Term Plan

It is vital to develop a long-term plan for the evolution of your site. This plan should take into account emerging technologies and demographics, as well as potential and actual competitors. It is important to consider some developing trends in formulating your plan. Following are some trends EarthWeb suggests you consider:

- The growing Internet audience will add millions of low-tech consumers to the Net
- Increased female and youth demographics will require new types of content and higher production and entertainment value on Web sites
- The increased audience will strain existing bandwidth and server capacity
- As the audience increases, advertising revenues will become more viable
- Standardization of online commerce technologies will allow safe and easy online shopping
- Emerging technologies will allow sophisticated animation and multimedia on Web sites
- Increased bandwidth to the home and office will allow larger file download sizes and real-time data and media streaming
- The Internet will be accessed on televisions via cable modems and on wireless portable devices
- Emerging technologies such as Java and ActiveX will allow sophisticated software functionality within Web sites
- The emergence of multicasting technologies will allow live broadcasting over the Internet to any size of audience using presently available bandwidth
- A number of "channels" are forming on the Internet around major technology providers (Netscape), directories (Yahoo), online services (America Online, Pointcast), and highly financed Web sites (Pathfinder, Sony).
- For any type of content you charge for, another site will give it away free as a loss leader for something else
- Due to security concerns, most ActiveX components will be useful only in the Internet space on Windows platforms, whereas more general and safer Java applets will function on all platforms and will be ubiquitous throughout the Internet space.
- Microsoft Internet Explorer will gain more market share than Netscape Navigator.
- Dedicated browsers will become irrelevant because the Web will be linked directly to the desktop and within applications
- The Windows NT platform will continually gain market share against UNIX platforms
- Digital cash will replace online credit-card transactions (but not until after the turn of the century)

- Almost all large Web sites will utilize some form of database by 1997
- Almost all large Web sites will utilize some form of search engine by 1998
- Almost all large Web sites will utilize some form of real-time content (animation, data streaming, multimedia) by 1999

These are just a few trends to be aware of and track. It is likely that they will figure into your long-term planning significantly over time.

Emerging Technologies

It is important that you consider emerging technologies carefully when designing and implementing a Web project. Generally, it is unwise to use emerging technologies in the critical functional elements of a Web site unless they have been thoroughly tested by the market for at least six months. On the other hand, the use of emerging technologies in user interfaces often differentiates a site and establishes it as leading-edge. On the down side, however, use of emerging technologies can often be a source of frustration among users who are not able to access them or when the technologies perform unreliably. Thus, the decision to use emerging technologies is as much a marketing issue as it is a technical one, because it has ramifications for the positioning and usability of a site as well as its functionality.

Some emerging technologies are much overblown, whereas others will become increasingly important on the Internet. The following sections give EarthWeb's predictions, for what they are worth.

Java

Poised to become the de facto programming language of the next decade, as well as the Internet, Java is already a standard. Java is quickly being adopted and supported by all the major players and is accessible to all Internet users today. Java enables the creation of both desktop applications and Web page applets. Built-in security features make Java safe for use on the Internet and on intranets. Java also is spreading out into other areas such as cellular phones, portable computing devices, set-top-boxes, game platforms, and dedicated network computer terminals.

ActiveX

Microsoft's ActiveX technology is a Windows-centric methodology for developing software components. ActiveX is based on the OLE framework, which is not well-supported on most non-Windows platforms. Whereas Java is a programming language and a new virtual platform for running platform-independent applications and applets, ActiveX is not a programming language—it is a way of writing programs. In fact, you can write ActiveX components using Java, C, C++, or other languages. The main advantage of writing programs according to ActiveX standards is that it integrates nicely with other OLE-compatible products and components, such as desktop applications software from Microsoft and other major vendors. This opens up the potential for a new era in "Web page to desktop application" data sharing. Unless you write ActiveX components in Java, they can't provide the level of built-in security that pure Java components offer and therefore are quite risky to use on the public Internet. It is likely that ActiveX components will be safe to use only within controlled, secure environments, such as intranets. Furthermore, because ActiveX components work only on Windows-compatible platforms, even if they were written in Java, they aren't ideal for non-Windows audiences. Therefore, if you're writing code for a multiplatform audience, ActiveX won't be of much use to you at this time. On the other hand, if your audience is primarily using Windows, ActiveX may be useful, especially if you want to make use of existing Windows OLE components or if you want to integrate with desktop applications.

VRML

Great advances have happened in VRML recently, but they still don't answer the main question of what it's good for. Very few if any compelling examples of VRML have been offered beyond virtual chat rooms. It remains to be seen whether VRML will become more important in years to come. Perhaps VRML will be most useful for online training or for the visualization of multidimensional information spaces. On the other hand, it might prove to be just a curiosity. In any case, it is now supported in major Web browsers, even though few sites use it.

Video Streaming

Video streaming will become increasingly prevalent, especially with increased bandwidth to the home from cable modems. A big question remains to be answered as to whether video on the Internet will be used mostly for multicasting the same data to many viewers at once or for narrow-casting video-on-demand data to particular users at different times. In any case, until the backbone bandwidth of the Internet increases dramatically, there will be severe limits on the amount of video traffic that can be supported. Better compression codecs also are emerging to allow near-full-motion video to slow modems. Video streaming will become most important within intranets, especially in the area of desktop training and enterprise-wide video-conferencing.

Audio Streaming

Audio streaming will not become entirely obsolete but will be ever less important over the next few years. By the next century, audio streaming will be relevant only to mobile applications where there are bandwidth limitations or when the user can listen but cannot watch a screen (such as when driving). Audio streaming will continue to be important to online music stores, however.

Data Streaming

We believe that by 1999 every major Web site will serve real-time data. From stock tickers to news feeds, from dynamic ads to live animation, from live data monitoring to multi-user interactive services, the Internet is coming alive. Although data streaming offers lower bandwidth than audio and video, it is just as important, and data streaming is easier to achieve on today's relatively low-bandwidth Internet. It is a key technology to watch.

Internet Phone

Here's a technology that is going to die off quickly. As soon as enough people start using Internet Phone services to create a bandwidth deficit on the backbone, they will no longer be free. When Internet Phones are not free, who will put up with their low signal quality and unreliability? Why not just use real phones? This is an example of technology as an end in itself. Only a few die-hard hackers will continue to use them.

Internet Video-Conferencing

This application is closely related to video streaming and will be feasible only within intranets or between users with high-bandwidth connections. It will become more common in the next decade.

Wireless Internet Connections

The Internet will go mobile as the cost of cellular communications goes down. In the next decade, most laptops and hand-held devices will routinely connect to the Internet via internal cellular modems. Wireless devices will open up new areas for Internet applications and will pose new challenges for Web site interface designers.

Intelligent Agents

Despite the General Magic disaster, intelligent agents are not dead. In fact, agent technologies will increase, especially in the area of personalizing databases.

Online Commerce

Online transactions will become commonplace and safe with the advent of digital cash and smartcards. But don't expect it to happen in a big way this decade. In the meantime, use credit-card transactions via SSL.

Advanced Topics

Part VIII

Outsourcing

Before concluding this chapter, I want to discuss outsourcing, because it often comes up in the context of large Web projects. Outsourcing can be a useful way to develop a large site when time is limited or when appropriate internal expertise and resources are not available. Outsourcing also can be detrimental, however, if not utilized properly. EarthWeb follows these rules when outsourcing or when advising clients and partners:

- Do not outsource project leadership
- Do outsource special projects
- Do not outsource business planning
- Do hire an Internet business expert to consult with your team
- Do not outsource all engineering for the project
- Do outsource engineering if you also have qualified internal lead engineers
- Do not outsource site maintenance and editorial functions indefinitely
- Do outsource servers, bandwidth, and 24/7 systems administration
- Do not outsource at the beginning of a project
- Do outsource after an in-house management team exists
- Do not exclude contractors from planning and decision making
- Do include contractors in team meetings and take their advice; they are the experts
- Do not assign more than one contractor to the same task
- Do assign different tasks to different contractors
- Do not allow contractors to finish without providing documentation
- Do attempt to retain as much project learning in-house as possible
- Do not micro-manage contractors
- Do empower contractors to work without constant supervision and reporting
- Do not under-manage contractors
- Do guide contractors by inviting them to regular reviews and team meetings
- Do not choose contractors on the basis of price alone
- Do choose contractors based on their previous work and their references

Outsourcing, when used appropriately, can rapidly speed up development and increase the technical sophistication of a project. On the other hand, if not managed carefully, outsourcing can lead to project fragmentation, delays, and technical incompatibilities.

EarthWeb recommends that outsourcing be used on the leading-edge of a project, and that day-to-day maintenance of the existing portions of the site be handled by an in-house team. Specialist contractors should be hired to add new state-of-the-art functionality to the site, because it is often unnecessary and expensive to hire such specialists full-time. On the other hand, external consultants are usually more expensive than full-time in-house employees, and they should not be used for content maintenance such as editing, content creation, Web page updates, and systems maintenance and administration.

One alternative to outsourcing is to hire internal consultants to work full-time within your organization. This provides the advantages of internal experts without the overhead of paying benefits. Also, you avoid the management overhead involved in outsourcing to a remote location. This alternative also can provide for better communication between the consultants and the in-house team; however, few Internet experts who are worth hiring will work on such terms for longer than a few months.

Summary

Management and planning for large Web sites is far more sophisticated than for small sites. As you have seen in this chapter, this work requires a significant team effort and a grasp of numerous business, technical, and marketing processes. With careful planning and appropriate use of expert advice, such projects can proceed very quickly. Without the benefit of experience and a model for developing large sites, many organizations fail without even knowing why. This chapter should provide useful guidance to those who are thinking of developing large Web sites.

The Future of Intranets

53

*by Frank Pappas
and
Clifford Majersik*

IN THIS CHAPTER

- Business trends **782**
- Information economy **785**
- Technology trends **789**
- Extranets **801**

One thing is certain in the uncertain world of computers and information-serving systems: Both business trends and evolving technologies will play important roles in shaping the future of intranets. Intranets will enable their users to conduct business more efficiently, communicate in a more rapid and effective manner, and generally facilitate nearly all manner of business, personal, and governmental interaction on almost any scale.

Now that you've made your way through a lot of technical, practical, and theoretical information on intranet design, it is time to discuss the future of the intranet concept: where the technologies, analysts, information systems (IS) managers—and, most importantly, the users—are channeling intranet development and viability. Essentially, this chapter is proffered as an intranet "road map" that will help you understand the trends and technologies that hold sway over the intranet scene. These trends include acceleration of the pace of business, movement toward a global information economy, enhanced telecommuting, the rise of virtual corporations, and significant outsourcing of traditionally in-house tasks. The technology trends include open architecture in application development and integration; increased bandwidth to support live, full-motion video and digital audio; intelligent agents to facilitate searches and indexing; and increased functionality of stand-alone applications to provide greater flexibility and utility to users.

Business Trends

The development of intranet and Internet systems—really, anything having to do with the integration of IS technology in the workplace—is linked inexorably with general trends in the business world, from revenue considerations to the whims of both managers and users when contemplating intranet functionality.

Many corporations are just now becoming aware of a fairly new concept: data mining. Data mining is essentially the analysis of an extremely large body of often ignored or undervalued data that has been collected as a result of the normal progression of business issues, such as sales figures, mailing lists, and product complaint information. By crunching numbers, putting the data up against different tests, and searching for new and perhaps unexplored indicators of viability in a product cycle, producers can reap significant insight into previously nebulous regions of their costs, markets for their products, and their products themselves.

Similarly, embedded processing technology and its potential is a trend that greatly influences both the implementation of current intranet systems and the direction in which such communication platforms will evolve over the next decade. Computer chips are falling in price dramatically, and one of the new uses for this resource is embedding processors everywhere—microwaves, cellular phones, soda machines. As an example, say a soda machine can call back to its distributor when it is empty. This is information technology that can help a company better satisfy customers and maximize profitability. This is also data that must be collected, tracked, stored, and manipulated. One way to distribute this data is through an intranet linked to a wide area network (WAN) or the Internet. Anyone at the soda company can access the average number of sales of Flying-Monkey soda around the country and can react accordingly, sending additional shipments to certain vendors, while simultaneously redirecting marketing and other promotional efforts to the regions where the product is not selling as well.

The bottom line is this: New technology is creating more information on services and products that must be analyzed, distributed, stored, and manipulated, and without the common framework of an intranet to support such activities, corporations will find themselves lost in a never-ending sea of data. As computer chip prices fall, many uses of these chips for collecting or processing information are becoming economically viable for the first time. As the use of embedded chips proliferates, more information is gathered. Much of this new information will be stored and accessed via intranets.

The growth of intranets is directly related to the information explosion. As information and technology become more accessible, we will begin to see them infiltrate every sector of our lives. For example, a power company only has so many trucks, but it needs to be more responsive to customers. In the past, the company would have had to buy more trucks and hire more drivers. Now, using computer chips and an intranet, the company can instead improve the management of its current fleet of service vehicles. Computer advances in general—and intranet technology specifically—have made it easier to track this data and provide it to the appropriate employees who can deal with it in an appropriate fashion.

Intranets offer a new and revolutionary way of communicating—both as a distribution channel and an information source. The most profound aspect of an intranet is that it can provide everyone in an organization equal access to information. It can also provide a soapbox from which disgruntled, enthusiastic, or otherwise motivated people can convey thoughts, ideas, and feelings. In order for organizations to take complete advantage of the new lines of communication made available by intranets, they must make a conscious effort to establish a corporate culture that is conducive or perhaps complementary to the atmosphere in which an intranet is designed to flourish. Although this is certainly not a simple task for any company, it is a necessity that must be undertaken if a corporation truly wants to maximize the possibilities of communication.

Essentially, organizations must flatten their hierarchies, which is the 1990s version of "Empower the workers." The power of intranets is that they give every employee easy access to up-to-date information. Such access dramatically increases the pool of employees who have the information on which to base intelligent decisions. By flattening their hierarchies and giving employees the authority and support with which to make decisions on their own, organizations will cut response times, streamline decisions, and thereby realize time and cost savings.

The important thing to remember is that a corporation's front line of employees are usually the best-positioned to efficiently manage its resources, resolve its problems, and advance its projects. By supporting employees with intranet-based information resources that are constantly available and consistently accurate, corporations will be able to service both corporate and client needs quickly, accurately, and successfully.

Reformatting the Workforce

With an intranet and various pieces of technology assembled in multiplatform, open architecture systems, some types of jobs will be eliminated, especially those that "repackage information," such as data entry, transcription, low-level oversight, filing, and basic research. Coupled with this decrease in one demographic of the corporate workforce, however, is an increase in another sector of jobs that will mushroom for those who draw on the intranet's resources in their daily work, as well as for those who have the background to support current and future technology advances. As this new technology proliferates, systems administrators and integrators, content developers, trends and data analysts, and front-line workers from salespeople to maintenance personnel will need to be empowered by ready access to information via intranets. Remember, though, that computers don't make anything but the most basic and mundane decisions (nor will they do much advanced decision-making in the near future), so employers won't be looking to replace decision makers with intranets or other information systems.

In addition, on a much grander scale, intranets will increase productivity and thereby potentially benefit the global economy. This will happen through both a general stimulation of trade as well as specific instances of corporate success due to advanced market planning based on such things as computerized analysis of market trends. All this will be made possible by virtue of the statistical business and other data collected and made available by intranet systems.

Workplace Communications

The technology of an intranet makes geography less important in a global economy. It's just as simple to send an e-mail message or post an event on a calendar for someone in another country as it is for someone in the cubicle down the hall. This makes it considerably more practical for people to report to managers in different locations, negating traditional concerns for departments to be in the same physical location. A traditional floor plan is no longer relevant with intranet technology. Individuals and companies can be connected despite geographic, time zone, or political (immigration) constraints. This fits in with the trend toward the internationalization of commerce and the specialization of business as in the virtual company, which is explained in "Virtual Corporations."

The organization of an intranet and its resources has the potential to be as important as the actual floor plan of an office. An intranet can link those who are far away from one another and can also allow those who normally are close to go far away, perhaps to work from home, while on an airplane, or in that favorite motel in Topeka, Kansas. For example, a firm in New

York City totally revamped its office strategy because of the way its communication systems facilitate new avenues of collaboration. It cut office space down to a third of its normal level, saving money and lots of space. Next, instead of everyone having a permanent office and space within the building, people now work from home or the road. They now use a system referred to as "hoteling," which means that their main office is administered somewhat akin to a hotel's management structure. Case in point: Bob George, John Smith, and Michael Alexander all have appointments with clients, so they'll need to reserve conference rooms for the following week. Each places a call to Patty McCormick, the office scheduler, and arranges for the appropriate rooms, equipment, and other resources necessary to satisfy their particular needs.

As more and more people work from home as telecommuters, intranets will provide the tools necessary to have a fully functional remote site offering access not only to the resources of the Internet but also corporate databases, documents, and workflow. An intranet offers a plausible solution to people who now do not need to physically be inside an office during the traditional 9-to-5 hours. Organizations save money on space rental, utilities, parking, and maintenance, and individuals save money on gas, clothing, and lunch. Individuals can also spend more time with their families, which often results in happier, more productive employees.

Information Economy

The most important thing that a company or an individual can possess in today's business world is information, in the form of either large sets of raw data or more refined, analyzed records. We will continue to experience the rise of the information economy as the prime motivator behind modern business transactions as the buying and selling of information grows in size to rival the trade in physical goods. Information is what distinguishes one company from another: It allows a company to understand its market, spot trends, and respond to crises or developing needs. In trying to position themselves for future growth and prosperity, corporations will strive to be one (preferably two) step ahead of the competition in gathering and analyzing infor-mation.

As more businesses have come to recognize the role that information plays in the workplace—and have begun to explore new, exciting, and powerful methods of collection, processing, and analysis—they are undergoing fundamental changes to the way that they conduct themselves in relation to not only their clients but the market as well. Although in the past such resources were only available to the largest and best-funded businesses and institutions, the many and varied technologies that intranets bring to bear on the system have the effect of leveling the playing field.

What's more, information can be purchased directly through news feeds—both conventional sources like Reuters and AP and those delivered primarily through the Internet such as Individual, Inc. (www.individual.com) or the PointCast Network (www.pointcast.com). For example, an organization could pay a service bureau $500 a month to stream targeted news feeds directly into its intranet, providing on-demand access to specialized information that is available to all employees. Each employee no longer has a subscription to newspapers and magazines, saving money, time, and frustration—and he or she will never again encounter articles missing from magazines, have to share subscriptions with coworkers, or deal with highlighted, dovetailed, and tattered paper-based information sources.

There are, of course, other complementary technologies that work to ensure the success and integration of the Internet within the workplace. For example, filtering technology exists to separate the important news from the trivial, depending on the needs of your employees in particular or the company as a whole. Organizations can purchase only financial or other job-specific information and subsequently route that data to all managers and employees with an urgent need for it. Whatever avenue you adopt, countless permutations are available that will allow you to implement a solution that matches your needs as closely as possible.

Again, instant access to all data—such as whether the Federal Reserve has raised the financial rate or consumer confidence reports—levels the playing field between the historically dominant companies and the smaller, specialty ones. Small organizations can buy news feeds as easily as big organizations. They no longer need in-house departments to clip news, copy news, distribute briefings and updates, or service the production of newsletters. All this frees up internal resources—from personnel to finances—to work on issues more vital to the well-being of the company.

News feeds can provide not only outside information but important inside information as well. For example, national sales figures can be made instantly and continuously available to employees—whether your organization is a $500,000-a-year startup or $5 billion giant. With this technology, people can see up-to-the-minute sales figures for the entire company or specific regions and departments, as well as all the other internal information that has traditionally allowed big companies to make both tactical and strategic decisions on corporate structure, budgeting, marketing, and so on. Large organizations have always been able to make these decisions with varying levels of success, but now the smaller companies are also able to leverage this information as an important internal resource and can compete more effectively in the global marketplace.

Businesses that sell information are tied into the rise of the information economy and the acceleration of business decisions. Significant amounts of information are time valued, essentially worthless if they don't reach the key players in a timely, efficient fashion. As more businesses are selling information, they are having to turn it around faster, placing a burden on both technology and personnel. An excellent example of time-valued information is the wire service. For example, a correspondent for a news organization in Hong Kong speaks Chinese and English. When she covers press conferences in Hong Kong, where Chinese officials speak, she translates it real-time into a cellular phone, while the person on the other line types it in and puts it immediately onto the wire service—there is no time wasted in her taking notes, writing them up, faxing them to the company, and so on. It is the succinct manner in which businesses can maximize their productivity that will separate the winners from the losers in the information arena.

Continuing with the wire service example, you'll often find that the people who subscribe to this wire need to have this information ASAP. Commodity and stock traders, for example, want the news first to make trades based on this information. The extra time it could take to type, translate, and fax the report could be the critical difference. In truth, time becomes the product you are selling. Primary source information is generally available to many people simultaneously—what you are selling is accuracy and time-to-market, and you can rely on intranet technology to keep ahead of the competition in many instances.

Intranets can create a divide between the technological haves and have-nots. A company that effectively utilizes intranet technology can be more responsive to changes; make rapid, well-informed decisions; produce higher-quality products more easily; and deliver to the customer more quickly, all the while reducing costs.

Granted, because large companies have the resources to buy the technology earlier, they will be afforded a competitive advantage. On the flip side, however, large organizations tend to move slowly, and it's hard for them to adapt to new technology. The smaller organizations that can move decisively and quickly to adopt and implement this new technology will have an advantage. However, intranet technology does not specifically help big or small organizations. It can provide real benefits to any company that can realize the importance of open systems information and communication management.

Virtual Corporations

One business trend that intranet systems help make possible is the advent of virtual corporations. A virtual corporation is born when several corporations, most often with different specialties and located in different geographic areas, work in concert as a single entity to service the needs of particular clients specific to the virtual corporation, or perhaps to support joint research efforts. Intranet technology is enabling virtual corporations to work more closely with one another, be better coordinated, and compete more directly with a single corporation. Virtual corporations can be defined as companies with little or no physical infrastructure. For example, during my company's first year of existence, the only building we gathered in was the restaurant we held meetings at. Almost all of our communication and collaboration was done using the Internet and our intranet. Even today, with more than 25 employees building complex software, more than two-thirds of our development is done at home. Only hard-core collaboration is done at the office.

The Global Economy

As the international walls of business disappear and trade barriers are lessened, domestic companies are shifting their focus from a national agenda to an international strategy. Today, companies are looking at international clients and evaluating the products and services that they can offer those clients. This includes everything from writing software in multiple languages to "westernizing" other cultures with U.S. products, or perhaps even to exporting U.S. marketing savvy abroad. To accomplish successful sales relationships on an international level, however, businesses first must begin to understand the trends that drive culture and business environments in particular countries. Intranets offer an ideal method to track issues worldwide because they can leverage companies' access to information.

Telecommuting and Hoteling

Telecommuting will continue to become more popular in the future, and hoteling, in some cases, will take the place of typical office arrangements. Recall that hoteling is the concept of employees reserving an office, cubicle, or conference room at a company's headquarters when they need space to work or to meet colleagues and clients, otherwise, conducting their work through the virtual floor plan of intranet technology. For the most part, an intranet eliminates the need for paper file storage in cumbersome file cabinets in an office. Electronic storage, therefore, eliminates the need to access files stored in a physical location, which in turn eliminates the need to conduct work near these files.

Similarly, telecommuting from home gives people access to all information stored on the intranet, leveling the playing field between employees working out of the office and employees working from home. Intranets will continue to open doors for employee collaboration, allowing all employees to participate fully, regardless of where in the city or world they are.

Outsourcing

Whether it is corporate downsizing, the decentralization of government, or the increasing hold of the computer in the workplace, more businesses are turning to "outsourcing," the hiring of short- or long-term consultants or contractors to accomplish a specific job once handled by a full-time employee. Consultants and contractors may not come cheap, but because they are not employees of the business (meaning that the business is not required to pay benefits, such as health insurance and pension plans, and even certain taxes for these employees), they often translate into significant savings. Thus, a business often gets more bang for the buck through consultants and contractors than it would with a full-time employee. Intranets will continue to play a role in outsourcing by offering a one-stop resource center for background information on the company or project, saving many hours that an employee might spend discussing information with a consultant or contractor. An intranet lets the employee put his or her energies elsewhere, while the consultant gets him or herself up to speed through the company's intranet.

If downsizing isn't in the company's present or future plans, new employees almost certainly are, whether they replace employees who leave or are hired for new positions. In either case, the company with an intranet in place is going to save perhaps thousands of dollars in training and retraining costs. For example, if Susan, a partner in a company, leaves, typically all her information and expertise leave with her. The information is in her head, in her files, on handwritten Rolodex cards, and in computer folders, most of which makes sense to no one but Susan.

Predesigned and systematically organized, an intranet should offer even first-time users a road map that includes every back-country turnoff and roadside attraction. Such an intranet will allow the new hire to easily access and clearly read Susan's work and projects. Susan doesn't need to be available for months to answer questions and interpret files. This also makes it difficult for individuals to create their own personal information fiefdoms, where only they understand and have access to the information. The very aspect that makes an intranet difficult also makes it invaluable. An intranet is an amorphous entity. It will die if it isn't used and updated. If it is used and updated, it creates a central data storage facility that lessens the impact of shifts in personnel and corporate structure.

Technology Trends

The technology trends that will both affect and be affected by intranets are many and varied, including open standards, bandwidth, wireless communication, single-client applications, increased integration of applications, voice mail and fax gateways, intelligent agents, and new applications. In the following sections we cover some of these topics, with the goal of empowering you with an excellent overview of the direction of intranet technology and the possibilities that loom on the horizon.

Open Standards

One of the most powerful technology trends in building intranets is open standards, also known as open protocols or open architecture. Open standards is an ideal that allows for the easiest and most fluid connection and communication between different corporations' applications. Intranets allow all software to be written using open standards; however, not all companies select this option, sometimes due to security concerns, although just as often due to a lack of useful information on the issue. The Open Standards Initiative allows applications to integrate with one another more easily and efficiently.

Advanced Topics

Part VIII

Open standards allow intranets to be built with standard protocols, which essentially means that all applications can speak in one language. The most important open standard is TCP/IP, which all intranets by definition use. This is opposed to a proprietary language only available with one application. Microsoft Word is a proprietary, or closed, standard, because Microsoft documents can only be read and written by Word. Special bridges can be put in place so that MS Word documents can be read by other applications, but this is essentially a workaround for those who don't have the native environment.

A lack of open standards is a great concern to consumers, who don't want to spend thousands of dollars setting up a network or intranet, only to find that future applications are designed in a different language and thus incompatible with present systems. Although open standards are not an absolute, it is as much of a guarantee for future functionality as consumers can expect, given the uncertainties of the computer industry. The Internet itself uses enormously powerful open standards; indeed, the fact that it uses open standards is why it is so powerful and popular.

Taking a cue from the Internet, anyone designing intranets should build them with open standards or risk being left behind in the intranet game. This will ensure a smoother transition from one intranet software application to another and will make life much easier for users and administrators alike. Intranets by their nature are partially open, and the more open standards an intranet is built on, the greater its compatibility. Few in the computer industry know with any degree of certainty what software will be developed three years from now, so keep your options open for future intranet technology.

As an example of a closed standard, assume an organization uses Microsoft Word for word processing, Lotus for spreadsheets, and Informix for its database. Not only does the organization have to be sure to get the right version of each platform, but often these applications don't even work together. To keep Informix running and to print a letter integrating Informix with Microsoft Word is impossible: game over. They are totally different and incompatible unless the company builds a software bridge between the two applications, which means you'd better be careful what you promise to your boss so that you don't end up on the unemployment line after assuring certain levels of functionality that are mission-critical to your organization.

Bandwidth

Bandwidth is probably the most rapidly developing technology. As recently as 1994, most people used 2,400- or 9,600-baud (bps) modems. Today, a majority of new modems transmit at 28,800 bps or faster, which means that telecommuting is becoming a viable option for corporate users. To illustrate the point, a document that I wrote a few weeks back in Word 7.0 for Windows was a whopping 18MB. At 2,400 bps, this file would take 18 hours to download—and that's assuming a solid, interference-free phone connection! At 28.8 Kbps, that same file (fortunately) would take only 90 minutes—still not fantastic (especially if you're used to a fast T-1 or T-3) but certainly much better than the 2,400-bps option. Currently research is progressing by leaps and bounds in several technologies on the bandwidth front, including cable modems, ISDN lines, and digital modems.

In the past there were small jumps in the time it took to access, view, and download information on the Internet in terms of modem access. The rate doubled but remained slow. Modem connect speeds went from 1,200 bps (.5MB/hour) to 2,400 bps (1MB/hour) to 9,600 bps (4MB/hour) to 14,400 bps(1MB/10 minutes) to 19,200 bps (2MB/15 minutes) to 28,800 (2MB/10 minutes) bps. The next big step in bandwidth will likely come soon, as new technologies are made available, and will take the form of cable modems, ISDN, or other "next-generation" communication systems.

That step is not going to be 56K or 128K—ISDN is already here and becoming widely available, although with the promise of cable-modem technology, ISDN will die hard when cable providers begin offering widespread service. However, prices on both hardware and service are dropping rapidly for ISDN connectivity, so more people will opt for the immediate connection option and will reevaluate their options at a later date. It is also possible that more bandwidth can be gleaned from an ISDN connection before cable or wireless providers get up to speed. If ISDN could offer more competitive transfer rates, it could be a much more popular and inexpensive alternative.

In truth, the next step will likely be 1.5 megabits (mbs) or even 10 mbs (just like the ethernet on your office network). This means there will be almost no waiting for Web pages or files to be downloaded, assuming you have a nonsaturated connection to the remote site and that the remote server is not overburdened. Real-time applications like audio- and video-conferencing and real-time video will be possible, even practical. Currently, people have to wait for images and very few can get video due to the limitations imposed by low-bandwidth 14.4 and 28.8 connections.

One or more of these methods are likely to prevail over other communications and data transmission technologies; but in any case it will be cheaper and easier to transmit data—text, images, sound, video—in the near future. However, successful intranet designers must design for the slowest speed at which someone may access an intranet. Today, users are often limited to how much can be transmitted over normal telephone lines: 14,400 or 28,800 bps with typical current modems. Even intranets designed to be accessed exclusively through a WAN with dedicated connections are often subject to severe bandwidth constraints, depending on usage. So remember, if you build a full multimedia intranet, chances are that people will ooh and ahh at first, and then make you rebuild it as a functional, minor-bandwidth site.

However, this will change. In the near future, medium bandwidths of up to 10 Mbps will become the norm, and following that we'll see a significant advance when broadband technologies become available, enabling up to 100 Mbps communication. At these speeds, real-time video can be transferred efficiently, VRML worlds fully developed—at this point anything is fair game.

Advanced Topics
Part VIII

When designing intranets and looking ahead at bandwidth, it's important to gain as accurate an idea of growth as possible on the basis of prevailing trends and technologies. Current and future intranet audiences must be able to access information quickly and efficiently, or they won't use intranets—regardless of how much you shout, kick, and scream. If Web pages will be designed in the future, consider how elaborate they will be, plus what types of A/V you might include (for example, ShockWave, RealAudio). Users might access the site if it's graphically pleasing, but they won't download information if their only access route is through a slow connection. Intranet designers must look into the future, because very soon, users will be able to buy more bandwidth at lower prices than are available today. An organization contemplating video-conferencing might want to postpone this application for a year or two. By comparison, intranet designers are already beginning to see audio bandwidth constraints easing, making new and exciting applications a reality.

LAN connections are another issue for intranet designers to consider. Typically, LAN connections are wide bandwidth (10 to 100 Mbps), whereas dial-up modem connections are narrow (28.8 Kbps). This is, as we've mentioned time and time again, an extremely important consideration. If, for example, your intranet will be accessed almost exclusively by LAN-based clients, you can safely design larger graphics, include multimedia options, use client/server apps—anything that needs tons of bandwidth to work efficiently becomes a viable option. There are also some intermediate options such as ISDN lines, T-1 lines, and frame relay, which can be part of a WAN. These are relatively expensive and significantly slower than ethernet connections. However, many local, regional, and national Internet Service Providers (ISPs) are increasing the availability of these services while reducing prices to stimulate sales, so the future looks promising for low-cost bandwidth access. In general, the technology that will survive and find popular acceptance will be inexpensive, fast, and simple to implement. The most promising options at this point are the range of cable modems, but until they're released to a significant number of people, it's difficult to get a true feel for the potential involved.

Frequently, intranets are designed to be useful to people connecting through dial-up modem connections. This will significantly affect what you can offer to your users. Video-conferencing is impossible, audio-conferencing is nearly impossible, and real-time applications are difficult. You cannot use large images as measured by file size. Thus, the actual dimensions, resolution, and color depth of images must be reduced so that they will download more quickly. Today it is expensive to connect remote locations with anything more powerful than ordinary dial-up connections, but the trend is that it will become cheaper, due to increased line/user capacities and the desire of ISPs to stimulate the market base.

In addition, telephone companies are becoming more adept at providing bandwidth; the relationship between Internet providers and phone companies is developing in a rather complementary fashion. At first phone companies didn't take the Internet seriously; now they are. Over the next few months and years, you will see more partnerships, acquisitions, and mergers in the communications industry. Every phone company, cable company, wireless service, and ISP will want to become your one-stop shop for data connectivity.

As a decrease in the price of high-speed Internet connections lures even more individuals and companies to the Internet, traffic jams may become unavoidable. When everyone has a cable modem in their house and is surfing at 1.5 mps, the Internet backbone may become overloaded and slow the pace of data transmitted over it to a crawl. If this happens, both individual users and businesses will spark widespread disenchantment with the Internet. Although this is a real danger, on the other side of the technology window is the rapid pace of developments in high-speed router technology. There is good reason to believe that the backbone can be upgraded fast enough to prevent traffic jams. However, if brownouts or traffic jams become a problem on the Internet, one logical solution posed by economists and scientists is to charge usage fees. Thus, audiences who use the most bandwidth would pay more than other user groups would. However, it seems unlikely that such a solution is in the near term, for two main reasons: First, because the Internet is so completely decentralized, it would be a fiasco for any one company, state, or nation to impose such fees without both users and other agencies objecting. Second, the task of monitoring every byte of data that is transmitted and then collecting, processing, and billing for the data (not unlike the process for billing long-distance service) would be a monumental task. Rest easy; this won't happen any time soon.

Wireless Communication

Wireless communication is becoming cheaper and more powerful, and this trend is unlikely to change for the worse any time soon. Currently, as well as for the foreseeable future, the ultimate bottleneck is wireless communications technology. The slowest link in your chain is wireless, and unless you have a wishing well of financial backing, there won't be much you can do to counter this. The slowest speed at which a user can connect to your intranet is through a wireless modem. This should be addressed by intranet designers: They shouldn't be planning for wireless users to download video and participate in video-conferencing any time soon. However, non-real-time applications shouldn't present much of a problem, such as accessing Web pages or corporate files or sending e-mail from one's car.

With palm-top computers, for example (which are discussed in more detail later), the biggest issue surrounding their acceptance is the success of wireless communication, which would subsequently make intranets more attractive to corporate managers and IS departments. People are more likely to invest in intranets if they know they can offer wireless access for field reps, salespeople, and managers who run the company from their yacht in the Caymans.

The future of technology is moving away from the desktop PC. When computers were first widely used as more than targeting computers for the Army, designers came out with the mainframe and dumb terminals that talked to the mainframe. All the applications were run on the mainframe, and the dumb terminal had no memory and performed no functions independent of the master. In the PC age all the applications run on the desktop—connectivity to the office LAN or other computers is minimal, generally just for e-mail or other transmission updates, or in response to specific requests for files, documents, or upgrades. In the future, we will see client/server technology become embraced as more and more machines are designed to handle specific tasks. Instead of a big, clunky, one-machine-does-it-all desktop or laptop computer, we will see many different types of machines, all with the ability to connect to the data source, or server, and all with the ability to perform specific tasks. For example, although you might need a keyboard for word processing, you might not need one to view documents or surf a database. Although you might need a big screen to view multimedia in your home or office, you might not need anything bigger than a watch face or a cellular phone to check your schedule or e-mail messages from the road. Although all these machines might access the same data source, they will become more specialized to meet specific needs.

Single-Client Applications

No one quite knows for sure who came up with the idea first, but Microsoft and Netscape are leading the charge for a one-stop Internet application. They decided to combine all the functionality of a Web browser, desktop browser, e-mail, FTP, and several other applications under one roof. This technology has been demonstrated in the beta releases of Microsoft's Internet Mail and News for Windows 95 and Windows NT 4.0, as well as Netscape 3.0. It is an extremely attractive proposition—not having to rely on perhaps a half-dozen or more separate applications to conduct your daily business. Of course, many users agree that single-client applications would be an ideal solution. Just think—less money involved—because you only have to purchase one system—less time involved in learning different applications, and one simple interface. However, there are a few problems. First, if you base an intranet on a proprietary client application (as opposed to an open standard such as TCP/IP and HTML), you'll be in trouble if the software vendor fails to release patches or new versions or ceases support for the product entirely. Second, in the past, when companies have tried to build many disparate functions into one product, the resulting product usually is a piece of garbage. The only really successful product of this type is the Swiss Army Knife. With computers, the closest example is that printer-fax-scanner-photocopier contraption that a few companies have on the market. Sounds great, and it's cheap, too—until you realize that these machines sacrifice things like speed and resolution in consideration of space, cost, and other issues. Not such a great idea, after all.

Although the idea does indeed have merit, and it may be that a successful single-client system is coming in the near future, it's a good idea to approach such products with extreme caution.

Voice Mail and Fax Gateways

Just as the introduction of high-end computer systems has drastically changed the daily operation of most offices, from policy to corporate culture to employee satisfaction, so too will that trend continue, eventually encompassing some of the intermediate technologies that have been present for some time, including voice mail and facsimile machines. It's important to realize that this is more than an "upgrading" of technology; it's more properly characterized as a paradigm shift (if you'll pardon the overused phrase) in the office workplace. This, of course, will occur over a somewhat extended period, but until then you will see gradual but consistent improvements and changes in both the systems themselves and their role in the professional environment.

In the short term, you can expect to find—or to implement, depending on your role in the office—voice mail and fax gateways integrated into LANs and intranets to provide both simplified in-house access to faxes as well as remote access from hotels, employee homes, and the like. As this trend continues, some or possibly all of the functionality of these services will be absorbed by information-serving systems that will be native to your intranet. Some examples are Internet Phone-based digital recording of voice transmission and a "virtual fax" machine that in place of (or in addition to) scanned, phone-line transmitted documents will be more tuned toward accepting "Internet faxes" of documents. This function is more like a hybrid of FTP and e-mail, and users will eventually accept this as a standard, distancing themselves from the "fax" and "voice mail" references.

Intelligent Agents

One of the things that will happen in the future of the intranet is the development of actual working intelligent agents, applications that can be given basic parameters for a search, CGI creation, or scheduling, and then complete at least an initial product for a manager to review or accept. The Internet is a huge resource, the biggest library in the world; unfortunately, a very large animal apparently ate the card catalog. An individual couldn't possibly find everything in the library in one sitting, but creating an intelligent agent makes it possible. In the future, advances in Natural Language Query processing and other complementary technologies, plus possibly some type of standardized Dewey Decimal-esque system for the Net, should result in faster, more powerful, and more effective search techniques, as well as other systems.

For example, a company that manages a mutual fund investing in a Turkish industry could have an intelligent agent that monitors news feeds and surfs the Net looking for Turkish financial news. The agent automatically stores relevant news items in the appropriate areas of its intranet. News items pertaining to stocks in the mutual fund's portfolio are immediately splashed across the fund managers' screens.

This allows users to have immediate access to the latest information all the time. Another new technology is software applications that can be programmed to check out your favorite sites in the middle of the night and download them to your computer so you can check them quickly and without having to wait while they are downloaded. These programs, including Freeloader and WebWhacker, help people who have bandwidth problems because they go out and download your favorite sites without you having to wait for the results; the next day they are there.

Whether one of these programs or a more sophisticated intelligent agent is used, retrieved information can be displayed on an intranet for all its users to refer to and so that it will be searchable.

Intelligent agents can visit the sites that the people on your intranet surf often and turn them into something useful like summaries of latest information. Intelligent agents are buffers between you and the sea of information that is the Internet.

The Future of Intranet Applications

The key to the success of intranets in the future is to integrate intranet functionality with systems that are currently installed on corporate networks, especially the icky legacy applications that are running on VAX, AS400, and other platforms. This can be accomplished most successfully through the use of gateways from intranets to desktop or server applications, thus allowing an organization or corporation full use of the most comprehensive set of internal resources available. Most organizations are PC based, meaning most applications are performed on the desktop; so the key is integrating this particular demographic.

Users are familiar with their desktop applications, and the organization has already invested in them, so it would seem obvious that a good medium-term solution is to keep using the desktop applications while enhancing them with the options available to intranet-based systems. The two players most likely to lead the way in this arena are Microsoft and Netscape, with a multitude of third-party software coming from random companies to support various applications and platforms.

For example, say an organization uses XYZ's legacy contact database system, and it is integrated into an intranet. Then if all the users upload their personal databases on XYZ, it will merge them into one large contact database for the organization as a whole. Ideally, each employee would have the choice of using a Web browser or continuing to use XYZ as their client application for interacting with the client database. The important thing is that the organization has all the information together and that all employees can access the full range of functions, including updating the database, from their computers.

Individual companies will most likely not build the gateways between their desktop applications and intranets, unless they use proprietary applications that have been developed or enhanced with in-house technology and programmers; they will most often look to the makers of the particular applications. The creators of these applications are working furiously to create gateway modules to make their applications compatible with TCP/IP protocols and aid in the exporting of data into more accessible formats. Gateway modules already constructed will allow companies to integrate intranets with the desktop applications with ease and speed. Getting information from desktop applications into an intranet is tough; it will require either excellent third-party software or a good bit of time, effort, and dedication by the company and its programming staff. It may be easier for large companies with involved applications to just start from scratch with a native intranet solution. Small, financially challenged companies will need to think long and hard about possible solutions so as to avoid huge IS debacles and wasted investment.

We're moving into a whole new arena with the advent of intranets. The applications are once again being performed on a server at a central location where computation processing and data storage is performed. The client or terminal used by the individual is just a window to the server. Today, far and away the most common window is the PC—but this could change with the commercial introduction of the network computer in fall 1996. The network computer will give people a stripped-down machine to serve as a window that allows entrance into an intranet; you may have heard the same product referred to as the "Internet Terminal." Some day this may be incorporated into a cellular phone or personal digital assistant that would serve as the window or gateway into an intranet, with the applications actually performed on the server and only output data being returned to the client.

Instead of having a PC with a traditional operating system on it (such as Windows 95, Linux, System7) you can have a machine that is tasked specifically to run network applications or TCP/IP services. The whole purpose of the machine is to access the server, get information, and somehow manipulate that information and send it back to the server. For example, such a network computer would have no hard drive. It would only be able to access the Internet, intranet, or network to which it was attached. It would download a Java applet to do any necessary client-side computations—for example, real-time graphic rendering of stock market transactions transmitted to it by a remote server. When the user was finished watching the stock market, the applet would be automatically flushed from the network computer's memory. That applet or any other would be reloaded as necessary to perform subsequent tasks.

The production of intranet software means an organization can buy integrated suites of software specifically designed for organizations to communicate internally. The suites have existing functions like asynchronous messaging, scheduling, and contact management.

Palm-Top Computers

A palm-top computer accesses your intranet's resources through a wireless modem and could also serve as a voice phone. Because you can pack all this technology together in one unit, your palm-top becomes your client; it doesn't need to sport particularly powerful features because all the resource-intensive work is done by the remote server. You just need a quick connection to the server to access your calendar, keep notes, browse your Rolodex, and so on.

Advanced Topics

Part VIII

Teleconferencing

Teleconferencing through intranets in the future will be free of long-distance telephone charges. Calls will be placed from intranets to the server, which in turn will dial a local phone exchange that completes the call or dial into software built into the recipient callers' software. In the latter exchange, the transmission becomes two computers "talking" to each other. This is an especially interesting case, because it raises several questions about who specifically would bear the cost of such systems—the phone company is in no way configured to monitor and bill for this system in an effective way. If the people who maintain the individual servers opt to charge for their services, the entire system would most likely be subject to numerous intrusive telecommunications regulations, which would seem to almost negate the efficacy of the system before it is even constructed. Of course, this second option is based on an extension of a nascent technology that is already circulating among Internet users, although not quite ready for the corporate world: Internet telephone software. Using this technology, user messages are recorded and converted into a particular format, say .WAV or .AU, and then piped to the receiving end where they are decoded and played. Currently, the sound quality is substandard, and it will be some time until an acceptable level is reached. However, when broadband transmission capabilities come into play, full-motion video and sound can be joined to provide powerful and affordable teleconferencing solutions.

As business becomes increasingly global, this intranet function aids in keeping the prices of global communication low. Software that can currently perform this task include IP Phone, Internet Phone, and WEB Phone (see Chapter 32, "Internet Phones: The Advanced Model").

Other evolving teleconferencing functions include recording call completion statistics in a central database that confirms that particular calls occurred and their duration, cost, and so on. There also could be a recording of the conference call saved and linked to a schedule so that someone could look back to that day, see what happened, and hear the contents of the call. As audio encoding becomes more advanced, you'll most likely see a rapid rush to store audio copies of all phone conversations and voice-mail messages on a server somewhere within your intranet. This has many legal implications that will have to be evaluated as case law becomes available.

The next step as this technology advances is real-time voice recognition, which would allow a transcript of the conversation to appear in real time on the screens of all the participants, or the conversation or transcript could be broadcast immediately to others who want to watch or listen to what happens with the call. This can be stored in a database or file that can be searched later. Everything can be recorded and used later, making everything a resource in and of itself. The conversation would not need to be transcribed by someone. It could be edited for use later in reports or to share with others in the organization. This technology exists in varying degrees but is neither efficient enough nor affordable for a general release to the public. In the near future, however, both hardware and software developments should make this type of system at least a possibility for midsize companies.

High-End Applications

At the high end, customized server-side intranet software will integrate more of the user's daily tasks—work flow, expense reports, time slips—and make it accessible through a single client. The client for this integration will increasingly be an ordinary Web browser.

If an organization uses client codes or project codes for time sheets, the codes could be integrated in intranet software. Then, when employees fill out time sheets on an intranet, a menu of project codes pops up so they can assign their time accurately. Using a Web browser as the client, users enter their time into a database, which can be fed into payroll and recorded so the organization can track costs.

The pop-up menu of client codes is one example of applications that can be built into a high-end customized intranet so users can input information directly into a decision-critical database—not just discussion group information, but information that goes into a database that can cause checks to be cut from payroll, generate expense reports, and monitor work flow. All will be accessible through the Web browser, which will be customized to the specific needs of an organization.

Ordinary users could do it, and it's automated so that it is being fed to the end user automatically—whether it is cutting a check, approving a design and automatically sending it on to the next person for his or her approval, or manufacturing for the product to be designed.

Mid-Range Applications

At the mid-range, there will not be quite as much customization. Off-the-shelf applications that offer more standardized functions will be the norm. Contact management, scheduling, and threaded messaging are the most common applications and likely will remain so. This is the one-size-fits-all approach, in which applications of general interest can be used by many organizations, from a membership organization to a bank to a zoo.

Another big step in mid-range applications will be building gateways between desktop applications and intranets. For example, MS Word allows a group of people connected through remote TCP/IP connections all to edit the same document at the same time. Soon, using Microsoft Excel, the user will be able to grab information from a database over the Internet and feed it into a spreadsheet.

The trend of the PC becoming more powerful adheres to Moore's Law, which states that computer chip performance doubles every 18 to 24 months. Moore's Law has proven remarkably accurate for more than 25 years, and most industry experts believe that computer chip innovation will continue at a similar pace for at least the next several years.

Groupware Tools: Not Ready for Prime Time

Although intranets and open-standards-based systems far overshadow groupware products, there are advances worthy of mention, though implementing these solutions may be less effective than you might imagine. Groupware products like Lotus Notes and Microsoft Exchange haven't taken off so well, partly because they are expensive to purchase, support, and use as development tools—and also because they offer very skewed functionality when compared with the wide range of possibilities available through standard HTML and CGI technologies. Lotus Notes is difficult to use because its user interface requires more training than a Web browser, and it is expensive for large organizations because they have to pay about $70 per desktop (just for the client software). It also takes special knowledge to install and upgrade, and it is a bandwidth hog. Rather than relying on the server database, these systems generally rely on replicated databases and are updated only periodically. You have to download the whole database to find the specific information, which means that your employees—who are depending on your intranet for vital, timely information—may be out of luck if you adopt one of these groupware products. This also applies to Microsoft Exchange as well.

Of course, both Lotus Corporation and Microsoft are working to ensure that their products play a prime role in the intranet business. The idea is that their databases will be accessible by the Web, and in addition to their basic specialty Web servers, these companies also make available intranet-specific packages designed to entice corporate IS managers to adopt new systems (prime example: Lotus Domino, a "gee-whiz" tool that looks great but offers significantly limited and extremely narrow functionality). To claim more of the system-savvy IS managers, these tools allow the users to utilize a Web browser as the primary method of viewing or changing Web information—a sort of tribute to the success and functionality of intranet systems. These are strong contenders—due mainly to the market share and financial backing of their parent companies—and they are not likely to go away any time soon, unless few people purchase the packages.

Lotus makes its money by selling Lotus Notes clients and servers, and it makes more money selling clients than servers; therefore, Lotus will be more aggressive in selling clients, because no one is paying them for the Web server; you can access data on Lotus Notes. (It was the first product to allow this interface with the Web.)

Microsoft's market power is so huge it's difficult to predict how it will fare in this arena. Lotus Notes has been around a lot longer and is perceived to have a much more complete background in this type of technology. Of course, Microsoft Exchange uses ActiveX, so if this takes off as a language, it will provide a big boost to Exchange as a collaboration platform. For Notes, anyone who has invested the time and applications will stick with it because it does the job well enough for companies willing to sacrifice some functionality for a fairly workable system.

Of course, because these types of systems generally rely on a ton of proprietary, resource-intensive, and prohibitively expensive client software packages, it is most likely that corporations will move en masse toward adopting systems that rely on multifunction viewers such as Web browsers in place of limited-use systems such as Notes or Exchange.

The impact of these systems is fairly impressive, though: They dramatically lower the cost of publishing information because they require little in the way of creativity or technical know-how to implement fairly substantial systems. The most prevalent consequence is that everyone will write and post HTML pages, just as everyone now writes memos using word processing. In the future, for mid- and high-range applications, the majority of personnel will publish through standard HTML and by using interactive intranet application message boards, human resources systems, and alert messaging features.

Extranets

Whew! All that being said, the truly remarkable thing about this technology is not what it can and will provide, but where it will take us. Everything you have just read about doesn't represent the ideal, all-encompassing use of this technology for a business or organization—it's merely a stepping-stone. The truth is, although an intranet will cut down on some redundancies and inefficiencies, many will remain. The true test of this technology will come when *all* the information in, about, and for an entity is integrated into a single storehouse with many different interfaces.

Consider a mouse manufacturer, for example. They have lots of information, from promotional materials to orders and invoices to earnings reports. Their information management system might look like this: They have a Web site with their contact information, promotional materials, and maybe spec sheets available to the public. They might have an intranet with their Human Resources information on it—maybe even inventory databases and collaboration applications. The rest, such as creating invoices and orders or tallying sales, is all done through independent applications.

Now consider an *extranet,* a clever mix between an Internet presence and an intranet. When a retailer wants mice, she looks at the Web site and sees that the specs are up to par, and then she clicks to check current prices and availability. As a new customer, she enters her store's information and places an order. That information is automatically entered into the mouse manufacturer's contact database, and the order is placed. The shipping label is printed, the transaction is logged in accounting, and the inventory database is updated. An invoice is created and sent. The parts suppliers are informed of the order, and new parts are on the way. Simple, efficient, quick. These are the kinds of information management techniques that will provide the most comprehensive change in the way we conduct business.

A simple cross-platform information storehouse that provides a different interface and different levels of access to different users is the next step in information technology. Redundant information, paper shuffling, and data entry are all outdated.

We will see fewer static Web sites and more online service-type sites, with interactivity and a place for vendors, customers, employees, and interested parties to log in, communicate, and exchange data with one another. The World Wide Web will become a doorway into a company or organization, and it will replace phone calls, faxes, FedExes, and even storefronts. You will no longer wait for papers in the mail or wait on hold to place an order.

As all these information stores become integrated, expect to see a shift in online activity. As savvy customers find savvy businesses, you will see the Internet become much more of a business and commerce tool than an entertainment medium. Expect to see a lot of small Internet or intranet software companies, including some mentioned in this book, lose hold of an ever-increasing market. Even big companies with current holds in the market might lose out to more nimble companies willing to take a risk on open standards technologies. Systems integrators and custom software developers might be the big winners. However it pans out, it will be exciting to watch!

Summary

Just as technological and business trends will affect the future of intranets, so will intranets have a major impact on these trends. The immense synergy between business and technological trends and intranets will continue to serve as a launching pad for new ideas and technological advances, all in the name of more productive businesses and workers. Intranets will allow businesses to change their concept of how business happens. Already, intranet audiences are accomplishing more just by using a Web browser, and the scales continue to tip toward smaller, cheaper, faster technology and technological devices. In the future, users may be walking around with their computers in their pockets. Whatever the size and shape of the next wave of computers, those workers who have unleashed the power of intranets will be ready to service their clients and step up to competition, no matter where in the world they are.

Resource Guide

Resource Guide
Appendix A

Here we have tried to arrange a quick resource guide of URLs (Uniform Resource Locators) so that you can quickly and easily find more information about the many companies, products, and individuals referenced in this book. On the accompanying CD-ROM, you will find Web pages with links to software and other Internet sites of interest.

Chapter 1

InTandem

http://intandem.intraactive.com

IntraActive's groupware intranet product will help you manage your time more efficiently.

Chapter 2

Audio and Video

RealAudio

http://www.realaudio.com

Progressive Networks' RealAudio gives your intranet the capability to deliver audio to all users.

Price: Free client. Server is $500+ depending on the intended number of simultaneous users.

Runs on Windows 3.x, Windows 95, Windows NT, MacOS, and UNIX.

VDOlive

http://www.vdo.net

VDOlive is a technology that allows for the distribution of audio and video content on your intranet for a price that is much lower than training videos.

Runs on Windows 3.x, Windows 95, Windows NT, and MacOS.

Databases

Oracle

http://www.oracle.com

Oracle is the leader in relational databases. These databases are often available on the Web.

Other Services

Internet Phone

http://www.vocaltec.com

Vocaltec's Internet Phone enables real-time voice communication over any TCP/IP network (like the Internet).

Chapter 3

Groupware

Lotus Notes

http://www.lotus.com

Lotus Notes was the premier groupware application before intranets took hold.

Netscape SuiteSpot

http://www.netscape.com

A group of server products designed with intranets in mind.

Act

http://www.symantec.com/act/index.html

Symantec's contact manager.

GroupWise

http://www.novell.com/groupwise/

Novell's group messaging and contact manager.

Web Browser

Netscape Navigator

http://www.netscape.com/comprod/products/navigator/

Netscape Navigator is the market leader of Web clients and is positioned as the interface for the next generation of applications, on and off the Web.

Databases

Sybase

http://www.sybase.com

A leader in the relational database market.

Oracle

http://www.oracle.com

A leader in the relational database market.

Chapter 4

Magazines

Boardwatch

http://www.boardwatch.com

The source for BBS information.

E-Mail Clients

Eudora

http://www.eudora.com

Qualcomm's e-mail program.

Free light version.

Runs on Windows 3.x, Windows 95, Windows NT, and MacOS.

File Transfer Programs

Fetch

http://www.dartmouth.edu/pages/softdev/fetch.html

FTP client for the Macintosh.

Free.

CuteFTP

http://www.cuteftp.com/

CuteFTP is an FTP client for Windows.

Servers

Solaris

http://www.sun.com/sunsoft/solaris/index.html

Solaris is Sun's version of UNIX.

Runs on SPARC, UltraSPARC, PowerPC, and x86 processors.

Windows NT Server

http://www.microsoft.com/ntserver/

Windows NT is a robust platform with a lot of support from Microsoft.

Price: $999.

Runs on x86, PowerPC, Alpha, and MIPS processors.

OS/2 Warp Server

http://www.software.ibm.com/os/warp-server/index.html

IBM's 32-bit multitasking environment.

Runs on x86 processors.

Appendix A

Operating Systems

SCO UNIX

http://www.sco.com/

Santa Cruz Operation's UNIX.

Runs on x86 processors.

Linux

http://www.linux.org

Linux is a free version of UNIX that has all of the necessary functions to run Web, mail, and other server software.

Runs on x86 processors.

Free BSD

http://www.freebsd.org/

A free version of UNIX that compares favorably to Linux.

Runs on x86 processors.

MacOS

http://www.macos.apple.com/macos8/

The OS for Apple's Macintosh line of computers.

Runs on Macintosh.

Novell NetWare

http://netware.novell.com/discover/disctoc2.htm

NetWare has been the dominant LAN OS for years.

Runs on x86 processors.

AIX

http://www.austin.ibm.com/software/OS/

IBM's version of UNIX for the RS/6000 line of servers.

Runs on PowerPC and select IBM RISC processors.

HP/UX

http://www.hp.com

Hewlett-Packard's version of UNIX.

Runs on the HP9000 line of servers.

Other Services

Stroud's Consummate Winsock Apps

http://www.stroud.com

Look here to fill all your Web, Telnet, FTP, IRC, and mail needs for Windows.

Chapter 5

Companies with Intranets

Ford

http://www.ford.com

Silicon Graphics

http://www.sgi.com

Servers

Netra Internet Server

http://www.sun.com/products-n-solutions/hw/servers/netrai/index.html

An all-in-one server solution.

Available through resellers around the world.

Comes with Netscape Enterprise Server, Navigator Gold, Solstice Firewall.

Runs on Solaris.

Microsoft Internet Information Server

http://www.microsoft.com/InfoServ/

Free download from Microsoft's Web site. It's scheduled to be included in Windows NT 4.0.

Runs on Windows NT only.

Netscape SuiteSpot

http://home.netscape.com/comprod/server_central/product/suite_spot/index.html

A group of applications for Web serving, mail, news, proxy, directory, catalog, and certificates.

Free demo from Netscape's Web site.

Price: $3,995.95.

Runs on Windows NT and many versions of UNIX.

NCSA httpd

http://hoohoo.ncsa.uiuc.edu/

A Web server from the same group that produced Mosaic.

Free.

Runs on many versions of UNIX. Source code is available.

Apache HTTP Server

http://www.apache.org/

An enhanced version of NCSA httpd 1.3.

Developed by the Internet community, it's much faster and more efficient than NCSA 1.3.

Free.

Runs on many versions of UNIX. Source code is available.

O'Reilly Software's WebSite

http://website.ora.com/

Noted for excellent documentation.

Free demo from their Web site.

Price: $249.

Runs on Windows 95 and Windows NT.

Intel

http://www.intel.com

Intel makes the x86 line of processors, which includes the 80386, 80486, Pentium, and Pentium Pro.

Digital Equipment Corp.

http://www.digital.com

The AltaVista search engine runs off digital hardware and its 64-bit versions of UNIX. It is an extremely fast system.

Operating Systems

Sun Microsystems

http://www.sun.com

Sun's workstations and servers are based on the SPARC architecture.

Linux

http://www.linux.org

Linux is a free version of UNIX that has all the necessary functions to run Web, mail, and other server software.

Modems

US Robotics

http://www.usrobotics.com

US Robotics is one of the leaders in modem technology. They have modems ranging from 14.4Kbps to Combo ISDN modems. Support is excellent.

Appendix A

Microcom

http://www.microcom.com

Microcom produces affordable modems that are often upgradable.

Supra

http://www.supra.com

Supra (now a part of Diamond Multimedia) produces a line of dependable modems.

Shiva

http://www.shiva.com

Shiva produces a range of modems specifically for the purpose of connecting a LAN to the outside world.

Sound Cards

Creative Labs

http://www.creaf.com

The maker of the SoundBlaster family of products is the industry leader in sound cards.

Advanced Gravis

http://www.gravis.com

The makers of the Gravis UltraSound line of sound cards.

E-Mail

Qualcomm

http://www.qualcomm.com

The makers of Eudora.

Runs on Windows and Macintosh.

Pine

http://www.cac.washington.edu/pine/

The University of Washington's excellent mail and news client. This is one of the first clients to support the IMAP protocol.

Free.

Runs on most versions of UNIX. Windows and DOS versions are in preliminary release.

Other Technology

Connectix

http://www.connectix.com

The Quickcam is a golf-ball-sized camera for color or black-and-white video-conferencing.

Price: $99-$150.

FreeLoader

http://www.freeloader.com

Freeloader is a service that downloads sites you set while your computer is unattended, for speedier viewing at a later time.

Chapter 7

Solaris

http://www.sun.com/sunsoft/solaris/index.html

Solaris is Sun's version of UNIX.

Runs on SPARC, UltraSPARC, PowerPC, and x86 processors.

SCO UNIX

http://www.sco.com/

Santa Cruz Operation's UNIX.

Runs on x86 processors.

Appendix A

Linux

http://www.linux.org

Linux is a free version of UNIX that has all of the necessary functions to run Web, mail, and other server software.

Runs on x86 processors.

Free BSD

http://www.freebsd.org/

A free version of UNIX that compares favorably to Linux.

Runs on x86 processors.

Windows NT Server

http://www.microsoft.com/ntserver/

Windows NT is a robust platform with a lot of support from Microsoft.

Price: $999.

Runs on x86, PowerPC, Alpha, and MIPS processors.

OS/2 Warp Server

http://www.software.ibm.com/os/warp-server/index.html

IBM's 32-bit multitasking environment.

Runs on x86 processors.

MacOS

http://www.macos.apple.com/macos8/

The OS for Apple's Macintosh line of computers.

Runs on Macintosh.

Novell NetWare

http://netware.novell.com/discover/disctoc2.htm

NetWare has been the dominant LAN OS for years.

Runs on x86 processors.

AIX

http://www.austin.ibm.com/software/OS/

IBM's version of UNIX for the RS/6000 line of servers.

Runs on PowerPC and select IBM RISC processors.

HP/UX

http://www.hp.com

Hewlett-Packard's version of UNIX.

Runs on the HP9000 line of servers.

Chapter 8

WebCompare's Server Features Comparison Page

http://www.webcompare.com/servers-main.html

Netscape Commerce Server

http://www.netscape.com/comprod/netscape_commerce.html

Runs on Windows NT and UNIX.

Netscape Navigator

http://www.netscape.com/comprod/products/navigator

Runs on Windows 3.x, Windows 95, Windows NT, MacOS, and UNIX.

Java

http://www.javasoft.com

Oracle WebServer

http://www.oracle.com/products/websystem/webserver/index.html

Integrates extremely well with Oracle databases.

Runs on UNIX.

Netscape LiveWire

http://www.netscape.com/comprod/products/tools/livewire_datasheet.html

Runs on Windows 95, Windows NT, and UNIX.

Microsoft Internet Information Server

http://www.microsoft.com/infoserv/

Runs on Windows NT.

O'Reilly Software's WebSite

http://website.ora.com/

Noted for excellent documentation.

Free demo from their Web site.

Price: $249.

Runs on Windows 95 and Windows NT.

Apple Internet Server

http://product.info.apple.com/productinfo/datasheets/ss/aiss.html

Runs on PowerMac.

NCSA httpd

http://hoohoo.ncsa.uiuc.edu/

A Web server from the same group that produced Mosaic.

Free.

Runs on many versions of UNIX. Source code is available.

Apache HTTP Server

http://www.apache.org/

An enhanced version of NCSA httpd 1.3.

Developed by the Internet community, it is much faster and more efficient than NCSA 1.3.

Free.

Runs on many versions of UNIX. Source code is available.

Sendmail

http://www.cis.ohio-state.edu/hypertext/faq/usenet/mail/sendmail-faq/faq.html

Frequently asked questions (FAQs) from `comp.mail.sendmail`.

Netscape Mail Server

http://www.netscape.com/comprod/server_central/product/mail/index.html

Runs on Windows NT and UNIX.

NT Mail

http://www.mortimer.com/ntmail/index.htm

Runs on Windows NT.

SL Mail

http://www.seattlelab.com

Runs on Windows 3.x, Windows 95, and Windows NT.

Netscape News Server

http://www.netscape.com/comprod/server_central/product/news/index.html

Runs on Windows NT and UNIX.

NNTP News Server

http://www.academ.com/academ/nntp/index.html

Runs on UNIX.

Progressive Networks RealAudio

http://www.realaudio.com

Runs on Windows 3.x, Windows 95, Windows NT, MacOS, and UNIX.

Xing StreamWorks

http://www.xingtech.com/streams/index.html

Runs on Windows, MacOS, and UNIX.

Appendix A

CoolTalk

`http://www.netscape.com/comprod/products/navigator/version_3.0/cooltalk/index.html`

CoolTalk is included with Netscape Navigator.

Runs on Windows and UNIX.

CU-SeeMe

`http://goliath.wpine.com/cu-seeme.html`

Runs on Windows and MacOS.

Lotus Notes

`http://www.lotus.com/allnotes/`

Runs on Windows, Windows 95, MacOS, and UNIX.

Chapter 12

Online Services

The List

`http://www.thelist.com`

This service provides a comprehensive list of ISPs across the U.S.

UUNet

`http://www.uunet.com`

UUNet was the first commercial ISP and is one of the leaders in Internet connectivity.

Price is on a monthly basis.

PSINet

`http://www.psi.com`

PSINet is one of the world's leading ISPs.

Price is on a monthly basis.

America Online

`http://www.aol.com`

America Online is the largest online service.

Price is based on the number of minutes spent online and is generally higher than an ISP, but the user is in a controlled environment.

Modems

Shiva

`http://www.shiva.com`

Shiva produces a range of modems specifically for the purpose of connecting a LAN to the outside world.

US Robotics

`http://www.usrobotics.com`

US Robotics is one of the leaders in modem technology. They have modems ranging from 14.4Kbps to Combo ISDN modems. Support is excellent.

Microcom

`http://www.microcom.com`

Microcom produces affordable modems that are often upgradable.

Supra

`http://www.supra.com`

Supra (now a part of Diamond Multimedia) produces a line of dependable modems.

Networking Hardware and Software

3Com

`http://www.3com.com`

3Com makes a range of quality networking products, including ISDN terminal adapters, NICs, and routers.

Appendix A

Bay Networks

http://www.baynetworks.com

Bay Networks produces network routers and networking hardware.

Cisco

http://www.cisco.com

Cisco is a router and networking hardware manufacturer.

Ascend

http://www.ascend.com

Ascend makes router and networking hardware.

Intranet Security

http://www.yahoo.com/Business_and_Economy/Companies/Computers/Security/

Many firms specialize in security and firewall products. This is a good list of companies.

Chameleon

http://www.netmanage.com/netmanage/nm3.html#cham

Netmanage's Chameleon is an integrated suite of client applications.

Runs on Windows, Windows 95, and MacOS.

PC/TCP

http://www.ftp.com/mkt_info/pctcp/pctcp4.html

FTP Software's PC/TCP provides a wide range of TCP/IP solutions for the PC.

Runs on Windows 3.1 and Windows 95.

Novell

http://www.novell.com

Novel produces a line of quality NIC cards that are often the basis for industry standards.

Chapter 13

Operating Systems

Windows 95

http://www.microsoft.com/windows/

Runs on 486 and higher.

Windows NT

http://www.microsoft.com/ntworkstation/

Runs on 486 and higher.

Windows 3.1 and Windows for Workgroups

http://www.microsoft.com/support/products/windows95/windows3x.htm

Runs on 386 and higher.

OS/2

http://www.austin.ibm.com/pspinfo/os2.html

Runs on 486 and higher.

MacOS

http://www.apple.com

Runs on Macintosh.

Linux

http://www.linux.org

Runs on 386 and higher.

Appendix A

TCP/IP Clients

Netcom's Netcruiser

http://www.netcom.com/software/join.html

Runs on Windows and MacOS.

SPRYMail

http://www.sprysoft.com/

Runs on Windows.

Netmanage Chameleon

http://www.netmanage.com

Runs on Windows 3.x, Windows 95, and MacOS.

FTP Software

http://www.ftp.com/mkt_info/

Runs on Windows 3.x, Windows 95, Windows NT, OS/2, and DOS.

Distinct

http://www.distinct.com

Spyglass

http://www.spyglass.com

Browsers

Netscape Navigator

http://www.netscape.com/comprod/products/navigator/index.html

Runs on Windows 3.x, Windows 95, Windows NT, MacOS, and UNIX.

Microsoft Internet Explorer

http://www.microsoft.com/ie/

Runs on Windows 3.x, Windows 95, Windows NT, and MacOS.

IBM WebExplorer

http://www.raleigh.ibm.com/WebExplorer/

Runs on OS/2.

Mosaic

http://www.ncsa.uiuc.edu/SDG/Software/Mosaic/NCSAMosaicHome.html

Runs on Windows 95, MacOS, and UNIX.

E-Mail

Eudora

http://www.eudora.com

Runs on Windows and MacOS.

Netscape Mail

http://www.netscape.com/comprod/products/navigator/index.html

Netscape Mail is part of Netscape Navigator.

Runs on Windows 3.x, Windows 95, Windows NT, MacOS, and UNIX.

Novell GroupWise

http://www.novell.com/groupwise/

Runs on Windows 3.x, Windows 95, Windows NT, MacOS, and UNIX.

SPRYMail

http://www.sprysoft.com

Runs on Windows 3.x and Windows 95.

Pine

http://www.cac.washington.edu/pine/

Runs on most versions of UNIX. Windows and DOS versions are in preliminary release.

FTP

CuteFTP

http://www.cuteftp.com

Runs on Windows 3.x and Windows 95.

Fetch

http://www.dartmouth.edu/pages/softdev/fetch.html

Runs on MacOS.

Telnet

NCSA Telnet

http://nethelp.tamu.edu/macintosh/tamunet/telnet/

Runs on MacOS.

Voice Communication

Internet Phone

http://www.vocaltec.com

Runs on Windows 3.x, Windows 95, Windows NT, and MacOS.

CoolTalk

http://www.netscape.com/comprod/products/navigator/version_3.0/cooltalk/index.html

CoolTalk is included with Netscape Navigator.

Runs on Windows and UNIX.

Chapter 14

Computer Emergency Response Team

http://www.cert.org

Chapter 17

Software

Novell

http://www.novell.com

Novell is the leading vendor of LAN server software and is the creator of IPX.

Netscape Navigator

http://www.netscape.com/comprod/products/navigator/

Navigator is the leading Web client.

Free to nonprofit organizations and schools. Others have a free trial.

Runs on Windows 3.x, Windows 95, Windows NT, MacOS, and UNIX.

Internet Explorer

http://www.microsoft.com

Internet Explorer is Navigator's main competition.

Free.

Runs on Windows 3.x, Windows 95, Windows NT, and MacOS.

Eudora

http://www.qualcomm.com

Qualcomm's Eudora is one of the best e-mail clients available.

Free light version.

Runs on Windows 3.x, Windows 95, Windows NT, and MacOS.

Modems

Shiva

http://www.shiva.com

Shiva makes a line of rack modems designed to provide connectivity to your intranet.

Internet Connections

Windows95.Com

http://www.windows95.com

This site contains excellent information on how to set up PPP, SLIP, and LAN connections in Windows 95.

Trumpet Winsock

http://www.trumpet.com

Trumpet Software produces the best 16-bit Winsock client.

Free demo.

Runs on Windows 3.x and Windows 95.

Chapter 19

Web Organizations

CERN

http://www.cern.ch/

World Wide Web Consortium

http://www.w3.org

Browsers

Netscape Navigator

http://www.netscape.com/comprod/products/navigator/

The world's most popular browser.

Runs on Windows 3.x, Windows 95, Windows NT, MacOS, and UNIX.

Microsoft Internet Explorer

http://www.microsoft.com/ie/

A close competitor to Navigator that is free.

Runs on Windows 3.x, Windows 95, Windows NT, and MacOS.

Mosaic

http://www.ncsa.uiuc.edu/SDG/Software/Mosaic/

The "original" Web client.

Runs on Windows 95, Windows NT, MacOS, and UNIX.

Oracle Power Browser

http://www.oracle.com/products/websystem/powerbrowser/

Not as fast or as capable as other browsers.

Runs on Windows 3.x, Windows 95, and Windows NT.

Web Technology

HTML

http://www.w3.org/pub/WWW/MarkUp/

Java

http://www.javasoft.com

Appendix A

JavaScript

http://www.netscape.com/comprod/products/navigator/version_2.0/script/index.html

http://www.microsoft.com/jscript/

VBScript

http://www.microsoft.com/vbscript/

Netscape's Plug-in Registry

http://home.netscape.com/comprod/products/navigator/version_2.0/plugins/index.html

ActiveX

http://www.microsoft.com/activex/

Chapter 20

Browsers

Netscape Navigator

http://www.netscape.com/comprod/products/navigator/

The world's most popular browser.

Runs on Windows 3.x, Windows 95, Windows NT, MacOS, and UNIX.

Microsoft Internet Explorer

http://www.microsoft.com/ie/

A close competitor to Navigator that is free.

Runs on Windows 3.x, Windows 95, Windows NT, and MacOS.

Mosaic

http://www.ncsa.uiuc.edu/SDG/Software/Mosaic/

The "original" Web client.

Runs on Windows 95, Windows NT, MacOS, and UNIX.

Oracle Power Browser

http://www.oracle.com/products/websystem/powerbrowser/

Not as fast or as capable as other browsers.

Runs on Windows 3.x, Windows 95, and Windows NT.

Authoring Tools

Microsoft Internet Assistant for Word

http://www.microsoft.com/msword/internet/ia/

Microsoft FrontPage

http://www.microsoft.com/frontpage/

Netscape Navigator Gold

http://www.netscape.com/comprod/products/navigator/gold/index.html

Sausage Hot Dog Pro

http://www.sausage.com/hotdog32.htm

SoftQuad HoTMetaL

http://www.sq.com/index.html

Chapter 23

Digital Document Formats

Adobe Portable Document Format

http://www.adobe.com/acrobat/prodinfo.html

http://www.adobe.com/Acrobat/PDF sites.html

Appendix A

WordPerfect Envoy

http://www.corel.com/products/wordperfect/envoy7/index.htm

PostScript

http://www.adobe.com/prodindex/postscript/main.html

Chapter 24

Standard Generalized Markup Language

http://www.w3.org/pub/WWW/MarkUp/SGML/

Hypertext Markup Language

http://www.w3.org/pub/WWW/MarkUp/

International Standards Organization

http://www.iso.ch/welcome.html

Chapter 25

Audio Formats

MPEG-Audio

http://www.mpeg.org/index.html/

Sound Format FAQ

http://www.cis.ohio-state.edu/hypertext/faq/usenet/audio-fmts/top.html

TrueSpeech

http://www.dspg.com/internet.htm

IWave

http://www.vocaltec.com/iwave.htm

ToolVox

http://www.voxware.com

Audio Editors

Macromedia SoundEdit Pro

http://www.macromedia.com/software/sound/index.html

Cakewalk Pro Audio

http://www.cakewalk.com/html/proaudio.html

Goldwave

http://web.cs.mun.ca/~chris3/goldwave/

CoolEdit

http://www.syntrillium.com/

Audio Servers

RealAudio

http://www.realaudio.com/products/server.html

StreamWorks

http://www.streamworks.com/

Appendix A

Voice Communication

Internet Phone

http://www.vocaltec.com

WebPhone

http://www.netspeak.com

CoolTalk

http://home.netscape.com/comprod/products/navigator/version_3.0/cooltalk/index.html

NetMeeting

http://www.microsoft.com/ie/ie3/netmtg.htm

Voice Recognition

Links to Voice Recognition Sites

http://www.kurz-ai.com/gen-vr.html

Chapter 26

Video Servers

Starlight Networks

http://www.starlight.com/

VDO Live

http://www.vdo.net

Xing StreamWorks

http://www.streamworks.com

Video Utilities

Adobe Premiere

http://www.adobe.com/prodindex/premiere/main.html

Apple QuickTime

http://quicktime.apple.com/

ppmtoyuvsplit

http://ltpwww.gsfc.nasa.gov:81/ltpcf/about/unix/Depotdoc/netpbm/

Mpeg

http://www.mpeg.org

Image Tools

Adobe Photoshop

http://www.adobe.com/prodindex/photoshop/main.html

Adobe Illustrator

http://www.adobe.com/prodindex/illustrator/main.html

PhotoCD

http://www.kodak.com/digitalImaging/aboutPhotoCD/aboutPCD.shtml

Sound Tools

Sound Designer

http://www.digidesign.com

SoundEdit

http://www.macromedia.com/software/sound/index.html

Appendix A

Goldwave

http://web.cs.mun.ca/~chris3/goldwave/

Chapter 27

FTP Clients

WS-FTP

http://www.csra.net/junodj/

CuteFTP

http://www.cuteftp.com

PC TCP

http://www.ftp.com

Fetch

http://www.dartmouth.edu/pages/softdev/fetch.html

FTP Servers

FTP Serv-U

http://catsoft.dorm.duke.edu/index.htm

WFTPD

ftp://ftp.simtel.net/pub/simtelnet/win95/inet/32wfd220.zip

(No Web site available)

Chapter 28

High-Level Databases

Oracle

http://www.oracle.com

Informix

http://www.informix.com

Sybase

http://www.sysbase.com

Microsoft SQL Server

http://www.microsoft.com/sql/

Mid-Level Databases

Borland Paradox

http://netserv.borland.com/paradox/

Microsoft Access

http://www.microsoft.com/msaccess/

Chapter 29

Telnet Clients

CRT

http://www.vandyke.com/vandyke/crt/

Appendix A

NetTerm

http://starbase.neosoft.com/~zkrr01/netterm.html

NCSA Telnet

http://www.ucalgary.ca/~gerke/desktop/macos/mactelnet.html

X Window Clients

Hummingbird Systems Exceed

http://www.hummingbird.com/products.html#exceed

NetManage XoftWare for MacOS

http://www.netmanage.com/netmanage/pcx/xoftware/xmac.html

Chapter 30

E-Mail Clients

Pine

http://www.cac.washington.edu/pine/

Eudora

http://www.eudora.com

SPRYMail

http://www.sprysoft.com

GroupWise

http://www.novell.com/groupwise/

Netscape Mail

http://www.netscape.com/comprod/products/navigator/index.html

Mail is part of Navigator.

Chapter 31

Chat Clients

Quarterdeck Global Stage

http://www.qdeck.com/chat/

Quarterdeck Global Chat

http://www.qdeck.com/chat/

iChat Realtime Object-Oriented Multimedia Server

http://www.ichat.com/

Ircle

http://www.xs4all.nl/~ircle/

Mirc

http://www.mirc.co.uk/

Chapter 32

Internet Telephones

Vocaltec Internet Phone

http://www.vocaltec.com

Resource Guide
Appendix A

Netspeak WebPhone

http://www.netspeak.com

Quarterdeck WebTalk

http://www.qdeck.com

Microsoft NetMeeting

http://www.microsoft.com/ie/ie3/netmtg.htm

Netscape CoolTalk

http://www.netscape.com/comprod/products/navigator/versions_3.0/cooltalk/index.html

Freetel

http://www.freetel.com

Free World Dialup

http://www.pulver.com/fwd/

Video-Conferencing

CU-SeeMe

http://www.wpine.com/

VDO Phone

http://www.vdo.net

Other Technology

Real-Time Protocol

http://www.fokus.gmd.de/step/rtp/

Vocaltec Telephony Gateway

http://www.vocaltec.com/telephon.htm

Chapter 33
Video-Conferencing

White Pine CU-SeeMe

http://www.wpine.com

PictureTel

http://www.pictel.com

VDO Phone

http://www.vdo.net

BBN Picture Window

http://www.bbn.com

Cinecom CineVideo

http://www.cinecom.cokm

Connectix Videophone

http://www.connectix.com

Other Technology

Internet Multicast Backbone

http://www.mbone.com

Chapter 34

Extending the Web

Extending Netscape's Server

http://home.netscape.com/comprod/server_central/server_add_ons.html

Netscape's Plug-In Directory

http://home.netscape.com/comprod/products/navigator/version_2.0/plugins/index.html

Databases

Oracle

http://www.oracle.com

Sybase

http://www.sybase.com

Microsoft SQL Server

http://www.microsoft.com/sql

Microsoft Access

http://www.microsoft.com/msaccess/

Borland Paradox

http://netserv.borland.com/paradox/

Languages

Java

http://www.javasoft.com

JavaScript

http://home.netscape.com/comprod/products/navigator/version_2.0/script/script_info/index.html

http://www.microsft.com/jscript/

Perl

http://www.bio.cam.ac.uk/cgi-lib/

Visual Basic

http://www.microsoft.com/vbasic

VBScript

http://www.microsoft.com/vbscript

Other Technology

Netscape CoolTalk

http://www.netscape.com/comprod/products/navigator/version_3.0/cooltalk/index.html

Point Cast Network

http://www.pointcast.com

VRML

http://www.sdsc.edu/SDSC/Partners/vrml/examples.html

Quickserver

http://www.wayfarer.com

Chapter 37

Message Board Examples

The Intranet Journal

http://www.brill.com/intranet/

The Well

http://www.well.com

David Wooley's Links

http://freenet.msp.mn.us/people/drwool/webconf.html

Time-Warner's Pathfinder

http://www.pathfinder.com

Message Board Utilities

IntraActive InTandem

http://www.intraactive.com

WebBoard

http://webboard.ora.com/

WebNotes

http://webnotes.ostech.com/

WebCrossing

http://lundeen.com

Resource Guide
Appendix A

Chapter 38

Intranet Suites

IntraActive InTandem

http://www.intraactive.com

Thuridion Crew

http://www.thuridion.com

Contact Management

GoldMine

http://www.goldminesw.com/

Symantec Act

http://www.symantec.com/act/index.html

Chapter 39

Alert Messaging

Quote.com

http://www.quote.com

Real-Time Chat

EarthWeb Gamelan

http://www.gamelan.com

Resource Guide

Appendix A

WBS WebChat

http://www.irsociety.com/wbs.html

WOO

SenseMedia The Sprawl

http://sensemedia.net/sprawl

Worlds Inc. AlphaWorld

http://www.worlds.net

Chapter 40
News Services

ClickShare

http://clickshare.com

Desktop Data NewsEdge

http:// www.desktopdata.com

Grayfire

http:// www.grayfire.com

IAC/SandPoint Hoover

http://www.iacnet.com

Individual First! Intranet

http://www.individual.com

Lexis-Nexis Trackers

http://www.lexis-nexis.com

Information, Inc.

http://www.information.com

News Alert

http://www.newsalert.com/

News Wires

Reuters

http://www.reuters.com

Bloomberg Personal

http://www.bloomberg.com

Business Wire

http://www.businesswire.com

PR Newswire

http://www.prnewswire.com

CNP Publications

http://www.cnp-inc.com/

Knight-Ridder

http://www.dialog.com/

Appendix A

Chapter 41

Intranet Suites

IntraActive InTandem

http://www.intraactive.com

Open Text Livelink

http://www.opentext.com

Chapter 43

Intranet Suites

IntraActive InTandem

http://www.intraactive.com

Open Text Livelink

http://www.opentext.com

Lotus Notes

http://www.lotus.com

Other Technology

Netscape Navigator

http://www.netscape.com/comprod/products/navigator/

Glossary

Glossary

access management   Controlling user accessibility of certain applications on intranets.

ActiveX   A standard for embedding into a Web page programs that enhance the capabilities of the browser. ActiveX used to be called OLE Controls or OCXs.

anonymous FTP   A special case of FTP (File Transfer Protocol) that provides a method of permitting anyone to attach to a system via FTP but allows them to have only very limited capabilities, thus enabling portions of the system to be available to the public while still maintaining some level of security.

ASCII FTP mode   One of two modes for data transfer via FTP. ASCII mode sets the transfer mode such that data is transferred ASCII character by ASCII character. Data is transferred faster in ASCII mode than in binary mode, but it will work only for raw text data; executable programs will not transfer correctly via ASCII FTP. See *binary FTP mode*.

ATM   Asynchronous Transfer Mode. A high-speed long-distance networking protocol.

.AU   The extension given to files stored in Sun's sound format. These files are common on the Web.

bandwidth   The volume of data per second that can pass through a network link, line, or device.

baud (bps)   Bits Per Second. Measures the speed that information flows over a given connection—usually a modem or an ethernet.

BBS   Bulletin Board System. A system that allows users to connect with other computers in remote locations.

beta group   The initial user group selected to test an intranet site when it is a functioning prototype.

binary FTP mode   One of two modes for transfer of data via FTP. Binary mode sets the transfer mode such that data is sent byte by byte. This is slower but more reliable than ASCII FTP mode. Any executable program should be sent via binary mode. See *ASCII FTP mode*.

BIOS   Basic Input/Output System. Generally refers to in an Intel-based PC. BIOS is a part of the system board that does basic system tests and configurations before starting any specific operating system.

Boolean search   A search based on using Boolean operators, usually AND or OR, that allows the user to narrow the information returned in a search to a comprehensible level. For example, a search for Cajun AND food would return only information pertaining to both "Cajun" and "food."

bridge   A hardware device used in local area networking to link LANs. Some bridges can pass data over a WAN, whereas others connect LANs directly. Bridges pass data packets using the ethernet or token ring card (hardware) addresses independent of the data inside the packets. Bridges are used in a LAN to make the it bigger or divide it into smaller sections.

browser   An application that allows the user to view a series of connected information—for example, the World Wide Web.

buffering   A process that stores data in memory for a set period of time before transmitting it to the recipient.

CGI   Common Gateway Interface. A program that can perform functions on a host machine and communicate with a World Wide Web server. CGI is typically used to create dynamic Web pages.

chat group   A group of people who can communicate with each other, usually through text messages, in real time through a network.

`chmod`   A UNIX command that changes the mode of a file. There are three modes a file can have turned on or off: read ability, write ability, and execute ability. Each mode can be set for either the owner, the members of the owner's group, or all users.

`chown`   A UNIX command that lets the user change the owner of a file. Only the person who owns the file or the superuser (the user with privileges over the entire system) can change the ownership of a file.

`chroot`   A UNIX systems command used when an anonymous FTP session is initiated. `chroot` allows a directory other than / to be set as the root directory, thereby making any directories above it inaccessible.

CIF/QCIF   Common Intermediate Format/Quarter Common Intermediate Format. Standards-based formats for communicating between video-conferencing systems from different vendors. CIF is a progressive format for computer animation with 360×288 pixels per frame at 30 frames per second. QCIF is a progressive format for computer animation with 180×144 pixels per frame at 30 frames per second. QCIF has one-quarter the resolution of FCIF (Full Common Intermediate Format).

circuit switching   A method of connecting to different sites within a phone company network based on the number called as opposed to packet switching, which is based on address. This is how your phone works: You dial a number associated with another location, and the numbers you press are used to route your call. This works for digital data networking just as it does for your phone. See *packet switching*.

client   An individual user's computer that is connected to a server.

coaxial cable   Two conductor cables almost identical to the wires used for cable TV.

contact database   The equivalent of electronic calendars and address books combined. It lets the user see the information needed to get in touch with others, and it shows the schedules of others so that meetings and appointments are managed more efficiently.

CU-SeeMe   An application for live video-conferencing over the Internet. The "CU" part stands for Cornell University, where CU-SeeMe was developed.

Glossary

daemon A server computer that becomes the host for an Internet protocol database.

data mining The analysis of extremely large, and often ignored or undervalued, data that has been collected as a result of the normal progression of business issues, such as sales figures, mailing lists, and product complaint information.

DCT Direct Connection Telephone. An Internet telephone program that does not use an operator but permits direct calls to fixed IP addresses.

DDF Digital Document Format. A way of storing information electronically. Adobe's Portable Document Format (PDF), Microsoft Word format, and HTML are examples.

DDS Digital Data Service. A channel on a T-1 circuit that generally refers to 56 Kbps circuits offered by the telephone carriers. The DDS circuit is usually a nailed circuit between two sites—that is, a circuit that is established all the time. A variation on the DDS service is the Switched 56 circuit, which can dial among several sites. See *circuit switching*.

dial-up analog service The way most non-LAN users access information. This is a complex way of referring to dialing in over a modem on regular telephone lines into some sort of server, such as a private LAN or the Internet.

disk mirroring A form of backup in which anything that is written to a disk is written simultaneously to a second disk.

domain name server A computer that matches up a domain address with an IP address.

DTD Document Type Definition. An electronic file linked to an SGML application that contains the attributes, elements, and entities that are assigned to the tags that mark up an SGML document. The DTD contains the rules for the structure of an SGML document. The DTD can exist separately from the document or be contained within it.

dumb terminal A terminal with only a keyboard and a monitor connected to a mainframe, a UNIX host, or even a PC. It has no capacity to process information itself.

e-mail Electronic mail. An electronic method of transferring information, usually from one computer to another.

envoy The electronic file format used with WordPerfect Envoy software. It allows electronic distribution of formatted documents.

ethernet A set of standards for local area networking. Also refers to the wire that connects computers on a LAN.

FAQ Frequently Asked Question. Typically a document available on a Gopher or World Wide Web site by e-mail, message board, or newsgroup. It's an information or fact sheet with answers to frequently asked questions regarding a particular application, software function, or anything related to the topic or technology at hand.

FDDI Fiber-Distributed Data Interface. A fiber-optic-based networking protocol that requires a dual-reign typology.

firewall software   Software that prevents unauthorized users from accessing a private network that is connected to a public network.

flat file   Used to describe data that is stored sequentially, usually in text format, as opposed to a database, which stores the data in a more organized manner.

flat file database   A database stored as a text file (or other method) that is nonrelational and contains a single table.

frame rate   The rate of playback for incoming video streams. Expressed in frames per second (fps).

frame relay   A data communication service that assembles data into groups called frames for transmission across a phone company's network. In a frame relay network, the groups or frames of data each have a source and destination address to facilitate correct routing through the network. Frame relay is an enhanced form of packet switching. Frame relay circuits transmit data at a rate between 56 Kbps and 1.54 Mbps.

frame size   The screen size of the video display, usually expressed in pixels.

FTP   File Transfer Protocol. The TCP/IP protocol that permits files to be moved from one system to another, regardless of whether the systems are the same.

full duplex   An asynchronous communications protocol that allows simultaneous two-way communication.

FWD   Free World Dialup. A nonprofit group that provides a gateway between Internet Phones and conventional phones around the world.

gateway   Also known as a router. An intermediate computer that directs packets of information over a network to their intended destination. Why don't the packets go to their intended destination in the first place? A direct connection between two computers on a network is a rare occurrence. Data is sent from one computer to the router, which sends the information in the direction of the intended computer. Over a large intranet or the Internet, data can pass through many routers before reaching its final destination.

GIF   Graphical Interchange Format. A popular image file format championed by CompuServe. It is one of two file formats supported by all Web servers. The other is JPEG.

GIX   Global Information eXchange. The whole idea of the global Internet.

grep   A utility that performs complex search-and-replace operations on files. Most commonly found on UNIX systems.

groupware   A type of software that allows group collaboration on and access to projects and access that are centralized on local or wide-area computer networks.

GUI   Graphic User Interface. Used to communicate with any graphically based program or tool. For example, it uses icons, "point-and-click" menus, or popup menus.

Glossary

half duplex An asynchronous communications protocol that allows one-way communication.

hardware platform Usually refers to the type of microprocessor used in a computer.

hoteling Refers to a company in which employees don't have traditional office space in a building but instead work from home or the road and reserve conference rooms or offices at a building, usually the company's headquarters, when they need to meet with clients, colleagues, or their departments.

HP-UX Hewlett-Packard's version of UNIX.

HTML HyperText Markup Language. The system of describing how information should be described on the Web. It is a scripting language that does not contain any branching or looping functionality. A browser such as Navigator or Mosaic simply loads an HTML file (designated by .HTML or .HTM) and interprets the information in it from beginning to end. All the information on the World Wide Web is stored in HTML files.

HTTP HyperText Transfer Protocol. A protocol used to create the World Wide Web.

hypertext A system of connecting information by associative links. The World Wide Web is the best-known example.

IDE Integrated Drive Electronics. A disk interface commonly used in Intel-based PCs. The interface is inexpensive and simple but is virtually nonexistent outside of the Intel PC world. Recently some CD-ROM drives and tape drives have appeared for the IDE interface. The IDE interface is generally limited to two devices.

IMAP Interactive Mail Access Protocol. A protocol that allows the manipulation of mail and mailboxes over the Internet.

intelligent agent A computer program that is given a specific task that can be done without user assistance. Programs that automatically search the Internet for information or know to defragment a hard disk at a certain time are examples.

interface A bridge either in hardware (such as a network card) or software (such as Windows) that allows for the conveying of information from one medium to another. Windows gives the user a graphical presentation of information in its graphical user interface (GUI). A network interface card changes data from its network form (usually ethernet) into a form usable by the computer.

Internet The worldwide computer network. The set of computers using the TCP/IP protocol suite connected to the successor of the Advanced Research Projects Agency Network (ARPANET) and the National Science Foundation Network (NSFNET).

Internet Phone A software program allowing real-time phone conversations over a computer network such as the Internet.

Internet terminal   A computer whose sole function is to connect to the Internet. Also known as a network computer, it has TCP/IP and Web-browsing functions. The rational for its existence is that the Web will become the platform for all computing, so that anyone with a browser can use remotely stored applications from anywhere in the world.

internetwork   One or more connected LANs.

intranet   A self-contained, internal network linking multiple users by means of Internet technology, usually within an organization. An intranet is typically used to enhance access to information, communication, and workflow between individual users and the organization. Using TCP/IP protocols, an intranet can be everything from a simple Web site that contains the employee handbook in HTML to a communication hub.

IP address   Internet Protocol address. The numerical port address of an Internet connection, expressed in numbers, such as `36.200.34.117`.

IP Phones   A class of products that allows users to speak over an IP network, such as the Internet or an intranet. Its benefit is its extremely low cost. All calls are free; all the user pays for is the IP phone software. Internet Phone, Web Phone, and Televox are examples.

IPX network   The traditional standard protocol that most LANs operate under.

IRC   Internet Relay Chat. A live, multiuser chat system in which people convene on "channels" that are based on a specific topic of conversation and exchange text messages that are displayed to everyone in the channel. Also a type of Internet Telephone program based on an "operator" program, which lists IP addresses and links them to complete phone calls.

ISDN   Integrated Services Digital Network. A medium capable of transmitting multimedia elements such as voice, video, audio, and data over networks.

ISO   International Standardization Organization. A worldwide federation founded to promote the development of international manufacturing, trade, and communications standards. It is composed of member bodies from some 100 countries.

ISP   Internet Service Provider. A company that provides access to the Internet. The ISP provides dial-in lines for modem users, as well as higher-speed lines for linking LANs to the Internet.

Java   A programming language similar to C++, developed by Sun Microsystems for use on the Internet. It is platform-independent, so any system that has the Java Virtual Machine (as does any Java-enabled application) can run Java applications. It has wide industry support because of the ease with which it allows developers to port their programs to many platforms.

Java applets   Binary files downloaded to a file and executed by a browser.

JavaScript   A scripting language based on Java that permits Web browsers and other JavaScript-enabled applications to run simple programs on a user's computer. JavaScript is often used for form validation.

Glossary

JPEG   Joint Photographic Experts Group. A popular image file format. It is one of two supported by all Web servers. The other is GIF.

Kbps   Kilobits per second. 1 Kbps equals 1,000 bps.

LAN   Local Area Network. A network that, through wiring, enables computers in the same building to communicate with each other.

Linux   A free version of UNIX designed to run on Intel x86 architecture chips.

listserv   An e-mail mailing list program that allows recipients to automatically subscribe to and/or cancel mailings.

masking data   To enforce the format of data as it is entered. For example, a telephone number in North America is of the form (*xxx*) *xxx-xxxx*, where *x* is an integer between 0 and 9. This is important to ensure that data collected is useable. It does not guarantee the validity of the data; that is, someone could enter a valid phone number that isn't necessarily his or her own.

MBONE   Multicast Backbone. A live audio and video multicast virtual network that sits on top of portions of the Internet. The MBONE network is made up of specially configured routers that support IP multicast with an "mrouted" multicast routing daemon.

Mbps   Megabits per second. 1 Mbps equals 1000 Kbps.

message board   An application that allows users to post and reply to messages from other users and review the flow of a discussion. Also known as a discussion group.

middleware   The server operating system, also known as the program or interface between the actual hardware and the application program.

modem   Short for modulator/demodulator. A device that enables a computer to communicate with other computers over telephone lines.

MOO   Multiuser Object-Oriented environment. Derived from MUD (Multiuser Dungeon), MOO offers people a way to communicate in real time with objects using just a shell account.

Mosaic   A browser used for exploring the World Wide Web.

MPEG   A video compression standard.

MUD   Multiuser Dungeon. A multiuser simulation environment, usually text-based. Some MUDs are purely for fun and flirting; others are used for serious software development or educational purposes. A significant feature of most MUDs is that users can create things that stay after they leave and that other users can interact with in their absence, thus allowing a "world" to be built gradually and collectively.

natural language query   A search based on human language parameters, such as "display all red cars made by Ford," instead of using SQL.

NCSA National Center for Supercomputing Applications. Located at the University of Illinois at Urbana-Champaign. It is where the first Web browser (Mosaic) was developed. The center continues to be at the forefront of developing Internet technology.

needs assessment The discipline applied to understanding the context from which an Intranet can add value.

Netscape A browser used for exploring the World Wide Web.

network-enabled application An application that needs or can use network resources.

NFS Network File System. A protocol for sharing file systems over a network.

NIC/MAC card Network Interface Card/Media Access Control. A device that connects a computer to a network.

NOS Network Operating Software. The software that controls the operations of a network, including user identification, file serving, security, and e-mail. The most well-known NOS is Novell Netware.

OLE standards Object Linking and Embedding standards. Microsoft's method of adding the functionality of objects to its products. OLE conforms to the Component Object Model (COM).

open standards Specifications that are public—that is, not owned by any company or individual. The Internet is based on open standards.

Oracle The second largest software manufacturer in the world. Its primary focus is high-end database software.

packet switching A data communications technique that packages data into groups called packets for transmission across phone company lines. In a packet-switched network, the groups or frames of data each have a source and destination address to facilitate correct routing through the network. Packet switching is the data communications equivalent of the postal system: Each letter or packet is sent and returned on the basis of the addresses on the packet. Packet switching transmission rates are usually low-speed circuits that operate at 1200 bps to 56 Kbps.

palm-top computer A very small computer that accesses a server or intranet's resources over a wireless modem. In the future, a palm-top computer may also serve as a telephone.

PDF Portable Document Format. The electronic file format used with Adobe Acrobat software. Allows electronic distribution of formatted documents.

Perl An interpreted language developed to process strings effectively that has become very popular with Web applications. It is well suited to the task of CGI applications.

PID Process Identification. The unique identification number assigned to a process by a microprocessor.

platform   A unique combination of a type of hardware and operating system. For example, a PC running Windows NT is a different platform than a Sun Microsystems SparcStation 20 running Solaris. It's safe to assume that most programs are not compatible across different platforms, with some notable exceptions. (For example, a Windows 3.1 application may be compatible with Windows NT.)

plug-in   A program that attaches to a larger application, such as Navigator, Internet Explorer, or Photoshop, and provides it with increased capabilities. RealAudio and Shockwave are examples.

POP3   Post Office Protocol 3. A protocol for retrieving messages across the Internet.

PostScript   A computer language that describes all the aspects of a document—text, graphics, and scanned images—to a printer or other output device.

PPP   Point-to-Point Protocol. One of the protocols that assigns an address to the client computer so that the server knows where to send the information.

protocol   A standard for interpretation of transmitted signals.

RAD   Rapid Application Development. Describes the process of in-house programmers building applications for use within the company. The main purpose of these applications is accessing databases of information.

RAID   Redundant Array of Inexpensive Disks. Normally used when performance or redundancy is necessary. There are several classes of RAID, from a simple mirroring of two drives to a controlled array of disks. In the more complex class, system data is spread over many drives such that all data is stored with parity on different drives for redundancy, and that when retrieving this data, many drives are working in tandem so that more data can be delivered to the system in a shorter amount of time.

RDBMS   Relational Database Management System. A program for manipulating relational databases.

real-time protocol   One of the proposed standards for transmitting audio and video content in an efficient manner over intranets and the Internet.

real-time video   Video that is being transmitted live.

reflector   A video server that intelligently routes multiple streams of data during a videoconference.

relational database   A database that contains multiple tables and other objects and has the information organized by defined relationships between tables.

remote network connection   A connection to a LAN or similar network from a site that is physically disconnected from the site of the network.

RISC processor   Reduced Instruction Set Computing. A school of chip design that places less-complex instructions on an integrated circuit, thereby allowing the chip to run at higher speeds. The PowerPC, Alpha, and SPARC chips are RISC-based.

rlogin   A remote access protocol that provides a mechanism for an individual at a remote computer system to establish a session with a computer that will respond exactly as if the user were using a terminal directly connected to the system. Unlike Telnet, rlogin provides a mechanism for logging in without supplying a password. See *trusted host*.

root   The top of a directory tree of a file system, as in "the root directory." Also, the superuser in the UNIX operating system (the user with privileges over the entire system).

router   A hardware device used in networking that looks inside the data packets to determine what kind of data is being sent. Routers read software addresses in the data packets in addition to hardware addresses to facilitate data routing. Routers are used for connecting different or separate LANs. If you are sending data to a computer that is not on your LAN or is on a different kind of LAN, you are using a router.

script   A form set up by the administrator to create something on an intranet that is used more than once, such as a conference.

SCSI   Small Computer Systems Interface. A small standard for connecting peripheral devices to a computer, such as disk drives, CD-ROMs, scanners, and tape drives. SCSI devices are linked to the computer in chains, and each device in a chain must have a unique ID number from 0 to 7. SCSIs are often used in high-end servers and workstations.

search engine   A utility that permits the user to find any word, concept, or file on a network using a variety of criteria, including date, size, and physical location.

server   A piece of hardware that receives, processes, and replies to a query from a client.

SGML   Standard Generalized Markup Language. A high-powered relative of HTML. It is a highly detailed and complex system of representing information that is designed to allow content to be platform-independent.

shareware/freeware   Software you can download from the Internet for free or on a trial basis. Usually, shareware or freeware is created by an individual, but lately, commercial entities have gotten into the game, offering stripped-down or beta versions of their software on the Internet for free.

shell account   A text-based account on a UNIX machine that allows the user to remotely access files, compile binaries, run programs, and generally do anything that can be done from a desktop computer in text mode.

shell script   A file containing operating system commands that are processed in a batch method, one at a time, until complete.

SLIP   Serial Line Interface Protocol. One of the protocols that assigns an address to the client computer so that the server knows where to send the information.

SMDS   Switched Multimegabit Data Service. A high-speed packet-switching service that is usually delivered over T-1—or, more often, T-3—circuits. It allows multiple sites to communicate with each other at high speeds. SMDS transmission rates start at 1.54 Mbps and run up to 45 Mbps.

Glossary

SMTP   Simple Mail Transfer Protocol. The protocol by which mail is sent from one computer to another on the Internet.

socket   A channel for communication between processes.

sonet   Synchronous Optical Network. The networking service that is replacing copper-based circuits in the phone companies' networks. Sonet is delivered over fiber optic cables. T-1 and T-3 circuits delivered on copper wires have been the standard wide-area networking medium for many years. T-1 circuits or DS-1 (Digital Signaling 1) operate at 1.544 Mbps. T-3 or DS-3 circuits operate at 45 Mbps. Sonet circuits are called OC-3 or OC-12. The OC-3 circuit is roughly equivalent to 3 T-3s, and the OC-12 is roughly 12 T-3s. The fiber optic cables are smaller, lighter, and more impervious to noise or static than their forebears.

SPARC   Scaleable Processor Architecture. A type of processor family that is used by Sun, SGI, and other companies.

SQL   Standard Query Language. A language that allows users to submit queries and perform actions on databases that support SQL.

SQL Server   A structured query language server, such as Microsoft's RDBMS. SQL Server is used to interact with a database. Recently, it has been widely used in Web applications involving a database back-end.

SSL   Secure Sockets Layer. A standard for transporting information over a network using encryption and validation.

stand-alone application   An application that does not need and cannot use network resources.

T-1   A long-distance fiber-optic circuit that transmits approximately 8,000 frames per second, or 1.54 Mbps.

tag   A standard marking in an SGML document that refers to a DTD for information on the structure of a document's elements. Tags are bracketed text at the beginning and end of a structural element that refer to that element's place within the structure of an SGML document (title, body text, header) and also its typographical attributes (type size, font, special characters).

TCP/IP   Transmission Control Protocol/Internet Protocol. A suite of networking protocols that forms the basis of the Internet.

Telnet   A remote access protocol that provides a mechanism for a person from a remote computer system to establish a session with a computer that will respond exactly as if the user were using a terminal directly connected to the system. It is similar to rlogin, except that Telnet always forces a user to supply a password to establish a connection, whereas rlogin does not always require a password.

thread   A trace of replies to messages in a message board. Threads often appear to trace the flow of a discussion and show how a topic was created.

token ring   A standard for local area networking analogous to ethernet.

trusted host   A computer not required to go through full authentication to gain access to your computer.

twisted pair   A wire used to network computers that looks identical to telephone wire and consists of smaller pairs of twisted wires.

UDP   User Datagram Protocol. A protocol that enables the sending of streams of information rather than packets.

UNIX   An operating system that runs on many different platforms. Originally developed by AT&T.

UNP   Universal Naming Procedure. Microsoft's solution to naming conventions.

URL   Universal Resource Locator. A mechanism to provide a unique naming convention across all points in the Web.

Usenet   The Internet news forum; an international discussion area that contains information on virtually every topic imaginable. Users access Usenet through applications such as tin, News Xpress, and NewsWatcher. Usenet also is known as newsgroups.

VAX   Virtual Address Extension. A type of mainframe made by Digital Equipment Corporation that runs the VMS operating system.

video compression   Reduces the number of bits required to store and/or transmit digital media. Compressed video can be transmitted more economically over a smaller carrier.

virtual corporation   A group of corporations, often with different specialties and located in different geographical areas, that work in concert as a single entity to serve the needs of particular clients.

Visual Basic Script   A scripting language based on Visual Basic that permits Web browsers and other Visual Basic Script-enabled applications to run simple programs on a user's computer. Visual Basic Script is often used for form validation. Also known as VBScript.

VMS   Virtual Memory System. Also known as OpenVMS. An operating system that runs on VAX- and Alpha-based computers.

VON   Voice/Video On the Net. The term used to describe products that allow for the transmission of audio or video over the Internet.

VRML   Virtual Reality Markup Language. A scripting language that allows for the creation of three-dimensional "worlds" that the user can explore.

WAN   Wide Area Network. A network spread over a large physical distance.

.WAV   The extension given to sound files saved in the Microsoft sound format. It is the standard format for Windows.

Glossary

Webchat   A live, multiuser chat system that uses HTTP instead of IRC. Text messages are displayed on a Web page that periodically reloads to include new content.

The Well   The Whole Earth 'Lectronic Link. An 11-year-old electronic community of Internet users that is based in California. It is one of the best examples of a virtual community.

WOO   Web-based multiuser Object-Oriented. An environment that presents a MOO in an easier-to-follow Web format.

WWW   World Wide Web. The multimedia segment of the Internet, developed in 1991 to facilitate communication between educational facilities. The WWW is now the fastest-growing part of the Internet.

WYSIWYG   What You See Is What You Get. The commonly used term to convey that the way a project looks on-screen in the development phase will be the same as when the project is done. For example, in most modern word-processing packages, the way the text looks on-screen is exactly the same as when it is printed.

INDEX

SYMBOLS

/ (slashes), home directories, 240
56K circuits (WANs), accessing, 159
56Kbps Digital Data Service (DDS), 152-153
802.3 (Ethernet), 133-134
   frames, 134

A

ABC Widgets Inc., 158
ac command, 446
Access America Web site, 389
access management, 848
access rights
   anonymous, 212
   databases, users, 719-721
   guests, 212
   LANs, 211-212
   universal access, 211
access.conf file, 236-237

accessing

accessing, 142
  applications, 286
  CGI scripts, 241
  FTP servers, 416-417
  intranets, 9
  LANs, 212-213
    resources, 213
  NewsAlert, 615
  online news services, 602-603
  security, 224-226
  SGML, 365
  sites, 290
  SSIs, 243-244
  WANs, 159
    56K circuits, 159
    ATM, 160-161
    frame relays, 160
    SMDS, 160
    Sonet, 160
    T-1 circuits, 160
    T-3 circuits, 160

accounts
  anonymous FTP, building, 406
  database users, tracking, 722-724
  PPP
    dial-up analog services, 166-167
    digital, 167
  shells, 857
    dial-up analog services, 166
  SLIP
    dial-up, 167
    dial-up analog services, 166-167
  users, 227
    Clickshare, 603

Acrobat, 355-356
  Excel, 356
  WordPerfect, 356
  workgroups, 356
  Web site, 354, 357

Acrobat Distiller, 356
Acrobat Pro, 356
Action Workflow Metro, 35
ActiveX, 305, 348-349, 427, 848
  Web sites, creating, 775-776

ActiveX SDK, 349
address routing protocol (ARP), 250
addresses
  DNS, 850
  e-mail
    help, 682-683
    messages, 461
  e-mail messages, 461
  Internet, 170-172
  IP, 853
    DCT, 850
    DNS, 850
    firewalls, 216
    restricting, 235
  listservs, 467

administering logs, 113
administrative groups
  databases, 720-721
    CGIs, 720
  UNIX, 720

administrators, 291
  archiving, 288-289
  communicating, 293
  e-mail, 289-290
  IDs, 286-287
  Internet systems administrators, 762-763
  organizing intranets, 291
  packet sniffers, 248
  passwords, 286-287
  role of, 290
  Sysops, 588
  systems, logs, 113
  technical support, 288, 292
  training, 293-295
  updating, 288-289, 292
  usage analysis, 287-288

Adobe Acrobat, *see* **Acrobat**
Adobe PostScript, 355, 856
Adobe Premiere, 383
Adobe Web site, 358
advantages of intranets, 7-8
advertising
  audio on intranets, 379
  FTP, 414

agents, 777
Airmail, e-mail, 199
alerts
  messages, 588
  messaging, 588-591
    Java applets, 590
    mailing, 591
    SGAA, 596

algorithms, encrypting, 251
aliasing, e-mail, 463-464
All-In-One, 702
AlphaWorld Web site, 594
AltaVista, 664-665
analog services (dial-up)
  connecting to the Internet, 166
    PPP accounts, 166-167
    shell accounts, 166
    SLIP accounts, 166-167

Index

anonymous access rights, 212
anonymous FTP, 395, 405, 417, 848
  accounts, building, 406
  commands, 405
  configuring, 405
  testing, 408
Apache Web site, 100
APIs (Application Programming Interfaces), 516-517
  HTTP servers, 517
  ISAPI, 517
  NSAPI, 517
AppleTalk LANs, 141-142
applets, 527
  alert messaging, 590
    mailing, 591
  Java, 346, 853
Application Programming Interfaces, *see* **APIs**
applications, 703-705
  access management, 848
  accessing, 286
  All-In-One, 702
  APIs, 516-517
  browsers, 300-301, 849
  CGI, 518-520
  Chat, 480-481
  client/servers, ATMs, 50
  commercial, 714-715
  CU-SeeMe, 849
  document collaborations, 627
    InTandem, 627
  frequency, 708
  functionality, 708
  graphics (X Windows), 443-444

groupware, converting to intranets, 39
help, 674
high-end, 799
history of, 702-703
hooks, 708
in-house, 716
integrating, 703-706, 710-711
  evaluation, 713-714
  feedback, 713-714
  implementation of, 712-713
  inventory, 711-712
Internet, 714
intranets, 714
  future of, 796-797
Locker, 627-628
message boards, 854
  creating, 566
mid-range, 799
networks, 708-709, 855
online scheduling, 553-555
  InTandem, 555-557
  WebShare Calendar, 557-558
plug-ins, 518, 856
purpose of, 707
RAD, 856
ranges, 707
security, 744-745
selecting, 514-515
single-client, 794
SSI, 515-516
stand-alone, 709-710, 858
StockWatcher, 532
TCP/IP, 530-531
video-conferencing, 503-504
Wayfarer QuickServer, 532-533

word processing
  PDFs, 352
architecture, Web sites, 767-769
archiving
  chats, 596
  files, 288-289
  message boards, 572
ARCnet
  LANs, 135-136
ARP (address routing protocol), 250
ARPANET, 852
Ascend routers, 173
ASCII
  BBSs, 45
  flat files databases, 330
  FTP mode, 848
ascii command (FTP), 398
assessing intranets, 536-539
  technical requirements, 539-540
Associated Press (AP), 605
associations (intranets), 28
  calendars, 29
  employees, 29
  organizing, 291
  publications, 30
  SGAA, 30-31
ATM (Asynchronous Transfer Mode), 156, 848
  LANs, 137-138
  WANs, accessing, 160-161
ATMs, client/servers, 50
attachments (e-mail), WANs, 468

AU file format, 371, 848
audio, 368-369, 376
  advertising, 379
  alert messaging, SGAA, 596
  bandwidths, 369-370
  dynamic sites, 323-325
  editing, 374-376
  files
    dynamic sites, 325
    streaming, 370
  formats, 370-371
    AU, 371, 848
    MPEG-Audio, 371
    WAV, 371, 859
  GIFs, 324
  GoldWave, 374
  hardware, 369-370
  Internet Phone, 376-377
  Internet telephones, 492
  IWave, 373
  JPEGs, 324
  MBONE, 854
  McKeon & Jeffries, 378
  metafiles, 376
  perceptual coding, 371
  Progressive Network, 615
  RealAudio, 372
  RealAudio Encoder, 376
  recording, 373-376
  servers, software, 372
  software, 106
  SoundEdit Pro, 371
  streaming, 372-373, 595
  StreamWorks, 372
  ToolVox, 373
  TrueSpeech, 373
  voices, 377-379
  WAV files, 375
  Web sites
    NetworkMusic, 370
    Webcorp, 370
audio chat, 591
audio conferencing, 379
audio streaming
  ToolVox, 373
  Web sites, creating, 776
Audio Video Interleave (AVI), 304
authenticating (security), 214
  CERN server, 229
  kerberos, 214-215
  NCSA server, 236
  passwords, 214-216, 227-229
  post name checks, 214
  smartcards, 215
  usernames, 214-215
authentication points (security), 207-208
AuthGroupFile directive, 236
AuthName directive, 236
authoring tools, 310
  near-WYSIWYG, 314
    HotDog Pro, 314-315
    HoTMetaL, 315-316
  WYSIWYG, 310
    FrontPage, 313
    Internet Assistant, 310-311
    Navigator Gold, 312-313
AuthType <auth scheme> directive, 231
AuthType directive, 236
AuthUserFile directive, 236
AVI (Audio Video Interleave), 304

B

back-end databases, search engines, 664
backups, disk mirroring, 850
bandwidths, 464-465, 790-793, 848
  audio, 369-370
  Internet telephones, 490
  software, 498
  video-conferencing, 503-506
baseline, 452
BASH shells, 336
Basic Rate Interfaces (BRIs), 167
batch processing, 336
baud, 848
BBSs (Bulletin Board Systems), 44-46, 848
  interfaces, 45
  modems, 46
  servers, 46
Because It's Time Network (BITNET), 48
beta groups, 848
betas
  PointCast, downloading software, 602-603
  testing, 542
  user input, 541-543
Bikes USA, intranet usage levels, 21
binary
  command (FTP), 398
  files, Java, 853
  FTP mode, 848
BIOS, 848
BITNET (Because It's Time Network), 48
Bloomberg Personal, 606

C

boards, *see* message boards
BoardWatch magazine, 46
bookmarks, building lists, 697
Boolean searches, 662-663, 848
Borland Paradox 7.0, 428
Bourne shells, 336
bps, 848
bridges, 157, 249, 848
   interfaces, 852
BRIs (Basic Rate Interfaces), 167
broadcast messaging, *see* alerts; messaging
BROWSE Web site, 343
browsers, 193, 300-301, 849
   ActiveX, 848
   Explorer, 193
   formats, interlacing, 302
   HTML, 300-302
      fonts, 302
   images, 302
   Internet Explorer, 301
   Java, 305
   JPEG, 302
   Live3D, 304
   McKeon & Jeffries, 306
   MOOs, building, 592
   MUDs, building, 592
   Navigator, 301, 304
   NCSA Mosaic, 195, 302, 854-855
   Netscape, 193, 301-304, 855
   OS/2, 195
   PowerBrowser, 305
   progressive rendering, 302
   SDK, 303
   SGAA, 306
   WWW, forms, 327
BSD/OS, 84-86
budgets, Web sites, 765-766
buffering, 849
   Internet telephones, 491
bugs, 223-224
building
   anonymous FTP accounts, 406
   bookmark lists, 697
   databases, 718-719
   FTP, home directories, 406-408
   intranets, 536-539
      technical requirements, 539-540
   MOOs, 592
   MUDs, 592
   security, 206-207
Bulletin Board Systems, *see* BBSs
buses
   Ethernet, 134
   tokens, 135
businesses
   BBSs, 45
   communicating, 784-785
   Grayfire news service, 611-612
   hoteling, 788, 852
   information, 785-787
   international, 788
   intranets, 9-10, 20-25, 37
      future of, 782-784
      goals, 12
   outsourcing, 788-789
   restructuring, 784
   telecommuting, 788
   teleconferencing, 798
   virtual corporations, 787
bye command (FTP), 398
bytes, binary, 848

C

C shells, 336
cables
   coaxial, 849
      LANs, 131
   fiber optics, 132
   LANs, 146
   twisted pair cabling, LANs, 131-132
Café version (Global Stage IRC chat server), 482
calendars
   association intranets, 29
   Crew, 558
   InTandem, 556
   WebShare, 557-558
calls (RPCs), security, 260
Cardfile, 582
Carnegie Mellon, Informedia, 691
Carrier Sensing Multiple Access Collision Detection system, 134
case sensitivity, JavaScript, 523
cd command (FTP), 399
CD-ROMs, video, 382
CERN
   authenticating passwords, 229
   Exec directive, 242
   WWW, 300
CERT (Computer Emergency Response Team), 219, 257

CGI (Common Gateway Interface), 328-330, 518-520, 849
  administrative groups, 720
  cgi-lib.pl, 340
  directories, 519
  nontextual data handling, 520
  scripts, 338
    accessing, 241
    directories, 241
    security, 222
    storing, 241
cgi-lib.pl, 340
challenge-and-response systems, 215
Chat, 479-480
  applications, 480-481
  Global Chat client, 483
  Global Stage IRC chat server, 481
    Café version, 482
    Stadium version, 482
    Theater version, 482
  groups, 849
  iChat, 483
  Internet Phone, 484
  IRC, 478-479, 853
    clients, 483-484
  Quarterdeck Web site, 480
  servers, 481-483
  video-conferencing, 484
  Webchat, 860
chat groups, 849
chat lines, help, 684
chats, 594-595
  audio, 591
  boards, 591
  MOOs, 592
  MUDs, 592
  real-time, 591
  group message boards, 591
  WBS, 591
  saving, 596
  SGAA, 30
  streaming audio, 595
checklist of intranets, 10-11
chmod command (FTP), 408
chmod command (UNIX), 849
chown command (UNIX), 849
chroot command (UNIX), 849
CIF/QCIF, 849
Cinepak, 388
CineVideo, 507
ciphertext, 251
circuit switching, 849
circuits
  56K, 159
  T-1, 160
  T-3, 160
Cisco, 173
cleaning up intranets, 288-289
Clickshare, 603
client/servers
  LANs, 139
  security, 257-258
clients, 53, 849
  applications, 794
  ATMs, 50
  BBSs, 44
  connecting, 69-70
  defined, 51
  e-mail
    Eudora, 472
    GroupWise, 474
    Netscape Mail, 474-476
    Pine, 472
    SPRYMail, 473
  Eudora, 53
  FTP, 408
    CuteFTP, 409
    DOS, 409
    Linux, 408
    MacOS, 410
    selecting, 411
    starting up, 409-410
    UNIX, 408
    versus FTP servers, 396-397
    Windows 3.x, 409
    Windows 95, 410
    Windows NT, 410
  Global Chat, 483
  hardware, 51, 69
  Internet telephones, 498-499
  IRC, 483-484
  Pine, 52
  protocols, 48
  servers, 48-49
  software, 51-53, 69
  Telnet, 440-441
  video-conferencing
    hardware, 507-508
    software, 507-508
clipping services, 604-608
close command (FTP), 399
coaxial cables, 849
  LANs, 131
coding, perceptual, 371
collaborative documents, 620-622, 630-631
  Exquisite Corpse game, 621-622
  InTandem, 627
  intranets, 623-626
  managers, 620-621
  McKeon & Jeffries, 625-626

online, 622-623
SamePage, 629-630
SGAA, 626
Collabra Share Web site, 38
colleges, video-conferencing, 504
COM (Component Object Model), 348
  applications, integrating, 710-711
comm ports, modems, 143
command line, Telnet, 442-443
commands
  ac, 446
  File menu, Mail Document, 696
  FTP
    anonymous, 405
    ascii, 398
    binary, 398
    bye, 398
    cd, 399
    chmod, 408
    close, 399
    dir, 399
    get, 396, 399
    hash, 399
    lcd, 400
    ls, 400
    mget, 400
    mput, 400
    open, 401
    put, 396, 401
    pwd, 401
    quit, 401
    user, 401
  FTP menu, Connection, 409
  last, 445-446
  PDF Writer menu, Print, 358
  ps, 447-450
  shells, 336
  UNIX
    chmod, 849
    chown, 849
    chroot, 849
    sendmail, 224
  who, 445
comments, contact databases, 579
commerce, SGAA, 31
commercial applications, 714-715
commercial Web servers, software, 93-94
Common Gateway Interface, *see* **CGI**
communicating, administrators, 293
communications, 38-39, 488
  WANs, 161-162
communications servers, 143
  LANs, 148-149
companies, 36
  communicating, 784-785
  hoteling, 788, 852
  information, 785-787
  international, 788
  intranets, 9-10, 37
    goals, 12
  organizing intranets, 291
  outsourcing, 788-789
  restructuring, 784
  telecommuting, 788
  teleconferencing, 798

compatibility
  FTP, 404
  hardware, 748
  software, 748
  operating systems, 188-189
compatibles (IBMs), 188
compilers, Perl, 339
compiling SGML documents, 365
Component Object Model, *see* **COM**
compressing
  video, 859
  video-conferencing, 505-506
CompuServe, Executive news service, 602
Computer Emergency Response Team, *see* **CERT**
Computer Science Research Network (CSNET), 48
computers, *see* **PCs**
concepts, Web sites, 763-765
conference calls, audio on intranets, 378
conferencing, *see* **video-conferencing**
configuration files
  HTTPd, 100
  logs, 111
configuring
  anonymous FTP, 405
  CERN, Exec directive, 242
  FTP, servers, 413
  NCSA, ScriptAlias directive, 242
  private message boards, software, 638-640

connecting
  BBSs, 848
  Internet, 165, 175-176
    addresses, 170-172
    dial-up analog services, 166-167
    digital PPP accounts, 167
    hardware, 172-173
    LANs, 167-169
    routers, 173-174
    security, 176
    SLIP dial-up accounts, 167
    software, 172-173
    workstations, 174
  intranet users, 264-268
  LANs, 131
    AppleTalk, 141-142
    ARCnet, 135-136
    ATM, 137-138
    cabling, 146
    client/servers, 139
    coaxial cables, 131
    communications servers, 143
    Ethernet, 133-134
    FDDI, 136-137
    fiber optic cables, 132
    file servers, 139, 147
    gateways, 143
    interfaces, 133
    ISDNs, 144-145
    LANtastic, 141
    MAC cards, 133
    modems, 142-144
    NetWare, 139-140
    NOSs, 138-139
    print servers, 148
    remote access, 142
    setting up LANs, 169-170
    TCP/IP, 141
    telecommuting, 142
    Token Ring, 135-136
    twisted pair cabling, 131-132
    Windows for Workgroups, 140
    Windows NT, 140
    wireless, 132-133
  networks
    hardware, 149-150
    servers, 145-147
  software, servers, 174-175
  WANs, 161
connecting to
  intranets, 69-70
  online news services, 602-603
Connection command (FTP menu), 409
connections
  Internet, wireless, 777
  remote network connection, 856
  security, 206
Connectix, 507
constructing
  intranets, 536-539
contact databases, 579, 849
  Cardfile, 582
  comments, 579
  corporate directories, 577
  Crew, 582
  fields, 578-579
  GoldMine, 582-583
  hyperlinked records, 580
  InTandem, 581
  intranets, 577-578
  LANs, 577
  profiles, 580-584
  search engines, 580
  shared resources, 576-577
  software contact management system, 578
  telephone lists, 579
contact lists, 24
contact management systems, 576
  software, 578
contact managers, *see* **contact databases**
converting groupware applications, intranets, 39
CoolTalk, 107, 204, 304, 507, 531
CoolView, 507
corporations, 36
  communicating, 784-785
  hoteling, 852
  information, 785-787
  intranets, 9-10
    goals, 12
  organizing intranets, 291
  restructuring, 784
copyrights, documents, 693
Cornell University Law Library Web site, 692
corporate directories, contact databases, 577
corporate e-mail, 465
corporations
  hoteling, 788
  international, 788
  intranets, 37
  outsourcing, 788-789
  servers, 62
  telecommuting, 788
  teleconferencing, 798

virtual, 787, 859
crackers, 223, 745
Crew
   contact databases, 582
   Locker, 627-628
Crew Calendar, 558
CSMA/CD system, 134
CSNET (Computer Science Research Network), 48
CU-SeeMe, 107, 495-496, 502, 507, 849
customer service, videoconferencing, 504
customized fields, contact databases, 578-579
customizing private message boards, software, 635-637
CuteFTP, 409
   e-mail, 200-201
Cybercash Web site, 636

D

daemons, 47, 174, 227, 850
   httpd, 61
DARPA (Defense Advanced Research Project Agency), 141
DAS (Dual Attached Station), 136
data
   availability, 432
   distribution, 429
   longevity, 432
   mining, 850
   streaming, creating Web sites, 777
   usage, 431-432
Data Definition Languages (DDLs), 343

Data Encrypt Standard (DES), 253
Data Manipulation Languages (DMLs), 343
databases, 420-435
   administrative groups, 720-721
   advanced issues, 429
   contact, 579, 849
      Cardfile, 582
      comments, 579
      contact management systems, 578
      corporate directories, 577
      Crew, 582
      fields, 578-579
      GoldMine, 582-583
      hyperlinked records, 580
      InTandem, 581
      intranets, 577-578
      LANs, 577
      profiles, 580-584
      search engines, 580
      shared resources, 576-577
      telephone lists, 579
   designing, 718-719
   e-mail, 723
   flat files, 330, 851
   gateways, 422
   Informix, 425
   integration, 433-435
   interactive, 520-521
   interfaces, 342
   management strategies, 431
   McKeon & Jeffries, tracking users, 723
   Microsoft SQL Server, 427-428
   object component, 425

   Oracle, 426-427
   Paradox 7.0, 428-429
   relational, 330-332, 425, 856
      Oracle, 668-670
      RDBMS, 856
   scaleability, 425
   search engines, Livelink, 664
   security, 722
   servers
      FTP, 721
      Web, 721-722
   SGAA, 31
   software
      documents, 652-653
      Oracle, 855
   storing data, 328
   submitting documents, 651-652
   Sybase, 425-426
   users
      access rights, 721
      flow charts, 723
      functions, 719
      groups, 719-720
      implementing, 721-724
      monitoring, 724-725
      passwords, 724
      tracking, 722-724
   vendors, 432
DataBlades, 425
dates, association intranets, 29
DBI (Database Interface), 342
DCT (Direct Connection), 850
DDF (Digital Document Format), 352, 850
DDLs (Data Definition Languages), 343

DDS (Digital Data Service), 152-153, 850
DECnet, LANs, 142
decrypting, 251
dedicated LANs, 167-169
Defense Advanced Research Project Agency (DARPA), 141
defining
   goals, creating Web sites, 763
   intranet priorities, 537-538
   LANs, paths, 211-212
   logs, 110-111
   Web sites, 774-775
      operating procedures, 770-772
DefProt directive, 230
deleting private message boards, 637
delivering (real-time messaging), 588
DES (Data Encrypt Standard), 253
design managers, Web sites, 760
designing
   databases, 718-719
   file structures, 729
   intranets, 536-539
      organizations, 17-19
      technical requirements, 539-540
      user input, 541
      user survey, 543-547
      users, 540-541
   servers, 117-119
      log books, 120
      troubleshooting, 123-125
      updating, 119

   Web sites
      architecture, 767-769
      Internet multimedia designers, 762
developing Web sites
   design managers, 760
   editorial managers, 760-761
   executive producers, 759
   product managers, 759-760
   production managers, 760
   program managers, 760
dial-up analog services, 166, 850
   PPP accounts, 166-167
   shell accounts, 166
   SLIP account, 166-167
dial-up LANs, 167-169
dialog boxes
   Message Composition, 696
   Password, 228
   TCP/IP Properties, 266
digests, e-mail, 607
Digital AltaVista, 664-665
Digital Data Service (DDS), 152-153, 850
Digital Document Format (DDF), 352, 850
digital documents
   Acrobat, 355-356
   creating, 356-358
   linking, 354-355
   PostScript, 355
digital PPP accounts, 167
dir command (FTP), 399
directives
   AuthGroupFile, 236

   AuthName, 236
   AuthType, 236
   AuthType <auth scheme>, 231
   AuthUserFile, 236
   DefProt, 230
   Exec, 242
   GetMask <group syntax>, 231
   GroupFile <filename>, 231
   GroupId <group>, 231
   Limit, 236-238
   Options, 236-238
   PasswordFile <filename>, 231
   Protect, 230
   Protection, 234
   protection setup files, 231
   ScriptAlias, 242
   security, 229
   ServerId <name>, 231
   UserDir, 240
   UserId <user>, 231
directories, 577
   / (slashes), 240
   CGI, 519
      scripts, 241
   FTP, building, 406-408
   HTML, personal, 240-241
   trees
      FTP, 410
      roots, 857
   UNIX, 732
      symbolic links, 732
discussion groups, *see* **message boards**
disk mirroring, 850
disks, IDE, 852

disseminating information through SGML, 365
Distiller, 356
Distinct, 184
distributing PDFs, 358
DMLs (Data Manipulation Languages), 343
DNS (Domain Name Server), 850
Document Type Definition (DTD), 364-365, 850
documents
    collaborative, 620-622, 630-631
        Exquisite Corpse game, 621-622
        InTandem, 627
        intranets, 623-626
        McKeon & Jeffries, 625-626
        online, 622-623
        SGAA, 626
    copyrights, 693
    databases, software, 652-653
    digital formats
        Acrobat, 355-356
        PostScript, 355
    distributing, envoy, 850
    downloading Locker, 627
    e-mail, 467
    FAQs, 850
    formats, PDFs, 855
    groups, 620
    instances, 364
    Internet Assistant, 310
    linking, 354-355
    Livelink Library, 654-655
    Locker, 627-628
    managers, 620-621, 624
    PDFs, 352-354, 692
        Acrobat, 355-356
        creating, 356-358
        embedding fonts, 357
        Times Fax, 354
    SamePage, 629-630
        creating, 629
    searchable Web pages, 623
    SGML, 364
        compiling, 365
        DTDs, 364-365
        tags, 858
    sharing, SGAA, 30
    submitting
        databases, 651-652
        FTP, 650
        InterNotes, 655
        Navigator, 656-657
    tracking, 620
    WebShare, 624
    WWW, 352
domains, names, 461-463
    finding, 462
    restricting, 235
DOS, FTP 409
    servers, 412
downloading
    binary files, Java, 853
    documents, Locker, 627
    Excite, 666
    files, FTP, 394-396
    freeware, 374
    SATAN, 746
    software
        MOOs, 594
        PointCast, 602-603
    Word, 704
downtime
    financial considerations, 80
    servers, 115
DowVision, 607
DSA (Dynamic Scaleable Architecture), 425
DSP, TrueSpeech, 373
DTD (Document Type Definition), 364-365, 850
Dual Attached Station (DAS), 136
dumb terminals, 42-43, 850
Dynamic Scaleable Architecture (DSA), 425
dynamic sites, 320-322
    e-mail, 325-326
    functions, 320
    inputting data, 322
        audio, 323-325
        images, 323-325
        static, 323
    inventory datasheets, 322
    WWW, forms, 327-328

E

e-mail (electronic mail), 325-326, 460, 464, 469, 850
    addresses, help, 682-683
    administrators, 289-290
    Airmail, 199
    aliasing, 463-464
    bandwidths, 464-465
    clients
        Eudora, 472
        GroupWise, 474
        Netscape Mail, 474-476
        Pine, 472
        SPRYMail, 473
    corporate, 465
    CuteFTP, 200-201

database users, tracking, 723
digests, 607
documents, 467
domain names, 461-463
Eudora, 197
FAQs, 467
Fetch, 200-201
files, 466-467
FTP, 200
FTP command-line, 201
GroupWise, 198, 469
history of, 460
host names, 461
IMAP, 469
intranets, 5
listservs, 854
mailbots, 467
mailing lists, 467-468
MailServer 2.0, 103
McKeon & Jeffries, 475
messages, addressing, 461
NetNotes, 570
Netscape, 197
passwords, 742
security, 216
Pine, 199
pipes, 464-465
POP3, 469, 856
remote messaging, 464
routers, help, 684
security, PGP, 744
Sendmail, 102
servers, 102-103, 469-470
  Exchange Server, 471
  LANs, 148
  Netscape, 470-471
  NTMAIL, 103
  Post Office, 470
  SLmail, 104

SGAA, 476
SMTP, 460, 469, 858
software, 196-197
transmissions, security, 246-247
WANs, 468
EarthWeb, 758
Web sites, 769
  agents, 777
  audio streaming, 776
  business planning, 763
  concepts, 763-765
  creating, 758, 766
  creating with ActiveX, 775-776
  creating with Internet Phone, 777
  creating with Internet video-conferencing, 777
  creating with Java, 775
  creating with VRML, 776
  data streaming, 777
  defining, 774-775
  defining goals, 763
  marketing, 772-773
  operating procedures, 770-772
  outsourcing, 778-779
  planning, 767
  production teams, 758-759
  site architecture, 767
  technical requirements, 770
  video streaming, 776
  wireless Internet connections, 777
EarthWeb Gamelan Web site, 346, 595

editing
  audio, 374-376
  files
    utmp, 446
    wtmp, 446
editorial managers, Web sites, 760-761, 769
editors (text), vi, 449
Edupage
  mailing list, 468
  Web site, 748
Elan Software Corporation GoldMine, 582-583
Electric Library Web site, 690
electronic clipping services, 604-606
electronic documents, *see* **digital documents**
electronic logs, 113
electronic mail, *see* **e-mail**
embedding
  ActiveX, 848
  fonts, PDFs, 357
  OLE, 855
  security, 234
  see also OLE
emergency startup procedures, logs, 111
employee handbooks, 270-271
employee tracking, 433
employees (associations), intranets, 29
enabling SSIs, 243-244
encoding audio, RealAudio Encoder, 376
encrypting, 251-252, 255-256
  algorithms, 251
  ciphertext, 251

decryptions, 251
DES, 253
file transmissions, 258
private keys, 252-253
public keys, 253-255
encryption, 453
Encyclopedia Brittanica Web site, 688
engines (search), 661-662
AltaVista, 664-665
defined, 660
Excite, 666, 683
help desk, 680
Livelink, 666-667
Pat, 666-667
selecting, 671
setting up, 663-664
Sybase SQL, 670
Verity, 670-671
entering FTP, 397
environmental variables, setting, 444
Envoy, 359, 850
errors, shell scripts, 338
Ethernet, 133-134
buses, 134
firewalls, 216
frames, 134
security, 451-454
star topology, 134
ethernet, 850
Eudora, 53, 197, 472
evaluating, integrating applications, 713-714
EveryWare Development Corp., 184
EVN Records Inc., WANs, 154
Excel, Acrobat, 356
Exchange Server, 471
Excite search engine, 666, 683, 695
Exec directive, 242

Executive news service, 602
executive producer, Web sites, 759
Explorer, 193
Web site, 194
Exquisite Corpse game, 621-622
extensions, files
.AU, 848
.WAV, 859
Extensions Manager, 112

F

FAQs (Frequently Asked Questions), 337, 467, 850
message boards, 562
writing, 679
WWW Security FAQs, 222
faxes, *Times Fax*, **354**
faxing, 794-795
FDDI (Fiber Distributed Data Interface), 850
DAS, 136
LANs, 136-137
SAS, 136
security, 137
feedback, integrating applications, 713-714
Fetch, e-mail, 200-201
Fiber Distributes Data Interface, *see* **FDDI**
fiber optic cables, 132
FDDI, 850
fields, contact databases, 578-579
File menu commands, Mail Document, 696
file servers, LANs, 139, 147

file structures
designing, 729
FTP, 735
hardware, 730-731
platforms, 732
servers, 729-730
storing, UNIX servers, 731
troubleshooting, 730-731
UNIX, 732-733
Web servers, 734-735
Windows NT, 733
File Transfer Protocol, *see* **FTP**
file transfers, security, 258
files
access.conf, 236-237
archiving, 288-289
audio, 368
dynamic sites, 325
streaming, 370
audio formats
AU, 371
MPEG-Audio, 371
perceptual coding, 371
WAV, 371
AVI, 304
collaborative documents, 620-621
configuration
logs, 111
files, HTTPd, 100
DTD, 850
e-mail, 466-467
WANs, 468
envoy, 850
extensions
.AU, 848
.WAV, 859
flat file databases, 851

files

formats
   GIFs, 851
   JPEG, 854
FTP, 394-396, 416
grep utility, 851
.htaccess, 236-237
.htgroup, 239
.htpasswd, 743
Java, 853
JPEG, 302
Locker, 628
NFS, 855
PDFs, 353-354
   Acrobat, 355-356
   creating, 356-358
   distributing, 358
   embedding fonts, 357
   Times Fax, 354
   viewing, 358
   WordPerfect Envoy, 359
permissions, 226
protection setup, 231
restricting, 235-236
sending, FTP, 326
servers, 25
   LANs, 39
   vs. PCs, 34-36
SGML, 363-364
shared file systems, LANs, 210
storing, 729
   user accounts, 735
storing data, 328
system startup, logs, 111
transmissions, security, 258
UNIX commands,
   chmod, 849
   chown, 849
   chroot, 849

updating, 288-289
utmp, editing, 446
WAV, 375
.www acl, 233

financial considerations
hardware, 182-183
Internet telephones, 493
   intranets, 494-495
intranets, 182
   maintenance costs, 186
   upgrading, 186
online transactions, 777
servers, 79-80
   downtime, 80
   hardware, 118
   maintenance costs, 118
   software, 118
SGML, 365
software, 183-185
Web sites, 765-766

finding
domain names, 462
online news services, 602-603

firewalls, 176-177, 207, 216, 496-498
FTP, 416
software, 851
WANs, 217-218

First! Intranet, 610
flat file databases, 330, 851
flow charts, database users, 723
folders (SamePage), opening, 629
fonts
embedding PDFs, 357
HTML, 302
PDFs, 353

footprints, 187
ForeFront RoundTable, 38
formats
audio, 370-371
   .WAV, 859
   AU, 371
   MPEG-Audio, 371
   WAV, 371
DDF, 850
digital documents
   Acrobat, 355-356
   PostScript, 355
files
   JPEG, 854
FTP, 415-416
GIFs, 851
graphics, 302
interlacing, 302
PDFs, 352-354, 692, 855
   Acrobat, 355-356
   creating, 356-358
   distributing, 358
   embedding fonts, 357
   Times Fax, 354
   viewing, 358
   WordPerfect Envoy, 359
sounds
   .AU, 848
video, 382-383
video-conferencing, CIF/QCIF, 849

formatting documents, envoy, 850
forms
message boards, 566
Perl, writing, 340-342
WWW, 327-328
   browsers, 327

Forum, 569

forums
  chats, 595
  WebChat Web site, 592
Forums.com, 640-642
frame relays
  WANs, 153-154
    accessing, 160
frames
  Ethernet, 134
  rates, 851
  relays, 851
  sizes, 851
Free World Dialup (FWD), 489, 851
FreeVue, 507
freeware, 183, 857
  downloading, 374
  Web servers, 99
Frequently Asked Questions, *see* **FAQs**
FrontPage, 313
FTP (File Transfer Protocol), 47, 258, 325-326, 394-396, 413-415, 851
  advertising, 414
  anonymous, 395, 405, 417, 848
    building accounts, 406
    commands, 405
    configuring, 405
    testing, 408
  ASCII, 848
  binary, 848
  clients, 396-397, 408
    CuteFTP, 409
    DOS, 409
    Linux, 408
    MacOS, 410
    selecting, 411
    starting up, 409-410
    UNIX, 408
    Windows 3.x, 409
    Windows 95, 410
    Windows NT, 410
  command-line, e-mail, 201
  commands
    ascii, 398
    binary, 398
    bye, 398
    cd, 399
    chmod, 408
    close, 399
    dir, 399
    get, 396, 399
    hash, 399
    lcd, 400
    ls, 400
    mget, 400
    mput, 400
    open, 401
    put, 396, 401
    pwd, 401
    quit, 401
    user, 401
  compatability, 404
  directory trees, 410
  documents, submitting, 650
  e-mail, 200
  entering, 397
  example, 404
  file structures, 735
  file systems, 416
  files, sending, 326
  firewalls, 416
  formats, 415-416
  help, 398
  history of, 394
  home directories, building, 406-408
  intranets, 415
  listing, 402-403
  security, 416
  servers, 396-397, 411, 721, 724
    accessing, 416-417
    configuring, 413
    DOS, 412
    Linux, 411
    Macintosh, 412
    UNIX, 411
    Windows 3.1, 412
    Windows 95, 412
    Windows NT, 412-413
  sharing files
    Internet, 414
  TCP/IP, 404, 413
FTP menu commands, Connection, 409
FTP Software, Inc., 185
full duplex, 851
functions
  databases, user groups, 719
  dynamic sites, 320
  security, 744-745
FWD (Free World Dialup), 489, 851

G

Gamelan Web site, 346, 595
games, Exquisite Corpse, 621-622
gateways, 143, 851
  CGI, 518, 849
  databases, 422
  faxing, 794-795
  FWD, 851
  see also CGI
Geffen/DGC Records Web site, 370
get command (FTP), 396, 399

**GetMask <group syntax>
directive, 231**
GIF89 format, 302
GIFs, 324, 851
GIX (Global Information eXchange), 851
Global Chat client, 483
Global Stage IRC chat server, 481
  Café version, 482
  Stadium version, 482
  Theater version, 482
goals for creating Web sites, 763
goals for intranets, 12
GoldMine, 582-583
GoldWave, 374
Goodbody Community Hospital, WANs, 155
Gopher, 106
Graphical User Interfaces (GUIs), 352
graphics
  applications, X Windows, 443-444
  formats
    interlacing, 302
    JPEG, 854
  GIFs, 324, 851
  help, 680-681
  interfaces, OpenWindows, 84
  JPEG, 302, 324
  Web browsers, 302
Grayfire, 611-612
grep utility, 851
GroupFile <filename> directive, 231
GroupId <group> directive, 231
groups
  administrative
    UNIX, 720

  betas, 848
  chats, 849
  conversations,
    moderators, 571-573
  creating, 232-233
    .www acl file, 233
  databases
    administrative, 720-721
    functions, 719
    users, 719-720
  documents, 620-622
  message boards, 591
  scheduling, 550-551
groupware, 36, 800-801, 851
  applications, converting to intranets, 39
  communicating with, 38-39
  defined, 34
  PCs vs. file servers, 34-36
GroupWise, 469, 474
  e-mail, 198
GroupWise WebAccess, 552
growth allowance, 432-433
guest access rights, 212
GUIs (Graphical User Interfaces), 352, 851
guiding users, 693
Gulf War IRC, 478

H

hackers (security), 222-223
Hackers Web site, 223
half duplex, 852

handbooks (employee), 270-271
hardware, 186, 748-749
  audio, 369-370
  bridges, 848
  clients, 51, 69
  compatibility, 748
  file structures, 730-731
  financial considerations, 182-183
  footprints, 187
  IBM compatibles, 188
  interfaces, 852
  Internet, 172-173
  Internet telephones, 488
  Macintosh, 187-188
  middleware, 854
  networks, 149-150
  operating systems, 82, 188-189, 192
    Linux, 191-192
    OS/2, 191
    Windows 3.1, 189
    Windows 95, 190
    Windows NT, 189-190
  platforms, 856
  routers, 857
  servers, 50, 60-63, 74, 125-126, 857
    financial considerations, 118
    Intel, 125-126
    Macintosh, 126
    network interfaces, 126
    upgrading, 749-750
  testing, 749
  video-conferencing, 507-508
hardware platform, 852
hash command (FTP), 399

Index

help, FTP, 398
help desks, 674-677
  chat lines, 684
  e-mail
    addresses, 682-683
    routers, 684
  FAQs, writing, 679
  images, 680-681
  Office, 675
  RealAudio Player, 676
  running, 681-682
  search engines, 680
  software, purchasing, 684-685
  Windows NT, 677
  WinZip, 675
  writing, 678-680
Hero Village, 592
high-end applications, 799
home directories
  / (slashes), 240
  FTP, building, 406-408
home pages, *see* **WWW, sites**
hooks, 708
Hoover, 604
host names, 461
hosts, trusted, 452, 859
  rlogin, 442
HotDog Pro, 314-315
hoteling, 788, 852
HoTMetaL, 315-316
HotWired **magazine, 562**
HP-UX, 852
.htaccess file, 236-237
htadm program, 231-232
  troubleshooting, 232
.htgroup file, 239
HTML (HyperText Markup Language), 352, 364, 514, 852
  browsers, 300
  directories, personal, 240-241
  fonts, 302
  SSI, 516
  static files, 323
  tags, <SCRIPT>, 523-525
  Web browsers, 302
htpasswd file, 743
HTTP, 852
  Mac HTTP, 98-99
  servers, APIs, 517
  Webchat, 860
HTTPd, 99
httpd (hypertext transfer protocol daemon), 61
HTTPd Web site, 99
Human Resources, 277
hyperlinked records, contact databases, 580
hyperlinks, NetNotes, 570
hypertext, 852
  help desk, writing, 678
  httpd, 61
HyperText Markup Language, *see* **HTML**

I

IBM compatibles, 188
  operating systems, 188-189
iChat, 483
IDE, 852
IDs, administrators, 286-287
IIS (MS-Internet Information Server), 427, 733
  Windows NT, 97-98
images
  dynamic sites, 323-325
  formats, interlacing, 302
  GIFs, 324, 851
  help, 680, 681
  JPEG, 324, 854
  Web browsers, 302
IMAP (Interactive Mail Access Protocol), 196, 469-470, 852
implementing
  application integration, 712-713
  databases
    FTP servers, 721
    security, 722
    Web servers, 721-722
  servers, 114-117
    log books, 120
  users, databases, 721-724
  video-conferencing, 508-509
  WANs, 156-157
in-house applications, 716
Individual, Inc., First! Intranet, 610
Infomatic Electric Library, 691
Information, Inc., 608-609
Informedia, 691
Informix, 425
initial capacity, servers, 74
initial parameters, log umbrellas, 111
input, users, 541
inputting data, dynamic sites, 322
  audio, 323-325
  images, 323-325

inventory data, 322
    static, 323
installing
    Netscape Enterprise
        Server, 94-95
    servers, 120-122
        hardware, 125-126
        instructions, 125
        *troubleshooting,
            123-125*
    software, logs, 112
    Web servers, software,
        94
**instances, documents,
    364**
**instructing intranet users,
    265**
instructions, servers, 125
**InTandem, 555-569, 627,
    639, 653**
    contact databases, 581
    Library, 654
**Integrated Services
    Digital Network,** *see*
    ISDN
integrating
    applications, 703-706,
        710-711
        evaluating, 713-714
        feedback, 713-714
        frequency, 708
        functionality, 708
        *implementing,
            712-713*
        networks, 708-709
        purpose of, 707
        stand-alone, 709-710
    databases, 433-435
    inventory, 711-712
Intel, 125-126
    servers, 76-77
**intelligent agents,
    795-796, 852**

interactive
    communications
    intranets, 25-28
**interactive databases,
    520-521**
**Interactive Mail Access
    Protocol (IMAP), 196,
    469, 852**
interactive sites, *see*
    dynamic sites
**interactive transmissions,
    259-260**
    security, 258
**intercepted transmissions,
    248**
interfaces, 852
    APIs, 516-517
    applications, hooks, 708
    BBSs, 45
    BRIs, 167
    CGI, 328-330,
        518-520, 849
        directories, 519
        scripts, 338
    databases, 342
    FDDI, 850
    GUIs, 352, 851
    IDE, 852
    interfaces, 133
    ISAPI, 517
    LANs, 133
        ARCnet, 135-136
        ATM, 137-138
        Ethernet, 133-134
        FDDI, 136-137
        Token Ring, 135-136
    middleware, 854
    networks, 126
    NIC/MAC, 855
    NSAPI, 517
    OpenWindows, 84
    PCN, 530
    Perl, 529-530

SCSI, 857
users, 769
WSAPI, 517
interlacing, 302
**internal message boards,
    566-567**
Internet, 47, 852
    addresses, 170-172
    applications, 714
    BITNET, 48
    connecting, 165,
        175-176
        *dial-up analog services,
            166-167*
        *digital PPP accounts,
            167*
        hardware, 172-173
        LANs, 167-169
        routers, 173-174
        *server software,
            174-175*
        *setting up LANs,
            169-170*
        *SLIP dial-up accounts,
            167*
        software, 172-173
        workstations, 174
    connections, wireless,
        777
    CSNET, 48
    DARPA, 47
    DCT, 850
    documents, copyrights,
        693
    e-mail, POP3, 856
    FTP, 47, 415
        sharing files, 414
    gateways, 851
        FWD, 851
    GIX, 851
    history of, 164-165
    ISPs, 853
        selecting, 165

systems integrators, 178-179
multimedia designers, 762
NCP, 47
needs assessment, 855
open standards, 855
protocols, real-time, 856
resources, 688-690
  linking, 690-693
  searching, 694
security, 176
  firewalls, 176-177
software developers, 761
systems administrators, 762-763
telephones, 488
  bandwidths, 490, 498
  bandwidths in intranets, 494
  buffering, 491
  clients, 498-499
  defined, 488-489
  financial considerations, 493
  financial considerations for intranets, 494-495
  firewalls, 497-498
  FWD, 489
  hardware requirements, 488
  history of, 491-493
  intranets, 493-494
  LANs, 491
  legal issues, 497
  operators, 489
  protocols in intranets, 493-494
  regulations, 497
  RTP, 489
  servers, 491, 496-497
  software, 492
  sound quality, 492
  speed in intranets, 493
  video-conferencing, 498
  video-phones, 495-496
  voice links on Web pages, 495
  WANs, 491
Usenet, 859
video, 382
video-conferencing, 509
voices, 377-379
VON, 859
WANs, 217
WWW, searching, 694-698
Internet Assistant, 310-311
Internet Chat, 203
Internet Explorer, 301, 304-305, 348
  ActiveX, 305
Internet Information Server, *see* **IIS**
Internet Information Server Web site, 98
Internet Mail Access Protocol, *see* **IMAP**
Internet Phone, 203, 376-377, 777, 852
  Chat, 484
Internet Relay Chat, *see* **IRC**
Internet Server API (ISAPI), 517
Internet terminal, 853
Internet Worm, sendmail command (UNIX), 224
internetworking devices, 249
internetworks, 853
InterNotes, 655

IntraActive
  InTandem, 555-557, 568-569, 627, 653
    contact databases, 581
IntraActive Web site, 92
Intranet Journal, 563
intranets, 5-6, 801-802
  accessing, 9
  applications
    future of, 796-797
    high-end, 799
    mid-range, 799
  associations, dates, 29
  bandwidths, 790-793
  businesses, 20-25
    future of, 782-784
  chats, 594-595
  checklists, 10-11
  collaborative documents, 623-626
  communicating with, 38-39
  contact databases, 577-578
  corporations, 37
  defined, 4-5, 853
  designing, 17-19, 536-539
    user input, 541
    user participating, 541-543
    users, 540-541
  e-mail, 5
  efficiency, 7-8
  financial considerations, 182
    maintenance costs, 186
    software, 183-185
    upgrading, 186
  First! Intranet, 610
  FTP, 415
  future of, 782
  goals, 12

intranets

groupware, 800-801
hardware, 186
Human Resources, 277
interactive communications, 25-28
Internet telephones, 493-494
  bandwidths, 494
  financial considerations, 494-495
  protocols, 493-494
  regulations, 497
  servers, 496-497
  speed of, 493
  video-phones, 495-496
LANs, 265-266
message boards, 567-571
online privacy, 646-647
open standards, 789-790
organizations, 9-10
posting materials to, 18
scheduling, 276-277
security, 70-71, 206, 222, 344-345
  authentication points, 207-208
  building, 206-207
servers, security, 227
software, training users, 268
starting, 13-14
technical requirements, 539-540
Internet telephones
  voice links on Web pages, 495
  legal issues, 497
  timeliness, 9
training users, 278-281
  McKeon & Jeffries, 281-283
  message boards, 282
  online, 282
  SGAA, 281-283
updating, 9
usage levels, 16
user survey, 543-547
users
  connecting, 264-268
  instruction sheets, 265
  online, 269-273
  training, 264
video, 383
WANs, 161
wireless, 793-794
workflow, 276-277
inventories, 434
  integrating, 711-712
inventory datasheets, 322
Investor's Business Daily, 690
IP addresses, 853
  DCT, 850
  DNS, 850
  firewalls, 216
  restricting, 235
IP Phones, 853
IPX network, 853
IRC (Internet Relay Chat), 478-480, 591, 853
  applications, 480-481
  Chat
    Global Chat client, 483
    Internet Phone, 484
    servers, 481-483
    video-conferencing, 484
  clients, 483-484

Global Stage IRC chat server
  Café version, 482
  Stadium version, 482
  Theater version, 482
Gulf War, 478
iChat, 483
Ircle, 483
Quarterdeck Web site, 480
software, 106
Ircle, 483
ISAPI (Internet Server API), 517
ISDN (Integrated Services Digital Network), 144-145, 267, 853
  BRIs, 167
ISO, 853
ISPs (Internet Service Providers), 46-47, 853
  history of, 164-165
  Internet
    connecting to, 165, 175-176
    dial-up analog services, 166
  Internet addresses, 170-172
  LANs
    dedicated, 167-169
    dial-up, 167-169
  PPP accounts, 166-167
    digital, 167
  routers, 173-174
  selecting, 164-165
  servers, software, 174-175
  shell accounts, 166
  SLIP, dial-up accounts, 166-167
  systems integrators, 178-179

workstations, 174
IWave, 373

J-K

Java, 305, 527-529, 853
  applets, 346, 527, 853
    alert messaging, 590
  defined, 345-346
  source code, 528
  tutorial, 345
  vs. JavaScript, 523
  Web sites, creating, 775

JavaScript, 346-348, 521-524, 853
  applets, 590
  case sensitive, 523
  listing, 346-347
  output, 524
  vs. Java, 523

Joint Photographic Experts Group (JPEG) files, 302, 324, 854

journalism, *see* **news services (online)**

JPEG (Joint Photographic Experts Group), 302, 324, 854

Kbps, 854
kerberos, 214-215
  servers, 259
keyword searches, 662-663
Korn shells, 336

L

languages
  Java, 527-529, 853
  JavaScript, 521-524, 853

  Perl, 529-530, 855
  PostScript, 856
  SGML, 857
  SQL, 858
  VBScript, 524-526, 859
  VRML, 526-527, 859

LANs (Local Area Networks), 130, 210, 854
  security, 208-209
  ABC Widgets Inc., 158
  access rights
    anonymous, 212
    guests, 212
  accessing, 212-213
    resources, 213
  AppleTalk, 141-142
  bridges, 157, 848
  buses, tokens, 135
  cabling, 146
  communications servers, 143, 148-149
  connecting, 131, 157
    coaxial cables, 131
    fiber optic cables, 132
    twisted pair cabling, 131-132
  contact databases, 577
  DECnet, 142
  dedicated, 167-169
  dial-up, 167-169
  dial-up analog services, 850
  ethernet, 850
  file servers, 39, 139, 147
  FTP, 394-396
  gateways, 143
  groupware, 39, 851
  hardware, 149-150
  interfaces, 133
    ARCnet, 135-136
    ATM, 137-138

    Ethernet, 133-134
    FDDI, 136-137
    Token Ring, 135-136
  Internet telephones, 491
  internetworks, 853
  intranets, 265-266
  ISDNs, 144-145
  LANtastic, 141
  MAC cards, 133
  modems, 142-144
  NetWare, 139-140
  networks, servers, 145-147
  NIC, 133
  NOSs, 138-139
  Novell, 158
  online scheduling, 551
  OSI, 142
  packet sniffers, 248-249
  paths, defining, 211-212
  PCs, 43
  PPP, 144
  Radio Frequency (RF), transmitters/receivers, 132
  remote access, 142
  remote network connections, 856
  resources, 209
  routers, 157-158, 173-174, 857
  security, 213
    access rights, 211-212
    passwords, 215-216
    paths, 211
    testing, 219-220
    universal access, 211
    usernames, 215
    users, 210-211
  servers
    e-mail, 148
    print, 148
    WWW, 149

LANs (Local Area Networks) UNLEASHED

setting up, 169-170
shared file systems, 210
TCP/IP, 141
telecommuting, 142
token rings, 859
users, resources, 210
Windows for
  Workgroups, 140
Windows NT, 140
wireless, 132-133
XNS, 142
LANtastic
  LANs, 141
last command, 445-446
lcd command (FTP), 400
legal issues, Internet telephones, 497
libraries
  cgi-lib.pl, 340
  DBI, 342
  Electric Library Web site, 690
  Informedia, 691
  InTandem, 653-654
  linking resources, 690-693
  Livelink, 654-655
  Perl, 529
  users, guiding, 693
Library of Congress Web site, 692
Limit directive, 236-238
linking, 768
  documents, 354-355
  networks, bandwidths, 848
  OLE, 855
  resources, 690-693
  see also OLE
links, 429
  UNIX, directories, 732
  voice, Web pages, 495

Linux, 65, 86, 191-192, 854
  FTP, 408
    servers, 411
Linux Web site, 191
listings
  The ac -d command, 446
  FTP, 402-403
  Initiating a Telnet session., 439
  JavaScript, 346-347
  The last command, 446
  Output from ps -aux command, 448
  Output from the ps -alx command, 449
  Perl, 340
    writing forms, 340-342
  ps -aux special program, 454
  The ps command, 448
  shell scripts, 337
  SQL, 343
  The who command, 445
listservs, 325-326, 467-468, 854
  addresses, 467
Live3D, 304
Livelink, 664-667
LiveLink Intranet, 36
Livelink Library, 654-655
Local Area Networks, *see* **LANs**
Locker, 627-628
  documents, downloading, 627
  files, 628
log books, 120
  servers, 119-120
    implementing, 120

log umbrellas, 110-111
  initial parameters, 111
logging on/off, usage analysis, 287-288
logins, monitoring (Telnet), 444-447
logs, 110-113
  administering, 113
  electronic, 113
  emergency startup procedures, 111
  software, installing, 112
  system administrators, 113
  system startup files, 111
  umbrellas, users with root access, 113
Lotus InterNotes, 655
ls command (FTP), 400
lurkers, 572
Lycos, online news services, 602

M

MAC (Media Access Control) cards, 133
Mac HTTP, 98-99
Macintosh, 64, 126, 187-188
  FTP, servers, 412
  Ircle, 483
  servers, 78-79, 127
  video
    compatibility, 384
    QuickTime, 385
    system requirements, 384
  video-conferencing, system requirements, 508
Macintosh Extensions Manager, 112

MacOS, 88, 410
Mail Document command (File menu), 696
mail, *see* e-mail
mailbots, 467
mailing
   alert messaging, 591
   lists, 467-468
      Edupage, 468
      listservs, 854
MailServer 2.0, 103
mainframes, 42-43
maintenace, servers, 92, 118, 186
man pages, 447
managers, documents, 620-621, 624
manuals, 24
mapping Web sites, 225
marketing
   video-conferencing, 504
   Web sites, 772-773
masking data, 854
MBONE, 505, 854
Mbps, 854
McKeon & Jeffries, 596, 625-626
   audio, 378
   authoring tools, 316
   browsers, 306
   contact databases, 584
   database users, tracking, 723
   e-mail, 475
   encrypting, 256
   firewalls, 177-178
   hardware, 186-187
   help desk, 678
   integrating applications, 706
   intranet usage levels, 23
   message boards, 573

online news services, 609
online scheduling, 554
online users, 274-275
operating systems, 90
PDFs, 359
private message boards, 638
search engines, 672
security, 218, 742-743
servers, 78, 102
   installing, 122
   operating systems, 66
software, upgrading, 752
submitting documents, 657
training administrators, 295
training intranet users, 268-269, 281
   online, 283
user space, 736
WANs, 162
workflow, 278
Media Access Control (MAC) cards, 133
Media Machine, LLC
   Forums.com, 640-642
medical services, video-conferencing, 504
memory
   buffering, 849
   financial considerations, 182
   VMS, 859
message boards, 24, 562, 566, 854
   archiving, 572
   chats, 591
      MOOs, 592
      MUDs, 592
   creating, 566

FAQs, 562
forms, 566
group conversations, 571-573
HotWired magazine, 562
InTandem, 568-569
internal, 566-567
intranets, 567-571
lurkers, 572
NetNotes, 570-571
O'Reilly WebBoard, 568
private, 31, 634-635
SGAA, 31
threads, 562, 858
training users, 282
Usenet, 563
Web Crossing, 563, 571
The Well, 563
Wooley's Web Conferencing Page, 564
WWW, 563-565
message boards (private)
   Forums.com, 640-642
   Motet Conferencing, 642
   removing, 637
   software
      configuring, 638-640
      customizing, 635-637
   WebShare, 644-646
Message Composition dialog box, 696
messages
   alerts, 588
   e-mail, 464
      addressing, 461
      aliasing, 463-464
      bandwidths, 464-465
      documents, 467
      domain names, 461-463

messages

pipes, 464-465
remote messaging, 464
group message boards, 591
POP3, 856
transmission security, 246-247
messaging
  alerts, 589-591
    Java applets, 590
    mailing, 591
    SGAA, 596
  real-time, 588-591
    Quote.com news service, 589-590
    stocks, 589
  remote, 464
metafiles, 376
mget command (FTP), 400
microprocessors
  hardware platform, 852
  PID, 855
Microsoft Internet Explorer, 301
Microsoft ActiveX, *see* **ActiveX**
Microsoft Exchange Server, *see* **Exchange Server**
Microsoft ISAPI Web site, 517
Microsoft SQL Server, 427-428
Microsoft Web site, 526
Microsoft Windows NT, *see* **Windows NT**
Microsoft Word, 310
  downloading, 704
mid-range applications, 799
Middleware, 53-54
middleware, 854

shell scripts, 338
minutes, applications, 704
mirroring, 430, 850
mission statements, Web sites, 765
modems, 854
  bandwidths, 790-793
  BBSs, 46
  bps, 848
  comm ports, 143
  dial-up analog service, 850
  LANs, 142-144
    communications servers, 143
    gateways, 143
moderators, group conversations, 571-573
modes
  ASCII, 848
  binary, 848
monitoring
  database users, 724-725
  logins, Telnet, 444-447
MOOs (MUDs Object Oriented), 854
  building, 592
  Hero Village, 592
  software, downloading, 594
Mosaic, 195, 302, 854-855
  Web site, 196
Motet Conferencing, 642
Moving Worlds (VRML), 304
MPEG, 854
MPEG-Audio file format, 371
mput command (FTP), 400
MS-Internet Information

Server, *see* IIS
MUDs (MultiUser Dimensions), 478, 854
  building, 592
MUDS Object-Oriented, *see* **MOOs**
multimedia, Internet multimedia designers, 762
  see also audio; sounds; video
multitasking, 440
MultiUser Dimensions, *see* **MUDs**

N

N-Plex, 36
  domain names, restricting, 235
National Center for Supercomputing, *see* **NCSA**
natural language query, 854
Navigator, 301-304, 518, 656-657
Navigator Gold, 312-313
NCompass, 348
NCP (Network Control Protocol), 47
NCSA, 855
  ScriptAlias directive, 242
  servers
    .htaccess file, 236-237
    access.conf file, 236-237
    authenticating, 236
    creating passwords, 239
    creating users, 239
  Telnet, 203

Index

NCSA Mosaic, 302
near-WYSIWYG, 314
    HotDog Pro, 314-315
    HoTMetaL, 315-316
needs assessment, 855
NETCOM On-line Communications, Inc., 185
NetManage, Inc., 185
NetNotes, 570-571
Netra, 76
Netsacpe
Netscape, 193, 301-304, 855
    API, 517
    Chat, 203
    CoolTalk, 107, 204
    e-mail, 197
        servers, 470-471
    Enterprise Server, 94-95
    Internet Explorer, 304-305
    Live3D, 304
    Mail, 474-476
    MailServer 2.0, 103
    Navigator, 301, 518, 656-657
    Navigator Gold, 312
    NCSA Mosaic, 302
    News Server, 105
    PDFs, 358
    plug-ins, 303
    PowerBrowser, 306
Netscape NSAPI Web site, 517
Netscape Web site, 194, 303
NetWare, 139-140
network administrators (Sysops), 588
Network Control Protocol (NCP), 47

Network File System (NFS), 210
Network Information System (NIS), 210
Network Interface Card (NIC), 133
Network Manager, StreamWorks, 386-387
Network News Corporation, 612-613
Network News Transport Protocol (NNTP), 104
Network Operating Systems, *see* NOSs
networking, ATM, 848
NetworkMusic Web site, 370
networks
    applications, 708-709, 855
        stand-alone, 709-710
    bandwidths, 848
    bridges, 249, 848
    circuit switching, 849
    FDDI, 850
    firewalls, software, 851
    frame relays, 851
    gateways, 851
    groupware, 851
    hardware, 149-150
    interfaces, 126
    Internet, 852
    IP Phones, 853
    IPX, 853
    IRC, clients, 483-484
    ISDN, 853
    ISPs, 853
    LANs, 130, 854
        access rights, 211-212
        accessing, 212-213
        AppleTalk, 141-142
        ARCnet, 135-136
        ATM, 137-138

        bridges, 157
        cabling, 146
        client/servers, 139
        coaxial cables, 131
        communications servers, 143, 148-149
        connecting, 131, 157
        contact databases, 577
        defining paths, 211-212
        e-mail servers, 148
        Ethernet, 133-134
        ethernet, 850
        FDDI, 136-137
        fiber optic cables, 132
        file servers, 139, 147
        gateways, 143
        interfaces, 133
        internetworks, 853
        ISDNs, 144-145
        LANtastic, 141
        MAC cards, 133
        modems, 142-144
        NetWare, 139-140
        NOSs, 138-139
        paths, 211
        print servers, 148
        remote access, 142
        resources, 209
        routers, 157-158
        security, 208-210, 213
        setting up, 169-170
        shared file systems, 210
        TCP/IP, 141
        telecommuting, 142
        Token Ring, 135-136
        twisted pair cabling, 131-132
        users, 210

Web servers, 149
Windows for Workgroups, 140
Windows NT, 140
wireless, 132-133
MBONE, 854
NFS, 855
NIC/MAC, 855
NOSs, 855
packet sniffers, 248-249
packet switching, 855
packet-switched, 47
peer, 709
post name checks, 214
remote network connection, 856
routers, 249
search engines, 857
security, 206-207, 260, 344-345
  authenticating, 214
  authentication points, 207-208
  crackers, 745
  firewalls, 216
  levels, 261
  passwords, 215-216, 742
  permissions, 207
  SATAN, 745-746
  testing, 219-220
  transmissions, 246-247
  troubleshooting, 257
  usernames, 215
servers
  defined, 49
  setting up, 145-147
software, Internet Phone, 852
sonets, 858
spoofing, 249-251
SSLs, 858
TCP/IP, 858
token rings, 859
transmissions
  defined, 247
  DES, 253
  encrypting, 251-252, 255-256
  files, 258
  interactive, 259-260
  intercepted messages, 248
  internetworking devices, 249
  private key encrypting, 252-253
  public key encrypting, 253-255
  security, 251
twisted pair cables, 859
VON, 304
WANs, 152, 468, 859
  56K circuits, 159
  accessing, 159-160
  ATM, 156, 160-161
  communications, 161-162
  connecting, 157, 161
  DDS, 152-153
  e-mail, 468
  firewalls, 217-218
  frame relays, 153-154, 160
  implementing, 156-157
  security, 161, 216-217
  SMDS, 155-156, 160
  Sonet, 155
  T-1 circuits, 153, 160
  T-1 services, 153
  T-3 circuits, 153, 160

new services, clipping services, 606-608
New York Times
  Times Fax, 354
news
  servers, 104-105
    Netscape News Server, 105
  Usenet, 859
news services (online), 600-604
  accessing, 602-603
  Associated Press (AP), 605
  Bloomberg Personal, 606
  Clickshare, 603
  clipping services, 604
  DowVision, 607
  e-mail digests, 607
  Executive, 602
  First! Intranet, 610
  Grayfire, 611-612
  Hoover, 604
  Information, Inc., 608-609
  Lycos, 602
  McKeon & Jeffries, 609
  Network News Corporation, 612-613
  NewsAlert, 614-616
  NewsEDGE, 613
  PointCast, 602-603
  Progressive Network, 615
  Quote.com, 589-590
  Reuters, 605
  Reuters Business Alert, 605
  SGAA, 30, 616
  subscribing, 604
  Timecast, 615

UPI, 605
Yahoo!, 602
NewsAlert, 614-616
  accessing, 615
NewsEDGE, 613
newsletters, 24
  intranets, 272
NFS (Network File System), 210, 855
NIC (Network Interface Card), 133
NIC/MAC card, 855
NIS (Network Information System), 210
NNTP (Network News Transport Protocol), 104
nontextual data handling, 520
NOSs (Network Operating Systems), 138, 855
  LANs, 138-139
    AppleTalk, 141-142
    client/servers, 139
    LANtastic, 141
    NetWare, 139-140
    TCP/IP, 141
    Windows NT, 140
    Windows Workgroups, 140
Novell, LANs, 158
Novell GroupWise WebAccess, 552

NSAPI (Netscape API), 517
NSFNET, 852
NTMAIL, 103

O

OAK, *see* **Java**
Object Linking and Embedding, *see* **OLE**
objects
  COM, 348
  MOO, 854
  OLE, 855
  WOO, 860
Office
  help, 675
OLE (Object Linking and Embedding), 348, 855
  applications, integrating, 710-711
one-time pads, 253
online
  audio, 368
  intranet users, 269-273
  multimedia libraries, Informedia, 691
  privacy, 646-647
  researching, 694
  scheduling, 551-552
    applications, 553-555
    InTandem, 555-557
    WebShare Calendar, 557-558
  transactions, 777
  users
    McKeon & Jeffries, 274-275
    SGAA, 275
    training, 282
  yellow pages, 692
online documents, collaborations, 622-623, 630-631
online news services, 600-604
  accessing, 602-603

  Associated Press (AP), 605
  Bloomberg Personal, 606
  Clickshare, 603
  clipping services, 604-608
  DowVision, 607
  e-mail digests, 607
  Executive, 602
  First! Intranet, 610
  Grayfire, 611-612
  Hoover, 604
  Information, Inc., 608-609
  Lycos, 602
  McKeon & Jeffries, 609
  Network News Corporation, 612-613
  NewsAlert, 614-616
  NewsEDGE, 613
  PointCast, 602-603
  Progressive Network, 615
  Reuters, 605
  Reuters Business Alert, 605
  SGAA, 616
  subscribing, 604
  Timecast, 615
  UPI, 605
  Yahoo!, 602
online private conferences, 634
online scheduling, Crew Calendar, 558
online services, 46-47
OOP (Object Oriented Programming), Java, 345
open command (FTP), 401

open standards, 789-790, 855
OpenDOC applications, integrating, 710-711
opening SamePage folders, 629
OpenVMS, 859
OpenWindows, 84
operating systems, 89, 192
   BIOS, 848
   BSD/OS, 84-86
   IBM compatibles, 188-189
   Linux, 86, 191-192
   Macintosh servers, 127
   MacOS, 88
   middleware, 854
   NOSs, 855
      LANs, 138-139
   OS/2, 88, 191
   platforms, 856
   SCO UNIX, 84-86
   selecting, 83
   servers, 63-67, 82-83
      Linux, 65
      Macintosh, 64
      McKeon & Jeffries, 66
      UNIX, 65
      Windows 3.1, 63
      Windows 95, 63
      Windows NT, 64
   shell scripts, 336-339
   Solaris, 84
   UNIX, 83, 859
      servers, 127
   users, 89
   VAX, 859
   VMS, 859
   Windows servers, 127
   Windows 3.1, 189
   Windows 95, 190
   Windows NT, 86-87, 189-190
operators, Internet telephones, 489
Options directive, 236-238
Oracle, 668-670, 855
   databases, 426-427
   PowerBrowser, 305
   servers, 95-97
Oracle7 Workgroup Server, 97
O'Reilly and Associates WSAPI Web site, 517
O'Reilly WebSite server, 98
O'Reilly WebSite Web site, 98
O'Reilly's WebBoard, 568
organizations, 36
   communicating, 784-785
   hoteling, 788, 852
   information, 785-787
   international, 788
   intranets, 9-10, 37
      designing, 17-19
      goals, 12
   ISO, 853
   outsourcing, 788-789
   restructuring, 784
   telecommuting, 788
   teleconferencing, 798
   virtual corporations, 787
organizing intranets, 291
OS/2, 88, 191
   browsers, 195
OS/2 Web site, 195
OSI LANs, 142
output, JavaScript, 524
outsourcing, 788-789
   Web sites, 778-779

P

packets
   filtering, 453
   sniffers, 248-249
   switching, 855
      SMDS, 857
packet-switched networks, 47
palm-top computers, 797, 855
Panorama, SGML, 362
Paper Software, Live3D, 304
Paradox 7.0, 428-429
parameters (initial), log umbrellas, 111
Password dialog box, 228
PasswordFile <filename> directive, 231
passwords, 215-216
   administrators, 286-287
   authenticating, 214, 227-229
      CERN server, 229
      kerberos, 215
   creating, 231-232, 239
   database users, 724
      tracking, 722-724
   e-mail, 216, 742
   O'Reilly WebBoard, 568
   security, 741-742
   WANs, 217
Pat, 666-667
Pathfinder Web site, 566
paths (LANs)
   defining, 211-212
   security, 211
PCN interfaces, 530
PCs, 43-44
   LANs, 43
   mainframes, 42-43

Index

palm-top, 797, 855
  vs. file servers, 34-36
PDAs (Personal Digital Assistants), 576
PDF (Portable Document Format), 692
PDF Writer menu commands, Print, 358
PDFs, 352-354, 855
  Acrobat, 355-356
  creating, 356-358
  distributing, 358
  fonts, 353
    embedding, 357
  Netscape, 358
  technical support, 353
  Times Fax, 354
  viewing, 358
  WordPerfect Envoy, 359
peer networking, 709
perceptual coding, 371
Perl (Practical Extraction and Report Language), 339-342, 529-530, 855
  cgi-lib.pl, 340
  compilers, 339
  libraries, 529
  listing, 340
  sources, 339
  writing forms (listing), 340-342
  Web site, 340
permissions
  files, 226
  security, 207
Personal Digital Assistants (PDAs), 576
personal HTML directories, 240-241
PGP (Pretty Good Privacy), 744

phone lists, 579
phones, *see* **telephones**
physical security, 740-741
PictureWindow, 507-508
PID (process ID), 448, 855
Pine, 52, 472
  e-mail, 199
pipes, 464-465
pixels, 383
planning
  intranets, 536-539
  servers, 114-115
platforms, 856
  file structures, 732
playback video, 388-389
plug-ins, 518, 856
  Netscape, 303
  Netscape CoolTalk, 204
  Netscape Navigator, 518
  RealAudio, 518
  WBS, 591
Point of Presence (POP), 170
Point-to-Point Protocol, *see* **PPP**
PointCast, 602-603
pointers, 429
POP (Point of Presence), 170
POP3, 469, 856
Portable Document Format (PDF), 692
portfolios, video-conferencing, 504
ports, 441
  comm, 143
  numbers, 441
post name checks, 214
Post Office, 470
posting material to intranets, 18
PostScript, 355, 856

PowerBrowser, 305
PPP (Point-to-Point Protocol), 266, 856
  accounts, dial-up analog services, 166-167
  digital, 167
  LANs, 144
Practical Extraction and Report Language, *see* **Perl**
Premiere, 383
Pretty Good Privacy (PGP), 744
prewritten TCP/IP applications, 530-531
Print command (PDF Writer menu), 358
print servers
  LANs, 148
  spooling jobs, 148
priorities of intranets, defining, 537-538
privacy on intranets, 291
privacy online, 646-647
private comments, contact databases, 579
private key encrypting, 252-253
  DES, 253
private message boards, 31, 634-635
  Forums.com, 640-642
  Motet Conferencing, 642
  removing, 637
  software
    configuring, 638-640
    customizing, 635-637
  WebShare, 644-646
privileges, accessing databases, 719-721
process control, 447-450

process ID (PID), 448
process table, 447-450, 453-454
processing batches, 336
processors, RISC, 856
product managers, Web sites, 759-760
production managers, Web sites, 760
production teams, Web sites
 creating, 758-759
 design managers, 760
 editorial managers, 760-761
 executive producers, 759
 product managers, 759-760
 production managers, 760
 program managers, 760
profiles, contact databases, 580-584
program managers, Web sites, 760
programming
 ActiveX, 348-349
 JavaScript, 346-348
Progressive Network, 615
 RealAudio, 372, 596
progressive rendering, 302
projects, *see* WWW, sites, 759
Protect directive, 230
protecting, *see* security
Protection directive, 234
protection setup files, 231
protocols, 856
 ATM, 848
 client/servers, 48
 daemons, 850

FDDI, 850
FTP, 258, 325-326, 851
 anonymous, 848
 entering, 397
 help, 398
 history of, 394
HTTP, 852
IMAP, 196, 469, 852
IMAP4, 470
Internet telephones, intranets, 493-494
NCP, 47
NFS, 855
POP3, 856
PPP, 266, 856
 LANs, 144
 real-time, 856
 rlogin, 857
RTP, 489
SLIP, 857
SMTP, 328, 469, 858
 e-mail, 460
TCP/IP, 858
 Internet telephones, 493
Telnet, 858
UDP, 504, 859
 Internet telephones, 493
 see also FTP
ps command, 447-450
public comments, contact databases, 579
public key encrypting, 253-255
publications, association intranets, 30
publishing newsletters, 272
purchasing help software, 684-685
purchasing information, 434

put command (FTP), 396, 401
pwd command (FTP), 401

Q-R

Quarterdeck
 Global Stage IRC chat server, 481
 Mac HTTP, 98-99
 Web site, 480
queries
 natural language query, 854
 search engines, 660
 SQL, 342-344
QuickServer, 532-533
QuickTime, 385
quit command (FTP), 401
Quote.com news service, 589-590

RAD, 856
Radio Frequency (RF) transmitters/receivers, 132
Radnet
 WebShare, 624, 644-646
 WebShare Calendar, 557-558
 Web site, 557
RAID, 856
ranges, applications, 707
rates, frames, 851
RDBMS, 856
real estates, video-conferencing, 504
Real Time Protocol (RTP), 489

Index

real-time
  chat, 591
    group message boards, 591
    saving, 596
    streaming audio, 595
    WBS, 591
  messaging, 588-591
    Quote.com news service, 589-590
    stocks, 589
  news, 612
  protocols, 856
  video, 856
  video-conferencing, 502-503
    CU-SeeMe, 502
RealAudio, 106, 325, 372, 595
  alert messaging, SGAA, 596
  Progressive Network, 615
RealAudio Player, help, 676
RealAudio plug-in, 518
RealAudio Web site, 107, 376, 615
receivers, RFs, 132
receiving e-mail, POP3, 469
recorded video, creating, 383-385
recording audio, 373-376
records (hyperlinked), contact databases, 580
Reference Desk
  guiding users, 693
  researching online, 694
references, 688-690
  SGAA, 31
reflectors, 505, 856

video-conferencing without, 505
video-phones, 496
registry, Netscape plug-ins, 303
regulations, Internet telephones, 497
relational databases, 330-332, 425, 856
  Oracle, 668-670
  RDBMS, 856
relays, frames, 851
  WANs, 153-160
remote access, LANs, 142
remote login, Telnet, 438-440
remote messaging, 464
remote network connection, 856
Remote Procedure Calls (RPCs), 260
remote systems, problems, 450-451
removing private message boards, 637
renderings, progressive, 302
replacing, grep utility, 851
replicating data, 430-432
replication, 430
requests, client/servers, 48
requirements
  hardware, Internet telephones, 488
  intranets, technical, 539-540
  Macintosh video, 384
  Web sites, 770
requisitions, 434

research, 25
researching online, 694
resources, 688-690
  LANs, 209
    accessing, 213
    users, 210
  linking, 690-693
restricting
  domain names, 235
  files, 235-236
  IP addresses, 235
  users, 235
Reuters, 605
Reuters Business Alert, 605
rights, accessing databases, 719-721
RISC processors, 856
rlogin, 438, 857
  compared to Telnet, 441-442
  trusted hosts, 442
root access, users (log umbrellas), 113
roots, 857
RoundTable, 38
routers, 157-158, 173-174, 249, 851, 857
  ARP, 250
  Ascend, 173
  Cisco, 173
  e-mail, help, 684
  security, 218
RPCs (Remote Procedure Calls), security, 260
RTP (Real Time Protocol), 489
running
  help desks, 681-682
  online news services, 602-603
  Timecast, 615

S

sales, video-conferencing, 504
SamePage, 629-630
    documents, creating, 629
    folders, opening, 629
SAP AMERICA, 504
SAS (Single Attached Station), 136
SATAN (Security Administrator Tool), 745-746
saving chats, 596
scalability, servers, 74-75
Scaleable Processor Architecture (SPARC) servers, 75
scheduling, 276-277, 550-551
    applications, 555
    Crew Calendar, 558
    InTandem, 555-557
    Novell GroupWise WebAccess, 552
    online, 551-552
        applications, 553-554
    WebShare Calendar, 557-558
SCO UNIX, 84-86
<SCRIPT> HTML tag, 523-525
ScriptAlias directive, 242
scripting languages
    Java, 345-346
        applets, 346
    JavaScript, 346-348, 521, 853
    Perl, 339-342
    PostScript, 856
    VBScript, 524-526, 859
    VRML, 859

scripting languages, ActiveX, 348-349
scripts, 857
    CGI, 338
        accessing, 241
        directories, 241
        security, 222
        storing, 241
    shells, 336-339, 857
        errors, 338
        listing, 337
    SQL, 342-344
    writing, 342
SCSI, 857
SDK (Software Development Kit), 303
    ActiveX, 349
search engines, 661-698, 857
    AltaVista, 664-665
    Boolean, 662-663, 848
    contact databases, 580
    defined, 660
    Excite, 666, 683, 695
    help desk, 680
    keyword searches, 662-663
    Livelink, 664-667
    Pat, 666-667
    selecting, 671
    setting up, 663-664
    Sybase SQL, 670
    Verity, 670-671
searching
    grep utility, 851
    Web, 694
    WWW
        building bookmark lists, 697
        source code, 696
secure sockets layers, *see* SSLs

security, 206, 224, 260, 344-345
    access rights, 224-226
        guests, 212
        universal access, 211
    applications, 744-745
    authenticating, 214
        kerberos, 214-215
        passwords, 214
        post name checks, 214
        smartcards, 215
        usernames, 214
    authentication points, 207-208
    bridges, 249
    bugs, 223-224
    building, 206-207
    CERT, 257
    CGI scripts, 222
    client/servers, 257-258
    crackers, 223, 745
    daemons, 227
    database users, monitoring, 724-725
    databases, 722
    directives, 229
        DefProt, 230
        Exec, 242
        Limit, 237-238
        Options, 238
        Protect, 230
        ScriptAlias, 242
    domain names, restricting, 235
    e-mail, PGP, 744
    embedding, 234
    Ethernet, 451-454
    FDDI, 137
    file transfers, 258
    files
        permissions, 226
        restricting, 235-236

Index

firewalls, 176-177, 216, 497
  software, 851
FTP, 416
  firewalls, 416
groups, creating, 232-233
hackers, 222-223
interactive transmissions, 258
Internet, 176
intranets, 70-71, 222
IP addresses, restricting, 235
kerberos, 259
LANs, 208-210, 213
  access rights, 211-212
  accessing, 212-213
  defining paths, 211-212
  paths, 211
  resources, 209
  shared file systems, 210
  users, 210-211
levels, 261
mapping sites, 225
NCSA server
  .htaccess file, 236-237
  access.conf file, 236-237
networks, packet sniffers, 248-249
online privacy, 646-647
passwords, 215-216, 741-742
  authenticating, 227-229
  CERN server, 229
  creating, 231-232, 239
  e-mail, 742
permissions, 207

physical, 740-741
protection setup files, 231
removing programs, 227
routers, 249
RPCs, 260
SATAN, 745-746
sendmail command (UNIX), 224
servers, 93, 115, 227
software, 744-745
SSIs, enabling, 243-244
SSLs, 260
testing, 219-220
transmissions, 246-247, 251
  DES, 253
  encrypting, 251-252, 255-256
  files, 258
  interactive, 259-260
  intercepted, 248
  internetworking devices, 249
  private key encrypting, 252-253
  public key encrypting, 253-255
  spoofing, 249-251
troubleshooting, 257
usernames, 215
users
  accounts, 227
  creating, 239
  restricting, 235
WANs, 161, 216-217
  firewalls, 217-218
  passwords, 217
  usernames, 217
Windows NT, FTP servers, 413
WWW, security, 743-744

WWW Security FAQs, 222
Security Administrator Tool (SATAN), 745-746
selecting
  applications, 514-515
  domain names, 461
  FTP, clients, 411
  ISPs, 164-165
  LANs, 130
  operating systems, 82-83
  search engines, 671
sending
  e-mail, SMTP, 469
  files, FTP, 326
  messages, transmission security, 246-247
Sendmail, 102
sendmail command (UNIX), 224
SenseMedia, Sprawl Web site, 592-593
SEQUEL, *see* SQL
Server-Side Includes, *see* SSIs
ServerId <name> directive, 231
servers, 74-78, 115, 857
  Apache, 100
  ATMs, 50
  audio, software, 372
  BBSs, 44-46
  CERN, authenticating passwords, 229
  Chat, 481-483
    Global Stage IRC chat server, 481
  client/servers
    LANs, 139
    security, 257-258
  clients, 48-49

communications, 143
  LANs, 148-149
connecting, 69-70
corporations, 62
daemons, 174, 850
defined, 49
designing, 117-119
DNS, 850
downtime, 115
e-mail, 102-103, 469-470
  Exchange Server, 471
  GroupWise, 469
  LANs, 148
  MailServer 2.0, 103
  Netscape, 470-471
  NTMAIL, 103
  Post Office, 470
  SLmail, 104
environments, 75
file structures, 729-730
  storing, 729
files, 25
  LANs, 39, 139, 147
  vs. PCs, 34-36
financial considerations, 79-80
  downtime, 80
  maintenance costs, 118
FTP, 411, 721, 724
  accessing, 416-417
  configuring, 413
  DOS, 412
  Linux, 411
  Macintosh, 412
  UNIX, 411
  versus FTP clients, 396-397
  Windows 3.1, 412
  Windows 95, 412
  Windows NT, 412-413

hardware, 50, 60-63, 125-126
  financial considerations, 118
  Intel, 125-126
  Macintosh, 126
  network interfaces, 126
  upgrading, 750
HTTP, APIs, 517
HTTPd, 99
IIS, 97-98
implementing, 114-117
  log books, 120
initial capacity, 74
installing, 120-122
  instructions, 125
Intel, 76-77
Internet telephones, 491, 496-497
kerberos, 259
log books, 119-120
log umbrellas, initial parameters, 110-111
Mac HTTP, 98-99
Macintosh, 78-79, 127
middleware, 854
NCSA
  .htaccess file, 236-237
  access.conf file, 236-237
  authenticating, 236
  creating passwords, 239
  creating users, 239
Netra, 76
Netscape Enterprise Server, 94-95
  installing, 94-95
networks, setting up, 145-147
news, 104-105
  Netscape News Server, 105

operating systems, Linux, 65
operating systems, 63-67, 82-83, 89
  BSD/OS, 84-86
  Linux, 86
  Macintosh, 64
  MacOS, 88
  McKeon & Jeffries, 66
  OS/2, 88
  SCO UNIX, 84-86
  selecting, 83
  Solaris, 84
  UNIX, 65
  users, 89
  Windows 3.1, 63
  Windows 95, 63
  Windows NT, 64, 86-87
Oracle, 95-97
Oracle Universal Server Suite, 426
PPP, 856
print
  LANs, 148
  spooling jobs, 148
protocols, 48
reflectors, 856
scalability, 74-75
security, 93, 115, 227, 740
  daemons, 227
  passwords, 741
setting up, 92
shells, 337
software, 50, 67, 92-93, 118, 174-175
  financial considerations, 118
  installing, 94
SPARC, 75-77
SQL Server, 858
SSLs, 744

technical support, 75, 115
Telnet, 440-441
   enabling, 444-447
trade organizations, 62
troubleshooting, 123-125, 733-734
UNIX, 127
   file structures, 732-733
   storage space, 731
updating, 119
upgrading, 116, 749-750
   software, 750
user space, 735-737
users, 92
VDOLive, 387
video-conferencing, 504-505, 509
Web, 721-724
   file structures, 734-735
Web servers
   freeware, 99
   LANs, 149
   security, 222, 743-744
   SGAA, 68
   software, 67-68, 92-94
WebSite, 98
Windows, 127
services, *see* **news services (online)**
setting up
   LANs, 169-170
   networks, servers, 145-147
   search engines, 663-664
   servers, 92, 117-122
      hardware, 125-126
      instructions, 125

   log books, 120
   troubleshooting, 123-125
SGAA
   alert messaging, 596
   association intranets, 30-31
   audio, 378
   authoring tools, 316
   browsers, 306
   collaborative documents, 626
   contact databases, 584
   database users, monitoring, 725
   e-mail, 476
   encrypting, 256
   firewalls, 178
   help desk, 678
   integrating applications, 706
   message boards, 573-574
   online news services, 616
   online scheduling, 554-555
   online users, 275
   operating systems, 90, 192
   PDFs, 359
   private message boards, 638
   search engines, 672
   security, 219, 743
   servers, 79, 102
      installing, 122-123
   software, upgrading, 752
   submitting documents, 657
   training administrators, 295

   training intranet users, 269, 281
      online, 283
   user space, 737
   WANs, 162
   Web servers, 68
   workflow, 278
SGML (Standard Generalized Markup Language), 300, 362-366, 857
   accessing, 365
   disseminating information, 365
   documents, 364
      compiling, 365
      DTDs, 364
      instances, 364
      tags, 858
   DTDs, 365, 850
   files, 363-364
   financial considerations, 365
   HTML, 364
   Panorama, 362
   tags, 363
   troubleshooting, 365-366
shared file systems, LANs, 210
shared resources, contact databases, 576-577
shareware, 183, 857
   CuteFTP, 409
   Linux, 86
sharing
   documents, SGAA, 30
   files
      e-mail, 466-467
      Locker, 628
shells
   accounts, 857
      dial-up analog services, 166

BASH, 336
Bourne, 336
C, 336
commands, 336
FAQs, 337
Korn, 336
scripts, 336-339, 857
    errors, 338
    listing, 337
servers, 337
Single Attached Station (SAS), 136
single-client applications, 794
sites
    dynamic, 320-322
        audio, 323-325
        e-mail, 325-326
        functions, 320
        images, 323-325
        inputting data, 322
        inputting static data, 323
        inventory datasheets, 322
        WWW forms, 327-328
    searching, 694-698
    Web sites, 769
        Access America, 389
        accessing, 290
        Acrobat, 354
        Adobe, 358
        agents, 777
        AlphaWorld, 594
        Apache, 100
        audio streaming, 776
        Bloomberg Personal, 606
        BROWSE, 343
        business planning, 763
        CERT, 257
        concepts, 763-765

Cornell University Law Library, 692
creating, 758-766
creating with ActiveX, 775-776
creating with Internet Phone, 777
creating with Internet video-conferencing, 777
creating with Java, 775
creating with VRML, 776
Cybercash, 636
data streaming, 777
defining, 774-775
defining goals, 763
design managers, 760
EarthWeb Gamelan, 595
editorial managers, 760-761
Edupage, 748
Electric Library, 690
Encyclopedia Brittanica, 688
executive producers, 759
Explorer, 194
financial considerations, 765-766
Gamelan, 346
Geffen/DGC Records, 370
Hackers, 223
HTTPd, 99
Internet Information Server, 98
Internet multimedia designers, 762

Internet software developers, 761
Internet systems administrators, 762-763
IntraActive, 92
IWave, 373
Library of Congress, 692
Linux, 191
mapping, 225
marketing, 772-773
Microsoft, 526
Microsoft ISAPI, 517
mission statements, 765
Mosaic, 196
Netscape, 194, 303
Netscape NSAPI, 517
NetworkMusic, 370
Novell GroupWise WebAccess, 552
operating procedures, 770-772
O'Reilly & Associates WSAPI, 517
O'Reilly WebSite, 98
OS/2, 195
outsourcing, 778-779
Pathfinder, 566
Perl, 340
planning, 767
product managers, 759-760
production managers, 760
production teams, 758-759
program managers, 760
Quarterdeck, 480
Radnet, 557

software Index

RealAudio, 107, 372, 376, 615
Reuters Business Alert, 605
security, 224
site architecture, 767-769
Software Engineering Institute and Carnegie-Mellon University, 219
Sprawl, 592-593
StreamWorks, 373
technical requirements, 770
time, 765-766
troubleshooting, 770-771
TrueSpeech, 373
user interfaces, 769
VDOLive, 387
video streaming, 776
Virtual Noise Audio Help Desk, 371
voices, 377
WBS, 591
Web Crossing, 571
WebChat, 591

WebCompare Server Features Comparison, 94
Webcorp, 370
Well, 564
wireless Internet connections, 777
Wooley's, 564
Word, 704
World Wildlife Fund, 696
yellow pages, 692
sizes, frames, 851

slashes (/), home directories, 240
SLIP, 857
 accounts, dial-up analog services, 166-167
 dial-up accounts, 167
SLmail, 104
smart keys, 215
smartcards, 215
SMDS (Switched Multimegabit Data Service), 155-156, 857
 WANs, accessing, 160
SMTP (Standard Mail Transfer Protocol), 328, 858
 e-mail, 460, 469
sniffers (packets), 248-249, 452
sockets, 441, 858
SoftQuad Panorama, SGML, 362
software, 105, 193, 748-749
 Adobe Premiere, 383
 audio
  editing, 374-376
  servers, 372
 bandwidths, 498
 BBSs, 44-46
 Bloomberg Personal, 606
 browsers, 193
  Explorer, 193
  Mosaic, 195
  Netscape, 193
  OS/2, 195
 bugs, 223-224
 clients, 51-53, 69
 compatibility, 748
 contact management systems, 578
 CoolTalk, 107

 CU-SeeMe, 107
 Distance, 184
 document databases, 652-653
 e-mail, 196-197
  Airmail, 199
  CuteFTP, 200-201
  Eudora, 197
  Fetch, 200-201
  FTP, 200
  FTP command-line, 201
  GroupWise, 198
  Netscape, 197
  Pine, 199
 Envoy, 850
 EveryWare Development Corp., 184
 financial considerations, 183-185
 firewalls, 498, 851
 FTP Software, Inc., 185
 Gopher, 106
 groupware, 851
 help, purchasing, 684-685
 help desk, 674-677
 installing logs, 112
 interfaces, 852
 Internet, 172-173
 Internet Chat, 203
 Internet Phone, 203, 852
 Internet software developers, 761
 Internet telephones, 488, 492
 intranets
  connecting users, 264
  training users, 268
 IRC, 106
 Linux, 854

message boards,
   creating, 566
MOOs, downloading,
   594
Motet Conferencing,
   642
MUDs, 854
NETCOM On-line
   Communications, Inc.,
   185
NetManage, Inc., 185
Oracle, 855
plug-ins, 518
PointCast, 602-603
private message boards
   configuring, 638-640
   customizing, 635-637
QuickTime, 385
routers, 857
security, 744-745
servers, 50, 67, 92-93,
   118, 174-175
   Apache, 100
   e-mail, 102-103
   financial
      considerations, 118
   freeware, 99
   HTTPd, 99
   IIS, 97-98
   installing, 94
   Mac HTTP, 98-99
   Netscape Enterprise
      Server, 94-95
   Oracle, 95-97
   security, 93
   upgrading, 749-750
   Web, 67-68
   WebSite, 98
   WWW, 93-94
shareware/freeware, 857
SPRY, 185
Spyglass, Inc., 185
streaming audio, 106

RealAudio, 106
streaming video, 106
Telnet, 202
   NCSA, 203
   Windows 95, 202
testing, 749
upgrading, 748-749
   servers, 750
video, Streamworks, 386
video-conferencing,
   498, 507-508
WebShare, 644-646
workstations, 174
Xing Streamworks, 107
**Software Development
Kit,** *see* **SDK**
**Software Engineering
Institute and Carnegie-
Mellon University Web
site, 219**
Solaris, 84
   OpenWindows, 84
**Sonet (Synchronous
Optical Network), 155**
   WANs, accessing, 160
sonets, 858
Sound Recorder, 371
SoundEdit Pro, 371
sounds, 368-369, 376
   advertising, 379
   bandwidths, 369-370
   editing, 374-376
   file extensions, .AU, 848
   formats, 370-371
      .WAV, 859
   GoldWave, 374
   hardware, 369-370
   Internet Phone,
      376-377
   Internet telephones, 492
   IWave, 373
   metafiles, 376

Progressive Network,
   615
RealAudio, 372
RealAudio Encoder, 376
recording, 373
servers, software, 372
SoundEdit Pro, 371
streaming, 372-373
StreamWorks, 372
ToolVox, 373
TrueSpeech, 373
voices, 377-379
WAV files, 375
**source code, searching
Web, 696**
source code for Java, 528
sources, Perl, 339
SPARC, 858
**SPARC (Scaleable
Processor Architecture)
servers, 75-77**
spoofing, 249-251
spooling printers, 148
**Sporting Goods and
Apparel Association,** *see*
SGAA, 725
Sprawl Web site, 592-593
SPRY, 185
SPRYMail, 473
Spyglass, Inc., 185
**SQL (Structured Query
Language), 342-344,
858**
   listing, 343
SQL Server, 858
**SSIs (Server-Side
Includes), 515-516**
   accessing, 243-244
   enabling, 243-244
   HTML, 516
**SSLs (secure sockets
layers), 260, 858**
   servers, 744

Stadium version (Global Stage IRC chat server), 482
stand-alone applications, 709-710, 858
Standard Generalized Markup Language, *see* SGML
Standard Mail, 460
star topology, Ethernet, 134
starting
   FTP, clients, 409-410
   intranets, 13-14
   networks, servers, 145-147
   online news services, 602-603
statements (mission), Web sites, 765
static data, dynamic sites, 323
stocks, real-time messaging, 589
StockWatcher, 532
storing
   CGI scripts, 241
   file structures, 730
   files, 729
      user accounts, 735
   UNIX servers, 731
storing data, 328
   CGIs, 328-330
   databases, relational, 330-332
   flat file databases, 330
streaming
   audio files, 370-373, 595
      Internet Phone, 376-377
      IWave, 373
      RealAudio, 106, 372
      RealAudio Encoder, 376
      servers, 372
      software, 106
      StreamWorks, 372
      TrueSpeech, 373
      voices, 377-379
      Web sites, creating, 776
   data, Web sites, creating, 777
   video
      software, 106
      Web sites, creating, 776
StreamWorks, 372, 386
   Network Manager, 386-387
   Web site, 387
Streamworks, 107
Structured Query Language, *see* SQL
submitting documents
   databases, 651-652
   FTP, 650
   InterNotes, 655
   Livelink Library, 654-655
   Navigator, 656-657
subscribing to online news services, 602-604
suites
   InTandem, 627
   SamePage, 629-630
   Thuridion Crew, 627-628
Sun Microsystems, Solaris, 84
Sun Systems, NIS, 210
Sun Yellow Pages, *see* NIS
support, *see* help
surveys (user input), designing intranets, 541
sustainable user databases, designing, 718-719
Switched Multimegabit Data Service, *see* SMDS
switching circuits, 849
Sybase
   databases, 425-426
   SQL, 670
symbolic links, UNIX directories, 732
Synchronous Optical Network (Sonet), 155
Sysops (network administrators), 588
   Telnet, 442
system requirements
   Macintosh
      video, 384
      video-conferencing, 508
   Windows
      video, 384
      video-conferencing, 509
system startup files, logs, 111
systems integrators, ISPs, 178-179

T

T-1 circuits, 858
   WANs, 153
      accessing, 160
T-1 services, WANs, 153
T-3 circuits, WANs, 153
   accessing, 160
Table Talk, 563

tables
   process table, 447-450, 453-454
   relational databases, 856

tags
   HTML, <SCRIPT>, 523-525
   SGML, 363, 858

TCP/IP, 858
   applications, 530-531
   daemons, 174
   DARPA, 141
   FTP, 404, 413
   Internet telephones, 493
   LANs, 141
   ports, 441
   sockets, 441
   Telnet, 441
   troubleshooting, 177
   Windows 95, configuring, 266

TCP/IP Properties dialog box, 266

technical requirements
   intranets, 539-540
   Web sites, 770

technical support
   administrators, 288, 292
   PDFs, 353
   servers, 75, 115
      installing, 121

telecommuting, 788
   LANs, 142

teleconferencing, 798

telephone lists, contact databases, 579

telephones (Internet), 488
   bandwidths, 490, 498
   buffering, 491
   clients, 498-499
   defined, 488-489
   financial considerations, 493
   firewalls, 497-498
   FWD, 489
   hardware requirements, 488
   history of, 491-493
   intranets, 493-494
      bandwidths, 494
      financial considerations, 494-495
      protocols, 493-494
      speed of, 493
      video-phones, 495-496
   LANs, 491
   legal issues, 497
   operators, 489
   regulations, 497
   RTP, 489
   servers, 491, 496-497
   software, 492
   sound quality, 492
   video-conferencing, 498
   WANs, 491
   Web pages, voice links, 495

Telnet, 202, 438, 858
   clients, 440-441
   command line, 442-443
   compared to rlogin, 441-442
   connectivity issues, 450-451
   enabling from server, 444-447
   monitoring logins, 444-447
   multitasking, 440
   NCSA, 203
   remote system problems, 450-451
   servers, 440-441
   sessions, initiating, 439
   system administrators, 442
   TCP/IP, 441
   tracking users, 444-447
   transmitting raw data, 453
   troubleshooting, 451
   Windows 95, 202

terminal sessions, virtual (Telnet), 438

terminals, Internet, 853

terminals (dumb), 850

testing
   anonymous FTP, 408
   betas, 542
   security, 219-220
   software, 749

text editors, vi, 449

Theater version (Global Stage IRC chat server), 482

threads, 562, 858

Thuridion Crew
   contact databases, 582
   Crew Calendar, 558
   Locker, 627-628

time Web sites, 765-766

time reporting, 434

Time-Warner's Pathfinder Web site, 566

Timecast, 615

timeliness of intranets, 9

Times Fax, 354

token buses, 135

Token Ring LANs, 135-136

token rings, 859

ToolVox, 373

Topic search engine, 670-671

tracking
   database users, 722-724
   documents, 620-622
   Telnet users, 444-447
trade organizations, servers, 62
training
   administrators, 293-295
   intranet users, 264, 278-281
      McKeon & Jeffries, 268-269, 281-283
      message boards, 282
      online, 282
      SGAA, 283
   SGAA, 269, 281
   software, 268
transactions
   online, 777
   port numbers, 441
transferring, ASCII files, 848
transmissions
   decrypting, 251
   defined, 247
   encrypting, 252, 255-256
      private keys, 252-253
      public keys, 253-255
   interactive, 259-260
      security, 258
   intercepted, 248
   security, 246-247, 251
      DES, 253
      encrypting, 251-252
      files, 258
      internetworking devices, 249
      spoofing, 249-251
   Telnet, raw data, 453
transmitters, RFs, 132
trees (directories) roots, 857

troubleshooting
   file structures, 730-731
   help desk, 674-677
      search engines, 680
      writing, 678-680
   help desks
      chat lines, 684
      e-mail addresses, 682-683
      e-mail routers, 684
      running, 681-682
   htadm program, 232
   lcd command (FTP), 401
   logs, 112
      emergency startup procedures, 111
      Macintosh Extensions Manager, 112
   Options directive, 238
   Protection directive, 234
   security, 257
   sendmail command (UNIX), 224
   servers, 123-125, 733-734
      installing, 121
   SGML, 365-366
   TCP/IP, 177
   Telnet, 451
   Web sites, 770-771
   .www acl file, 233
TrueSpeech, 373
trusted hosts, 452, 859
   rlogin, 442
tutorial, Java, 345
twisted pair cables, 131-132, 859
Type I data, 431
Type II data, 431
Type III data, 431
Type IV data, 432

U

UDP (User Datagram Protocol), 504, 859
   Internet telephones, 493
   bandwidths in intranets, 494
umbrellas (logs), 110-111
   electronic, 113
   initial parameters, 111
   software, installing, 112
   system startup files, 111
   users, root access, 113
United Press International (UPI), 605
universal access, 211
University of Virginia, Hero Village, 592
UNIX, 65, 83, 89, 859
   administrative groups, 720
   commands
      chmod, 849
      chown, 849
      chroot, 849
      sendmail, 224
   directories, 732
      symbolic links, 732
   file structures, 732-733
   FTP, 408
      servers, 411
   grep utility, 851
   Hero Village, 592
   HP-UX, 852
   Linux, 854
   Netscape Enterprise Server, 94-95
   Post Office e-mail server, 470
   SCO UNIX, 84-86
   servers, 127
      storage space, 731

Unix-to-Unix Copy Protocol (UUCP), 48
UNP, 859
updating
   administrators, 292
   business data, 20-25
   files, 288-289
   intranets, 9
   servers, 119
upgrading
   intranets, financial considerations, 186
   servers, 116, 749-750
      hardware, 750
      software, 750
   software, 748-749
   workstations, 750-752
UPI (United Press International), 605
URLs, 859
usage analysis, 287-288
usage levels, intranets, 16
Usenet, 104-105, 563, 859
   message boards, 567
   NNTP, 104
user command (FTP), 401
User Datagram Protocol, *see* **UDP**
user survey for designing intranets, 543-547
User/Password dialog box, 228
UserDir directive, 240
UserId <user> directive, 231
usernames, 215
   authenticating, 214
      kerberos, 215
   O'Reilly WebBoard, 568
   WANs, 217

users
   access management, 848
   accounts, 227
      Clickshare, 603
      storing files, 735
   CGI scripts, accessing, 241
   clients, 849
   creating, 231-232, 239
   databases, 718-719
      access rights, 721
      administrative groups, 720-721
      flow charts, 723
      functions, 719
      groups, 719-720
      implementing, 721-724
      monitoring, 724-725
      passwords, 724
      security, 722
      tracking, 722-724
   FTP, advertising, 414
   guiding, 693
   input, 541
   interfaces, 769
   intranets
      connecting, 264-268
      designing, 540-541
      instruction sheets, 265
      participating, 541-543
      software, 268
      surveys, 541
      training, 264
   ISDN, 267
   LANs
      resources, 210
      security, 210-211
   message boards, 282
   online, 269-273
      McKeon & Jeffries, 274-275
      SGAA, 275

   operating systems, 89
   restricting, 235
   root access, log umbrellas, 113
   security, 207
   server space, 735-737
   servers, 92
   tracking, Telnet, 444-447
   training, 278-281
      McKeon & Jeffries, 268-269, 281-283
      online, 282
      SGAA, 269, 281-283
   usage analysis, 287-288
utmp files, 446
UUCP (Unix-to-Unix Copy Protocol), 48

V

variables (environmental), setting, 444
VAX, 859
VBA (Visual Basic for Applications), 526
VBScript, 305, 524-526
VDOLive, 387-388
   Web site, 387
VDOLive Player, 387
VDOLive Server, 387
Verity, 670-671
vi text editor, 449
video, 382-383
   Adobe Premiere, 383
   Cinepak, 388
   compressing, 859
   frames, rates, 851
   intranets, 383
   Macintosh
      compatibility, 384
      system requirements, 384

MBONE, 854
MPEG, 854
pixels, 383
playback, 388-389
QuickTime, 385
real-time, 856
recorded, creating, 383-385
servers, reflectors, 856
software, 106
StreamWorks, 386
Network Manager, 386-387
VDOLive, 387-388
Windows
*compatibility, 385
system requirements, 384*
video streaming, creating Web sites, 776
video-conferencing, 502, 508-509, 777
applications, 503-504
audio, 379
bandwidths, 503-506
Chat, 484
clients
*hardware, 507-508
software, 507-508*
colleges, 504
compressions, 505-506
CU-SeeMe, 502, 849
customer service, 504
formats, CIF/QCIF, 849
Forums.com, 640
Internet, 509
Macintosh, system requirements, 508
marketing, 504
medical services, 504

Motet Conferencing, 642
portfolio, 504
real estates, 504
real-time, 502-503
reflectors, 505
sales, 504
servers, 504-505, 509
software, 498
UDP, 504
WebShare, 644
Windows, system requirements, 509
without reflectors, 505
video-phones
CU-SeeMe, 495-496
Internet telephones, 495-496
reflectors, 496
VideoPhone, 507
VideoPix, 508
viewing PDFs, 358
virtual corporations, 787, 859
Virtual Garden, 566
Virtual Noise Audio Help Desk Web site, 371
Virtual Reality Markup Language, *see* **VRML**
virtual terminal session, 438
Visual Basic, 526
StockWatcher, 532
Visual Basic for Applications (VBA), 526
Visual Basic Script, *see* **VBScript**
VMS, 859
VocalChat, 491-493
VocalTec, IWave, 373
voice links (WWW), Internet telephones, 495

voice mail, 794-795
Voice Over Network (VON), CoolTalk, 304, 859
voices, 377-379
Voxware, ToolVox, 373
VRML (Virtual Reality Markup Language), 304, 526-527, 859
Web sites, creating, 776

W

WANs (Wide Area Networks), 152, 216-217, 468, 859
56K circuits, accessing, 159
ATM, 137, 156
accessing, 160-161
bridges, 848
communications, 161-162
connecting, 161
to LANs, 157
DDS, 152-153
e-mail, 468
EVN Records, Inc., 154
firewalls, 217-218
frame relays, 153-154
accessing, 160
FTP, 394-396
Goodbody Community Hospital, 155
groupware, 851
implementing, 156-157
Internet telephones, 491
intranets, 161
LANs
*bridges, 157
routers, 157-158*

security, 161
   passwords, 217
   testing, 219-220
   usernames, 217
SMDS, 155-156
   accessing, 160
Sonet, 155
   accessing, 160
T-1 circuits, 153
   accessing, 160
T-1 services, 153
T-3 circuits, 153, 160
   accessing, 160
WAV files, 371, 375, 859
Wave Systems, Network News Corporation, 612-613
Wayfarer QuickServer, 532-533
WBS (Web Broadcasting Service) Web site, 591
Web Crossing, 563
   Web site, 571
WebAccess, 552
WebBoard, 568
WebChat, 480
Webchat, 860
WebChat Web site, 591
WebCompare Server Features
   Comparison Web site, 94
Webcorp Web site, 370
Webmaster audio
   bandwidths, 369-370
   hardware, 369-370
WebShare, 624, 644-646
WebShare Calendar, 557-558
WebSite, 98
WebSite API (WSAPI), 517

The Well, 636, 860
   Table Talk, 563
Well Web site, 564
who command, 445
Wide Area Networks, *see* **WANs**
Windows
   configuration files, logs, 111
   servers, 127
   video
     compatibility, 385
     system requirements, 384
   video-conferencing, system requirements, 509
Windows 3.1, 63, 189
   FTP servers, 412
Windows 3.x FTP, 409
Windows 95, 63, 190
   FTP, 410
     servers, 412
   Internet Explorer, 301
   TCP/IP, configuring, 266
   Telnet, 202
Windows for Workgroups, LANs, 140
Windows NT, 64, 86-87, 189-190
   file structures, 733
   FTP, 410
     servers, 412-413
   help, 677
   IIS, 97-98
   LANs, 140
   N-Plex, 36
   Netscape Enterprise Server, 94-95
   Post Office e-mail server, 470

WinZip, help, 675
wireless
   intranets, 793-794
   LANs, 132-133
wireless Internet connections, 777
WOO, 860
Wooley's Web site, 564
WOOs, Sprawl Web site, 592-593
Word
   downloading, 704
   Internet Assistant, 310-311
word processing applications, PDFs, 352
WordPerfect
   Acrobat, 356
   Envoy, 359
workflow, 276-277
   scheduling, 276-277
workgroups
   Acrobat, 356
   Windows for Workgroups, LANs, 140
workstations
   software, 174
   upgrading, 750-752
World Inc., AlphaWorld Web site, 594
World Wildlife Fund Web site, 696
Worm, 224
writing
   help, 678-680
   scripts, 342
     SQL, 342-344
writing Perl forms (listing), 340-342
WSAPI (WebSite API), 517

Index

wtmp files, 446
WWW, 860
  bookmarks, building
    lists, 697
  browsers, 300-301, 849
    Explorer, 193
    fonts, 302
    forms, 327
    HTML, 300-302
    images, 302
    interlacing, 302
    Internet Explorer, 301
    Java, 305
    JPEG, 302
    Live3D, 304
    McKeon & Jeffries,
     306
    MOOs, 592
    Mosaic, 195, 854
    MUDs, 592
    Navigator, 301, 304
    NCSA Mosaic, 302
    Netscape, 193,
     301-304, 855
    OS/2, 195
    PowerBrowser, 305
    progressive rendering,
     302
    SDK, 303
    SGAA, 306
  CERN, 300
  CGI, 849
  chats, boards, 591
  digests, online news
    services, 608
  documents, 352
    searchable pages, 623
  embedding ActiveX,
    848
  FAQs, 850
  forms, 327-328
  history of, 300

  HTML, 852
  HTTP, 852
  hypertext, 852
  message boards,
    563-565
  NewsAlert, accessing,
    615
  pages, voice links with
    Internet telephones,
    495
  Perl, 339-342
  private message boards,
    635
  search engines, 661-662
    AltaVista, 664-665
    Boolean, 662-663,
     848
    defined, 660
    Excite, 666, 683
    keyword searches,
     662-663
    Livelink, 666-667
    Pat, 666-667
    selecting, 671
    setting up, 663-664
    Sybase SQL, 670
    Verity, 670-671
  searching, 694-698
    source code, 696
  servers, 721-724
    file structures,
     734-735
    freeware, 99
    LANs, 149
    security, 222,
     743-744
    SGAA, 68
    software, 67-68,
     92-94
  sites, 769
    Access America, 389
    accessing, 290

    Acrobat, 354
    Adobe, 358
    Adobe Acrobat, 357
    agents, 777
    AlphaWorld, 594
    Apache, 100
    audio streaming, 776
    Bloomberg Personal,
     606
    BROWSE, 343
    business planning, 763
    CERT, 257
    Collabra Share, 38
    concepts, 763-765
    Cornell University
     Law Library, 692
    creating, 758, 766
    creating with ActiveX,
     775-776
    creating with Internet
     Phone, 777
    creating with Internet
     video-conferencing,
     777
    creating with Java,
     775
    creating with VRML,
     776
    Cybercash, 636
    data streaming, 777
    defining, 774-775
    defining goals, 763
    design managers, 760
    EarthWeb Gamelan,
     595
    editorial managers,
     760-761
    Edupage, 748
    Electric Library, 690
    Encyclopedia
     Brittanica, 688
    executive producers,
     759

Explorer, 194
financial considerations, 765-766
Gamelan, 346
Geffen/DGC Records, 370
Hackers, 223
HTTPd, 99
Internet Information Server, 98
Internet multimedia designers, 762
Internet software developers, 761
Internet systems administrators, 762-763
IntraActive, 92
IWave, 373
Library of Congress, 692
Linux, 191
mapping, 225
marketing, 772-773
Microsoft, 526
Microsoft ISAPI, 517
mission statements, 765
Mosaic, 196
Netscape, 194, 303
Netscape NSAPI, 517
NetworkMusic, 370
Novell GroupWise WebAccess, 552
operating procedures, 770-772
O'Reilly & Associates WSAPI, 517
O'Reilly WebSite, 98
OS/2, 195
outsourcing, 778-779
Pathfinder, 566
Perl, 340
planning, 767
product managers, 759-760
production managers, 760
production teams, 758-759
program managers, 760
Quarterdeck, 480
Radnet, 557
RealAudio, 107, 372, 376, 615
Reuters Business Alert, 605
security, 224
site architecture, 767-769
Software Engineering Institute and Carnegie-Mellon University, 219
Sprawl, 592-593
StreamWorks, 373
technical requirements, 770
time, 765-766
troubleshooting, 770-771
TrueSpeech, 373
user interfaces, 769
VDOLive, 387
video streaming, 776
Virtual Noise Audio Help Desk, 371
voices, 377
WBS, 591
Web Crossing, 571
WebChat, 591
WebCompare Server Features Comparison, 94
Webcorp, 370
Well, 564
wireless Internet connections, 777
Wooley's, 564
Word, 704
World Wildlife Fund, 696
yellow pages, 692
URLs, 859
.www acl file, 233
WWW Security FAQs, 222
WYSIWYG, 860
authoring tools, 310
FrontPage, 313
Internet Assistant, 310-311
Navigator Gold, 312-313

X-Y-Z

X Windows, 443-444
Xing
StreamWorks, 372
Streamworks, 386
Xing Streamworks, 107
XingMPEG Player
playback, 388-389
XNS, LANs, 142

Yahoo!, online news services, 602
yellow pages, 692

A VIACOM SERVICE

The Information SuperLibrary™

Bookstore   **Search**   **What's New**   **Reference**   **Software**   **Newsletter**   **Company Overviews**

Yellow Pages   **Internet Starter Kit**   **HTML Workshop**   **Win a Free T-Shirt!**   **Macmillan Computer Publishing**   **Site Map**   **Talk to Us**

CHECK OUT THE BOOKS IN THIS LIBRARY.

You'll find thousands of shareware files and over 1600 computer books designed for both technowizards and technophobes. You can browse through 700 sample chapters, get the latest news on the Net, and find just about anything using our massive search directories.

All Macmillan Computer Publishing books are available at your local bookstore.

We're open 24-hours a day, 365 days a year.

You don't need a card.

We don't charge fines.

And you can be as **LOUD** as you want.

The Information SuperLibrary
http://www.mcp.com/mcp/   ftp.mcp.com

Copyright © 1996, Macmillan Computer Publishing-USA, A Simon & Schuster Company

Building an Intranet

—Tim Evans   *Internet/Intranets*

This is the first book to focus on using Web technology to provide information for a company internally. The reader will learn how to choose hardware and software, how to set up a secure Web server, and how to make his company's applications Web-aware.

- Teaches how to design, build, and deploy information and applications within an organization
- Covers security issues

Price: $55.00 USA/$74.95 CDN   User Level: Casual - Accomplished
ISBN: 1-57521-071-1   720 pp.   7 3/8 × 9 1/8   Publication date 4/1/96

Building an Intranet with Windows NT 4

—Scott Zimmerman and Tim Evans   *Internet/Intranets*

This hands-on guide teaches readers how to set up and maintain an efficient intranet with Windows NT. It comes complete with a selection of the best software for setting up a server, creating content, and developing intranet applications.

- CD-ROM includes a complete Windows NT intranet toolkit with a full-featured Web server, Web content development tools, and ready-to-use intranet applications
- Includes complete specifications for several of the most popular intranet applications, group scheduling, discussions, database access, and more

Price: $49.99 USA/$70.95 CDN   User Level: Casual - Accomplished
ISBN: 1-57521-137-8   600 pp   7 3/8 × 9 1/8   Publication date 7/1/96

Netscape 3 Unleashed, Second Edition

—Dick Oliver   *Internet/Online Communications*

Readers learn how to fully exploit the new features of this latest version of Netscape—the most popular Web browser in use today.

- Teaches how to install, configure, and use Netscape Navigator 3.0
- Covers how to add interactivity to Web pages with Netscape

Price: $49.99 USA/$70.95 CDN   User Level: Accomplished - Expert
ISBN: 1-57521-164-5   1,000 pp.   7 3/8 × 9 1/8   Publication date 7/1/96

World Wide Web Database Developer's Guide

—Swank and Kittle   *Internet Programming*

Teaches readers how to quickly and professionally create a database and connect it to the Internet. Real-world database problems and solutions explain how to manage information. Includes HTML, Java, and the newest Netscape 2.0 features to help organize information.

- Explores ways to convert and present database information quickly and professionally

Price: $59.99 USA/$84.95 CDN   User Level: Accomplished - Expert
ISBN: 1-57521-048-7   800 pp.   7 3/8 × 9 1/8   Publication date 8/1/96

Teach Yourself Web Publishing with HTML 3.2 in 14 Days, Professional Reference Edition

—*Laura Lemay*　　　　　　　　　　　　　　　　　　　*Internet/Web Publishing*

This is the updated edition of Lemay's previous bestseller, *Teach Yourself Web Publishing with HTML in 14 Days, Premier Edition*. In it readers will find advanced topics and updates—including adding audio, video, and animation to Web pages.

- Explores the use of CGI scripts, tables, HTML 3.2, the Netscape and Internet Explorer extensions, Java applets and JavaScript, and VRML

Price: $59.99 USA/$81.95 CDN　　*User Level: New - Casual - Accomplished*
ISBN: 1-57521-096-7　　*1,104 pp.*　　*7 3/8 × 9 1/8*　　*Publication date 6/1/96*

Programming Netscape Plug-Ins

—*Zan Oliphant*　　　　　　　　　　　　　　　　　　　*Internet/Programming*

This book provides the reader with an understanding of what plug-ins are and how they can and should be used. Design information is discussed in detail, giving readers the knowledge they need to program and design effective Web pages with Netscape.

- Details ways to develop plug-ins that can be used with the Netscape browser
- Defines various APIs that can be used to create plug-ins

Price: $39.99 USA/$56.95 CDN　　*User Level: Accomplished - Expert*
ISBN: 1-57521-098-3　　*400 pp.*　　*7 3/8 × 9 1/8*　　*Publication date 8/1/96*

Microsoft SQL Server 6.5 DBA Survival Guide, Second Edition

—*Mark Spenik and Orryn Sledge*　　　　　　　　　　　　　　　　　*Client/Server*

This book will turn a mediocre administrator into an effective, skilled leader in charge of a well-tuned RDBMS. Time-saving techniques show how to maximize Microsoft SQL Server.

- Teaches how to implement day-to-day preventive maintenance tasks
- Updated to cover new features—including the new transaction wizard and the latest version of SQL Server

Price: $49.99 USA/$67.99 CDN　　*User Level: Accomplished - Expert*
ISBN: 0-672-30959-9　　*912 pp.*　　*7 3/8 × 9 1/8*　　*Publication date 6/1/96*

Designing and Implementing Microsoft Internet Information Server 2

—*Arthur Knowles and Sanjaya Hettihewa*　　　　　　　*Internet Communications/Online*

This book details the specific tasks involved in setting up and running a Microsoft Internet Information Server. Readers will learn troubleshooting, network design, security, and cross-platform integration procedures.

- Readers learn everything from planning to implementation

Price: $39.99 USA/$56.95 CDN　　*User Level: Casual - Expert*
ISBN: 1-57521-168-8　　*336 pp.*　　*7 3/8 × 9 1/8*　　*Publication date 7/1/96*

Add to Your Sams.net Library Today with the Best Books for Internet Technologies

ISBN	Quantity	Description of Item	Unit Cost	Total Cost
1-57521-071-1		Building an Intranet (book/CD-ROM)	$55.00	
1-57521-137-8		Building an Intranet with Windows NT 4 (book/CD-ROM)	$49.99	
1-57521-164-5		Netscape 3 Unleashed, Second Edition (book/CD-ROM)	$49.99	
1-57521-048-7		World Wide Web Database Developer's Guide (book/CD-ROM)	$59.99	
1-57521-096-7		Teach Yourself Web Publishing with HTML 3.2 in 14 Days, Professional Reference Edition (book/CD-ROM)	$59.99	
1-57521-098-3		Programming Netscape Plug-Ins (book/CD-ROM)	$39.99	
0-672-30959-9		Microsoft SQL Server 6.5 DBA Survival Guide, Second Edition (book/CD-ROM)	$49.99	
1-57521-168-8		Designing and Implementing Microsoft Internet Information Server 2	$39.99	
		Shipping and Handling: See information below.		
		TOTAL		

Shipping and Handling: $4.00 for the first book, and $1.75 for each additional book. If you need to have it NOW, we can ship the product to you in 24 hours for an additional charge of approximately $18.00, and you will receive your item overnight or in two days. Overseas shipping and handling adds $2.00. Prices subject to change. Call between 9:00 a.m. and 5:00 p.m. EST for availability and pricing information on latest editions.

201 W. 103rd Street, Indianapolis, Indiana 46290

1-800-428-5331 — Orders   1-800-835-3202 — Fax   1-800-858-7674 — Customer Service

Book ISBN 1-57521-115-7

What's on the CD-ROM

The companion CD-ROM contains software developed by the authors, plus an assortment of third-party tools and product demos. The disc is designed to be explored using a CD-ROM menu program. Using the menu program, you can view information concerning products and companies, and install programs with a single click of the mouse. To run the menu program, follow the steps listed next.

Windows 95 Installation Instructions

> **NOTE**
>
> If you have the AutoPlay feature of Windows 95 enabled, the Guide to the CD-ROM program will start automatically. If you have disabled the AutoPlay feature, please follow the instructions listed next.

1. Insert the CD-ROM into your CD-ROM drive.
2. From the Windows 95 desktop, double-click the My Computer icon.
3. Double-click the icon representing your CD-ROM drive.
4. Double-click the Setup.exe icon to run the Guide to the CD-ROM program.

Windows NT and Windows 3.1 Installation Instructions

1. Insert the CD-ROM into your CD-ROM drive.
2. From File Manager or Program Manager, choose File | Run.
3. Type *drive*\setup and press Enter. *drive* corresponds to the drive letter of your CD-ROM. For example, if your CD-ROM is drive D:, type D:\SETUP and press Enter.
4. Follow the on-screen instructions in the Guide to the CD-ROM program.